I0146164

Adorno's Critique of Political Economy

Historical Materialism Book Series

T he Historical Materialism Book Series is a major publishing initiative of the radical left. The capitalist crisis of the twenty-first century has been met by a resurgence of interest in critical Marxist theory. At the same time, the publishing institutions committed to Marxism have contracted markedly since the high point of the 1970s. The Historical Materialism Book Series is dedicated to addressing this situation by making available important works of Marxist theory. The aim of the series is to publish important theoretical contributions as the basis for vigorous intellectual debate and exchange on the left.

The peer-reviewed series publishes original monographs, translated texts, and reprints of classics across the bounds of academic disciplinary agendas and across the divisions of the left. The series is particularly concerned to encourage the internationalization of Marxist debate and aims to translate significant studies from beyond the English-speaking world.

For a full list of titles in the Historical Materialism Book Series available in paperback from Haymarket Books, visit: www.haymarketbooks.org/series_collections/1-historical-materialism.

Adorno's Critique of Political Economy

Dirk Braunstein

Translated by
Adam Baltner

Haymarket Books
Chicago, IL

First published in 2022 by Brill Academic Publishers, The Netherlands
© 2022 Koninklijke Brill NV, Leiden, The Netherlands

Published in paperback in 2023 by
Haymarket Books
P.O. Box 180165
Chicago, IL 60618
773-583-7884
www.haymarketbooks.org

ISBN: 978-1-64259-992-3

Distributed to the trade in the US through Consortium Book Sales and
Distribution (www.cbsd.com) and internationally through Ingram
Publisher Services International (www.ingramcontent.com).

This book was published with the generous support of Lannan
Foundation, Wallace Action Fund, and the Marguerite Casey Foundation.

Special discounts are available for bulk purchases by organizations and
institutions. Please call 773-583-7884 or email info@haymarketbooks.org
for more information.

Cover design by David Mabb. Cover art is a detail of *Construct 57, John
Henry Dearle for Morris & Co. Compton, / Kasimir Malevich, Suprematist
Composition (18th Construction)*, paint and wallpaper mounted on linen
(2006).

Printed in the United States.

10 9 8 7 6 5 4 3 2 1

Library of Congress Cataloging-in-Publication data is available.

Contents

Translator's Note

With *Adorno's Critique of Political Economy*, Dirk Braunstein has produced one of the most comprehensive accounts to date of both the historical development of Adorno's concept of economy, and of the importance of the critique of political economy to his philosophy. In doing so, Braunstein quotes Adorno extensively in order to refute a tendency in the secondary literature to play down or disparage this aspect of his thought.

In translating Braunstein's study from German into English, I have had the fortune of being able to draw upon the work of numerous translators, thanks to whom a great deal of Adorno's writings have already been made accessible in English. Unless otherwise noted in the footnotes, any use of brackets in quoted passages from translated texts mark modifications or insertions I have made, either to avoid ambiguity or correct translation errors. Otherwise, I have faithfully reproduced existing translations – hence, the coexistence of British and American spellings in this book, and of some other minor inconsistencies in some technical terms (for example, 'class-conscious' versus 'class consciousness', 'use-value' versus 'use value', 'praxis' versus 'practice', and so on). All direct quotations from non-English sources were translated by myself. Whenever sources are referred to in the body of the text which have not been translated into English, I have reproduced their German titles and given English translations of these in parentheses.

My warmest thanks are due to the Historical Materialism Book Series team for asking me to be involved with this project and providing support and encouragement throughout, and to Dirk Braunstein for his immensely helpful feedback and suggestions – although it goes without saying that any errors in this final English version are my fault alone.

Adam Baltner
Vienna, September 2022

Acknowledgements

There, in baroque formulations, thanks are no longer only given to the respective doctoral supervisor, the alma mater, the patrons, librarians and archivists, but of course also to parents, grandparents, great grandparents, spouses, children, cousins, lovers, roommates, landlords, neighbours, friends, maids, copy-shop employees, more-or-less fleeting holiday acquaintances, and in the meantime even to pets – indeed, by now, this too has been repeatedly substantiated and corroborated.

GERHARD HENSCHEL, Danksagung

• •
•

I would like to express my thanks to Dagmar Börner-Klein, Beate Hepprich, Ursula Marx, Stephen Roeper, Gudrun Schwarz, Michael Schwarz, Martina Schwörke, Rolf Voigt and Christoph Ziermann.

In particular, I owe a debt of gratitude to Viola Braunstein, Simon Duckheim and Christoph Hesse.

In accordance with time-honoured tradition and entirely deservingly, the first edition of this book was dedicated to my parents, Monika Braunstein and Willi Braunstein. The second edition was dedicated to Rolf Tiedemann in friendship.

CHAPTER 1

Attempting a Critique of Political Economy

... each of the chapters is decorated ...
with a motto, and as always these are
weighty words of famous men.

HANNELORE SCHLAFFER, Eine Träne für den Vater

∴

'Adorno was not bothered with political economy',[1] claims Jürgen Habermas, when in fact the opposite is true. In *The Dialectical Imagination*, Martin Jay deploys the same stereotype, writing that 'Horkheimer and Adorno, however broad the scope of their interests and knowledge, were never really serious students of economics, Marxist or otherwise'.[2] Setting aside the question of what it means to qualify as a serious student or critic of economics, it is true that '[i]n private conversation, Adorno made no secret of his aversion to dealing with the economy'.[3] After all, as Jürgen Ritsert notes, '[e]conomics were certainly not his thing!'[4] Yet Karl Marx, himself not an economist, also made no secret of his aversion to dealing with 'economic stuff' (*ökonomische Scheiße*).[5] Indeed, for Adorno, '[t]he genius of Marx consisted precisely in the fact that, filled with disgust, he tackled exactly that which he found disgusting: the economy'.[6] 'People who champion critical theory', Adorno claims in a seminar from 1968, 'should not let the predominance of the economic deter them from attempting a critique of political economy'.[7] One year later, Iring Fetscher reports, Adorno 'betrayed to a student that the study of economy simply repelled him, but that

---

1   Habermas 1991, p. 109.
2   Jay 1996, p. 152; cf. von Wussow 2007, p. 146, n. 375.
3   Reichelt 2007, p. 4.
4   Ritsert 1998, p. 331.
5   Letter from Marx to Engels, 2 April 1851 (Marx and Engels 1982, p. 325). Translator's note: although the German *Scheiße* is not as vulgar as the English 'shit', some of the pathos is lost in this translation from the *Marx/Engels Collected Works*, as this passage can indeed also be translated as 'economic shit'.
6   Adorno 2018c, p. 164.
7   Adorno 2021a, vol. 4, p. 548.

he also knew the critique of political economy would have to be the basis of a revolutionary theory and practice which invokes Marx'.[8]

Having said that: the present study is about neither Marx nor his critique of political economy. Nor is it primarily concerned with Adorno's reception of Marx, which will be referred to only insofar as is necessary to reproduce the genuinely Adornian critique of political economy. That this critique exists (and that one misses the best it has to offer by measuring it simply against the Marxian critique of political economy) is the central thesis of this study, which aims to depict the shape, goals and course of development of Adorno's critique.

Indication is the predominant gesture of this study for two reasons. First, the difficulties encountered by Adorno in attaining an adequate understanding of the critique of political economy cannot be erased with witty paraphrases which simply recapitulate them. As such, Adorno will be directly quoted whenever possible. Second, many of the materials supporting the notion of a specifically Adornian critique of economy have until now remained unpublished and thus largely unknown. These materials include numerous sketches, remarks and at times also quotations and references which only assume the contours of a critique of economy when contextualised and interpreted. Hence, Adorno's critique of political economy can only exist as 'secondary literature'. The fact that Adorno himself never attempted or even planned to issue this critique in, for example, the form of a monograph cannot simply be attributed to a feeling of incompetence in economics-proper, but rather must also be viewed as a result of the pronounced tendency of his critique of political economy to evade systematic exposition. As far as is possible, Adorno's own work remains free of an explicit critique of economy. What Adorno offers his readers is almost exclusively the result of his own thinking, minus insight into this thinking itself.[9]

It goes without saying that there is no Adorno the economist to be (re-)discovered. Yet there is certainly a critic of political economy who in many respects goes beyond Marx, even while often lagging behind the latter's economic subject knowledge. In any case, Adorno was never under any illusions regarding the importance of economy to the functioning of the wrong society.[10] 'The

---

8   Fetscher 1971, p. 93.
9   An exception to this rule is *Negative Dialectics*, in which Adorno announces that he '[t]o the best of his ability ... means to put his cards on the table' (Adorno 2007b, p. xix). Bracing himself accordingly for the reactions, Adorno adds that he 'feels no rancor and does not begrudge the joy of those in either camp who will proclaim that they knew it all the time and now he was confessing' (Adorno 2007b, p. xxi).
10 Translator's note: 'wrong society' (*falsche Gesellschaft*) recalls Adorno's oft-quoted saying, '[e]s *gibt kein richtiges Leben im Falschen*' (Adorno 2003r, p. 43). While the standard

categories of the critique of political economy form ... the constantly present although rarely visible substrate upon which the Adornian critique of political economy takes place'.[11] As Rolf Johannes notes, although the critique of economy is central for Adorno, it is a centre which is almost completely omitted.[12] Indeed, as extensive as Adorno's work is, it contains very few explicit engagements with the critique of political economy: these occur first in the posthumously published 'Reflections on Class Theory', then in his contribution to the so-called positivism dispute and finally in 'Late Capitalism or Industrial Society', his opening address to the Sixteenth German Sociological Congress in 1968.

For this reason, notes from Adorno's lectures and transcripts from his seminars will be referred to throughout this book. These sources reveal 'how intensively Adorno must have engaged with the Marxian critique of political economy. The Marxian texts were permanent points of reference [in his seminars], and communicating the basic categories of the critique of political economy must have been one of Adorno's main concerns'.[13] From the mid-1950s onwards, transcripts from Adorno's seminars, some of which were co-taught with Horkheimer, were regularly taken down by participants and archived at the Institute for Social Research.[14] Some of these transcripts have already been

---

print translation of this passage by Edmund Jephcott reads '[w]rong life cannot be lived rightly' (Adorno 2005b, p. 39), Dennis Redmond's translation at marxists.org, '[t]here is no right life in the wrong one' (Adorno 2005c) is syntactically closer to the original. Alternatively, recalling the millennia-old philosophical concern with 'the good life', Rodney Livingstone's translation of *Problems of Moral Philosophy* renders this saying as 'there can be no good life within the bad one' (Adorno 2000c, p. 166).

11   Würger-Donitza 1996, p. 170.

12   Cf. Johannes 1995. Johannes's central thesis is that Adorno 'in his works from the post-war period took aim at the economic critique at the centre of materialist theory' but rarely took it up as a specific theme: 'What he developed was a *critical theory with the centre left out*', and 'with the concept of constellation' Adorno's *Negative Dialectics* 'formulates almost a methodology of critical theory with the centre left out' (Johannes 1995, p. 60). However, this assumption rests on a misunderstanding. The 'methodology' that Johannes claims to recognise does not derive from a method which would constitute 'a singularly necessary consequence if critical-theoretical work were no longer organised according to the Horkheimerian institutional idea' (Johannes 1995, p. 61). After all, the centre of a constellation is not left out due to theoretical or institutional deficiencies, but rather because it cannot be named conceptually without thereby being destroyed: at its centre is not something relating to economy, but rather an epistemological antinomy.

13   Grigat 2007, p. 146. For his own part, Adorno discusses the pitfalls associated with the notion of 'concern' (*Anliegen*) – not in a seminar transcript, but in *The Jargon of Authenticity* (cf. Adorno 1973, pp. 6, 79, 80, n. 62).

14   At the time of the present study, the transcripts were located in the social sciences library

analysed by Alex Demirović in a chapter on the Frankfurt School's 'teaching practice' from his German-language monograph on the Frankfurt School, *Der nonkonformistische Intellektuelle (The Nonconformist Intellectual)*.[15]

On the question of the relationship between his spontaneous utterances and written work, Adorno stated unambiguously that it would be 'impossible to make something printed out of a free improvisation, unless the standards involved were lower than mine':[16] 'As much as I know about their mediation, I keep the genres strictly separate, and I mean, not without reason'.[17] That being said, for the purpose of the present study, both 'genres' appear indispensable. 'We have nothing else', one wants to say – also a quotation from one of the 'unauthorised texts', namely, from the transcript of a conversation between Adorno and Horkheimer from 1956, as Horkheimer reciprocates Adorno's comment that they 'must not abandon Marxist terminology'.[18]

When Adorno's grasp of economy is called into question, Marxian theory is invariably presented as the benchmark against which Adorno's social critique must be measured. Every deviation is pedantically marked up as false or at least as a vulgar misunderstanding in order ultimately to portray Adorno as the victim of a naive fallacy. Answering the question of the nature of Adorno's theoretical relationship to Marx from the latter's perspective, a widespread assumption is affirmed: that Adorno, for the most part, simply came up short in his critique of political economy. The sparse amount of secondary literature which takes Adorno seriously as a critic of economy at all[19] hardly contradicts this view. Yet for his own part, Adorno was less scrupulous when it came to further developing or even modifying or abandoning Marxian theorems. This can be seen in his response to Herbert Marcuse's essay on existentialism, in which he takes particular issue with Marcuse's claims that '[i]n so far as Existentialism is a doctrine, it remains an idealistic doctrine: it hypostasises specific historical

---

of the Goethe University of Frankfurt, and it is here where they were accessed. Since then they have been relocated to the university's archive, where as a 'discovery' (Herrschaft 2010a, p. 4) they are finally getting the attention they deserve (cf. Herrschaft 2009). In the archive, the 'sociological' minutes from Adorno's seminars are listed in a stock overview (cf. Herrschaft 2010b, p. 223). The complete minutes from Adorno's seminars from 1949–69 have now been published in a series of four volumes, edited by the author of the present study (Braunstein 2021, cf. Braunstein 2014).

15   Demirović 1999a, pp. 429–78, especially p. 439, n. 337.
16   Letter from Adorno to Kaufmann, 9 December 1968 (Kaufmann 1993, p. 294).
17   Letter from Adorno to Kaufmann, 27 February 1968 (Kaufmann 1993, p. 279).
18   Adorno and Horkheimer 2019, p. 25.
19   In addition to Johannes 1995, notable recent papers in this vein include Koltan 1999, Hafner 1993 and Lindner 2007.

conditions of human existence into ontological and metaphysical character-
istics', and that existentialism 'thus becomes part of the very ideology which it
attacks, and its radicalism is illusory'.[20] Writing to Marcuse, Adorno points out
that it 'gives too much credit to the bourgeois concept of philosophy' to offhandedly equate 'all philosophy with thinking in invariants, with ontologism'.
Regarding this equation, Adorno poses the following question: 'I know it is good
Marx, but is it also true?'[21]

The present study[22] consists of three parts. By and large, these are structured
chronologically in order to trace the development of Adorno's critique of economy within his philosophy.

Generally biographical-narrative in character, the first part takes up the
question of how Adorno arrives as his critique of economy in the first place. As
will become apparent, it is primarily through his study of Georg Lukács's writings (Chapter 2) as well as his engagement with Walter Benjamin and to a lesser
extent Alfred Sohn-Rethel (Chapter 3) that Adorno comes to the conviction
that society can only be conceptualised with the help of economic categories.
Having appropriated these categories, Adorno is led at the end of the 1930s to
apply them explicitly for the first time as part of his own philosophy, which at
the time was already pursuing socio-critical goals (Chapter 4).

Adorno's American exile not only constitutes a caesura in his biography, but
also in the development of his critique of economy. The second part of this
work explores the debate concerning the concept of state capitalism in which
Adorno participates during this period (Chapter 5). Adorno's exile also sees –
once he had lain important groundwork with his 'Reflections on Class Theory' –
the genesis of *Dialectic of Enlightenment*, co-authored with Max Horkheimer
(Chapter 6), followed by *Minima Moralia* (Chapter 7). These texts are placed
within the development of Adorno's critique of political economy alongside
three conversations in which Adorno and Horkheimer affirm the political content of their Critical Theory (Chapter 9).

The third and most actively theoretical part of this study engages with
Adorno's return to the critique of economy following his move back to Frankfurt in the post-war period. Adorno's renewed engagement with Marx during
this time stands at the centre of his work on the philosophy he would ultimately propound in *Negative Dialectics* (Chapter 10). It is within this work

---

20   Marcuse 1973, p. 161.
21   Letter from Adorno to Marcuse, 25 June 1948 (Adorno and Horkheimer 2005, p. 427).
22   Some sections of this study have already been published in slightly modified form; cf.
      Braunstein 2009; cf. Braunstein 2010a; cf. Braunstein 2010b.

that Adorno arrives at a concept of economy which refers to the relationship between nature and society on the one hand (Chapter 11), and to the relationship of society to itself on the other (Chapter 12). The critique of economy understood in this way ultimately gestures towards the utopia of a humanity no longer fated to languish under economic coercion (Chapter 13).

PART 1

CHAPTER 2

The Most Important Marxist Publication on Hegel

... a dispute is at least permissible,
because here the truth can be said.

NIETZSCHE, Human, All Too Human

∙∙
∙

1 The Universal Category of Society as a Whole

At the beginning of the 'short' twentieth century,

> [i]t seemed obvious that the old world was doomed. The old society, the
> old economy, the old political systems had, as the Chinese phrase put it,
> 'lost the mandate of heaven'. Humanity was waiting for an alternative.
> Such an alternative was familiar in 1914.

The tremor unleashed by the October Revolution is difficult to overestimate.
This event, Eric J. Hobsbawm notes,

> had far more profound and global repercussions than its ancestor. For,
> if the ideas of the French revolution have, as is now evident, outlasted
> Bolshevism, the practical consequences of 1917 were far greater and more
> lasting than those of 1789. The October revolution produced by far the
> most formidable organized revolutionary movement in modern history.
> Its global expansion has no parallel since the conquests of Islam in its
> first century.[1]

In a 1967 conversation with Iring Fetscher, Ernst Bloch recounts that he and
Georg Lukács 'both viewed the October Revolution as a *fulfilment*, Lukács in
an even more theological sense back then than I'.[2]

---

1 Hobsbawm 1995, p. 55.
2 Bloch, Fetscher and Lukács 1975, p. 36.

Lukács's 1923 essay collection *History and Class Consciousness* appeared as a theoretical reaction to this upheaval that '– at last! at last! –'[3] had arrived. Among others, it was addressed to the 'proponents of the orthodox reception of Marx within the Second International'[4] around Karl Kautsky, a group whose 'dogmatisation of the Marxist conception of history' had transformed this conception 'into an objective historical law of motion'.[5] With the pathos of a 'freshly-baked Marxist',[6] Lukács contrasts this objectivistic approach against his own theory, according to which the worker 'becomes aware of himself as a commodity' insofar as he 'recognises himself and his own relations with capital', and in doing so becomes capable of overcoming the prevailing order.[7] 'The telos of world history, the redemption of humanity, is for Lukács doubtless identical with the emancipation of the proletariat in the successful world revolution'.[8]

As was the case for many intellectuals of his time, reading *History and Class Consciousness* was a foundational educational experience for Adorno.[9] He had long been familiar with the name Lukács, claiming to have encountered the latter's 1916 *The Theory of the Novel*, itself 'a reaction to the outbreak of the First World War',[10] during his final year of secondary school in 1921.[11] With that early work, an outline of a philosophy of history written before his turn to Marx, Lukács sought to show how, in spite of the progressive loss of meaning in modernity, epic poetry might still lead to a rational transformation of the existing order. Even in 1958, quite some time after he had ceased being a follower of Lukács, Adorno would describe *The Theory of the Novel* as having 'a brilliance and profundity of conception which was quite extraordinary

---

3   Lukács 1972b, p. xi.

4   Doyé 2005, p. 123; cf. for example Lukács 1972a, p. 221, n. 59.

5   Gmünder 1985, p. 9; cf. also Behrens and Hafner 1993, p. 91.

6   Dannemann 1997, p. 32. In his 'Preface to the New Edition' of *History and Class Consciousness*, Lukács writes of 'the idealism and utopianism of my revolutionary messianism' (Lukács 1972b, p. xv), a messianism whose 'intellectual passion' (Lukács 1972b, p. xiv) was the genesis of all his works.

7   Lukács 1972a, p. 168.

8   Tietz and Caysa 2005, p. 95.

9   Cf. Demirović 1999b, p. 35; cf. editorial note by Tiedemann (Adorno 2008, p. 252, n. 2). Michael Krätke argues that reading Marx's *Paris Manuscripts* following their initial publication in 1932 constituted another 'foundational educational experience' for the Frankfurt School (see Krätke 2004, p. 217). However, at least in Adorno's case, this would not have been true. For him, 'the young Marx was not a decisive influence' (Wiggershaus 1995, p. 5).

10 Heiniger 1990, p. 398.

11 See Adorno 2019m, p. 466.

at the time, so much so that it set a standard for philosophical aesthetics which has been maintained ever since'.[12]

History and Class Consciousness is not only concerned with class-consciousness, as its title suggests, but also with the concepts of second nature, commodity fetishism,[13] reification[14] and totality.[15] Following Marxian theory, Lukács seeks to put these concepts in the service of a renewed philosophy of practice. At the centre of his social critique stands the category of the commodity: while there were commodities in antiquity, the universality of the category of the commodity in developed capitalism, a category which by now 'shapes the entirety of reality',[16] is qualitatively new. As Lukács writes, '[t]he commodity can only be understood in its undistorted essence when it becomes the universal category of society as a whole'.[17] Moreover, when this happens, Lukács sees the arrival of an historical moment in which a knowledge capable of fundamentally transforming reality becomes possible. After all, 'when the commodity form has become universal, it must then also be possible to grasp the totality of reality',[18] provided that the knowing subject is itself able to adopt the commodity form and thus come to know itself. In any case, the experience

---

12   Adorno 2006c, p. 151; on the implicit critique that Adorno would later level against *The Theory of the Novel* in his *Aesthetic Theory* cf. Hohendahl 1981, p. 138.

13   'Marx's theory of commodity fetishism has only been understood insufficiently in the traditions of the labour movement and of Marxism. It plays a role neither in the theoretical considerations of Luxemburg and Kautsky, nor of Lenin. The reason for this is the agent-theoretical conception of ideology which reduces the latter to the ruling-class partisanship of the scholar. It is not until Lukács's *History and Class Struggle* [sic] (1923) that commodity fetishism is regarded as the quintessence of Marxism. Yet this concept underwent a personification in Lukács's work. Lukács conceives of it as a reification of human relationships which degrades the human being to a commodity, thereby alienating it from its human essence. The proletarians who grasp their alienation discover the human core behind the reified curtain. This is the condition of possibility for which the alienated human can return to his true essence. Lukács conducts the critique of commodity fetishism on the basis of anthropological essentialism' (Iber 2005, pp. 71–2; cf. Backhaus 2004b, p. 128).

14   Recommending the 'chapter on reification in *History and Class Consciousness* by Lukács' to Ernst Krenek, Adorno argues that it shows 'that the materialist method is suited to the deepest questions of philosophy – more so, I'm convinced, than the organologists of today' (letter from Adorno to Krenek, 7 October 1934 [Adorno and Krenek 1974, p. 47]).

15   Whereas Lukács's social analysis is based on a normative concept of totality, Adorno recognises social totality as objectively negative (cf. König and Markl 2001). As Adorno writes, '[t]otality is not an affirmative but rather a critical category' (Adorno 1976a, p. 12).

16   Scheible 1999, p. 58.

17   Lukács 1972, p. 86.

18   Scheible 1999, p. 58.

of being 'turned into a commodity'[19] is something which must be endured by the worker, whose

> immediate existence integrates him as a pure, naked object into the pro-
> duction process. Once this immediacy turns out to be the consequence of
> a multiplicity of mediations, once it becomes evident how much it pre-
> supposes, then the fetishistic forms of the commodity system begin to
> dissolve: in the commodity the worker recognises himself and his own
> relations with capital. Inasmuch as he is incapable in practice of raising
> himself above the role of object his consciousness is the *self-consciousness
> of the commodity*; or in other words it is the self-knowledge, the self-
> revelation of the capitalist society founded upon the production and
> exchange of commodities.

If the proletarian now 'becomes aware of himself as a commodity',[20] this self-knowledge already becomes practical because the proletarian recognises himself as 'identical subject-object, the subject of action',[21] or in other words, as the actual reproducer of the social order.

> [W]hen the worker knows himself as a commodity his knowledge is prac-
> tical. *That is to say, this knowledge brings about an objective structural
> change in the object of knowledge.* In this consciousness and through it the
> special objective character of labour as a commodity, its 'use-value' (i.e. its
> ability to yield surplus produce) which like every use-value is submerged
> without a trace in the quantitative exchange categories of capitalism, now
> awakens and becomes *social reality*. The special nature of labour as a
> commodity which in the absence of this consciousness acts as an unac-
> knowledged driving wheel in the economic process now objectifies itself
> by means of this consciousness. The specific nature of this kind of com-
> modity had consisted in the fact that beneath the cloak of the thing lay
> a relation between men, that beneath the quantifying crust there was a
> qualitative, living core. Now that this core is revealed it becomes pos-
> sible to recognise the fetish character *of every commodity* based on the
> commodity character of labour power: in every case we find its core, the
> relation between men, entering into the evolution of society.[22]

---

19   Lukács 1972, p. 166.
20   Lukács 1972, p. 168.
21   Lukács 1972, p. 149.
22   Lukács 1972, p. 169.

In this way, Lukács 'links the self-consciousness of the proletariat with perspectives which are world-historical in scope' by adopting the speculative conviction 'that the subjectivity of the subject consists of its ability to take being-in-itself from what is tangible, from what opposes it as existing in itself and outside of consciousness, and to idealise this being-in-itself and make it conscious, make it being-for-itself, so that in the end all otherness is abolished while knowledge and certainty become identical in the sense of absolute knowledge. This Hegelian notion of progress, according to which the idea encounters itself, is the progress of the world spirit at the final stage of the objective spirit – a world spirit whose rational and necessary course is world history'.[23] According to Lukács's eschatological vision, the proletariat will necessarily precipitate the telos of history once it causes the objective appearance of second nature to fall away.

However, the concept of class-consciousness is already highly problematic in Lukács's work insofar as it imputes the existence of the proletariat as a collective subject. In contrast to Marx, Lukács does not explain how proletarians become a proletariat with reference to the position of individuals relative to the means of production, but rather by borrowing Max Weber's assumption that the rationalisation of the labour-process would continue apace:[24] 'The fate of the worker becomes the fate of society as a whole; indeed, this fate must become universal as otherwise industrialisation could not develop in this direction' – that is, could never become 'rationally mechanised'. After all, the rational mechanisation of the labour-process 'depends on the emergence of the "free" worker who is freely able to take his labour-power to market and offer it for sale as a commodity "belonging" to him, a thing that he "possesses"'.[25] As convincing as this assumption may be, it does not itself imply, either logically or historically, that proletarians will join together and form a collective subject, which would require them to be conscious of themselves in the capitalist process of production. Lukács is only able to outline the logical synthesis of proletarians into his collective-subject proletariat by postulating the Com-

---

23   Doyé 2005, p. 137.

24   'Rationality can be understood as a central concept of the recent historical era, a period we call modernity. The concept of reification denotes the result of a miscarried, misdirected rationalisation – a notion which was initially preconceived in Hegel's concept of diremption: diremption for Hegel is a signature aspect of modernity, even though modernity is connected to the principle of self-conscious subjectivity, the bearer of which is reason; diremption therefore becomes the source of the need for a philosophy which elevates reason to understanding and thereby operates under the guiding concept of reconciliation' (Doyé 2005, p. 121; cf. Hegel 1977, p. 90).

25   Lukács 1972, pp. 90–1, cf. also p. 88.

munist Party as an intermediary between the two which would consolidate class-interest and convert it into an allegedly objective species-interest.[26] Yet the problem 'of the Lukácsian concept of an objective interest ... is that it is ambiguous insofar as a class-interest attributed thusly has its basis in real social relations, that is, is socially underpinned, while an alleged interest in emancipation requires premises from the philosophy of history and anthropology'.[27] Martin Blumentritt notes correctly that Lukács's version of proletarian thinking is in fact not at all 'the thinking of the proletariat, but rather of the idea of the proletariat'. The result of the latter mode of thinking is that 'the practical consequence of the dictatorship of the proletariat becomes not the proletarianisation of the state, but rather the nationalisation of the proletariat'.[28]

2   The Reflexive Form of False Objectivity

Second nature, an 'extremely important concept'[29] for Adorno, and one which Lukács himself adopts from Hegel,[30] is already employed by Lukács in *The Theory of the Novel*. Here, it refers to a social construct which appears natural;[31] it is the 'world of things created by man, yet lost to him'.[32] In *History and Class*

---

26   Cf. Jay 1977, pp. 127–8.

27   Behrens and Hafner 1993, p. 93, cf. p. 202, n. 28.

28   Blumentritt 1992, p. 299.

29   Adorno and Benjamin 1999, p. 101.

30   In § 4 of Hegel's *Elements of the Philosophy of Right*, second nature is described thusly: 'The basis [*Boden*] of right is the *realm of spirit* in general and its precise location and point of departure is the *will*; the will is *free*, so that freedom constitutes its substance and destiny [*Bestimmung*] and the system of right is the realm of actualized freedom, the world of spirit produced from within itself as a second nature' (Hegel 1991, p. 35, brackets in original; cf. also Doyé 2005, pp. 143–4).

31   As Lukács writes, '[t]he second nature, the nature of man-made structures, has no lyrical substantiality; its forms are too rigid to adapt themselves to the symbol-creating moment; the contend of the second nature, precipitated by its own laws, is too definite to be able to rid itself of those elements which, in lyric poetry, are bound to become essayistic; furthermore, these elements are so much at the mercy of laws, are so absolutely devoid of any sensuous valency of existence independent from laws, that without them they can only disintegrate into nothingness. This second nature is not dumb, sensuous and yet senseless like the first: it is a complex of senses – meanings – which has become rigid and strange, and which no longer awakens interiority; it is a charnel-house of long-dead interiorities; this second nature could only be brought to life if this were possible – by the metaphysical act of reawakening the souls which, in an early or ideal existence, created or preserved it; it can never be animated by another interiority' (Lukács 1974, p. 64).

32   Adorno 1984, p. 117.

Consciousness, this concept is further developed into a description of the modern state of society in which, 'on the one hand, men are constantly smashing, replacing and leaving behind them the "natural", irrational and actually existing bonds, while, on the other hand, they erect around themselves in the reality they have created and "made", a kind of second nature which evolves with exactly the same inexorable necessity as was the case earlier on with irrational forces of nature (more exactly: the social relations which appear in this form)'.[33]

Already from his reading of *History and Class Consciousness*, Adorno derives the idea of the *Selbstbeherrschung* of the modern individual, a term which can be translated into English as self-control or self-mastery, but also as self-domination. This idea constitutes a highly important insight for the further development of Adorno's Critical Theory. Judging by the handwritten comments and underlining in his copy of *History and Class Consciousness*, Adorno evidently studied the following longer passages especially intensively:

> What is of central importance [in the case of the basic phenomenon of reification] is that ... a man's own activity, his own labour becomes something objective and independent of him, something that controls him by virtue of an autonomy alien to man. There is both an objective and a subjective side to this phenomenon. Objectively a world of objects and relations between things springs into being (the world of commodities and their movements on the market). The laws governing these objects are indeed gradually discovered by man, but even so they confront him as invisible forces that generate their own power. The individual can use his knowledge of these laws to his own advantage, but he is not able to modify the process by his own activity. Subjectively – where the market economy has been fully developed – a man's activity becomes estranged from himself, it turns into a commodity which, subject to the non-human objectivity of the natural laws of society, must go its own way independently of man just like any consumer article. 'What is characteristic of the capitalist age', says Marx, 'is that in the eyes of the labourer himself labour-power assumes the form of a commodity belonging to him. On the other hand it is only at this moment that the commodity form of the products of labour becomes general'.[34]

---

33   Lukács 1972, p. 128. Together with Horkheimer, Adorno would later produce an analysis in *Dialectic of Enlightenment* which goes back even further: all the way back to prehistory, in order to use pre-social, or mythical relationships between nature and humans to decipher social relations themselves.

34   Lukács 1972, pp. 86–7; quoted from Marx 1982a, p. 274, n. 4.

In a margin next to this passage, Adorno notes that 'man "dominates" himself. "Revolutionary" lack of restraint initially – albeit incorrectly – yields the commodity-character of one's own productivity'.[35] For Adorno, the submission of human beings to society's so-called natural laws, that is, to a compulsion which they themselves have created, is the decisive element in Lukács's analysis of the all-encompassing process by which they are 'turned into a commodity'.

Lukács's analysis continues as follows:[36]

> the universality of the commodity form is responsible both objectively and subjectively for the abstraction of the human labour incorporated in commodities. (On the other hand, this universality becomes historically possible because this process of abstraction has been completed.) Objectively, in so far as the commodity form facilitates the equal exchange of qualitatively different objects, it can only exist if that formal equality is in fact recognised – at any rate in this relation, which indeed confers upon them their commodity nature. Subjectively, this formal equality of human labour in the abstract is not only the common factor to which the various commodities are reduced; it also becomes the real principle governing the actual production of commodities. Clearly, it cannot be our aim here to describe even in outline the growth of the modern process of labour, of the isolated, 'free' labourer and of the division of labour. Here we need only establish that labour, abstract, equal, comparable labour, measurable with increasing precision according to the time socially necessary for its accomplishment, the labour of the capitalist division of labour existing both as the presupposition and the product of capitalist production, is born only in the course of the development of the capitalist system. Only then does it become a category of society influencing decisively the objective form of things and people in the society thus emerging, their relation to nature and the possible relations of men to each other.[37]

In this passage, Lukács of course does not pursue 'in detail, as Marx does in *Capital*, how the money-form develops as the result of viewing the commodity analytically' but rather 'establishes as a basic insight in its own right that the "commodity-form" must be viewed as a "formal equality" which emerges from the abstracting reduction of heterogenous qualities into undifferentiated,

---

35   TWA, NB 422, pp. 98–9, legibility of the last word 'discarded' (*abgeworfen*) is uncertain.
36   The underlined passages in the following excerpt correspond to the underlining in Adorno's copy of *History and Class Consciousness* (TWA, NB 422).
37   Lukács 1972, pp. 87–8.

abstract labour'.[38] That being said, in view of Adorno's future deployment of the concept of reification, Lukács's last two sentences do appear programmatic if only the sections underlined by Adorno are read: 'Here we need ... [to] establish that labour ... measurable ... according to the time socially necessary for its accomplishment ... become[s] a category of society influencing decisively the objective form of things and people in the society thus emerging'. Yet Adorno has a correspondingly more thorough – which is to say, more radical – grasp of the implications of reification than Lukács:

> The commodity-form as total reification, including of knowledge and of the subject, renders the general forms of consciousness problematic. In contrast to Lukács's account, consciousness and subjectivity do not have to adhere to their own objective albeit alienated essence and interest for society to nevertheless ultimately arrive at a definitively rational reason. For *Adorno*, subjectivity and reason must turn against themselves and directly ... carry out *their own* critique.[39]

Various authors take the problem of reification as the centre of their social critiques.[40] However, in *Negative Dialectics*, Adorno himself rejects any theorist who imagines that 'in the dissolution of reification, of the [commodity-character], he possesses the philosophers' stone'. After all,

> reification itself is the reflexive form of false objectivity; centering theory around reification, a form of consciousness, makes the critical theory idealistically acceptable to the reigning consciousness and to the collective unconscious. This is what raised Marx's early writings – in contradistinction to *Das Kapital* – to their present popularity, notably with theologians.
>
> There is a good deal of irony in the fact that the brutal and primitive functionaries who more than forty years back damned Lukács as a heretic, because of the reification chapter in his important *History and Class Consciousness*, did sense the idealistic nature of his conception. We can no more reduce dialectics to reification than we can reduce it to any other isolated category, however polemical. The cause of human suffering, meanwhile, will be glossed over rather than denounced in the lament

---

38   Dannemann 1997, p. 46.
39   Engster 2006, p. 136.
40   Cf. for example Brandt 1981, especially p. 24.

about reification. The trouble is with the conditions that condemn mankind to impotence and apathy and would yet be changeable by human action; it is not primarily with people and with the way conditions appear to people. Considering the possibility of total disaster, reification is an epiphenomenon, and even more so is the alienation coupled with this reification, the subjective state of consciousness that corresponds to it.[41]

Here it can be seen that Adorno does not in fact take up the concept of 'the authentic individual', but rather 'holds alienation and reification as unsuitable concepts for a critical theory of society'[42] and 'attack[s] philosophical concentration on alienation and reification as a fashionable ideology, susceptible to religious usage; the cult of the works of the young Marx at the expense of *Capital*; anthropocentric conceptions of history, and the emollient rhetoric of humanism accompanying them'.[43] As Adorno warns in a letter to Wilhelm Alff,

> one has to be careful in turning 'to the *young* Marx'. It is no coincidence and not due to forgetfulness that Marx in his later development no longer expressly referred back to humanism, but instead completely remoulded the 'anthropological' concepts into economic-dialectical ones and did not crystallise something like a positive doctrine of the right life. I'm the last to fail to recognise that within this development itself lie quite dubious elements which find their expression in things such as the fetishisation of products and similar Russian abominations. But for all that, the young Marx is too popular among the religious socialists and those who believe that socialism has to be given a 'meaning', which then always simply amounts to ideology. I'm sure you know what I mean.[44]

However, from his reading of *History and Class Consciousness*, Adorno not only adopts the originally Hegelian conceptions of totality, reification and second nature, but also picks up a certain imprecision in his use of Marxist terminology. Such imprecision can be seen when Lukács identifies the 'transformation *of labour* into a commodity' as the cause of the removal of 'every "human" element from the immediate existence of the proletariat'[45] in one passage, only to shortly thereafter portray *the worker* himself 'as commodity, as ... at best

---

41   Adorno 2007b, p. 190.
42   Demirović 2004, p. 21; cf. Jay 1984, p. 66.
43   Anderson 1987, pp. 72–3.
44   Letter from Adorno to Wilhelm Alff, 29 August 1951 (TWA, Br 14/1).
45   Lukács 1972, p. 176, emphasis added.

a mechanical driving wheel in the machine'[46] of uninterrupted social reproduction. It bears noting that the claim that the worker turns into a commodity can be seen as deriving from an early formulation of Marx and Engels: 'in
the words of the *Communist Manifesto*, "these labourers, who must sell themselves piecemeal, are a commodity, like every other article of commerce"'.[47]
However, as Thomas Kuczynski correctly comments, if this assessment from
the *Manifesto* is valid, then 'either labour or the worker would need to be sold',
whereas, as Marx would later demonstrate in his critique of political economy,
'neither in fact occurs'.[48] Rather, it is labour-*power* which becomes a commodity
under capital. Thus, if the worker really does 'see through' himself or his labour
(or both simultaneously), as Lukács anticipates, he actually crassly misunderstands economic reality – precisely because he does *not* see the fundamental
mediation between labour and capital, which is founded on the exchange of
the commodity of labour-power for wages. 'Lukács's reckless use of the expression "the commodity of labour" and his implicit equation of it with the expression "the commodity of labour-power" shows that he is apparently unable to
understand Marx's distinction between the substance and the economic form
of labour, and is thus unable to define the specific character of the capitalist
production of commodities with respect to reification in the Marxian sense'.[49]

3   My Ramshackle Luxury Hotel

Adorno's rejection of Lukács – his development, as Martin Jay put it, into
the latter's 'most radical antipode'[50] – began in the spring of 1925. While living in Vienna to study composition with Alban Berg, Adorno had a lengthy
encounter with 'the Marxist thinker Lukács, ... whom, as you know', – Adorno
writes in a letter to Berg – 'I greatly revere'. However, their conversation ended
for Adorno in disillusionment, presumably in the most literal sense of the
word: 'in intellectual terms communication proved impossible, which of course
pained me particularly in the case of Lukács, who has had a more profound
intellectual influence on me than almost anyone else'.[51] In a letter to Siegfried

46   Lukács 1972, p. 181.
47   Lukács 1972, p. 173; quoted from Marx and Engels 2010, p. 73.
48   Kuczynski 1990, p. 211.
49   Tietz and Caysa 2005, p. 107. According to Doyé, 'Lukács' susceptibility to the concept of
      reification has its basis in the fact that Lukács largely ignores the Marxian ... analysis of
      the value-form' (Doyé 2005, p. 132, n. 22).
50   Jay 1977, p. 117.
51   Letter from Adorno to Alban Berg, 21 June 1925 (Adorno and Berg 2005, p. 9).

Kracauer written shortly after the meeting, Adorno gives a more detailed account of the content of his discussion with Lukács:

> I sensed at once that he was beyond any kind of possible human relation-
> ship, and so I too behaved accordingly and maintained a certain reserve
> during our conversation, which lasted over three hours. Our exchange,
> therefore, assumed the form of an interview rather than a conversation.
> ... first of all, he roundly disavowed the theory of the novel, saying that
> it was 'idealistic and mythological'. He contrasted it with the 'conversion
> into content' of history by means of Marxist dialectics. To my objection
> that this too was idealism (a criticism which he did not understand prop-
> erly), he retorted that 1) it was precisely by means of dialectics that the
> object was 'included and created in its nature of being in and for itself'
> (something which I shall never comprehend); 2) Nature would only be
> perceptible in a 'classless society'. ... He declared himself in favour of
> Feuerbach's anthropomorphism, which left only because Hegel's 'logic of
> appearances' our of consideration – i.e. his claim that because God had
> operated as a historical entity, he was real (terrible!). ... He did shock me
> at one point when he declared to me that, in his conflict with the Third
> International, his opponents were in the right, in actual terms, and in dia-
> lectical ones all that was required of him was an absolute approach to
> dialectics. His human greatness and the tragedy of her reversal of fortune
> are rooted in this nonsensical error.[52]

---

52   Letter from Adorno to Siegfried Kracauer, 17–18 June 1925 (Adorno and Kracauer 2020,
      pp. 50–1). In a subsequent letter to Kracauer, Adorno expresses his 'annoyance with
      Lukács' (letter from Adorno to Kracauer, 29 June 1925 [Adorno and Kracauer 2020, p. 53])
      following the meeting, which a letter from the following year shows was not their only
      one. Therein, Adorno reports that he had 'two conversations with Lukács, from whom I
      wrung a lot, which does not take much effort, however. Conversation without brilliance –
      how bored you would have been!' (letter from Adorno to Kracauer, 4 May 1926 [Adorno
      and Kracauer 2020, p. 80]). A 'small Lukács archive' set up by Adorno and consisting of
      'drafts of dramas by Lukács and of lecture notebooks, of letters from Paul Ernst, of piano
      receipts, library loan slips and letters from landladies, as well as ... pre-World War love let-
      ters' (Benseler et al. 1970, pp. 5–6, cf. p. 9, n. 12) also likely dates from this period. In another
      letter to Kracauer composed some years later, Adorno writes upon re-reading *History and
      Class Consciousness* that the book had 'leaves a shocking number of loose ends and dif-
      fuses a kind of Heidelberg local colour in an unbearable fashion; it is only a step to [Karl]
      Mannheim, most of all in the wholly abstract conception of the concept of ideology which
      cannot be handled in this schematic way of deducing it in idealistic terms. In spite of this
      there are a few outstanding passages in his work. These days, though, we have advanced a
      considerable way beyond that' (letter from Adorno to Kracauer, 12 May 1930 [Adorno and
      Kracauer 2020, p. 140]).

Adorno takes particular issue with 'the idea of a dialectic which is immanent within "the object" itself and has a correspondingly trans-subjective character'.[53] He would later maintain that 'primacy of the ob[ject]' is possible 'only *in* dialectics'. Dialectics is not a thing-in-itself, and neither is the category of mediation. While the 'possibility of a negative dialectics depends on the proof of the primacy of the object', this proof 'cannot be an absolute principle for dialectics or a reprise for naïve realism: it is valid exclusively in the interrelationship. If the primacy of the object were to break free of the dialectic and be positively postulated – accompanied by the triumphant howls of the complicit – then philosophy would regress to the fatuous dogma of the reproduction or reflection [of reality] that we see in the late writings of Georg Lukács'.[54]

In any case, already in Adorno and Lukács's conversation, personal aversions and theoretical differences emerge which would never again be overcome. Here, one can discern not only 'the germ of Lukács's future rejection of ontological realism',[55] but also Adorno's recurring 'critique of Lukács's "party-conformism"'.[56] As late as his course *Lectures on Negative Dialectics* from the winter semester of 1965–6, Adorno brings up his encounter with Lukács to clarify the differences between their respective positions:

This mechanism of coercion binds subjectivity and thought into the objectivity that stands opposed to it. In view of this dependency and of what we might call the logic of the facts, a logic that leads to the triumph of objectivity, it is not obvious why an insight into this mechanism should mean that this objectivity must itself be in the right. The situation suggests pangs of conscience imposed from outside. This is something I experienced most tellingly in my dealings with a Hegelian Marxist in my youth, namely with Georg Lukács, who at the time had just quarrelled with his party. In connection with that he explained to me that the party was in the right, even though his ideas and arguments were better than the party's. The party was in the right because it embodied the object-

---

53   Tertulian 2005, p. 70.
54   Adorno 2008, pp. 154–6, brackets in original.
55   Tertulian 2005, p. 70.
56   Müller-Doohm 2000, p. 227, n. 37; cf. also Jay 1984, pp. 28–9. Adorno would later write that Lukács 'took the crudest criticisms from the Party hierarchy to heart, twisting Hegelian motifs and turning them against himself; and for decades on end he laboured in a series of books and essays to adapt his obviously unimpaired talents to the unrelieved sterility of Soviet claptrap' (Adorno 2006c, p. 151).

ive state of history, while his own position, which was more advanced
both in his view and in terms of the sheer logic of the ideas involved,
lagged behind that objective state of affairs. I believe that I do not have
to spell out for you the implications of such a statement. It would imply
simply that, with the assistance of the dialectic, whatever has greater success, whatever comes to prevail, to be generally accepted, has a higher
degree of truth than the consciousness that can see through its fraudulent
nature. In actual fact, ideology in the Eastern bloc is largely determined
by this idea. A further implication is that mind would amputate itself, that
it would abdicate its own freedom and simply adapt to the needs of the
big battalions [*sich einfach an die stärkeren Bataillone anpaßt.*]. To accept
such a course of action does not appear possible to me.[57]

Here, Lukács appears as an apologist for the Hegelian understanding of history,
as well as for the process by which the universal asserts itself at the expense of
the particular, the identical at the expense of the non-identical.

In turn, Lukács strikes back against Adorno with a praxis-philosopher's
scorn in the 1963 reissue of *The Theory of the Novel*. In its new preface, Lukács
accuses Adorno – the intellectual who maintains 'that a theory is much more
capable of having practical consequences owing to the strength of its own
objectivity than if it had subjected itself to praxis from the start'[58] – of having
'taken up residence in the "Grand Hotel Abyss" … a beautiful hotel, equipped
with every comfort, on the edge of an abyss, of nothingness, of absurdity. And
the daily contemplation of the abyss between excellent meals or artistic enter-
tainments, can only heighten the enjoyment of the subtle comforts offered'.[59]
Unsurprisingly upset by this, Adorno writes to Kracauer that Lukács 'blackens
my name in the most ridiculous and servile fashion by calling me a nihilist'.[60]
'Well where should I live?' Adorno asks in a subsequent note:

---

57   Adorno 2008, pp. 16–17. Adorno's allegation that Lukács's philosophy 'sides with the big
      guns' [*marschiert mit den stärkeren Bataillonen*] is already contained in *Hegel: Three Stud-
      ies*. There, he alleges that Lukács revives 'one of Hegel's most dubious theses, that of the
      rationality of the real', thereby adopting 'the judgement of a reality that always destroys
      what could be different' (Adorno 1993d, pp. 83–4; cf. also Adorno and von Haselberg 1983,
      p. 102).
58   Adorno 2002b, p. 15.
59   Lukács 1974, p. 22.
60   Adorno and Kracauer 2020, pp. 398–9. Following his death, Adorno was again accused of
      choosing nihilism over hope, this time from Bloch: 'There's been enough nihilism from
      Adorno. He may pay lip service to hope, but that alone doesn't paint a positive picture'
      (Bloch 1975, p. 234).

In the must of shelteredness? I'd prefer that to my ramshackle luxury hotel. Its luxury is nothing other than happiness in articulating the utmost negativity; and one is begrudged even that.[61]

Adorno's polemical invocation of shelteredness – a word which, after the events to which history had just borne witness, he regards as obsolete and even obscene[62] – alludes to Heidegger's notion of fundamental ontology, which he accuses Lukács of having appropriated as early as his 1949 essay 'Heidegger redivivus'.[63] For Adorno, 'Heidegger redivivus' defames 'the attempt to mediate between subject and object – the core of all dialectics, and a core which is most certainly taken up by Marxian dialectics'[64] – and relapses 'into reified consciousness out of fear of ontology'.[65] Lukács's critique, Adorno claims, constitutes 'a textbook case of the inadequacy of transcendental critique' because it must first adopt a normative standpoint: in this case, that 'an idealist thinks being is brought forth by consciousness', whereas dialectical materialism, in keeping with its maxims,[66] assumes 'that being has priority over consciousness'.[67] With this one-sided decision in favour of the primacy of being having been made in advance, the dialectical mediation between being and consciousness which is only made comprehensible by theory is replaced by a simple choice between materialism or idealism. According to Adorno, to completely and fully side with the objective while discounting the subjective as peripheral is simultaneously 'to mock the dialectical principle itself, because without a subject, without an element of reflection and negativity, discourse on the dialectical process becomes hopelessly entangled'. Given that Lukács lacks such an element of negativity, Adorno argues, he falls victim to an originary philo-

---

61   Adorno 2003k, p. 36.
62   Cf. Adorno 1973, pp. 26–7.
63   See Lukács 1949.
64   Adorno 2003a, p. 252.
65   Adorno 2003a, p. 255.
66   As Adorno notes, '[t]he Marxian theory that being has priority over consciousness precisely does not want to be understood ontologically but rather as an expression of a negative, namely of the supremacy of reification, of the relations of production into which human beings "enter involuntarily"' (Adorno 2003a, pp. 252–3).
67   Adorno 2003a, p. 251. The relevant passage from Lukács reads as follows: 'We know: Heidegger and his followers would above all protest vehemently against label of idealism here. Yet Heidegger keeps claiming to be neither idealist nor materialist, but rather to have discovered a relationship to being which stands beyond this alleged dilemma. What he consistently means by this dilemma is the clear, sharp and correct Engelian juxtaposition: a materialist believes that being has priority over consciousness, an idealist thinks being is brought forth by consciousness' (Lukács 1949, p. 44).

sophy (*Ursprungsphilosophie*), or in other words, to 'precisely the very reified
thinking to which he once dedicated such vivid analyses in *History and Class
Consciousness*', almost as if 'the discourse on dialectics within Marxism were
not at all meant to be taken seriously. Indeed, any attempt to view the relationship between subject and object dialectically – the only possible method to
move beyond philosophical reification theoretically – is banished'.[68] Adorno
sees Lukács' formerly unorthodox Marxism as having been betrayed to official party *Diamat* (the Stalinist abbreviation for dialectical materialism),[69] with
objective problems being decided from above to benefit a doctrine rather than
thought through. For Adorno, Lukács has come to embody 'the incarnation of a
theoretical regression following the conforming of his thought to the demands
of Communist orthodoxy'.[70]

Following the publication of Lukács's book *The Young Hegel* in 1948, Adorno
writes of his evidently irrevocable disappointment with its author[71] in a letter
to Thomas Mann:

---

68   Adorno 2003a, pp. 251–2.
69   Adorno becomes more explicit at the end of his note 'Ad Lukács' when he criticises the
      language of Lukács's essay on Heidegger: 'When Lukács quite rightly counters the blown-
      out lie about the authenticity of youth, that abhorrent residue of the youth movement
      which still haunts Heidegger's solemn expectorations, he says of the young Germans who
      participated in Hitler's military campaigns that they "in the best case were witnesses, pass-
      ive participants in the plunder and murder, the rapes of women and children, etc. on the
      part of Hitler's army ...". The "best case" is a bloody joke, the "etc." after the "rapes", however,
      followed by the bureaucratic "on the part of", does conceptually to the victims through the
      inhumanity of discourse yet again what the fascist hordes committed in reality. It's a mat-
      ter of whether the atrocities perpetrated by the German army exceeded what militarism
      brings about everywhere pending the beheading of the last marshal; but it is telling that
      Lukács's outrage limits itself to the army without referring to the SS, which carried out the
      most gruesome work, or to the extermination camps. He is allowed to speak out against
      the Wehrmacht precisely because it was the enemy of the Red Army; yet the security ser-
      vice is taboo, lest one stumble upon subversive analogies' (Adorno 2003a, p. 256; quoted
      from Lukács 1949, p. 39).
70   Tertulian 2005, p. 71.
71   While on a ship to New York, Horkheimer wrote the following to Adorno in Europe regard-
      ing *The Young Hegel*: 'Yet the people have the same hard faces. I don't think this changes
      with the form of a society. People have to coerce people to coerce nature, otherwise nature
      coerces people. This is the concept of society. Our specific task is to recognise it precisely
      in its contingency, without positing spirit like Hegel. Critique of sociology is critique of
      the entire concept of society to which all have been beholden since Hegel, even the 'good
      Europeans'. The narrow-mindedness of the Lukács book consists in its complete reduction
      of Hegel to this concept. Yet with all that, one has the feeling that society in the concise
      sense has been played out today. What everyone understood by it actually doesn't exist at
      all anymore – it exists as little as Europe does. As society elevated itself to a science, soci-

I am afraid I must regard Lukács's big book on Hegel, which I have worked through from beginning to end, as among my most depressing recent experiences. One can hardly credit such reification of consciousness in the very man who coined this concept in the first place. Heidegger's essay in *Off the Beaten Track* on the *Phenomenology of Spirit* is almost dialectical by comparison.[72]

On the same topic, Adorno expresses himself even more harshly in a letter to Peter von Haselberg:

> *Ad vocem* dialectics, so it is that there are indeed now two more or less official statements from the Communist and fascist wings: from Lukács the tome on the young Hegel, rubbish in which the essential achievements of the young Hegel are depicted as his excerpting of [James] Steuart and Adam Smith, and which otherwise oscillates between the party-bureaucratic necessity of reclaiming Hegel as a great man, and the equally official necessity of identifying him as having been refuted by Marx and refuting him again and without any grace. Compared with this, Heidegger's chapter in *Off the Beaten Track* at least displays the rigorous exertion of the concept (*Anstrengung des Begriffs*),[73] even though the reappraisal of Hegel as an ontologist is just as nonsensical as the attempt to construe the economic motif as his central motif.[74]

---

ety disappeared within science. But the coercion has remained' (letter from Horkheimer to Adorno, 8 May 1949 [Adorno and Horkheimer 2005, pp. 248–9]).

72 Letter from Adorno to Mann, 3 June 1950 (Adorno and Mann 2006, p. 47). In his lecture course *Ontology and Dialectics* from 1960–61, Adorno brings up Heidegger's objectivism, which, Adorno argues, 'effectively neutralizes the subject'. Having done so, Adorno continues, this objectivism 'has led to a situation in which all of these aspects which originally provoked such interest in this philosophy now have completely retreated into the background. Hence this thinking profits to this day from a certain interest, namely the interest in responding to essential questions, which it has actually long since ceased to respond to them. There is something very peculiar here which reveals a strange cultural and historical parallel with another figure who is radically opposed to Heidegger and yet in several respects not entirely unlike him. I am talking about Lukács, who in all work from around 1925 onwards, if not slightly earlier, has completely retracted and repudiated all the things to which he owes his intellectual reputation. Yet this turn has done nothing to damage this reputation. On the contrary, the reputation has now been transferred to products which no longer justify anything of the kind' (Adorno 2019h, pp. 142–3).

73 Translator's note: cf. Hegel 2018, p. 36: 'What thus matters to the *study* of *science* is that one take the rigorous exertion of the concept upon oneself'.

74 Letter from Adorno to von Haselberg, 23 May 1950 (TWA, Br 599/9). The aptness of Adorno's classification of Heidegger is supported by a letter from 1966 in which the latter

In a report produced for Horkheimer[75] upon reading *The Young Hegel*,[76] Adorno draws the following conclusion:

> Lukács sees himself faced with double necessity of both having to appropriate the 'great thinker' Hegel *directly* for economic materialism and, because Marx refuted him, having to refute him again. Thus, good and bad marks are given to him alternately. However, out of fear of the mandarins [i.e., the party functionaries], Lukács doesn't dare to search for the materialist motifs in Hegelian logic and metaphysics themselves, but rather clings to that which is more or less excerpted from classical national economy and is overjoyed when the application of the dialectical method in the subject area of economy occasionally yields results which are reminiscent of Marx and Engels.[77]

Lukács's 1954 book *The Destruction of Reason* also plays a significant role in the dispute between himself and Adorno, who claimed it was actually a crass manifestation of 'the destruction of Lukács's own'.[78] Among other things, this work portrays Nietzsche as the 'founder of irrationalism in the imperialist period':[79] as Lukács argues, '[w]hat determined Nietzsche's particular position in the development of modern irrationalism, was partly the historical situation at the time of his appearance' – something doubtless true of every theoretical posi-

---

complains about 'Wiesengrund-Adorno' having undertaken 'to smear me'. The recipient of this letter, Ernst Jünger, would have understood what Heidegger was implying here (Heidegger and Jünger 2016, p. 37). For his own part, Adorno responded to antisemites of this sort with remarkable composure: 'When one adds to my name Adorno the name Wiesengrund which I went by earlier, that may well be meant antisemitically. But I myself have never denied my previous name, I took the maiden name of my mother only because the other was unpronounceable in America, and I can't bring myself to take offence at being called by my father's name' (letter from Adorno to Hans Naumann, 22 November 1955 [TWA, Br 1069/5]).

75   According to the Theodor W. Adorno Archiv, the untitled two-page typescript was written in 1949 or at the beginning of 1950; on this report cf. also Tertulian 1984. The report is reprinted in its entirety in Braunstein and Duckheim 2015, pp. 50–2.

76   In 1950 Adorno writes to Hermann Lübbe about Lukács's 'schoolmasterly verbosity': 'The content of the whole tome [*The Young Hegel*], which I've read through from start to finish, could have been presented comfortably in a 40-page journal article if Mr Lukács didn't need to stage such a delicate performance (*Eiertanz*) to avoid losing his head over some of those statements' (letter from Adorno to Hermann Lübbe, 18 January 1955 [Braunstein and Duckheim 2015, p. 53]).

77   Adorno quoted in Braunstein and Duckheim 2015, p. 52, brackets in original.

78   Adorno 2006c, p. 152.

79   This is the title of the third chapter of *The Destruction of Reason* (see Lukács 1980, p. 309).

tion – 'and partly his unusual personal gifts'. From this specific 'historical situation' arose for Nietzsche 'a favourable opportunity to conjecture and to solve in mythical form – on the reactionary bourgeoisie's terms – the main problems of the subsequent period'. Yet here Lukács disregards the fact that Nietzsche could only become the 'leading philosopher'[80] of reaction because reaction distorted him into his opposite, misconstruing him as its prophet and even as an intellectual precursor of National Socialism.[81] According to Adorno, rather than side with Nietzsche – who was horrified by *völkisch* Germanness and anti-semitism[82] – Lukács refers to him, 'in the condescending tones of a provincial Wilhelminian school inspector, as a man "of above-average abilities". Under the mantle of an ostensibly radical critique of society [Lukács] surreptitiously reintroduced the most threadbare clichés of the very conformism which that social criticism had once attacked'.[83] Thus, Nietzsche is portrayed as possessing a not insignificant gift, only to immediately thereafter and all the more resolutely be grouped together with those against whom he consistently albeit unsuccessfully philosophised throughout his entire life. 'Apparently nineteenth-century intellectual history only knows two kinds of poets and thinkers', writes Henning Ottmann in his critique of Lukács's Nietzsche critique: 'the apologists for capitalism on the one hand, and the followers of socialism on the other'.[84] Because Lukács is 'blind for dialectical reversals' in this matter, he must systematically counterpose Nietzsche to reason, which for its own part is viewed as 'shin[ing] in the bright light of democracy and progress'.[85]

When Lucien Goldmann asks Adorno at the beginning of the 1960s why he is so intent on attacking Lukács given their quite similar positions, Adorno responds as follows:

> Regarding the person of Lukács: it was not I who first directed a sharp attack against him, but rather he who attacked and distorted me simul-

---

80   Lukács 1980, pp. 314–15.

81   Cf. Montinari 2003.

82   Cf. for example the following note from late in Nietzsche's life: 'Ah what a relief a Jew is among German horned cattle! ... The Messrs. antisemites underestimate this. What actually distinguishes a Jew from an antisemite: the Jew knows *that* he lies *when* he lies; the antisemite doesn't know that he always lies' (Nietzsche 1999, p. 580); cf. also especially Brömsel 2000.

83   Adorno 2006c, p. 152.

84   Ottmann 1984, p. 571.

85   Ottmann 1984, pp. 573–4. In a posthumous work from the materials for *The Destruction of Reason* Lukács defends the thinkers 'of the unstoppability of human progress' against Nietzsche's conception of history (Lukács 2004, p. 12).

taneously. If you take a look at my long essay from the second volume of *Notes to Literature* ['Reconciliation under Duress'], you will see expressed my respect for the works of his which you also esteem highly, and you will realise that I afford this respect to him as a person. Of course, this cannot change the fact that I regard his later works, and above all the book *The Destruction of Reason*, as pure rubbish, and I can't imagine that we wouldn't agree here. Yet I think that these works – you'll understand what I mean – have retroactive power and also subtly affect much of the early works. The concept of the meaningful era, which summarily disregards – from the elevated vantage point of his philosophy of history – all of humanity's suffering in periods of closed society, is already in a way the model of what even in his orthodox Communist phase could most fittingly be called right-wing Hegelianism. I do not exaggerate when I tell you that my experience of Lukács's early writings, above all of his *The Theory of the Novel*, essentially brought me to philosophy, and I will certainly never forget that about him. But on the other hand, the limits of these works are showing themselves quite clearly today – in the novel theory the romantic *laudatio temporis acta*, in *History and Class Consciousness* the metaphysical glorification of the party as the world spirit.[86]

In later years, the significance of *History and Class Consciousness* for Adorno would become entirely historical. In his lecture course *'Fragen der Dialektik (Questions of Dialectics)'* from the winter semester of 1963–4, he refers to it as 'the most important Marxist publication on Hegel':

[it] is, and this chapter is quite interesting, the attempt, one could indeed say, of a maximal Hegelianisation of Marxian dialectics, and it is quite peculiar that precisely in this book the closest connection was forged between apparently idealist theses and what are officially professed to be extreme Communist positions .... Let me say straight away that the universality which is derived from the concept of reification precisely in this book, and the transmission of the problem of the concepts of reification and alienation to the broader field of epistemology, are eminently fruitful, and that hardly anyone who has never once learned what happens to the concept of reification in this book by Lukács can seriously reflect upon questions of dialectics. On the other hand, let me say that precisely the

---

86   Letter from Adorno to Lucien Goldmann, 15 October 1963 (Braunstein and Duckheim 2015, p. 45).

overdone Hegelianism, or in other words, what one could call the idealistic extreme of this book, led to the highly outlandish construction of the
Communist Party – which in Lukács's later works is still to some extent
identified with the world spirit – along with all the disastrous political
consequences you know of.[87]

In a 1968 seminar transcript, Adorno brings up *History and Class Consciousness* once again. Here, he develops the argument that while Lukács 'believed
in 1922–3 that revolution was imminent, he had not really comprehended the
problem of essence and appearance, of objective class-situation and subjective class-consciousness. The accusation of idealism refers above all to the fact
that Lukács, following Hegel, apparently believed that the Hegelian world spirit
had possessed the proletariat: moreover, because its turn had objectively come,
the proletariat would automatically also become the subject of history and of
revolution'. Adorno is just as unwilling to participate in this idealisation as he is
to abstain from the concept of class, for '[n]either should the proletariat (in the
sense of a straightforward identification of subjective and objective situation)
be fetishised, not the category of "class" simply abandoned'.[88]

Adorno's early work largely adopts Lukácsian social critique's focus on the
commodity-form. As will now be seen, this is made evident 'by both his 1936
"On Jazz" and 1938 "On the Fetish-Character in Music and the Regression of
Listening", two works of music criticism in which Adorno becomes the first
Marxist theoretician following Lukács to harness the possibilities of commod-
ity-form analysis'.[89]

---

87   Adorno 2021b, pp. 19–20; cf. Braunstein, and Duckheim 2015, pp. 58–9.
88   Adorno 2021a, vol. 4, p. 544.
89   Breuer 1985, p. 24.

CHAPTER 3

Objection to the *Intérieur* and the Sociology of Interiority

> We shall work our way laboriously through wild hedges
> and thick underbrush, like the unfortunate suitors
> of the Sleeping Beauty, to find at last –
>
> E. MARLITT, Gold Elsie

∴

1 A World That Comes into Focus as a Mere Commodity

In 1927, Adorno submitted *Der Begriff des Unbewußten in der transzendentalen Seelenlehre* (*The Concept of the Unconscious in the Transcendental Theory of Mind*)[1] for consideration as a habilitation – the post-doctoral manuscript one must write in Germany to teach one's own academic research at the university level, and thus to pursue a career as a professor. This was all for naught: the work was 'determined to be too insubstantial and withdrawn by Adorno'.[2] Interestingly, however, its 'concluding remarks' are already 'committed to Marxism ..., a Marxism, of course, which to some extent Adorno has not yet completely processed'.[3] Compared with 'the framework of transcendental-philosophical preconditions' Adorno had imposed upon himself and faithfully followed until then, these remarks constitute a fundamental break occurring 'immediate-

---

1 This work, which was never published by Adorno himself, can now be found in Volume 1 of the *Gesammelte Schriften* (Adorno 2003f).

2 Wiggershaus 1987, p. 17. Adorno submitted this manuscript to Hans Cornelius, who previously had accepted his dissertation. Cornelius, the founder of an 'immanent-philosophical approach of strict epistemology between neo-Kantianism and phenomenology' (Lang 1995, p. 8), expresses a negative opinion of Adorno's work in an assessment written to the faculty of philosophy at the University of Frankfurt: 'I must therefore submit that Mr Wiesengrund be advised to withdraw his application, as his work, in its present form at any rate, does not meet the necessary requirements' (quoted in Maaser 2003, pp. 50–1).

3 Pettazzi 1983, p. 33.

ly within the text' and facilitating a critique of ideology also present in Adorno's later works.[4]

Regarding the predominant theories of the unconscious at the time, Adorno assigns them an ideological function within the general sphere of the social and the particular sphere of the economic:

> These theories of the dominant mode of economics, and of the suprem-
> acy of the economic in general, primarily seek to distract when they attest
> that, in addition to economic forces, there are other equally potent forces
> which are independent of consciousness in every sense, and thus free
> from the economic tendency towards rationalisation. That is, they seek to
> distract when they attest that islands remain to which the individual can
> retreat to escape economic competition. Such realities existing independ-
> ently from the economic process of production are held to be nothing
> other than the unconscious powers of the mind, powers into which one
> only need retreat to find respite from economic coercion through con-
> templation or enjoyment, as if they were summer resorts for one's con-
> sciousness.[5]

Adorno sees the theory of the unconscious as both having a sedative function, and as being unable to account for the way in which this function is
socially mediated. Rejecting this and anticipating later developments in Critical Theory – which would come to view 'scholarship as one force of production
among others in society, and as intertwined with relations of production'[6] –
he defines the general function of theory as 'always itself social', and therefore
as 'based in social relations'.[7] While Adorno's 1924 doctoral dissertation[8] 'unreservedly adopts the version of transcendental idealism espoused by [his doc-

---

4 Alker 2007, p. 55.
5 Adorno 2003f, p. 318.
6 Letter from Adorno to Horkheimer, 31 March 1969 (Theodor W. Adorno Archiv 2003, p. 292).
7 Adorno 2003f, pp. 317–18.
8 Like *Der Begriff des Unbewußten in der transzendentalen Seelenlehre*, Adorno's doctoral dissertation would remain unpublished during his lifetime. The fact that he never submitted either
   text for publication later in life was 'not accidental, not due to a lack of opportunity to do so
   ..., but rather because they appeared to him to be lacking only shortly after their composition'
   (Tiedemann 2003a, p. 381). The dissertation is now located in Adorno's *Gesammelte Schriften*
   under the title *Die Transzendenz des Dinglichen und Noematischen in Husserls Phänomenologie* (*The Transcendence of the Material and the Noematic in Husserl's Phenomenology*) (Adorno
   2003h).

toral advisor] Hans Cornelius',[9] his would-be habilitation marks a final break with the conventions of transcendental philosophy. Adorno had become a proponent of a materialist critique of society and economy, albeit a critique which had yet to be articulated.[10]

After his first habilitation attempt, Adorno composed *Kierkegaard: Construction of the Aesthetic* in 1929–30 and saw the manuscript accepted in 1931.[11] Finding it to be an 'extremely interesting and most significant piece of work',[12] Walter Benjamin claims in a letter to Adorno that it left him with the impression that 'there are still sentences which allow one individual to stand in for and represent another'.[13] A laudatory review written later by Benjamin would prove strikingly prophetic:

> This book contains much in a small space. The author's subsequent writings may someday emerge from it. It is, in any case, one of those rare first books in which inspiration manifests itself in the guise of criticism.[14]

Benjamin's endorsement of this debut work is not entirely coincidental: beyond its original Adornian ideas, *Kierkegaard* bears the lasting impression of Benjamin's own *The Origin of German Tragic Drama*.[15] Originally written as a habilitation and submitted unsuccessfully in 1925 – 'not least due to the antisemitism of the German university'[16] – to the faculty of philosophy at the University of Frankfurt (where Adorno's own first habilitation attempt would also end in failure), *The Origin of German Tragic Drama* was published as a book in 1928. '[A]mong Benjamin's completed works probably the most substantial',[17] it exerted an immense influence on Adorno in the 1930s.[18] In a letter

---

9   Tiedemann 2003a, p. 382.

10   Cf. ibid.

11   Cf. Adorno 2003t, p. 263.

12   Letter from Benjamin to Adorno, 1 December 1932 (Adorno and Benjamin 1999, p. 20).

13   Letter from Benjamin to Adorno, 1 December 1932 (Adorno and Benjamin 1999, p. 21); cf. Buck-Morss 1977, pp. 268–9, n. 23.

14   Benjamin 2005c, p. 705.

15   Benjamin's book is mentioned explicitly at one point in Adorno's debut (Adorno 1999a, p. 62).

16   Menke 2006, p. 210; on Benjamin's rejected habilitation attempt cf. Lindner 1985.

17   Tiedemann and Schweppenhäuser 2001, p. 868. In contrast, Adorno writes to Horkheimer in 1937 that he 'still regard[s] Benjamin's work on Goethe's *Elective Affinities* as his best work' (letter from Adorno to Horkheimer, 25 January 1937 [Adorno and Horkheimer 2003b, p. 281]; cf. Benjamin 2004b).

18   On the particular influence of the book's 'Epistemo-Critical Prologue' on Adorno's treatment of questions of representation cf. Lehr 2000, pp. 24–33, 50–62.

written after having read Adorno's book on Kierkegaard, Gershom Scholem describes it to Benjamin as 'a sublime plagiarism of your thought'.[19]

Adorno would dedicate his first two semesters of teaching respectively to works by the two most important theorists for him at the time. In the summer semester of 1932, he held a seminar on Benjamin's *The Origin of German Tragic Drama*,[20] followed by a seminar in the winter semester on Lukács's *The Theory of the Novel*.[21]

As Susan Buck-Morss notes regarding the theoretical background of Adorno's engagement with Kierkegaard,

> Kierkegaard's critique of Hegel was the bourgeois alternative to that of Marx. Although both rejected Hegel's identity theory because it lost sight of lived reality, Kierkegaard rested his case on the reality of individual existence, whereas for Marx existence was a social category. For Kierkegaard, the riddle of philosophy was ontological: the meaninglessness of human existence.[22]

As an author's note in the new German edition attests, *Kierkegaard* addresses a constantly prevalent motif in Adorno's later work: that of 'the critique of the domination of nature and of the reason which dominates nature, that of reconciliation with nature and of the self-consciousness of spirit as an element of nature'.[23] While the ideology-critical element of the rejected habilitation only emerges at its very end, and in a quasi-underhanded manner as something external to be considered from the perspective of transcendental philosophy, a critique articulated in a Marxist vocabulary – or in what was at the time really a Lukácsian vocabulary – occupies a central position in *Kierkegaard*. From a socio-critical perspective, Adorno rejects Kierkegaard's ethics and their invocation of the Christian motif of neighbourly love, arguing that to love thy neighbour is a meaningless notion 'when human relations are so preformed by the domination of exchange-value, the division and commodity form of labor that one "neighbor" can no more respond spontaneously to the other for more than an instant than the individual's kindness suffices to do him any good, let alone

19   Letter from Scholem to Benjamin, 24 October 1933 (Benjamin and Scholem 1992, p. 84).
20   Some of the transcripts from this seminar have been preserved and can be found in Adorno 1995a, pp. 52–77; cf. also Brodersen 1986.
21   Cf. the introduction to Adorno 1995a, pp. 52–3.
22   Buck-Morss 1977, p. 114.
23   Adorno 2003t, p. 262. Romano Pocai argues that Adorno is already moving 'towards the horizon of *Dialectic of Enlightenment*' (Pocai 2006, p. 16) in *Kierkegaard* via the concept 'of a dialectic in the mythical fundament of nature itself' (Adorno 1999a, p. 58).

have an effect on the social structure'.[24] For Adorno, Kierkegaard's Protestant ethic is merely liberal ideology in the guise of religion – an ideology which claims that the allegedly free subject which is individually virtuous according to a higher-order justice is always rewarded in kind:

> The possibility that a person, faultless in terms of private ethics, could act infamously in his objective social function, a function not reducible to inwardness, is a thought that Kierkegaard does not allow to occur. In fact neither this immediacy nor its semblance exist in the framework of common class interests; the rupture of immediacy is identical with that between the classes. Kierkegaard's ethics of concrete-meaningful life is therefore a poor and deceptive class moral.[25]

According to Adorno, rather than criticise the social conditions responsible for impoverished individuality, for the isolation of individuals (*die Vereinzelung der Einzelnen*), Kierkegaard seeks a solution to the problem of injustice between human beings within individuality itself. The 'universality of the moral law' proclaimed by Kierkegaard, a law whose 'universality' he immediately restricts to the bourgeoisie, has both its genesis and limits in his own unenlightened 'class consciousness': Kierkegaard produces his theory not arbitrarily but as a representative of the interests of his class, interests which disguise themselves as the public interest.[26] One need not desire to discover, as does Lorenz Jäger, a 'praise of class struggle'[27] in *Kierkegaard* to see that Adorno here makes capitalism on the whole responsible for 'the reification of social life, the alienation of the individual from a world that comes into focus as a mere commodity'. Following Lukács, the experience of being turned into a commodity is taken as a totalising experience: 'in a society dominated by exchange-value, things are "immediately" accessible to the person' no longer.[28] Thus, at the same time, every philosophy which assumes an individual-in-itself, or assumes within the individual a pure essence of subjectivity unaffected by objective social reality, has become obsolete.

---

24   Adorno 1999a, p. 51. '[T]hrough unfolding commodity relations, the social basis of the tran-
     scendentally grounded ethic of fraternity is destroyed' (Schiller 1993b, p. 66).
25   Adorno 1999a, p. 50.
26   Adorno 1999a, p. 49.
27   Jäger 2004, p. 71.
28   Adorno 1999a, p. 39.

2   The Historical Figure of the Commodity

In May 1931, after finally having qualified to work as a professor, Adorno delivered his *Antrittsvorlesung*, or inaugural lecture, a tradition for newly-quali-
fied professors in Germany. Programmatically titled 'The Actuality of Philosophy',[29] Adorno attempts within it 'a comparative critical consideration of
contemporary philosophical schools of thought (such as idealism, neo-Kantianism, positivism, phenomenology and *Lebensphilosophie*)' in order 'to establish his own concept of philosophy as the science of interpretation'.[30] Here to
an even greater extent than in *Kierkegaard*, and with explicit reference to both
Lukács and materialism, the commodity-form becomes the central element of
social knowledge.[31]

Entirely following Benjamin,[32] Adorno's lecture begins with a 'bold denial'[33]
which simultaneously implies a renunciation of Lukács: 'Whoever chooses
philosophy as a profession today must first reject the illusion that earlier philosophical enterprises began with: that the power of thought is sufficient to grasp
the totality of the real. No justifying reason could rediscover itself in a reality whose order and form suppresses every claim to reason; only polemically
does reason present itself to the knower as total reality, while only in traces
and ruins is it prepared to hope that it will ever come across correct and just
reality'. Against both Hegel's assumption of an absolute spirit, and Lukács's
assumption of a proletariat capable as history's subject-object of grasping totality given the right conditions, Adorno maintains that what must be grasped

---

29   'The Actuality of Philosophy' is also a response to Marx's *The Poverty of Philosophy*, 'which
      included the first systematic account of historical materialism; in the second part, espe-
      cially, it comprised a critique of philosophy as practised by the Hegelian school, which
      Marx confronted with the sense of history which Hegel himself had possessed. Whereas
      Marx drew from the poverty of philosophy the conclusion that it should be replaced by his-
      tory, for Adorno, who held fast to philosophy in a changed historical situation, the "poverty
      of philosophy" consisted ... in the objective compulsion linking thought to the discursive
      sphere, from which, nevertheless, it must detach itself if it is to become materialist in
      earnest' (editorial note by Tiedemann [Adorno 2000b, p. 162, n. 3]; cf. Marx 1976).
30   Müller-Doohm 2006, p. 90.
31   As Peter von Haselberg would later recall, '[i]t was a real inaugural lecture, polemical
      against all the dominant philosophemes .... Dialectics, materialism, even the commodity-
      form itself came up, but no doctrine whatsoever. Instead, apparently turning quite modest
      again, at the end there was the optimism that spirit, even if it does not yet grasp the
      entirety of the real, might still penetrate it within the small – might shatter, within the
      small, the dimensions of the merely existing' (von Haselberg 1983, p. 9).
32   'The inaugural lecture appears to be a – not unoriginal – exposition of Benjaminian gnos-
      eology' (Pettazzi 1983, p. 41; cf. Adorno 1977, p. 127, n. 2).
33   Jay 1981, p. 75.

does not even correspond to reason. For him, a philosophy which continues to view reality as rational 'only veils reality and eternalizes its present condition'.[34] Hegel's verdict that '[w]hat is rational is actual; and what is actual is rational'[35] – in Adorno's words, an imperative justified with reason 'to capitulate before reality'[36] – is categorical, and claims to be valid independently from all historical and social variables in order to permanently brand any critique of existing conditions as unreasonable. In contrast, Adorno regards the notion that history teleologically propels itself towards the realisation of a reason contained within itself as foolish in light of irrational reality. 'Not by interpreting the historical process as an irresistible power pressing toward a messianic break with the present', as in *History and Class Consciousness*, 'but by focusing on the breaks, the gaps within the present – here was where Adorno saw the hope of a new future, but never its guarantee'.[37]

Here, Adorno is in complete agreement with Horkheimer's critique of the philosophy of history. In the book *Beginnings of the Bourgeois Philosophy of History*, composed 'on the basis of lecture scripts'[38] 'one year before Adorno's inaugural lecture, Horkheimer writes that history in itself '*has* no reason, nor is it an "essence" in the usual sense; it is neither "Spirit" before which we must genuflect nor "power", but rather a comprehensible collection of events resulting from the social life processes of human beings. ... The pantheistic promotion of history to the status of an autonomous, unitary, substantial being is nothing other than dogmatic metaphysics'.[39] Adorno adopts the epistemological assumption that one cannot grasp reality by identifying it with spirit or with the subject, but rather only by means of the material of society. The task of theory is to configure this material so that objectivity itself can speak.

Benjamin's conception of philosophical contemplation as resembling mosaics – '[b]oth are made up of the distinct and disparate; and nothing could bear more powerful testimony to the transcendent force of the sacred image and the truth itself'[40] – is taken by Adorno as the starting point of a philosophy of interpretation:

---

34   Adorno 1977, p. 120.

35   Hegel 1991, p. 20.

36   Adorno 2005a, p. 282.

37   Buck-Morss 1977, p. 47.

38   Schmid Noerr 1987, p. 456. The lecture course in question was held by Horkheimer in the summer semester of 1928 (see Horkheimer's 'Verzeichnis der Vorlesungen und Seminare' ['Index of Lecture Courses and Seminars'] [Horkheimer 1996b, p. 218]).

39   Horkheimer 1993a, p. 375.

40   Benjamin 2009, pp. 28–9; cf. Ponzi 2004, p. 116.

He who interprets by searching behind the phenomenal world for a world-in-itself (*Welt an sich*) which forms its foundation and support, acts mistakenly like someone who wants to find in the riddle the reflection of a being which lies behind it, a being mirrored in the riddle, in which it is contained. Instead, the function of riddle-solving is to light up the riddle-*Gestalt* like lightning and to negate it (*aufzuheben*), not to persist and imitate it. Authentic philosophic interpretation does not meet up with a fixed meaning which already lies behind the question, but lights it up suddenly and momentarily, and consumes it at the same time. Just as riddle-solving is constituted, in that the singular and dispersed elements of the question are brought into various groupings long enough for them to close together in a figure out of which the solution springs forth, while the question disappears – so philosophy has to bring its elements, which it receives from the sciences, into changing constellations, or, to say it with less astrological and scientifically more current expression, into changing trial combinations, until they fall into a figure which can be read as an answer, while at the same time the question disappears.[41]

Next, Adorno's conception of reality as unintentional leads him to a materialism which clearly stems from Lukács:

> The task of philosophy is not to search for concealed and [existing] intentions of reality, but to interpret unintentional reality, in that, by the power of constructing figures, or images (*Bilder*), out of the isolated elements of reality, it negates (*aufhebt*) questions, the exact articulation of which is the task of science .... Here one can discover what appears as such an astounding and strange affinity existing between interpretive philosophy and that type of thinking which most strongly rejects the concept of the intentional, the meaningful: the thinking of materialism. Interpretation of the unintentional through a juxtaposition of the analytically isolated elements and illumination of the real by the power of such interpretation is the program of every authentically materialist knowledge, a program to which the materialist procedure does all the more justice, the more it

---

41   Adorno 1977, p. 127. 'If true interpretation succeeds only through a juxtaposition of the smallest elements, then it no longer has a [stake] in the great problems in the traditional sense, or only in the sense that it [suppresses] within a concrete finding the total question which that finding previously seemed to represent symbolically. Construction out of small and unintentional elements thus counts among the basic assumptions of philosophic interpretation' (Adorno 1977, pp. 127–8).

distances itself from every 'meaning' of its objects and the less it relates
itself to an implicit, quasi-religious meaning. For long ago, interpretation
divorced itself from all questions of meaning or, in other words, the sym-
bols of philosophy are decayed. If philosophy must learn to renounce the
question of totality, then [this] implies that it must learn to do without the
symbolic function, in which for a long time, at least in idealism, the particular appeared to represent the general. It must give up the great problems,
the size of which once hoped to guarantee the totality, whereas today
between the wide meshes of big questions, interpretation slips away.[42]

Down to the linguistic detail, Adorno appropriates Benjamin's epistemological
aspiration 'to discover in the analysis of the small individual moment the crys-
tal of the total event'.[43] This aspiration represents a break with the 'nineteenth-
century concept of system', which submits itself 'to a syncretism which weaves
a spider's web between separate kinds of knowledge in an attempt to ensnare
the truth as if it were something which came flying in from the outside'.[44]

Adorno uses Benjamin's category of the riddle (*Rätsel*)[45] to expound upon
his vision of a dialectic which transforms philosophical theory into an element
of practice:

I said that the riddle's answer was not the 'meaning' of the riddle in the
sense that both could exist at the same time[, or in the sense that t]he
answer was contained within the riddle, and the riddle portrayed only its
own appearance and contained the answer within itself as intention. Far
more, the answer stands in strict antithesis to the riddle, needs to be constructed out of the riddle's elements, and destroys the riddle, which is not
meaningful, but meaningless, as soon as the answer is decisively given
to it. The movement which [executes itself] in this [game] is executed in

---

42   Adorno 1977, p. 127. 'In art, the *smallest element* determines the total ... as incidentally also
     in philosophy' (Adorno 2006d, p. 139).
43   Benjamin 2002c, p. 461; cf. Schlette 2000, column 548. As Adorno writes in *Minima Mo-
     ralia*, 'Benjamin's writings are an attempt in ever new ways to make philosophically fruitful
     what has not yet been foreclosed by great intentions. The task he bequeathed was not to
     abandon such an attempt to the estranging enigmas of thought alone, but to bring the
     intentionless within the realm of concepts: the obligation to think at the same time dia-
     lectically and undialectically' (Adorno 2005b, pp. 151–2).
44   Benjamin 2009, p. 28.
45   Translator's note: in the standard English translation of *The Origin of German Tragic
     Drama* (Benjamin 2009), the German term *Rätsel* is also rendered in various places as
     'enigma'.

earnest by materialism. Earnestness means here that the answer does not remain mistakenly in the closed area of knowledge, but that [it is spread by praxis]. The interpretation of given reality and its abolition are connected to each other, not, of course, in the sense that reality is negated by the concept, but that out of the construction of a configuration of reality the demand for its real change always follows promptly. The [changing] gesture of the [game of the riddle] – not its mere resolution as such – provides the [archetype] of resolutions to which materialist praxis alone has access. Materialism has named this relationship with a name that is philosophically certified: dialectic. Only dialectically, it seems to me, is philosophic interpretation possible. When Marx reproached the philosophers, saying that they had only variously interpreted the world, and contraposed to them that the point was to change it, then the sentence receives its legitimacy not only out of political praxis, but also out of philosophic theory. Only in the annihilation of the question is the authenticity of philosophic interpretation first successfully proven, and mere thought by itself cannot accomplish this: therefore the annihilation of the question compels praxis. It is superfluous to separate out explicitly a conception of pragmatism, in which theory and praxis entwine with each other as they do in the dialectic.[46]

Flash back to 1915, as Sigmund Freud addresses an audience of listeners with the following:

It is true that psycho-analysis cannot boast that it has never concerned itself with trivialities. On the contrary, the material for its observations is usually provided by the inconsiderable events which have been put aside by the other sciences as being too unimportant – the dregs, one might say, of the world of phenomena. But are you not making a confusion in your criticism between the vastness of the problems and the conspicuousness of what points to them? Are there not very important things which can only reveal themselves, under certain conditions and at certain times, by quite feeble indications?[47]

For Adorno, Freud's proclaimed turn to the dregs of the world of phenomena 'has validity beyond the realm of psychoanalysis, just as the turning of progress-

---

46   Adorno 1977, p. 129.
47   Freud 2001a, pp. 26–7.

ive social philosophy to economics has validity not merely due to the empirical superiority of economics, but just as much because of the immanent requirements of philosophic interpretation itself'.[48]

Adorno designates the economy as a suitable place for the possibility of 'authentically materialist knowledge' insofar as a figure can emerge within it which contains all 'the elements of a social analysis', one 'which certainly does not lie before us organically, but which must first be posited: the commodity structure'. Yet even if the figure of the commodity-structure were to emerge, '[t]his would hardly solve the thing-in-itself problem, not even in the sense that somehow the social conditions might be revealed under which the thing-in-itself problem came into existence, as Lukács even thought the solution to be; for the truth content of a problem is in principle different from the historical and psychological conditions out of which it grows'.[49] For Adorno, Lukács's attempt 'to collapse truth into class origin was ultimately untenable, because genesis and truth value are unrelated'.[50] Against this, Adorno maintains that it 'might be possible that, from a sufficient construction of the commodity structure, the thing-in-itself problem absolutely disappeared. Like a source of light, the historical figure of the commodity and of exchange value may free the form of a reality, the hidden meaning of which remained closed to investigation of the thing-in-itself problem, because there is no hidden meaning which could be redeemable from its one-time and first-time historical appearance'.[51] The 'historical images' with which Adorno is concerned

---

48   Adorno 1977, p. 128. Adorno writes of turning to the 'dregs of the world of phenomena' (*Abhub der Erscheinungswelt*) in several places throughout his work, the first occurring as early as *Der Begriff des Unbewußten in der transzendentalen Seelenlehre* (Adorno 2003f, p. 232). Translator's note: this phrase has also been translated as 'refuse of the physical world' (Adorno 1977, p. 128), 'refuse of the world of phenomena' (Adorno 2005c), 'offal of the phenomenal world' (Adorno 2005b, p. 240) and 'dross of the phenomenal world' (Adorno 2007b, p. 170).

49   Adorno 1977, p. 128.

50   Jay 1981, p. 77.

51   Adorno 1977, p. 128. Hermann Schweppenhäuser observes that the 'construct of Critical Theory ... is formed following the Kantian construct' (Schweppenhäuser 2003, p. 43, n. 81). In the preface to the second edition of *Critique of Pure Reason*, Kant writes: 'A new light broke upon the first person who demonstrated the isosceles triangle. For he found that what he had to do was not to trace what he saw in this figure, or even trace its mere concept, and read off, as it were, from the properties of the figure; but rather that he had to produce the latter from what he himself thought into the object and presented (through construction) according to a priori concepts, and that in order to know something securely a priori he had to ascribe to the thing nothing except what followed necessarily from what he himself had put into it in accordance with its concept' (Kant 1998, p. 108).

do not lie organically ready in history; not showing (*Schau*) or intuition is required to become aware of them. They are not magically sent by the gods to be taken in and venerated. Rather, they must be produced by human beings and are legitimated in the last analysis alone by the fact that reality crystallises about them in striking conclusiveness (*Evidenz*).[52]

As an instrument for constructing those images which are supposed to 'dissolve and resolve' the questions of being, Adorno identifies an 'exact fantasy; fantasy which abides strictly within the material which sciences present to it, and reaches beyond them only in the smallest aspects of their arrangement: aspects, granted, which fantasy itself must originally generate. If the idea of philosophic interpretation which I tried to develop for you is valid', Adorno continues his lecture, 'then it can be expressed as the demand to answer the questions of a pre-given reality each time, through a fantasy which rearranges the elements of the question without going beyond the circumference of the elements, the exactitude of which has its control in the disappearance of the question'.[53]

In a letter to Kracauer written a few weeks after his lecture, Adorno recounts the 'scandal' it caused among the listeners.[54] By his account, he

decided on the relatively programmatic form (which is not at all up my alley) for no other reason than that everyone kept wanting to hear in clear and concise words what my expectations of philosophy actually were. But when it came to the point, it wasn't to anybody's liking. [Max] Wertheimer had a convulsive fit of weeping from rage and excitement; [Adorno's habilitation supervisor Paul] Tillich was repelled by the form because of its definitive tone; [Karl] Mannheim cursed; and Horkheimer (together with Leo [Löwenthal], who has metamorphosed completely into one of his swarm of tsetse flies and satellites) thought it not Marxist enough. You can have no idea of the wrath – the flood of hatred, opposition and malice – that the lecture brought down on me. It would be too tedious to go into individual details, but not a single stage was lacking – from 'salon

---

52   Adorno 1977, p. 131; as noted in the original translation, *Schau* and *Evidenz* allude to the work of Edmund Husserl. In *One-Way Street*, Benjamin defines the 'faculty of imagination' as 'the gift of interpolating into the infinitely small, of inventing, for every intensity, an extensiveness to contain its new, compressed fullness-in short, of receiving each image as if it were that of the folded fan' (Benjamin 2004c, p. 466).

53   Adorno 1977, p. 131.

54   Letter from Adorno to Kracauer, 29 May 1931 (Adorno and Kracauer 2020, p. 187); cf. Müller-Doohm 2005, p. 139.

philosophy' and baseless arguments to abstruseness and complete crazi-
ness. (Leo found the whole thing 'inhuman'; he is planning to qualify as
a lecturer.) None of this is at all surprising. I don't fit in. I have no wish
to forge a 'science' or 'world view'; I want something that is fundamentally different – something which is entirely incompatible with academic
categories and embitters people who basically want to enquire into the
meaning of existence in Aristotelian or Hegelian terms. This was clear to
me from the outset, and I believed that on this occasion I really ought to
say what I think.[55]

3   To Speed Up the Completion

Benjamin's familiarity with the Marxian critique of political economy developed in a similar manner to Adorno's. Only after becoming acquainted with
this critique in the form conveyed by Lukács did Benjamin turn to texts by Marx
himself.[56] Just as was the case for Adorno, 'it was the earlier writings of Lukács's
which made the strongest impression'[57] on Benjamin. In 'Bücher, die lebendig
geblieben sind' ('Books Which Have Remained Alive'), an article published in
the literary weekly *Die literarische Welt* three years after the appearance of *History and Class Consciousness*, Benjamin refers to the latter as the 'most cohesive
philosophical work of Marxist literature'. According to him, '[i]ts uniqueness
rests on the certainty with which, in the critical situation of philosophy, it has
perceived the critical situation of class struggle, and with which, in the over-
due concrete revolution, it has perceived the absolute precondition, indeed, the
absolute consummation and final say of theoretical knowledge. The polemic
which has been published against this work by the authorities of the Communist Party under Deborin's leadership confirms in its own way the work's
import'.[58]

55   Letter from Adorno to Kracauer, 29 May 1931 (Adorno and Kracauer 2020, pp. 186–7).
56   Benjamin had already come into contact with an exoteric Marxism of practice through
      Asja Lacis, whom he describes as a 'Bolshevist Latvian woman from Riga who performs
      in the theater and directs' and 'one of the most splendid women I have ever met' (letter
      from Benjamin to Scholem, 7 July 1924 [Benjamin 2012, pp. 242, 245]). In an autobiography,
      Lacis describes herself as a 'good soldier of the revolution' (Lacis 1976, p. 24). On the bio-
      graphical and theoretical relationship between her and Benjamin cf. Kaulen 1995; cf. also
      Tiedemann, Gödde and Lonitz 1991, pp. 161–70.
57   Editorial note by Tiedemann (Adorno 2019h, p. 281, n. 3); on the relationship between Ben-
      jamin and Lukács cf. Feher 1985.
58   Benjamin 2001a, p. 171. In a polemic from 1924, Abram Deborin (cf. Hedeler 1997) accuses

Benjamin's reception of *History and Class Consciousness* appears to have occurred somewhat gradually, however. Although he writes in a June 1924 letter to Gershom Scholem that 'the book itself is very important, especially for me',[59] he had still only read Ernst Bloch's review[60] of it by the following September: 'By the way', he writes Scholem again, 'I want to study Lukács's book as soon as possible and I would be surprised if the foundations of my nihilism were not to manifest themselves against communism in an antagonistic confrontation with the concepts and assertions of Hegelian dialectics'.[61] As can be seen from Benjamin's fastidiously maintained index of his readings, he did not ultimately read *History and Class Consciousness* until 1925.[62] And only ten years later, in June 1935, could he report to Adorno that he had begun 'to explore the first volume of "Capital"',[63] an exploration whose results can be found in part in his posthumously published *Arcades Project*.[64]

An *exposé*,[65] or research proposal, for *The Arcades Project* – a long-planned yet never-completed 'primal history of the nineteenth century' through which

---

Lukács of pitting Marx against Engels in order to revert to an idealist, 'deviationist' position 'in full agreement with the bourgeois critics of Marxism' (Deborin 1924, p. 617): 'Any even modestly trained Marxist will upon some reflection easily recognise the idealist tendencies which rise to the surface in a sea of muddled phrases' (Deborin 1924, p. 615; cf. Kapferer 1993, p. 94). As Lukács would later note, 'the official critics of the time (Deborin, [László] Rudas, etc.) erroneously criticized erroneous statements in the book, and thus also directed "the fire of criticism" at those traits that were – unconsciously – of a progressive and forward-looking tendency' (Lukács quoted in Fekete and Karáci 1981, p. 130). The custom of discrediting Lukács as a revisionist or falsifier of Engels's theoretical role lasted throughout Marxism-Leninism. As late as 1971, the East Berlin philosophy journal *Deutsche Zeitschrift für Philosophie* would accuse him of a 'falsifying representation of Marxist dialectics', claiming that Adorno's reception of Lukács's writings had led to him view 'dialectics as virtually the natural law of a still unconscious society' instead of as a trans-historical, positive-materialist principle (Bauermann and Rötscher 1971, pp. 1450–1).

59   Letter from Benjamin to Scholem, 13 June 1924 (Benjamin 2012, p. 244).

60   See Bloch 2020; cf. Kaulen 1995, p. 98; cf. letter from Benjamin to Scholem, 16 September 1924 (Benjamin 2012, p. 246).

61   Letter from Benjamin to Scholem, 16 September 1924 (Benjamin 2012, p. 248).

62   See Benjamin's 'Verzeichnis der gelesenen Schriften' ('Index of Works Read') (Benjamin 2001e, p. 456).

63   Letter from Benjamin to Adorno, 10 June 1935 (Adorno and Benjamin 1999, p. 101). It should be noted that *Capital* is not included in the aforementioned index. The only two works by Marx which are cited therein are *The Eighteenth Brumaire of Louis Napoleon* and 'Critique of the Gotha Programme', which Benjamin read between June and October 1938, see Benjamin's 'Verzeichnis der gelesenen Schriften' ('Index of Works Read') (Benjamin 2001e, p. 474). 'From Benjamin's carefully maintained reading list it is clear that his passion was not philosophy, and certainly not Marxism, but rather literature' (Schneider 2006, p. 678).

64   See Benjamin 2002c, pp. 651–670.

65   Benjamin 2002a. Translator's note: Benjamin produced several drafts of the 1935 *exposé*,

Benjamin believed himself to have gradually 'reached solid ground [in] the Marxist discussion'[66] – is the subject of Adorno's so-called Hornberger letter. Written between 2–5 August 1935, this letter addresses Benjamin's use of the Marxian critique of economy in an extremely critical and, in Adorno's own words, 'carping' manner.[67] Thus, it provides contemporary readers with valuable insight into Adorno's own understanding of the subject. Described by Adorno himself as 'an extremely detailed counter-*exposé*'[68] and by Martin Vialon as 'an act of friendship, ... comparable to Schiller's role in compelling Goethe to speed up the completion of his *Faust* project',[69] the Hornberg letter constitutes an attempt to keep Benjamin from accepting the worldview of dialectical materialism 'with closed eyes'.[70] Here, Adorno's aim is not only to speed up the completion of the *Arcades Project*, but also to rescue Benjamin's original intention – to preserve the 'general approach' upon which they had agreed.[71]

In a 1967 letter to Helmut Heißenbüttel, Adorno responds to the former's accusations that he had made serious omissions in his capacity as the editor of a volume of selected works by Benjamin.[72] Expounding on his view of Benjamin's misunderstanding of Marx and how it manifested itself in their discussions, Adorno writes:

> You appear to suspect I wanted, for whatever reason, to curtail Benjamin's Marxist intentions. My motive in the controversy was actually much more complex. While on the one hand, I specifically wanted to defend Benjamin's metaphysical impulses from himself, I also wanted just as much to defend dialectical materialism from him, which he appeared to me, in a word, to misinterpret. Not he alone, but also Brecht. I like to think I know my Marx quite precisely, as you certainly also grant me implicitly. For this reason, I could not overlook that although Benjamin may have professed Marxism, he did not understand the essential content

---

and Braunstein cites an earlier version which has not been translated into English (Benjamin 2001c). Here, the existing English translation of the 'final' 1935 version is cited, as variations between the two versions are negligible in the passages quoted by Braunstein.

66   Letter from Benjamin to Adorno, 31 May 1935 (Adorno and Benjamin 1999, p. 89).
67   Letter from Adorno to Benjamin, 2–5 August 1935 (Adorno and Benjamin 1999, p. 114).
68   Letter from Adorno to Horkheimer, 21 October 1935 (Adorno and Horkheimer 2003b, p. 150).
69   Vialon 2004, p. 119.
70   Adorno 2007b, p. 18.
71   Letter from Adorno to Benjamin, 18 March 1936 (Adorno and Benjamin 1999, p. 128); cf. Gödde and Lonitz 2006, p. 95.
72   Cf. Küpper and Skrandies 2006.

of Marxian theory. God knows I sing Brecht's merits highly enough, but his ignorance of Marxism, even of notorious matters such as the theory of surplus-value, was simply beyond words. Neither studied Marx seriously, but rather, to modify Hobbes's saying about religion, swallowed Marx like a pill; and this appeared dubious to me: heteronomous and irrational, in contrast to materialist dialectics as a theory. If Benjamin had really learned this theory, it would have been better for his own approach.[73]

Already in a letter to Benjamin from 5 June 1935, Adorno criticises the former's use of the category of the commodity, arguing that this category 'is rather too generally expressed in the *exposé* (as indeed it also was in my Kierkegaard book) if it is supposed to disclose something *specific* about the character of the nineteenth century; and it is not really enough to define the category in purely technological terms – in terms of "fabrication" say – since it is necessary above all to enquire into the economic function of the same, that is, into the laws of the market within early high capitalism precisely as the "modern" age in the strict sense'.[74] In one passage in *Kierkegaard* which Benjamin praised enthusiastically for its 'ground-breaking analysis'[75] after a first reading, Adorno reflects on both the interiors of upper-class homes[76] in which one must fear 'being turned into a thing oneself',[77] and on the alienation of the self from things caused by the commodity-character more generally:

---

73   Letter from Adorno to Heißenbüttel, 14 March 1967 (Heißenbüttel 2006, pp. 183–4); on the relationship between Benjamin and Brecht cf. Wizisla 2016 and Müller-Schöll 2006; on Adorno's aversion to Brecht cf. for example his reference to 'the figure of Brecht' in a letter to Benjamin (letter from Adorno to Benjamin, 6 November 1934 [Adorno and Benjamin 1999, p. 53]).

74   Letter from Adorno to Benjamin, 5 June 1935 (Adorno and Benjamin 1999, p. 92).

75   Letter from Benjamin to Adorno, 1 December 1932 (Adorno and Benjamin 1999, p. 20).

76   For his own part, it was Benjamin 'who first focussed on the bourgeois *intérieur* as an expression of bourgeois decay' (Buck-Morss 1977, p. 270, n. 45): as he writes in *One-Way Street*, '[t]he bourgeois interior of the 1860s to the 1890s-with its gigantic sideboards distended with carvings, the sunless corners where potted palms sit, the balcony embattled behind its balustrade, and the long corridors with their singing gas flames-fittingly houses only the corpse. "On this sofa the aunt cannot but be murdered". The soulless luxury of the furnishings becomes true comfort only in the presence of a dead body' (Benjamin 2004c, p. 447). For the *Arcades Project*, Benjamin had planned an entire section (*Konvolut*) on this topic, the notes for which include the passage quoted here from Adorno's *Kierkegaard* (cf. Benjamin 2002c, pp. 220–1); cf. also Tiedemann, Gödde and Lonitz 1991, pp. 9–10 for a photo of a salon of 'a "lordly" residence in Berlin'.

77   Palmier 2006, p. 81.

The contents of the *intérieur* are mere decoration, alienated from the purposes they represent, deprived of their own use-value, engendered solely by the isolated apartment that is created in the first place by their juxtaposition. The 'lamp shaped like a flower'; the dream orient, fit together out of a cut paper lampshade hung over its crown and a rug made of osier; the room an officer's cabin, full of precious decorations, greedily collected across the seas – the complete *fata morgana* of decadent ornaments receives its meaning not from the material of which they are made, but from the *intérieur* that unifies the imposture of things in the form of a still life. Here, in the image, lost objects are conjured. The self is overwhelmed in its own domain by commodities and their historical essence. Their illusory quality is historically-economically produced by the alienation of thing from use-value.[78]

According to Adorno, alienation causes objects to no longer serve use in a strong sense. The need fulfilled by use no longer precedes things, which now tend first to be produced and only subsequently assigned some use. Already here, a highly problematic conception of use-value emerges which can be seen throughout Adorno's work. This conception assumes a transhistorical 'use-value-in-itself' inherent to things beyond economic determinants, while effectively denying that certain things lend themselves to being used in various ways: hence, Adorno's claim that the 'contents of the *intérieur*' are 'alienated from the purposes they represent' and therefore 'deprived of their own use-value'. Setting aside the assumption that there could exist something like a 'genuine' use-value which certain commodities have lost – an assumption absolutely incompatible with Marxian theory – the notion of 'use-value-in-itself' leads to Adorno's inability in this passage to trace the need for ornamental embellishment manifested in the bourgeois *intérieur* back to socio-economic causes. What he views as 'real need' is simply need which has been socially deformed in the concept of use-value.

Adorno's second objection concerns Benjamin's deployment of the concept of collective consciousness. In the *exposé*, the new means of production of the nineteenth century are said to correspond in their form to 'wish images' (*Wunschbilder*) in the collective consciousness, images with which 'the collective seeks both to overcome and to transfigure the immaturity of the social product and the inadequacies in the social organization of production'.[79] In a

---

78   Adorno 1999a, pp. 43–4.
79   Benjamin 2002a, p. 4.

letter to Horkheimer, Adorno claims he 'could not accept this concept without an extremely precise articulation of its class character'.[80] As he elaborates shortly thereafter in a letter to Benjamin,

> [t]he idea of collective consciousness was invented to distract attention from true objectivity, and from alienated subjectivity as its correlate. Our task is to polarize and dissolve this 'consciousness' dialectically in terms of society and singular subjects, not to galvanize it as the imagistic correlate of the commodity character. The fact that such a dreaming collective serves to erase the differences between classes should already act as a clear and sufficient warning in this respect.[81]

As the 'subject of the collective dream',[82] the class-antagonism of soberly alert reality gets lost among the masses. Therefore, Adorno wants Benjamin to treat the dialectical image more dialectically in order to avoid prematurely reconciling the class-antagonism of existing society. Such a reconciliation would portray the opposition between the classes, in spite of its social – that is, objective – causes, as a mere idealist construct. In turn, this would give the impression that this opposition could be overcome idealistically, through recourse to a kind of ultimate intersubjective inwardness not requiring a confrontation with empirical social reality.[83]

In this context, Adorno also regards as problematic Benjamin's anthropological invocation of an actually existing prehistory in which humanity lived in a 'classless society'.[84] 'On the one hand, these dream images include the collective idea of a classless society as an anthropological representation of the origin of human history. On the other hand, they acquire a reactionary tinge when mixed with daily impressions in the form of capitalist commodities'.[85] In contrast, already in 'The Actuality of Philosophy', Adorno calls for 'the avoidance of invariant general concepts, also perhaps the concept of man'.[86]

---

80 Letter from Adorno to Horkheimer, 8 June 1935 (Adorno and Horkheimer 2003b, p. 73).

81 Letter from Adorno to Benjamin, 2–5 August 1935 (Adorno and Benjamin 1999, p. 107).

82 Freytag 1992, p. 25.

83 Cf. Wiggershaus 1995, p. 194; cf. Weber 1999, columns 708–9.

84 Benjamin 2002a, p. 4.

85 Vialon 2004, p. 121.

86 Adorno 1977, p. 129; cf. also letter from Adorno to Benjamin, 6 September 1936 (Adorno and Benjamin 1999, p. 146): 'all those points in which ... I differ from you could be summed up and characterized as an *anthropological materialism* that I cannot accept. It is as if for you the human body represents the measure of all concreteness. But the latter is an "invariant"

Also out of the question for Adorno is Benjamin's solution, to 'transpose the dialectical image into consciousness as a "dream"'.[87]

> In accordance with your immanent vision of the dialectical image (with which, to employ a positive term, I would contrast your earlier conception of a model), you interpret the relationship between the oldest and the newest, one which was already central to your first draft, in terms of a utopian reference to the 'classless society'. The archaic thereby becomes a complementary addition to the new, instead of actually being 'the newest' itself, and is therefore rendered undialectical. However, at the same time, and equally undialectically, the image of classlessness is projected back into mythology ... instead of becoming properly transparent as the phantasmagoria of Hell. Thus the category in which the archaic fuses with the modern seems to me more like a catastrophe than a Golden Age. I once remarked how the recent past always presents itself as though it had been destroyed by catastrophes. *Hic et nunc*, I would say that this is how it presents itself as pre-history.[88]

Yet there is another reason why Adorno takes issue with transposing the wish-image, or dream-image, into consciousness. Benjamin designates the world's fairs of the nineteenth century as the physical manifestation of such images of the collective consciousness, characterising them as 'places of pilgrimage to the commodity fetish'.[89] At the same time, in direct contradiction to Marxism, he locates the fetish-character of the commodity in the consciousness of the dreaming collective.[90] In response, Adorno writes the following:

---

factor which, as I believe, distorts the decisively concrete (that is, precisely the *dialectical* rather than the archaic image)'.

87   Letter from Adorno to Benjamin, 2–5 August 1935 (Adorno and Benjamin 1999, p. 105).
88   Letter from Adorno to Benjamin, 2–5 August 1935 (Adorno and Benjamin 1999, p. 106). The note to which Adorno refers here is located in *Minima Moralia* (Adorno 2005b, p. 45).
89   Benjamin 2002a, p. 7.
90   In a letter to Scholem, Benjamin writes the following: 'Otherwise, I periodically succumb to the temptations of visualizing analogies with the Baroque book in the book's inner construction, although its external construction decidedly diverges from that of the former. And I want to give you this much of a hint: Here as well the focus will be on the unfolding of a handed-down concept. Whereas in the former it was the concept of *Trauerspiel*, here it is likely to be the fetish character of commodities. Whereas the Baroque book mobilized its own theory of knowledge, this will be the case for "Arcades" at least to the same extent, though I can foresee neither whether it will find a form of representation of its own, nor to what extent I may succeed in such a representation. The title "Paris Arcades" has finally been discarded and the draft is entitled "Paris, Capital of the Nineteenth Cen-

The fetish character of the commodity is not a fact of consciousness; rather it is dialectical in character, in the eminent sense that it produces consciousness. But if so, then neither consciousness nor unconsciousness can simply replicate it as a dream, but must respond to it rather with desire and fear in equal measure. But it is precisely this dialectical power of the fetish character that is forfeited in the replica realism (*sit venia verbo*) of your current immanent version of the dialectical image. ... To return to the magnificent language of the first draft of the Arcades project: if the dialectical image is nothing but the way in which the fetish character is perceived in the collective consciousness, then the Saint-Simonian conception of the commodity world might well reveal itself as Utopia, but hardly as the reverse – namely as a dialectical image of the nineteenth century as *Hell*. ... The dialectical image must therefore not be transferred into consciousness as a dream, but rather the dream should be externalized through dialectical interpretation and the immanence of consciousness itself understood as a constellation of reality – the astronomical phase, as it were, Hell wanders through mankind. It seems to me that it is only a map of such a journey through the stars which could provide a perspicuous vision of history as pre-history.[91]

Regarding another passage in the *exposé* – which he would cite at unusual length in his 1950 essay 'Portrait of Walter Benjamin', presumably because it appeared exemplary to him[92] – Adorno becomes more explicit. In this passage, Benjamin discusses the 1844 lithograph 'Le pont des planètes' by Grandville:[93]

World exhibitions propagate the universe of commodities. Grandville's fantasies confer a commodity character on the universe. They modernize it. Saturn's ring becomes a cast-iron balcony on which the inhabitants of Saturn take the evening air. ... Fashion prescribes the ritual according to which the commodity fetish demands to be worshipped. Grandville extends the authority of fashion to objects of every day use, as well as

---

tury". Privately I call it "Paris, capitale du XIXe siecle", implying a further analogy: just as the Baroque book dealt with the seventeenth century from the perspective of Germany, this book will unravel the nineteenth century from France's perspective' (letter from Benjamin to Scholem, 20 May 1935 [Benjamin and Scholem 1992, p. 159]).

91 Letter from Adorno to Benjamin, 2–5 August 1935 (Adorno and Benjamin 1999, pp. 105–6).
92 See Adorno 1988b, pp. 236–7.
93 See Benjamin 2002c, p. 65 for a reproduction of Grandville's lithograph; cf. also Benjamin's essay 'The King of Saturn or Some Remarks on Iron Construction' from 1928 or 1929, where he already mentions this image (Benjamin 2002d, p. 885).

to the cosmos. In taking it to an extreme, he reveals its nature. Fashion stands in opposition to the organic. It couples the living body to the inorganic world. To the living, it defends the rights of the corpse. The fetishism that succumbs to the sex appeal of the inorganic is its vital nerve. The cult of the commodity presses such fetishism into its service.[94]

On the one hand, Adorno objects to Benjamin that in a real fetishistic inversion, '[t]he ring of Saturn should not become a cast-iron balcony, but the balcony should become the real ring of Saturn', and that on the other, '[a]s was probably your own intention, the conception of the commodity fetish must be documented with appropriate passages from the man who discovered it' – that is, with passages from Marx's *Capital*.[95]

In attempting to write a *primal* history of the nineteenth century, Adorno continues, Benjamin would need to work out '[t]he specific commodity character of the nineteenth century, in other words, the industrial production of commodities ... much more clearly and substantively', given that '[a]ll references to the commodity form "as such" lend that history a certain metaphorical character which in this crucial case cannot be permitted'.[96] And yet again, Adorno explicitly expresses his misgivings – not without repeatedly emphasising the failure of his own first habilitation in this regard as well – about 'the overly abstract use of the commodity category':

> I am doubtful whether this category appeared 'for the first time' as such in the nineteenth century. (Incidentally, I would say the same objection also applies to the *intérieur* and the sociology of interiority in my Kierkegaard book, and every criticism I have made of your draft also holds for my own earlier study.) I believe that the commodity category could be rendered much more concrete by reference to the specifically modern categories of world trade and imperialism.[97]

---

94 Benjamin 2002a, p. 8.
95 Letter from Adorno to Benjamin, 2–5 August 1935 (Adorno and Benjamin 1999, p. 111). What Benjamin understands by the term 'fetishism' becomes clear among other places in *The Arcades Project*: 'The property appertaining to the commodity as its fetish character attaches as well to the commodity-producing society – not as it is in itself, to be sure, but more as it represents itself and thinks to understand itself whenever it abstracts from the fact that it produces precisely commodities' (Benjamin 2002c, p. 669). On the (redemptive) criticism of this understanding of the commodity's fetish-character cf. Tiedemann 2001, p. 28.
96 Letter from Adorno to Benjamin, 2–5 August 1935 (Adorno and Benjamin 1999, p. 108).
97 Letter from Adorno to Benjamin, 2–5 August 1935 (Adorno and Benjamin 1999, pp. 111–12). The passage criticised here by Adorno is located in Benjamin 2002a, pp. 8–9.

4   Masochism

Benjamin's essay 'The Work of Art in the Age of Its Technological Reproducibility' presents a further source of controversy. Described by Perry Anderson as
'Benjamin's most significant theoretical legacy within Marxism',[98] this text first
appeared in French in a 1936 issue of the *Zeitschrift für Sozialforschung*,[99] the
academic journal of the Institute for Social Research (a German version of the
essay was later published in 1955).[100]

Asked by Horkheimer for an assessment of Benjamin's work in January
1936,[101] Adorno responds with ambivalence: 'many of the details specifically
on art, as well as some on politics (such as the digression on the concept of
the "masses"), are quite brilliant, and I quite agree with the de-mythologisation
of art. My only issue is ... the fundamental objection that [Benjamin] mytholo-
gises this de-mythologisation and ... thus fashions a veritable ontology out of all
conceivable abominations'.[102] Although Adorno claims in a letter to Benjamin
that he finds the latter's 'masses' digression 'to be among the most profound
and most powerful statements of political theory I have encountered since I
read *State and Revolution*',[103] he nevertheless views Benjamin's mythologisation
of de-mythologisation as grounded in a 'masochism'[104] stemming from fear of
the proletarian element of proletarian revolution – a fear comparable to 'the
bourgeois artist's fear of the "philistinism" of revolution'. Believing Benjamin
knows that 'this attitude is reactionary', Adorno sees him drawing an undialectical conclusion: the abstract negation of all that is bourgeois and not genuinely
proletarian.[105]

---

98   Anderson 1987, p. 76.
99   Originally published as 'L'œuvre d'art à l'epoque de sa reproduction méchanisée', *Zeit-
       schrift für Sozialforschung*, 5, 1: 40–68, this French version is now available in Benjamin's
       Gesammelte Schiften (see Benjamin 2001f).
100   On the work's origins cf. Tiedemann and Schweppenhäuser 2001 and Schöttker 2007.
101   See letter from Horkheimer to Adorno, 29 January 1936 (Adorno and Horkheimer 2003b,
       p. 113).
102   Letter from Adorno to Horkheimer, 21 March 1936 (Adorno and Horkheimer 2003b, p. 130).
103   Letter from Adorno to Benjamin, 18 March 1936 (Adorno and Benjamin 1999, pp. 132–
       3; Adorno's library does not contain a copy of *State and Revolution*). The 'digression' is
       located in Benjamin 2006d, pp. 129–30, n. 24. This digression was omitted in the version
       published in the *Zeitschrift für Sozialforschung* – apparently 'due to time pressure during
       the translation' (Schöttker 2007, p. 127) – and in the final version from 1939 (see Benjamin
       2006e).
104   Letter from Adorno to Horkheimer, 21 March 1936 (Adorno and Horkheimer 2003b, p. 132).
105   Letter from Adorno to Horkheimer, 21 March 1936 (Adorno and Horkheimer 2003b, p. 130).
       In 'The Present Social Situation of the French Writer', his first essay published in the

Invoking Marx, Benjamin's essay formulates 'theses defining the tendencies of the development of art under the present conditions of production'[106] – theses which Benjamin explicitly claims stand to 'contribute to the political struggle', not least by being *useful for the formulation of revolutionary demands in the politics of art*.[107] According to Benjamin, the work of art previously sustained itself on aura, yet this is precisely what 'withers in the age of technological reproducibility'.[108] The aura of so-called autonomous artworks was rooted in their authenticity, the 'here and now of the original';[109] and although the aura now finds itself in a time of crisis, ostensibly autonomous artworks – the descendants of 'the earliest artworks', which themselves 'originated in the service of rituals, first magical, then religious'[110] – still continue to invoke the magical-religious aura: this can be seen with the advent of photography, to which art 'reacted with the doctrine of *l'art pour l'art* – that is, with a theology of art. This in turn gave rise to a negative theology, in the form of an idea of "pure" art, which rejects not only any social function but any definition in terms of a representational content'.[111] Here, Benjamin wants to indicate 'a future state of the world, liberated from magic'.[112] However, Adorno accuses him of prematurely surrendering magic to irrationality without reflecting on magic's enlightening substance:[113]

Zeitschrift für Sozialforschung, Benjamin writes of the difficulty of turning towards the proletariat as an intellectual: 'The fact that these intellectuals have abandoned their own class in order to make common cause with the proletariat does not mean that the latter have accepted them into their ranks. Nor have they' (Benjamin 2005e, p. 761). Additionally, in a 1930 conversation with Brecht, Benjamin claimed that '[t]oday's situation precedes the seizure of power by the proletariat', which Brecht objected '[c]annot be assumed' (quoted in Wizisla 2016, p. 204). During a discussion at the Sixteenth German Sociological Congress, Adorno confirmed that Benjamin believed, 'as did Marx, that a radical transformation of the world through powerful social forces was imminent' (quoted in Kluth 1969, p. 142).

106   Benjamin 2006d, p. 101. This second version of 'The Work of Art in the Age of Its Technological Reproducibility' is the one which Adorno would read first (cf. Schöttker 2007, p. 204) and criticise to Benjamin and Horkheimer.

107   Benjamin 2006d, pp. 101–2.

108   Benjamin 2006d, p. 104.

109   Benjamin 2006d, p. 103.

110   Benjamin 2006d, p. 105.

111   Benjamin 2006d, p. 106.

112   Letter from Benjamin to Werner Kraft, 28 October 1935 (Benjamin 2012, p. 516).

113   In doing so, Adorno already gestures towards a central insight of *Dialectic of Enlightenment* as well as the phenomenon described by its title: 'Myth is already enlightenment, and enlightenment reverts to mythology' (Adorno and Horkheimer 2002, p. xviii).

I now find it somewhat disturbing – and here I can see a sublimated rem-
nant of certain Brechtian themes – that you have now rather casually
transferred the concept of the magical aura to the 'autonomous work of
art' and flatly assigned a counter-revolutionary function to the latter. I do
not need to assure you just how aware I am of the magical element that
persists in the bourgeois work of art .... However, it seems to me that the
heart of the autonomous work of art does not itself belong to the dimension of myth – forgive my topical manner of speaking – but is inherently
dialectical, that is, compounds within itself the magical element with the
sign of freedom.[114]

Writing to Horkheimer in March 1936, Adorno claims that Benjamin's 'masochism' allows him to 'forget the dialectical counterpart' of the magical and
the mythical in their entirety. Benjamin 'first throws out the baby with the
bath water, and ... then worships the empty tub' – that is, de-mythologised
artworks which have been de-rationalised precisely through their de-mythologisation:

On the one hand, Benjamin perceives far too little the progressive intentions of 'autonomous' art, intentions which aim at good rationality and
technological empowerment. When it comes to such intentions, he completely forsakes dialectics while liquidating them with a promptness and
a terseness which seem to me to damage the liquid assets. On the other
hand, in the realm of technologised capitalist art, the realm of the cinema – ultimately the most alienated art of all – Benjamin invents theories which stand to serve the most base capitalist practice .... I certainly
share his view that the lowest things are dialectical through and through –

---

114   Letter from Adorno to Benjamin, 18 March 1936 (Adorno and Benjamin 1999, p. 128).
      Bernhard Reich also criticises the 'Work of Art' essay's one-sided account of aura in a letter
      to Benjamin: 'In your work, the shattering of aura appears as something positive, although
      you make an effort to support your claim thusly: the uniqueness of the artwork is bound
      up with ritual, which means that the destruction of aura is a destruction of rituals. / No
      doubt, in times when art is most closely bound up with the religious, ... ritual penetrates
      all characteristics of the artwork, and hence also its uniqueness. In my opinion, you make
      a mistake by only and always wanting to see a particular concentration of the ritualistic in
      the uniqueness of the artwork. I think that the highly personal relationship to the work of
      art, and the expression of the highly personal within it, will also take place under social-
      ism, and will even grow more intense' (letter from Reich to Benjamin, 19 February 1936
      [Benjamin 2007, p. 58]).

but this would just as well require a dialectics of the highest production (something I long ago expressed by explaining that, in music, it comes down to Schönberg and *Schlager*[115]).[116]

Adorno regards the essay's approach as 'masochistic' because he sees Benjamin attempting within it 'to outdo Brecht in radicalism',[117] and then – after having dared to master his bourgeois fear of the proletariat and the proletarian revolution – 'tightly shut[ting] his eyes, stick[ing] cotton in his ears and emphatically scream[ing] all the things he is afraid of'. However, for Adorno, 'the issue runs deeper: namely to fear itself':

> Revolution is supposed to eliminate anxiety and barbarity, and we need not fear it, but rather what currently exists. Yet although we need not fear revolution, we also do not have to revere it ... in abstract overexcitement. Politically speaking, this means simply that the proletariat needs the intellectuals for revolution just as much as the latter need the proletariat – whereas Benjamin, and this is in fact the worst of Brecht, places his trust in the proletariat as though it were a blind world spirit, tolerating specifically those characteristics of it which were produced by bourgeois machinery, characteristics which our precise task is to transform with knowledge.[118]

Adorno expresses his criticism of the theses for the first time in a letter to Benjamin also written in March 1936. Here, Adorno primarily takes issue with the application of the concept of the magical aura to the autonomous artwork, which he claims is thereby assigned a counter-revolutionary function.[119] As he had already written two years prior to Ernst Krenek, the 'redemption of art from liturgical function' is a process

---

115   Translator's note: a style of German popular music with folk origins; originated in the early twentieth century.

116   Letter from Adorno to Horkheimer, 21 March 1936 (Adorno and Horkheimer 2003b, pp. 131–2).

117   Palmier 2006, p. 313. In a letter to Scholem from the mid-1960s, Siegfried Kracauer writes the following: 'I once had a heated confrontation with Benjamin in Berlin regarding his slavish-masochistic attitude towards Brecht. But it's better if I tell you about it sometime in person' (letter from Kracauer to Scholem, 23 May 1965 [Puttnies and Smith 1991, pp. 118–19]). A subsequent meeting between Kracauer and Scholem would never come about.

118   Letter from Adorno to Horkheimer, 21 March 1936 (Adorno and Horkheimer 2003b, pp. 130–1); cf. Palmier 2006, p. 315.

119   See letter from Adorno to Benjamin, 18 March 1936 (Adorno and Benjamin 1999, p. 128).

which, since the middle of the sixteenth century, has thoroughly belonged to the bourgeois world, and has fallen under the category of 'reification'. Yet it is a quite superficial view, one at best held by sociologists of [Hanns] Eisler's crudity, that this 'reification' is undialectically 'negative', socially irrelevant and arbitrarily correctable through some sort of community art. 'Reification' is itself much more an expression of a fundamental social fact – one which can be discerned from the model of economy, specific- ally from the character of the commodity and the division of labour, and which necessarily remains in effect as long as the old 'immediacy' in the relationship between human being and thing (and our artworks are unavoidably things) has not been restored. While this restoration may be constantly desired by some anarchism-infected Marxists who have not understood Marx, I regard it as base and reactionary, and therefore regard attempts to modify the purpose of art as base and reactionary as well. Here, I am clearly opposed to Brecht and also to certain intentions of Ben- jamin.[120]

In contrast to Benjamin, who in the tradition of expressionism upholds the world of dreams as an antipode to base reality, Adorno views 'dreamworld and counter-world, phantasmagoria and aesthetic fundamentalism, as inextricably woven together'.[121]

'The Work of Art' essay renewed Adorno's misgivings about Benjamin's work. Just as with the *exposé* to *The Arcades Project*, Adorno criticises in a letter to Benjamin the lack of 'dialectical penetration'[122] of the subject matter – in this case, 'the autonomy of the work of art, and therefore its material form'. For Adorno, an artwork's autonomy and material form are

> not identical with the magical element within it. The reification of a great work of art is not simply a matter of loss, any more than the reification of the cinema is all loss. It would be a reactionary bourgeois gesture to negate the reification of the cinema in the name of the ego, and it would border on anarchism to revoke the reification of a great work of art in the spirit of an immediate appeal to use-value. *Les extrèmes me touchent*, as they do you – but only if the dialectic of the lowest has the same value as the dialectic of the highest, and not if the latter is simply left to decay.

---

120   Letter from Adorno to Ernst Krenek, 7 October 1934 (Adorno and Krenek 1974, p. 45).
121   Klein 2006, p. 40.
122   Letter from Adorno to Benjamin, 18 March 1936 (Adorno and Benjamin 1999, p. 131).

Both bear the stigmata of capitalism, both contain elements of change
.... Both are torn halves of an integral freedom, to which, however, they
do not add up. It would be romantic to sacrifice one to the other, either
with that bourgeois romanticism which seeks to uphold the 'personality'
and such-like mystification, or with that anarchistic romanticism which
places blind trust in the spontaneous powers of the proletariat within the
historical process – a proletariat which is itself a product of bourgeois
society.[123]

Whereas Benjamin sees in the proletariat 'the most enlightened form of class
consciousness',[124] Adorno urges, in an entirely un-Lukácsian manner, against
relying on revolutionary proletarian self-consciousness: workers 'in fact enjoy
no advantage over their bourgeois counterparts apart from their interest in the
revolution, and otherwise bear all the marks of mutilation of the typical bourgeois character'. While intellectuals such as Benjamin and himself must, 'in
full knowledge and without intellectual inhibitions, ... maintain our solidarity with the proletariat', they must also refrain from 'making our necessity into
a virtue of the proletariat as we are constantly tempted to do – that proletariat
which itself experiences the same necessity, and needs us for knowledge just as
much as we need the proletariat for the revolution'. Furthermore, just as he had
done previously in his letter to Horkheimer, Adorno writes to Benjamin that the
'goal of revolution is the elimination of anxiety. That is why we need not fear
the former, and need not ontologize the latter.'[125] In 'Theorie der Gesellschaft'
('Theory of Society'), his lecture course from the winter semester of 1949–50,
Adorno would still adhere to the idea that if society were genuinely transcended, this would benefit *everyone* – that is, that this would only be possible if

---

123   Letter from Adorno to Benjamin, 18 March 1936 (Adorno and Benjamin 1999, pp. 129–30).
       Here, Adorno is supported by the following passage from the *Communist Manifesto*: 'But
       not only has the bourgeoisie forged the weapons that bring death to itself; it has also
       called into existence the men who are to wield those weapons – the modern working
       class – the proletarians' (Marx and Engels 2010, p. 73; cf. also Marx 1976, p. 176.) Apro-
       pos *'Les extrèmes me touchent'*: at the beginning of the introduction to his 1948 *Philosophy
       of New Music*, Adorno quotes a sentence from Benjamin's *The Origin of German Tra-
       gic Drama*: 'Philosophical history as the research of origin is the form that, in the most
       remote extremes, in the apparent excesses of development, reveals the configuration of
       the idea as the configuration of the totality, characterized by the possibility of a mean-
       ingful juxtaposition of these extremes' (Adorno 2007c, p. 7; quoted from Benjamin 2009,
       p. 47).
124   Benjamin 2006d, p. 129, n. 24.
125   Letter from Adorno to Benjamin, 18 March 1936 (Adorno and Benjamin 1999, p. 131).

all forms of domination were transcended: 'If critique of society were only the interest of a class and not humanity specifically, it would not be deserving of one shot's worth of gunpowder'.[126]

5   Arcades Orthodoxy

A third controversy over Benjamin's use of Marxian terminology is connected to Adorno's reception of 'The Paris of the Second Empire in Baudelaire'.[127] At Horkheimer's request, Benjamin wrote this text in 1938 for publication in the *Zeitschrift für Sozialforschung*,[128] although the journal rejected the first draft. In a letter from November 1938, Adorno asks Benjamin to 'forego publication of the present version',[129] citing similar misgivings to those he had expressed regarding the *exposé* to *The Arcades Project* as well as 'The Work of Art in the Age of Its Technological Reproducibility'. Above all, Adorno alleges 'a lack of mediation between pragmatic substance and Marxian theory leading to a "materialistic-historiographical evocation" of socio-historical motifs'.[130] The missing mediation of which Adorno writes is mediation between 'conspicuous individual features from the realm of the superstructure' and the 'corresponding features of the substructure' – a mediation that can only be achieved theoretically, however, 'through the total social process'. This means unpacking 'the overall social and economic tendencies of the age' rather than 'imput[ing] to phenomena precisely the kind of spontaneity, tangibility and density which they have lost under capitalism'.

To express this another way: the theological motif of calling things by their names tends to switch into the wide-eyed presentation of mere facts. If one wanted to put it rather drastically, one could say that your study is located at the crossroads of magic and positivism. This spot is bewitched. Only theory could break this spell – your own resolute and

---

126   Adorno 2003ab, p. 124; cf. Bredtmann 2015, p. 279.

127   Benjamin 2006c.

128   Cf. letters from Adorno to Benjamin, 2 July 1937 and 13 September 1937 (Adorno and Benjamin 1999, pp. 196, 208); cf. letter from Horkheimer to Benjamin, 6 May 1938 (Tiedemann and Schweppenhäuser 2001, p. 1075); cf. letter from Gretel Adorno to Benjamin, 3 August 1938 (Adorno and Benjamin 2008, p. 236).

129   Letter from Adorno to Benjamin, 10 November 1938 (Adorno and Benjamin 1999, p. 285).

130   Schmider and Werner 2006, p. 568; quoted from letter from Adorno to Benjamin, 10 November 1938 (Adorno and Benjamin 1999, p. 283).

salutarily speculative theory. It is simply the claim of this theory that I bring against you here.[131]

Having expected the Baudelaire essay to provide 'a model for the Arcades project', Adorno must now recognise that Benjamin had written nothing more than 'a prelude to the latter. Motifs are assembled but they are not elaborated'.[132] Once again, Adorno involves his own work in his criticism, this time referring to his essay on Wagner: 'No one is more aware of the problems involved here than I am; the phantasmagoria chapter of my book on Wagner has certainly not succeeded in resolving them yet'.[133]

Moreover, precisely with regards to the Baudelaire essay, it is quite evident that Adorno is trying 'to defend Benjamin's metaphysical impulses from himself', as he would later write to Heißenbüttel. In his own words, Adorno brings his 'Arcades orthodoxy'[134] to bear against Benjamin in order to remind the latter of his own intentions, and to keep him from sacrificing these to an ostensible yet in reality quite superficial Marxism:

> Your solidarity with the Institute [for Social Research], which pleases no one more than myself, has led you to pay the kind of tributes to Marxism which are appropriate neither to Marxism nor to yourself. Not appropriate to Marxism because the mediation through the entire social process is missing, and because of a superstitious tendency to attribute to mere material enumeration a power of illumination which really belongs to theoretical construction alone rather than to purely pragmatic allusions. Not appropriate to your own individual nature because you have denied yourself your boldest and most fruitful ideas through a kind of pre-censorship in accordance with materialist categories (which by no means correspond to Marxist ones) .... God knows, there is only one truth, and if your powers of intelligence can seize this one truth through categor-

131   Letter from Adorno to Benjamin, 10 November 1938 (Adorno and Benjamin 1999, p. 283).

132   Letter from Adorno to Benjamin, 10 November 1938 (Adorno and Benjamin 1999, p. 281); cf. Buck-Morss 1977, p. 156.

133   Letter from Adorno to Benjamin, 10 November 1938 (Adorno and Benjamin 1999, p. 283).

134   Letter from Adorno to Benjamin, 10 November 1938 (Adorno and Benjamin 1999, p. 284). Continuing, Adorno writes that his wife Gretel 'once jokingly remarked that you [Benjamin] dwell in the cavernous depths of your Arcades and that you shrink from completing the study because you are afraid of leaving what you have built. We would exhort you to offer us some access to the Holy of Holies. I am sure you do not have to worry either about the stability of the structure or its profanation' (Adorno and Benjamin 1999, p. 285).

ies which may seem apocryphal to you given your conception of materialism, then you will capture more of this one truth than you will ever
do by employing conceptual tools that merely resist your grip at every
turn.[135]

By way of example, Adorno refers to the following passage from Benjamin's
essay: 'If there were such a thing as a commodity-soul (a notion that Marx occasionally mentions in jest), it would be the most empathetic ever encountered
in the realm of souls, for it would be bound to see every individual as a buyer
in whose hand and house it wants to nestle. Empathy is the nature of the
intoxication to which the flaneur abandons himself in the crowd'.[136] Regarding
this claim, Adorno suggests that Benjamin 'once again pay particularly careful
attention to this theory and compare it with the chapter on commodity fetishism in the first volume [of *Capital*]'.[137] In other words, here again, another
self-proclaimed Marxist thesis of Benjamin's 'must be documented with appropriate passages' from the man who first articulated the fetish-character of commodities.

'You may be confident that we are prepared to make your most extreme theoretical experiments our own', Adorno assures Benjamin. 'But we are equally
confident on our part that you will actually carry out these experiments'.[138]
So it was that Benjamin embarked on a new Baudelaire essay for the *Zeit-*

---

135 Letter from Adorno to Benjamin, 10 November 1938 (Adorno and Benjamin 1999, p. 284).
136 Benjamin 2006c, p. 31. In *Capital*, Marx writes the following: 'If commodities could speak,
they would say this: our use-value may interest men, but it does not belong to us as objects.
What does belong to us as objects, however, is our value. Our own intercourse as commodities proves it. We relate to each other merely as exchange-values. Now listen how
these commodities speak through the mouth of the economist' (Marx 1982a, pp. 176–7);
Marx subsequently quotes two economists. In *The Arcades Project*, Benjamin notes that
'[e]mpathy with the commodity is fundamentally empathy with exchange value itself.
The flâneur is the virtuoso of this empathy. He takes the concept of marketability itself
for a stroll. Just as his final ambit is the department store, his last incarnation is the
sandwich-man' (Benjamin 2002c, p. 448). 'Here, Benjamin implicitly references Lukács's
model of a revolutionary transcendence the of the capitalist form of objectivity through
the ... proletariat which has arrived via class-consciousness at the "*self-consciousness of the
commodity*": as precursor of this self-consciousness, empathy with the commodity gives
form to the distorted dream "in which each epoch entertains images of its successor";
the action of the f[lâneur] objects to reified rationality by internalising its principle of
bringing all that is social into object form, and specifically into the form of atomised experiences' (Schlette 2000, column 556; quoted from Lukács 1972a, p. 168 and Benjamin 2002a,
p. 4).
137 Letter from Adorno to Benjamin, 1 February 1939 (Adorno and Benjamin 1999, p. 304).
138 Letter from Adorno to Benjamin, 10 November 1938 (Adorno and Benjamin 1999, p. 285).

schrift für Sozialforschung, which Adorno and Horkheimer would enthusiastically accept[139] for publication in the journal's first issue of 1939.[140]

Philosophically, Adorno doubtlessly owes more to Benjamin than anyone
else (more indeed than even to Horkheimer). 'Every comparative reading of
their writings makes evident the heretofore insufficiently researched degree to
which Adorno took up concepts and motifs of thought from his older friend.
These are reflected only indirectly by Adorno's texts with their anti-academic
renunciation of footnotes and references. Adornian concepts such as nucleus
of time (*Zeitkern*), truth content (*Wahrheitsgehalt*), myth (*Mythos*), monad
(*Monade*), guilt-context (*Schuldzusammenhang*), language (*Sprache*), writing
(*Schrift*), redemption (*Erlösung*), remembrance (*Eingedenken*), natural history
(*Naturgeschichte*) and mimetic comportment (*mimetisches Verhalten*), originate – regardless of how they are altered – from the context of Benjamin's
writings'.[141] Nevertheless, it is also the case that a development in Adorno's
critique of political economy – one in which he was able to explicate and
substantiate his own insight as a Marxist philosopher – took place in direct confrontation with Benjamin, and that studying the writings of Benjamin
was not instructive for him in this development. Not only does Adorno's letter to Heißenbüttel attest to the fact that *in question of political economy*, the
relationship between him and Benjamin was not one of mutual learning and
teaching;[142] in his correspondence with Benjamin himself, Adorno was also
much more of a '[critical] partner'[143] who did not hold back his judgements:

---

139   In a letter to Benjamin following the arrival of the new version, Adorno writes that his
      'enthusiasm about the Baudelaire increases steadily!' (letter from Gretel and Theodor
      W. Adorno to Benjamin, 21 November 1939 [Adorno and Benjamin 1999, p. 318, original
      letter in English]).

140   Originally published as 'Über einige Motive bei Baudelaire', *Zeitschrift für Sozialforschung*,
      8, 1/2: 50–91; see Benjamin 2006a for English translation.

141   Lindner 1983, pp. 78–9.

142   Brodersen indicates that 'the intellectual relationship between Adorno and Benjamin ...
      was probably at times viewed by the two men themselves through the categories of "stu-
      dent" and "teacher", with the roles corresponding to their ages'. However, the fact that
      Adorno – to whom friendship did not mean withholding criticism when discussing the
      questions dealt with here – did not want to play a 'role' towards Benjamin, is characterised
      negatively by Brodersen: 'And when the relationship between them later (but still during
      Benjamin's lifetime) virtually reversed, with the former student bringing himself to criti-
      cise his teacher (Adorno's letters to Benjamin and others are a sad example of this), this
      circumstance was certainly not least the result of the fact that Adorno was never prepared
      to draw from the historical experiences of his time similar consequences to those drawn
      by Benjamin: Benjamin's rejection of an esoteric style of thinking and writing, which was
      already elevated to programme with the conclusion of the book on tragic drama, was
      something Adorno wanted neither to comprehend nor just accept' (Brodersen 1986, p. 13).

143   Habermas 1991, p. 129.

so it is that Adorno comments in a note from his final years that Benjamin's 'knowledge and understanding of Marx were extremely limited'.[144] At the same time, however, Adorno's critique of Benjamin takes a redemptive turn. This can be seen when he refers to Benjamin's 'form of Marxism, which he wanted to take over in orthodox form, as doctrine, without any inkling of the kind of productive misunderstanding he thereby set in motion'.[145] '[I]t would be unfair to juxtapose' this form of Marxism – which is hardly orthodox but rather had been 'worked out' by Benjamin himself – 'to Marx's own theory'.[146]

'With his emancipation from Benjamin, the phase in which Adorno's basic philosophical positions were formulated can be viewed as complete. His American emigration marks the beginning of his truly productive time, during which the manifold impulses from the interwar period reach maturity'.[147]

6   So'n-Rätsel (Such-a-Riddle)

However, though it has been claimed that Adorno was 'fascinated by Benjamin's elaborations on the "commodity-fetish", and specifically by the idea of "real abstraction" as presented in Sohn-Rethel's apocrypha',[148] this assumption is incorrect.

In discussions of Adorno's understanding of economy, Alfred Sohn-Rethel is often pointed to as the very first person to familiarise Adorno with the critique of political economy, and as the decisive influence on Adorno's philosophy in general. This claim is primarily supported by an enthusiastic letter from Adorno to Sohn-Rethel,[149] and by the fact that the latter is mentioned in a passage in *Negative Dialectics*.[150] However, the relationship between the two – both biographically and intellectually – was not nearly as harmonious as it may at times appear.

---

144   Adorno, 'Zur Interpretation Benjamins' (Tiedemann, Gödde and Lonitz 1991, p. 338). This text is a note recorded in Adorno's 'Manusktiptheft "Z" 1967/68'.

145   Adorno 2019c, p. 483.

146   Adorno 2006a, p. 90.

147   Pettazzi 1983, p. 42.

148   Hafner 2005, p. 141.

149   Among others, Alfred Sohn-Rethel himself repeatedly refers back to this letter, lastly in *Intellectual and Manual Labour* (Sohn-Rethel 2020, p. xxii). However, Tiedemann correctly notes that this particular letter 'does not come close to adequately representing either Adorno's objective position ... or his personal relationship' to Sohn-Rethel, 'as is documented more or less by their entire correspondence' (Tiedemann quoted in Höge 2008).

150   See Adorno 2007b, p. 177.

Adorno met Sohn-Rethel in September 1925 during a stay in Capri; Benjamin, Bloch and Kracauer were also there at the time.[151] One year later, in hopes of gaining the financial support of the Institute for Social Research, Sohn-Rethel sent a document titled 'Exposé zum theoretischen Kommentar der Marxschen Gesellschaftslehre' ('*Exposé* on the Theoretical Commentary of Marxian Social Theory') to Adorno and Kracauer in Frankfurt. Still unpublished to this day, this typescript

> begins with a bold preliminary remark: 'If one critically examines the theoretical foundation of Marxian social theory – *Capital* – it is evident that none of its elements stand up to thorough consideration. This means that none of the basic intentions which define the system as a whole find their identical, coherent realisation in Marxian concepts, or that when expressed in Marxian concepts, these intentions stand everywhere askance to the objective nature of things'. Sohn-Rethel wants to conceptually clarify Marx and to construct a 'rationalised parallel-system to *Capital*'. He wants to untangle the 'inextricable knot' produced by Marx. Marx – who 'through his errors glossed over the erroneousness of the world, only to recognise its other form in the twilight of the mist which has become transparent' – is said to need Sohn-Rethel's commentary to translate 'his theory from its violent language into the lesser, nonviolent, yet identical language of things'. However, the concluding sentence of the *exposé* – 'This is how we want at present to build philosophy into the stronghold of our last hope!' – gives the impression that a systematic philosophy of the kind Sohn-Rethel is proposing tends to keep its distance from the world and to be at home in a defensive stronghold.[152]

Moreover, this sentence also implies that Benjamin, who was sceptical of Sohn-Rethel,[153] had been acquainted with latter's 'rationalised parallel-system': in a letter to Adorno, Benjamin sardonically refers to Sohn-Rethel as the 'High Priest of Economics in his misty stronghold'.[154]

---

151   Cf. Freytag 2006, p. 79; cf. also van Reijen and van Doorn 2001, pp. 89–90.
152   Freytag 2006, p. 81.
153   Not unlike Horkheimer, Benjamin was above all sceptical of Sohn-Rethel's terminology, calling it 'the language of a pimp' (see letter from Adorno to Benjamin, 29 February 1940 [Adorno and Benjamin 1999, p. 322]).
154   Letter from Benjamin to Adorno, 11 February 1938 (Adorno and Benjamin 1999, p. 238); cf. also letter from Benjamin to Adorno, 1 March 1937 (Adorno and Benjamin 1999, p. 169)

In any case, Adorno was unimpressed by Sohn-Rethel's *éxpose*. His opinion was shared by Kracauer, whom he sent a devastating critique of the text:

> the framework, like the basis, is completely inadequate ... And what a murky Bloch-like confusion he stirs up with his concept of the transcendental! And how wrong – at least like Benjaminian ideas – and how unbroken are the metaphysics perching on top of it! He misses the entire content of Marxism in Heidelberg fashion and gives it the spuriously profound quality of a dilettante. ... The banal rejection [of Sohn] by every communist would [be even more justified than the rejection of] Lukács, of whom he is a goyish-pastoral incarnation minus the mask. No, this book is no use.[155]

Ten years later, Sohn-Rethel sent Adorno his so-called 'Lucerne *exposé*',[156] a lengthy letter expounding on lines of thought for a further draft. In contrast to the earlier *exposé*, it elicited an enthusiastic response in which Adorno calls it 'the greatest intellectual shock I experienced in philosophy since my first encounter with Benjamin's work – in 1923!'[157]

It is possible to distinguish between four areas of work Sohn-Rethel pursued during his life:[158]

1) the discovery of the 'transcendental subject'[159] in the commodity-form;
2) the common genesis of the commodity-form and forms of thought in the logic of exploitation and appropriation;
3) the separation of intellectual and manual labour;[160]
4) fascism theory.[161]

---

and letter from Benjamin to Adorno, 4 December 1937 (Adorno and Benjamin 1999, p. 235).

155   Letter from Adorno to Kracauer, 17 September 1926 (Adorno and Kracauer 2020, p. 92); cf. Freytag 2006, p. 82.
156   Later published under the title *Soziologische Theorie der Erkenntnis* (Sohn-Rethel 1985).
157   Letter from Adorno to Sohn-Rethel, 17 November 1936 (Adorno and Sohn-Rethel 1991, p. 32).
158   According to Engster 2009, p. 9.
159   Sohn-Rethel 2020, p. xxi; cf. Hörisch 1978, p. 45.
160   Lastly expounded upon in *Intellectual and Manual Labour* (Sohn-Rethel 2020). Demirović criticises this aspect of Sohn-Rethel's work: 'Sohn-Rethel's considerations tend towards an abstract theory of derivation which easily becomes unhistorical insofar as its sole concentration on the form of the commodity means that it cannot address different stages of capitalist social formation and of the relationship between intellectual and manual labour' (Demirović 2001, column 135).
161   See Sohn-Rethel 1987.

The letter by Sohn-Rethel which so excited Adorno primarily relates to the second point while presenting 'two insights'[162] which the *exposé* itself pursues.

The first insight consists of the claim 'that the historical development of *theory* independent from the practical-material being of humans and endowed with the appearance of logical autonomy – that is, the historical development of "knowledge" in every idealistic sense – can ultimately be explained alone by a unique and extremely profound break in the *practice* of human existence'.[163] This break is said to be 'the fact of exploitation in the elementary sense that one part of society lives on the products of the labour of the other part'.[164]

Sohn-Rethel's second insight can be summarised with his concept of 'functional socialisation', which for him 'is the decisive approach for analysing and dialectically bursting open the "commodity-form" and the relationships which hide it'.[165] As he writes, functional socialisation is a form of socialisation which

> is based on absolutely no natural human relationship ..., but rather on the exploitation of humans with respect to their relationship to nature; it occurs only in relationships between humans, while of course requiring that exploited humans relate to nature as producers, but in a way that involves their relationship to nature in their entirely different order, and in doing so transforms all internal features of this relationship. Hence, functional socialisation is the interweaving of human existence through exploitation, and is always materially mediated, that is, mediated through appropriated products as things existing identically. This socialising form through which things are mediated, or even more precisely, the essential identity of these things as objects appropriated in an exploitative relationship, is the foundation of the 'commodity-form'.[166]

In a letter to Benjamin, Adorno reports that 'from a quite different angle, [Sohn-Rethel] has arrived at certain conclusions which are remarkably similar to those of my own current efforts'.[167] Here, Adorno refers to his work on Husserl,

---

162   Letter from Sohn-Rethel to Adorno, 12 November 1936 (Adorno and Sohn-Rethel 1991, p. 13).

163   Ibid.

164   Letter from Sohn-Rethel to Adorno, 12 November 1936 (Adorno and Sohn-Rethel 1991, p. 16).

165   Letter from Sohn-Rethel to Adorno, 12 November 1936 (Adorno and Sohn-Rethel 1991, p. 18).

166   Letter from Sohn-Rethel to Adorno, 12 November 1936 (Adorno and Sohn-Rethel 1991, p. 20).

167   Letter from Adorno to Benjamin, 28 November 1936 (Adorno and Benjamin 1999, p. 162). In

which he was pursuing at the time under the auspices of obtaining a PhD from Oxford in order to teach there.[168] Responding to Sohn-Rethel directly, Adorno praises the 'greatness and might' of his idea before promising 'that I at the Institute will do *everything* I can for your work!'.[169] However, this would not amount to much.

Adorno '*urgently*'[170] advises Horkheimer to materially enable Sohn-Rethel to develop his *exposé*. However, Horkheimer replies that his and Adorno's 'opinions on Sohn-Rethel's work unfortunately diverge'.[171] Suspecting Adorno has 'simply let himself be blinded by Sohn-Rethel's great intelligence', Horkheimer himself claims to find 'Sohn-Rethel's perpetual assurance that whatever odd proofs must be provided revealing whatever odd "geneses" – from existence, or from history, or from the development of man's existence, or from the deepest roots of the existence of man in his history – to be synonymous with the truth-problem of consciousness, or with the question of knowledge's validity or with the practice of society ... to be infinitely tedious and uninteresting'.[172] Ultimately, Horkheimer maintains that 'this Sohn-Rethel absolutely does not stand

---

a letter to Horkheimer, Benjamin reports that Sohn-Rethel's 'two most important' theses are 'the derivation of commodity exchange from exploitation and the derivation of purely theoretical thought from the commodity economy', noting that Adorno is 'in his most recent works particularly wedded to Sohn-Rethel's second thesis, which the difficulties of articulating seem to me to be the greatest' (letter from Benjamin to Horkheimer, 28 March 1937 [Benjamin 1999, pp. 492–3]).

168   Cf. Theodor W. Adorno Archive 2003, pp. 130–52. Provisionally titled 'The Doctrines of Intellectual Intuition and Intentionality in the "Phenomenological" Philosophy of Edmund Husserl', this work was never completed due to Adorno's move to the United States. Written between 1934–7, the manuscript provided Adorno with material for his book *Against Epistemology: A Metacritique*, which he wrote after returning to Germany (cf. Adorno's own account of the book's origins in Adorno 2013, pp. 1–2 as well as that of Rolf Tiedemann in Tiedemann 2003b, pp. 385–6). According to Alfred Schmidt, this book is 'not actually a contribution to Husserl research, but rather a study occasioned by Husserl: it is the ingenious attempt to convey the idealist character of all originary philosophy (*Ursprungsphilosophie*), even that which gestures materialistically' (Schmidt 1983, pp. 20–1).

169   Letter from Adorno to Sohn-Rethel, 17 November 1936 (Adorno and Sohn-Rethel 1991, p. 32).

170   Letter from Adorno to Horkheimer, 23 November 1936 (Adorno and Horkheimer 2003b, p. 227).

171   Letter from Horkheimer to Adorno, 8 December 1936 (Adorno and Horkheimer 2003b, p. 248); cf. Horkheimer's diplomatic yet thoroughly critical letter to Sohn-Rethel regarding his *exposé*: letter from Horkheimer to Sohn-Rethel, 25 November 1936 (Horkheimer 1995b, p. 745).

172   Letter from Horkheimer to Adorno, 8 December 1936 (Adorno and Horkheimer 2003b, pp. 248–9).

in real contrast to what we hate'.[173] Referring specifically here to Sohn-Rethel's
'entirely formal' use of 'the concept of exploitation', Horkheimer continues that
'[i]t would be a mistake to believe that idealism can be overcome by simply
replacing idealist terms with those from a materialist theory. This merely gives
the appearance of actuality without actually changing anything'.[174] However,
Horkheimer mainly objects to Sohn-Rethel for another reason: namely, 'that
Sohn-Rethel constantly submits his thesis as articulations of problems for
future explorations, thereby giving the impression that everything he says will
eventually find scholarly support, and that he is only dealing provisionally in
hypotheses. Yet the scientific credit which he claims in this way must be dis-
counted if one realises that precisely Sohn-Rethel's method testifies in various
résumés against the expectations of such future evidence'. For Horkheimer, the
difficulty involved in setting down in a work what Sohn-Rethel's various *exposés*
only ever gesture towards is the result of 'a deep internal ambiguity which will
not diminish over time'.[175]

After his initial enthusiasm, Adorno increasingly adopted Horkheimer's
opinion of Sohn-Rethel. In a 1937 letter to Benjamin, Adorno reveals himself
to be disillusioned that 'So'n-Rätsel' – his new nickname for Benjamin's 'High
Priest of Economics', a slight corruption of Sohn-Rethel translating to 'Such-a-
Riddle' – 'is eagerly trying to rediscover the man who first started on the work
in order to disable him completely, and that he is far more interested in spin-
ning things out into the indeterminate future than he is in completing anything
within a foreseeable period of time'.[176] In light of ever newer *exposés*[177] arriving at lengthy intervals,[178] Horkheimer's scepticism of Sohn-Rethel's ability to
follow his own programme appeared to have been confirmed.

---

173   Letter from Horkheimer to Adorno, 11 January 1937 (Adorno and Horkheimer 2003b,
       p. 269).
174   Letter from Horkheimer to Adorno, 11 January 1937 (Adorno and Horkheimer 2003b,
       p. 268).
175   Letter from Horkheimer to Adorno, 24 May 1937 (Adorno and Horkheimer 2003b, pp. 370–
       1).
176   Letter from Adorno to Benjamin, 27 November 1937 (Adorno and Benjamin 1999, p. 230).
       On this point, Philipp von Wussow refers laconically to Sohn-Rethel's 'laziness' (von Wus-
       sow 2007, p. 42, n. 101).
177   Sohn-Rethel himself counts seven *exposés*, the last of which was written for the last Ger-
       man edition of *Intellectual and Manual Labour* and 'still leaves many questions open'
       (Sohn-Rethel 1989b, p. vi). 'My entire path is plastered with these elaborations bearing
       the name *exposés*, the majority of which still rot in my drawer' (Sohn-Rethel 1989a, p. 145).
178   'I would like to know what's happening with Alfred Sohn. Of course, his expose still has
       not arrived' (letter from Adorno to Benjamin, 20 April 1937 [Adorno and Benjamin 1999,
       p. 176]). Referring to Sohn-Rethel's work in a letter from the following year, Gretel Adorno

Following the failure of Sohn-Rethel's attempt to work out a final version of the Lucerne *exposé*, contact between him and Adorno largely broke off, only to be resumed on occasion.[179] Adorno himself barely continued to follow Sohn-Rethel's project 'to derive the Kantian deduction of the categories from the commodity-form and its dialectic'.[180] In a 1965 letter to Lucien Goldmann, who had never heard of Sohn-Rethel, Adorno writes that the latter 'has been working for many a long year on a problem with which he is downright obsessed: the derivation of the Western tradition's epistemological categories from the exchange-relation'. After describing this work as 'the quite energetic and manifold attempt to push further certain approaches from the reification chapter from *History and Class Consciousness* into a Marxian epistemology', Adorno notes: 'Just now, Sohn-Rethel submitted to me his most recent draft from the complex [the lecture 'Warenform und Denkform' ('Commodity-Form and Thought-Form')];[181] tomorrow he will visit me here'.[182] The correspondence between Adorno and Sohn-Rethel during this time suggests that the former never read the draft in question.

On balance, Sohn-Rethel is for Adorno a '*Stichwortgeber*',[183] a giver of catchwords. His aspirations, which at times run parallel to Adorno's own, provide the latter with 'an additional support'[184] for forming his own understanding of the theory of value. In the years following his exchange with Sohn-Rethel, Adorno would adopt an ideology-critical approach in order to explore the mediation between the principle of identity and exchange. This can be seen in a passage in *Negative Dialectics* which directly addresses the transcendental subject:

---

writes to Benjamin that 'naturally we do not get to see any of the results' (letter from Gretel Adorno to Benjamin, 1 February 1938 [Adorno and Benjamin 2008, p. 209]).

179   In a letter from August 1944, Sohn-Rethel laments to Adorno: 'I have written you letters and sent you two m[anu]s[cript]s and have never had from you a proper reply. ... Nothing about your work and plans, as you had led me to hope, and not a word of criticism of my own stuff. I don't consider this very comradely, and for the life of me I can't see the reason' (letter from Sohn-Rethel to Adorno, 20 August 1944 [Adorno and Sohn-Rethel 1991, p. 111, original in English and with brackets]). Adorno's next letter to Sohn-Rethel is dated 1958 (cf. Hentschel 2006, p. 35).

180   Letter from Adorno to Horkheimer, 23 November 1936 (Adorno and Horkheimer 2003b, p. 226).

181   See Sohn-Rethel 1961.

182   Letter from Adorno to Goldmann, 29 March 1965 (Theodor W. Adorno Archive, Br 484/51); on Sohn-Rethels visit and the course it took, see letter from Sohn-Rethel to Adorno, 27 April 1965 (Adorno and Sohn-Rethel 1991, p. 142); see also Christoph Gödde's editorial comments (Adorno and Sohn-Rethel 1991, p. 144).

183   Grigat 2007, p. 167.

184   Breuer in Sohn-Rethel, Breuer and von Greiff 1986, p. 315.

As the extreme borderline case of ideology, the transcendental subject comes close to truth. The transcendental generality is no mere narcissist self-exaltation of the I, not the *hubris* of an autonomy of the I. Its reality lies in the domination that prevails and perpetuates itself by means of the principle of equivalence. The process of abstraction – which philosophy transfigures, and which it ascribes to the knowing subject alone – is taking place in the factual [exchange] society.[185]

Again, in his subsequent theoretical work, Adorno is less interested in the common historical genesis of knowledge and social domination than in the factual mediation of both in the here-and-now. While Sohn-Rethel pursues the question of how 'objectivity and the claim to truth of the natural sciences'[186] are possible in the first place, Adorno can set aside this issue aside with a simple observation: 'The concept of objectivity is formed in society'.[187] In spite of Friedemann Grenz's claim to the contrary, Adorno precisely does not trace back 'the principle of domination' established by the intellect 'to the division between intellectual and manual labour'.[188] 'For a dialectician of Adorno's rank, causal-mechanical interpretations of the relationship between commodity-form and form of thought are simply forbidden'.[189] In the question of 'which comes first, the socially necessary separation of physical and mental labour or the usurpatory privilege of the medicine man', Adorno ultimately recognises the mere 'debate over the chicken and the egg. In any case, the shaman requires ideology and without him it would not be possible'.[190] On this point, he is even more explicit in a subsequent lecture, claiming that humans as 'functionaries' of exchange-processes are already ruled by domination, and that this is why he 'does not base theoretical analyses ... on some ideal-typical and ahistorical models of a pure exchange act from which this and that follow'.[191]

Incidentally, the passage in *Negative Dialectics* which refers to Sohn-Rethel reads as follows: 'Alfred Sohn-Rethel was the first to point out that hidden in this principle, in the general and necessary activity of the mind, lies work of an inalienably social nature'.[192] This reference is problematic. Sohn-Rethel would later claim in conversation never to have said 'what is cited there ... in that

185   Adorno 2007b, p. 178.
186   Engster 2009, p. 11.
187   Adorno 1993b, p. 18.
188   Grenz 1974, p. 149; cf. Kager 1988, p. 254, n. 176.
189   Ritsert 1998, p. 333.
190   Adorno 1976a, p. 64; cf. Kager 1988, p. 254, n. 176.
191   Adorno 2019i, p. 58.
192   Adorno 2007b, p. 177.

way, that abstract labour was contained within the transcendental subject. I would never be able to justify that'.[193] This misunderstanding never came up between Adorno and Sohn-Rethel, yet political differences did, which were at the same time also theoretical differences. These differences are manifest in two letters from 1966. After receiving *Negative Dialectics* from Adorno just after its release, Sohn-Rethel thanks him: 'Your book just arrived! Wonderful! What a Xmas gift!'. However, he then immediately takes issue with the claim in the second sentence of the introduction:

> '... after the attempt to change the world miscarried'. That reads like the summary of a concluded past. Are you so sure of that? For the Soviet Union and its annexation I admit you're right, but even for China I'm not so sure. And if things fail there as well, there will be further attempts, not only among the latecomers, and I still hold the devout conviction that the world will either shatter or need to be changed by humans. For this task, 'indefinite time' does not exist. And do negative dialectics have no relationship to changing the world? Does all that fall under the 'affirmative essence' from which 'the book seeks to free dialectics'? Or is it the case that you don't view the necessary changes to the world as impossible, but rather their ability to contribute to the 'realisation of philosophy'? In that case, wouldn't the forms of thought *not* be determined by social being, while we would have arrived back at dialectical idealism?
>
> Without answers here, I'll hardly know how to get my bearings. Do you still remember the philosophical conversation between Walter Benjamin and yourself and Kracauer in Naples in 1924 (or 1925?) for which I was also present?[194]

Adorno does in fact remember: 'The Benjamin conversation you bring up – my god, how the World Spirit or whatever it's called passed over everything. One should really try to learn from one's mistakes without betraying one's motivations – you'll believe me that I and especially I am not betraying my motivations'.[195] Furthermore, Adorno defends himself

---

193   Sohn-Rethel quoted in Höge 2008.
194   Letter from Sohn-Rethel to Adorno, 18 December 1966 (Adorno and Sohn-Rethel 1991, pp. 150–1). Translator's note: Sohn-Rethel 'Wonderful! What a Xmas gift!' written in English in the original.
195   Letter from Adorno to Sohn-Rethel, 23 December 1966 (Adorno and Sohn-Rethel 1991, pp. 152–3).

against official Marxism's moral coercion, which consists of a particular kind of positivity .... The notion that this match must end well in all circumstances is indeed only one of the reasons, but nonetheless one of them, why it will probably be lost. I can't deny to myself that a deep injury to theory itself bears a degree of blame here. ... I can't believe there could be some hope in what is taking place in China – I'd need to disavow everything I've thought my whole life if I wanted to profess to feel anything other than dread.[196]

Concerning the 'realisation of philosophy' which Sohn-Rethel feels to be a return to idealism, Adorno responds thusly:

I believe the problem is posed incorrectly. It interprets Marxism *totally*, which is to say: idealistically. There is no continuum – no identity of theory and practice. In a certain sense, practice is *more modest* than philosophy, and philosophy in turn doesn't assimilate into Marxism.[197]

This barely concealed rejection of Sohn-Rethel's understanding of theory indicates his diminished influence on Adorno, who was 'probably only interested in Sohn-Rethel's actual idea in the mid-thirties'.[198] Yet this interest is attested to by the fact that

a *systematic* usage of the apparatus of value-form analysis can first be registered in the period after 1936–7, and most clearly in the study 'On the Fetish-Character in Music and the Regression of Listening', which emerged in the summer of 1938. However, this study's thesis of the substitution of use-value through exchange-value also shows that Adorno did not settle for a materialist version of transcendental logic, but rather pressed on in a thoroughly independent way towards a theory of negative *totality*. A future history of Critical Theory may well view this transition from a Kantian to a Hegelian problem as the decisive step by which Adorno moved beyond Horkheimer as well as Sohn-Rethel.[199]

---

196 Letter from Adorno to Sohn-Rethel, 23 December 1966 (Adorno and Sohn-Rethel 1991, p. 152). Regarding China, Adorno is referring to the so-called Cultural Revolution.
197 Letter from Adorno to Sohn-Rethel, 23 December 1966 (Adorno and Sohn-Rethel 1991, p. 153).
198 Engster 2009, p. 6, n. 6.
199 Breuer in Sohn-Rethel, Breuer and von Greiff 1986, p. 319.

CHAPTER 4

Familiarity with Its First Chapter

'I've already been to Bidjan, you weren't even born, you foetus!'
'Fetishist!'
'Fake! You use expressions without knowing what they mean. Give up, Falstaff.'

TIERNO MONÉNEMBO, Un attiéké pour Elgass

．．
．

1   A Music That Has Become Incomprehensible

In 1936, the *Zeitschrift für Sozialforschung* published 'On Jazz', an essay written by Adorno under the pseudonym Hektor Rottweiler.[1] Situating this text within the ongoing debate initiated by 'The Work of Art in the Age of its Technological Reproducibility', Adorno describes it in a letter to Benjamin as extremely closely related to the latter's own article, even going so far as 'to insist that the entire conception of my essay ... goes back to a time before I became acquainted with your work'.[2] Benjamin in turn attributes their independently originating engagements with a similar topic to 'a profound and spontaneous inner communication between our thoughts' causing their respective investigations to be 'like two different headlamps trained upon the same object from opposite directions'.[3] Yet to use Benjamin's metaphor, Adorno's contribution appears to cast a decidedly brighter light on the object in question. Regarding Benjamin's 'masochism' in 'The Work of Art' (an issue discussed in the previous chapter of this study), Adorno writes the following to Horkheimer:

> [The Parisian brothel] Sphinx is a (more) appropriate place for masochism than Marxist theory. Same goes for the professorially romantic

---

1   Originally published as 'Über Jazz', *Zeitschrift für Sozialforschung*, 5, 2: 235–59; see Adorno 2019e for English translation.
2   Letter from Adorno to Benjamin, 28 May 1936 (Adorno and Benjamin 1999, p. 135).
3   Letter from Benjamin to Adorno, 30 June 1936 (Adorno and Benjamin 1999, p. 144).

notions of technology. It really does have something of a *Wandervogel*[4] gone insane, and Benjamin has long failed to emancipate himself from Brecht. But as a basis for discussion, the work is very useful in spite of everything, and must absolutely be published, of course. My jazz essay should already contain some correctives.[5]

Adorno acknowledges several inadequacies of 'On Jazz' at various places in his writings. In a 1959 letter to the music critic Baldur Bockhoff, he admits that the essay 'indeed has the flaw that the decisive American experiences are still not processed in it, and is in more than one respect primitive, yet contains the core of certain categories which are implicitly required by the later work you are familiar with from *Prisms*'.[6] Subsequently, in his 1964 *Moments musicaux*, a collection of essays on music in which 'On Jazz' is republished, Adorno confesses an 'insufficient knowledge of the specifically American aspects of jazz, especially that of standardization' while noting 'the obsolescence of some characteristics of European jazz in the 1930s'.[7]

That being said, shortly after composing 'On Jazz', Adorno locates the essay's 'primary flaw' elsewhere: namely, in its lack of 'concrete economic categories', a lack he nevertheless 'neither could nor wanted to paper over'.[8] This flaw is evident in the editorial revisions made to Adorno's manuscript by Horkheimer and Friedrich Pollock. In one passage, Adorno does in fact employ the concept of surplus value: while innovation sometimes 'leads to a piece's great success', he writes, such pieces are 'mostly pressed against the will of the publishers, as they

---

4 Translator's note: here, *Wandervogel* (an antiquated word for 'migratory bird') denotes a member of an early twentieth-century German youth movement (*Die Wandervogelbewegung*) which romanticised nature and folk culture.

5 Letter from Adorno to Horkheimer, 21 March 1936 (Adorno and Horkheimer 2003b, p. 132).

6 Letter from Adorno to Bockhoff, 29 September 1959 (TWA, Br 151/2). The work to which Adorno is referring is the essay 'Perennial Fashion – Jazz' (Adorno 1988e), which was first published in 1953 before being then republished in the essay collection *Prisms* in 1955. In his extensive study on the significance of jazz for Adorno, Heinz Steinert concludes that Adorno informed himself about jazz while in the United States 'mainly by listening to the radio and reading two books' (Steinert 2003b, p. 65).

7 Adorno 2019e, p. 5.

8 Letter from Adorno to Horkheimer, 26 January 1936 (Adorno and Horkheimer 2003b, p. 111). Adorno makes a quite similar claim in his lecture course *Fragen der Dialektik* (*Questions of Dialectics*): 'Now in the little booklet *Moments musicaux*, one can find a work on jazz which is now almost 30 years old yet nevertheless very programmatic for me. This ... work, partially due to the fact that it was written in Europe before I had lived in America, has a certain ignorance of its material, is disputable in its premise, so to speak, and I absolutely would not want to defend ... its substance or put myself on the line for every sentence it contains' (Adorno 2021b, pp. 311–12.).

involve a clear risk; ~~surplus-value prevails against the entrepreneur~~'.[9] However, as the strikethrough in the above quotation from the edited manuscript indicates, the final clause was removed in the editorial process, with even Adorno acknowledging that his 'own formulation was awkward in its economic inexactitude'.[10] Elsewhere, Adorno's use of Marxian terminology was refined by the *Zeitschrift für Sozialforschung*. For example, one sentence from the manuscript reads: 'Jazz is a commodity in the strict sense: in musical production, its suitability for everyday use establishes itself in no other form than ~~its exchange-value~~ its saleability'.[11] Regarding the replacement of the Marxian 'exchange-value' with 'saleability' (*Absatzfähigkeit*), Horkheimer remarks that Pollock is 'of the opinion that the concept of "exchange-value" belongs on another theoretical level as that on which it is used in the essay. This passage could thus give the impression of mere "coquetry" with Marxian terminology, which at any rate should be avoided'.[12]

Several years prior in 1932, the very first issue of the *Zeitschrift für Sozialforschung* published a two-part essay by Adorno titled 'On the Social Situation of Music'.[13] The piece can be regarded as a kind of precursor to 'On Jazz' in many respects, including in its use of economic categories. Already within it, Adorno identifies the 'role of music in the social process' as

> exclusively that of a commodity; its value is that determined by the market. Music no longer serves direct needs nor benefits from direct application, but rather adjusts to the pressures of the exchange of abstract units. Its value – wherever such value still exists at all – is determined by use: it subordinates itself to the process of exchange.

In this passage, Adorno evidently still believes there could potentially be commodities for which use-value no longer in fact 'still exists at all'. However, he also asserts that '[t]hrough total absorption of both musical production and consumption by the capitalist process, the alienation of music from man has become complete'.[14] According to Adorno, for music to 'intervene in the social

---

9   Cited from editorial note by Tiedemann (Adorno and Horkheimer 2003b, p. 151); for the final English version of the sentence cf. Adorno 2019e, p. 92.

10   Letter from Adorno to Horkheimer, 26 May 1936 (Adorno and Horkheimer 2003b, p. 147).

11   Cited from editorial note by Tiedemann (Adorno and Horkheimer 2003b, p. 160); for the final English version of the sentence cf. Adorno 2019e, p. 84.

12   Letter from Horkheimer to Adorno, 15 June 1936 (Adorno and Horkheimer 2003b, p. 159).

13   Originally published as 'Zur gesellschaftlichen Lage der Musik', *Zeitschrift für Sozialforschung*, 1, 1/2 and 3: pp. 103–24, 356–78; see Adorno 2009d for English translation.

14   Adorno 2009d, p. 391.

process', it has to be 'in a position to intervene as *art*'. Yet for music to be able to intervene as art in the first place, it cannot simply be counterposed to society as 'a "spiritual" phenomenon, abstract and far-removed from actual social conditions': this would result in nothing more than a 'sanction of the fetish character of music which is the major difficulty and most basic problem to be represented by music today'.[15] Thus, there emerges for Adorno the problem of how music and society can be theoretically mediated:

> The short circuit: such music is incomprehensible, esoteric-private, thus reactionary, and must, therefore be rejected: such music is constructed upon the foundation of a romantic concept of primitive musical immediacy, which gives rise to the opinion that the empirical consciousness of present-day society – a consciousness promoted in unenlightened narrow-mindedness and, indeed, promoted even to the point of neurotic stupidity in the face of class domination for the purpose of the preservation of this consciousness – might be taken as the positive measure of a music no longer alienated, but rather the property of free men. Politics must not be permitted to draw abstractions from this state of consciousness which is necessarily of central concern to the social dialectic, nor is cognition to allow the definition of its boundaries by a consciousness produced by class domination and which further as the class consciousness of the proletariat extends the wounds of mutilation by means of the class mechanism.[16]

In a letter written after receiving 'On the Social Situation of Music' directly from Adorno himself, Ernst Krenek responds by criticising its central thesis: 'that music first assumed a commodity-character in the capitalist world'. For Krenek, the true novelty of music under capitalism lies in the fact that

---

15   Adorno 2009d, p. 393.

16   Adorno 2009d, pp. 393–4. 'Was an essential component of the materialist conception of history not being finally abandoned here, with only the concept of a mechanics of the development of productive forces and productive relations remaining? In none of the articles did the expression "monopoly capitalism" occur as often as in Adorno's. He even saw "Fazism", as he called it (he was the only one to mention it at all), as being controlled by monopoly capitalists, in accordance with the communist dogma of the time. This gave the impression that, by declaring his belief in the key concepts and thought processes of dogmatic Marxism, he was trying to create a favourable climate for his own interpretation of modern music for himself and for the left, from which he most expected sympathy for the new music' (Wiggershaus 1995, p. 122).

music, like all art, has become autonomous. The place where it is consumed and paid for no longer exists, because music no longer desires
to conform to existing needs .... Yet as the autonomous composer still
wishes to live off the income from his work, that which we call isolation
emerges. ... Certainly, the autonomisation of art can be explained from
social transformations. However, capitalism did not turn art into a commodity, but rather at most transformed humans in such a way that they
no longer desired the commodity which music always already was, and
which had once been gladly purchased. If we judge a humanity interested
in this commodity more highly than one which is disinterested, which is
something I am willing to do, then we have delivered a verdict on the capitalist world. It has destroyed human dignity by exorcising from man the
wish for spiritual goods. By this, I do not intend any criticism of these
goods themselves, and on this point I do not understand, for example,
Benjamin's polemic against the 'creative'.[17]

In the final sentence of this passage, Krenek refers to a review by Benjamin from
the same year which takes issue with the concepts of 'the creative' and 'the productive'. Although Benjamin views these concepts as 'by nature nothing other
than the expression of humane relationships between humans', he also argues
that they are,

> to the degree that they have died in the life of the community, reified,
> ... emblems on private man. To want to place ... an already by definition
> amorphous mass of private people at the helm politically, in a parliament
> of intellectuals, for example, is outright quixotism. Today it may still be
> amiable, but by tomorrow it could be harmful.[18]

In a response letter of his own, Adorno clarifies to Krenek that

> music does not take on the character of a commodity because it is ex-
> changed in general, but rather because it is exchanged *abstractly*, in the
> sense of the commodity-form explicated by Marx, which is to say that
> instead of an immediate relation of exchange taking place, a 'reified' one
> occurs instead. When you identify art's 'autonomisation' as the decisive

---

17   Letter from Krenek to Adorno, 11 September 1932 (Adorno and Krenek 1974, pp. 29–30).
18   Benjamin 2001b, p. 352.

transformation, this is in reality nothing other than what I mean by commodity-character; it is just the same phenomenon described not from the perspective of the *relations* of production, but rather from that of the *forces* of production. This of course can be done, it is just not the subject of my work; just as with the musician, the *positive* element of autonomisation is what I have accentuated here as well. If one understands capitalism not merely as 'pro money', but namely as the *totality* of a social process defined by abstract labour-time as a unit of exchange, then capitalism has, in a precise sense, most certainly made art into a commodity *along with* man. The commodity-character of art as the objective side of this process, and the destruction of 'human dignity' as its subjective side, are equivalent and cannot be wrested free from each other. And if Benjamin ... attacked 'creative' man, he did so because the pathos of 'spirit' does not strengthen the true pathos opposed to the reified state of humans and objects, but rather obscures this state by presenting an illusory, provisional possibility – one that is merely subjective, in fact, and undialectical – as sufficient for overcoming it. In other words, Benjamin attacked 'creative' man because the latter regards the world precisely in a 'bourgeois' manner as produced by spirit and correctible through it, whereas world and spirit are intertwined with each other, and the corrective can only be surmised in their dialectic.[19]

In 'On Jazz', Adorno subsequently turns towards exposing 'the subject of jazz as eccentricity and sham-opponent'.[20] '[W]ritten on a double defensive: first against jazz as music, yet even more so against its positive appraisal, against "jazz ideology"',[21] the essay argues that jazz is 'pseudo-democratic' because its 'attitude of immediacy ... hides class differences'. Listeners are given what they desire, but at the same time their desire is *merely* satisfied. In turn, this desire has already been shaped in advance by what is on offer: 'the irresistible propaganda machine belabours the masses with the songs it likes, which are usually

---

19   Letter from Adorno to Krenek, 30 September 1932 (Adorno and Krenek 1974, pp. 36–7). On the '*positive* element of autonomisation', Adorno had previously written that 'the autonomy of art itself, through which it opposes the machinery, is according to its innermost sense already the negation of fossilised relations. Whoever therefore blurs the boundary of the aesthetic realm into contemporary practice, levels it to this practice and thus to the prevailing reification' (Adorno 2003p, pp. 70–1).

20   Letter from Adorno to Horkheimer, 31 January 1936 (Adorno and Horkheimer 2003b, p. 115).

21   Fahlbusch 2006a, p. 19; the phrase 'jazz ideology' appears in Adorno 2019e, p. 96.

the bad ones, until their tired memory is defenceless and at their mercy – and this fatigue of the memory in turn affects further production'.[22]

And despite the lack of strict economic categories, Adorno does define the functionality of jazz from an economic perspective as well. 'Jazz is a commodity in the strict sense', he writes: 'in musical production, its suitability for everyday use establishes itself in no other form than its saleability, which stands in the most extreme opposition not only to the immediacy of its use but also to that of the work process itself; it is subject to the rules – as well as the arbitrariness – of the market, just as its distribution is subject to those of competition or even its heir'.[23]

Anticipating a topos of critique of the culture industry, a concept which was lacking in 1936, Adorno describes jazz as *Gebrauchsmusik*, or use-music – that is, music which takes on the character of a commodity due to its mode of production, thereby acquiescing to the status quo. Given its function in upholding the status quo, jazz fosters alienation, which Adorno believes it must nevertheless 'cloak' along with its commodity-character in order not to jeopardise 'its own success on the market'.[24] In seemingly direct opposition to Benjamin's 'Work of Art' essay and its hope for an emancipatory mass-produced art, Adorno issues his verdict against jazz's capacity to subordinate itself to utilitarian ends:

> For if, as has often been the case, one wished to view the usability of jazz, its suitability as a mass item, as a dialectically advanced corrective of the bourgeois isolation of autonomous art, and even to accept its usability as a motive for the abolition of music's object-character, one would be lapsing into that latest form of Romanticism which desperately seeks to escape the fatal character of capitalism by affirming the object of fear itself as some ghastly allegory of imminent freedom, and by sanctifying negativity – a sanctity in which, incidentally, jazz would like to make us believe. Whatever the situation of art might be in a future order of things, whether its autonomy and reity will survive or not – and the economic perspective supplies various reasons why the right form of society will not be centred on the creation of pure immediacy – this much is certain: the usability of jazz does not negate alienation but, rather, reinforces it.[25]

---

22   Adorno 2019e, pp. 86–7.
23   Adorno 2019e, p. 84.
24   Ibid.
25   Adorno 2019e, pp. 83–4.

Adorno views the variety of avant-garde musical currents collectively referred to as *Neue Musik* as a model for emancipatory art. In contrast, while
listeners may initially turn towards jazz in search of such a model, it is precisely this of which they are defrauded. 'Whoever flees to jazz from a music
that has become incomprehensible, or from the alienation of everyday life,
becomes caught up in a system of musical commodities whose only advantage, compared with others, is that of not being immediately transparent; but
which, in its decisive aspects – namely the unimprovised ones – crushes precisely those hopes for humanity with which the fugitive comes to it. With jazz,
powerless subjectivity leaps from the world of commodities into the world of
commodities; the system permits no escape'.[26] After all, Adorno argues, jazz's
commodity-character demands that it conform to the rule that 'an element of
the market is as good as one of myth: jazz must therefore always be the same
while always feigning novelty'.[27]

2   Torn Away from All Functions

In 1938, the *Zeitschrift für Sozialforschung* published Adorno's essay 'On the
Fetish-Character in Music and the Regression of Listening'. A revised version
was included in his 1956 essay collection *Dissonanzen. Musik in der verwalteten
Welt (Dissonances: Music in the Administered World)*.[28] In a letter to Benjamin,
Adorno describes the piece as 'a kind of counterpart'[29] to 'On Jazz', which had
appeared two years earlier. Although he had arrived at the idea for a work on the
fetish-character in music as early as 1936,[30] the realisation of his plan was initially delayed on account of timing: 'Publishing an essay on music and the fetish
character now, so soon after the jazz essay, doesn't seem appropriate to me',[31]
Horkheimer comments in a letter from the time. Not until 1938 does Adorno
mention his idea to Kracauer: 'In connection with the Wagner, I have been read-

---

26   Adorno 2019e, p. 90.
27   Adorno 2019e, p. 91.
28   Originally published as 'Über den Fetischcharakter in der Musik und die Regression des
     Hörens', *Zeitschrift für Sozialforschung*, 7: 321–356 (Adorno 1938); the English version
     (Adorno 2009c) is a translation of the revised version from *Dissonanzen*; on the origin
     of the essay in the Princeton radio project cf. Müller-Doohm 2009, p. 251.
29   Letter from Adorno to Benjamin, 4 May 1938 (Adorno and Benjamin 1999, p. 251).
30   See letter from Adorno to Horkheimer, 30 October 1936 (Adorno and Horkheimer 2003b,
     p. 209).
31   Letter from Horkheimer to Adorno, 14 November 1936 (Horkheimer 2007, p. 80).

ing a great deal of Schopenhauer with considerable interest. I am thinking of writing something about the general regression in listening and the character-istics of fetishism in music'.[32]

Here, Adorno is referring to his book-length essay *In Search of Wagner*, written 'between autumn 1937 and spring 1938'.[33] This text clearly draws on Benjamin's understanding of phantasmagoria and fetish as expressed in the preliminary studies to the *Arcades Project*: 'The property appertaining to the commodity as its fetish character', Benjamin writes, 'attaches as well to the commodity-producing society – not as it is in itself, to be sure, but more as it represents itself and thinks to understand itself whenever it abstracts from the fact that it produces precisely commodities'.[34] Presumably following Marx's use of the concept,[35] Benjamin seeks to convert the commodity's fetish-character into an aesthetics of phantasmagoria,[36] arguing that 'the creations and forms of life based above all on the production of commodities ... are "illumin-ated" not primarily ideologically by theorisation, but rather sensuously by their immediate presence. They are manifest as phantasmagorias'.[37] These so-called

---

32   Letter from Adorno to Kracauer, 3 May 1938 (Adorno and Kracauer 2020, p. 263). Schopen-hauer famously describes music thusly: 'In fact, music is an unmediated objectivation and copy of the entire will, just as the world itself is, just as in fact the Ideas themselves are, whose multiplied appearance constitutes the world of particular things. Therefore, unlike the other arts, music is in no way a copy of the Ideas; instead, it is a copy of the will itself, whose objecthood the Ideas are as well: this is precisely why the effect of music is so much more powerful and urgent than that of the other arts: the other arts speak only of shadows while music speaks of the essence' (Schopenhauer 2010, p. 285). Adorno refers to this pas-sage in his 1958 essay 'Some Ideas on the Sociology of Music': 'By virtue of its basic material, music is the art in which the prerational, mimetic impulses ineluctably find their voice, even as they enter into a pact with the processes leading to the progressive domination of matter and nature. This is the material to which music owes its ability to transcend the business of mere self-preservation, an ability that led Schopenhauer to define it as the immediate objectification of the will and to place it at the apex of the hierarchy of the arts' (Adorno 1999b, p. 6).

33   Adorno 2009a, xxviii. An excerpt from this work was originally published as 'Fragmente über Wagner', *Studies in Philosophy and Social Sciences* [*Zeitschrift für Sozialforschung*], 8, 1: 1–49.

34   Benjamin 2002c, p. 669.

35   See Marx 1982a, p. 163; cf. Tiedemann 2002, p. 938. Translator's note: in Marx's work, '*der Fetischcharakter der Ware*' ('the fetish-character of the commodity') has been translated as 'the fetishism of the commodity'.

36   See Benjamin 2002c, p. 669; cf. Freytag 1992.

37   Benjamin 2001g, p. 1256. Translator's note: here, Braunstein quotes from a 1939 version of Benjamin's *éxpose* to *The Arcades Project*. Although a 'final' version of the 1939 *exposé*, writ-ten in French, has been translated into English, I have chosen to quote from the earlier

phantasmagorias are described as such not due to 'their economic and social function, but as an expression of *collective space*'.[38]

In *Wagner*, Adorno further develops this interpretation of the concept of fetish:

> If we leave aside the dubious notion of 'truth in the artistic sense' and discard the category of interiorization as irrelevant to Wagner, the concept of illusion as the absolute reality of the unreal grows in importance. It sums up the unromantic side of the phantasmagoria: phantasmagoria as the point at which aesthetic appearance becomes a function of the character of the commodity. As a commodity it purveys illusions. The absolute reality of the unreal is nothing but the reality of a phenomenon that not only strives unceasingly to spirit away its own origins in human labor, but also, inseparably from this process and in thrall to exchange value, assiduously emphasizes its use value, stressing that this is its authentic reality, that it is 'no imitation' – and all this in order to further the cause of exchange value. In Wagner's day the consumer goods on display turned their phenomenal side seductively towards the mass of customers while diverting attention from their merely phenomenal character, from the fact that they were beyond reach. Similarly, in the phantasmagoria, Wagner's operas tend to become commodities.[39]

Here, it might be objected that by equating phantasmagoria with the desire for commodities whose origins in human labour are hidden, Adorno invokes a myth of authenticity while assigning commodities an appearance one-sidedly declared to be inauthentic. However, it appears possible that this problem is not lost on him. In a letter to Benjamin from the same year in which he composed *Wagner* – the same letter in which he criticises the first draft of Benjamin's Baudelaire essay – Adorno admits that 'the phantasmagoria chapter of my book on Wagner has certainly not succeeded in resolving [the difficulty of commodity-form analysis] yet'.[40]

In 'On the Social Situation of Music' and 'On Jazz', Adorno still evidently speaks a language received from Lukács and Benjamin. However, with 'On

---

version cited by Braunstein given differences between the two versions. For an English translation of the equivalent passage in the 'final' 1939 *exposé*, cf. Benjamin 2002b, p. 14.

38   Freytag 1992, p. 25.
39   Adorno 2009a, p. 79.
40   Letter from Adorno to Benjamin, 10 November 1938 (Adorno and Benjamin 1999, p. 283).

the Fetish-Character in Music', he claims to have treated 'the recent musical-sociological observations I had made in America'[41] with the help of distinctly Marxian categories – that is, he claims to have remedied his observations' lack of 'concrete economic categories'. Adorno apparently tackled the required reading for this undertaking only shortly beforehand: in a 1937 letter, he writes to Benjamin that '[o]ne of the first things I have planned to do is to undertake the systematic study of *Capital*',[42] and one of the two copies of the first volume of *Capital* from his personal library bears the date 10 June 1938 handwritten on its endpaper.[43]

Adorno's experiences of music in the United States were first and foremost experiences of music on the radio. Shortly after arriving in his New York exile in late February 1938, he began working on the Princeton Radio Research Project[44] headed by Austrian émigré sociologist Paul F. Lazarsfeld. The goal of the project was to investigate 'the preferences and habits of American radio listeners'.[45]

> Benjamin's thesis that the mechanical reproduction of art would extract art treasures from the aura of their politically burdensome authority by demolishing their claim to being one-of-a-kind – by annulling the spell they cast from their perpetually sacred distance – had been conceived exclusively in terms of print media and the visual arts, most of all cinema and photography. The Music Study of the Princeton project, however, under Adorno's directorship, examined the claims of Benjamin's seminal essay with regard to the reproduction of music. And the results of this study illuminated it in an altogether new way. Adorno had observed in listening to radio music that the humanizing content of the music that he had spent his life composing, reflecting on, and studying had vanished. Radio music, to Adorno's ears, was no longer *that* music.[46]

After all, the mass-reproduction of what once carried the promise of universal happiness degrades the individual's aspiration for happiness: 'The man who in the subway triumphantly whistles loudly the theme of the finale of Brahms's

---

41   Adorno 2005h, p. 218.

42   Letter from Adorno to Benjamin, 13 September 1937 (Adorno and Benjamin 1999, p. 210).

43   The edition in question here was published in 1932 by the *Verlag für Literatur und Politik*, Vienna and Berlin (TWA, NB 279).

44   Cf. Levin and von der Linn 1994.

45   Fahlbusch 2006b, p. 22.

46   Hullot-Kentor 2009, pp. 15–16.

First is already primarily involved with its debris'.[47] In a letter to the project's co-directors from around the same time, Lazarsfeld relates the following about his first impression of Adorno:

> He looks exactly as you would imagine a very absent-minded German professor, and he behaves so foreign that I feel like a member of the May-flower Society. When you start to talk with him, however, he has an enorm-ous amount of interesting ideas. As every newcomer, he tries to reform everything, but if you listen to him, most of what he says makes sense.[48]

Looking back, Lazarsfeld notes the 'brilliance and importance of Adorno's ideas' when discussing a controversy surrounding the concept of fetishism:

> To straighten out the situation, I asked Adorno to summarize his ideas in a memorandum which I planned to circulate among various experts to secure a broader basis of support for his work. In June 1938 he delivered a memorandum of 160 single-spaced pages, entitled 'Music in Radio'. But it seemed to me that the distribution of this text would only have made the situation more difficult, for in English his writing had the same tan-talizing attraction and elusiveness that it had in German. The notion of 'fetish' played – as could be expected from a neo-Marxist – a central role.[49]

This retrospective account tends to read like the report of a productive en-counter between two quite different theorists. However, the events surround-ing the publication of 'Fetish-Character' in 1938 actually unfolded in a much more controversial and conflictual manner. This can be seen in a letter by Lazarsfeld in which, having received the aforementioned memorandum, he accuses Adorno himself of the very fetishism he claims to recognise in others:

---

47   Adorno 2009c, p. 298. Hullot-Kentor writes that despite Benjamin's claim, reproduction had not 'made art music slough off its auratic cocoon. On the contrary, radio reproduction, Adorno would show, subjects the broadcast remnants of the artwork to a new spell; the remaindered husk becomes a new fetish. Mechanical reproduction does not destroy the primacy of the original, as Benjamin asserted, but rather it changes music into nothing but the search for an original to be possessed' (Hullot-Kentor 2009, p. 16). While all emphatic originality is rendered anachronistic by the process of production, products still present themselves as if each were the latest novelty.

48   Lazarsfeld 1969, p. 301.

49   Lazarsfeld 1969, p. 323.

Don't you think that it is perfect fetishism the way you use Latin words all through your text? The pages are full of: 'prima facie'; 'e contrario'; 'conditio sine qua non'; and so on. There is no doubt that the words 'necessary condition' express everything which the corresponding Latin word can express. But you evidently feel magically more secure if you use words which symbolize your education although they are a trouble for any stenographer and a hidden offence against any American colleague; just because American professionals are not brought up to use Latin words unnecessarily we are not yet better than they are. Isn't your attitude exactly what you call fetishism?[50]

Evidently, Lazarsfeld 'had probably selected the person least likely to be of any plausible use to him in completing a study on improving radio reception'.[51] And although he expresses hope in a subsequent letter that Adorno 'just has a queer way of behaving of which he might be cured',[52] private communications from the 'very absent-minded German professor' show him as far less concerned with 'being cured' than with 'throwing in the towel' (*den Bettel vor die Füße zu werfen*)[53] on his collaboration with the 'nuisance' (*Plagegeist*)[54] Lazarsfeld. Their collaboration finally did end in autumn 1939.[55]

'Fetish-Character' reflects both Adorno's experience of music on the radio (as well as of concert performance) in the United States and his predilection for the concept of fetishism. According to the film scholar Christoph Hesse, the essay 'throws together, indeed remarkably, the Marxian concept of fetish and the Freudian one', something which can be seen in its very title.[56] Yet while Hesse's claim may be true of the first version of 'Fetish-Character', it is only partially so of its republication. In the former, Adorno refers a total of eighteen times to the 'pleasure' (*Lust*) he claims music – 'the immediate manifestation of instinct and the locus of its taming'[57] – offers listeners. Through its consideration of pleasure and instinct, and of the natural-somatic as the ultimate

50   Letter from Lazarsfeld to Adorno, ca. early September 1938 (Adorno and Horkheimer 2004, p. 445); on Lazarsfeld's view of the controversy between himself and Adorno cf. Lazarsfeld 1969.
51   Hullot-Kentor 2009, p. 14.
52   Letter from Lazarsfeld to Frank Stanton, 14 December 1938 (Hullot-Kentor 2009, p. 30).
53   Letter from Adorno to Horkheimer, 6 January 1939 (Adorno and Horkheimer 2004, p. 51).
54   Letter from Adorno to Horkheimer, 15 August 1938 (Adorno and Horkheimer 2004, pp. 42–3).
55   Cf. Morrison 1978.
56   Hesse 2006, p. 214.
57   Adorno 2009c, p. 288.

point of reference for music's reception, the piece evidently gestures towards a sociology of music based on the theoretical tools of psychoanalysis.[58] And when Adorno explicitly mentions the mediation implied by its title, he does so by laconically stating that the 'counterpart to the fetishism of music is a regression of listening'[59] – 'regression' is a 'purely descriptive' concept for the subjective-psychological phenomenon of an individual 'return from a higher to a lower stage of development'.[60] In the original version of 'Fetish-Character' from 1938, there is a clear interplay – what Hesse offhandedly refers to as a 'throw[ing] together' – between the Marxian and Freudian concepts of fetishism. It is precisely fetishism, Adorno writes in a 1937 letter to Erich Fromm, which is supposed to serve as the mediating element for converting the relationship between Marxian theory and psychoanalysis from one of analogy to one of genuine synthesis:

> I am increasingly convinced that the actual coincidence of Marxist theory and psychoanalysis does not lie in analogies such as that between superstructure and base versus ego and id, etc. Rather, it lies in the *fetish-character* of commodities and in the fetishistic character of humans. I also believe that the methodological opposition between Marxism and psychoanalysis can first be manoeuvred dialectically at the moment in which one manages to concretely prove that the economic fetish-character is the rule of psychological fetishisations. Incidentally, this also implies tracing the economic fetish-character back beyond capitalist society and potentially back to the prehistory in which the primordial facts of economic fetishisation left their first inner-human deposits.[61]

Psychoanalysis uses the concept of fetishism to describe the neurotic displacement of desire for a sexual object onto a part of the actual object – which thereby becomes fetishised – as a psychopathology: 'The *fetishist* achieves sexual arousal and satisfaction by putting particular objects – that is, inanimate objects (such as pieces of clothing or shoes) or even body parts (the foot) – in the place of an entire love object'.[62] For Marx, however, the fetish-character

---

58   'We regard instinct as being the concept on the frontier-line between the somatic and the mental, and see in it the psychical representative of organic forces' (Freud 2001c, p. 74).
59   Adorno 2009c, p. 303.
60   Freud 2001a, p. 342.
61   Letter from Adorno to Erich Fromm, 16 November 1937 (Adorno and Horkheimer 2003b, p. 540).
62   Mentzos 1984, p. 205.

of commodities (as well as of money[63] and capital[64]) describes the fact that the economic – that is, the social – form of value emerges in the guise of things whose value is not regarded as socially mediated. Such things appear as if they always had value in themselves: their thoroughly social essence hides behind their material appearance.

> The mysterious character of the commodity-form consists therefore simply in the fact that the commodity reflects the social characteristics of men's own labour as objective characteristics of the products of labour themselves, as the socio-natural properties of these things. Hence it also reflects the social relation of the producers to the sum total of labour as a social relation between objects, a relation which exists apart from and outside the producers. Through this substitution, the products of labour become commodities, sensuous things which are at the same time supra-sensible or social.[65]

At the same time, this also means that fetish-character in the Marxian sense can only be spoken of in a society in which the commodity-form dominates the entirety of production – that is, in a capitalist society. In other words, Adorno's description of his programme to Fromm as 'tracing the economic fetish-character back beyond capitalist society' is a contradiction in terms, as Marxian fetish-character cannot grasp pre-capitalist modes of production. In his letter to Fromm and his 'Fetish-Character' essay, Adorno has not yet come to appreciate the specific relevance of Marx's critique of political economy to capitalism. Thus, in the pages of the essay, he can only master his self-imposed programme in a superficial sense, namely by watering down both the Marxian and Freudian concepts of fetishism. Among other places, this can be seen in

---

63   'Men are henceforth related to each other in their social process of production in a purely atomistic way. Their own relations of production therefore assume a material shape which is independent of their control and their conscious individual action. This situation is manifested first by the fact that the products of men's labour universally take on the form of commodities. The riddle of the money fetish is therefore the riddle of the commodity fetish, now become visible and dazzling to our eyes' (Marx 1982a, p. 187).

64   As Marx claims – with critical distance – '[c]apital is conceived as a thing, not as a relation' (Marx 1993, p. 258).

65   Marx 1982a, pp. 164–5. In Adorno's copy of Capital (TWA, NB Adorno 279), this passage is marked by an 'X' at its beginning and its end respectively. It is underlined five times, and an 'ff' for fortissimo is written in the margin (on the meaning of this marginalia, cf. Tiedemann 1994, p. 76, n. 36).

Adorno's reference to society's 'auto[mobile] religion'.[66] Here, the invocation of
a discourse on industrial society's fetishisation of cars suggests that Adorno's
concept of fetishism corresponds not to a technical usage of the term, but
rather to a common one – a usage no doubt indebted to a vulgarised version
of Freud's concept of fetish[67] (which Freud himself fashioned out of what was
originally a religious concept),[68] yet one whose meaning is already quite distinct from Freud's, let alone from Marx's.[69] Tellingly, even when Adorno pro-
fesses what Schmid Noerr describes as a 'pronounced libidinal relationship'[70]
to his own texts in a letter to Horkheimer concerning potential changes to
summary of 'On Jazz', it is still apparent that his concept of fetishism owes
far less to Marx and psychoanalysis than to popular discourse: when Adorno
writes to Horkheimer that '[m]y fetishism only applies to the grand German
text, not the summaries',[71] it is difficult to interpret him as referencing Marx's
fetish-character of the commodity-form or wanting to diagnose himself with
a psychopathology. Rather, Adorno's particular use of the concept of fetishism
here can be seen as illustrating a point he would subsequently make in 1954 –
not without unintentional irony – regarding the use of psychological concepts:
'As soon as one removes concepts from the theoretical context in which their
meaning is rooted and reduces them to the level of alleged common sense,
they change their meaning and no longer achieve their formerly intended purpose'.[72]

66   Adorno 2009c, p. 297.
67   Freud's first mention of the concept of fetish in 1905 is accompanied by the following
      description: 'The substitute for the sexual object is some part of the body (such as the foot
      or hair) which is generally hardly appropriate for sexual purposes; or it is some inanimate
      object in some demonstrable relation to the person whom it replaces, and preferably to
      that person's sexuality (e.g., items of clothing, or underwear)' (Freud 2016, p. 16).
68   Cf. Marxhausen 1999, columns 343–4.
69   A revealing misunderstanding can be seen in a text from the 1970s in which an ostenta-
      tious car, its decadent appearance and a nefarious capitalist meld together into a nexus
      of manipulation referred to as 'fetishism': 'In the fetishism of the sports car owners – as
      aptly as psychoanalytic categories may describe it – no small role is played by the fetish-
      ism fermented by capital owners with the exchange value of commodities – that is, with
      the appearance abstracted from the material, with the simulated beauty' (Kreimeier 1971,
      pp. 81–2). This passage simply has nothing to do with Marx's fetish-character of commod-
      ities.
70   Schmid Noerr 1995, p. 71.
71   Letter from Adorno to Horkheimer, 15 May 1936 (Adorno and Horkheimer 2003b, p. 144).
72   Adorno 2003d, p. 436. In the essay's republication, Adorno does in fact considerably qual-
      ify the relevance of psychoanalysis to a critical portrayal of the fetish-character in music.
      In this updated version, the thesis that the fetishism of music entails a regression of listen-
      ing is followed by the explanation that this regression 'does not mean a relapse of the

Adorno's understanding of fetishism in the mid-1930s is further exemplified by his concept of 'vocal fetishism'.[73] In a letter to Horkheimer from 28 November 1936, Adorno mentions his intention to investigate the 'valuation of "beautiful voices" as commodities'[74] in 'Fetish-Character', which at the time was still in its planning stages. Ultimately, the essay would read as follows:

> At its most passionate, musical fetishism takes possession of the public valuation of singing voices. Their sensuous magic[75] is traditional as is the close relation between success and the person endowed with 'material'. But today it is forgotten that it is material. For musical vulgar materialists, it is synonymous to have a voice and to be a singer. In earlier epochs, technical virtuosity, at least, was demanded of singing stats, the castrati and prima donnas. Today, the material as such, destitute of any function, is celebrated. One need not even ask about capacity for musical performance. Even mechanical control of the instrument is no longer really expected. To legitimate the fame of its owner, a voice need only be especially voluminous or especially high. If one dares even in conversation to question the decisive importance of the voice and to assert that it is just as possible to make beautiful music with a moderately good voice as it is on a moder-

---

individual listener into an earlier phase of his own development, nor a decline in the collective general level, since the millions who are reached musically for the first time by today's mass communications cannot be compared with the audience of the past. Rather, it is contemporary listening which has regressed, arrested at the infantile stage' (Adorno 2009c, p. 303). In all but two places, the term '*Lust*' ('pleasure') is replaced with the softer term '*Genuß*' (enjoyment) or simply removed (cf. Adorno 1938 and Adorno 2003ad).

73 'Productive critique should be applied, through the directional tendency of the work, to the reigning culinary ideas, especially to vocal fetishism. In doing so, one touches upon what is probably the trickiest point of the opera problematic. That opera listeners are interested in voices is also legitimate. Through the voice, living humans engage with music in the most immediate sense. ... Yet one should not content oneself with voice, should not elevate voice to an end in itself. Something of its inherent right must also be preserved in its shaping through musical intention, but through its specific qualities it must ultimately serve music as an instrument. As a higher understanding of opera instructs, the voice should be appreciated in its musical function' (Adorno 2003o, pp. 509–10). The term vocal fetishism also occurs in Adorno 2006d, p. 6. The same text also contains the following note: '*Songs* are almost always presented at much too slow a tempo, because singers want to display their voices and give expression, often at the music's expense' (Adorno 2006d, p. 88). As opposed to this, Adorno argues that music 'must be allowed to linger, – but not to listen to itself' (Adorno 2006d, p. 104).

74 Letter from Adorno to Horkheimer, 28 November 1936 (Adorno and Horkheimer 2003b, p. 238).

75 Like Marx, Adorno too is no stranger to 'the misty realm of religion' (Marx 1982a, p. 165).

ately good piano, one will immediately find oneself faced with a situation of hostility and aversion whose emotional roots go far deeper than the occasion. Voices are holy properties like a national factory trademark.[76]

Adorno draws an analogy between singing voices and 'factory-brands' (*Fabrikmarken*) or 'commodity-brands' (*Warenmarken*)[77] – that is, commodities – in order to articulate the objective inadequacy of the absolutist view of singing voices promoted by commodity fetishism. According to him, concertgoers who hold this view do not perceive voice as an instrument for performing the particular content of a particular piece,[78] but rather measure voice out of context against an idealised 'absolute' voice.[79] In this way, voice is 'torn away from [all] functions which could give [it] meaning'.[80] The audience in turn judges the quality of a voice solely by it virtuosity – as if this were a value in itself – and the quality of a musical composition by its success. However, while it may be true that the 'ever more senselessly cutthroat competition between ... the most mar-

---

76   Adorno 2009c, pp. 294–5.
77   Adorno 2003g, p. 393; cf. Adorno 2003e, p. 381: 'If success today does in fact demand the commodity-mark of the emotional type, this reveals nothing about musical thinking in particular. Rather, it says something about the prevailing enterprise'.
78   Along these lines, Adorno writes elsewhere that '[i]f you say from the musical point of view, for example, that even in opera beautiful voices are means of presenting the composition rather than ends in themselves, you will be answered in a tone of outrage out of all proportion to the rational gist of the controversy. The study of such outbursts and of their psychogenesis promises more insights into the function of musical activities in the psychological household of society than will result from inquiries about immediate likes or dislikes' (Adorno 1976b, p. 222).
79   In *Introduction to the Sociology of Music*, Adorno speaks of the archetype of the '*culture consumer*' who 'lies in wait for specific elements, for supposedly beautiful melodies, for grandiose moments' (Adorno 1976b, pp. 6–7). As he continues, a certain tentativeness emerges in his use of the concept of fetishism: 'On the whole, his relation to music has a fetishistic touch. The standard he consumes by is the prominence of the consumed. The joy of the composition, of that which – in his language – music "gives" to him, outweighs his enjoyment of the music itself as a work of art that makes demands on him. / Two or three generations ago this type used to pose as a Wagnerian; today he is more likely to call Wagner names. At a violinist's concert his interest will focus on what he calls "tone production", if not indeed on the violin itself. In a singer's case it is the voice that interests this type; in a pianist's, it may be the tuning of the grand. Such people are appraisers. The one thing they primarily respond to is an exorbitant and, so to speak, measurable performance-breakneck virtuosity, for instance, wholly in the sense of the "show" ideal. Technique, the means, impresses them as an end in itself; in this respect they are quite close to the presently widespread mass audience' (Adorno 1976b, p. 7).
80   Adorno 2009c, p. 295.

FAMILIARITY WITH ITS FIRST CHAPTER

ketable voices'[81] transforms voice from a means to an end into an end-in-itself, to identify every quid pro quo as simply an expression of commodity fetishism is to use the concept of fetishism as 'the left's prestige catch-all term of abuse'.[82] And indeed, it is precisely this kind of conceptual watering down in which '[m]any of the well-known misinterpretations and over-interpretations of commodity-fetishism ... have their origin'[83] – not only in Adorno's work, but in Marxist literature in general.[84] At times, it seems that practically everything disagreeable can be written off as fetishism: in self-professed Marxist literature, references can be found to 'equality-fetishism', 'market-fetishism', 'party-fetishism', 'plan-fetishism', 'council-fetishism', 'immediacy-fetishism', 'object-fetishism', 'position-fetishism', 'praxis-fetishism', 'science-fetishism', 'balance-fetishism', 'legality-fetishism', 'clerical-fetishism', 'data-fetishism', '"facts, facts, facts"-fetishism', 'document-fetishism', 'costuming-fetishism', and so on.[85] Tracing these 'fetishisms' back to the argumentation generating them – an argumentation which ultimately always says that 'fetishism' is the basis of an inversion of means and ends, the mistaken positing of a being-in-itself – one would have to diagnose a 'fetish-fetishism': 'The most stubborn of all fetishisations appears to be the overestimation of the concept of fetish'.[86]

---

81   Henscheid 1999, p. 164.
82   Henscheid 2005, p. 655.
83   Hesse 2006, p. 215. For his own part, Hesse enriches the discussion on 'form-fetish' (Hesse 2006, p. 206).
84   Just how trivial the use of the Marxian concept of fetishism has become is demonstrated by an anecdote from the not-quite-scholarly literature on the subject. In his work *Kennen Sie Marx?* (*Do You Know Marx?*) the philosopher Günter Schulte uses a 'splendour of analogy-intimation' (*Analogieahnungspracht*) (Henscheid 2003, p. 615) combining Talmudic exegesis with thoroughly vulgarised psychoanalysis to arrive at an exceedingly unique interpretation of Marx's fetish-character. Drawing a comparison between the figure of Lilith – in the Jewish mythological tradition, Adam's first wife – and the Marxian image of the inverted table (see Marx 1982a, pp. 163–4) from the 'fetish chapter' in *Capital*, Schulte argues in short that Marx, as someone allegedly familiar with the Talmud, envisions with his table metaphor nothing other than the image of Lilith, the 'bearer of desire and undoing'. After all, according to the mythology, Lilith 'turned the table' – that is, herself during sex with Adam – 'around'. As the author graphically depicts with his own handmade drawings, the naked woman, turned around on all fours, presents herself – voilà! – as a *FeTisch* (translator's note: this is a play on the German words for table [*Tisch*] and fetish [*Fetisch*]) (Schulte 1991, pp. 210–11).
85   The fetishisms identified here are located in Trenkle 1992, p. 99; Trampert 2002, p. 151; Wolf 1999, p. 10; Kurz 1987, p. 45; Dauvé 2002, p. 40; Wenzel and Amzoll 1997, p. 36; Schenk 1992, p. 175; Schandl 2001, p. 46; Liessmann 2003, p. 16; Gross 2003, p. 48; Zademach 2003, p. 946; Niemann 1999, p. 20; Lange 1978, p. 42; Stock 1996, p. 37; Helmes-Conzett and Knab 1999, p. 139; Hofmann 1999, p. 52; Schütrumpf 2008, p. 21.
86   Erckenbrecht 1976, p. 7.

In addition to the commodity-fetish, Adorno views the category of success as another mediating economic element in the production and consumption of music:

> Marx defines the fetish-character of the commodity as the veneration of the thing made by oneself which, as exchange-value, simultaneously alienates itself from producer to consumer – 'human beings'. 'A commodity is therefore a mysterious thing, simply because in it the social character of men's labor appears to them as an objective character stamped upon the product of that labor; because the relation of the producers to the sum total of their own labor is presented to them as a social relation, existing not between themselves, but between the products of their labor'. This is the real secret of success. It is the mere reflection of what one pays in the market for the product. The consumer is really worshipping the money that he himself has paid for the ticket to the Toscanini concert. He has literally 'made' the success which he reifies and accepts as an objective criterion, without recognizing himself in it. But he has not 'made' it by liking the concert, but rather by buying the ticket.[87]

Thus, according to Adorno, success no longer depends on objective factors relating to musicians (ability, performance, talent, etc.), but instead on the consumers of musical products, who alone determine the success of producers: while musicians produce music, consumers produce success. At the same time, consumers fail to recognise the social character of this success they 'achieve', which appears to them in a reified form bearing no recognisable trace of origin in human labour. In this way, humans are alienated from themselves, no longer able to perceive the results of their actions as such.

Against Adorno's attempt to analyse commodity-fetishism sociologically, one might object that the passage he cites from Marx refers to the products of labour, and that the acquisition of a concert ticket does not constitute labour in the Marxian sense. In other words, while Marx's work already characterises the concept of fetishism as mere 'analogy', Adorno analogises it yet again.[88] Also problematic is Adorno's assumption that the fetish-character of the com-

---

87   Adorno 2009c, p. 296; quoted from Marx 1982a, pp. 164–5.

88   Cf. Tiedemann 1998, p. 30. Adorno's library contains a copy of an edition of the first volume of *Capital* edited by Hans-Joachim Lieber and Peter Furth (the fourth volume of the collection *Karl Marx. Werke, Schriften, Briefe*, edited by Hans-Joachim Lieber and Benedikt Kautsky) and published by Cotta in Stuttgart. The only sign of it having been read is an underlining of the word 'analogy' (TWA, NB Adorno 288) in the famous sentence from the

modity is the expression of a falsehood per se. After all, according to Marx, it is precisely under existing capitalist conditions that the commodity's fetish-character is not false: 'That [individuals'] social relationship to one another appears as a social relationship between things is ... not at all an illusion';[89] rather, to individuals as producers, 'the social relations between their private labours appear as *what they are*'.[90] The fetish-character of the commodity pertains to 'the commodity itself as a form of relations, not a set of relations "behind" the commodity'.[91]

Without a doubt, Adorno's understanding of commodity-fetishism is problematic and worthy of critique from the perspective of the Marxian concept. At the same time, his description of the commodity's fetish-character as 'the veneration of the thing made by oneself' is the genesis of a constantly recurring element of his philosophy. The 'veneration of the thing made by oneself',[92] that is, the religiously overinflated worship of the non-natural – how Adorno wants to understand the fetish-character – is for him the expression of the contemporary treatment of cultural products of all kinds, from autonomous works of art to the most insipid popular music. 'Deluded, man sets up something artificial as a primal phenomenon, and prays to it; an authentic instance of fetishism'.[93] The artwork, 'a man-made social product', is thereby transfigured into an 'in-itself',[94] even while 'the immediate datum itself is inherently mediated'.[95] Against this fetishism, 'art as a consumer commodity' is actually 'a corrective' insofar as it is 'appraised ... according to the consistent exchange principle which values any being as "for something else"'.[96] The fetishism which adheres to artworks cannot be criticised or transcended abstractly, as

---

fetish chapter: 'In order, therefore, to find an analogy we must take flight into the misty realm of religion' (Marx 1982a, p. 165).

89   Heinrich 2012, p. 73.
90   Marx 1982a, p. 166, emphasis added.
91   Postone 2003, p. 276, n. 41.
92   It is not unlikely that Adorno borrowed the term 'veneration' (translator's note: '*Venera-tion*' in the original) – which is highly uncommon in German – from the following passage in Kierkegaard's *Either/Or*: 'The individual rests with confident security in the assurance that his life is ethically structured, and therefore he does not torment himself and others with quibbling anxiety about this or that. / I find it quite in order that the person who lives ethically has a whole territory for inconsequentials, and being unwilling to force it into every triviality is precisely a veneration for the ethical' (Kierkegaard 1987, p. 257).
93   Adorno 2009e, p. 194.
94   Adorno 1976b, p. 173.
95   Adorno 1976b, p. 142.
96   Adorno 1976b, p. 173.

the truth of all artworks would, on the other hand, not exist without the fetishism that now verges on becoming art's untruth. The quality of artworks depends essentially on the degree of their fetishism, on the veneration that the process of production pays to what lays claim to being self-produced, to the seriousness that forgets the pleasure taken in it. Only through fetishism, the blinding of the artwork vis-a-vis the reality of which it is part, does the work transcend the spell of the reality principle as something spiritual.[97]

Although the art-commodity which is *solely* a commodity 'produces its own pretense of immediacy and intimacy',[98] the autonomous artwork which elicits from the pseudo-sophisticate the classic response that he 'cannot understand modern art'[99] also refuses to appear immediately accessible to the more generous recipient. 'Taste is the ability to keep in balance the contradiction in art between the made and the apparent not-having-become; true works of art, however, never at one with taste, are those which push this contradiction to the extreme, and realize themselves in their resultant downfall'.[100] This fetishisation 'expresses the paradox of all art that is no longer self-evident to itself: the paradox that something made exists for its own sake; precisely this paradox is the vital nerve of new art. By exigency, the new must be something willed; as what is other, however, it could not be what was willed':[101] 'Autonomy and fetishism are two sides of the *same* truth'.[102]

Not long before writing 'On the Fetish-Character in Music and the Regression of Listening', Adorno warned Benjamin that 'the conception of the commodity fetish must be documented with appropriate passages from the man who discovered it'.[103] However, through a productive misunderstanding, Adorno's own essay transforms the concept into one which describes the reception of artworks under conditions relating to the dominant mode of production.

---

97   Adorno 2002a, p. 341.
98   Adorno 2009c, p. 299.
99   Adorno 1988a, p. 100.
100   Adorno 2005b, p. 227.
101   Adorno 2002a, p. 22.
102   Adorno 2006d, p. 53.
103   Letter from Adorno to Benjamin, 2–5 August 1935 (Adorno and Benjamin 1999, p. 111).

3   Pure Use-Value

According to Adorno, when the importance of music's quality is supplanted by its economic success, when music's social function is dependent on sales and profit, then it indeed follows that music itself must be viewed as a commodity. As he writes in the original version of 'Fetish-Character' from the *Zeitschrift für Sozialforschung*, '[t]he application of the category of the commodity to music is not an analogy. Yes, the exchange of "cultural goods", however it occurs, terminates in material matters: opera and concert tickets, piano compositions of popular songs, gramophone records, radio sets and – especially in America – articles advertised with the aid of musical executions'.[104]

Although Adorno's earlier work 'On the Social Situation of Music' echoes the view expressed in his habilitation on Kierkegaard that it is possible for commodities to exist which have been 'deprived of their own use-value',[105] 'Fetish-Character' appears to revise this position:

> To be sure, exchange-value exerts its power in a special way in the realm of cultural goods. For in the world of commodities this realm appears to be exempted from the power of exchange, to be in an immediate relationship with the goods, and it is this appearance in turn which alone gives cultural goods their exchange-value. But they nevertheless simultaneously fall completely into the world of commodities, are produced for the market, and are aimed at the market. The appearance of immediacy is as strong as the compulsion of exchange-value is inexorable. The social compact harmonizes the contradiction. The appearance of immediacy takes possession of the mediated, exchange-value itself. If the commodity in general combines exchange-value and use-value, then the pure use-value, whose illusion the cultural goods must preserve in completely capitalist society, must be replaced by pure exchange-value, which precisely in its capacity as exchange-value deceptively takes over the function of use-value. The specific fetish character of music lies in this quid pro quo. The feelings which go to the exchange-value create the appearance of immediacy at the same time as the absence of a relation to the object belies it. It has its basis in the abstract character of exchange-value. Every 'psychological' aspect, every ersatz satisfaction, depends on such social substitution.

---

104   Adorno 1938, p. 330.
105   Adorno 1999a, p. 43.

In this way, Adorno continues, the 'appearance of exchange-value in com-modities has taken on a specific cohesive function'.[106] Although it is acknow-ledged here that commodities have exchange-value *and* use-value, Adorno still continues to regard use-value as a condition of possibility for the pleasure music offers listeners. Use-value is conceptualised as where 'the feelings' would have to go, if only it were not 'replaced by pure exchange-value'.

Using cultural phenomena such as music – among others – Adorno attempts to provide an exemplary illustration of an historic situation of inversion be-tween use-value and exchange-value. 'The more inexorably the principle of exchange-value destroys use-values for human beings, the more deeply does exchange-value disguise itself as the object of enjoyment [or object of pleas-ure, according to the 1938 version of the essay]'.[107] Yet if use-value were indeed destroyed for 'human beings', music would no longer be a commodity in the Marxian sense, according to which a commodity without use-value cannot exist. On the other hand, if music *is* a commodity – if it does have a use-value – then it is not clear why the recipients of music, that is, the consumers of the commodity of music, would not consume this commodity by consuming its use-value, as is the case with every other commodity.

Adorno claims that '[t]he woman who has money with which to buy is intox-icated by the act of buying'. While this statement may be true, it does not describe a genuinely economic phenomenon. It is not exchange-value which 'the woman' enjoys, but rather, if anything, the prestige she acquires from the commodity or its purchase, or it is the pastime of shopping she enjoys, or the real or imagined sense of *'Dabeisein'* – of being present or a participant – in a crowd of consumers, as Adorno himself notes immediately thereafter: 'In American conventional speech, *having a good time* means being present at the enjoyment of others, which in its turn has at its only content being present'.[108] Here, Adorno invokes a situation which appears to him as the unfortunate rule in what he describes elsewhere as 'Toscanini's America'.[109] Seeing in Toscanini's

---

106   Adorno 2009c, p. 296.
107   Adorno 2009c, p. 296; Adorno 1938, p. 332.
108   Adorno 2009c, p. 297; *'having a good time'* written in English in the German version (Adorno 2003ad, p. 26).
109   Adorno 2006d, p. 39; cf. Bahr 2007, pp. 66–7. In their early days, American radio stations 'founded their own symphonic orchestras out of artistic and practical considerations. When the New York Symphony Orchestra dissolved, its director Walter Damrosch foun-ded the NBC Symphony Orchestra in 1927. In 1937, this orchestra was newly organised and entrusted to the 70-year-old Arturo Toscanini. For 16 and a half years, he remained the leader of this outstanding musical body' (Mattfeld 1966, columns 1482–3).

'music-making' a 'dreadful streamline',[110] Adorno identifies 'streamlining' as the 'fetishism of smooth functioning without musical sense and construction. ... Functioning comes to replace function'.[111] Just as *Dabeisein*[112] comes to replace participation, functioning and *Dabeisein* detached from any substance exist merely for their own sake. Although the quid pro quo which Adorno evokes in another example also invoking 'women' – 'in moments of intimacy, women attach greater importance to the hairdressers and cosmeticians than to the situation for the sake of which the hairdressers and cosmeticians are employed' – does describe an inversion of means and ends, it does not describe an inversion of use-value and exchange-value.

Here, a tentativeness in Adorno's approach to commodity-analysis reveals itself. When he remarks that the exchange-value of cultural goods 'exerts its power in a special way' because these goods take on 'the appearance of immediacy', he fails to recognise that it is precisely this appearance which Marx attempts to capture with his concept of the commodity's fetish-character. By Marx's definition, *every* commodity has a corresponding fetish-character, not simply those to which an immediacy is ascribed externally and possibly for cultural reasons – such as music. Once music has become a commodity, it has the same immediacy as any other profane commodity: namely, an immediacy in appearance only. Therefore, it is not the appearance of immediacy 'which alone gives cultural goods their exchange-value'; this appearance is the result of the commodity-form of cultural goods, that is, is logically proceeded by their exchange-value. Rather, once again: as is the case with *every* commodity, cultural goods gain their exchange-value from the way in which they are produced. The insight that economic value, and hence also exchange-value, is not imposed on a commodity by ideology, but rather emerges objectively in the production of commodities, is the core of the Marxian labour theory of value. Although Adorno does write that 'the commodity in general combines exchange-value and use-value', he overlooks that *both* forms of value have their origins in capitalist production. And as a consequence of this misunderstanding of the economic essence of use-value, use-value acts in 'Fetish-Character' as the arbiter of immediacy and authenticity. Yet in reality, if use-value is merely the precondition for commodities to be able to be consumed at all – even in a way which is regarded as 'false' – then it is precisely use-value

---

110   Adorno 2006d, p. 6.
111   Adorno 2006d, p. 4.
112   Elsewhere, Adorno writes of the 'illusion of "being with" [of *Dabeisein*] no matter what' (Adorno 1976b, p. 16) which radio produces.

which is *not* 'destroyed' for human beings, and the claim that exchange-value 'deceptively takes over the function of use-value' is false. Both use-value and exchange-value have fixed economic functions independent of the psychology of subjects. While it is entirely possible that 'every pleasure which emancipates itself from exchange-value takes on subversive features',[113] emancipation from exchange-value would necessarily also be emancipation from use-value, that is, from commodities altogether; and this would mean: from capitalism entirely.

Writing to Benjamin about 'Fetish-Character', Adorno expresses his particular eagerness to hear the former's 'response to the theory that today exchange-value itself is being consumed. The tension between this theory and your own concerning the buyer's empathy with the soul of the commodity, could prove to be a very fruitful one'. Agreeing in his reply with Adorno's remark that the essay 'certainly bears the marks of haste in composition; but perhaps that is not entirely a bad thing',[114] Benjamin compares his own first essay on Baudelaire with Adorno's work:

> Basically, however, empathy with the commodity is probably empathy with exchange-value itself. And in fact, one can hardly imagine the 'consumption' of exchange-value as anything else but an empathy with it. You write: 'The consumer really worships the money which he has spent on a ticket for a Toscanini concert'. Empathy with exchange-value can turn guns into articles of consumption more attractive than butter. When in popular parlance someone is said to be 'loaded to the tune of five million', then the entire national community also feels itself loaded with millions more; and it empathizes with those millions.[115]

Adorno responds with reservation:

> it does still seem to me that the concept of empathy with inorganic matter does not provide the decisive resources. Of course, one is treading on extremely delicate ground here, particularly as far as the journal is concerned, since a kind of absolute Marxist competence is rightly postulated for every claim that is made. I have now reformulated my own position

---

113 Ibid.
114 Letter from Adorno to Benjamin, 10 November 1938 (Adorno and Benjamin 1999, p. 286).
115 Letter from Benjamin to Adorno, 9 December 1938 (Adorno and Benjamin 1999, pp. 295–6).

concerning the substitution of exchange-value, with enormous effort and the assistance of Max, as compared with its rather more audacious version in the first draft ....[116]

4   Blank Spaces in the Mediation

Adorno did not have to wait long for criticism of 'Fetish-Character' to arrive. On 23 January 1939, Hans Mayer, a Marxist literary scholar in contact with the Institute for Social Research at the time, sent Horkheimer an essay titled 'Bemerkungen zu einer kritischen Musiktheorie' ('Remarks on a Critical Music Theory').[117] First, this essay sharply criticises Adorno's inadequate use of economic categories. 'Adorno chose as the foundation of his analysis (and signalled as much with the title of his work) the famous concept of commodity-fetishism, which was developed by Marx to inquire into the secret of the commodity-*form*, and later expanded by Luk[á]cs in his famous considerations of the problem of "reification" and then applied to the formation of consciousness. Yet everything depends on whether this category is well-chosen in the present case, on whether it is "fruitful"'.[118] Mayer forthrightly concludes that it is not. According to him, 'Fetish-Character' takes 'formulations such as "reification" and "fetishism", which are gradually becoming catchwords',[119] out of the context of Marx's *Capital*, only to place them 'anywhere at random'.[120] Ultimately, he argues, Adorno's 'reading of *Capital* appears to be limited to familiarity with its first chapter on the secret of the commodity-form'.[121] This criticism must have stuck a nerve: while Adorno's essay claims to introduce Marxian categories into the analysis of the reception of music, nowhere in its discussion of the categories of commodity, use-value, exchange-value and fetishism does it pose the question of the specific form of socialisation – the very question which leads Marx to attend to these categories in the first place.

Mayer does not take long to address the '"substitution" of use-value by exchange-value'[122] alleged by Adorno:

116   Letter from Adorno to Benjamin, 1 February 1938 (Adorno and Benjamin 1999, p. 304).
117   Cf. editorial note by Gunzelin Schmid Noerr (Horkheimer 1995, p. 581, n. 1).
118   Mayer 1998, pp. 371–2.
119   Mayer 1998, p. 372.
120   Mayer 1998, p. 374.
121   Mayer 1998, p. 375.
122   Ibid.

One is first puzzled by the use of the economic categories of use-value and
exchange-value, and then especially when one learns that 'the application
of the category of commodity to music is not' supposed to be 'merely an
analogy' ..., that is, when one learns that these categories are supposed
to be understood literally. Here, the objections arise immediately. First
and foremost, there is the unfortunate use of the term use-value as a
description of the specifically musical values of a tonal work, and thus
as the opposite of the character of exchange-value which accumulated
success has. Use-value, that is, the use-vale of a *commodity*, is by nature
an economic category. In this respect, it by no means stands opposed to
exchange-value, another economic category.

Although Marx describes use-value as the opposite of value in *Capital*, this
dichotomy is intra-economic:

> Therefore, the concept of use-value can only be applied to an economic
> approach ..., outside of the economic sphere, it loses all meaning. This
> is particularly true in the present case, an ostensible description of the
> genuine musical-artistic substance of Schubert's B Minor symphony –
> and an attempt to show that this source of value is increasingly repressed
> by the numbers hype around 'The Unfinished'. The social phenomenon
> is accurately described, but its construal in the formulation 'substitution
> of use-value by exchange-value' is clumsy. There is no 'use-value' in this
> sphere; what could appear as such, namely the 'marketability' of this
> symphony or that Chopin étude, has nothing to do with musical value.
> Marketability is also not suppressed by 'exchange-value', but rather is a
> part of this realm, the sphere of the quantitative, of measurable suc-
> cess.[123]

Mayer recognises clearly that the Marxian designations of exchange-value and
use-value as respectively quantitative and qualitative elements of the defin-
itionally economic category 'commodity' are not observed in Adorno's work.
Given this ambiguity, he criticises Adorno for failing to provide evidence 'that
all of his examples deal with *more* than analogies. If it is true that the laws of
commodity production also directly generate and shape the world of contem-

---

123   Mayer 1998, pp. 377–8. Adorno writes that 'the world of music' which extends 'to Schubert's
      B Minor Symphony, labeled *The Unfinished*, is one of fetishes' (Adorno 2009c, p. 293). The
      allegedly unfinished symphony is Schubert's seventh, from 1822.

porary musical life in all of its manifestations, then Adorno has at least failed to provide us with concrete evidence of the *mediations* which produce such relations between the economic and musical spheres'.[124] As a consequence, 'instead of concrete mediations, a somewhat homely economism is given':[125] 'The problem bursts ... the framework of purely economic categories'.[126]

Following Mayer's critique, Adorno himself drafted a memorandum titled 'Notizen zu Mayer'[127] ('Notes to Mayer') which Horkheimer used to compose his response letter to Mayer, partially quoting it verbatim.[128] In this memorandum, Adorno attempts once again to defend his analysis of the present state of music with Marxian categories:

> Paramount among Mayer's theoretical objections is the claim that I haphazardly isolated out the fetish chapter of *Capital*, or the antitheses of use-value and exchange-value, thereby producing a rigid musical-sociological schema while disregarding other important motifs of Marxian analysis, and particularly the theory of circulation. As far as the Marxist question is concerned, I would just like to note that I do not in fact believe that the analysis of the commodity-form in Marx's work is simply one among a number of equally important motifs (what a pluralist sociologist would believe). Rather, what I believe is that the category of the commodity is indeed the category which illuminates the entire realm of Marxism like a headlamp. Horkheimer himself recently went so far as to illustrate the concept of ideology with the capitalist who, for reasons of necessary social appearance, attributes surplus-value not merely to v [variable capital][129] but also to c, constant capital, that is, to congealed rather than living labour. At heart, this motif is identical with the critique of reification, and I believe it would not be difficult to show that *Capital* is dominated

124 Mayer, 'Bemerkungen zu einer kritischen Musiktheorie' (MHA I 18.81); the two emphases are omitted from the transcription of the typescript (Mayer 1998, p. 379).
125 Mayer 1998, p. 379.
126 Mayer 1998, p. 385.
127 Adorno, 'Notizen zu Mayer' (MHA I 18.41).
128 As Horkheimer writes to Mayer, '[t]he following intimations correspond to the common standpoint of Wiesengrund and myself' (letter from Horkheimer to Mayer, 23 March 1939 [Horkheimer 1995c, p. 576]).
129 Cf. the chapter in *Capital* on 'The Rate of Surplus-Value': 'The capital C is made up of two components, one the sum of money c laid out on means of production, and the other the sum of money v expended upon labour-power; c represents the portion of value which has been turned into constant capital, v that turned into variable capital' (Marx 1982a, p. 320).

down to the most intimate economic details – for example, the theory of the falling rate of profit – by the theory of reification, which has a precisely defined economic meaning.[130]

Here, Adorno refers to a comment made by Horkheimer in a discussion between the two on 3 February 1939, shortly before Adorno drafted his memorandum on Mayer's letter. In this discussion, Horkheimer 'expresses ... the economic formulation for the objective origin of ideology as one of necessary appearance: by virtue of his social position, the entrepreneur must be of the conviction that the social surplus also comes from c and not merely from v'.[131]
   Adorno continues:

> Therefore, by focusing on these concepts, I believe I am not following a fetishistic whim or Lukács's example, but rather the spirit of the Marxist method itself. I would claim the same for the other point on which Mayer accuses me of obstinacy, namely for starting from production. To start principally from circulation would immediately summon the danger of precisely the very psychologism which the work opposes in principle. This is the same consideration which determines the particular stance of my work on the problem of mediation. I am quite well aware of the demand for economic mediation. Equally so, I am aware of the immense difficulties standing in its way. However, replacing it with an intellectual-historical demand of the kind Mayer suggests would mean regressing from the entire approach and taking up psychological-historical explanations where political economy does not deliver. I for one would rather leave the blank spaces in the mediation like white spots on a map and pose the problem firmly as an objectively social one.[132]

To make his thesis of the substitution of use-value by exchange-value more precise, Adorno again invokes his postulation of the phenomenon of 'vocal fetishism': while Adorno claims that 'the cult of the voice, of mere virtuosity, of incursion, of the so-called sensuous harmony and any manner of similar things are unique to the entire epoch of developed bourgeois music dating at least as far back as the middle of the nineteenth century', he believes it should be noted that

---

130   Adorno, 'Notizen zu Mayer' (MHA I 18.42).
131   Adorno and Horkheimer 1985a, p. 470.
132   Adorno, 'Notizen zu Mayer' (MHA I 18.42–3); cf. letter from Horkheimer to Mayer, 23 March 1939 (Horkheimer 1995c, p. 576).

there has been a decisive change today insofar as these elements are no longer even enjoyed anymore, I almost want to say no longer even perceived. Rather, it is actually their mere reflection in prevailing enterprise which is perceived and enjoyed .... What is decisive for the contemporary state of affairs is not externality or superficiality, nor is it even the old-fashioned worship of success, but rather the very process of substitution which I attempt to describe with the thesis that exchange-value is consumed in place of use-value. I have the impression that Herr Mayer does not see the real scope of this thesis, but rather constantly reduces it to much more harmless, older phenomena. Although these may be 'the same' in a certain sense, they are entirely different in another, namely in the sense of totality, of the alteration of the individual by a totality of commodities between which there is no choice and to which, deep down, there is no longer even any relationship. While all of these elements used to contribute to a progressive tendency, today they serve a regressive one. This is because they are not really even themselves anymore, but rather only the stylistic reflection of themselves, and also because the delights that they allegedly bring today are actually reducible to their entirely abstract exchange-value. To emphasise this idea, I prefaced my work by examining the concept of musical taste and its liquidation, and I thought that the rest of the work made it clear enough.[133]

In other words, Adorno maintains that consumers desire things not for their inherent worth, but rather because they are viewed as valuable (in a non-economic sense) by the general public. However, this has an effect on the economy of things, which is why commodities do in fact have a mediating function between individuals. Although essentially social rather than economic by nature, this function appears to belong to commodities themselves: a particular commodity confers a particular prestige which can be acquired through its purchase.

Concluding by addressing the 'purely economic categories' decried by Mayer, Adorno claims to be misunderstood by the former insofar as he

views the meaning of economic categories in the framework of Marxist theory as specifically limited to economic science. He believes that this meaning must be 'mediated' by categories from other sciences, whereas

---

133   Adorno, 'Notizen zu Mayer' (MHA I 18.43–4); cf. letter from Horkheimer to Mayer, 23 March
       1939 (Horkheimer 1995c, pp. 577–8).

the essence of the Marxist method is precisely to turn to the process of
production itself in order to dismantle all of the obfuscations reflected in
other bourgeois sciences' concepts of mediation. If my work has a fundamental deficiency, it is that it is not economic enough, that is, that the
economic categories used in it are insufficiently distinguished as such to
achieve what they are burdened with .... If Herr Mayer sensed something
of this deficiency, he certainly interprets it backwards, which is to say he
believes that this distinction can be achieved through the introduction
of non-economic categories, whereas in truth only the ongoing distinction of the economic categories themselves would have the power to dismantle the intellectual-historical blanket-concepts, among which I must
of course count his concept of the historical.[134]

Adorno argues that the mediations demanded by Mayer are all already present
given that music is *produced* as a commodity. Whoever recognises this can use
Marx to explore the status of music *as a commodity* in existing society.

Far more problematic is Adorno's critique of a 'commodity-listening' to
which serious music is sold out 'for the price of its wages'.[135] Even if this characteristic of the reception of music is supposed to be purely descriptive – see,
for example, when Adorno writes of 'ears trained [in commodity-listening]'[136]
in his monograph on Mahler – one might ask which mediations determine the
difference in reception of a piece of music depending on whether or not it was
produced as a commodity. Whatever these mediations may be, it is hardly conceivable that they would be economic in nature.

Having received from Horkheimer the response prepared by Adorno to his
objections, Mayer again inquires about the 'concrete mediations' in another
letter:

It was never my intention to deny the central importance of the problem
of reification to the analysis of capitalist society. However, I do protest
against a certain tendency which I though I perceived in Adorno's work,
namely the tendency to separate the problem of commodity-fetishism
from the ensemble of *Capital*, to absolutise and thus to remain stuck in
the first volume, instead of advancing to the 'process of capitalist production as a whole'. Against me, it is objected that Adorno did not 'economise'

---

134 Adorno, 'Notizen zu Mayer' (MHA I 18.47); cf. letter from Horkheimer to Mayer, 23 March
     1939 (Horkheimer 1995, pp. 579–80).
135 Adorno 2009c, p. 293.
136 Adorno 1996, p. 73.

too much, but rather too little. As paradoxical as it may appear to sound, to this I reply that this is precisely what I meant. The apparent contradiction is only a matter of differing usages of the word 'economic'. If my critics agree ... that Adorno's essay juxtaposes certain economic categories with corresponding 'superstructural' phenomena too abruptly and without accounting for the economic mediations in detail, this was precisely the core of my critique. I simply conceived of the term 'economic' in a narrower sense, which I contrasted with the necessary, extremely nuanced overall analysis. In its own right, this analysis admittedly struck me too as by no means an amorphous stringing together of psychology plus sociology plus history etc., or otherwise as pluralist, but rather as conceived strictly structurally around a central thesis. Objectively, I therefore see no differences here. Yet the fact remains that Adorno did not depict in detail the (economic or socioeconomic) *process as a whole* – the concrete mediations are missing. Whether this can be avoided given the manner in which he addresses the problems methodologically is another question. I still regard the application of the concept of 'use-value' to the material of the tonal work as inadequate and unproductive. This is not to say I am for an analysis which starts from the sphere of circulation. Yet here we arrive at the points where also still today, it seems to me, differences exist.[137]

Mayer later recalls that the debate was not carried on further: the lead-up to and arrival of war meant that 'scholarly contacts between Europe and America could no longer be maintained'. Looking back on the epistolary dispute, he adopts a thoroughly conciliatory tone:

At the time, there had already been an initial theoretical dispute between Adorno and myself. It started with a musical-sociological analysis of the 'Fetish-Character in Music' and of the process of a 'Regression of Listening' which he had published in the *Zeitschrift für Sozialforschung*. While today I would describe this analysis as quite correct and prescient, I was embittered by it at the time and felt I had to identify a misunderstanding of facts of music history and an absolutisation of the positions of the Arnold Schönberg school. Thus, I wrote an extensive counter-analysis in the form of a letter-essay, which was followed by a theoretical counter-statement from the Institute for Social Research, drafted by Horkheimer

---

137   Letter from Mayer to Horkheimer, 23 April 1939 (Horkheimer 1995c, pp. 590–1).

and Adorno as a joint opinion. It in turn accused my insistence on historical concreteness of embodying the standpoint of historicism and intellectual history.[138]

In the version of 'Fetish-Character' published in the essay collection *Dissonanzen*, the passage criticised by Mayer which claims that 'application of the commodity category to music is not an analogy' is omitted. This prompts Wolfram
Ette to speculate: 'Nothing ... could have possibly been less like Adorno than to
assume an analogy between art and commodity. Art is commodity: hence, the
commodity character encompasses everything related to art'. In reality, 'Fetish-
Character' is not about an analogy, but rather

> a structural affinity based on real relations of participation, that is, a
> homology which differs from analogy precisely in the existence of a rela-
> tion of participation. Thus, it appears all the more puzzling that Adorno
> deleted the corresponding passage in the revision of the text. Perhaps
> the critique appeared graver in his memory than it actually was on this
> point.[139]

However, it is more likely that Adorno would not agree with Ette's claim that
although the 'totalitarian principle means a society as a whole and in all of its
parts is composed according to the same principle', a 'mediation between these
parts is absent'.[140] Again, a totality whose elements do not do justice to their
mediacy with the whole can only be misunderstood as analogy. The concept of
totality states nothing more 'than the triviality that everything is linked with
everything else'[141] while saying 'nothing about the nature of the linkage'.[142]

Adorno's retrospective also comes off as distanced and self-critical when, in
his lecture course *Philosophical Elements of a Theory of Society* held 26 years
later during the summer semester of 1964, he concedes that his thesis that
'people do not only consume or attach themselves to use-values' but rather
'are attached to exchange values' was 'perhaps not completely economically
ironclad'. Likewise, he admits that the essay's theory was 'developed somewhat
blithely ... especially because something like the enjoyment of exchange values
can only truly be grasped socio-psychologically, in terms of certain Freudian

---

138   Mayer 1971, p. 147.
139   Ette 1998, p. 438.
140   Ette 1998, p. 423.
141   Adorno 1976a, p. 13.
142   Reemtsma 1995, p. 94.

categories, and is thus, strictly speaking, not actually social. So I am very much aware of the deficiencies of such a theory'.[143] Adorno's estimation of his own thesis as 'blithe' here shows that he has realised the objective inadequacy of the way in which it uses Marxian terminology: 'a thinking that blithely begins afresh, heedless of the historic form of its problems, will so much more be their prey'.[144]

Curiously, however, in *Aesthetic Theory*, a posthumously edited work which Adorno was not able to bring to completion himself, this exact thesis reappears: 'in monopoly capitalism it is primarily exchange value, not use value, that is consumed'.[145] As to whether this passage was meant to be deleted or revised before the final draft, one can only speculate. Yet it is certainly also possible that Adorno wanted to claim for himself that which he recognised both aphoristically of psychology, where 'nothing is true except the exaggerations',[146] as well as more generally: 'only exaggeration per se today can be the medium of truth'.[147]

---

143 Adorno 2019i, p. 45.
144 Adorno 2007b, p. 17. Adorno identifies the ahistoricity of this ostensible 'beginning afresh' in 'blithely advancing positivism' (Adorno 1976b, p. 182) as well.
145 Adorno 2002a, p. 21; cf. Adorno and Horkheimer 2002, p. 128: 'What might be called use value in the reception of cultural assets is being replaced by exchange value; enjoyment is giving way to being there and being in the know, connoisseurship by enhanced prestige'.
146 Adorno 2005b, p. 45.
147 Adorno 2005i, p. 99.

PART 2

CHAPTER 5

The Theoretically Useless Concept of State Capitalism

> The director of the Progress Insurance Company was always greatly dissatisfied with his employees. Now every director is dissatisfied with his employees; the difference between employees and directors is too vast to be bridged by means of mere commands on the part of the director and mere obedience on the part of the employees. Only mutual hatred can bridge the gap and give the whole enterprise meaning.
>
> FRANZ KAFKA, Diary Entry from 30 July 1914

∴

1 The Present State of Affairs in Our Soviet Republic

In 1924, the Austrian Marxist Carl Grünberg became the head of the newly established Institute for Social Research in Frankfurt am Main.[1] Grünberg 'brought with him from Vienna the periodical he had published since 1911, *Archiv für die Geschichte des Sozialismus und der Arbeiterbewegung* (*Archive for the History of Socialism and the Labour Movement*), which subsequently figured as the Institute's official journal' until 1930.[2] By the time Horkheimer succeeded Grünberg that same year, the Institute had come to stand in the 'tradition of the critical Marxism of the 1920s, which opposed itself to the Stalinisation and

---

1 For an extensive overview of the beginnings of the Institute see Migdal 1981.
2 Gödde and Lonitz 2006, p. 92. Grünberg presents his understanding of the tasks of the Institute for Social Research in a speech from 1924: 'One generation ago I still thought that I had to have reservations against the materialist conception of history, the main pillar of scientific socialism. Taught by developments since, however, I have given up my reservations. It is therefore understandable that I approach scientific tasks in my specialty equipped with the Marxist method of research. Insofar as projects in the Institute for Social Research are conducted under my supervision, this method shall be brought to application' (Grünberg 1986, p. 7).

Bolshevisation of the Communist movement'.[3] At the same time, however, the Institute also criticised Marxism's turn towards Social Democracy as well as its degeneration into an eternally valid theory of absent revolution. 'In contrast to the Kautskyist Marx-orthodoxy of the Second International and the Leninist Marx-orthodoxy of the Third International, two instances of Marxist theory having coagulated into a "scientific worldview" of the proletariat and a doctrine of the general "dialectical" laws of nature and history',[4] the Institute's employees had as their goal the 'supposedly viable adaptation of Marxian theory to the real development of late capitalism'.[5]

Yet this adaptation would not come about soon. In a memorandum from late 1935, Horkheimer details a conversation between himself and Kurt Mandelbaum[6] concerning 'the activation of the economics department at the Institute for Social Research':

> We were both convinced that a representative statement from the Institute on this matter was to be justifiably expected. As our actual economists Pollock, [Julian] Gumperz and Mandelbaum spend most of their time with administrative matters, they can work on theory but are unable to tackle the writing. We discussed the plan of initially producing a 100–120-page critical examination of the most advanced contemporary currents within the bourgeois study of national economy. Here, the goal would certainly not be an exhaustive account, but rather a critique of those elements which exert a simultaneously fascinating and misleading influence in conventional circles. By no means should the critique merely remain negative; instead, it should make our positive position visible. A main task would be to show why we regard a large portion of contemporary national economy as irrelevant, and why this conviction is not arbitrary. Like many other contemporary scholarly fields, the ideological aspect of national economy is often not even a matter of objective falsehoods and confusions, but rather a matter of its focus on the *inessential*.[7]

---

3 Demirović 1999b, p. 35. Karl Korsch, who occasionally did work for the Institute, describes the other theorists there in a letter to Paul Mattick as follows: 'Internally, they are all without exception, to varying degrees, anti-Stalinists' (letter from Korsch to Mattick, 20 October 1938 [Korsch 2001, p. 684]). On the relationship between Korsch and the Institute cf. Blank 2005.
4 Wiggershaus 1998, p. 54.
5 Dubiel 1981, p. 900. 'The authors of the older critical theory believed that capitalism's liberal high-period had given way to the catastrophe-ridden stage of late capitalism' (Demirović 2003b, p. 5).
6 Cf. Jay 1979.
7 Horkheimer 1995a, p. 422, n. 2.

In a letter written just under a year later to Henryk Grossmann, another economist at the Institute,[8] Horkheimer acknowledges that '[i]t pains me that the economic section of our journal so often comes up short'.[9] Grossmann answers as follows:

> You mention that the volumes contain 'no *principally* economic contributions'. This is correct. But how often can 'principal' problems be posed, and how many can be posed? I believe that national economy has reached a stage at which there are enough theory-*constructions* which lead nowhere. Now, the *examination* of the validity of these theoretical constructions is more necessary than *research*! That is my conviction. For one hundred years, *all* positions have been taken up only to be claimed again and again in new variations. Now is the time for the results of the great experiments of the last fifty years to be examined.[10]

Two years later in 1938, Adorno became a permanent employee at the Institute for Social Research, which had been relocated to New York. There, he encountered a controversy 'over the relationship between politics and eco-

---

8   'In his 1929 book *Law of Accumulation and Breakdown of the Capitalist System*, Institute for Social Research employee Henryk Grossmann delivered what was until that point the most comprehensive critique of both the harmonious interpretation of the models according to which capitalism reproduces itself, and of the theory of underconsumption's justification of capitalism's necessary breakdown .... Yet at the same time, he attempted to demonstrate capitalism's inevitable breakdown with an argumentation based on over-accumulation theory. On the basis of ... a reproduction model, Grossmann showed that when value composition increases, the tendency of profit to fall – which he took as necessary – is at first accompanied by accelerated accumulation, that is, by an increase in the mass of profit. However, the process of accumulation eventually leads to an absolute decline in the mass of profit until the point at which further accumulation becomes impossible .... Grossmann does concede that this development has countervailing tendencies, which amount to a change in the preconditions he identifies (constant rate of surplus value, continuous growth of constant capital). However, his discussion of these countervailing tendencies is unconvincing. What has been said above regarding the "laws" of the accumulation of capital applies here. Grossmann's methodological error consists of an inappropriate use of the models of reproduction. These have the ability to show that capitalist reproduction is only possible in the first place if certain sectoral conditions of proportionality are met. Yet the real course of the process of accumulation can be neither predicted nor logged theoretically' (Sablowski 2003, p. 109). For an overview of Grossmann's national-economic theory see Braeuer 1954.
9   Letter from Horkheimer to Grossmann, 12 October 1936 (Horkheimer 1995b, p. 661).
10   Letter from Grossmann to Horkheimer, 6 November 1936 (Horkheimer 1995b, p. 713).

nomy in fascism',[11] and over whether contemporary social changes meant that
the political sphere had superseded the economic as the primary source of
domination. In short, what was at stake was how to assess the respective political and economic results of the 'great experiments' – that is, the experiments
of fascism and National Socialism in Germany and Italy, of a planned economy in the Soviet Union and of the politics of the New Deal[12] in the United
States.

In light of National Socialism, the question emerged as to whether the 'command economy'[13] of Nazi Germany had rendered capitalism as such inoperative. While some of the members of the Institute – Franz L. Neumann,[14]
A.R.L. Gurland,[15] Otto Kirchheimer[16] and Herbert Marcuse[17] – championed the
thesis 'that the fascist state merely represented the political form appropriate
to advanced monopoly capitalism',[18] Friedrich Pollock and Horkheimer maintained that the contemporary political-economic order of both Nazi Germany
and the United States was aptly described by the term 'state capitalism'. As
Helmut Dubiel writes in the introduction to a German translation of a volume
of the former's collected writings from his time in America, 'Friedrich Pollock,
together with his colleagues Gerhardt Meyer and Kurt Mandelbaum, represents the economic expression of Critical Theory'. Pollock first engages with the
Russian mode of production in detail in his 1929 study *Die planwirtschaftlichen
Versuche in der Sowjetunion 1917–1927* (*Economic Planning Attempts in the Soviet
Union 1917–1927*). 'This work, the fruit of an extensive scholarly journey in the

---

11   Dubiel 1975, p. 16.
12   'It will easily be seen that in the absence of a single posture and definition, the genesis of
       a version of state capitalism represented by the New Deal was also conceived differently
       (as "democratic" or "manipulated"). Those theorists who concentrated on the manipu-
       lated, closed, authoritarian features of the system (Horkheimer, Adorno, Kirchheimer and
       the later Marcuse) focused on the objectively necessary response of capitalism to crisis
       and the conquest of the subjective factor by the political organizations of pluralist mass
       democracy and by the culture industry (in a manner analogous to the fascist "psychoana-
       lysis in reverse"). The theorists who insisted on the juridical-legal protection of civil rights
       and the survival of some residues of popular political participation under late capital-
       ism (Neumann and Pollock) postulated a New Deal type of system as the achievement of
       the democratic forces (unions, reformist parties etc.) battling against the other historical
       alternative, fascism' (Arato 1978, p. 21).
13   Türcke and Bolte 1994, p. 45.
14   See Neumann 2009.
15   See Gurland 1941.
16   See Kirchheimer 1939.
17   See Marcuse 2009.
18   Dubiel 1975, p. 17; cf. van Reijen and Bransen 2002, pp. 248–9.

Soviet Union, still ranks ... among the seminal non-Russian works on the beginning of the planned economy in Russia'.[19]

> Pollock's study of the development of capitalism had been a permanent part of the Institute's work since the early 1930s. In his early essays he followed Marx in locating the contradictions threatening the capitalist system in the growing tension between productive forces and the relations of production. He argued that the quality of the new economic crisis demonstrated that liberal capitalism, with its attempts to regulate crises through the market, must fail. It was therefore time for a transition to a new economic order which, although based on the old one and therefore to be seen as a development of it, exhibited the novel quality of a planned economy. ... Pollock contradicted the Marxian theory of the collapse of capitalism and went still further in prophesying its permanence: 'What is coming to an end is not capitalism but only its liberal phase'.[20]

Pollock's visions of state capitalism refer to Rudolf Hilferding's 1910 study *Finance Capital*. As Perry Anderson writes, this work presents 'a full-scale "updating" of [*Capital*], to take account of the global changes in the capitalist mode of production as such, in the new epoch of trusts, tariffs and trade wars. Centring his analysis on the growing ascendancy of banks, the accelerating thrust of monopolization, and the increasing use of state machinery for the aggressive expansion of capital, Hilferding stressed the mounting international tension and anarchy that was the concomitant of the tightening organization and centralization of each national capitalism'.[21] To Hilferding, with whom Pollock had come into contact[22] during the Institute for Social Research's collaboration on the first *Marx-Engels-Gesamtausgabe*,[23] the 'most characteristic features of "modern capitalism"' are 'those processes of concentration which, on the one hand, "eliminate free competition" through the formation of cartels and trusts,

---

19   Dubiel 1975, pp. 8–9.
20   van Reijen and Bransen 2002, pp. 248–9; quoted from Pollock 1933, p. 350.
21   Anderson 1987, pp. 9–10.
22   'During the twenties, the Institute of Social Research ... had both Communists and Social-Democrats on its staff, and maintained a regular liaison with the Marx-Engels Institute in Moscow, dispatching archival material to [David] Ryazanov for the first scientific edition of the works of Marx and Engels. The inaugural volume of the Marx-Engels Gesamtausgabe (MEGA) was, in fact, published in Frankfurt in 1927 under the joint auspices of the two institutions' (Anderson 1987, pp. 21–2; on the work of Ryazanov cf. Kolpinskij 1997). Cf. Hecker 2000.
23   See letter from Pollock to Hilferding, 21. November 1924 (Hecker 2000, pp. 174–5).

and on the other, bring bank and industrial capital into an ever more intimate relationship'.[24] As a result, Hilferding traces 'the formation of a general cartel dominating society's production ... to the dissolution of the market and of wage-labour, so that surplus-value and wage alike are reduced to variables of distribution'.[25] These assumptions in turn stem from Engels's *Herr Eugen Dühring's Revolution in Science*, more commonly known as *Anti-Dühring*. As Engels writes therein, the 'modern state ... is only the organisation that bourgeois society takes on in order to support the general external conditions of the capitalist mode of production against the encroachments as well of the workers as of individual capitalists. The modern state, no matter what its form, is essentially a capitalist machine, the state of the capitalists, the ideal personification of the total national capital'.[26]

Pollock draws not only on Hilferding's theses, but also on Lenin's considerations of 'state capitalism in the proletarian state'.[27] On the one hand, Lenin cautions that '[t]he proletarian state may, without changing its own nature, permit freedom to trade and the development of capitalism only within certain bounds, and only on the condition that the state regulates (supervises, controls, determines the forms and methods of, etc.) private trade and private capitalism'.[28] However, Lenin also refers more affirmatively to state capitalism elsewhere: 'The whole problem – in theoretical and practical terms – is to find the correct methods of directing the development of capitalism (which is to some extent and for some time inevitable) into the channels of state capitalism, and to determine how we are to hedge it about with conditions to ensure its transformation into socialism in the near future'.[29] For Lenin, 'state capitalism' meant the limited sanctioning of capitalism by the 'proletarian state' progressing towards socialism. According to him, as long as 'transport and large-scale industry remain in the hands of the proletariat',[30] the dynamism inherent in capitalism can only be of use, which is why he greets the fear of 'Left Communists' concerning the 'threat of an "evolution towards state capitalism"' with 'nothing short of Homeric laughter':

24   Hilferding 1981, p. 21.
25   Robelin 1988, p. 1248; cf. especially Chapter 15 of *Finance Capital*: 'Price determination by the capitalist monopolies and the historical tendency of finance capital' (Hilferding 1981, pp. 227–35).
26   Engels 1987a, p. 266; for the critique of Engels's conception cf. Elbe 2008, pp. 23–4.
27   Lenin 1973a, p. 185.
28   Lenin 1973a, p. 185; cf. Blank 2005, p. 103, n. 306.
29   Lenin 1973b, p. 345.
30   Lenin 1973c, p. 457.

They have really frightened us this time! ... It has not occurred to them that state capitalism would be a *step forward* as compared with the present state of affairs in our Soviet Republic. If in approximately six months' time state capitalism became established in our Republic, this would be a great success and a sure guarantee that within a year socialism will have gained a permanently firm hold and will have become invincible in our country.[31]

However, in this polemic, Lenin 'fatefully neglects the connection between the formal determinants of politics and economy'.[32] Assuming that 'capitalism contains a quasi-neutral, technical rationality of nature-appropriation which, once liberated from class-domination, would enable a free and emancipatory form of social production',[33] he is able to refer positively to the allegedly socialist-affirming elements of capitalism – as if these could be separated from their functional context within capitalism and implemented within socialism while maintaining their functionality.

For Pollock, the term state capitalism 'indicates four items better'[34] than do all other apparently related expressions:[35] 'that state capitalism is the successor of private capitalism, that the state assumes important functions of the private capitalist, that profit interests still play a significant role, and that it is not socialism'.[36]

2   Mere Problems of Administration

Over the course of several essays, Pollock engages with the question of 'whether in capitalism as well' – just as was the plan in the state socialism of Soviet Russia – 'continuous growth and full employment might only be achievable through a quasi-planned regulation of the entire economic process'.[37] His conclusion is entirely affirmative.

---

31   Lenin 1972, pp. 334–5.
32   Blank 2005, p. 103, n. 306.
33   Bruch 2003, p. 178.
34   Pollock 1941b, p. 201.
35   '"State organized private-property monopoly capitalism", "managerial society", "administrative capitalism", "bureaucratic collectivism", "totalitarian state economy", "status capitalism", "neo-mercantilism", "economy of force", "state socialism"' (Pollock 1941b, p. 201).
36   Pollock 1941, p. 201.
37   Dubiel 1975, p. 12.

Pollock's theory of state capitalism 'as a superior form of society to liberal capitalism'[38] is presented as a 'model'[39] 'in the sense of Max Weber's "ideal type"'.[40] This model 'represents a consequent systematisation of trends [Pollock] believes to recognise particularly in National Socialism, but also in the United States',[41] respective manifestations of the 'two most typical varieties' of state capitalism: 'its totalitarian and its democratic form'.[42]

In the preface to the second issue of the 1941 volume of the *Zeitschrift für Sozialforschung*, produced during the Institute's American exile, Horkheimer writes:

> For more than eight years, the government of this country has attempted to overcome the difficulties of the prevailing economy by incorporating into it the elements of planning, in the industrial as well as the agricultural sector. The alarming predicament of agriculture in Germany under the Weimar Republic was an important factor in the rise of fascism. In this the government of the United States has recognized the danger and has attempted to bring agriculture under its control. The same holds true for other sectors of economic life.[43]

According to Pollock, these trends suggest that the restoration of full employment and overall well-being would necessitate a 'general plan'[44] resulting in the fixing of the prices of most commodities[45] and the subordination of the production and distribution of commodities to the control of the state.[46] Individual interests – the motor of economic liberalism – would become meaningless, superseded by the maxim '*Gemeinnutz geht vor Eigennutz*' (public interest

---

38   Sablowski 2003, p. 115.

39   Pollock 1941b, p. 200.

40   Pollock 1941b, p. 200, n. 1.

41   Dubiel 1975, p. 14; cf. also Marramao 1975, p. 67.

42   Pollock 1941b, p. 201.

43   Horkheimer 1941a, p. 198; for the critique of this position cf. Neumann 2009, p. 225.

44   Pollock 1941b, p. 204.

45   Cf. Pollock 1941b, pp. 208–15. Marramao points out that the prospects recognised by Pollock for a reorganisation of the economy around planning 'indicate ... only a tendential direction which in itself not necessary' (Marramao 1975, p. 65). Already in 1933, Horkheimer writes that the 'knowledge of tendencies' afforded by materialist theory 'offers no clear prognosis of historical development' (Horkheimer 1993a, p. 44). Cf. Gmünder 1985, p. 27.

46   See Pollock 1941b, pp. 204–5. However, in his essay 'Is National Socialism a New Order', Pollock is clear on the following point: 'It seems certain that no master plan exists for the Nazi economy and it is unlikely that detailed figures have been worked out for the various branches of industry' (Pollock 1941a, p. 445).

before self-interest).[47] '[S]tate activity' would expand to 'all spheres of social life as a whole',[48] with formerly economic processes being replaced to the greatest possible extent by political processes – that is, by controllable ones. Given the suppression of the sphere of circulation in state capitalism, even exchange would yield its role as central mediator to a controlled distribution of commodities.[49] Whereas in the liberal market economy, 'the individuals and strata communicate with each other through the medium of exchange as legally equal partners', National Socialism as a command economy 'has abolished the last vestiges of such free economic subjects'.[50]

In light of the major economic crises of the recent past – and above all the global economic crisis of 1929–33 – Pollock enthusiastically welcomes the democratic form of command economy he sees as existing in the United States. To him, this type of economy represents an instrument for regulating those processes which classical liberalism has left to run their course in an uncontrolled manner:[51]

---

47   Pollock 1941b, p. 205 (translator's note: the German '*Gemeinnutz geht vor Eigennutz*' appears in Pollock's original English essay). Pollock argues that this maxim also applies within the ruling elite: 'The interest of the ruling group as a whole is decisive, not the individual interests of those who form the group' (ibid.).

48   Pollock 1941b, p. 206.

49   'Under private capitalism, all social relations are mediated by the market; men meet each other as agents of the exchange process, as buyers or sellers. The source of one's income, the size of one's property are decisive for one's social position. The profit motive keeps the economic mechanism of society moving. Under state capitalism men meet each other as commander or commanded; the extent to which one can command or has to obey depends in the first place upon one's position in the political set-up and only in a secondary way upon the extent of one's property. Labor is appropriated directly instead of by the "roundabout" way of the market' (Pollock 1941b, p. 207).

50   Pollock 1941a, p. 443; cf. Gangl 1987, p. 205, n. 1.

51   Regarding how depression and global economic crisis changed the general assessment of capitalism's stability, Hobsbawm writes the following: 'In the past, waves and cycles, long, medium and short, had been accepted by businessmen and economists rather as farmers accept the weather, which also has its ups and downs. There was nothing to be done about them: they created opportunities or problems, they could lead to bonanzas or bankruptcy for individuals or industries, but only socialists who, with Karl Marx, believed that cycles were part of a process by which capitalism generated what would in the end prove insuperable internal contradictions, thought they put the existence of the economic system as such at risk. The world economy was expected to go on growing and advancing, as it had patently done, except for the sudden and short-lived catastrophes of cyclical slumps, for over a century. What was novel about the new situation was that, probably for the first, and so far the only, time in the history of capitalism, its fluctuations seemed to be genuinely system-endangering' (Hobsbawm 1995, p. 87).

Replacement of the mechanics of *laissez faire* by governmental command does not imply the end of private initiative and personal responsibility, which might even be put on a broader basis but will be integrated within the framework of the general plan. During the non-monopolistic phase of private capitalism, the capitalist ... had power over his property within the limits of the market laws. Under state capitalism, this power has been transferred to the government which is still limited by certain 'natural' restrictions but free from the tyranny of an uncontrolled market. The replacement of the economic means by political means as the last guarantee for the reproduction of economic life, changes the character of the whole historic period. It signifies the transition from a predominantly economic to an essentially political era.[52]

What Grossmann takes to be 'absolutely impossible in a capitalist system',[53] Pollock sees as the way out of economic depression:

Government control of production and distribution furnishes the means for eliminating the economic causes of depressions, cumulative destructive processes and unemployment of capital and labor. We may even say that under state capitalism economics as a social science has lost its object. Economic problems in the old sense no longer exist when the coordination of all economic activities is effected by conscious plan instead of by the natural laws of the market. Where the economist formerly racked his brain to solve the puzzle of the exchange process, he meets, under state capitalism, with mere problems of administration.[54]

Pollock draws a sobering consequence from his description of economic conditions: society faces a choice 'between democratic and authoritarian versions of state capitalism, rather than between capitalism per se and socialism'.[55] However, the sobriety with which Pollock resigns himself to this theoretical insight[56] amounts to its affirmation: when Pollock advocates 'eliminating' the

---

52   Pollock 1941b, p. 207.

53   Marramao 1975, p. 71.

54   Pollock 1941b, p. 217 (cf. van Reijen and Bransen 2002, pp. 249–50). Elsewhere, Pollock writes that '[i]f the democracies can show that economic security must not be tied up with the loss of liberty but can be achieved under democratic conditions, then I dare forecast that the new order of National Socialism will be followed in Germany and elsewhere by an infinitely superior democratic new order' (Pollock 1941a, p. 455).

55   Jay 1984, p. 37.

56   In general, Pollock's recurring analyses of prevailing economic relations are much more

'unemployment of capital and labor', it becomes clear that he is concerned not with a *critique* of economy,[57] but rather with considerations of regulatory policy, such as how capitalism's vulnerability to crisis can be redressed. Whether intentionally or not, Pollock marvels in these considerations at the very machinery which, especially in Germany at the time, was already starting to run so powerfully. In doing so, he grants legitimacy to the 'National Socialist regime's self-conception'[58] as a command economy for overcoming capitalist crises.[59] It seems his ideal state is no longer simply the Engelsian 'ideal personification of the total national capital', but rather the total capitalist in real and unrivalled form. Pollock ends up in this position due to his assumption that 'capitalism is capable of conclusively leaving its competition phase and developing in the direction of a planned economy', an assumption which 'marks the fundamental difference between Pollock's theory and that of the most important economist of the *Zeitschrift für Sozialforschung*, Henryk Grossmann'.[60] That being said, Engels's thesis that the more the state 'proceeds to the taking over of productive forces, the more does it actually become the national capitalist'[61] is untenable in its own right: 'Although the state does indeed become a real capitalist by taking over capitalist production processes, it does not become the *total* capitalist. As a capitalist producer the state is subject to the contradictions of individual capitals among themselves, as are other *large* individual capitals'.[62]

---

focused on description than critique (cf. Marramao 1975, p. 73). Pollock would remain loyal to this approach. In the postwar era, his interest was 'claimed almost exclusively' by his 'studies of the social forms of automation of work processes' (Marramao 1975, p. 74, n. 70); cf. above all Pollock's book on automation, where the concept of state capitalism is taken up again when Pollock claims 'that a policy of public works can act effectively against technological mass unemployment only if they are introduced on a sufficiently large scale and for a sufficiently long period of time to achieve their object. And if they were introduced on a large scale for a sufficient number of years they would represent an important step in the direction of State [Capitalism]' (Pollock 1957, p. 74).

57   Thus, Gangl comments from an economy-critical perspective that this position is based 'on a certain state illusionism which Pollock shared with other Social Democratic theorists' (Gangl 1987, p. 202).

58   Cf. Brandt 1981, p. 28.

59   Cf. Neumann 2009, pp. 293–361.

60   Marramao 1975, p. 57; for Kurt Martin's recollections of the debate cf. Martin 1981, p. 904. Martin is 'the later name of Kurt Mandelbaum, which he adopted over the course of his emigration to England' (editorial comment by Schmid Noerr [Horkheimer 1995b, p. 422, n. 1]).

61   Engels 1987a, p. 266.

62   Altvater 1978, p. 186, n. 7.

In an earlier essay from 1932, 'Die gegenwärtige Lage des Kapitalismus und die Aussichten einer planwirtschaftlichen Neuordnung' ('The Contemporary State of Capitalism and the Prospects of a Planned Economy Reorganisation'), Pollock makes a strong argument for a socialist planned economy before writing the following: 'A *capitalist* planned economy could not be tolerated by the owners of the means of production, simply because they ... would have to be stripped of their economic function and reduced to mere rentiers. But there has never been a social order in which the mere collection of rents from tenants at society's expense without visible service in return was viable in the long run'.[63] However, in 'Bemerkungen zur Wirtschaftskrise' ('Observations on the Economic Crisis'), an essay written the following year after the Nazi seizure of power, Pollock revises this position: 'Earlier, we expressed the view that the degradation of the owner of capital to mere rentier status renders a capitalist planned economy inadmissible .... In light of the possibilities for controlling the masses which have become visible in the meantime, we can no longer count this view among the serious objections'.[64] Pollock would henceforth concede 'that the prospects for a capitalist planned economy would be good'.[65] Within the grouping around him, a discussion emerged of his new assessment of economic relations. Kurt Martin recalls that he and Gerhard Mayer were among those 'not convinced'[66] and that other employees of the Institute also remained sceptical, 'especially those with a background in economics'.[67] This was particularly true of Neumann, the 'dogged political-economic objectivist among the members of the former New York Institute for Social Research'[68] who would later help establish the discipline of political science in the Federal Republic of Germany.[69] As a critic of the theory of state capitalism, Neumann recognised that while 'politics had gained dominance over economics',[70] the envisaged immobilisation of market dynamics in state capitalism had actually resulted in an 'economy without economics'[71] – a capitalism without a market eco-

---

63   Pollock 1932, p. 27.
64   Pollock 1933, p. 349, n. 2.
65   Wiggershaus 1995, p. 280.
66   Martin 1981, p. 905. 'Mandelbaum and Meyer interpreted Pollock's remarks so that they amounted "in practical terms to a strengthening of monopoly capitalist tendencies"' (Gangl 1987, p. 206; quoted from Mandelbaum and Meyer 1934, p. 232).
67   Martin 1981, p. 905.
68   Söllner 1983, p. 339.
69   Cf. Funke 2004, p. 80.
70   van Reijen and Bransen 2002, p. 251.
71   Neumann 2009, p. 221.

nomy. And if, as per Pollock, all of the 'essential constituents of a capitalist economy' – 'the law of value, the market, competition, the law of accumulation and the profit motive of individual economic subjects'[72] – were invalidated and replaced by a 'general plan',[73] the resulting form of society would no longer be capitalism: 'The very term "state capitalism" is a *contradictio in adiecto*'.[74]

Yet Neumann 'did not need ... to spend much time at all addressing the systematic weaknesses of the thesis of state capitalism'.[75] As he conclusively demonstrates empirically in his 1942 book *Behemoth: The Structure and Praxis of National Socialism*, the National Socialist command economy 'certainly [was] not' state capitalism:[76]

> there is no reason to speak of nationalization in Germany – on the contrary, there is a definite trend away from nationalization. All industrial positions held by public authorities had been established prior to National Socialism. ... The power of private capital is certainly not threatened or broken by public capital – on the contrary, in the control of public corporations, private capital plays a decisive part.[77]

Neumann also articulates a detailed critique of Pollock's essay on state capitalism in a letter to Horkheimer from July 1941, writing among other things that '[m]y objection to the essay should surprise neither Pollock nor yourself. From the first page to the last, he contradicts the theory of the Institute'. Once again, Neumann explains that it is fundamentally incorrect to speak of state capitalism in Nazi Germany:

> I want to concede to Pollock that his system is coherent. But I am completely missing the proof of how not-capitalism can appear out of capitalism. According to my view, such proof can only be furnished on the basis of a very material-rich analysis of, for example, Germany, whereby this analysis would also need to contain a theory of transition from monopoly capitalism to state capitalism. The theory is not present, and the material contradicts Pollock's thesis. For one year, I've done nothing other than

---

72   Türcke and Bolte 1994, p. 46.
73   Martin 1981, p. 905.
74   Neumann 2009, p. 224.
75   Türcke and Bolte 1994, p. 47.
76   Neumann 2009, p. 295.
77   Neumann 2009, p. 298.

study the economic processes in Germany, and so far, I haven't found the slightest indication that Germany is even approaching a state-capitalist condition.[78]

Horkheimer's response to Neumann's critique is ambivalent. On the one hand, he has to acknowledge the empirical weaknesses in Pollock's essay, but on the other, he does not want to simply abandon the theoretical concept of state capitalism. He answers as follows:

> As I have absolute confidence in your study of the economic processes in Germany, I trust your disclosure that Germany is also not approaching a state-capitalist condition. At the same time, I cannot get away from the Engelsian view that society is striving in precisely this direction. I must therefore assume that this [state-capitalist] period still threatens us with great probability, which is why the value of Pollock's construction, in spite of all deficiencies, appears largely justified to me as a basis for discussion concerning a current problem.[79]

From the numerous qualifiers in this formulation – the construct of state capitalism, 'in spite of all deficiencies', 'appears' 'largely' justified, at least as a 'basis for discussion' – it can be seen that Horkheimer by no means unreservedly endorses Pollock's thesis.

3   The Last Stage Offered by Bourgeois Society

In a March 1941 letter to Harold Laski – at the time the 'star political scientist'[80] of the London School of Economics[81] and subsequently the leader of the Labour Party from 1945–46 – Horkheimer mentions his recent essay 'The Authoritarian State',[82] claiming it 'pursues the line'[83] of his article 'The Jews

---

78   Letter from Neumann to Horkheimer, 23 July 1941 (Horkheimer 1996a, pp. 103–4).

79   Letter from Horkheimer to Neumann, 2 August 1941 (Horkheimer 1996a, p. 116).

80   Phelps and Sweezy 1999, p. 34.

81   Cf. Dahrendorf 1995.

82   The essay dates from February 1940 but was first published the following year in the hectographic typescript *Walter Benjamin zum Gedächtnis* (*In Memory of Walter Benjamin*): cf. Horkheimer's 'Verzeichnis der Vorträge und Erstveröffentlichungen' ('Index of Lectures and First Publications') (Horkheimer 1987, p. 461) and Breines 1973, p. 2.

83   Letter from Horkheimer to Laski, 10 March 1941 (Horkheimer 2007, p. 173); cf. Blank 2005, p. 104, n. 311.

and Europe'. According to a letter from Adorno to Benjamin, this earlier piece 'essentially presents the first outline of a theory of fascism' on which Adorno himself had 'intensely collaborated'.[84] First appearing in the *Zeitschrift für Sozialforschung* in 1939,[85] 'The Jews and Europe' explains 'the phenomenon of anti-semitism largely as a superstructural phenomenon of totalitarian monopoly capitalism'.[86] Meanwhile, its main focus is the 'obsolescence of the market economy'[87] caused by the 'totalitarian rule of particular interests over the entire people advancing throughout Europe'.[88] It portrays fascism as nothing short of the economic and ideological consummation and transcendence of 'final phase of liberalism':[89] 'To appeal today to the liberal mentality of the nineteenth century against fascism means appealing to what brought fascism to power',[90] for 'the totalitarian order differs from its bourgeois predecessor only in that it has lost its inhibitions'.[91] To Horkheimer, liberalism no longer appears to be anything other than an 'interlude', after which 'the upper class in the fascist countries has returned to its basic insights'.[92]

Horkheimer outlines the terrible vision of a 'fascism as world system' whose end from an economic perspective would be unforeseeable. Under its new relations, exploitation of the weak would not simply reproduce itself through blind mechanisms, but rather 'through the conscious exertion of domination'. Methodical violence would be strived for in order to 'directly master social antagonisms'. While this would not cause the categories of Marxian economy to lose their 'real validity', it would – ironically – mean the realisation of their predicted consequence: 'the end of political economy'.[93]

---

84 Adorno and Benjamin 1999, p. 313.

85 Originally published as 'Die Juden und Europa', *Studies in Philosophy and Social Science* [*Zeitschrift für Sozialforschung*], 8, 1: 115–37.

86 Dubiel 1975, p. 18. 'Horkheimer later distanced himself from this essay. After co-authoring the book *Dialectic of Enlightenment* with Adorno, he no longer viewed the relationship between productive forces and relations of production as the driving element of the historical process, but rather the instrumental-technological reason which has prevailed throughout history in the form of irrational and anonymous bureaucratic superstructures' (ibid).

87 Horkheimer 1989, p. 79.

88 Horkheimer 1989, p. 80.

89 Horkheimer 1989, p. 79.

90 Horkheimer 1989, p. 91.

91 Horkheimer 1989, p. 78.

92 Horkheimer 1989, p. 82.

93 Schmidt 1988, p. 228. It should be noted that there is no positive 'Marxian economy', only a Marxian *critique* of economy.

This same vision is articulated in 'The Authoritarian State', albeit with a modified theoretical language: 'Even though the term state capitalism is not explicitly used in ["The Jews and Europe"], its argumentation is based on the same theoretical assumptions as "The Authoritarian State"'.[94]

As with 'The Jews and Europe', Adorno evidently also contributed to 'The Authoritarian State': in a letter to his parents from early 1940, he describes the text as a 'critique of contemporary Marxism' he needs to 'sort out' with Horkheimer and Gretel Adorno;[95] writing to Horkheimer around the same time, he refers to it as the essay 'we wrote'.[96] During this period, which would continue through *Dialectic of Enlightenment*, Adorno and Horkheimer's collaboration was so intense that the latter even considered publishing his 1942 essay 'The End of Reason'[97] 'under both of our names',[98] although he ultimately did not do so.

In 'The Authoritarian State' – which initially also bore the working title 'State Capitalism', like Pollock's article[99] – Horkheimer develops the idea he had formed on the basis of Engels and in opposition to Neumann 'that the state would necessarily have to take over the management of production as a consequence of the monopolisation process'.[100] As Engels writes in 'Socialism: Utopian and Scientific':

> In any case, with trusts or without, the official representative of capitalist society – the State – will ultimately have to undertake the direction of production. ... All the social functions of the capitalist are now performed by salaried employees. ... And the modern State, again, is only the organisation that bourgeois society takes on in order to support the external conditions of the capitalist mode of production against the encroachments, as well of the workers as of individual capitalists. ... The more it proceeds to the taking over of productive forces, the more does it actually become the national capitalist, the more citizens does

94   Blank 2005, p. 104.
95   Letter from Adorno to his parents, 7 February 1940 (Adorno 2006b, p. 37).
96   Letter from Adorno to Horkheimer, ca. spring 1940 (Adorno and Horkheimer 2004, p. 67).
97   See Horkheimer 1942.
98   Letter from Horkheimer to Löwenthal, 11 February 1942 (Horkheimer 1996a, p. 268); cf. Blank 2005, p. 24.
99   Cf. editorial note by Schmid Noerr (Horkheimer 1996a, p. 270, n. 6) and Blank 2005, p. 102, n. 303.
100 Blank 2005, p. 103.

it exploit. The workers remain wage-workers – proletarians. The capitalist relation is not done away with.[101]

Horkheimer cites this passage at the very beginning of his essay before concluding as follows: 'In the transition from monopoly to state capitalism, the last stage offered by bourgeois society is "the appropriation of the large productive and commercial organisms, first by joint-stock companies, later by trusts and then by the state". *State capitalism is the authoritarian state of the present*'.[102] However, in contrast to the consequences Pollock draws from the supposed progression towards state capitalism, Horkheimer's assessment contains no affirmative element whatsoever.[103] 'The authoritarian state is repressive in all of its forms'.[104] Writing to Pollock regarding his essay 'State Capitalism', Horkheimer urges the former to 'avoid being misunderstood as overly sympathetic to state capitalism',[105] apparently failing to recognise that Pollock's apparent sympathy can hardly be attributed to a simple misunderstanding.

Horkheimer agrees with Pollock that capitalism has outlived the market economy, and that this fact 'was heralded long ago by the fate of working-class organisations'. Trade unions and labour parties 'integrated themselves into the transformations of the economy', improving conditions for the working population, but also causing 'the critique of work as drudgery, which was the only way the past had seen it', to be largely forgotten. Meanwhile, '[w]ork was transformed from the bourgeois' badge of merit into the longing of the disinherited'. The more thoroughly integration occurred, Horkheimer argues, the more working-class organisations adapted to the status quo, as part of which they could finally assert themselves. However, this entailed a risk: '*Whatever seeks to extend itself under domination runs the danger of reproducing it*'.[106] Concretely, Horkheimer perceives this reproduction of domination in the replacement of

---

101   Engels 1989, pp. 318–19.
102   Horkheimer 1973, p. 3; quoted from Engels 1988, p. 325.
103   'However, Horkheimer did not want the authoritarian state to be understood as a stable formation; he emphasised the repressive, exploitative and antagonistic character of all of its variants without denying the potentially decisive implications for individuals entailed by reformism, Bolshevism and fascism respectively' (Sablowski 2003, p. 116).
104   Horkheimer 1973, p. 8.
105   Letter from Horkheimer to Pollock, 1 July 1941 (Horkheimer 1996a, p. 91). Horkheimer had already pointed out to Pollock the need to avoid the 'mistake of endorsing the "totalitarian answer"' (letter from Horkheimer to Pollock, 30 May 1941 [Horkheimer 1996a, p. 46]); cf. Wiggershaus 1995, p. 282.
106   Horkheimer 1973, pp. 4–5.

class-domination with 'the bureaucratic-technocratic apparatus of the state',[107] and in the replacement of class struggle with inequalities of distribution: qualitative differences regulated through appeals from trade unions and similar organisations which co-constitute capitalist society.

According to Horkheimer, what applies to fascism and 'integral statism, or state socialism',[108] also applies to a lesser extent to the remaining democracies. In the latter,

> the leaders of the big working-class organizations find themselves in the same relationship to their membership as the executives of integral statism have to the society as a whole: they keep the masses, whom they take care of, under strict discipline, maintain them in hermetic seclusion from uncontrolled elements, and tolerate spontaneity only as the result of their own power. Far more than the pre-fascist statesmen who mediated between the monopolists of labor and industry and who could never extricate themselves from the utopia of a humanitarian version of the authoritarian state, these labor leaders strive for their own kind of national community (*Volksgemeinschaft*).[109]

Just as he does in 'The Jews and Europe', Horkheimer explicitly indicates in 'The Authoritarian State' that there can be no return to liberalism which would not simply lead back to the prevailing barbarism of the present:

> [One claims i]t would be sentimental to remain opposed to state capitalism merely because of those who have been slain. [It is said] that the Jews were for the most part capitalists, and that the small nations have no justification for their existence. State capitalism is said to be the only thing possible today. As long as the proletariat does not make its own revolution, [it is argued,] there remains no choice for it and its theoreticians but to follow the *Weltgeist* on the path it has chosen. Such opinions, and there are plenty of them, are neither the most stupid nor the most dishonest. This much is true, that with the return to the old private enterprise system, the entire horror would start again from the beginning under new management. But the historical outlook of such reasoning recognizes only the dimension of the cycle of progress and regression; it ignores the active intervention of men. It values men only

---

107   Lindner 1983, p. 90, n. 11.
108   Horkheimer 1973, p. 8.
109   Horkheimer 1973, p. 5.

for what they are under capitalism: as social quantities, as things. [A]s long as world history follows its logical course, it fails to fulfil its human destiny.[110]

Adorno puts his own spin on the last thesis of this passage by pointing out the hypocrisy of the claim that the existence of the capitalist order 'depends solely on humans'.[111] Pithily formulated, capitalism does not exist for humans; rather, under capitalism, humans only exist to serve a function. When Pollock observes that state capitalism is 'quite capable of securing the imperatives of all modern economic policies, such as continuous growth and full employment',[112] he overlooks that it was never 'capitalism's purpose to deliver full employment and well-being'.[113] This oversight stems from an unsophisticated concept of economic crisis which fails to account for the fact that depression, unemployment and poverty by no means inevitably constitute a crisis for capital. On the contrary, a critique which takes individuals as its starting point must consider 'that capitalism in its very existence *is* the crisis, that it therefore cannot enter into crisis'[114] – an insight which seems to indicate a limit of practical critique, for a 'permanent crisis is not a crisis, and a critique with nothing to determine remains only a pose of determination'.[115] This is a problem which Adorno and Horkheimer would yet have to confront over multiple conversations.[116]

4   An Inversion of Kafka

The controversy 'over the primacy of politics or economics in postliberal capitalism ... impinged deeply on the theoretical self-understanding of the members of the Institute for Social Research'.[117] Nevertheless, in spite of all of the potentially theory-rich discussions of economic questions he may have had with Pollock – and with other employees of the Institute – during this time, Adorno did not adopt Pollock's position. On the contrary, in correspondences with Horkheimer from the summer of 1941, he voices extreme dissatisfaction

110   Horkheimer 1973, p. 20.
111   Adorno 2003l, p. 452.
112   Dubiel 1975, p. 15.
113   Heinrich 2007, p. 17.
114   Initiative Sozialistisches Forum 2000, p. 105.
115   Bröckling 2006, p. 97.
116   Cf. Chapter 9 of the present study.
117   van Reijen and Bransen 2002, p. 248.

over preliminary excerpts from Pollock's 'State Capitalism', and even expresses doubt as to whether the essay should be published the *Zeitschrift für Sozialforschung* at all. In one letter, he writes the following:

> I can best summarise my views on this essay by saying that it represents an inversion of Kafka. Kafka portrayed bureaucratic hierarchy as hell. Here, hell is transformed into a bureaucratic hierarchy. Additionally, the whole thing is so full of theses and so formulated 'from above' in a Husserlian sense that it fully dispenses with urgency. This is to say nothing of its undialectical assumption that in an antagonistic society, a non-antagonistic economy would be possible.

For Adorno, the hell of capitalism must be overcome, not bureaucratically administered. Yet it must be noted that Adorno takes issue not merely with Pollock's subjective account of capitalism, but also with his economic analysis. However, 'as a non-economist', Adorno lacks the confidence to express his misgivings to Pollock directly, unsure that he possesses 'the necessary authority to cast such doubt'.[118] As he writes in a subsequent letter to Horkheimer, '[s]ubstantively, I view the central problem of [Pollock's "State Capitalism"] to be the question of whether the tendency it discerns towards a crisis-free economy guided from above actually does express the objective tendency of reality, or whether the antagonistic state of the present means that the ideal purity of this construction is also foreclosed for the future. I feel unable to answer this question'.[119]

If Adorno had agreed with Pollock's thesis that state capitalism had overcome monopoly capitalism, he no longer would have had to (or have been able to) pursue the critique of economy for the sake of social critique. Instead, he could have focused solely on a critique of hierarchised administrative hell – a critique expressed extensively throughout his and Horkheimer's work by the concept of the 'administered world'.[120] At the same time, the Marxian critique

---

118 Letter from Adorno to Horkheimer, 8 June 1941 (Adorno and Horkheimer 2004, p. 139). As the 'only resort' for salvaging Pollock's essay for publication, Adorno suggests that Horkheimer re-write it himself 'using the motifs in *your* "State Capitalism" [that is, "The Authoritarian State"] and in collaboration with [Edward M.] David. That would even make it quite plausible. After all, the motifs of the essay by Fritz [Pollock] apparently originate from yours, and are only simplified and made non-dialectical in a way which transforms them into their opposite' (letter from Adorno to Horkheimer, 8 June 1941 [Adorno and Horkheimer 2004, p. 140]).

119 Letter from Adorno to Horkheimer, 2 July 1941 (Adorno and Horkheimer 2004, p. 160).

120 Cf. for example Adorno 2019i, p. 132.

of political economy was becoming increasingly central to Adorno's interests. He was coming to see the concept of state capitalism as useful for describing the relations in Soviet Russia and the Eastern Bloc states. This can be seen in the transcript of a July–August 1942 seminar on the theory of needs – the other participants included Horkheimer, Pollock, Günther Anders, Bertolt Brecht, Hanns Eisler and Herbert Marcuse – when Adorno offers a reading of Aldous Huxley's *Brave New World* not as a critique of socialism in general, but rather as a 'critique of the condition of the society which has perhaps reached a stage in which socialism has been cut off. ... Hence, the critique applies to state capitalism'.[121] Regarding this seminar, Brecht notes the following in an entry in his 'Work Journal' from 13 August 1942:

> at adorno's horkheimer, pollock, adorno, marcuse, eisler, stern, reichenbach and steuermann discuss HUXLEY'S 'brave new world'. huxley is disturbed at certain modern phenomena. he establishes a certain lowering of cultural needs. the more *iceboxes*, the less huxley. when physical needs have been satiated ... spiritual needs suffer. suffering has been created by culture; so is barbarism likely to ensue if they put a stop to suffering? dr pollock, the economist from the institute for social research (formerly frankfurt, now hollywood) is convinced that capitalism can rid itself of crises simply by means of public works. marx could not predict that governments would one day just build roads. – eisler and i, somewhat tired of the way things are going, lose patience and then 'get across everyone' for lack of anywhere else to go.[122]

Here, it becomes clear that Brecht fundamentally misunderstands the Institute for Social Research 'Tuis' – his made-up term of abuse for pseudo-revolutionary intellectuals – from a glance at 'On the Problem of Needs', a collection of theses which Horkheimer formulated himself over the course of the seminar. As Horkheimer writes:

> It is ridiculous to blame chewing gum for damaging our predisposition for metaphysics [as Huxley seems to do], but it could probably be shown that [chewing-gum industrialist William] Wrigley's profits and his palace

121   Adorno, Anders, Brecht, Eisler, Horkheimer, Marcuse, Marcuse, Nbg., Pollock, Reichenbach and Viertel 1985, p. 573; cf. Adorno 2001d, p. 97, n. 9.
122   Brecht 1993, p. 252; Stern refers to Günther Anders, Reichenbach to Hans Reichenbach and Steuermann to Eduard Steuermann.

in Chicago [that is, the baseball stadium Wrigley Field] are the result of the social function that reconciles human beings with their bad relations and dissuades them from criticizing them. It is not that chewing gum is damaging to metaphysics; on the contrary, it is rather that chewing gum is metaphysics – this is what has to be made clear. We criticize mass culture not because it provides us with too much or because it makes our lives too secure – we can leave that to Lutheran theology. Rather, we criticize mass culture because it contributes to a situation in which we receive too little and in which what we receive is too bad; because broad swathes of society live in terrible misery, both inwardly and outwardly; and because people end up resigning themselves to injustice. In short, we criticize mass culture because it keeps the world in a state in which we have to expect large-scale catastrophes, on the one hand, and a conspiracy on the part of infernally cunning elites to broker a hellish peace, on the other.[123]

In his lecture course *Fragen der Dialektik* (*Questions of Dialectics*) from the winter semester of 1963–4, Adorno would again speak of the 'negative utopias of state capitalism illustrated by people such as Orwell and Aldous Huxley'.[124] Such negative utopias, Adorno writes in his 1966 *Negative Dialectics*, are far removed from the vision advocated by Marx and Engels, who 'could not foresee what would become apparent later, in the revolution's failure even where it succeeded: that domination may outlast the planned economy, *which the two of them, of course, had not confused with state capitalism*'.[125] Nevertheless, in his undated 'Diskussionsbemerkung ad Aufsatz über Staatskapitalismus' ('Discussion Comment Regarding the Essay on State Capitalism'), Adorno does draw a point of distinction between his own position and that of Marx:

> A formulation is needed which more or less says the following: in contrast to the anarchists, we are not against planning. The planned economy is realised and transcended in socialism. Yet in contrast to Marx, we are against an overemphasis on implementing plans with the apparatus of power – against the identification of the organisational form of economic planning with forms of political domination.[126]

---

123   Horkheimer 2019, pp. 96–7. Adorno cites the entirety of this passage in his essay 'Aldous Huxley and Utopia' (Adorno 1988a, p. 108).

124   Adorno 2021b, p. 265.

125   Adorno 2007b, p. 322, emphasis added.

126   Adorno, 'Diskussionsbemerkung ad Aufsatz über Staatskapitalismus' (TWA, Ts 52519). (It is

Pollock's theory has an additional consequence: in light of the historical 'shift from economic to political dominance'[127] Pollock sees fascism as having revealed, he believes that the class-antagonisms necessary to the functioning of capitalism have ceased to exist. In his writings, these antagonisms are 'not even ... merely hinted at anymore'.[128] The economically rooted dominance of the capitalist class is regarded as though it were transferred to the immediate discretionary power of politically operating 'gang[s] and rackets'.[129] Thus, the chief social antagonism is viewed no longer as existing between the bourgeoisie and the proletariat, but rather between immanently political rulers and their immanently political subjects.

In this way the economic 'base' loses its role in supporting the social totality. National Socialism and bureaucratic socialism or, more generally, a new 'integral statism', can no longer be described only in terms of economic basic categories. Political analysis takes on greater importance to the extent that liberalism appears as an historical episode, after the downfall of which society reverts to direct methods of domination no longer mediated via the market. The fundamental economic factors leading to crisis are tending to become controllable by measures of state intervention, which can range from compensatory welfare legislation to overt terror.[130]

---

unclear which 'State Capitalism' essay is meant, and who the other participants in the discussion were: consisting of only one typewritten page, the note simply summarises a conversation). Regarding the emphasis on implementing plans, Adorno can above all invoke the *Communist Manifesto*, which makes the following claim: 'The proletariat will use its political supremacy to wrest, by degrees, all capital from the bourgeoisie, to centralise all instruments of production in the hands of the State, i.e., of the proletariat organised as the ruling class; and to increase the total of productive forces as rapidly as possible. / Of course, in the beginning, this cannot be effected except by means of despotic inroads on the rights of property, and on the conditions of bourgeois production; by means of measures, therefore, which appear economically insufficient and untenable, but which, in the course of the movement, outstrip themselves, necessitate further inroads upon the old social order, and are unavoidable as a means of entirely revolutionising the mode of production' (Marx and Engels 2010, p. 86).

127   Brandt 1981, p. 17.
128   Olle 1974, p. 100.
129   Adorno 2003x, p. 100. Writing to Horkheimer, Pollock refers to the 'gangsters ruling in the dictator countries' (letter from Pollock to Horkheimer, 7 September 1937 [Horkheimer 1996a, p. 231]).
130   Schmid Noerr 2002, p. 234.

Horkheimer's acceptance of the theory of state capitalism is the cornerstone of his – ultimately never elaborated – political theory of the 'racket'.[131] In a 1943 letter to Grossman, he describes his interest in developing such a theory as follows:

> my purpose here is a very specific one, namely to attempt a real and concrete elaboration of the theory of classes, something which, as I hardly need to tell you, we do not really have at the moment. What's really at issue here is the dialectic of legitimacy, with all which this implies for property relations. An explanation of why class has always been the epitome of rackets is not something different from proving that the universality of justice in this society is heading increasingly in the direction of unmitigated domination – the rationalisation of which has in any case been the very function of this ostensible 'justice' since time immemorial. It is this belief that extends the critique of the reality of free and fair exchange finally to the entire realm which bourgeois science calls Sociology, meaning to the entirety of the societal forms under which people nowadays have to live. To what extent it's actually going to be possible to do this I don't want to try to anticipate, but I am of the opinion that it is necessary for us to explore this seriously. An investigation of the type 'the influence of rackets' – aiming for example at the old institutions of European Democracy – is, compared to the above, of secondary importance, since the rackets should not be conceptualised as a power over and above the system but as the essential determinate form of class domination itself. It was in the sense of the above that I'd understood, from the outset, your original proposal for a specific investigation, and not at all in the sense of an empirical-sociological study of the type that would – for instance – examine how illegal interests supposedly 'influence' legal ones. That is how I had understood you originally, that you intended to investigate how the concept of original accumulation applied not merely to a supposedly early period, but – rather – to each and every phase of the bourgeois economy altogether. The Subject of this original accumulation would then be – thus conceived – the various groups within the classes, modelled on the rackets, tearing at each other over the extorted surplus value, in con-

---

131   Schmid Noerr 2002, p. 233. Horkheimer deploys the concept of the racket for the first time in his posthumously published text 'Die Rackets und der Geist' ('Rackets and Spirit'), written between 1939–40 (Horkheimer 1985a, pp. 287–91; cf. Lindemann 2000).

trast to the individual dominant groups, as this has manifested itself in so many wars in history.[132]

While Horkheimer stood by the concept of racket and the theory associated with it throughout his life, he distanced himself from 'the theoretically useless concept of state capitalism' in the postwar era, ultimately concluding that 'Grossmann's conception goes further' than Pollock's.[133] For his part, Adorno would recommend Neumann's *Behemoth* to his students in an introductory sociology lecture course during 1968, referring to it as 'the most apposite socioeconomic account of fascism that has yet been produced'.[134]

In a letter to Horkheimer from the spring of 1940, the same period in which Horkheimer's 'Authoritarian State' originated, Adorno brings up 'the question of the general cartel'. According to him, the concept is 'entirely undialectical' insofar as neither the 'survival of pseudo-competition between the monopolies', nor a ban on trusts, would be sufficient to ensure continued adherence to the '"unrational" form' of 'sham-competition between the concerns' existing at the time 'in monopolised America'. This assumption leads Adorno 'to a much more principal observation': 'It is apparently the case that, economically, only this quasi-artificially maintained competition still makes it possible to appropriate surplus-value at all, whereas, socially, the moment this competition were to disappear, the pretence for exploitation and domination would also disappear'.[135]

A problem with Adorno's consideration of monopoly capitalism is that he sees it as a concentration of firms leading to fewer concerns dominating the market, yet also perceives that firms within monopoly capitalism only differ from each other 'in the composition of their administrations and in their property titles, whereas their mode of production and products themselves are completely equivalent'.[136] Both observations are doubtless true; competition does in fact consist of these two aspects: competition between concerns regarding the cost of the production of products, and competition of concerns on the market, that is, competition between their products – between

---

132   Letter from Horkheimer to Grossmann, 20 January 1942 (Horkheimer 2014); on Horkheimer's theory of the racket cf. above all Horkheimer 1985a, pp. 287–91 and also Horkheimer 2016.

133   Horkheimer 1988b, p. 322; cf. Blank 2005, p. 116.

134   Adorno 2000a, p. 44.

135   Letter from Adorno to Horkheimer, ca. spring 1940 (Adorno and Horkheimer 2004, pp. 66–7).

136   Letter from Adorno to Horkheimer, ca. spring 1940 (Adorno and Horkheimer 2004, p. 67).

how well these sell and for how much. However, competition between concerns is not artificial, but rather emerged 'primordially' – that is, in accordance
with political-economic necessities as a functionally essential element within
capitalism. Additionally, competition is also not maintained by regulation for
the purpose of legitimating exploitation and domination. While class antagonism and domination continually reproduce each other, the state is tasked
with regulating monopolisation to the extent that no sole producer of a particular kind of product can determine its price independently from 'economic
competition'. Domination is not merely reproduced by ideology, but rather,
as always, is bound to control over the means of production. Competition
is

> the form of implementation of the immanent laws of capital. It is there-
> fore not a mere instrument, indifferent to content, but a real and [concep-
> tually] necessary [element] of the establishment of capital as total social
> capital. ... In the realm of competition capital can only become total social
> capital to the extent that the individual capitals *really* relate to each other.
> But this they can only do to the extent that they act capitalistically, that
> is, as surplus-value-producing capitals.[137]

Later, Adorno writes the following:

> While we [Adorno and Horkheimer] have written [in 'The Authoritarian
> State'] that the chance of integral statism consists not of a general capit-
> alism, but rather in the formation of two competing state blocs of vary-
> ing composition, this principle strikes me as already prefigured at least
> within the most monopolistically advanced country insofar as the con-
> tinued existence of its monopolies is bound to the continued existence
> of struggle between them. It seems to me that denoting the precise eco-
> nomic reason for the continued existence of the competitive principle is
> decisively important for the formulation of the question of state capital-
> ism – even if the form in which the competitive principle continues to
> exist is largely emancipated from the market, hovering at every moment
> between unmediated, naked power struggles and the liquidation of con-
> flicts between mere sham-opponents.[138]

---

137 Altvater 1978, p. 41.
138 Letter from Adorno to Horkheimer, ca. spring 1940 (Adorno and Horkheimer 2004, pp. 67–
     8). The passage in 'The Authoritarian State' referred to by Adorno reads as follows: 'The few
     big monopolies, which maintain their competition despite identical manufacturing meth-

Adorno would develop this thesis further, yet without the concept of state capitalism, which he would henceforth only deploy in reference to the state economy of the Soviet Union and its allies 'in the east':[139]

> To those who do not want [it to reach its potential], materialism has [now] done [them] the favor [of] debas[ing] itself. The [immaturity] that caused this is not mankind's own fault, as Kant thought. [Rather, i]n the mean-time, at least, it has come to be systematically reproduced by men in power. The objective spirit, which they maneuver because they need its restraint, adjusts to a consciousness that has been restrained over thou-sands of years. A materialism come to political power is no less sold on such practices than the world it once wanted to change; it keeps fettering the human consciousness instead of comprehending it and changing it on its part. On the threadbare pretext of a dictatorship (now half a cen-tury old) of the proletariat (long bureaucratically administered), govern-mental terror machines entrench themselves as permanent institutions, mocking the theory they carry on their lips. They chain their vassals to their most direct concerns and keep them stupid.
>
> Yet the depravation of theory could not have happened, had there been no apocryphal dregs in it.[140]

The meaning of 'apocrypha' here is clarified in a subsequent note by Adorno on the 'dictatorship of the proletariat':

> The assumption that any revolutionary mode of conduct must orient itself towards the contemporary state of the proletariat's consciousness is ambiguous at the very least. Abstracting from this state of consciousness,

---

ods, and products, furnish a model for future international constellations. Two friendly-hostile blocks of varying composition could rule the entire world; they could offer their followers, in addition to the *fasci*, better merchandise, at the expense of colonial and semi-colonial populations. As mutual threats they could always find new reasons to continue military armament. The increase in production, which would first be accelerated and later slowed by bourgeois property relations, in itself corresponds in no way to human needs. Today this increased production serves only the ruling class. Trees should not grow up in the sky. As long as there exists in the world a scarcity of necessary needs, in fact even a scarcity of luxury articles, the rulers will take advantage of the opportunity to isolate from one another individuals and groups, and national and social classes, and thus reproduce [their] own ruling position' (Horkheimer 1973, p. 14).

139 Adorno 2019i, p. 75.
140 Adorno 2007b, p. 204.

it is certainly true that no political activity can proceed according to the predefined outline of a correct social order, provided that one does not want to neglect practice and backslide into stale utopianism. Yet on the other hand, the state of consciousness of the proletariat must not be made absolute and simply elevated to the canon of revolutionary action. After all, this consciousness is produced by class-society and bears its marks; to proclaim the 'proletarian state' means nothing less than to immortalise these marks, to eliminate class-domination in order to preserve its bleak result. The idea of dictatorship and of eliminating the proletariat are inextricably bound up with each other; to abandon one of them means to fall short of the Marxist concept of dialectics.[141]

In his early years, Adorno regarded 'The State and Revolution' as among the 'most powerful statements of political theory'.[142] Like Lenin, he viewed the state as an instrument of the ruling class.[143] However, the unity of subjects and rulers in their identification with the state – already apparent in the 1920s, and especially so in light of National Socialism – rendered implausible and obsolete the view of the state as an instrument for violently subordinating individual interests to its own general interest. While Adorno could not have been familiar with Gramsci's concept of hegemony while the debate on state capitalism at the Institute for Social Research was unfolding, he began to take his own concept of ideology in a similar direction. Whereas there used to be rulers who 'simply' dominated, now there are subjects who are dominated in a variety of ways. Individuals and even rulers dominate themselves from within. For Adorno, states and their governments are functions of the impersonal domin-

---

141   Adorno 2003w, pp. 150–1. Marx's comments on the relationship between the state and politics are quite fragmentary (cf. Heinrich 2009). In Marxist debates on this topic, three major trends in the theory of the state can be distinguished: first, Marxism-Leninism, which is mainly oriented towards Engels' instrumental concept of the state (cf. Elbe 2009); second, the so-called state derivation debate, in which the essence of the state is derived from the capital-relation using formal analysis (cf. Elbe 2008, pp. 319–443); and finally, the theory of the state apparatuses from Gramsci via Louis Althusser (cf. Wolf 1994) to Nicos Poulantzas (cf. Demirović 2007). A helpful overview of the debate on the state as it took place in the Federal Republic of Germany can be found in Rudel 1981. Discussions of the question of state capitalism at the Institute for Social Research responded to political developments of the day and concerned concrete economic and political issues. A form-analytical derivation of the capitalist state as such was never debated.

142   Letter from Adorno to Benjamin, 18 March 1936 (Adorno and Benjamin 1999, p. 133).

143   Lenin justified his alternative position 'to the petty-bourgeois theory of the "reconciliation" of classes by "the state"' (Lenin 1992, p. 9) with the claim that the state is 'an instrument for the exploitation of the oppressed class' (Lenin 1992, p. 12).

ation of the capital-relation, and the late-capitalist state creates order through administration – just as is favoured today by the very liberal ideology which puts forth neoliberalism as the best possible reality. The state need only function as a coercive apparatus when it wants to stem practical resistance from its dependants. Yet when individuals acting on their own initiative push for 'a common accord between the various wills',[144] ideology functions less as hierarchised manipulation than as collective belief resulting in unanimous consent to the state's domination, as the state itself comes to be seen as the quasi-natural form for regulating coexistence and conflict.

144   Gramsci 2000, p. 127; cf. Haug 2004, column 8.

Hatched a National-Economic (!!) Theory

The first progress was
out of paradise.

ALBRECHT FABRI, Sätze

∙∙
∙

1　What Has Become of the Proletariat?

Already in a letter to Horkheimer from November 1936, Adorno reveals what strikes him as 'the most important task towards which the Institute should put the theory of dialectical materialism to use, namely, a theoretical analysis of the contemporary situation of class struggle'.[1] Prompted by his collaboration with Horkheimer on their work *Dialectic of Enlightenment*, Adorno would take up this task himself in 1942, penning a set of theses later published under the title 'Reflections on Class Theory'.

Earlier that same year, Horkheimer and Adorno composed a four-page 'Memorandum über Teile des Los Angeles Arbeitsprogramms, die von den Philosophen nicht durchgeführt werden können' ('Memorandum on Parts of the Los Angeles Programme of Work Which Cannot Be Carried Out by the Philosophers')[2] – a request addressed to the economists of the Institute for Social Research for assistance with their work-in-progress, *Dialectic of Enlightenment*. This brief text provides insight into precisely those economic questions which its authors saw as being 'related to the theory of class'[3] and apparently felt unable to answer themselves.

Only shortly beforehand, Horkheimer suggested to Felix Weil that he and Pollock take over the economic portion of *Dialectic of Enlightenment*:

1　Letter from Adorno to Horkheimer, 28 November 1936 (Adorno and Horkheimer 2003b, p. 238).
2　Adorno and Horkheimer, 'Memorandum über Teile des Los Angeles Arbeitsprogramms, die von den Philosophen nicht durchgeführt werden können' (henceforth cited as 'Memorandum') (MHA VI.33.1–33.4); cf. also Wiggershaus 1995, pp. 314–15.
3　Adorno and Horkheimer, 'Memorandum' (MHA VI.33.1).

In this I was thinking that Fritz and you should, in the future, work here for at least four or five months out of the year and the rest of the year in New York, with the intention that this longer portion of the year will be used to work on our theoretical agenda. Here you would participate in the determination and structuring of the major parts; there you'd work on the economic sections in detail so that, after a few years, our interpretation of the current phase will be completed. It is, of course, nonsense to think that I could lend the project the necessary precision and concreteness even in cooperation with Teddie. It has to be stuffed to the bursting point with historical and economic material; otherwise it will give the impression of being [speculation].[4]

Adorno and Horkheimer's memorandum begins with a series of questions:

What has become of the proletariat in the monopolistic-fascistic phase? Can it still be defined as it is in *Capital*? What effect has monopolisation had on distinctions within the proletariat? To what extent do changes in these distinctions mean changes in class-consciousness and in the structure and role of the party?[5]

The question of what has happened to the proletariat – a question Adorno would later describe in *Minima Moralia* as a 'grimly comic riddle'[6] for sociologists – is taken up by Horkheimer at least as early as his 1937 'Traditional and Critical Theory'. According to Burkhardt Lindner, in addition to presenting 'exchange as an epistemological category', this essay by the future co-author of *Dialectic of Enlightenment* cites 'the class-relation as the "basic economic structure" of all social change, yet no longer in view of the organised proletariat'.[7] In a passage clearly motivated by 'the revolution's failure even where it succeeded',[8] Horkheimer writes the following:

The idea of a transformed society ... does not have the advantage of widespread acceptance, as long as the idea has not yet had its real possibility tested. To strive for a state of affairs in which there will be no exploitation or oppression, in which an all-embracing subject, namely self-aware

---

4   Letter from Horkheimer to Felix Weil, 10 March 1942 (Horkheimer 2007, p. 204).
5   Adorno and Horkheimer, 'Memorandum' (MHA VI.33.2).
6   Adorno 2005b, p. 194.
7   Lindner 1983, p. 90, n. 4; quoted from Horkheimer 2002, p. 234; cf. Gmünder 1985, p. 19.
8   Adorno 2007b, p. 322.

mankind, exists, and in which it is possible to speak of a unified theoretical creation and a thinking that transcends individuals – to strive for all this is not yet to bring it to pass. The transmission of the critical theory in its strictest possible form is, of course, a condition of its historical success. But the transmission will not take place via solidly established practice and fixed ways of acting but via concern for social transformation. Such a concern will necessarily be aroused ever anew by prevailing injustice, but it must be shaped and guided by the theory itself and in turn react upon the theory.

The circle of transmitters of this tradition is neither limited nor renewed by organic or sociological laws. It is constituted and maintained not by biological or testamentary inheritance, but by a knowledge which brings its own obligations with it. And even this knowledge guarantees only a contemporary, not a future community of transmitters. The theory may be stamped with the approval of every logical criterion, but to the end of the age it will lack the seal of approval which victory brings. Until then, too, the struggle will continue to grasp it aright and to apply it. A version of it which has the propaganda apparatus and a majority on its side is not therefore the better one. In the general historical upheaval the truth may reside with numerically small groups of men. History teaches us that such groups, hardly noticed even by those opposed to the status quo, outlawed but imperturbable, may at the decisive moment become the leaders because of their deeper insight.[9]

Adorno develops a similar idea in a 1941 letter to Edward M. David, the English translator of his essay on Oswald Spengler, while clarifying the meaning of a passage of that text:

---

9   Horkheimer 2002, p. 241. In a letter to Pollock from the same year, Horkheimer writes the following: 'The few people in whom the truth has taken refuge appear as ridiculous dogmatists who speak a bombastic language with nothing to back them up. The consolation that things were the same for certain figures in the Old Testament is all the less helpful given that the success of the prophets was not exactly overwhelming in the long run. The most unpleasant discovery to which materialism leads is that reason only exists insofar as it is backed up by a natural subject. The subject possesses reason according to how it wants to make use of reason. It can also lose reason through no fault of its own. The retroactive effect of reason on the subject is never so intense and sustained that the subject would lose its natural character. In other words, that famous identity from which idealism lives never comes into being. Of course, as far as is possible, we must attempt to produce this identity. But ultimately, there will be waters over which no spirit hovers' (Letter from Horkheimer to Pollock, 20 September 1937 [Horkheimer 1996a, p. 235]).

The non-identical element must not be nature alone, it also can be man. The German reads: *Freiheit entfaltet sich bloß am Widerstand des Seienden: wird sie absolut gesetzt und das Seelentum zum herrschenden Weltprinzip erhoben, so verfällt es selber dem bloßen Dasein.* [Freedom unfolds merely in resistance to what is: if freedom is made absolute and the life of the soul elevated to a reigning universal principle, then freedom itself falls victim to mere existence.] I have inserted one sentence later: 'freedom postulates the existence of something non-identical'. I hope this makes the meaning clearer.[10]

Just as the status of the proletariat changed under monopoly capitalism, so too did that of the capitalist class. In a subsequent section of their memorandum, Adorno and Horkheimer ask the following:

> What has become of the capitalist class? To what extent today is the capitalist class nationally and internationally unified? Relationship of trade, finance, heavy industry and manufacturing industry. Which changes has capitalist class-consciousness undergone, and how do capitalists relate to dominant ideologies such as individualism and collectivism?[11]

Adorno and Horkheimer also inquire about the 'bureaucracy' as a potential third class:

> We should arrive at a concrete position on the contemporary controversy. This probably requires tracing bureaucratisation back to its various roots (civil service, the corporation, etc.). Particular attention is to be paid to the problem of separation – or fusion – of ownership titles and discretionary power. Emphasis will continue to be placed on the influence of technical changes, on the transition from immediate to mediated domin-

---

10   Letter from Adorno to David, 3 July 1941 (MHA VI.1B.95); cf. Wiggershaus 1995, p. 312; cf. Claussen 2008, p. 141. This correspondence reveals that Adorno did not intend 'must not be' in the sense of 'is not allowed to be' but in the sense of 'does not have to be'. In the English version of Adorno's essay on Spengler, published shortly thereafter, the passage reads: 'What we may call the freedom of man consists only in the human attempts to break the rule imposed by nature. If that is ignored and the historical world is made a mere product of human essence, freedom will be lost in the resulting all-humanity (*Allmenschlichkeit*) of history. Freedom postulates the existence of something non-identical' (Adorno 1941, p. 322).

11   Adorno and Horkheimer, 'Memorandum', MHA VI.33.2.

ation. The factory turns from a business into an institution complete with its own 'form of life', consciously created 'community', fraternal mythology and hierarchy. Supervisory role of the manager in various cultural areas.[12]

A further question refers to the contemporary state of Marxist discussion:

What is the state of the academic and extra-academic discussion of Marxist theory? It would be extremely important to first gain an overview which could then be critically assessed. What is the status of important trade union leaders in Marxist and non-Marxist theory? Have there been any advances in Marxist economics which deserve to be taken seriously? Which other important theorems should be considered today?

The section following this one provides a glimpse into Adorno's search for material for his essay 'The Schema of Mass Culture' and for the 'Culture Industry' chapter of *Dialectic of Enlightenment*:

One question relatively … separate from the above questions refers to the immediate control of mass culture by monopoly. It would be extremely important for the work to have a clear picture of the economic and personal mechanisms of control through which each of the important spheres and the cultivation of the next generation is regulated. This is quite easy to determine for film, but essential data should also be compiled for other areas (radio, newspapers, magazines, universities and scholarly foundations). This also includes the interconnections between the individual branches of the culture industries.[13]

---

12   Ibid. The 'Memorandum' (and not, as assumed by the editors of Horkheimer's collected works, the essay 'On the Sociology of Class Relations' [see Horkheimer 1996a, p. 285, n. 1]) appears to be the text which, in a letter to Pollock from 21 April 1942, Horkheimer says he will send to the latter in a few weeks. In this letter, Horkheimer writes the following regarding the problems involved with *Dialectic of Enlightenment*: 'I think that these problems will be close enough to your own theoretical concerns. As far as I can see now they are mostly related to the problem of classes. Which changes have taken place in the structure of the well-to-do-classes as well as among the workers and unemployed in the last decades? Is it still possible to speak of the "proletariat" in the sense it played a role in the old theories? What does "bureaucracy" in the modern sense really mean, how did it come about, and what is its real function?' (letter from Horkheimer to Pollock, 21 April 1942 [Horkheimer 1996a, pp. 283–4]).

13   Adorno and Horkheimer, 'Memorandum' (MHA VI.33.3).

No deeper knowledge of the standard work practices at the Institute for Social Research is needed to recognise that the memorandum – assuming it was distributed among the Institute's employees as planned – could not have had its intended effect. No responses have been found, at any rate. Rolf Wiggershaus suspects that this was due not least to the manner in which it was written. While the memorandum 'made it clear that Horkheimer was still convinced of the necessity of interdisciplinary collaboration ..., it remained unclear in what sense "interdisciplinary collaboration" was intended'.[14] For this reason, Adorno would subsequently tackle some of the problems which were 'particularly close to our [his and Horkheimer's] hearts'[15] on his own.[16]

Regarding his 'Reflections on Class Theory', which would first appear in his posthumously published collected works in May 1971,[17] Adorno writes to his parents in September 1942 that he has '[hatched] a national-economic (!!) theory in order to bring Marx's doctrine of [pauperisation] up to date'.[18] Two weeks later, he gives Horkheimer a similar update:

> Otherwise, I have worked on the theoretical aspect[19] and written new 'reflections on class theory' – which are partially formulations of common things with a view towards the theory of the racket, and partially formulations of entirely new ones. This manuscript is constructed so that it will be able to be assimilated into the work as is, taken up as needed in entirely different passages of the final product. A paragraph about pauperisation and one about formal sociology are also included.[20]

---

14   Wiggershaus 1995, p. 315.
15   Adorno and Horkheimer, 'Memorandum' (MHA VI.33.1).
16   Cf. Wiggershaus 1995, p. 318.
17   See Adorno 2003x for English translation.
18   Adorno 2006b, p. 67.
19   Adorno is referring to 'The Schema of Mass Culture', which was originally supposed to be part of *Dialectic of Enlightenment*.
20   Letter from Adorno to Horkheimer, 15 September 1942 (Adorno and Horkheimer 2004, p. 288). According to Gödde and Lonitz, at the time, Horkheimer and Adorno were planning 'a "sociology of the racket" which they wanted to elaborate with Grossmann, Löwenthal, Pollock and Weil, and they apparently also considered devoting a part of this work to the transformation of capitalism and the resulting critique of the concept of class-society. In *Dialectic of Enlightenment*, such motifs are located in the chapter "The Concept of Enlightenment" and in the two excursuses. The following year, Horkheimer wrote his essay "On the Sociology of Class Relations"' (editorial note by Gödde and Lonitz [Adorno and Horkheimer 2004, p. 290]; for Horkheimer's essay see Horkheimer 2016). In a letter from later that same month, Horkheimer suggests to Adorno that after finishing *Dialectic*

2   Now They Are United

The 'Reflections on Class Theory' Adorno 'hatched' represent a transition – and by no means only in a temporal sense – from the debate on state capitalism at the Institute and in the *Zeitschrift für Sozialforschung* towards *Dialectic of Enlightenment*.[21] Indeed, Horkheimer and Adorno take up several theses of the 'Reflections' in the final product *Dialectic of Enlightenment* – albeit in a thoroughly modified and usually less economy-critical form (and while eschewing any and all explicit reference to Marx). The former text 'in many respects provides the key' to the latter.[22]

The treatment of pauperisation theory Adorno mentions in the letters to his parents and Horkheimer constitutes only *one* section of the 'Reflections' in which Adorno refers directly the *Communist Manifesto* and its militant conclusion: 'Let the ruling classes tremble at a communistic revolution. The proletarians have nothing to lose but their chains. They have a world to win'.[23] From Adorno's perspective just under a century after those words were written, the proletariat seems to hardly resemble how it had been depicted in them:

> The proletariat does have more to lose than its chains. ... Shorter working hours; better food, housing, and clothing; protection for family members and for the worker in his old age; an average increase in life expectancy – all these things have come to the workers with the development of the technical forces of production. There can be no question of their being driven by hunger to join forces and make a revolution.[24]

---

of Enlightenment, they 'should do some work in connection with the economic projects (sociology of rackets). Very soon in the new year we should start either with what you wrote on mass culture or with some other subject with which we can proceed a little faster than with our first paragraphs' (Letter from Horkheimer to Adorno, 17 September 1942 [Adorno and Horkheimer 2004, pp. 294–5]).

21   'It is in any case unthinkable that "Reflections on Class Theory" would have come about if not for Horkheimer's studies on "The Jews and Europe", "The Authoritarian State" and "The End of Reason"' (Breuer 1985, p. 31).

22   Münz-Koenen 1997, p. 97. The 'Reflections' provide the key for understanding not only the refusal of utopia in *Dialectic of Enlightenment*, but also the latter's economy-critical implications.

23   Marx and Engels 2010, p. 98.

24   Adorno 2003x, p. 103.

Adorno believes that the integration of the proletariat and the absence of revolution had cast 'a dubious light'[25] on the Marxian theory of history, which is summarised in the third volume of *Capital* as follows:

> each particular historical form of this process further develops the material foundations and social forms. Once a certain level of maturity is attained, the particular historical form is shed and makes way for a higher form. The sign that the moment of such a crisis has arrived is that the contradiction and antithesis between, on the one hand, the relations of distribution, hence also the specific historical form of relations of production corresponding to them, and, on the other hand, the productive forces, productivity, and the development of its agents, gains in breadth and depth.[26]

In retrospect, Adorno is left to conclude that the development of the forces of production have 'had the opposite effect of the Marxian prognosis and led to an increase in worker living standards':[27]

> Marx's insight that the system produces the proletariat has been fulfilled on a scale that was absolutely unforeseeable. By virtue of their needs and the omnipresent requirements of the system, men have truly become its products: under the monopoly system the process of dehumanization is perfected on the backs of the civilized as an all-encompassing reification, not as naked coercion; indeed, this dehumanization is what that civilization is. The totalizing character of society proves itself in the fact that it does not just take utter possession of its members but creates them in its own image.[28]

However, Adorno believes that the dehumanising effects of capitalist civilisation apply not only to the proletariat, but to all members of society in equal measure – to capitalists and intellectuals, to the dominant and the dominated. 'Pauperization does exist to the degree that the bourgeois class really is an anonymous and unconscious class, and that both it and the proletariat are dominated by the system'.[29] This 'blind system *is* the domination itself';[30] in

---

25   Kager 1988, p. 93.
26   Marx 1991, pp. 1023–4.
27   Kager 1988, p. 251, n. 152.
28   Adorno 2003x, p. 109
29   Adorno 2003x, p. 104.
30   Adorno 2003x, p. 106, emphasis added.

its incessant reproduction, it is one in the same with domination. As Adorno remarks in a note from 1943, '[i]f I were to sum up in one sentence the secret of both contemporary monopolistic and totalitarian society, I would say: that today the apparatus of life's reproduction directly coincides with the apparatus of its domination'.[31]

The integration of the proletariat is a negative integration. Rather than being achieved by workers overcoming the class-antagonism with the help of a revolutionary class-consciousness forged through collective misery, it came about when those who had more to lose than their chains became equally as organised through the class-relation as the class struggle itself. Meanwhile, class struggle has been confined to limits set by capital in the interest of its own continued existence.

> The immeasurable pressure of domination has so fragmented the masses that it has even dissipated the negative unity of being oppressed that forged them into a class in the nineteenth century. In exchange, they find they have been directly absorbed into the unity of the system that is oppressing them. Class rule is set to survive the anonymous, objective form of class.[32]

Unity among proletarians was thus established as a negation of a negation – yet one with no positive upshot. After all, society under capital reproduces itself no differently than it did so before: social reproduction still occurs under coercion from authority. 'Hierarchy had always been a coercive organisation designed for the appropriation of the labor of others. Natural law' – here, 'natural' ironically refers to the appearance of naturalness which is 'both an actuality *and* at the same time a socially necessary illusion'[33] – 'is historical injustice that has become obsolete; the articulated organism is a system of divisiveness'.[34] In this respect, as long society itself has existed, so too have there been classes: not in the Marxian sense of groups defined by their control or lack thereof over the means of production, but in the sense of a sorting of society into the dominant and the dominated. However, only under capitalism does the evidence of domination dissolve, yielding the apparent 'classless society of car drivers, cinema goers, and [*Volksgenossen*]':[35]

---

31   Adorno 2003k, p. 11.
32   Adorno 2003x, p. 97.
33   Adorno 2006a.
34   Adorno 2003x, p. 93.
35   Adorno 2003x, p. 97. Translator's note: the term '*Volksgenosse*' – compatriot, or more liter-

Proletarians of all countries, unite. Now they are united. But that does not mean anything other than that the significance of the Marxian proposition has been superceded.[36]

In his theses, Adorno reflects on how economic pauperisation has largely failed to materialise, whereas a pauperisation of the individual has triumphed completely – a thesis which would be developed in *Minima Moralia*. Additionally, he also revisits a subject he addressed in 'On the Social Situation of Music', namely the Lukácsian false absolutisation of proletarian class-consciousness as a phenomenon 'to be understood positively here and now'.[37] Although Adorno still espouses the concept of class in 'Reflections' given that 'its basis, the division of society into exploiters and exploited, not only continues unabated but is increasing in coercion and solidity', he abandons the assumption of a proletarian class-*consciousness*, arguing that 'the oppressed who today, as predicted by the [Marxian] theory, constitute the overwhelming majority of mankind are unable to experience themselves as a class'.[38] For this reason, Adorno claims, '[m]embership in the same class by no means translates into equality of interests and action',[39] and 'the idea that the oppressed, the workers of the world, might unite as a class and put an end to the horror seems doomed in the light of the present distribution of power and impotence'.[40]

According to Adorno, under monopoly capitalism, 'the untrue aspect of the concept of class'[41] – that is, the impossibility of an overarching proletarian class-consciousness – has become visible. Yet at the same time, the objective persistence of classes has been made 'virtually invisible';[42] '[b]ourgeois sociology of all nations' no longer recognises their existence. Apparently against Karl Mannheim, Adorno continues as follows:

> The skepticism toward the so-called metaphysics of class becomes the norm in the realm of formal sociology: classes are said not to exist because of the unshakable facts. The facts are unshakable because they are made

---

ally, national or racial comrade – came to be associated with National Socialism. Rodney Livingstone translates the term here simply as 'comrade', which entirely erases the allusion to National Socialism.

36   Adorno, 'Diskussionsbemerkung ad Aufsatz über Staatskapitalismus' (TWA, Ts 52519).
37   Adorno 2009d, p. 410.
38   Adorno 2003x, p. 97.
39   Ibid.
40   Adorno 2003x, p. 96.
41   Adorno 2003x, p. 99.
42   Adorno 2003b, p. 183.

to take the place of class, and wherever the sociological gaze seeks the stones of class, it discovers only the bread of the elites, and learns daily that you simply cannot dispense with ideology. And since sociology always acts in this way, the cleverest thing it can do is to leave the forms of socialization unscathed and, perhaps with bleeding heart, adopt the cause of the unavoidable elite as one's own ideology.[43]

3   Handout

A meta-economic precondition of the existence of classes is the validity of the 'principle of sovereign ownership' as well as the 'law of the exchange of equivalents'. Although classes exist objectively, they are 'also ideology in equal measure'[44] as far as their function is concerned, given that the social condition of possibility on which they are based – the extremely longstanding validity of the ownership and equivalence principles[45] – is effaced by their objective existence. Subordinated to capital, the law of the exchange of equivalents derives its legitimacy from the liberal principle of justice. However, according to Adorno, if the Marxian critical theory 'shows that there is something questionable about the idea of fair exchange, bourgeois freedom, and humanity, this sheds light on the dual nature of the class. This duality consists in the fact that its formal equality has the function both of oppressing the class with which it is contrasted and of using the strongest to control members of its own'.[46] Adorno's claim here echoes Marx and Engels's portrayal of class in *The German Ideology* as 'the negative unity of all of its individuals', a portrayal which suggests that 'class struggle should not be fetishised, but rather that classes should be abolished':[47] 'separate individuals form a class only insofar as they have to carry on a com-

43   Adorno 2003x, p. 101.

44   Adorno 2003x, p. 98.

45   This does not mean that pre-capitalist *exchanges* were equivalent, but rather that the *principle* of equivalence, as a stipulated means of quantifying equality for different qualities, is at least as old as the oldest records from ancient history. 'Counting, measurement and calculation are a universal language used by man in his interaction with nature and his own. With them, he links part and whole. He had already discovered "quantising" during that time from which we have access to archaeological traces but no textual sources. The facts and findings from the study of measurement's prehistory help us to understand that the first texts on measurement, from the epoch of early high cultures, are themselves based on several millennia of oral and material-practical tradition' (Haustein 2004, p. 1).

46   Adorno 2003x, p. 98.

47   Blumentritt 1992, p. 302, n. 3.

mon battle against another class; in other respects they are on hostile terms with each other as competitors'.[48] In reality, the alleged novelty introduced by capitalism with its specific form of class domination is merely the continuation of domination's triumphant history.

Adorno believes that

> [t]heory's prognosis of a few owners and an overwhelming mass of the expropriated has come true, but instead of becoming glaringly obvious, this has been conjured out of existence by the mass society in which class society has culminated. The ruling class disappears behind the concentration of capital. This latter has reached a magnitude and acquired a weight of its own that enables capital to present itself as an institution, as the expression of society as a whole. By virtue of its omnipotence, the particular is able to usurp the totality: this overall social aspect of capital is the endpoint of the old fetish character of the commodity according to which relations between men are reflected back to them as relations between things. Today, the entire order of existence has turned into such things.

However, rather than conclude from this that class-domination, blind and indifferent to the individual, always asserts itself quasi-naturally through the capital-relation, Adorno sees class-formation – that is, the formation of class-consciousness – as 'closed off by the conscious will and practical measures of the rulers in the name of the great totality [which they themselves are]'.[49] Adorno recognises one such practical measure, necessary for preventing the material pauperisation of the proletariat, in an 'extraeconomic improvement of the standard of living'[50] through an irregular 'handout' (*Trinkgeld*) from the rulers, paid not as part of one's salary, but rather 'out of income or monopoly profits'. 'The dynamics of poverty are brought to a halt by the process of accumulation. The improvement or stabilization of the economic situation of the lower classes is extraeconomic'. This is to say that the ruling class had made the economic stabilisation of the working class its own private concern, albeit certainly not out of kindness: 'Goodwill and psychology have nothing to do with it'. Rather, the ruling class ultimately has to provide for workers, the sole guarantors of its own existence – it has to '"secure for the slaves their existence within slavery" in order to consolidate its own'.[51] In this phase of capitalism, Adorno

---

48 Marx and Engels 1976, p. 77; cf. Kager 1988, p. 97.
49 Adorno 2003x, pp. 99–100.
50 Adorno 2003x, p. 107.
51 Adorno 2003x, pp. 104–5. This dynamic was described in the *Communist Manifesto*: 'And

sees the organisation of workers, the double-negative unity of proletarians of all countries, not merely as the consequence of a fated triumph of the capital-relation or its blind, automatic adaptation to contemporary challenges to its continued existence, but rather as the deliberate maintenance of domination by the dominant. Given that not even members of the ruling class are secure in their status as such, they too must maintain the class-antagonism which makes others workers and themselves non-workers.

According to Adorno, this 'process of liquidating the economy'[52] does not lead to state capitalism. Instead, he sees it as helping monopoly capitalism become completely established for the first time, resulting in both the greatest possible standardisation of the economic sphere – of the process of production and of consumption – as well as of the formerly extra-economic sphere, that is, of culture in the broadest sense. In this way, the liquidation of the economy leads to everything, including life itself, becoming the economy.

4   As in Myth

'According to the theory' – *Marxian* theory, that is – 'history is the history of class struggles. But the concept of class is bound up with the emergence of the proletariat'[53] because the proletariat is the first class able to experience itself as a class. History up to the present is the history of the dominant and the dominated. 'The archaic silence of pyramids and ruins becomes conscious of itself in materialist thought: it is the echo of factory noise in the landscape of the immutable'.[54] The hardship of the proletariat as an exploited class is seen

---

here it becomes evident that the bourgeoisie is unfit any longer to be the ruling class in society, and to impose its conditions of existence upon society as an overriding law. It is unfit to rule because it is incompetent to assure an existence to its slave within his slavery, because it cannot help letting him sink into such a state that it has to feed him, instead of being fed by him. Society can no longer live under this bourgeoisie, in other words, its existence is no longer compatible with society' (Marx and Engels 2010, pp. 78–9). Here, Adorno largely follows Horkheimer's considerations in 'The Authoritarian State': 'The institutionalization of the top ranks of capital and labor have the same basis: the change in the means of production. Monopolized industry, which makes the mass of stockholders into victims and parasites, pushes the masses of workers into supporting passivity. They have more to expect from the protection and assistance of the organizations than from their work' (Horkheimer 1973, p. 5).

52   Adorno 2003x, p. 104.
53   Adorno 2003x, p. 93. For the most prominent description of history as one of class struggles, see Marx and Engels 2010, p. 67.
54   Adorno 2003x, p. 93.

by Adorno as a modern counterpart to the grinding down of humans which enabled the construction of monumental gravesites for the rulers of ancient Egypt.

This suggests that while it is impossible to trace a universal history from past to present, it is certainly possible to trace the emergence of the class-antagonism as the highest stage which perpetual domination has reached thus far. 'No universal history leads from savagery to humanitarianism, but there is one leading from the slingshot to the megaton bomb'.[55] From this insight, Adorno draws consequences for the view of all previous history as a 'prehistory', which as a history of domination is both ancient and still current. 'By exposing the historical necessity that had brought capitalism into being, [the critique of] political economy became the critique of history as a whole, whose immutable nature was the source of the privileged status of capitalism as well as its forbears. To recognize the catastrophic violence in the latest form of injustice, that is to say, the latent injustice contained in fair exchange, means simply to identify it with the prehistory that it destroyed'.[56] Much later on, in *Aesthetic Theory*, Adorno would take up this idea again: 'Social antagonisms are as old as the hills; only desultorily did they become class struggles: where market economies related to bourgeois society began to take shape. For this reason the interpretation of everything historical as class struggle has a slightly anachronistic air, just as the model of Marx's constructions and extrapolations was that of liberal entrepreneurial capitalism'.[57] The description of history as the history of class struggles ontologises history as what 'was always the same',[58] statically defining it as what has been until now – as what Marx himself terms prehistory '[w]ith a kind of hope born of despair'. However, this always still current prehistory is 'no less than the entire stretch of [known] history ..., the realm of bondage'.[59] Its 'forms and structures' are

> eternally transitory because, as blind products of nature, they are subject to natural decay. Marx's dialectic includes, therefore, a doctrine of invariance, [a] negative ontology of a society which advances through internal conflict. [Society's dynamism, the energetic dissonance, the antagonism, is its stasis – is what has not changed at all until today and what

---

55   Adorno 2007b, p. 320; cf. Tiedemann 1998, pp. 23–4 and Bolte 2003, p. 23, n. 22.
56   Adorno 2003x, pp. 93–4.
57   Adorno 2002a, p. 255.
58   Adorno 2003x, p. 94.
59   Adorno 1961, p. 45.

has caused every relation of production to spoil.] The urge to expand, to absorb more and more [new sectors], and to leave out less and less, had so far remained static or invariant. In this way, [fate continues to reproduce itself. To avoid being destroyed, each and every form of society unconsciously works towards its destruction as well as the destruction of the whole that keeps itself alive within it.] This was [its] eternity. [Progress, which Marx claims brought prehistory to an end, would be the end of this dynamic, which becomes entangled with stasis according to its own contradictory substance. A right society would transcend both.] It [would] not seek to preserve what [merely exists], to tie men down for the sake of order [which would no longer need such ties as soon as it became united with the interests of humanity]. Nor [would] it seek to perpetuate blind [movement], which is the opposite of Kant's aim of history – eternal peace.

The interpretation of previous history as 'prehistory' occurs throughout Marx's work, and probably most explicitly in the preface to *A Contribution to the Critique of Political Economy*:

> The bourgeois relations of production are the last antagonistic form of the social process of production – antagonistic not in the sense of individual antagonism but of an antagonism that emanates from the individuals' social conditions of existence – but the productive forces developing within bourgeois society create also the material conditions for a solution of this antagonism. The prehistory of human society accordingly closes with this social formation.[60]

By ascribing to it the status of a natural law – some are dominated by others, that is just the way of the world – the particular injustice of the ruling class becomes flattened. In this way, real history becomes the tireless proclaimer 'of the unspeakable commandment to submit'.[61] – 'The widely lamented immaturity of the masses simply reflects the fact that they are now no more the autonomous masters of their lives than they ever were. As in myth, their lives befall them, like fate'.[62]

---

60   Marx 1987a, pp. 263–4; regarding this passage, cf. letter from Adorno to Horkheimer, 2 July 1949 (Adorno and Horkheimer 2005, pp. 282–3).
61   Adorno 2007b, p. 336.
62   Adorno 2003q, p. 116.

And from today's perspective, only once history indeed cannot be deciphered as anything other than a constantly regenerating prehistory whose expression is 'revealed in conditions and things' – however these might become manifest – 'as the trace of former suffering', does the conceptualisation of history as the history of class struggles have an element of truth.[63] On this point, Adorno is able to follow Marx's understanding of history as expressed in an oft-cited comment from the 'Methods' chapter of the *Grundrisse*: 'Human anatomy contains a key to the anatomy of the ape. The intimations of higher development among the subordinate animal species, however, can be understood only after the higher development is already known'.[64] In a 1967 seminar, Adorno would claim that Marx 'conceives of the whole of history from its beginning and projected the antagonistic structure of bourgeois society onto pre-capitalist history' in order 'to show that domination could only be deduced from the vital process of society'.[65] If this is so, it can also be claimed that Adorno himself conceives of history as the history of suffering, believing that the key to power relations of the past must be sought in the current way in which humans dominate each other and nature. 'From the most recent form of injustice, a steady light reflects back on history as a whole'.[66] This whole, the course of history thus far, is radiant with injustice as the 'persistent suffering of humanity',[67] just as 'the wholly enlightened earth is radiant with triumphant calamity'.[68] As Horkheimer remarks incisively in a letter to Adorno from May 1949, '[h]umans must compel humans to compel nature, otherwise nature compels humans. This is the concept of society'.[69] And this means: of *every* society which has existed. 'The irreconcilable power of the negative that sets history in motion is the power of what exploiters do to the victims. As a shackle binding one generation to the next, it functions as an obstacle to both freedom and history'.[70] History has, just like progress, 'so far failed to take place'.[71] What appears as

---

63   Adorno 2003x, p. 94.
64   Marx 1993, p. 105. Cf.: 'Reflection on the forms of human life, hence also scientific analysis of those forms, takes a course directly opposite to their real development. Reflection begins *post festum*, and therefore with the results of the process of development ready to hand' (Marx 1982a, p. 168). 'In contrast, genetic reconstruction understood as a model representation of history would amount to declaring the anatomy of the ape as the key to the anatomy of the human' (Heinrich 2003, p. 402, n. 6).
65   Adorno 2021a, vol. 4, p. 332.
66   Adorno 2003x, p. 94.
67   Kager 1988, p. 102.
68   Adorno and Horkheimer 2002, p. 1.
69   Letter from Horkheimer to Adorno, 8 May 1949 (Adorno and Horkheimer 2005, p. 248).
70   Adorno 2003x, p. 95.
71   Adorno 1961, p. 41.

progress is deciphered by Adorno as the eternal return of 'the old terror'[72] in
the figure of the novel and the cutting-edge – of the myth under which the
entirety of the Enlightenment was still spellbound, and which consists of 'that
blind continuum of time that continually retracts itself'.[73] The dynamism of
Marxism, for which '[m]embers of the bourgeoisie and their supporters' have
at times 'been loud in their praise',[74] is a dynamism within constant sameness;
it accomplishes nothing new by itself: 'The new does not add itself to the old
but remains the old in distress' as long as 'the ever-new is also the old lying
close at hand'.[75] The whole course of history thus far, Adorno would later claim
in his lecture course *History and Freedom*, 'is constructed like a gigantic process involving the exchange of cause and effect', and 'in this sense history never
escapes from the bonds of *myth*'.[76] Instead, history is a 'vast analytic proposition'[77] which always only validates that which 'exists in this manner and not in
any other'.[78]

This manner of looking back at what has been, one which recognises history's negative tendency towards degradation, recalls – and certainly not by
accident – Benjamin's 'historical-philosophical theses',[79] and especially his

---

72   Adorno 2003x, p. 95. Cf. the following passage from the text 'Imperial Panorama' in Ben-
      jamin's *One-Way Street*: 'A curious paradox: people have only the narrowest private interest
      in mind when they act, yet they are at the same time more than ever determined in their
      behavior by the instincts of the mass. And mass instincts have become confused and
      estranged from life more than ever. Whereas the obscure impulse of the animal (as innu-
      merable anecdotes relate) detects, as danger approaches, a way of escape that still seems
      invisible, this society, each of whose members cares only for his own abject well-being,
      falls victim – with animal insensibility but without the insensate intuition of animals –
      as a blind mass, to even the most obvious danger, and the diversity of individual goals is
      immaterial in face of the identity of the determining forces. Again and again it has been
      shown that society's attachment to its familiar and long-since-forfeited life is so rigid as
      to nullify the genuinely human application of intellect, forethought, even in dire peril. So
      that in this society the picture of imbecility is complete: uncertainty, indeed perversion,
      of vital instincts; and impotence, indeed decay, of the intellect. This is the condition of the
      entire German bourgeoisie' (Benjamin 2004c, p. 451).
73   Adorno 2003x, p. 95.
74   Adorno 2003x, p. 94.
75   Adorno 2003x, p. 95.
76   Adorno 2006a, p. 93; cf. editorial note by Tiedemann (Adorno 2006a, p. 288, n. 13).
77   Adorno 2003x, p. 95.
78   Adorno 1976a, p. 64.
79   Benjamin's theses were published under the title 'On the Concept of History'; for Eng-
      lish translation see Benjamin 2006b. While writing 'Reflections on Class Theory', Adorno
      was already familiar with Benjamin's theses. In a letter to Horkheimer from June 1941, he
      writes that he has received a copy of them from Hannah Arendt (see letter from Adorno to

tenth thesis about the 'angel of history'.[80] The 'one single catastrophe' this angel recognises in the 'chain of events appear[ing] before us'[81] is perceived by Adorno as well as Benjamin in the reduction of progress to methods of perfecting domination – a version of progress which, as nothing other than base myth, makes a mockery of its very concept.[82] 'Within the sphere of influence of the system, the new – progress – is, like the old, a constant source of new disaster'.[83]

In one passage in *Composing for the Films*, a book co-authored by Adorno and Hanns Eisler in 1944, bourgeois music is described as follows: 'On the one hand, it is in a certain sense precapitalistic, "direct", a vague evocation of togetherness; on the other hand, because it has shared in the progress of civilization, it has become reified, indirect, and ultimately a "means" among many others'.[84] Yet manipulation no longer occurs deceptively and coercively as the instilling of ideologies in defenceless victims of domination. On the contrary, society itself has become its own ideology:[85] 'in the name of realism', people acquiesce to coercion and misfortune, to the 'overwhelming power of the existing conditions', which come to be tolerated as normality while it is assumed that things

---

Horkheimer, 12 June 1941 [Adorno and Horkheimer 2004, p. 144; cf. Schöttker and Wizisla 2006]).

80   Cf. Tiedemann 1983, pp. 73–4.

81   Benjamin 2006b, p. 392.

82   Nietzsche already recognises that 'progress' often means progress in making things controllable. In a posthumous fragment cited by Adorno in the introduction to *Dialectic of Enlightenment* (see Adorno and Horkheimer 2002, p. 36), he writes the following: '*Spiritual enlightenment* is an infallible means for making men unsure, weaker in will, so they are more in need of company and support – in short, for developing the *herd animal* in man. Therefore all great artists of government so far (Confucius in China, the *imperium Romanum*, Napoleon, the papacy at the time when it took an interest in power and not merely in the world), in the places where the dominant instincts have culminated so far, also employed spiritual enlightenment – at least let it have its way (like the popes of the Renaissance). The self-deception of the mass concerning this point, e.g., in every democracy, is extremely valuable: making men smaller and more governable is desired as "progress"!' (Nietzsche 1968, p. 79).

83   Adorno 2003x, p. 95.

84   Adorno and Eisler 2005, p. 22.

85   'Ideology loses the very characteristic of being something conscious. It is said there is no dominant ideology anymore because homogenous interests have dissolved and no particular interest presents itself as general. Power relations are taken as self-evident. While it is assumed that the remnants of former ideology could no longer count as such, the sorry state of society becomes ideology itself. This is because the conformity which it openly preaches makes unnecessary that ideology which was once supposed to cover up class oppositions' (Demirović 1999a, p. 453; quoted from transcript by Sok-Zin Lim, 28 Mai 1957, cf. Adorno 2021a, vol. 1, p. 542).

simply 'are the way they are'.[86] As an instrument for implementing this 'down-right morbidly reality-addicted'[87] fatalism, Adorno recognised that which he would shortly thereafter describe as 'the culture industry'.

> [D]omination becomes an integral part of human beings. They do not need to be 'influenced', as liberals with their ideas of the market are wont to imagine. Mass culture simply makes them yet again what they already are thanks to the coercion of the system. It keeps a watchful eye on the anomalies, introduces the official complement of practice in the shape of 'public morality', and provides people with models for imitation.[88]

The calibration of the self-mastery of individuals to the domination imposed on them externally corresponds to the calibration between ideology and reality. 'However, because ideology and reality are converging in this manner, because reality, due to the lack of any other convincing ideology, becomes its own ideology, it requires only a small effort of mind to throw off this all-powerful and at the same time empty illusion; but to make this effort seems to be the most difficult thing of all'.[89] Adorno regards it as possible that a domination which has become total would do away with itself. 'The power which openly admits its own irresistibility', Frank Böckelmann writes in his study on Marx and Adorno, 'lives off of the belief that openness could not be a lie. Yet to a society which de facto identifies reality with appearance, freedom can only "appear" when masked as unfreedom'.[90] Where domination verges on totality, it undermines its own condition of possibility: the existence of something external to it which can be dominated in the first place.[91]

> [D]ehumanization is also its opposite. In reified human beings reification finds its outer limits. They catch up with the technical forces of production in which the relations of production lie hidden: in this way these relations lose the shock of their alien nature because the alienation is so complete. But they may soon also lose their power. Only when the vic-

86   Adorno 1972, p. 202.
87   Demirović 2005, p. 144.
88   Adorno 2003x, p. 109.
89   Adorno 1972, pp. 202–3.
90   Böckelmann 1998, p. 41.
91   'The truth of ideology first disappears when domination no longer needs to deny its own existence and the function of false consciousness has become abstract. Potentially expendable, ideology degenerates into an imitation of that which exists either way' (Böckelmann 1998, p. 40).

tims completely assume the features of the ruling civilization will they be capable of wresting them from the dominant power. The only remaining differentiating factor is reduced to naked usurpation. Only in its blind anonymity could the economy appear as fate: its spell is broken by the horror of the seeing dictatorship. The mimicking of the classless society by class society has been so successful that, while the oppressed have all been co-opted, the futility of all oppression becomes manifest. The ancient myth proves to be quite feeble in its new omnipotence. Even if the dynamic at work was always the same, its end today is not the end.[92]

Economy in the sense criticised by Marx 'is a special case of [economy]'[93] as a form of domination. This is the rule which knows no exceptions. 'While Marx attempted to extrapolate the antagonisms of capitalist society from the dialectics of the rationality of exchange, Horkheimer and Adorno expand these antagonisms in *Dialectic of Enlightenment* – their decisive turn against Marxian theory – while integrating them into a general dialects of human self-preservation which allows them to account for extra-economic elements of domination'.[94] Adorno's 'Reflections on Class Theory' lays the economy-theoretical foundations for *Dialectic of Enlightenment* by conceiving of the economy as an element of a meta-economy which is itself domination, and at times asserts itself in the form of the capital-relation.

---

92   Adorno 2003x, p. 110.

93   Adorno 2003x, p. 100. Translator's note: the original German '*Ökonomie ist ein Sonderfall der Ökonomie*' ('economy is a special case of economy') is translated by Rodney Livingstone as '[e]conomics is a special case of economizing'.

94   Kager 1988, p. 98.

Humanity Had to Inflict Terrible Injuries on Itself

Other than that, the horizon is bleak: the situation in Germany is more than serious. ... A disaster looms large over this country, and I'm certain that it's not just capitalism. There's no way that capitalism becoming so bestial has only economic causes. (How could I begin to formulate what these are? I just keep noticing time and again in France, where there is certainly much to criticise, everything which has been destroyed in our country: basic decency, good nature in its entirety and with it all sense of mutual trust.) However, given that a revolution in Germany would not give a boost to an unspent 'people', unlike perhaps in Russia, I don't believe in the healing powers of upheaval. I only perceive a general mess, and I'd almost prefer if it would be possible to continue muddling through like this.

Letter from KRACAUER to Adorno, 24 August 1930

∴

1   A Provisional Close

Horkheimer's idea for a 'book collaboration on dialectical materialism'[1] went back to as early as the 1930s.[2] Over the course of its planning, not only was Adorno to be involved, but also Korsch,[3] Löwenthal[4] and Herbert Marcuse[5] in alternating constellations, and only in exile did it finally become a reality. In a March 1941 letter to Horkheimer, Adorno reports that he has completed a preliminary draft of his work *Philosophy of New Music*.[6] Although he admits

---

1 Letter from Adorno to Horkheimer, 2 March 1937 (Adorno and Horkheimer 2003b, p. 310).
2 Cf. Krätke 2004, p. 218.
3 Cf. letter from Korsch to Horkheimer, 13 September 1938 (Horkheimer 1995c, p. 482) and Wiggershaus 1995, p. 147.
4 Cf. Adorno and Horkheimer 2002, p. xix.
5 Cf. Wiggershaus 1995, pp. 147, 263.
6 On Adorno and Horkheimer's 'Work on the Dialectic Project' cf. the chapter of that title in

that it might initially be hard to imagine 'anything so absurd as the philosophical examination of the most subtle details of an art about which no human
wants to know anything', it is 'in spite of this, or ... precisely because of this'
that he feels confident promising Horkheimer that the 'excessive undertaking
in prose' would benefit their collaborative work: 'It is a kind of crossroads of
many motifs'.[7] Upon receiving from Adorno the revised manuscript in August,[8]
Horkheimer responds ecstatically:

> If ever in my life I have been enthusiastic, it was while reading this book.
> ... I can't begin to tell you how pleased and happy I am that this docu-
> ment exists. If we're so successful in projecting an incorruptible view that,
> might I say, is the force of the passivity with which you experience new
> music, if in doing so we are successful in confronting the categories that
> guide your presentation with reality in spite of all receptivity for the sub-
> ject, then we'll have accomplished what theory can expect of us at this
> time.[9]

22 July of that same year saw the beginning of the German assault on the
Soviet Union, and with it, of the mass murder of the population of Eastern
Europe committed over the course of the war. On 1 September, four days after
Horkheimer penned his ecstatic reply to Adorno, a police ordinance was issued
forbidding all Jews from the age of six from appearing in public without a
so-called *Judenstern*, or yellow badge – as had already happened in German-
occupied Poland. The legally underwritten public discrimination against Jews
also marked the beginning of their extermination: on 3 September, two days
after the police ordinance took effect, gassings of Jews began in Auschwitz.[10]
Reports of what had occurred 'could be found, for example, in the extensive
"Chronicles" section of *Contemporary Jewish Record*, published by the American Jewish Committee. But it was also possible to find information on the
terrible events in Europe even in the main newspapers in the USA'.[11]

———

    Wiggershaus 1995, pp. 302–26, which further elaborates the origin of *Dialectic of Enlight-
enment* merely outlined in the present study.

7   Letter from Adorno to Horkheimer, 20 May 1941 (Adorno and Horkheimer 2004, p. 116).
Individual passages from *Philosophy of New Music* would be taken up in Thomas Mann's
Doctor Faustus 'almost word-for-word' (cf. Tiedemann 1992).

8   Cf. letter from Adorno to Horkheimer, 10 August 1941 (Adorno and Horkheimer 2004,
p. 184).

9   Letter from Horkheimer to Adorno, 28 August 1941 (Horkheimer 2007, p. 189).

10   Cf. Overesch 1983, pp. 202–3 and Kwiet 1998, p. 535.

11   Wiggershaus 1995, p. 310.

At the time 'delighted' by Horkheimer's letter, Adorno expresses doubts to his colleague over whether they 'really want to focus our collaborative work on art as planned, or rather for god's sake to finally talk about society itself'.[12] For his own part, in his letter from August, Horkheimer already mentions the problem of antisemitism,[13] which Adorno then takes up in light of the prevailing circumstances:

> How would it be if the book ... were to crystallize around antisemitism? This would bring with it the concretization and limitation which we have been looking for. It would also be possible for the topic to motivate most of the Institute's associates, whereas if we write something like a critique of the present judged by the category of the individual, my nightmare is that Marcuse would then prove that the category of the individual has contained both progressive and reactionary elements since the early days of the bourgeoisie. Then again, antisemitism is today really the central injustice, and our form of physiognomy must attend to the world where it shows its face at its most gruesome. Finally, the question of antisemitism is the one in which what we are writing would be most likely to find an effective context, without our having to lose anything by it. And I can imagine, even without any illusory optimism, that a work of this sort would come over to the outside world in a way that would help us. For my part, I would give up years to produce it without a moment's hesitation.[14]

The problem of antisemitism would ultimately be explicitly dealt with in the 'Elements of Anti-Semitism' chapter of *Dialectic of Enlightenment*, although

---

12 Letter from Adorno to Horkheimer, 4 September 1941 (Adorno and Horkheimer 2004, pp. 220–1).

13 Regarding his own reflections on the subject, Horkheimer writes Adorno the following: 'The ridiculous loyalty to one god makes the Jews (in the view of the antisemite, not in reality) simultaneously clumsy and dangerous. The murder of the mad contains the key to the pogrom of the Jews. / Of course, the view that monotheistic consciousness is folly contains a deep reverence. Or rather a superstitious dread that one's own actions are perverse and pernicious. Because they are less spellbound than the sane by the means and ends in whose service life today happens, the mad are rendered uncanny spectators who must be gotten rid of. ... The investigation of antisemitism leads back to mythology and ultimately to physiology' (letter from Horkheimer to Adorno, 28 August 1941 [Adorno and Horkheimer 2004, pp. 217–18]).

14 Letter from Adorno to Horkheimer, 2 October 1941 (Adorno and Horkheimer 2004, pp. 255–6; translation from Wiggershaus 1995, p. 309).

this section is not central, insofar as the book's critique of reason does not take antisemitism as its ultimate benchmark.

It bears mentioning that *Dialectic of Enlightenment* is a book only in a formal sense; the published product would ultimately remain incomplete. The essays are as disparate next to each other as they are internally fragmentary, a feature related to the theory they elaborate. In this sense, the preface to the 1944 edition notes that '[s]till more than the others, the section on the culture industry is fragmentary. Large parts, written long before, need only final editing'.[15] Even in the 1947 edition, the essay on the culture industry still concludes with the following injunction: '(to be continued)'.[16]

In a letter from March 1943, Adorno informs his parents that he and Horkheimer do not intend to complete the 'big theoretical works' with which they are engaged, a prospect which was 'out of the question for lack of time alone'. However, he does state that they at least want to bring these works 'to a provisional close and mimeograph'.[17] This took the form of a 1944 hectographic typescript titled *Philosophical Fragments*. No effort was made to deny the provisional nature of this collection, and the designation of its texts as fragments was doubtless meant seriously. Later in the 1947 edition, the description *Philosophical Fragments* became the subtitle and was replaced by the new title *Dialectic of Enlightenment* as it became clear that no further drafts would be forthcoming. Even still, Adorno would later contemplate the possibility of a sequel from time to time. In a 1949 letter to Hans Paeschke, the publisher of the cultural journal *Merkur*, Adorno reports that he and Horkheimer are working on a 'second volume of *Dialectic*'.[18] Seven years after that, Adorno informs the music educator Erich Doflein that he hopes 'to finally write with Horkheimer the second volume of our *Dialectic*'.[19] Yet another letter by Adorno, written to Wilhelm Melchior Meyer slightly over a year later, reads as follows: 'I can disclose to you that Horkheimer and I hope to finally get to a substantial work which will take the idea of *Dialectic of Enlightenment* further, and which will have at its centre the concept of praxis itself'.[20]

---

15   Adorno and Horkheimer 2002, pp. xix, 254.

16   Adorno and Horkheimer 2002, p. 272.

17   Adorno 2006b, p. 130.

18   Letter from Adorno to Paeschke, 12 December 1949 (Adorno and Horkheimer 2003b, p. 438). This work does not appear to have progressed very far: aside from Adorno's posthumously published note 'Ad Lukács', no evidence of it exists.

19   Letter from Adorno to Erich Doflein, 7 January 1956 (Adorno and Doflein 2006, p. 203).

20   Adorno to Wilhelm Melchior Meyer, 19 March 1957 (TWA, Br 1009/6).

2   The Magic Schema of Rational Exchange

In 'Reflections on Class Theory', Adorno alludes to the natural tendency of history thus far, a tendency which leads him to follow Marx in designating all previous history as mere prehistory. At the same time, Adorno believes that natural tendencies have to be conceptualised dialectically. On the one hand, repeated attempts to dominate nature have in fact brought about advancement and enabled humans to escape their prehistoric enslavement to nature, yet on the other, this escape has led back to an existence at nature's mercy: 'In the mastery of nature, without which mind does not exist, enslavement to nature persists'.[21]

Using the conception of history whose foundations Adorno had lain in 'Reflections on Class Theory', the authors of *Dialectic of Enlightenment* examine why history has led to 'a new kind of barbarism',[22] that is, to fascism and National Socialism. For this purpose, they take as their starting point the origin of the secular promise of salvation in enlightenment – understood not as a term for an historical era,[23] but rather as the attempt to replace nature's domination over humans with human domination over nature. According to Horkheimer and Adorno, humanity's historical departure from its enslavement to nature was marked by human beings using myth to assign nature animistic qualities, which helped humans apprehend nature. Moreover, to truly understand this departure as a process rather than simply account for its grim results, the authors interpret the primal history of enlightenment so that the latter always contains the potential to transform into its opposite, unfettered barbarism. On this point, Horkheimer and particularly Adorno[24] perceive the role played by exchange and its preconditions – namely, the claim of equivalence and the phenomenon of identity thinking, which Adorno would later describe in his

---

21   Adorno and Horkheimer 2002, p. 31.

22   Adorno and Horkheimer 2002, p. xiv.

23   The failure of enlightenment 'goes all the way back to its earliest prefigurations, and demands the term be re-conceptualised: no longer as simply an epoch, but rather as a law of motion in the development of human thought; not simply as a mental process, but rather as a social process whose institutions and technical achievements are just as much manifestations of the human spirit as are philosophical ideas or artworks' (Türcke and Bolte 1994, p. 60).

24   Based on a conversation on the subject with Gretel Adorno, Habermas confirms which of the two authors did most of the writing for which chapter, something which was previously assumed and has since become common knowledge. Horkheimer was chiefly responsible for the title essay and on the chapter on Sade, Adorno for the Odysseus and culture industry chapters. Only 'Elements of Anti-Semitism' and 'Notes and Sketches' were actually written together (cf. Habermas 1993, p. 69).

1957 lecture 'Sociology and Empirical Research' as the law determining 'how the fatality of mankind unfolds'.[25] This analysis made *Dialectic of Enlightenment* the first text in which Adorno not only criticises exchange in a Marxian sense as an economic category and structural principle of capitalist society, but *also* attempts to define exchange as a meta-economic principle whose primal history coincides with that of abstraction, identity and conceptuality – that is, with the primal history of reason itself.

According to Horkheimer and Adorno, while mimetic behaviour was succeeded in its day by mythic behaviour[26] – 'the incantatory practices of the magician by the carefully graduated sacrifice and the labor of enslaved men mediated by command'[27] – the latter was in turn replaced in the Enlightenment by the exchange of equivalents and its mediating services. This ushered in the pre-eminence of exchange's particular form of rationality, which Horkheimer and Adorno recognise as a rationality of domination. In this sense, as Andreas Benl correctly observes, although the 'fundamental difference between the concept of exchange in Horkheimer/Adorno versus in the Marxian critique of political economy' is frequently invoked as a 'reproach against Critical Theory', this is unjustified: after all, *'Dialectic of Enlightenment* is not a sequel novel in the *Capital* series, but rather a radical critique of the forms of bourgeois rationality'.[28]

The fundamental difference between Marx's and Adorno's respective concepts of exchange has been invoked in precisely this manner by Gerhard Brandt:

> Adorno certainly did not avert the danger of a 'generalization in the field of philosophy of history of the critique of political economy'. ... While he did not transpose the paradigm of the Marxian theory of capitalism onto the history of humanity, he did transpose it onto the history of modernity beginning with the overcoming of myth in ancient Greece, arguing that both the abstraction of immediate needs and instinctual impulses as well as reification – manifestations of commodity exchange – were ... already inherent in the early advanced civilisations. Yet however compelling and legitimate it may be to interpret developments prior to capitalism as the prehistory of capitalism ..., and as much as the regression of bourgeois society to apparently pre-capitalist forms of political domination

---

25   Adorno 1976d, p. 80.
26   Cf. Adorno and Horkheimer 2002, p. 148.
27   Adorno and Horkheimer 2002, p. 5.
28   Benl 1999, p. 69.

supports such an interpretation, so too does a generalisation and overextension of historical categories threaten to weaken the analytical power of the theory with regards to how it apprehends both new structural changes in contemporary capitalism as well as past phases of development.[29]

Yet Brandt misreads the significance of *Dialectic of Enlightenment*. Following Marx, Adorno views previous history from the immediate present, differing from the former by conceptualising capitalism not as a new form of domination, but as a variety of the very oldest form of domination. And from Adorno's perspective – the perspective of wars of extermination and concentration camps – the history of humanity does appear as the history of human extermination. In all their scientific, technological and cultural achievements, modern human beings stand not on the shoulders of giants who show them the way, but rather on a gigantic mountain of corpses – the price of all progress thus far.[30] This is what Horkheimer and Adorno allude to with the claim that '[h]umanity had to inflict terrible injuries on itself before the self – the identical, purpose-directed, masculine character of human beings – was created, and something of this process is repeated in every childhood'.[31]

Yet the invocation of childhood here gives rise to a terrifying question: what exactly is *not* repeated in every childhood? Here, one might draw upon an observation made by Emile Durkheim, one which is particularly remarkable considering the time in which it was written. Presented by Durkheim as a substantiation of his definition of social constraint, this observation reads as follows:

> If one views the facts as they are and indeed as they have always been, it is patently obvious that all education consists of a continual effort to impose upon the child ways of seeing, thinking and acting which he himself would not have arrived at spontaneously. From his earliest years we oblige him to eat, drink and sleep at regular hours, and to observe cleanliness, calm and obedience; later we force him to learn how to be mindful of others, to respect customers and conventions, and to work, etc. If this

---

29 Brandt 1981, pp. 24–5; quoted from Habermas 1991, p. 109.
30 Cf. Benjamin's fourth historical-philosophical thesis, in which it is alleged that the historical materialist views 'cultural treasures' with 'cautious detachment': 'For in every case these treasures have a lineage which he cannot contemplate without horror. They owe their existence not only to the efforts of the great geniuses who created them, but also to the anonymous toil of others who lived in the same period. There is no document of culture which is not at the same time a document of barbarism' (Benjamin 2006b, pp. 391–2).
31 Adorno and Horkheimer 2002, p. 26.

constraint in time ceases to be felt it is because it gradually gives rise to habits, to inner tendencies which render it superfluous; but they supplant the constraint only because they are derived from it.[32]

Meanwhile, when a child preserves his idiosyncrasies amidst this process of constrictive socialisation – experiencing joy, worry and even fright without the cause of his expressions being immediately clear to others – he is simply diagnosed with an emotional adjustment disorder. Individual experience simultaneously stamps out individuality, making it all too ready to submit to the self-denial or 'renunciation within thought that extends even into its purely formal character',[33] and ultimately to the asceticism of a pure philosophy – one which aspires to be nothing other than philosophy, and no longer cares to know anything about the subject and its experiences. Philosophy of this kind extends the socially produced poverty of experience, a poverty which afflicts subjects even in said philosophy's absence.[34]

In any case, the above passage from *Dialectic of Enlightenment* takes aim 'directly at Freud, for whom a rational process of social rationalisation entails a model of socialisation in which the "compulsive", narcissistic child entangled in illusions is refined into an adult who speaks and acts straightforwardly'.[35] As opposed to this, a reconciled society 'would not have to remove children from a happy situation and place them in an unhappy one',[36] as the reality-principle would no longer entail conformity to a reality envisioned as self-denial.

Horkheimer and Adorno describe capitalism, humanity's most advanced stage thus far, as an historical moment within an overarching prehistory. After all, as Christoph Türcke and Gerhard Bolte write, capitalism '*is* prehistory and *has* a prehistory, and one cannot sufficiently grasp capitalism without simultaneously grasping the prehistory it contains, without discerning the structure of its prehistory from its own structure, and thereby discerning the deep structure of prehistory in its entirety. According to Horkheimer and Adorno, only in this way is it possible to grasp the horrors of fascism at all: it was not simply capitalism which erupted into fascism; rather, fascism absorbed the entire mythical violence of prehistory and endowed it with maximum technological resources'.[37] The 'deep structure of prehistory' Türcke and Bolte mention

---

32   Durkheim 1982, pp. 53–4.
33   Adorno 2019i, p. 212.
34   This paragraph is also located in Braunstein 2015, pp. 46–7.
35   Lohmann 2006, p. 378.
36   Jornitz 2003, p. 102.
37   Türcke and Bolte 1994, pp. 63–4.

here is domination – domination over nature, others and oneself, which openly reveals itself in National Socialism as unfettered horror. In the chapter in *Dialectic of Enlightenment* titled 'Odysseus or Myth and Enlightenment',[38] Adorno attempts to uncover this historically constant structure of domination in order to reveal contemporary domination, whether in the form of monopoly capitalism or fascism, as an element of a more general phenomenon.

An exemplary misunderstanding of the economy-critical intentions of *Dialectic of Enlightenment* can also be seen in Michael T. Koltan's essay 'Adorno, gegen seine Liebhaber verteidigt' ('Adorno Defended Against His Fans').[39] Koltan addresses the function of exchange in Horkheimer and Adorno's work as follows:

> For obvious reasons, Adorno and Horkheimer expounded upon the relationship between exchange and sacrifice in *Dialectic of Enlightenment*. The outward historical grounds for this are easy to establish. Yet it should be remembered that the philosophical fragments of *Dialectic of Enlightenment* attempted first and foremost to put into words the catastrophe of National Socialism. By emphasising the close relationship between sacrifice and exchange, Horkheimer and Adorno criticise the ideology of National Socialism, an ideology in which the sacrificial cult plays an essential role.[40]

Contrary to this account, the authors of *Dialectic of Enlightenment* most certainly do not intend 'to put into words the catastrophe of National Social-

---

38   '[N]o work bears more eloquent witness to the intertwinement of enlightenment and myth than that of Homer, the basic text of European civilization' (Adorno and Horkheimer 2002, p. 37).

39   With this essay, Koltan seeks to both criticise Adorno while also defending him against his critics and his misappropriation by a 'species of Adorno disciples who defuse him precisely by unconditionally subjugating themselves to his texts' (Koltan 1999, p. 15). It is no coincidence that the substantive shortcomings of this essay are clearly reflected in its language, one which speaks of a 'perspective ... drafted' (ibid.), a 'centrality ... unfolded' (Koltan 1999, p. 16), a point of 'importance ... underscored' (Koltan 1999, p. 17), of 'considerations ... grown dear to heart' (Koltan 1999, p. 20), of 'the ideology of sacrifice ... nullified' (ibid.), of 'structures ... established' (ibid.), of an 'illusion' which can 'seep into minds'. Over Odysseus 'floats the sword of Damocles' (Koltan 1999, p. 21), things end up 'on the opposite pole of the subject-object dualism' (Koltan 1999, p. 22) and 'commodity exchange ... accompanies humanity ... for part of its journey' (Koltan 1999, p. 24). That being said, the essay is important as a rare instance of a text which actually takes Adorno seriously as a critic of economy.

40   Koltan 1999, p. 17.

ism'[41] in order to make it accessible to rationality, something which the culture industry does nonstop.[42] In view of National Socialism, they do not conceive of sacrifice as an act of economic exchange, but rather as the sacrifice of individuals to the individual, a 'sacrifice of the self' following from the 'denial of nature in the human being for the sake of mastery over extrahuman nature and over other human beings'.[43] In this regard, the concept of sacrifice relies on that of self-denial.[44] Through these concepts, 'both the difference between and the unity of mythical nature and enlightened mastery of nature become apparent'.[45]

Concerning the *economy* of sacrifice in *Dialectic of Enlightenment*, Koltan is also incorrect to say that 'the concept of exchange is developed out of the concept of *sacrifice*'.[46] On the contrary, the book treats exchange as the 'secularization of sacrifice', as 'the magic schema of rational exchange',[47] which is to say nothing other than that it examines sacrifice in its demythologised form in order to discover traces of the formerly mythical in the currently secular: 'Myth is already enlightenment, and enlightenment reverts to mythology'.[48] Koltan's formulation is wrong in the same way as it would be wrong to claim that the secularised Greece of today 'developed out of' ancient Greece. That being said, traces of the latter can be found within the former, something which is also the case in other countries. While secularisation does constitute the

---

41   Cf. Adorno 2004b, p. 63.

42   In Germany, the personalisation of Holocaust history has been executed by Guido Knopp, who Wolfgang Nitschke describes as the 'the reprocessing plant for both factual and funny stories (*Sach- und Lachgeschichten*) from the dark period' (Nitschke 1999, p. 42), and by Knopp's helpers. 'The re-examination of Hitler's actions – collected, edited and neatly taken apart in thousands of books – allows nothing to be felt except that general emotion which ... accompanies a neighbour's misfortune: complacence. The more subtly and seriously that scholarliness itself operates and differentiates, the more it downplays. The denser the materials, the more conclusive the analysis, the more barbaric the subjects: the more cosy and comfortable the reader feels. Is this what the creator intended?' (Henscheid 2003, p. 516).

43   Adorno and Horkheimer 2002, p. 42.

44   In a letter to his parents during work on *Dialectic of Enlightenment*, Adorno writes that 'the Homer study is a critique of self-denial' (Adorno 2006b, p. 131). Adorno had already addressed the relationship between sacrifice and self-denial in *Kierkegaard* (cf. Adorno 1999a, p. 121).

45   Adorno and Horkheimer 2002, p. xviii.

46   Koltan 1999, p. 16.

47   Adorno and Horkheimer 2002, p. 40.

48   Adorno and Horkheimer 2002, p. xviii. 'But the myths which fell victim to the Enlightenment were themselves its products. The scientific calculation of events annuls the account

negation of religiosity in society, this negation can only take place determinately as long as history has not experienced an absolute (that is, an ultimate
revolutionary) break. This is also true of the relationship between sacrifice
and exchange. Exchange under capital is certainly different from exchange in
pre-capitalist societies, which is itself different from sacrifice. However, what
remains constant is that something is given in order for something else to be
received. Exchange does not need to be theoretically 'developed out of' sacrifice, as sacrifice was *itself* already exchange.[49] This was the rational aspect of
irrational, mythical sacrifice, a ritual whose irrational, mythical element persists within fully rational exchange: 'If the principle of sacrifice was proved
transient by its irrationality, at the same time it survives through its rationality'.[50]

   In a late note written during his work on *Aesthetic Theory*, Adorno substanti-
ates his definition of myth, arguing that myth is not a long obsolete explanation
of the world, '*not* what is not the case', but rather base reality – 'what is always
constant in the world, its baked-togetherness (*das Immergleiche, Zusammenge-
backene, der Welt*)'. Myth is 'the stuff of world: how it is, how it will remain, how
it should be'.[51] Hence, in the exchange of equivalents – the exchange which permits neither more nor less than equivalency – Adorno recognises this myth of
the always constant: 'as long as domination persists through exchange, myth
will dominate as well'.[52]

3   Ruled by Equivalence

Both sacrifice and exchange are rational insofar as they result in a utility which
is experienced as just. In the case of sacrifice, both the sacrificer and the deity
to whom the sacrifice is made gain what is rightfully theirs through the observance of ritual, whereas in the case of exchange in a more narrowly economic
sense, equal values are exchanged. The principle common to both is justice,

---

of them which thought had once given in myth. Myth sought to report, to name, to tell of
origins – but therefore also to narrate, record, explain. This tendency was reinforced by
the recording and collecting of myths. From a record, they soon became a teaching. Each
ritual contains a representation of how things happen and of the specific process which
is to be influenced by magic' (Adorno and Horkheimer 2002, p. 5).

49   Cf. Adorno and Horkheimer 2002, p. 42.
50   Ibid.
51   Adorno 2003k, p. 35.
52   Adorno 2005f, p. 159.

which also distinguishes sacrifice from forms of offering or gift-giving in which nothing is expected in return.[53] Justice is unthinkable without the idea of equivalence because the medium of justice is equality.

The failure of *Dialectic of Enlightenment* to account for the difference between pre-capitalist and capitalist exchange in its models does in fact lead to confusion in some passages, such as when Adorno and Horkheimer write that '[t]he seafarer Odysseus outwits the natural deities as the civilized traveler was later to swindle savages, offering them colored beads for ivory'.[54] Setting aside whether the exchange of glass beads for ivory actually happened on a large enough scale to produce anything more than anecdotes, this example indicates an objective problem with determining unjust advantage in exchange. After all, in the particular exchange it depicts, there *is* no unjust advantage. Both parties can count themselves as 'winners' – both the traveller who exchanges beads which are worthless to him for ivory he can sell for money, and the 'savages' who receive the beads they desire for the ivory in which they have no or only limited interest. This is a win-win situation of a kind which does not occur in capitalism-proper. Moreover, insofar as the exchange detailed by Adorno is a circumstantial exchange, as opposed to an instance of an exchange relationship generalised throughout society, it does not follow the principle of equivalence.[55] And when it is noted that 'the gift to the host anticipates the principle of equivalence', this 'anticipation' also marks the limits of what can be accomplished by deciphering Homeric epic poetry as the primal history of enlightenment with respect to the exchange of equivalents. For with

---

53   In what has become a work of 'classic rank' (Ritsert 1998 p. 326) on gift giving, Marcel Mauss concludes from his analysis of Polynesian potlatches that 'there has never existed ... anything that might resemble what is called a "natural" economy' (Mauss 2002, p. 6), and that there is an 'absolute obligation to reciprocate' gifts given at potlatches (Mauss 2002, p. 11). Thus, he argues that apparently long-institutionalised forms of gift-giving 'express one fact alone, one social system, one precise state of mind: everything – food, women, children, property, talismans, land, labour services, priestly functions, and ranks – is there for passing on, and for balancing accounts. Everything passes to and fro as if there were a constant exchange of a spiritual matter, including things and men, between clans and individuals, distributed between social ranks, the sexes, and the generations' (Mauss 2002, p. 18).

54   Adorno and Horkheimer 2002, p. 39.

55   'Odysseus's defenselessness against the foaming sea sounds like a legitimation of the enrichment of the voyager at the expense of indigenous inhabitants. Bourgeois economics later enshrined this principle in the concept of risk: the possibility of foundering is seen as a moral justification for profit. From the standpoint of the developed exchange society and its individuals, the adventures of Odysseus are no more than a depiction of the risks which line the path to success' (Adorno and Horkheimer 2002, p. 48).

the assertion that 'the host receives really or symbolically the equivalent value of the service he has performed, while the guest takes away provisions which, in principle, are intended to enable him to reach home',[56] it becomes clear not only that the ostensible equivalence here is constructed, but even more so that there is no objective standard by which this equivalence could be measured in the first place. Equivalence is not produced when participants in an exchange are reasonably satisfied at its conclusion, but rather when the socially determined value is equal on both sides of the exchange equation. The example in question does not demonstrate that prehistoric trade already involved the exchange of equivalents, but rather that it occurred in a way which saw each of the parties involved make a subjective gain. Yet according to Adorno, this gain remains dependent on a subjective theory of value, something he himself would later deem 'ideological'.[57] Adorno would only be able to solve the problem of simultaneous compliance and non-compliance with the exchange of equivalents in his subsequent examination of class-antagonism. Front a strictly economic viewpoint, the meaning of equivalence and comparability in the Odysseus chapter of *Dialectic of Enlightenment* remains restricted to the unmediated exchange act. Nevertheless, this restriction also allows Adorno to trace exchange and rational logic back to equivalence, and thus, to identity.

The unshakeable 'principle of give and take',[58] whose origins are located in sacrifice, and which under capitalism no longer occurs in isolated incidents, but rather systematically through the billions of exchanges of goods for money (and vice versa) made everyday,

> does not lead outside the circle of existence. The world controlled by mana, and even the worlds of Indian and Greek myth, are issueless and eternally the same. All birth is paid for with death, all fortune with misfortune. While men and gods may attempt in their short span to assess their fates by a measure other than blind destiny, existence triumphs over them in the end. Even their justice, wrested from calamity, bears its features; it corresponds to the way in which human beings, primitives no less than Greeks and barbarians, looked upon their world from within a society of oppression and poverty. Hence, for both mythical and enlightened justice, guilt and atonement, happiness and misfortune, are seen as the two sides of an equation. Justice gives way to law.[59]

---

56 Adorno and Horkheimer 2002, p. 39.
57 Adorno 1967, p. 73; cf. Backhaus 2004a, p. 31.
58 Adorno 1974b, p. 70.
59 Adorno and Horkheimer 2002, pp. 11–12.

In *Negative Dialectics*, Adorno would again return to this motif – that of the 'universal exchange of equivalents' as the law 'which flouts justice':[60]

> Law is the primal phenomenon of irrational rationality. In law the formal principle of equivalence becomes the norm; everyone is treated alike. An equality in which differences perish secretly serves to promote inequality; it becomes the myth that survives amidst an only seemingly demythologized mankind. For the sake of an unbroken systematic, the legal norms cut short what is not covered, every specific experience that has not been shaped in advance; and then they raise the instrumental rationality to the rank of a second reality *sui generis*. The total legal realm is one of definitions. Its systematic forbids the admission of anything that eludes their closed circle, of anything *quod non est in actis*. These bounds, ideological in themselves, turn into real violence as they are sanctioned by law as the socially controlling authority, in the administered world in particular.[61]

Jochen Bung takes this passage as an opportunity to demonstrate

> that Adorno's outline of that which he refers to as the 'ideology of positive law' or the 'untruth of positive law' is at least incomplete, and even goes amiss in places. Why should the destructive side of the law, its 'destructiveness', follow specifically from its creation of systems? It is by no means inevitable that the replacement of that which Adorno refers to as the 'bounds' created by legal definitions with case reports or judicial decision in the style of free law would produce a better or fairer practice of law.[62]

Yet Adorno would have shared this assessment, and indeed nowhere advocates for an alternative legal practice. However, the fact that such an alternative may be even worse than current practices is neither a positive justification for law, nor for its scalable version of justice. Law's formation of systems 'specifically' relates to its 'destructiveness' because its systematisation omits individual interests

> The step from chaos to civilization, in which natural conditions exert their power no longer directly but through the consciousness of human beings, changed nothing in the principle of equivalence. Indeed, human beings

---

60   Letter from Adorno to Horkheimer, 10 January 1945 (Adorno and Horkheimer 2005, p. 12).
61   Adorno 2007b, p. 309.
62   Bung 2007, p. 157; quoted from Adorno 2007b, pp. 309–10; cf. also Buckel 2008, p. 110.

atoned for this very step by worshipping that to which previously, like all other creatures, they had been merely subjected. Earlier, fetishes had been subject to the law of equivalence. Now equivalence itself becomes a fetish. The blindfold over the eyes of Justitia means not only that justice brooks no interference but that it does not originate in freedom.[63]

Only through self-imposed blindness is law able to let justice prevail. All are only seen as equal insofar as they are not seen at all; to do justice to the individual is only possible by negating individuality. It is not individuals who count as equal, but rather 'the individual'. In this way, justice degenerates into tautology: an individual is what corresponds to the concept of the individual, which is in turn abstracted from individuals.[64]

As humanity civilised itself with rationality, a form of rational domination simultaneously asserted itself, drawing on the same principle as the former: equality. Responsible for 'regulat[ing] punishment and reward within civilization',[65] equality – or equivalence – is the ubiquitous principle of civilised, that is, of rational domination:

> Bourgeois society is ruled by equivalence. It makes dissimilar things comparable by reducing them to abstract quantities. For the Enlightenment, anything which cannot be resolved into numbers, and ultimately into one, is illusion; modern positivism consigns it to poetry. Unity remains the watchword from Parmenides to Russell. All gods and qualities must be destroyed.[66]

In other words, Horkheimer and Adorno's conception of bourgeois society is broad enough to include the city-state of antiquity. From there, they trace the

---

63 Adorno and Horkheimer 2002, p. 12. It should also be mentioned that Adorno leaves another insignia of Justitia unmentioned here: the scale. This scale certainly does not 'weigh', as is implied by the application of reason to individual cases. Rather, its sole function is to measure according to a predetermined *absolute*, as does a ruler, for example, which is no more inherently just than the scale.
64 Cf. Reuss 2007, pp. 135–48; cf. Adorno 2019d, p. 41.
65 Adorno and Horkheimer 2002, p. 12.
66 Adorno and Horkheimer 2002, pp. 4–5. Adorno writes elsewhere that Parmenides was 'astounded by the composition of the object of exchange, substance; Heraclitus by the balance in the continuous motion which happens in exchange, the unity of the chaotic and the regulated; Pythagoras from the dimensional ratio, etc.' (Adorno and Sohn-Rethel 1989, p. 222). On Adorno's treatment of the pre-Socratics, cf. Adorno 2008, p. 159; cf. Adorno 1974a, p. 80; cf. Adorno 1998.

history of the domination of equivalence, a history still in progress today. The way in which the world is understood conforms to the 'requirement of scientific security',[67] which can only be met through appropriation. An 'enlightenment through tabulation'[68] is running its course, rejecting everything which cannot be measured and sorted as unverifiable and therefore irrational. 'The true instrument of domination is the ruler'[69] – as Adorno notes, this insight is already present in the work of Hegel, who suggests that 'a critique of the kind of tabulating thought which in the era of the administered world today has indeed almost become the universal form of science in general, a form of thought against which language itself now obviously occupies a hopelessly defensive position'.[70] This critique can be seen in the preface to *Phenomenology of Spirit*, in which Hegel describes the form of the 'tabular chart' as follows:

> it is itself a little bit like a skeleton with small bits of paper stuck all over it, or maybe a bit like the rows of sealed and labeled boxes in a grocer's stall. Either of these makes just as much sense as the other, and, as in the former case, where there are only bones with the flesh and blood stripped off of them, and as in the latter case, where something equally lifeless has been hidden away in those boxes, ... the living essence of what is at stake has been omitted or concealed. ... The monochromatic nature of the schema and its lifeless determinations, together with this absolute identity and the transition from one to the other, are each and everyone the result of the same lifeless intellect and external cognition.[71]

Because they assume their form under capital, the French Revolution's ideals of liberty and justice through equality – ideals which first became established as bourgeois values and then as bourgeois law – transform into their opposites. Individual freedom under capital consists of the freedom to sell and buy, including to sell and buy labour-power. Equality results from disregarding the particular people who carry out these transactions: on the one hand, the value of commodities and money does not depend on their owners, yet on the other – according to the ideology of liberalism – the amount of money every individual has is dependent on individual achievement. Justice prevails due to the validity

---

67   Letter from Adorno to Horkheimer, 28 November 1936 (Adorno and Horkheimer 2003b, p. 240).
68   Henscheid 2007, p. 570.
69   Fabri 2000, p. 698.
70   Adorno 2017a, p. 47.
71   Hegel 2018, p. 32; cf. editorial note by Christoph Ziermann (Adorno 2017a, p. 268, n. 7).

of the universally performed exchange of equivalents. Ideally, all members of society enjoy an equal amount of formal freedom to face off against each other in formally just competition.

Yet this competition is always also a competition for the opportunity to acquire commodities – that is, a competition for money – and people must earn money to survive because it is a universal equivalent. For workers, therefore, freedom transforms into the unfreedom of submitting to the material necessity of earning money (read: of submitting to wage-labour), as circumstances demand that ostensibly free subjects coerce themselves into unfreedom for the sake of their existence. Equality as free competition becomes an existential struggle, one occurring within classes yet primarily between them. Meanwhile, regardless of the level of wages and other labour conditions, the working class is always at a disadvantage in this supposedly free competition because it has already sold the surplus-value it has created to the capitalist class – in accordance with justice, as ensured though the observance of the principle of equivalence. Whoever is committed to this justice must *coerce himself* to comply with the principle which works to his disadvantage: labour-power for wages. This means that the individual, who is statutorily regulated by force, must give himself over to struggle with other virtually superfluous individuals, or in short, that freedom, equality and justice assert themselves as mechanisms of coercion – of *de facto* coercion to *personally* submit to the capitalist mechanisms of reproduction. In this way, the particular individual becomes subsumed into the universality of a society which never grants him the choice of rejecting this form of freedom, equality and justice.[72] According to Marx, here it is revealed 'that exchange-value or, more precisely, the money system is in fact the system of equality and freedom, and that the disturbances which they encounter in the further development of the system are disturbances inherent in it, are merely the realization of *equality and freedom*, which prove to be inequality and unfreedom'.[73] Engels already points

---

72   'We know today ... that this eternal Right found its realisation in bourgeois justice; that this equality reproduced itself to bourgeois equality before the law; that bourgeois property was proclaimed as one of the essential rights of man; and that the government of reason, the Contrat Social of Rousseau, came into being, and only could come into being, as a democratic bourgeois republic. The great thinkers of the eighteenth century could no more than their predecessors, go beyond the limits imposed upon them by their epoch' (Engels 1987a, p. 190).

73   Marx 1993, pp. 248–9. In a reflection from 1851, Marx wrote the following regarding the 'equality' of the classes: 'The gilding or silvering blurs class character and whitewashes it. This is the origin of the apparent equality – minus the money – in bourgeois society. On the other hand, this is also the origin of the real bourgeois equality of individuals in

out the historicity of these principles when he claims that 'to represent equal-ity = justice as the highest principle and ultimate truth is absurd. Equality exists only in opposition to inequality, justice in opposition to injustice; hence they are still saddled with the opposition to old, past history, and hence to old society itself'.[74] When these revolutionary principles were proclaimed in the eighteenth century while the world appeared to stand 'upon its head',[75] they were already a reflection of what already existed. As Adorno himself observes,

> at the time when the Great French Revolution broke out, the crucial eco-nomic levers were already in the hands of the middle class. This means that production was already under the control of the manufacturing and the incipient industrial middle class. At the same time ... the feudal class and the groups associated with it in the absolutist system had ceased almost entirely to have any influence over production in the sense of socially useful labour. This weakness of the absolutist system was the pre-condition for the outbreak of the revolution, and it will be difficult to deny ... that what appeared in the self-glorifying accounts of bourgeois histori-ography to be an indescribable act of liberation was in reality more like the confirmation of an already existing situation. ... And this is connected with the fact that, because all bourgeois revolutions merely make official or *de jure* something that already existed *de facto*, they all have an element of illusion, of ideology, about them.[76]

The concepts of freedom, justice and equality are historically determined by the context of their specific genesis, namely by the early capitalist form of society. Having already been internalised by human beings in fully developed capitalism, these principles can hardly still serve as the standard for a critique

---

a society in which the money system is fully developed, as long as those individuals have money which is also a source of income. No longer is it like in antiquity, where the priv-ileged could exchange this or that; rather, everything can be had by all, every metabolism carried out by everyone according to the amount of money into which one's income can be converted; whores, science, protection, awards, sycophants – all exchangeable products, just like coffee and sugar and earrings. With estates, individual consumption depends on the particular division of labour into which it is subsumed. With classes, it depends only on the general medium of exchange which the individual knows to acquire' (Marx 1977, pp. 508–9).

74   Engels 1987b, p. 603.
75   Engels 1987a, p. 16.
76   Adorno 2006a, pp. 34–5.

which goes beyond mere morality and allows itself to be guided by the 'contradictory nature of its object'.[77] Such a critique would have to take aim at these principles as well.

The more freely, justly and closely to formal equality that individuals under capital can labour in its service, the simpler it becomes for society to ensure capital's politico-economic parameters. The more this happens, the more individuals themselves behave as market agents, as executors of their own unfreedom, injustice and inequality. This leads Marx to adopt a critical stance towards allegedly emancipatory principles which provide an opening for the economic domination of capital,[78] and thus to reject the idea of justice as inadequate. In contrast, Adorno takes the mere hypostatised idea of justice – as well as that of freedom – at face value. Ironically, by distancing himself from the idea of justice – which became ubiquitous as an ineluctable principle under the capitalist mode of production – because it had gone unfulfilled, Marx treats it as if its intent were utopian (versus merely formal). Adorno, however, seeks to redeem the utopian element *also* contained in the concepts of justice and freedom. While he recognises the ideological character of these principles just as Marx does, he nevertheless ascribes to them an element of truth in spite of their falseness. He views them as at least containing the potentiality for emancipatory practice, even though they do not yet constitute this practice themselves.

> According to Adorno, the non-foreshortened element of truth consists of the ideals of bourgeois society, even though these ideals are not honoured in reality. This dimension of Adorno's definition of the critique of ideology – the assessing of bourgeois society's reality according to its unrealised ideals, later a decisive element of Critical Theory – differentiates it from the Marxian definition, which identifies deficiencies of these ideals themselves. For Marx, there is no undeformed element of truth in bourgeois ideals. He criticises both the reality and the ideality of bourgeois society by indicating its contradictory determination.[79]

Yet Adorno recognises not only the 'contradictory determination' of bourgeois society, but also the basic absence of 'a non-foreshortened' or 'undeformed element of truth' within existing society. Society's element of truth is thoroughly particular, and therefore deformed, but this does not mean it is any less true.

---

77   Adorno 1976a, p. 17.
78   Cf. Iber 2005, p. 15.
79   Iber 2005, p. 73.

Human rights, for example, may very well be ideology, yet for people living in countries committed to the appearance of upholding them, ideology can have real, emancipatory effects:

> Freedom and equality are appearances which mediate the relations of exchange and capital. But for someone forced to flee from a dictatorship, the existence of these appearances is a matter of life and death. Appearance itself is a reality, for its existence determines whether survival in a bourgeois society is possible. This led the representatives of Critical Theory to reflect on how to move beyond the concept of dialectically mediated totality, that is, the notion that superstructure is always simply an expression.[80]

Returning once again to the French Revolution, Adorno remarks as follows in his 1958 lecture course *Introduction to Dialectics*:

> if the men who brought about the liberation of bourgeois society during the French Revolution had not seriously regarded this bourgeois society as the realization of a just society as something absolute, if their own limited intellectual perspective in this regard were not effectively at work as an explosive force, then the revolution as a whole would never have come to pass. But, at the same time, this defective understanding involved in turn that particular limitation which made this into a merely relative historical achievement after all.[81]

4   No Shepherd

In *Dialectic of Enlightenment*, economic or economy-critical motifs emerge most clearly in Adorno's chapter on the culture industry. 'The term culture industry was perhaps used for the first time in the book *Dialectic of Enlightenment*', Adorno recalls in a 1963 lecture titled 'Culture Industry Reconsidered'.[82] The culture industry 'fuses the old and familiar into a new quality',[83] for it is the new form assumed by traditional domination at the level of currently exist-

80   Demirović 1999b, p. 44.
81   Adorno 2017a, p. 34.
82   Horkheimer and Adorno had in fact already used this term in the 'Memorandum über Teile des Los Angeles Arbeitsprogramms' (see Chapter 6 of the present study).
83   Adorno 1975, p. 12.

ing relations of production. As he wrote Benjamin, Adorno was affected by extremes,[84] and this can be seen here as well insofar as he examines the persistent element of domination on the basis of domination's 'historically most distant source – myth – and its most current – "the culture industry"'.[85]

In all branches of the culture industry,

> products which are tailored for consumption by masses, and which to a great extent determine the nature of that consumption, are manufactured more or less according to plan. The individual branches are similar in structure or at least fit into each other, ordering themselves into a system almost without a gap. This is made possible by contemporary technical capabilities as well as by economic and administrative concentration. ... Thus, although the culture industry undeniably speculates on the conscious and unconscious state of the millions towards which it is directed, the masses are not primary, but secondary, they are an object of calculation; an appendage of the machinery. The customer is not king, as the culture industry would like to have us believe, not its subject but its object. The very word mass-media, specially honed for the culture industry, already shifts the accent onto harmless terrain. Neither is it a question of primary concern for the masses, nor of the techniques of communication as such, but of the spirit which sufflates them, their master's voice.[86]

With this claim, Adorno by no means seeks to describe the assertion of a subjective will to domination as a conspiracy. Rather, the culture industry produces its effects 'with or without the conscious will of those in control' as defined as 'both those who carry out directives as well as those who hold the power'. This is because

> [u]ltimately, the culture industry no longer even needs to directly pursue everywhere the profit interests from which it originated. These interests have become objectified in its ideology and have even made themselves independent of the compulsion to sell the cultural commodities which must be swallowed anyway. The culture industry turns into public relations, the manufacturing of 'good will' per se, without regard for particular

---

84   Letter from Adorno to Benjamin, 18 March 1936 (Adorno and Benjamin 1999, p. 130).
85   Reemtsma 1995, p. 95.
86   Adorno 1975, p. 12.

firms of saleable objects. Brought to bear is a general uncritical consensus, advertisements produced for the world, so that each product of the culture industry becomes its own advertisement.[87]

On this point, Burkhardt Lindner has criticised Adorno for mostly referring 'to "the dominant" (*den Herrschenden*) in a mythical manner, as if to an unknown royal house or race of gods'. As a result, 'the partially used categories of the critique of political economy lose their analytical power', while 'the culture industry as mass deception is denounced in a posture of late-bourgeois enlightenment'.[88] However, Adorno's consideration of the culture industry is not as simple as Lindner implies. Adorno views the manipulation by the culture industry not as driven by the interest of individuals, but rather as unfolding structurally 'for the depersonalised and anonymous apparatus of power in an administrated society. After all, it is directed precisely against the interests of its recipients, whom it turns into victims'.[89] Hence, the culture industry is a function of capitalism. 'The result of the culture industry is ultimately the destruction of the individual. Domination is no longer externally imposed on the individual; rather, in Horkheimer's words, it has already been "internalised" by human beings'.[90] Humans dominate themselves, and the culture industry supports them in doing so. However, it would be wrong to say that the culture industry violates humans: 'In reality, a cycle of manipulation and retroactive need is unifying the system ever more tightly'.[91] In an unpublished note, Adorno describes this dynamic as follows:

> Not only do human beings have masses of commodities pushed on them to the point of psychological coercion by the apparatus of distribution, which is integrated with the apparatus of production and thus made distant from them; not only is the advertisement pitched in the name of that reason which could instruct consumers that they do not need and probably do not even want these commodities. Beyond that, needs are already so preformed, as are human beings themselves, that the former have an illusory character and stand in frequent contradiction to the latter's interests, not only because humans beings gain what they did not need while frequently lacking what they need the most, but also because

87   Adorno 1975, p. 13.
88   Lindner 1972, pp. 24–5.
89   Kausch 1988, p. 85.
90   Kausch 1988, p. 90; quoted from Horkheimer 2004, p. 64.
91   Adorno and Horkheimer 2002, p. 95.

the sedimented interest in what is being sold distracts them from what could allow them to escape a delusion in which they are now involved.[92]

In this way, the masses are 'manipulated while pursuing their own interests',[93] and capitalist society reproduces itself – a society whose 'total domination likes to keep itself invisible: "No shepherd and a herd"'.[94] This image taken up from Nietzsche[95] of a herd with no shepherd standing before it suggests that the herd only qualifies as such because it dominates itself. Under capital, a section of the herd – which has been abandoned by princes and gods – assumes the position of the shepherd. *Who* assumes this position is unimportant for the perpetuation of domination, as long as the position is simply occupied.

According to Adorno, the commodities created by the culture industry are devoid of use-value – or in other words, useless. However, these commodities disguise their uselessness. 'In reality, the utility gained by recipients from their culture industry consumption is a fetish, just as the commodities of the cultural industry are themselves fetishes'. For this reason, Adorno rejects the common objection to the critique of the culture industry that 'life is chaotic, and the media orient individuals, helping them to overcome the chaos by structuring it':[96]

The most ambitious defense of the culture industry today celebrates its spirit, which might safely be called ideology, as an ordering factor. In a supposedly chaotic world it provides human beings with something like standards for orientation, and that alone seems worthy of approval. However, what its defenders imagine is preserved by the culture industry is in fact all the more thoroughly destroyed by it. ... The idea of an object-

---

92   Adorno, '2. Fassung / Frankfurt, 2. März 1968. / Weiter 3. III. 68' (TWA, Ts 48147–8, note written as a typescript with hand-made underlinings [probably to mark repetitions of words]; all crossed out). It appears that this note was to follow a passage in 'Late Capitalism or Industrial Society'; it would have come after 'seem to be under a curse' (Adorno 2003q, p. 121). Adorno presumably revisited the older text for the purpose of self-reflection before the reissue of *Dialectic of Enlightenment*, which he probably wanted to revise more than he ultimately did.

93   Haug 1986, p. 6.

94   Adorno 2004b, p. 94; cf. Adorno 2003q, p. 116. 'In this way, Adorno views Nietzsche's thought on autonomy as superseded by history, which is itself subject to the dialectic of enlightenment. For Adorno, even Nietzsche's radical critique of the flattening tendencies of the modern age, encapsulated in the saying "[n]o shepherd and a herd", has become a matter of course for omnipresent domination' (Maras 2002, p. 71).

95   'No shepherd and one herd! Each wants the same, each is the same, and whoever feels differently goes voluntarily into the insane asylum' (Nietzsche 2006, p. 10).

96   Kausch 1988, p. 108.

ively binding order, huckstered to people because it is so lacking for them, has no claims if it does not prove itself internally and in confrontation with human beings. But this is precisely what no product of the culture industry would engage in. The concepts of order which it hammers into human beings are always those of the status quo.[97]

From the start, the culture industry classifies the detailed and heterogenous, subordinating them to its own liquidating schematism; the expectation that subjects 'should, from the first, relate sensuous multiplicity to fundamental concepts ... is denied to the subject by industry'.[98] The aspiration for uniqueness is standardised, satisfied with standard commodities which adorn themselves with attributes of exclusivity and individuality.[99]

The question of use-value, of the subjective utility of a commodity, involves the question of the needs of that commodity's consumers. 'Need is a social category; nature as "drive" is contained within it', Adorno claims. Yet this drive 'is so socially mediated that its natural side never appears immediately, but always only as socially produced. The appeal to nature in relation to this or that need is always merely the mask of denial and domination'.[100] The capitalist mode of production enables both the spatial and temporal separation of need from the reshaping of nature necessary to fulfil need, making it possible for this process to be socialised. 'Need, in contrast to the action which satisfies it, is already an historical product',[101] and has emancipated itself from the immediate compulsion of nature: 'It is precisely not need that constitutes the commodity. Commodity value is not derived from need but from objective conditions of production of which need is an element but only in the last instance, that is, mediated by the interest to get rid of the stuff'.[102]

Mass consumption of the culture industry's commodities prompts their makers and apologists to point out the inevitability of 'standard products' being

---

97   Adorno 1975, pp. 16–17. 'The culture industry, whose products ... cause consumers to
      remain perpetually fixed in their essence, produces the status quo as a tranquilliser. It
      is a status quo industry' (Glasenapp 2006, p. 174).

98   Adorno and Horkheimer 2002, p. 98.

99   One contribution of the oft-cited media critic Neil Postman was to show on the basis of
      the medium of television that an essential function of offerings by the mass media is to
      avoid division into programme areas: 'The problem is not that television presents us with
      entertaining subject matter but that all subject matter is presented as entertaining, which
      is another issue altogether' (Postman 2005, p. 87).

100   Adorno 2017c, p. 102.

101   Pohrt 1995, p. 118.

102   Adorno 2018c, p. 159.

used 'to meet the same needs at countless locations'.[103] However, Adorno's critique concerns not only standardised production, but the very needs it ostensibly fulfils: 'these needs – which are not really needs at all – are bad insofar as they are directed towards a fulfilment that cheats us out of this very fulfilment. The social mediation of need – as mediated by capitalist society – has reached a point where need comes into contradiction with itself'.[104] Adorno identifies this situation as one of 'mass deception'[105] and 'total social delusion'.[106] The deception in question here is less of a case of directed manipulation than of the eager promotion of the misconception that mass culture is the culture of the masses.[107] The concept of mass culture Adorno uses in 'The Schema of Mass Culture' is ultimately dropped in *Dialectic of Enlightenment* 'in order to exclude from the outset the interpretation agreeable to its advocates: that it is a matter of something like a culture that arises spontaneously from the masses themselves, the contemporary form of popular art. From the latter, the culture industry must be distinguished in the extreme'.[108]

'Because, therefore, on one hand, one cannot become aware of the ideologies of people merely by the technique of questioning them; and because, on the other, one must take into account that the ideologies themselves are largely functions of the influence exerted on them by supposed or real mental structures', Adorno calls for 'concern with the relationship between the content of social stimuli and social reactions'.[109] Understood thusly, all sociological research into cause and effect[110] would be futile 'in view of the favourite question of what television actually does to human beings, given that not a single study on the effect of a programme or episode would be able to demonstrate measurable changes in the victims. Yet even overrated common sense would have to recognise that cumulative effect stands in proportion to stimuli'.[111] Elsewhere, Adorno writes the following regarding empirical research into the effects of the media:

---

103 Adorno and Horkheimer 2002, p. 95; cf. also Adorno 2005g, pp. 55–6.
104 Adorno 2017c, pp. 102–3.
105 Adorno and Horkheimer 2002, p. 94.
106 Adorno 2005f, p. 206.
107 In a lecture from 1964, Adorno emphasised again 'that by apparently being allowed to partake in so-called cultural goods, the masses are actually cheated out of what these goods are about' (Adorno 1964, p. 57).
108 Adorno 1975, p. 12; cf. Glasenapp 2006, pp. 170–1.
109 Adorno 2000a, p. 85.
110 Cf. Kausch 1988, pp. 218–23.
111 Adorno 2003u, p. 242.

Since the material aspires to affect the unconscious, direct questioning would not help. Preconscious or unconscious effects are inaccessible
to direct verbalization by those being questioned. They would produce
either rationalizations [in a psychoanalytic sense] or abstract statements
to the effect that television 'entertains' them.[112]

When research focuses solely on reaction, it forgets that 'reactions, being something mediated, derivative and secondary, do not have anything like the certainty ascribed to them'.[113] Produced on a mass-scale and for the masses under
capital, the products of the culture industry and all cultural commodities are
hopeless copies of art. According to Adorno, the central element of art and
its works is autonomy, which, 'having freed itself from cultic function and its
images, was nourished by the idea of humanity'.[114] In spite of existing in a society already reshaped by economy, early-bourgeois autonomous art was anti-
economic, de-mythologising and enlightening. Its goal was 'to wipe out the
power of images over man'[115] and to use creative freedom to deliver altern-
atives to the prevailing conditions of the day in a form which would enable
an experience beyond the realm of the purely factual. Where culture produces autonomous artworks as epiphenomena, it maintains its own contradiction from within, continuing to exist as 'the social antithesis of society'[116]
which points beyond the objective appearance of what is given: 'Artworks
detach themselves from the empirical world and bring forth another world, one
opposed to the empirical world as if this other world too were an autonomous
entity'.[117]

If art was once at least ideally autonomous with its works standing in contradiction to bourgeois society, it has lost this essential purpose in late capitalism:
'Nothing remains of the autonomy of art – that artworks should be considered
better than they consider themselves to be arouses indignation in culture customers – other than the fetish character of the commodity, regression to the
archaic fetishism in the origin of art: To this extent the contemporary attitude
to art is regressive'.[118] Having lost even its contingent autonomy, the artwork
now submits affirmatively to the society of which it is still merely an element.

---

112   Adorno 2005g, pp. 53–4.
113   Adorno 2000a, p. 85.
114   Adorno 2002a, p. 1.
115   Adorno 2005b, p. 140.
116   Adorno 2002a, p. 8.
117   Adorno 2002a, p. 1.
118   Adorno 2002a, p. 17.

Moreover, because it is made into 'something merely factual, even art's mimetic element, itself incompatible with whatever is purely a thing, is bartered off as a commodity'.[119]

At the same time, Adorno believes that art did possess the character of a commodity even before the onset of capitalism:

> That character is not new: it is the fact that art now dutifully admits to being a commodity, abjures its autonomy and proudly takes its place among consumer goods, that has the charm of novelty. ... Pure works of art, which negated the commodity character of society by simply follow-ing their own inherent laws, were at the same time always commodities. To the extent that, up to the eighteenth century, artists were protected from the market by patronage, they were subject to the patrons and their purposes instead. The purposelessness of the great modern work of art is sustained by the anonymity of the market. The latter's demands are so diversely mediated that the artist is exempted from any particular claim, although only to a certain degree, since his autonomy, being merely tol-erated, has been attended throughout bourgeois history by a moment of untruth, which has culminated now in the social liquidation of art.[120]

What is novel about the culture industry is that it opposes itself with an all-encompassing tolerance to what could be better: to both better artworks and a better world, a world which autonomous artworks aim for:

> The successful fusion of waking life and dream life however can allow itself a certain tolerance with regard to ideals. They are accepted as an ahistorical given along with others and the honour which they owe to their opposition to life becomes a means of vindicating them as legitim-ate and successful elements of real life. A great poet is almost as good as a great inventor or talent scout, just as long as the standing of the work protects us from having to read any of it.
>
> With the liquidation of its opposition to empirical reality art assumes a parasitic character. Inasmuch as it now appears itself as reality, which is supposed to stand in for the reality out there, it tends to relate back to culture as its own object.

---

119   Ibid.; on Adorno's concept of mimesis see for example Kausch 1988, pp. 145–6.
120   Adorno and Horkheimer 2002, p. 127.

In self-described postmodernity, where self-examination takes precedence over all else, the art-products regarded as particularly intelligent and successful are precisely those which refer to themselves or other art-products. This is often done with an ironic gesture, as if to say: don't take any of this too seriously! Mass-produced art 'has taken that alienation of the masses from art, blindly sustained in life by society, up into the process of production as its presupposition, lives from it and deliberately reproduces it. The work of art becomes its own material and forms the technique of reproduction and presentation, actually a technique for the distribution of a real object'.[121] Art itself responded to this with pop art, before the latter was equated with pop itself in a deliberate misunderstanding.[122]

> The self-reflection of culture brings a levelling down process in its wake. Inasmuch as any and every product refers back to what has already been preformed, the mechanism of adjustment towards which business interest drives it anyway is imposed upon it once again. Whatever is to pass muster must already have been handled, manipulated and approved by hundreds of thousands of people before anyone can enjoy it.[123]

In place of alternative concepts to existing reality, the culture industry merely presents what is always the same in the guise of the eternally new. In doing so, it makes 'even escape from a world determined by the principle of realistic self-denial into a part of that world', passing off 'a dreamless art as the fulfilment of dreams, and smiling or jovial renunciation as a compensation for renunciation'.[124]

Adorno already addresses the relationship between success and self-denial in a passage of the original version of 'On the Fetish-Character in Music and the Regression of Listening'. Although omitted from the version of the essay republished in *Dissonanzen*, this passage is helpful for assessing Horkheimer and Adorno's understanding of the fetish-character of the commodity:

---

121 Adorno 2004b, pp. 64–5.
122 Many artworks indeed 'seem to have been conceived by their authors as ironic goods' (Palmier 2006, p. 10). Pop art's original intention of using an ironic concept of art as commodity production and of artworks as commodities in order to get to the heart of the world of commodities did not ultimately work in its favour. Instead, pop art saw the inversion of its argument become legitimated, which maintains that if all art is equally commodity, then all commodities are also art.
123 Adorno 2004b, p. 67.
124 Wiggershaus 1995, p. 337.

Scarcity also always guarantees child prodigies their market. Yet it is precisely this market in its new condition which does not appear to be free from opposing tendencies .... The reason is probably that because success here is achieved without arduous labour by those who do not yet count as legal persons in competition, the prevailing fetishisation of success appears compromised: Why buy the expensive [Fritz] Kreisler ticket when there is someone who can play just as well and only legally perform for free? Not to mention that the values of maturity, interiority and personality in musical reproduction must amount to hot air if the designer is still playing with cars instead of reverently buying them.[125]

It is possible that Hans Mayer's misunderstanding of Adorno's essay, which took issue with precisely this passage (see Chapter Four of the present study), was the reason the latter was omitted from the republication. Mayer wrote that '[t]he cult of the child prodigy certainly points to entirely different phenomena than Adorno would lead one to believe. The notion that that the child prodigy "compromises the fetishisation of success" ... hardly evokes anything tangible'.[126] In response, Adorno again clarified what he meant with the passage: 'It's not clear to me why Herr Mayer doesn't want to understand the claim that the child prodigy compromises the fetishisation. The point is simply that the amount of exertion and labour demanded by the bourgeois as proof of the dignity of any given achievement is apparently not produced by the child prodigy, and that the bourgeois is deeply suspicious given that from the start, the achievement of the child prodigy cannot be represented as a labour-equivalent'.[127]

What Adorno described in 1938 as the 'fetishisation of success' is referred to in the culture industry chapter of *Dialectic of Enlightenment* as the 'myth of success'.[128] In retrospect, it appears Adorno had used the term fetish to

---

125   Adorno 1938, p. 329. In 1929, Benjamin expressed precisely this sentiment in 'On the Image of Proust', an essay with which Adorno was familiar (cf. Letter from Adorno to Benjamin, 10 November 1938 [Adorno and Benjamin 1999, p. 281]): 'After all, nothing makes more sense to the model pupils of life than the notion that a great achievement is the fruit of toil, misery, and disappointment. The idea that happiness could have a share in beauty would be too much of a good thing, something that their *ressentiment* would never get over' (Benjamin 2005d, p. 239).

126   Mayer 1998, pp. 384–5.

127   Adorno, 'Notizen zu Mayer' (MHA 1.47–8). Gerhard Henschel points out that under National Socialism, pre-existing aversion to so-called child prodigies was exploited by none other than Alfred Rosenberg, chief Nazi ideologue for anti-Semitic propaganda (cf. Henschel 2008, p. 95).

128   Adorno and Horkheimer 2002, p. 106.

describe nothing other than the persistence of an irrational residue on the wholly enlightened earth.

In any case, the culture industry appropriates the notion that things could be different and creates a pale copy of it: if art is the 'promise of happiness which gets broken',[129] then the culture industry provides its customers with a happiness surrogate – hence, the cynical running gag in the advertising industry of perpetual escape from perpetual routine. Yet this surrogate carries just as little credibility as a source of happiness for the culture industry itself as it does for its recipients.[130]

> [Anything which] resists can survive only by being incorporated. Once registered as diverging from the culture industry, it belongs to it as the land reformer does to capitalism. [Righteous] indignation [at reality] is the trademark of those with a new idea to sell.[131]

This idea, of course, does not stay new for long, let alone continue to resist. Rather, it obeys 'the general laws of capital':[132] 'What is new in the phase of mass culture compared to that of late liberalism is the exclusion of the new. The machine is rotating on the spot'.[133] After all, 'once industrial management of all cultural goods was established as a totality, it also won control over the aesthetically nonconforming'.[134] If successful, today's artistic avant-garde becomes tomorrow's design, whether it wants to be or not: 'It's hailing impositions and permanent design'.[135] The banalisation of this prognosis owes to a culture industry which fabricates fashions in the same manner in which the fashion industry fabricates clothing: *if* the commodity is sold, a new one must be produced; *because* it is sold constantly, it must be produced anew just as constantly. Culture is *manufactured* under the primacy of capitalism, which stipulates that everything be available in abundance and that everything be desired, and hence acquired and consumed, for the purpose of turnover and economic growth.

When what was once regarded as art became valorised economically, all cultural expressions conformed to the market and its demands. If autonom-

---

129   Adorno 2002a, p. 136.
130   Cf. Steinert 2003a, p. 138 and Auer, Bonacker and Müller-Doohm 1999, p. 125.
131   Adorno and Horkheimer 2002, p. 104.
132   Adorno and Horkheimer 2002, p. 105.
133   Adorno and Horkheimer 2002, p. 106.
134   Adorno 2007c, p. 9.
135   Kapielski 1999, p. 33.

ous artworks also existed as commodities in early capitalism, they only did so in circulation, whereas under the totality of the capital-relation, cultural commodities are already produced as commodities. The recipient of autonomous artworks could give himself over to these objects, which is to say he could 'do justice to the object's qualitative moments'.[136] In contrast, Adorno claims, '[s]ince the beginning of the industrial era an art has been in vogue which is adept at promoting the right attitudes and which has entered into alliance with reification insofar as it proffers precisely for a disenchanted world, for the realm of the prosaic and even the banausic, a poetry of its own nourished upon the work ethic'.[137] Having come to be manufactured in a mode of production involving the division of labour, the autonomy of the artificial degrades because it no longer exhibits the autonomous features of an artistically engaged subject, a 'social agent'[138] who objectifies his experience in the artwork. 'A reproducing collective is generally not able to convey "subjective" experience'.[139] After all, '[w]hat falls victim to the elimination process is not just individual randomness, but also everything that only the thinking individual has by way of objective insight'.[140] The degradation of the artwork's autonomy results in an obliteration of the 'qualitative element', which Adorno defined as the artwork's use-value: the 'essence'[141] of art.

From the perspective of the theory of economy, the elimination of the qualitative leads Adorno to a problem which would later become acute in *Negative Dialectics*, namely, the question of the relationship between use-value as a qualitative phenomenon and exchange-value as a quantitative one. In *Dialectic of Enlightenment*, this problem of use-value – aptly described by Kornelia Hafner as 'the fetishism of use-value'[142] – is only made explicit in a few passages. One such passage occurs in a discussion of cultural goods in the culture industry chapter, when Adorno writes that 'in the nineteenth or early twentieth century … use value was not dragged along as a mere appendage by exchange value but was developed as a precondition of the latter, to the social benefit of works of

---

136   Adorno 2007b, p. 43.
137   Adorno 2004b, p. 61.
138   Adorno 2002a, p. 43.
139   Kausch 1988, p. 173.
140   Adorno 2003aa, p. 496.
141   Adorno and Horkheimer 2002, p. 128.
142   Hafner 1993. This description is apt insofar as use-value appears as a real entity even though it is actually the conceptual result of an economic – that is, a social – relation; it is not the commodity itself, but rather an aspect of the commodity which it inseparable from the commodity-form.

art'.[143] Here, it again becomes evident that Adorno does not conceive of *both* use-value and exchange-value as strictly economic categories, something for which Hans Mayer had already criticised him,[144] but rather one-sidedly views use-value as a precondition of exchange-value. Once again, Adorno neglects the opportunity to conceptualise the relationship between exchange-value and use-value in a decisively dialectical manner, and once again – as he had already done in his 'Fetish-Character' essay with regards to music specifically, and which he now does with regards to art in general – he insists upon the possibility of a 'paradoxical commodity ... so completely subject to the law of exchange that it is no longer exchanged', a commodity 'so blindly equated with use that it can no longer be used'.[145]

It is Adorno's intention to ascribe to culture – and especially art – a role which would enable it, in spite of its status as an element of capitalist totality, to also preserve a redemptive aspect external to capitalism. In order to do so, he needed to appeal to cultural commodities' appearance of immediacy,[146] which he sees as simultaneously untrue and true. The fact that the culture industry 'reduces' its products to the 'mere promise'[147] of enjoyment through advertising is abundantly clear. Yet this does not permit the conclusion that use-value 'is being replaced in the reception of cultural assets by exchange value', that 'enjoyment is giving way to being there and being in the know, connoisseurship by enhanced prestige',[148] as is claimed in the first edition of *Dialectic of Enlightenment*. Likely suspecting the inadmissibility of equating use-value with the way in which a commodity is used, Adorno and Horkheimer modify the first part of this sentence in the 1947 version, incorporating a more cautious phrasing: 'What *might be called* use value in the reception of cultural assets is being replaced by exchange value; enjoyment is giving way to being there and being in the know, connoisseurship by enhanced prestige'.[149]

---

143   Adorno and Horkheimer 2002, p. 130.
144   See Chapter 4, n. 123 of the present study.
145   Adorno and Horkheimer 2002, p. 131.
146   Cf. Adorno 2009c, p. 296.
147   Adorno and Horkheimer 2002, p. 131.
148   Adorno and Horkheimer 2002, pp. 128, 271.
149   Adorno and Horkheimer 2002, p. 128, emphasis added.

5   The Authors Have Not Mastered This Dilemma

On the occasion of the 1969 republication of *Dialectic of Enlightenment*, Adorno composed a draft for a new preface, which he sent to Horkheimer with a 'request for trashing'[150] – that is, for editing. 'Although the book did not hide its origin in materialist dialectics', Adorno writes therein, 'it had already let go of their orthodoxy. Without recourse to elaborated economic analyses, which would be necessary in many places, the concept of domination was used, a heresy against Engels's polemic in *Anti-Dühring*'.[151]

In *Anti-Dühring*, Engels polemicised against Eugen Dühring's idea that a theory of society could be based solely on the categories of domination and violence.[152] For Engels, domination is the result of economic relations. Entirely in the spirit of the *Communist Manifesto*, he stipulates 'that *all* past history was the history of class struggles; that these warring classes of society are always the products of the modes of production and of exchange – in a word, of the *economic* conditions of their time; that the economic structure of society always furnishes the real basis, starting from which we can alone work out the ultimate explanation of the whole superstructure of juridical and political institutions as well as of the religious, philosophical and other ideas of a given historical period'.[153] In contrast, Adorno insists that the question of domination be addressed on its own terms:

> It would seem to me that the revival of the category of domination, which notoriously stands in sharp opposition to Engels's *Anti-Dühring*, goes back to *Dialectic of Enlightenment* by Horkheimer and myself. Yet theory did not merely regress, in spite of accusations occasionally made against us. Rather, this revival expresses something very real and serious ...: the tendency – and I explicitly mean tendency – for contemporary society, if its political forms are compelled to radically follow the economic ones, to head directly, in a word, towards meta-economic forms, forms which are no longer defined according to the classical mechanism of exchange.

---

150   Letter from Adorno to Horkheimer, 24 January 1969 (Adorno and Horkheimer 2006, p. 838).

151   Adorno 2003c, p. 7.

152   Cf. Engels 1987a, pp. 165–6, 171; Vollgraf 1988 offers an overview of the reasons which occasioned Engels to compose this book (with Marx's support), as do Dowe and Tenfelde 1980.

153   Engels 1987a, p. 26; cf. letter from Engels to Joseph Bloch, 21 September 1890 (Engels 2001, p. 34): 'According to the materialist view of history, the determining factor in history is, *in the final analysis*, the production and reproduction of actual life'.

The existence of such tendencies should not be particularly controversial among us. Yet this means the concept of domination gains a new preponderance with respect to purely economic processes. Structurally, an immanent socio-economic movement seems to produce or reveal forms which in turn emerge from the determinative context of pure economy and pure immanent social dialectics. To a certain extent, these forms become independent, and in no way for the better.[154]

In his draft for the preface to the new edition of *Dialectic of Enlightenment*, Adorno elaborates:

The deviation from purely economic thinking nevertheless has an economic reason. The object of Marxian political economy was liberalism as reality and ideology. With its progression to an economy which does leave intact the pseudo-market, yet otherwise depends on the powers which both rule over production and determine circulation and distribution, liberal laws of the market lose their meaning. Therefore, so too does the economic concept of economy.[155]

Here, Adorno takes up an insight from 'Reflections on Class Theory': economy as market-mediated exchange is a particular case of economy more generally, one which became totalising in late capitalism and encroached upon realms which had previously existed outside of the formerly limited sphere of economy.

Adorno develops this insight as follows:

Domination was always contained within political economy. The sale of the commodity of labour-power, from which Marx deduces the class-relation, actually presupposes the class-relation as compulsion to sell labour-power. Thus, no longer is domination unexplainable due to its abstractness; rather, it is the form assumed by economic reason long corroded by irrationality. ... As a consequence, it would seem that categories of political economy such as surplus-value, pauperisation and even class must be redefined. Critical theory today faces the dilemma of either strictly adhering to these categories and thereby blatantly missing what is obviously the case, or weakening the theoretical skeleton in an attempt

---

154   Adorno 2003i, pp. 583–4.
155   Adorno 2003c, p. 7.

to accommodate changes in reality and thereby falling victim to conceptual positivism, as numerous contemporary theorists have done. The authors have not mastered this dilemma; it is the limit of this book and remains the limit of critical theory. Blind actionism is encouraged as long as these categories are not formulated both radically and prudently, in a manner which is appropriate yet not accommodating. The ever more apparent irrational elements of prevailing reality addressed by the book raise doubts as to whether what is demanded can be accomplished at all. Regarding the dilemma, which they do not obscure, the authors believe they are most likely to account for it by using the once-valid critical concepts, not for the purpose of erecting them as invariants, which they cannot be on their own terms, but rather to exhaust them in the process of reflection and perhaps take them forward.[156]

Two months after receiving this draft from Adorno, Horkheimer answers as follows: 'The elaborations of the concept of domination still seem a bit unsuitable to me, above all because they would require us to mention a series of other aspects which necessitate the editor's note today. In my opinion, we should definitely drop the sentence on Engels's polemic against Dühring, "Without recourse to elaborated economic analyses ..."'.[157] Apparently, Horkheimer believes either that the economic analysis of *Dialectic of Enlightenment* is already sufficient, or alternatively – and this is more likely given the direction Horkheimer's thought had taken in the meantime – that the critique of economy is no longer a suitable instrument for the critique and ultimate overcoming of existing society.

A number of critics of the Adornian understanding of economy might have been able to save themselves the trouble of proving that the authors of *Dialectic of Enlightenment* were unable to unambiguously define their economic categories. After all, Adorno himself openly admits here that they have 'not mastered' the dilemma of 'either strictly adhering' to the categories of political economy or 'weakening the theoretical skeleton'. This dilemma gave rise to doubts about 'whether what is demanded can be accomplished at all', while also demarcating, in the words of Hans-Georg Backhaus, 'a limit in the state of knowledge, not only with regards to economics in the narrower sense, but also with regards to social theory in general'.[158]

---

156   Ibid.
157   Letter from Horkheimer to Adorno, 25 March 1969 (Adorno and Horkheimer 2006, p. 838).
158   Backhaus 2004a, p. 29.

In his lecture 'Late Capitalism or Industrial Society' from 1968, one year before the draft of the new preface to *Dialectic of Enlightenment* was composed, Adorno already expresses scepticism regarding the possibility of adequate knowledge of society:

> It is conceivable that contemporary society [resists coherent theorization]. Marx had it easier [insofar as the elaborated system of liberalism lay before him in scholarship]. He needed only to inquire whether capitalism in its own dynamic categories fit into this system in order to produce a quasi-systematic theory of his own, in determinate negation of the system he found before him. In the meantime, the market economy has become so full of holes as to [make a mockery of] any such confrontation. The irrational nature of contemporary society inhibits a rational account of it in the realm of theory.[159]

Society has become total; a place outside of it can no longer be assumed, not even theoretically. Society therefore precludes thoughts which would critically transcend it by eluding totality's grasp.

---

159   Adorno 2003q, p. 115.

CHAPTER 8

Garbage

> Zum Beispiel, daß man beinah nichts / bekommt, wenn man nicht
> zahlt / daß niemand jemand irgendetwas / glaubt, wenn man nicht
> prahlt // Auch wenn der pünktlich Gereifte / mich laut dafür ver-
> höhnt – / noch hab ich mich / noch hab ich mich / an nichts /
> gewöhnt
> (Take, for example, that you get basically nothing if you don't pay, or
> that no one ever takes your word for anything if you don't show off.
> Even though people who act their age might make fun of me, I've
> never gotten used to anything)
>
> HEINZ-RUDOLF KUNZE, Noch hab' ich mich an nichts gewöhnt

∴

1   Not a Single Missing Link

In a letter from October 1947, Adorno writes to his parents regarding his work
on 'a very long manuscript written in the Nietzschean aphoristic form, relating
to a relatively wide range of philosophical objects, but above all the question
of what has fundamentally become of "life" under the conditions of monopoly
capitalism'.[1] After all, as Adorno states in *Minima Moralia: Reflections on the
Damaged Life* – the title under which the 'very long manuscript' was eventually published – the 'perspective of life', formerly the genuine substance of all
philosophy, 'has passed into an ideology which conceals the fact that there is
life no longer'.[2] A comparison of Adorno's aphorism 'Vandals' with the aphorism 'Leisure and Idleness' by Nietzsche reveals *Minima Moralia* not only to be
formally the 'most Nietzschean'[3] of Adorno's works, but also at times to come
quite close substantively to Nietzsche as well. In 'Vandals', Adorno writes the
following:

---

1   Letter from Adorno to his parents, 31 October 1945 (Adorno 2006b, p. 236).
2   Adorno 2005b, p. 15.
3   Jay 1984, p. 42.

Everybody must have projects all the time. The maximum must be extrac-
ted from leisure. This is planned, used for undertakings, crammed with
visits to every conceivable site or spectacle, or just with the fastest possible locomotion. The shadow of all this falls on intellectual work. It is
done with a bad conscience, as if it had been poached from some urgent,
even if only imaginary occupation.[4]

This echoes an observation Nietzsche made in the nineteenth century:

Already one is ashamed of keeping still; long reflection almost gives
people a bad conscience. One thinks with a watch in hand, as one eats
lunch with an eye on the financial pages – one lives like someone who
might always 'miss out on something'. 'Rather do anything than nothing' –
even this principle is a cord to strangle all culture and all higher taste. ...
For life in a hunt for profit constantly forces people to expend their spirit
to the point of exhaustion .... More and more, work gets all good conscience on its side; the desire for joy already calls itself a 'need to recuper-
ate' and is starting to be ashamed of itself. 'One owes it to one's health' –
that is what one says when caught on an excursion in the countryside.
Soon we may well reach the point where one can't give in to the desire for
a *vita contemplativa* (that is, taking a walk with ideas and friends) without
self-contempt and a bad conscience.[5]

In general, the substantive proximity between Adorno and Nietzsche can be
described thusly: both understand modernity along with its capitalist forms of
intercourse not as an open opportunity for genuine enlightenment, but as one
which has already been wasted. Just like Adorno, Nietzsche views the course of
human history from the standpoint of the immediate present in order to interpret it as a failed attempt at self-liberation from mythology. In other words, he
too recognises the dialectic in enlightenment.[6]

---

4 Adorno 2005b, p. 138. Elsewhere, Adorno remarks along these lines that '[t]he principle
   of [conduct] as "doing", [as accomplishing, ultimately as] society's production process [is]
   finally traceable back to the [figure of *the busy person*]', even going so far as to say that '[f]or
   the bourgeois: [vitality = business in getting something done]' (Adorno 2007a, pp. 37–8).
5 Nietzsche 2001, pp. 183–4.
6 Henning Ottmann identifies three developmental phases in Nietzsche's philosophy of enlightenment: '1) the freethinking (*Freigeisterei*) which becomes 2) the critique of enlightenment by enlightenment in order to ultimately give way to 3) an ambiguous "new enlightenment", which is to be understood as both the critique of enlightenment as well as its regener-
   ation' (Ottmann 1985, p. 10).

Nietzsche had pushed the idea of the enlightenment to the limit and to its reversal. He obscured nothing, but cried to the world that no argument against murder could be deduced from unfettered reason. Like critical theory, he recognized that enlightenment had turned into its opposite, and he then attempted to master chaos with an exaggerated individualism.[7]

In his lecture course *Problems of Moral Philosophy*, Adorno says of Nietzsche that 'of all the so-called great philosophers I owe him by far the greatest debt – more even than to Hegel'.[8] Adorno does criticise Nietzsche for having 'lacked the concept of determinate negation', arguing that 'if one counterposes an other to that which is recognised as negative, this other must contain in a new form that which is negated'. Nevertheless, he also maintains that Nietzsche's work 'really does involve the attempt – born out of despair over what was once recognised as bad – to simultaneously conjure up and counterpose a new order, new values as he always referred to it, out of nothing. One can say that it is a thinking which relentlessly sprouts aerial roots'.[9] Adorno's verdict on Nietzsche in this passage is probably not quite correct, for as Henning Ottmann emphasises, Nietzsche's late theory 'lends itself to being misunderstood in two ways: as mere anti-enlightenment, and as mere scientific anti-mythology', whereas it 'should be regarded as enlightening the "fallacies" of religion, metaphysics and morality on the one hand, and as drawing upon the power of myth on the other'.[10] The tendency to fundamentally misunderstand Nietzsche would seem to have far more to do with Nietzsche's own failure to recognise that what 'he himself called life'[11] is inadequate for achieving what Adorno refers to as determinate negation – something which can only be accomplished via the whole which dominates 'life'.

7   Pütz 1981, p. 107; cf. Adorno and Horkheimer 2002, p. 106.
8   Adorno 2000c, p. 172; cf. Demirović 1999a, p. 648. On his own appropriation of Nietzsche's philosophy and especially of the latter's critique of metaphysics cf. Adorno 2000b, p. 2: 'I recall my own early experience as a schoolboy when I first came across Nietzsche, who, as any of you who are familiar with his work will know, is not sparing in his complaints about metaphysics .... When I sought the advice of someone considerably older than myself, I was told that it was too early for me to understand metaphysics but that I would be able to do so one day. ... So that the naive postponement and procrastination that I experienced is not really so accidental; it seems to have something to do with the subject matter itself, and especially with the general procedure which philosophy adopts in relation to metaphysics'.
9   Adorno quoted in Adorno, Gadamer and Horkheimer 1989, p. 116; along similar lines cf. Schmidt 1963.
10   Ottmann 1985, pp. 32–3.
11   Adorno quoted in Adorno, Gadamer and Horkheimer 1989, p. 112.

Marx discovered the overarching coercive mechanisms in effect between all individuals in society, mechanisms which classify individuals and which in doing so ultimately give society its specific, capitalist form. From here, Adorno goes on to examine both the manner in which society's coercion of socialised individuals takes place and the results of this coercion. This marks a shift in focus onto questions concerning individuality's conditions and possibilities – its expressions in professional life, leisure time, culture, art, sport, consumption and daily routine, and the ways in which it relates to science, reason, philosophy and art. In short: Adorno is concerned with the remaining possibilities for self-determination, for unregulated experience which is neither standardised nor determined in advance, for accessing and generating culture and for social knowledge – that is, with the remaining possibilities for living life, given that the vision of life offered by bourgeois society as an individual promise of happiness is rendered *de facto* unliveable by the existence of bourgeois society, where the prevailing and totalising capital-relation forms the backdrop of socially mediated domination, repression and restriction both in general and particular. 'Private life is, more than we can even imagine, mere reprivatization; the realities to which men hold have become unreal. "Life itself is a lifeless thing" [*Das Leben lebt nicht*]'.[12]

'*Das Leben lebt nicht*' is placed as a motto before the first section of *Minima Moralia*;[13] in the authorised English translation of the book, it is rendered as '[l]ife does not live'. This sentence is taken from a novel by the eighteenth-century Austrian writer Ferdinand Kürnberger titled *Der Amerikamüde* (*The One Who Grew Tired of America*) – a particularly resonant title for the situation in which Adorno found himself while working on *Minima Moralia*.[14] Alexander García Düttmann notes that this motto's 'almost corny yet also emotionally moving turn against itself' can also be readily understood as a 'statement against *Lebensphilosophie*'.[15] Kürnberger's sentence, which 'sounds vitalistic and presumably was also once meant as such ... becomes in the context of Adorno's philosophy the (self-)knowledge that the return of what is always the same can only be recognised from the perspective of what is different'.[16] In

---

12 Adorno 1989, p. 273.
13 Adorno 2005b, p. 19.
14 See Kürnberger 1985, p. 420.
15 García Düttmann 2004, p. 26.
16 Scheit 2003, p. 25. The insight that life doesn't live any longer can be found almost word-for-word in Nietzsche's work: 'Life, equal vitality, the vibration and exuberance of life pushed back into the smallest structures, all the rest impoverished of life. ... The whole does not live at all any more: it is cobbled together, calculated, synthetic, an artifact' (Nietzsche 2007, p. 245; cf. Fischer 1999, p. 147, n. 208).

a 1952 letter to Leo Löwenthal, Adorno explains that his concern is with 'the concept of life as a meaningful unity unfolding from within itself', which for him

> has ceased to possess any reality, much like the individual himself, and the ideological function of biographies consists in demonstrating to people with reference to various models that something like life still exists, with all the strong qualities of life. And the task of biography is to prove this in particular empirical contexts which those people who no longer have any life can easily claim as their own. Life itself, in a highly abstract form, has become ideology, and the very abstractness that distinguishes it from older, fuller conceptions of life is what makes it practicable (the vitalist and existentialist concepts of life are stages on this path).[17]

Eight years later, in October 1960, Adorno mentions that he is beginning

> to question whether the sentence 'life does not live', whether the non-existence of experience, really applies today. Won't the explosion of catastrophe now release a much older horror? Is it not rather the case that what's new is the *self-consciousness* of these things rather than the things themselves? ... Standardisation is the newest historical form of old untruth, of unreconciled generality, ultimately of mythical repetition, but only the fire of what is newest illuminates the darkness of what is ancient.[18]

The old ever-sameness, which Adorno refers to as myth, stands opposed to a strong concept of experience which would demand novelty – would demand that what is be more than merely what has always been, even when the latter appears in fashionable costume.

As Adorno writes at the beginning of *Minima Moralia*,

> the relation between life and production, which in reality debases the former to an ephemeral appearance of the latter, is totally absurd. Means and end are inverted. A dim awareness of this perverse *quid pro quo* has still not been quite eradicated from life. Reduced and degraded essence tenaciously resists the magic that transforms it into a façade. The change

---

17   Letter from Adorno to Löwenthal, 25. November 1942 (Adorno and Löwenthal 1984, pp. 158–9; translation from Claussen 2008, pp. 5–6).
18   Adorno quoted in Tiedemann 1994, p. 32.

in the relations of production themselves depends largely on what takes place in the 'sphere of consumption', the mere reflection of production and the caricature of true life: in the consciousness and unconsciousness of individuals. Only by virtue of opposition to production, as still not wholly encompassed by this order, can men bring about another more worthy of human beings. Should the appearance of life, which the sphere of consumption itself defends for such bad reasons, be once entirely effaced, then the monstrosity of absolute production will triumph.[19]

As a consequence, Adorno describes the 'specific approach of *Minima Moralia*' as the attempt to present aspects of philosophy 'from the standpoint of subjective experience'.[20] According to this approach, 'the state of society dominated by the instrumental rationality of economic calculation is measured with regards to the compromised and submerged possibilities of subjective reaction, possibilities to which subjects themselves are subordinated'.[21]

Most of the aphorisms published in *Minima Moralia* in 1951 were written between 1944–5; these are located in the first two sections of the book. Also included in the final publication are another set of aphorisms originating between 1946–7, composing its third section.[22] Together, these aphorisms explore the question of 'whether man was made merely to exchange'[23] along with exchange itself – both as an action, but also primarily as a principle which has come to undergird the thinking and feeling of individuals, shaping them in its own image all the way down to their innermost being. In this way, the book also presents a model of solidarity with 'metaphysics at the time of its fall', which Adorno later advocates in *Negative Dialectics*: 'The smallest intramundane traits would be of relevance to the absolute, for the micrological view cracks the shells of what, measured by the subsuming cover concept, is helplessly isolated and explodes its identity, the delusion that it is but a specimen'.[24] In this passage, 'mere specimen' refers not only to the object of know-

---

19   Adorno 2005b, p. 15.
20   Adorno 2005b, p. 18.
21   Seel 2006, p. 35.
22   In a 1950 letter to his publisher Peter Suhrkamp, Adorno writes that he views this third part as 'incidentally by far the most important today' (letter from Adorno to Suhrkamp, 29 September 1950 [Adorno 2003z, p. 18]). On the origin of *Minima Moralia* cf. García Düttmann 2004, pp. 24–5.
23   Adorno 2005b, p. 195.
24   Adorno 2007h, p. 408.

ledge, but also to the individual who is defined as a social object, an element
of a negative totality. 'It has long been demonstrated that wage labour formed
the masses of the modern epoch, indeed created the worker himself'.[25] Taking this insight from Marx and Engels,[26] Adorno applies it to the individual
in general under existing conditions: this individual is 'not merely the biological basis, but the reflection of the social process; his consciousness of himself
as something in-itself is the illusion needed to raise his level of performance,
whereas in fact the individuated function in the modern economy as mere
agents of the law of value'.[27] In the 'modern economy' – that is, in capitalism[28] – the 'law of value', which features in Adorno's writings 'mainly in metaphorical form',[29] uses individuals as a means to override individuals. For its
own part, this law has become total 'with the complete hegemony of exchange
value';[30] its principle is that exchange of like for like which extends itself all
the way into 'the inner constitution of the individual', going beyond 'merely
his social role'. 'Only when the process that begins with the metamorphosis of
labour-power into a commodity has permeated men through and through and
objectified each of their impulses as formally commensurable variations of the
exchange relationship, is it possible for life to reproduce itself under the prevailing relations of production'.[31] In *Minima Moralia*, Adorno takes this insight
as the economy-theoretical explanation of the preponderance of the general
over the particular, which he would later criticise in *Negative Dialectics*: 'The
objective and ultimately absolute Hegelian spirit; the Marxist law of value that
comes into force without men being conscious of it – to an unleashed experience these are more evident than the prepared facts of a positivistic scientific
bustle which today extends to the naive prescientific consciousness. Only, to
the greater glory of objective cognition, that activity breaks men of the habit
of experiencing the real objectivity to which they are subjected in themselves
as well'.[32] Before the 'general course of the whole',[33] the individual is merely

---

25   Adorno 2005b, p. 228.
26   In *Anti-Dühring*, for example, Engels writes 'that modern large-scale industry has called
      into being on the one hand a proletariat, a class' (Engels 1987a, p. 145).
27   Adorno 2005b, pp. 228–9.
28   In *Negative Dialectics*, Adorno writes more specifically of 'Marx's Hegelian-trained the-
      ory of the law of value, which capitalism realizes over the heads of men' (Adorno 2007b,
      p. 199).
29   Editorial note by Tiedemann (Adorno 2006, p. 280, n. 2).
30   Adorno 2009a, p. 72.
31   Adorno 2005b, p. 229.
32   Adorno 2007b, pp. 300–1.
33   Adorno and Horkheimer 2002, p. 184.

a function of the principle of exchange; universal exchange limits the individual's actions (as well as his impulses and feelings) to the realm of the economic.

Under the dictate of the exchange of equivalents, the arbitrary injury caused by this exchange necessarily has 'something nonsensical and implausible about it'. For example, someone who gives a gift without expecting anything in return comes to be viewed with some suspicion, 'as if the gift were merely a trick'.[34] The ostensible friendliness appears as effrontery, as something that will in fact have to be paid back at some point, even if only because the recipient is 'unwilling to tolerate, in the chain of exchange acts whereby expenses are recovered, a single missing link'.[35] The irritating gap caused by this missing link serves as a reminder of the not yet fully integrated particular, of the individual's individuality. Yet at the same time, it is precisely the gapless 'chain of exchange acts' – the constant circulation of values, niceties and emotions – which constitutes the remaining life of individuals, whose purpose is exhausted in their function as agents of the law of value. To cite one example of this, the president of Germany 'summoned an extraordinary meeting in Bellevue Palace consisting of twelve philosophers, sociologists, political scientists and theologians from all the world's important cultural spheres. For one whole day, they discussed what it is that still holds the world together in the first place' before reaching the following conclusion: 'society is dependent on giving and taking'.[36] On the one hand, this anecdote may sound like a mockery of the efforts of those theorists 'from all the world's important cultural spheres', given that all they ultimately discovered was that the world is 'still' held together by what has always forced it together at the expense of any number of victims. Adorno also recognises this basic insight, but the point for him is 'to escape from this process of exchanging like for like'.[37] Yet on the other hand, the *Realpolitiker*-president obviously revealed himself to be a rationalist: the instrumental deployment of giving wants to be equivalently remunerated; the means should not contain a 'surplus' with respect to the ends. At the same time, however, no 'surplus' at all is expected from the ends with respect to the means either. The idea of something achieved which does not offset the investment in its achievement, but is nonetheless rewarding, is regarded as irrational – and presumably even is. Not even rationality escapes blind application unscathed.

---

34   Adorno 2005b, p. 42.
35   Adorno 2005b, p. 15.
36   Kornelius 2008, p. 13.
37   Adorno 2006a, p. 93.

2   No Happiness without Fetishism

If the economy was once a means to the end of social reproduction, the two
are one and the same today. By now, members of society are members of an
economy which is synonymous with everything, even with the relationships of
individuals to themselves and others. Hence, as mentioned above, friendliness
exists under '*a priori* saleability', where 'the living has made itself, as something
living, a thing, equipment'. '[F]rom genuine kindness to the hysterical fit of
rage', everything previously alive has become 'capable of manipulation'[38] in
order that that the gift which has nothing to do with own concept – something
freely given with nothing gained in return (as Nietzsche claims, 'we acquire no
rights by making gifts'[39]) – will yield the return already implied in its giving. Yet
in contrast to how cultural pessimism would have it, this does not mean that all
friendliness is simply fake – the situation actually is more dire. Although friendliness is indeed severed both from its 'instinctual basis and from the self',[40] it
is still 'genuine'; what alone stands in doubt is genuineness itself. 'Among the
concepts to which, after the dissolution of its religious and the formalization
of its autonomous norms, bourgeois morality has shrunk, that of genuineness
ranks highest. If nothing else can be bindingly required of man, then at the
least he should be wholly and entirely what he is'.[41] The word genuine should
not stand 'unquestioned, exempt from conceptual development';[42] it is not
simply a constant, but rather something which changes depending on what

---

38   Adorno 2005b, p. 230.

39   Nietzsche 1995, p. 200.

40   Adorno 2005b, p. 230.

41   Adorno 2005b, p. 152. A quotation from the 1950s reveals just how patronising and authoritarian one patriarch was while seeking to instruct the following generation how to
become a 'real person': 'Confronted with the *effective recognition of authority*, the task of
critique becomes to restrict this recognition in a rational manner in accordance with the
intellectual growth of the recogniser. In all areas where critique is in effect, the mature
human being is driven to revise opinions he has assumed due to his recognition of the
authority of parents, friends, books, comportment in his surroundings, etc. However, there
are also particular areas of life in which a free statement of personality must be able to
come into effect to the greatest possible extent. Precisely the important decisions in the
life of the human being cannot simply be handed over to the doctrines or advice of an
authority. Self-reflection and self-determination must, for example, become the source of
a human being's actual choice of religion, if this choice is to be the foundation of a genuine and responsible personality. For such decisions, critique must clear the way; in any
number of other cases, it is critique's task to set boundaries on the influence of authority'
(Strohal 1959, p. 405).

42   Adorno 2005b, p. 152.

it attempts to describe. While human beings may bear a number of deformities, they have 'no substratum beneath such "deformations", no ontic interior on which social mechanisms merely act externally: the deformation is not a sickness in men but in the society which begets its children with the "hereditary taint" that biologism projects on to nature'.[43] If society has become its own ideology, then human beings are the way they are under capital precisely because this benefits capital. In the aphorism 'Gold assay', Adorno expressed this idea as follows:

> The more tightly the world is enclosed by the net of man-made things, the more stridently those who are responsible for this condition proclaim their natural primitiveness. The discovery of genuineness as a last bulwark of individualistic ethics is a reflection of industrial mass-production. Only when countless standardized commodities project, for the sake of profit, the illusion of being unique, does the idea take shape, as their antithesis yet in keeping with the same criteria, that the non-reproducible is the truly genuine.[44]

The possibility of leading an extra-capitalist 'niche existence' within society (among leftists, the desire to lead such an existence finds expression in the notorious fantasy of 'moving off the grid' as well as in the notion of 'authenticity',[45] which imagines 'that if I live in accordance with my own ethos, my own nature, or if, to use the fine phrase of our own time, I realize myself, then this will be enough to bring about the good life. And this is nothing but pure illusion and ideology'[46]), if such a possibility ever even existed at all, has finally become history under the fully developed capital-relation. 'Although the alternative islands of bliss – that is, practical self-organisation as the pedagogical boondocks of capitalism – soon came in on the waves of the environmental move-

---

43 Adorno 2005b, p. 229.
44 Adorno 2005b, p. 155. This is also an objection to Benjamin's 'The Work of Art in the Age of its Technological Reproducibility', which declares precisely that the authenticity of the autonomous artwork has been rendered obsolete by reproducibility.
45 By now, this concept has degenerated into an overused phrase. René Martens perceives in it 'the entire perspective of cultural pessimism held by those who no longer expect anything good from human beings, and therefore above all hold themselves to be good. What it demands is that which is original and natural, the unspoilt state, the primordial – in other words, all which has yet to be manipulated and fiddled around with by human hands. Back to the roots, instead of moving as far away from them as possible' (Martens 1995, p. 22).
46 Adorno 2000c, p. 10.

ment, they escaped neither the practical critique of more advanced corporate policy, nor the far less destructive critical social theorists'.[47] To borrow Adorno's words, these islands were 'washed away'[48] by the totality of capitalism.

It would seem that only what is of no use to capital, that is, what cannot be valorised, offers a way out by not letting itself be subsumed: 'The only cure for the half-uselessness of a life which does not live would be its entire inutility'.[49] In existing society, where everything made has a purpose for which it was made in the first place, the inutility which resists all instrumental absorption through its uselessness 'occupies the place of that which can no longer be distorted by profit'.[50] And for its own part, knowledge 'must be guided by what exchange has not maimed or – since there is nothing left unmaimed anymore – by what is concealed within the exchange processes'.[51] Things are 'maimed' by their purposeful production, and so, according to Adorno,

> amid universal fungibility happiness attaches without exception to the non-fungible. No humane exertions, no formal reasoning, can sever happiness from the fact that the ravishing dress is worn by only one, and not by twenty thousand. The utopia of the qualitative – the things which through their difference and uniqueness cannot be absorbed into the prevalent exchange relationships – takes refuge under capitalism in the [fetish-character].[52]

---

47   Hafner 1993, p. 61. Uwe Kurzbein does not want to accept this and would rather broadcast 'signals from the niche', which is supposed to secure him a certain independence from society – typical of the 'off-the-grid-ism' (*Aussteigertum*) described by Hafner. However, he suffers from a lack of money. According to him, 'socialising the land' and creating 'means of production, hierarchy-free structures, self-responsibility and self-determination' against a 'predatory capitalism' demands an embrace of 'ecology, the economy and social togetherness'. Yet because he envisions this embrace not as an overcoming of the capital-relation, but rather as taking place within it, it cannot happen without money: 'The critics tell me broadly and overwhelmingly that the communities also need money', Kurzbein writes. On this point, he agrees: 'Of course they need money, and because they latently' – and certainly also quite manifestly – 'have little money, many conversations revolve around acquiring money'. How socially typical: people talking about money! 'However', Kurzbein reassures us, 'great care is taken not to restrict voluntary activity' (Kurzbein 2003, pp. 10–11). Such activity is voluntary in the same sense that working is voluntary when one has to do so to earn money (and thus to operate as a member of capitalist society, which one already is anyway), a necessity for survival.
48   Adorno 2009d, p. 391.
49   Adorno 1988d, p. 271.
50   Adorno 1978a, p. 98.
51   Adorno 2005d, p. 253.
52   Adorno 2005b, p. 120.

In times when no other happiness can be experienced besides that which is damaged by the false whole, the reflection of falseness in happiness must be taken as a given.

Here, Adorno uses the term fetish-character to refer to an aesthetic fetishism which is at times levelled as an accusation against the proponents of art for art's sake due to their 'concept of a pure, exclusively self-sufficient artwork'. According to Adorno, this accusation may indeed be quite apt, yet the 'truth content of artworks, which is indeed their social truth, is predicated on their fetish character'.[53] Although artworks' truth-content may also have something guilty about it, 'the guilt they bear of fetishism does not disqualify art, any more so than it disqualifies anything culpable; for in the universally, socially mediated world nothing stands external to its nexus of guilt [*Schuldzusammenhang*]'.[54] For this reason, artworks are

> plenipotentiaries of things that are no longer distorted by exchange, profit, and the false needs of a degraded humanity. In the context of total semblance, art's semblance of being-in-itself is the mask of truth. ... A liberated society would be beyond the irrationality of its *faux frais* and

---

53   Adorno 2002a, p. 228.

54   Adorno 2002a, p. 227. According to Rolf Tiedemann, '[t]he "web or context of guilt" [*Schuldzusammenhang*] and "web or context of delusion" [*Verblendungszusammenhang*] are concepts frequently used by Adorno in his theory of society. Their meaning is sketched in his Metaphysics, for example, in the course of a critique of the Stoics' (editorial note by Tiedemann [Adorno 2006a, p. 296, n. 8]). The passage mentioned by Tiedemann reads as follows: 'But I would say that even this standpoint ... nevertheless has a moment of narrow-mindedness in the sense that it renders absolute the entrapment of human beings by the totality, and thus sees no other possibility than to submit. The possibility of seeing through this situation as a context of guilt [*Schuldzusammenhang*] concealed through blinding [*Verblendungszusammenhang*], and thus of breaking through it, did not occur to that entire philosophy. Stoicism did, it is true, conceive for the first time the idea of the all-encompassing context of guilt, but it did not discern the moment of necessary illusion in that context – and that, I would say, is the small advantage that we, with our social and philosophical knowledge, enjoy over the Stoic position' (Adorno 2000b, p. 112). 'The concept of *Schuldzusammenhang* may incidentally go back to Benjamin' (editorial note by Tiedemann [Adorno 2001e, p. 415, n. 156 – translator's note: this final comment by Tiedemann appears to have been mistakenly admitted from the English translation of *History and Freedom* quoted above, hence the reference to the German original here]). As Benjamin writes in 'Fate and Character', '[l]aw condemns not to punishment but to guilt. Fate is the guilt context of the living. It corresponds to the natural condition of the living – that semblance, not yet wholly dispelled, from which man is so far removed that, under its rule, he was never wholly immersed in it but only invisible in his best part' (Benjamin 2004a, p. 204).

beyond the ends-means-rationality of utility. This is enciphered in art and is the source of art's social explosiveness. Although the magic fetishes are one of the historical roots of art, a fetishistic element remains admixed in artworks, an element that goes beyond commodity fetishism.[55]

Adorno interprets this element as the precondition for breaking out of the ever-sameness of what has always been determined in advance – there can be 'no happiness without fetishism',[56] for 'autonomy and fetishism are two sides of the *same* truth'.[57] Something of this view appears in René Magritte's dictum that a 'superior life cannot be conceived of without genuine luxury'.[58] However, the 'promise of happiness in luxury' also mentioned by Adorno in *Minima Moralia* also refers to the economic realm which it cannot escape, given that luxury

> pre-supposes privilege, economic inequality, a society based on fungibility. Thus the qualitative itself becomes a special case of quantification, the non-fungible becomes fungible, luxury turns into comfort and finally into a senseless gadget. This vicious circle would put an end to luxury even without the levelling tendency of mass society, over which reactionaries wax sentimentally indignant. The inner constitution of luxury is not unaffected by what happens to the useless in its total incorporation into the realm of use. Its remnants, even objects of the highest quality, already look like junk.[59]

As long as luxury continues to be eliminated 'but not by declaring privilege a human right'[60] (and by realising it as such), as long as the subjectively ashamed and objectively guilty aspect of luxury does not become obsolete with luxury becoming accessible to all, so too will the capital-relation deform luxuriousness when former luxury articles are mass-produced as standardised commodities – which is why even the genuine luxury article, whose lavishness is only certified by its price tag, appears just as ridiculous as the mass-produced commodities – like how formerly useless activities were integrated into the process of production as value-producing labour. However, if happiness 'attaches without exception to the non-fungible', yet the formerly non-fungible has become fun-

---

55   Adorno 2002a, p. 227.
56   Adorno 2005b, p. 121.
57   Adorno 2006d, p. 53.
58   Magritte 2016, p. 133.
59   Adorno 2005b, p. 120.
60   Adorno 2005b, p. 119.

gible with 'luxury turn[ing] into comfort and finally into a senseless gadget', the question emerges as to what happiness might be able to attach to for longer.

That being said, usefulness 'cannot be separated from the process of integral socialization': society still integrates efforts to escape its totality – the usefulness of which 'can be defined only in terms of [its] negation'[61] – as strength-through-joy (*Kraft durch Freude*)[62] escapism. In this way, even autonomous artworks which might transcend appropriation by the culture industry are already just as damaged by it as happiness is by horror. 'Wrong life cannot be lived rightly'.[63] Moreover, whoever attempts to live rightly after what history has borne witness to[64] is already living wrongly or no longer living at all, if life is to be more than simply the ability to live, or a cheerful disposition, or 'an endless procession of bent figures chained to each other, no longer able to raise their heads under the burden of what is'[65] – a procession entered into for the sake of sheer survival, even though it is a procession of the damned 'trotting towards the grave'.[66]

Nevertheless, Adorno holds fast to the possibility of happiness in times of its impossibility:

> What beauty still flourishes under terror is a mockery and ugliness to itself. Yet its fleeting shape attests to the avoidability of terror. Something of this paradox is fundamental to all art; today it appears in the fact that

---

61   Adorno 1978a, p. 103.
62   Translator's note: *Kraft durch Freude* was a state-operated recreational organisation in Nazi Germany.
63   Adorno 2005b, p. 39. 'Incidentally, long after I formulated this sentence', Adorno comments in his lecture course *Problems of Moral Philosophy*, 'I discovered a similar statement in Nietzsche, although it is very differently phrased' (Adorno 2000c, p. 167). On the occasion of Adorno's 100th birthday, the literary writer Christiane Scherer mistakenly claimed that Adorno – the namesake of her pen name Thea Dorn – was 'clever enough to create a legitimation for anything and everything with his notorious "wrong life cannot be lived rightly"' (Dorn 2003). One can of course read (and ultimately propagate) Adorno this way, but Adorno's dictum does not in fact imply 'compromise with reality, but simply a recognition of it' (Liessmann 1998, p. 37).
64   Ulrich Raulff's thesis that Adorno 'gifted the Germans one of their very few and probably their last philosophical book of folk tales [*philosophischen Volksbücher*]' (Raulff 2003, pp. 123–4) is grotesque. Hermann Krings captured *Minima Moralia*'s gesture and substance far better when he wrote in a 1953 review that it 'could also have been titled *The Damned Society* or even *The Last Judgment*' (Krings 1953, p. 363). For a contemporary critique of *Minima Moralia*, cf. Demirović 1989.
65   Adorno 2007b, p. 345.
66   Busch 2008, p. 51.

art still exists at all. The captive idea of beauty strives at once to reject happiness and to assert it.[67]

After all, 'there is no longer beauty or consolation except in the gaze falling on horror, withstanding it, and in unalleviated consciousness of negativity holding fast to the possibility of what is better'.[68] Blemished by the ubiquitous necessity of valorisation and no longer possible as a state of blissful, thoughtless intoxication,[69] happiness bears the antagonistic traits of the society which at once facilitates and obstructs it. Thus, happiness can only be found in the remembrance of constantly self-perpetuating disaster, as long as this remembrance does not also pessimistically renounce the happiness which still wants to be everything. 'Without historical remembrance there would be no beauty'.[70]

What fetishism is to art, lie is to truth: 'scattered traces ... from the negative whole'.[71] 'Rationalization is not yet rational; the universality of mediation has yet to be transformed into living life; and this endows the traces of immediacy, however dubious and antiquated, with an element of corrective justice'.[72] It may be true that '[a]ll post-Auschwitz culture, including its urgent critique, is garbage',[73] yet in the cultural sphere, ideas of freedom and justice that, unlike economy, are not based on the precondition of a relentless rationality which has led to terrible disaster seem to have formed anyway. If 'free and honest exchange is itself a lie, to deny it is at the same time to speak for truth: in face of the lie of the commodity world, even the lie that denounces it becomes a corrective. That culture so far has failed is no justification for furthering

---

67   Adorno 2005b, p. 121.

68   Adorno 2005b, p. 25.

69   'Of course, the demand of soberness ... takes something away: the happiness gained through drunken ecstasy. But does not this happiness only cheat us of another happiness which is absolutely denied to us in the world as it is? Kierkegaard's demand for sobriety is not that of the Philistine. It attacks the shams of mere individuality, the making absolute of accidental "differences", and all the false happiness connected with them. Behind this sobriety lies the profound knowledge that in the last analysis the differences between men are not decisive. For all the features of individualization and specification owe their very existence to the universal injustice which makes this man thus and not otherwise – whereas he could be different' (Adorno 1999a, p. 425; cf. also Adorno and Horkheimer 2002, p. 52).

70   Adorno 2002a, p. 65.

71   Adorno 2007b, pp. 377–8.

72   Adorno 2002a, p. 64.

73   Adorno 2007b, p. 367; cf. Adorno 2002a, p. 310: 'Culture is refuse, yet art – one of its sectors – is nevertheless serious as the appearance of truth. This is implicit in the double character of fetishism'.

its failure'[74] by taking up the position of cultural pessimism, which since the dawn of civilisation has predicted civilisation's demise is but a day away.[75] A far more valid task would be to redeem from culture what it can *also* stand for.

> Culture is only true when implicitly critical, and the mind which forgets this revenges itself in the critics it breeds. Criticism is an indispensable element of culture which is itself contradictory: in all its untruth still as true as culture is untrue. Criticism is not unjust when it dissects – this can be its greatest virtue – but rather when it parries by not parrying.[76]

That being said, culture's truth is not positive. Rather, it can only be established in culture's absence; the only avenue remaining is the critique of untruth. In his introductory lecture course *Erkenntnistheorie (Epistemology)*, Adorno addresses the question of 'what the deal might be with my concept of truth anyway' by explaining that it 'consists of the fact that simply everything that exists at all is understood in terms of the tension or the contradictions between the existence of the phenomenon which is spoken of, and the concept it has of itself, or – if this manner of speaking is too subjective for you – of the concept under which it appears. And the difference which emerges through this confrontation, or in other words, the proof that no thing does justice to its concept – this difference, this negative, is the only way at all in which we can become aware of truth if we don't want to absolutise a finite, if we don't want to hypostasise a conditional'. That is,

> if on the one hand, truth must be conceptualised as socially mediated, ... but on the other hand, society can't do justice its own concept – namely the concept of justice – then truth would indeed consist precisely of the fact that this proof is not held up against society abstractly and as something outside of it, as something from a fully furnished abstract utopia. Instead, truth involves society being confronted with its own concept of justice in the form which it has as ideology, so to speak, a movement from which society's own untruth emerges. In actuality, in the movement of these concepts, in the transition of the concept and ultimately in the

---

74 Adorno 2005b, p. 44.
75 Gerhard Henschel has succinctly demonstrated with select materials that the constantly necessary updating of the apocalyptic worldview – the world persists, even after apocalypse was prophesied – does not make it more plausible (see Henschel 2010).
76 Adorno 1988c, p. 22.

course of a praxis which wants to go beyond society's untruth, something like an idea of truth is actually constituted.[77]

Critique of untruth thus becomes the task of a theory suited to '[t]he almost insoluble task' of letting 'neither the power of others, nor our own powerlessness, stupefy us'.[78] After all, '[f]ear of the impotence of theory supplies a pretext for bowing to the almighty production process, and so fully admitting the impotence of theory'. Even in Marx's work, signs can be found of an unacknowledged capitulation before overwhelming circumstances, and a theory which escapes both immediate valorisability and rote acquiescence must criticise this capitulation. 'Traits of malice are not alien even to authentic Marxist language'.[79]

3   What is Deceptive about Dialogue

In one of his very last notes, written in July 1969,[80] Adorno comments as follows:

> Long have Marx's mannerisms of speech been suspect to me. If only an incisive critique of the whole theory on the basis of language would be made. For example, the derivative rhetoric and imagery – does this not bear witness against him *from the perspective of the philosophy of history*? According to his and Hegel's logic, his inability to find the words for what he meant would have to prove that the world spirit they trusted was not with him.[81]

The most illustrious example of the 'derivative rhetoric' Adorno criticises here may well be located in the 'fetish chapter' of *Capital*, where Marx reveals himself to be unable to expound upon the fetish-character of the commodity without resorting to unclear metaphors and analogies. The problematic, metaphoricising adoption of the term fetish from ethnology[82] can itself be seen as the first instance of this. Moreover, where precise phrasing would seem to

---

77   Adorno 2018b, p. 345.
78   Adorno 2005b, p. 57.
79   Adorno 2005b, p. 44.
80   Cf. Backhaus 2004a, p. 27.
81   Adorno 2003k, p. 38.
82   Cf. Marxhausen 1999, column 343.

be in order, one finds puns[83] and personifications,[84] somewhat ambiguous imagery,[85] anti-bourgeois rancour[86] and a schoolmasterly rhetoric with which Marx repeatedly strives to uncover so-called economic 'secrets'. As justified as Marx's critique, and as revolutionary as the substance of his theory may be, they sometimes amount linguistically to an overwrought polemic. An example of this can be seen in Marx's treatment of other authors in *The German Ideology*, many of whom are 'maliciously embarrassed'[87] therein.[88]

Adorno's note continues as follows:

> The fact, probably noted by Lukács, that the proletariat was not the most advanced class, but rather, as a dehumanised class, was regressive and backwards, would only fit all too well here. Just take a look at the hymns and the revolutionary poetry. Moreover, the backwardness of the proletariat allowed its integration into bourgeois society.[89]

Indeed, as Marx and Engels themselves note in *The Holy Family*, private property 'produces the proletariat *as* proletariat, poverty which is conscious of its

---

83 In examining the relative form of value, Marx claimed that 'the coat' – selected as a general example along with the linen out of which it was made – is a '"bearer of value", although this property never shows through, even when the coat is at its most threadbare. In its value-relation with the linen, the coat counts only under this aspect, counts therefore as embodied value, as the body of value [*Wertkörper*]. Despite its buttoned-up appearance, the linen recognizes in it a splendid kindred soul, the soul of value' (Marx 1982a, p. 143).

84 See for example the claim that 'commodities are in love with money' (Marx 1982a, p. 202).

85 Take, for example, the claim that '[w]e perceive straight away the insufficiency of the simple form of value: it is an embryonic form which must undergo a series of metamorphoses before it can ripen into the price-form' (Marx 1982a, p. 154), or that '[t]he price or money-form of commodities is, like their form of value generally, quite distinct from their palpable and real bodily form; it is therefore a purely ideal or notational form. Although invisible, the value of iron, linen, and corn exists in these very articles: it is signified through their equality with gold even though this relation with gold exists only in their heads, so to speak. The guardian of the commodities must therefore lend them his tongue, or hang a ticket on them, in order to communicate their prices to the outside world' (Marx 1982a, p. 189).

86 See for example Marx's mention of the 'crude bourgeois vision of the political economist' (Marx 1982a, p. 149).

87 Iorio 2003, p. 9.

88 Indeed, more than a few Marx researchers have appropriated this hostile style of argumentation while mutually accusing each other of not having understood Marx, even though they allege he propounded his theory as clear as day. These philological disputes regarding the perfect reading of Marx are probably less useful to social critique than to the formation of factions in which it is possible to be indisputably correct.

89 Adorno 2003k, p. 38.

spiritual and physical poverty, dehumanisation which is conscious of its dehumanisation, and therefore self-abolishing'.[90] The evident consequence from the perspective of the philosophy of history that the proletariat would not be suited for revolution was abandoned by Marx and Engels in favour of the thesis that the proletariat would overturn existing relations once it finally championed its own interests. However, they neglected to interrogate which imposed interests it might have in the first place.

Writing to Thomas Mann in 1952, Adorno suspects that

> [p]erhaps it was the inconspicuous weakness of Marx, though one of the implications of which can hardly be exaggerated, that he did not truly and substantially embody in himself the culture against which he struggled. His language, particularly in the period of his maturity, strongly suggests something of the kind. And when he effectively dissolves the tension between the utopian and positivist elements of his thought in favour of the latter, thus anticipating the way in which socialism itself would eventually become another part of the machinery of production, this is surely connected with a curious blindness to the moment of semblance without which there can be no truth. I fear that this is where the Church Fathers of dialectical materialism proved to be all too bourgeois themselves, ... But one can hardly say this sort of thing today without inviting misunderstanding, and if one does say it, one is immediately likely to be misused by those who simply claim to defend culture against materialism.[91]

Culture has to be negated not abstractly, but rather determinately: as reconciliation with nature. This requires a dialectic which Adorno views as lacking in Marx's work, particularly in his later writings on the critique of economy. When Marx – who Adorno believes 'fought against utopias ... maybe even more

---

90   Marx and Engels 1975, p. 36.

91   Letter from Adorno to Mann, 1 December 1952 (Adorno and Mann 2006, p. 96). Adorno elaborates on his view of Marx as 'all too bourgeois' in his lecture course *Philosophische Terminologie* (*Philosophical Terminology*) from the 1962–3 winter semester. According to him, Marx had 'in the bourgeois, egalitarian traits which he inherited, just as above all in his idea of increasing productive forces – that is, in the reckless domination of nature – certain ascetic traits himself. These are manifested particularly crudely in certain astounding formulations in the *Communist Manifesto* on erotic matters' (Adorno 1974a, pp. 187–8). See for example the following passage from the *Manifesto*: 'Our bourgeois, not content with having the wives and daughters of their proletarians at their disposal, not to speak of common prostitutes, take the greatest pleasure in seducing each other's wives' (Marx and Engels 2010, p. 84).

than was good'[92] – 'used philosophical motifs to complete the transition from philosophy to economy', he became for Adorno 'in a certain sense more positivist, scientistic and undialectical than he was in his writings from his youth, the *Manifesto* included'.[93] As Michael Heinrich emphasises, Marx 'places *Capital* among the "*scientific* attempts to revolutionise a science"',[94] and hence did not criticise 'the so-called positive sciences, but rather believed himself to be in agreement with them'.[95] This stands in contrast to the conception of science in Critical Theory, for which, according to Adorno,

> science is one among other societal forces of production and interwoven with the conditions of production. It itself is subject to that reification against which Critical Theory is arrayed. It cannot be the measure of Critical Theory, and Critical Theory cannot be science as Marx and Engels postulated it.[96]

Of all things, critique cannot spare the rationality according to which both the understanding of science as well as society as such are constituted.

On the one hand, science is itself a productive force, yet on the other, it is essentially a part of culture. For Adorno, insofar as Marx does not reflect upon this, Marxian theory stands in danger of itself becoming part of that ideology which is inseparable form society:

> The less ideology stands out, the more directly it becomes the objective spirit under which we are living. So it is no longer a theoretical construct; it is now neither the idealization of something existent nor its complement but, rather, the existent as appearance, the existent in the guise reflected in the total social consciousness, and thus objective spirit. This spirit is now infiltrating language most of all, which is why, if I may just say something subjective about my own approach, I think – and the work of Karl Kraus is already an excellent example – that ideology critique today is not so much a critique of an explicit, theoretically false content as simply

---

92   Adorno 2017b, p. 296.
93   Letter from Adorno to Jürgen von Kempski, 27 January 1950 (TWA, BR 740/8).
94   Heinrich 2021, p. 36; quoted from letter from Marx to Ludwig Kugelmann, 28 December 1862 (Marx and Engels 1985, p. 436).
95   Adorno 1974a, p. 172.
96   Adorno, 'On the Specification of Critical Theory', unpublished translation by Henry Pickford, available at: https://www.academia.edu/37619108/THEODOR_W._ADORNO 1903-69; originally part of a letter from Adorno to Horkheimer, 31 March 1969 (Adorno and Horkheimer 2006, p. 848).

a critique of the form in which certain content is expressed in the social consciousness, a form that contradicts the actual issue in question. And that, I would think, is why language critique is now really the appropriate form, or at least one of the appropriate forms, of ideology critique.[97]

According to Adorno, Kraus's critique of language is essentially true of 'liberal speech', or in other words,

> of the malediction that everyone having the same right to communicate became injustice in fact and in expression. Certainly, Kraus limited himself to criticising liberal speech just as little as the society in which he lived was purely liberal. Not only did he perceive the process of putrefaction under both total domination and the forms of objective spirit which imitate it. *The Third Walpurgis Night* already contains the phrase 'it's alright' ('*Geht in Ordnung*'), a self-contentedly inhuman form of communication which only today, after Hitler's downfall, has transformed into popular speech.[98]

In language, bourgeois coldness condenses as an indifference towards every interaction, which stems from the fact that no instance of speech, regardless of its substance, is presumed to be any different from any other. Under the banner of legitimacy of domination-free speech, a German interior minister –

---

97   Adorno 2019i, p. 137. 'The analyses micrologically attained by Kraus, are my no means so "unconnected" with science as would be acceptable to the latter. More specifically, his language-analytical theses on the mentality of the commercial traveller – of the future office worker – must, as a neo-barbaric norm, concur with those aspects of Weber's theory of the dawning of bureaucratic domination which are relevant to the sociology of education. In addition, Kraus' analyses also concur with the decline of education explained by Weber's theory. The strict relation of Kraus' analyses to language and their objectivity lead them beyond the promptly and automatically recorded fortuitousness of merely subjective forms of reaction. The analyses extrapolate from the individual phenomena a whole which comparative generalization cannot master, and which is co-experienced as pre-existent in the approach adopted in Kraus' analysis' (Adorno 1976a, p. 46).

98   Adorno 2003m, p. 515. '[B]etter for those campaigning for autarchy to speak bad German than to use foreign words they can never really understand. (For Example: "dynamic" or "synthesis".) It is precisely the attempt to replace them that has led to that enrichment of German vocabulary which is the envy of other nations. But this enrichment also results from the expanding needs of trade and commerce, a development which – at the end of the day – justifies the unthinking adoption of Jewish idioms and an acceptance of the inflated patois of profiteers already in vogue among republican authors. So now all variants of the primal soul's awakening can claim to be "one hundred percent guaranteed" – with "expedited delivery"' (Kraus 2020, p. 86).

whose job should involve checking right-wing extremism with the resources of the state – can respond to a question about how to deal with neo-Nazis by asking the following question: 'When was the last time you or I spoke with a right-wing radical?'[99] This reinterprets a social problems as a failure of speech while conceiving of communication[100] as an end in itself, as therapy and service in one. In the process, linguistic '[s]hoddiness that drifts with the flow of familiar speech is taken as a sign of relevance and contact: people know what they want because they know what other people want. Regard for the object, rather than for communication, is suspect'.[101] Communication is itself shot through with the coercive principle of like for like even when it presents itself as non-coercive and free from domination, given that '[t]he word communication itself implicitly contains a neutralization which makes it appear to refer to nothing more than that some people communicate something to others, inform them of something, regardless of the fact that in the forms of this communication the entire historical relationships of power are constitutively contained'.[102] The hypocrisy of communication, 'what is deceptive about dialogue',[103] results from the ideology of free togetherness (*freies Miteinander*). However, under given conditions, togetherness is no more free than its value inherent:

> Declaring togetherness as such the goal indicates that one has forgotten about the substance of community: a humane arrangement of the world. The cult of community as an end-in-itself belongs to the National Socialists and the people's democracies in the Russian style. It is essentially totalitarian: within it, the tendency towards the oppression of the individual constantly resonates. However, a real community would be one of free human beings.[104]

The delusion that community is already real is evident among other places in one pseudo-democratic admonition which poorly disguises itself as a request

---

99   Former Interior Minister of Saxony Heinz Eggert quoted in Droste 1995, p. 139.

100   'A magic word, indeed *the* magic word, and apparently the cloudy remains of the legacy of the Christian concept of *communio* and the socialist concept of communism' (Henscheid 1993, p. 114).

101   Adorno 2005b, p. 101.

102   Adorno 2000a, p. 148. In his aphorism 'How nice of you, Doctor', Adorno issues what probably his clearest statement regarding the recurring demand for nonviolent and non-hierarchical communication (Adorno 2005b, 25–6).

103   Adorno 2019n, p. 263.

104   Adorno 2003ac, p. 438.

while legitimating every appeal to inhumanity as free speech: 'the stock phrase "wouldyouletmefinish" [*Darfichmalausreden*]'.[105] Woe betide us if not! For this would namely expose the 'so-called democratic common sense, which is neither democratic nor common sense',[106] for what it always was: a 'deal' in which someone demands to have his opinions heard in return for allowing another in good faith to speak; *Pacta sunt servanda*. Free expression requires free individuals, which do not exist at present. What instead exists are subjects who exchange opinions, and when people speak of exchanging opinions or information, this is not merely a metaphor. Exchange really does take place, and this means that the relevant rules must be followed – rules which, among their other functions, uphold the illusion that language as well must bow to the dictate of rationality if it wants to mean something. '[N]ow that demythologization has led to the destruction of language itself',[107] all speech which does not positivistically consent to reality is consigned 'to poetry',[108] while only a 'threadbare language'[109] remains. As the 'difference between language as a means of communication and language as the precise expression of the matter under consideration'[110] has been flattened, this threadbare language is sup-

---

105   Schulz 2001, pp. 228–9; see Braunstein 2008, p. 40.
106   Letter from Horkheimer to Pollock, 7 May 1946 (Horkheimer 1996, p. 728).
107   Adorno 2005b, p. 222.
108   Adorno and Horkheimer 2002, p. 5; cf. the following passage from Adorno's 'Theses on the Language of the Philosopher' from the early 1930s: 'The demand for the "understandability" of philosophical language – for its societal communicability – is idealist, necessarily predicated on the significative character of language. It posits that language is separable from the object, insofar as the same object could be adequately given in various ways. Objects, however, are not at all adequately given through language, but rather adhere to language and stand in a historical unity with it. In homogeneous society the communicability of philosophical language is never demanded; it is nevertheless everywhere imposed, if the ontological power of words is so extensive that objective dignity is attributed to them in society. This objectivity never results from an adjustment of philosophical language to societal communicability. Rather, objectivity, which renders language "communicable", is the same as that which unambiguously assigns words to the philosopher. It [*die Objektivität*] cannot be demanded; where it has become problematic, it is essentially non-existent and as little predetermined for the philosopher as is only to be registered in society. The abstract, idealist demand for the adequation of language to object and society is the exact opposite of linguistic reality. In atomized, disintegrated society, constituting language by taking audible being into consideration romanticizes a state of the ontological obligation of words to feign, [a state] that is instantly denied by the impotence of the words themselves. In the absence of unified society there is no objective language and therefore no truthfully communicative language' (Adorno 2007d, p. 36).
109   Adorno and Horkheimer 2002, p. xv.
110   Adorno 2005e, p. 28.

posed to be equally suited to everything – hence the 'unfortunate existence of a word for everything',[111] even for the unspeakable. In reality, however, it simply obscures everything. Meanwhile 'public life has reached a state in which thought is being turned inescapably into a commodity and language into celebration of the commodity'.[112] This has resulted in a 'highly gelatinous heap made of new-agey and zeitgeisty rubbish, of pretentious verbal muddle intended to simultaneously obfuscate and mock, or alternatively, made of fear'[113] – or in other words, in a language which reflects both the social and the private, both the objective coercion to work and the simultaneously objective superfluity of the individual:

> It wants to seem impressive – this language in which work and leisure slide into each other. It wants to be meaningful and relaxed, very, very relaxed, downright forcibly relaxed. It makes one casual and confident, suggests superiority, yet is nevertheless subject to the most hideous trends. Everything sounds like advertising: 'we're paving the way', 'it's well under way', 'we have a handle on it'. Precisely: language is kept in a stranglehold by people who perform the role of acting (*handelnde*),[114] determining subjects.[115]

Subjects use mutilated language to present themselves as individuals while merely fulfilling their function as 'users of stock phrases'.[116] This has led Michael Rudolf to view as historically superseded Adorno's observation that for many people – that is, for those who have been completely absorbed in their social determinacy – 'it is already an impertinence to say "I"':[117]

> We used to be able to justifiably find fault with the fact that many people found it presumptuous to say 'I'. This has taken on a new quality in that these people can no longer even unambiguously say 'yes' or 'no'. Today, 'exactly', 'correct', or 'nope, not really' sputters out of them.[118]

---

111   Schmidt 1990, p. 440.
112   Adorno and Horkheimer 2002, p. xiv.
113   Henscheid 1993, p. 8.
114   Translator's note: the play on words between the German word *handeln* (to act), and the references to 'having a handle' on something and to 'a stranglehold', is lost in translation.
115   Droste 2007, p. 25.
116   Rudolf 2007, p. 61.
117   Adorno 2005h, p. 50.
118   Rudolf 2007, p. 6.

Language expresses a social stupidity which presents itself as desirable cunning. After all,

> in present society, the ego or self has become such a burden to many
> people because, by thinking too consistently and vigorously, they cause
> themselves all kinds of inconvenience. They avoid being 'too clever by
> half', and find it more appropriate to reality not to develop their ego
> too far, in keeping with the old Berlin saying: 'You're lucky – you're stu-
> pid'.[119]

The 'public now only communicates in phrases', and 'the inflationary accumulation of imposing and intimidatory blather' reveals 'human beings' panic at their own insignificance, at not being able to keep up in the everyday hamster wheel of post-industrial debasement'.[120] The panic is justified, and in the struggle of each against all, language too is a weapon both in the general struggle, and in the struggle against one's own downfall.

Stupidity, including the stupidity of language, 'is not a natural quality, but one socially produced and reinforced'.[121] However, 'stultification is caused not by the oppressed but by oppression, and it affects not only the oppressed but, in their essentials, the oppressors as well'.[122] Adorno sees the world as immersed

> in a gloomy flood of nonsense, the fallen form of language. Karl Kraus
> compressed that fact into the thesis that today the phrase gives birth to
> reality – especially to that reality which arose, after the catastrophe, under
> the name of culture. To a great extent that reality is ... only there to keep
> men away from what is of importance to them.[123]

---

119   Adorno 2000a, p. 57; on the thesis that '[stupidity] itself has been taken over by fungibility' cf. Adorno 2007a, p. 36.
120   Rudolf 2007, pp. 5–6.
121   Adorno 2005b, pp. 105–6. Adorno thus stood in the humanistic tradition of great French enlightenment thinkers such as Helvétius, who wrote that '[m]an is born ignorant; he is not born a fool; and it is not even without labour that he is made one' (Helvétius 1810, p. 6).
122   Adorno 1988f, p. 41.
123   Adorno 1973, pp. 100–1. As Kraus wrote, '[t]he world is deaf from intonation. I am convinced that events no longer even happen anymore, but rather that clichés keep working automatically. Or if events should actually happen without being repelled by clichés, then the events will stop once the clichés are shattered. Matters have gone rotten from language. The age already stinks of the phrase' (Kraus 1986, p. 229).

The dialectic of language, another essential 'element of the total process of enlightenment',[124] entails language's double character 'as a means of discursive signification – of communication first and foremost – on the one hand and as expression on the other'.[125] Meanwhile, Adorno's attempt to find a language which does not reduce itself to one of these functions is itself dialectical:

> Best able to meet the demands of this predicament would be a philosophical language that would strive for intelligibility without confusing it with clarity. As an expression of the thing itself, language is not fully reducible to communication with others. Nor, however ... is it simply independent of communication. Otherwise it would elude all critique, even in its relationship to the matter at hand, and would reduce that relationship to an arbitrary presumption. Language as expression of the thing itself and language as communication are interwoven. The ability to name the matter at hand is developed under the compulsion to communicate it, and that element of coercion is preserved in it; conversely, it could not communicate anything that it did not have as its own intention, undistracted by other considerations. This dialectic plays itself out within the medium of language itself; it is not merely a fall from grace on the part of an inhumane social zeal that watches to make sure that no one thinks anything that cannot be communicated.[126]

---

124   Adorno and Horkheimer 2002, p. 133.
125   Adorno 2019j, p. 98.
126   Adorno 1993c, p. 105.

CHAPTER 9

The Curse of Writing Today

99 % of the readership wants not to have a copy of reality, but rather to partake in a perfectly formed celebration in honour of an existential stability *which does not exist.*

ARNO SCHMIDT, 'Funfzehn'. Vom Wunderkind der Sinnlosigkeit

∴

1   Everything Is Quite Simple

The problems of linguistic mediation between theory and practice confront Adorno and Horkheimer in three illustrative groups of conversations from 1939, 1945 and 1956 respectively. Each one revolves around the topic of a manifesto the two intended to write.

The first of these groups of conversations, titled 'Diskussionen über Sprache und Erkenntnis, Naturbeherrschung am Menschen, politische Aspekte des Marxismus' ('Discussions on Language and Knowledge, Domination of Nature in Humans, Political Aspects of Marxism')[1] by editor Gunzelin Schmid Noerr, took place in the fall of 1939. Already, it concerns 'the political perspective of Critical Theory in view of the National Socialist war, with the interlocutors immediately thematising the cultural and political hindrances to what they take to be the obvious goal of proletarian revolution'.[2]

> HORKHEIMER: The German proletarians are tasked with toppling their government .... The task of all proletarians is to eliminate the impediments standing in the way of a rational ordering of the world. ...
> These things are really quite simple. One ought to say: 'Over the last twenty years, it's been drilled into you that the world is not ready for socialism. Yet you didn't want to believe this in 1918, and it's even less true today.' The time is now or in a hundred years.

---

1   Adorno and Horkheimer 1985b.
2   Schmid Noerr 1996, p. 34.

ADORNO: So you're of the opinion that existing relations of political power shouldn't factor into setting political goals?

HORKHEIMER: Revolution always appears completely impossible and insane until it happens. ... Bearing in mind the aforementioned complexity, I just meant that what the proletariat ought to do is extremely simple to describe. The perspective is that if the world weren't struck by blindness, the proletariat could put things in order immediately.[3]

Adorno is apparently interested in a theory which would reflect experience – presumed to be general – in such a way that its account would be resoundingly evident. To him, enlightenment is in order not concerning the 'wholly enlightened'[4] earth, but rather the practical consequences stemming from the knowledge thereof. The result of knowledge should be to indicate a pending triumph over prevailing circumstances.

ADORNO: The individual insights must not be blind. In the theory, each must be equally close to the midpoint.

HORKHEIMER: So, like in the *Communist Manifesto*. The sentences capture experiences. We should try to write a text with those tendencies.[5]

One week later, Adorno and Horkheimer attempt to 'establish individual points for the schema of the "Manifesto".'[6] The fourteen points[7] they lay out include the stipulation that '[e]very single sentence' of the manifesto should 'articulate something which everyone has already thought himself'.[8] Adorno reiterates Horkheimer's notion that what needs to be said is simple: 'Basically, everyone

---

3 Adorno and Horkheimer 1985b, pp. 513–14.
4 Adorno and Horkheimer 2002, p. 2.
5 Adorno and Horkheimer 1985b, p. 509.
6 Adorno and Horkheimer 1985b, p. 512.
7 These points are as follows: '1) actuality of Marxism / 2) orientation in this situation. ... / 3) Every single sentence must articulate something which everyone has already thought himself. ... / 4) The knowledge of complex individual relationships is one of the most important tricks used to sabotage real insight. ... / 5) The political situation. / 6) The question of political theory. /) Together with 6), certain philosophical things, questions of culture and science. ... 8) The political programme. ... / 9) Critique of the proletariat / 10) Anthropology. ... / 11) Concept of reason ... / 12) To what extent happiness can no longer exist in this society, and to what extent the image of happiness is distorted by its orientation on this society. ... / 13) Socialism and administration. ... / 12) Socialism and domination of nature' (Adorno and Horkheimer 1985b, pp. 512–15).
8 Adorno and Horkheimer 1985b, p. 512.

has to know that the world today is hell',[9] and it is this knowledge to which he and Horkheimer seek to appeal.

> ADORNO: Additionally, every sentence must break through the façade.
> HORKHEIMER: Isn't opacity a façade?
> ADORNO: The whole thing has to have a tenor of 'fear-mongering is invalid'.
> HORKHEIMER: Basically, things today are simpler than under liberalism.
> ADORNO: The complexity is just a veil to conceal the simplicity.[10]

The last of the 'Diskussionen über Sprache und Erkenntnis', held in November 1939, returns to the question of 'a possible beginning of the "Manifesto"'. Adorno establishes their position as follows: 'Everyone says that Marxism is finished. We reject this: not only is Marxism not finished, the point is to stay faithful to it' – at the moment of its demise, so to speak – for '[t]o really stay faithful is to further advance the dialectical process'. Moreover, Adorno once again emphasises

> [t]hat in reality everything is quite simple. Basically everyone knows how it is, but no one wants to say it. So, first Marxism, fidelity. Solidarity as fidelity to theory, synonymous with the particular transformation preordained by matters. Then political analysis with a double aspect: both Marxist and a blow to the face of political and theoretical stabilisations.[11]

Horkheimer replies that the issue is 'not simplicity, but opacity'.[12] To him, an opacity mystifying the evident nature of simple matters is what the manifesto has to overcome: 'Liberating knowledge is only separated from human beings by a thin partition'.[13] As would be made clear in *Dialectic of Enlightenment*, this 'partition' is taken to be a function of culture. Yet already in the discussion, Adorno voices his suspicion that the reasons for revolution's absence are located 'in the cultural sphere', arguing that 'culture is absorbed into advertising'.[14] At the conclusion of the discussion, Adorno poses the question of whether experience, 'given that it yields no happiness, points back to the capit-

---

9   Adorno and Horkheimer 1985b, p. 515.
10   Adorno and Horkheimer 1985b, p. 512.
11   Adorno and Horkheimer 1985b, p. 524.
12   Adorno and Horkheimer 1985b, p. 525.
13   Adorno and Horkheimer 1985b, p. 515.
14   Adorno and Horkheimer 1985b, p. 514.

alist process of labour' and refers to a 'fun-theory',[15] which, although no longer mentioned, would later be condensed into the thesis that '[f]un is a medicinal bath'[16] in the 'Culture Industry' chapter of *Dialectic of Enlightenment*. Horkheimer answers with resignation: 'The entire labour movement which fights for fun has become base'.[17]

2   **That Quite Interesting Critique by H. and A.**

The state of the world in 1945 was fundamentally different from when these discussions had taken place. Unable to compel itself to overthrow its government, the German proletariat had instead put its service towards honouring the *Führer*, the *Volk* and the *Vaterland*. Meanwhile, fascism had not left language unscathed. In the words of Adorno and Horkheimer, '[t]oday language calculates, designates, betrays, initiates death; it does not express'.[18]

A summary of a conversation between Adorno and Horkheimer from 1945[19] illustrates their shared resignation in view of the difficulties facing the public mediation of Critical Theory's insights. 'If we criticise psychoanalysis today and call for incest, Herr Schapiro will say to Herr Kohn: have you already read that quite interesting critique by H. and A.?'[20] In contrast to their own situation, Adorno and Horkheimer believe that if the *Communist Manifesto* could have counted on making an impact in its own time, this was because it was able to

---

15   Adorno and Horkheimer 1985b, p. 525, English word 'fun' used in the German original here and in the following quotations.

16   Adorno and Horkheimer 2002, p. 112.

17   Adorno and Horkheimer 1985b, p. 525.

18   Adorno and Horkheimer 2002, p. 209; cf. Adorno 2005b, p. 25: 'The chance conversation in the train, when, to avoid dispute, one consents to a few statements that one knows ultimately to implicate murder, is already a betrayal; no thought is immune against communication, and to utter it in the wrong place and in wrong agreement is enough to undermine its truth'.

19   This summary exists as an untitled six-page typescript with handwritten corrections (Adorno and Horkheimer, TWA, Ts 52528–33).

20   Adorno and Horkheimer, TWA, Ts 52528. 'Herr Schapiro' refers to the Marxist art historian Meyer Schapiro, who at the time taught at Columbia University and was in contact with Adorno and Horkheimer (cf. letter from Adorno to Kracauer, 3 May 1938 [Adorno and Kracauer 2020, p. 262] and letter from Theodor and Gretel Adorno to Benjamin, 10 August 1938 [Adorno and Benjamin 1999, pp. 269–70]). 'Herr Kohn' may refer to Elliot E. Cohen, the publisher of Commentary Magazine upon its establishment by the American Jewish Committee in 1945, and someone else with whom Adorno and Horkheimer maintained contact (cf. letter from Adorno to Horkheimer, 28 August 1945 [Adorno and Horkheimer 2005, pp. 145]).

address itself to an 'unintegrated society' in which the proletariat 'was not yet completely "on the inside"': insofar as the proletariat 'has no stake in society's humanity, it is all the better off in its own dehumanisation'. With the apparent disappearance of a proletariat which still saw itself as dominated by an external force, all theory became obsolete which regarded itself as able to appeal in an immediate and enlightened manner to an addressee with a practical interest in changing what exists. 'The curse of writing today is that however it turns out, it no longer rouses anyone anymore. The *Communist Manifesto* still set something in motion'.[21]

Adorno and Horkheimer now see themselves confronted with antinomies relating not only to the philosophy of language, but to society itself: assisted not least by the culture industry, the integrative force of society has disavowed the entire appellatory character of linguistic expression in favour of the mere exchange of information. The mediating linguistic relationship between theory and practice has been abrogated by the latter. 'We believe that the relationship of what is written to the world must be consciously included in the theoretical formulation as something co-determinative of the truth of the matter. Yet this relationship is suspect to us'.[22] Adorno and Horkheimer view the relationship between theory and practice as truncated by a practice which only permits statements about what exists. 'No terms are available which do not tend toward complicity with the prevailing intellectual trends'.[23] A call for anything at all, even for something like incest, is treated as literature, as something to be judged not according to some standard of truth, but by opinion if at all. No immediacy to reality can be asserted anymore, even though such immediacy is precisely what a manifesto would need to claim for itself in order to be effective. Theoretical statements not content to list facts degrade objectively into the 'the non-committal character of a private *Weltanschauung*'.[24]

Instead of being approached as interventions which deserve to be taken seriously, texts tend to be treated with 'indifference or condescension, or at most, with irony'[25] by their recipients, who prefer to maintain their distance where judgment would be in order. Meanwhile, what texts themselves say comes to stand in for judgement, with the author being seen as already having made and communicated a judgement. When language itself is 'taken as plot, as communication (*Mitteilung*)' in this way, it loses its appellatory character: 'How one

---

21   Adorno and Horkheimer, TWA, Ts 52528.
22   Ibid.
23   Adorno and Horkheimer 2002, p. xv.
24   Adorno 2005b, p. 68.
25   Willemsen 1999, p. 8.

gives someone else an axe, shares an axe with that person (*eine Axt mit-teilt*)[26] so that he can fell a tree, is also how one gives someone else a formula to wipe out the entire forest. The criterion of the deed becomes the criterion of the thought: the expedience, the effect'.[27] As Adorno and Horkheimer conclude,

> [t]he only way forward we now see, and upon which we will not back-slide behind Marx, is to take up his categories. In this, we currently have in mind concepts such as class and labour. With class, we are envision-ing a critique which has as its subject class's absorption into rackets. In a strict sense, perhaps no class has ever existed.[28]

Here, class is used not in the objective sense of the critique of political eco-nomy, but rather as a synonym for the class-consciousness of the proletariat. Although proletarians of course exist, Horkheimer and Adorno see themselves confronted with the question of whether 'the proletariat' can be said to exist in a strong sense – the very question which Lukács enthusiastically answered in the affirmative more than twenty years prior. In arriving at their own answer, Horkheimer and Adorno turn to the concept of labour.

As Horkheimer and Adorno explain,

> [t]he process of demythologisation, which we described in *Dialectic of Enlightenment*, should be developed from the concept of labour. Enlight-enment means the decoupling of labour from its substance. The process is essentially mediated through trade unions. They detach the worker from his objective interests. The point is to reveal the dialectic of this process, and hence, of the labour union and concept of the proletariat.[29]

---

26 Translator's note: the original German passage involves a play on words: with root words which mean 'with' (*mit*) and 'sharing' (*Teilung*), the German word for message (*Mitteilung*) can be read as 'sharing-with'.

27 Letter from Horkheimer to Adorno, 12 May 1945 (Adorno and Horkheimer 2005, p. 109). In his response to this letter, Adorno writes of his 'unbridled excitement that we will soon return these things' (Adorno and Horkheimer 2005, p. 118). One of these 'things' would have been the conversation about the manifesto.

28 Adorno and Horkheimer, TWA, Ts 52528.

29 Ibid. Here as well, trade unions are discussed a hindrance to class-consciousness. In his earlier 'Reflections on Class Theory', Adorno writes that trade unions have become 'monopolies, and their officials ... bandits', for the 'division between leader and led to be found in the ruling class reproduces itself compulsively' in the proletariat (Adorno 2003x, p. 100). In *Dialectic of Enlightenment*, Horkheimer and Adorno draw from this the fol-lowing conclusion: 'Even for a union boss, to say nothing of a manager, a proletarian is no more than a superfluous specimen, should he catch his notice at all, while the union

Domination, the principle undergirding the entirety of society, also asserts itself within the latter's individual spheres. Staying faithful to 'Reflections on Class Theory', Horkheimer and Adorno note that the proletariat has become subordinated to its own command as well – that domination by others has become domination by the self. And just as in Adorno's 'Reflections', '[gangs] and rackets'[30] – even those aligned with the labour movement – are said to function as mediators of this domination:

> As reluctant as we are to do so, we should ... probably broach a critique of international organisations. As squalid, bloated rackets, they are the caricature of what could be. Already visible in them are the collective interests of the bureaus of various national rackets.[31]

Adorno and Horkheimer observe that the 'increasing integration of society has made the concept of nonconformism problematic in the sense that no theoretical and hardly any practical utterance can be imagined anymore which does not in one form or another get caught in the mesh of the system'. Thus, they feel compelled to

> develop alternative forms of resistance to those which presuppose something transcendent to society, such as still existed in the time of Marx among the poor who were pressed into factories. Instead, resistance today is a matter of bringing into self-consciousness those countervailing tendencies (*Tendenzen zum Umschlag*) which are maturing within integrated society itself, helping them to their reversal (*ihrem Umschlag zu helfen*).

---

boss in turn must live in terror of his own liquidation' (Adorno and Horkheimer 2002, p. 30).

30   Adorno 2003x, p. 100. The summary of Adorno and Horkheimer's discussion continues as follows: 'We are not sure whether the assumption of Marxian categories today vouches for the inner actuality of our theoretical achievement. Yet it appears for the time being to continue to drive the movement, almost like an attack on the repressive role of those rackets (religious, political, military, industrial and trade-union) which superficially conflict but actually agree with each other. At the same time, it must be kept in mind above all that while the attack will refer to the national rackets, substantively it must keep current the transposition of the class-relation onto the international scene. In an age of transition from the national class-relation to the oppression of peoples by peoples, the leaders of peoples and all gangsters of the world join together under the star of fame into an international union. One example of an exponent of this union is Harold Laski' (Adorno and Horkheimer, TWA, Ts 52529–30). Laski was the leader of the British Labour Party at the time.

31   Adorno and Horkheimer, TWA, Ts 52531.

When taken together with the human being's radical self-alienation, and hence, with the absolutely negative, the process of the radical alienation of labour brought about by the extreme domination of nature also portends an 'almost-utopia' at the same time. The fully reified society is infinitely close to the concept of humanity. The ant colony is a projection of those who prepare it yet repress it from consciousness. Its conscious realisation could coincide with its abolition.[32]

Here, Adorno and Horkheimer follow in 'that tradition of enlightenment which reaches from the Homeric myth to Hegel and Marx, in whom the spontaneous deed, the act of freedom, coincides with the culmination of the objective trend'.[33] This tradition is present in the notion that society, conceived of as 'infinitely close to the concept of humanity', shall navigate through the 'absolutely negative' to find refuge within the latter, with theory helping society – which already produces its own 'countervailing tendencies' – to its own reversal.[34] Yet this theory, which wants to help transcend what exists, contains the same dialectic recognised by Adorno in *Minima Moralia* as existing within Marxian theory, namely the dialectic which maintains 'that the proletariat as the absolute object of history is capable of becoming its first social subject, and realizing the conscious self-determination of mankind':

> Negative philosophy, dissolving everything, dissolves even the dissolvent. But the new form in which it claims to suspend and preserve both, dissolved and dissolvent, can never emerge in a pure state from an antagonistic society. As long as domination reproduces itself, the old quality reappears unrefined in the dissolving of the dissolvent: in a radical sense no leap is made at all. That would happen only with the liberating event. Because the dialectical determination of the new quality always finds itself referred back to the violence of the objective tendency that propagates domination, it is placed under the almost inescapable compulsion, whenever it has conceptually achieved the negation of the negation, to substitute, even in thought, the bad old order for the non-existent alternative. The depth to which it penetrates objectivity is bought with complicity in the lie that objectivity is truth. By strictly limiting itself to extra-

---

32   Adorno and Horkheimer, TWA, Ts 52529.

33   Adorno 1988d, p. 270.

34   The *Communist Manifesto* also ultimately claims that the bourgeoisie produces above all 'its own grave-diggers. Its fall and the victory of the proletariat are equally inevitable' (Marx and Engels 2010, p. 79).

polating the image of a privilege-free state, from that which owes to the historical process the privilege of existing, it bows to restoration. This is registered by private existence.[35]

For the intellectual, fleeing from this privilege would simultaneously mean the betrayal of theory. Adorno and Horkheimer saw themselves tasked with theorising the contingent luxury of the possibility of theoretical practice, or in other words, the privilege which, following the 'separation of mental and manual labor, ... reserves mental labor, ... despite all assertions to the contrary ... the easier [form of labor], for itself'.[36]

> Our predicament has a dual nature: we don't simply want to become third persons again. This doesn't mean that we have something against 'the parasitic'. On the contrary, freedom from the coercion of production within degenerated bourgeois society was accompanied precisely by the survival of autonomy. Yet following the Marxian era, one can no longer seek to amuse the bourgeoisie as a third person, be it through critique or glorification. We have to be clear about this, even while we certainly know that for us, intellectual pursuit is still the natural mode of existence for the sons of rich parents. Thus, as 'philosophers of existence', we want to reflect on our own existence.[37]

---

35   Adorno 2005b, p. 245.
36   Adorno 1993a, p. 25. Adorno writes about intellectuals – that is, about himself – in two similar passages in *Minima Moralia*: 'In still permitting themselves to think at all in the face of the naked reproduction of existence, they act as a privileged group; in letting matters rest there, they declare the nullity of their privilege. Private existence, in striving to resemble one worthy of man, betrays the latter, since any resemblance is withdrawn from general realization, which yet more than ever before has need of independent thought. There is no way out of entanglement. The only responsible course is to deny oneself the ideological misuse of one's own existence, and for the rest to conduct oneself in private as modestly, unobtrusively and unpretentiously as is required, no longer by good upbringing, but by the shame of still having air to breathe, in hell' (Adorno 2005b, pp. 27–8); 'Intellectual business is helped, by the isolation of intellect from business, to become a comfortable ideology. This dilemma is communicated to intellectual behaviour even in its subtlest reactions. Only someone who keeps himself in some measure pure has hatred, nerves, freedom and mobility enough to oppose the world, but just because of the illusion of purity – for he lives as a "third person" – he allows the world to triumph not merely externally, but in his innermost thoughts' (Adorno 2005b, pp. 132–3).
37   Adorno and Horkheimer, TWA, Ts 52530.

Here, the term 'third person' refers to those who 'live on profit that has been diverted to them',[38] or in Marx's words, to those members of that 'idle surplus population' which 'does not work'[39] – people described by Adorno and Horkheimer as '"the parasitic"' insofar as they stand outside the economic process of reproduction: intellectuals. As Adorno writes in his 1960 essay 'Valéry's Deviations',

> [w]hile [third persons] perform no 'socially useful work' and contribute nothing to the material reproduction of life, it is they alone who represent theory and all consciousness that points beyond the blind coercion of material circumstances. They are defenseless against the distrust both of the status quo, which they live on without serving it dependably, and its enemies, for whom they are nothing but impotent agents of power.

From this insight, Adorno draws the same conclusion from fifteen years prior: if one is to defend third persons, 'it cannot be by praising the mind abstractly but only by expressing the negative element in them as well. Only when the ideological husk of their own existence falls away, only in a process of merciless self-reflection that would be the self-reflection of society as well, would they attain their social truth'.[40]

Later in their conversation from 1945, Adorno and Horkheimer turn their considerations towards 'the right state of humanity, which would already be possible today', arguing that Marx 'essentially defined this state with the concept of leisure',[41] inasmuch as leisure 'stands for the "true realm of freedom, the development of human powers as an end in itself"'.[42] In *Theories of Surplus Value*, Marx describes 'real wealth' as time which is not 'absorbed in direct productive labour', but instead 'available for enjoyment, for leisure, thus giving scope for free activity and development'.[43] Adorno and Horkheimer seek to 'draw on' this conception of leisure, which they see as 'deeply connected with that of the third person'[44] insofar as Marx conceives of 'third persons' – those

---

38   Adorno 2019o, p. 158.
39   Marx 1993, p. 608.
40   Adorno 2019o, p. 158.
41   Adorno and Horkheimer, TWA, Ts 52531.
42   Schürmann 2003, p. 9; quoted from Marx 1991, p. 959.
43   Marx 1989, p. 390. Originally published by Karl Kautsky between 1905–10, the collection of Marx's writings known as *Theories of Surplus Value* can now be found in English in *Marx/Engels Collected Works*, vols. 30–32.
44   Adorno and Horkheimer, TWA, Ts 52531.

'idlers, whose business it is to consume alien products'[45] – as people who are capable of leading the very life which should exist as a utopia for all.

Adorno and Horkheimer claim that 'under monopoly capitalism', the concept of leisure changed as fundamentally as the concept of the individual itself – understood as someone who is still able to partake in leisure after monopoly capitalism's rise:

> The concept of dehumanisation has changed in its composition. In Marx's work, it meant non-participation in culture, brutalisation (*Vertiertsein*). Today it amounts to being completely occupied by culture, to the Hegelian identity of the human with its being-for-itself being ironically fulfilled by the human's social substance. This development applies to the concept of leisure. Under monopoly capitalism, working hours are indeed already degraded by the total dematerialisation of labour. But precisely this disqualification of labour has claimed as a victim what in the Marxian sense makes humans in leisure human. The individual that, following Hegel, can only realise itself within the general social parameters has realised itself so fundamentally therein that in fact nothing individual is taken seriously anymore .... Yet this involves the dialectic that the individual, by realising its substance in the Hegelian sense, forfeits all substance: the parameter of being the chief of police is just as external to the individual as is, in the Hegelian sense, the question of whether it prefers veal or mutton. The less additional work humans have to do, the more they become a mere appendage of the machinery.[46]

Not only does this passage recapitulate insights expressed in *Minima Moralia*, it also revisits the notion from *Dialectic of Enlightenment* that contemporary culture forges a 'false identity of universal and particular'.[47]

'The other difficulty' with which Adorno and Horkheimer have to contend involves 'the concept of practice, the opposite of the fetishised spirit'. This difficulty 'follows from the state of the labour movement',[48] for if the labour movement as an entity no longer functions by helping the class-consciousness

---

45   Marx 1993, p. 608.
46   Adorno and Horkheimer, TWA, Ts 52531; cf. Adorno 1975, p. 12: 'the masses are not primary, but secondary, they are an object of calculation; an appendage of the machinery'. The 'appendage of the machinery'-motif occurs almost verbatim in multiple passages in Adorno's work: cf. Adorno 1989, p. 129; cf. Adorno 1974b, p. 71; cf. Adorno 2003q, p. 117; cf. Adorno 2001a, p. 189; cf. Adorno and Eisler 2005, p. 59.
47   Adorno and Horkheimer 2002, p. 95.
48   Adorno and Horkheimer, TWA, Ts 52530.

of the proletariat to assert itself, then it is insufficient to simply promote the Communist Party or 'to toe the Communist Party line'[49] (as Adorno put it in *Aesthetic Theory*).

> We do not believe that one should join those for whom the alternatives are being for or against the Communist Party. ... The unconditional accept-ance of the alternative itself already contains the acknowledgement that the revolution has failed. On the contrary, we believe that the opposition, that the Communist Party itself above all, belongs to the world which must be overcome by the revolution.[50]

However, in their discussion from 1956, Adorno and Horkheimer modify their position on the utility of a revolutionary party yet again.

3   A Strictly Leninist Manifesto

Adorno and Horkheimer's last surviving series of conversations about writing a manifesto dates from 1956. A discussion on theory and practice[51] in view of 'the constellation of the two antagonistic world blocs', it attempts to chart a course for Critical Theory 'between utopia and politically concrete position-taking'.[52]

When the relationship between labour and free time in both the West and the East is brought up on 12 March 1956, Horkheimer expresses the idea that he and Adorno 'ought to construct a kind of programme for a new form of prac-tice'. Adorno responds by suggesting 'the *Communist Manifesto* as a theme for variations'.[53] Notably, no mention is made of their earlier discussions on the necessity of composing a manifesto.[54] Apparently, the idea for a manifesto kept resurfacing during the war years and in the early post-war period, only to be rejected time and again due to a similar set of problems:

---

49   Adorno 2002a, p. 254.
50   Adorno and Horkheimer, TWA, Ts 52530.
51   Originally appearing under the title 'Diskusson über Theorie und Praxis' ('Discussion on Theory and Practice') in Volume 19 of Horkheimer's *Gesammelte Schriften*, an English translation of the series of conversations has since been published in *Towards a New Mani-festo* (Adorno and Horkheimer 2019).
52   Schmid Noerr 1996, p. 34.
53   Adorno and Horkheimer 2019, pp. 22 3.
54   At any rate, reflections on previous debates on the topic have not survived.

ADORNO: On the other hand, we must not abandon Marxist termino-
    logy.
HORKHEIMER: We have nothing else. But I am not sure how far we must
    retain it. Is the political question still relevant at a time when you
    cannot act politically?
ADORNO: On the one hand, it is ideology, on the other, all processes that
    might lead to change are political processes. Politics is both ideology
    and genuine reality.[55]

The notion that politics has become obsolete is already present in a conversation between Adorno and Horkheimer from eleven years prior: 'In a certain
sense, politics is no longer current, given that it has become clear to everyone what it involves, what the political goal would be'.[56] Just as Adorno and
Horkheimer address the evident nature of what is in 1945, a motif of their 1939
conversations as well, so too does this motif recur on 25 March 1956 when the
idea of composing a manifesto comes up yet again – and yet again spontaneously, as if for the first time:

ADORNO: Shouldn't we really have to think everything out from the
    beginning? Write a manifesto that will do justice to the current situ-
    ation. In Marx's day it could not yet be seen that the immanence of
    society had become total. That means, on the one hand, that one
    might almost need to do no more than strip off the outer shell; on the
    other hand, that no one really wants things to be otherwise.
HORKHEIMER: We still have something of a breathing space. We must
    not lose sight of that in our discussion of theory. We cannot be act-
    ive politically and yet every word we write is political. We have to say
    clearly that the Communist Party is not a whit superior to the lib-
    eral politicians in the Federal Republic. ... It must become quite clear
    from our general position why one can be a communist and yet des-
    pise the Russians.
ADORNO: We must be against Adenauer.
HORKHEIMER: But that is only true as long as we list the reasons that
    make it possible to keep on living in the West. An appeal for the re-
    establishment of a socialist party.
ADORNO: With a strictly Leninist manifesto.[57]

---

55   Adorno and Horkheimer 2019, pp. 25–6.
56   Adorno and Horkheimer, TWA, Ts 52532.
57   Adorno and Horkheimer 2019, pp. 62–4.

Against this, Horkheimer argues that 'we would be told that such a manifesto could not appear in Russia, while in the United States and Germany it would be worthless. At best, it might have some success in France and Italy'. Hedging himself again, he then adds that '[w]e are not calling on anyone to take action'.[58] Shortly thereafter on 30 March, in a conversation on the relationship between theory and practice, Adorno clarifies what he envisions under a 'strictly Leninist manifesto':

> What irritates me so much about the entire relationship between theory and practice is something quite obvious, namely the experience that everything the Russians write slips into ideology, into crude, stupid twaddle, that culture is rubbish and that somewhere, at the very same spot as in Marx and Engels, there is an element of re-barbarization. Thinking in their [the Russians'] writings is more reified than in the most advanced bourgeois thought. I have always wanted to rectify that and develop a theory that remains faithful to Marx, Engels and Lenin, while keeping up with culture at its most advanced.[59]

Horkheimer's surprising and immediately abandoned suggestion to compose an 'appeal for the re-establishment of a socialist party' is rejected by Adorno, who explicitly does not want to hand over revolutionary theory to a political party:

> Any appeal to form a left-wing socialist party is not on the agenda. Such a party would either be dragged along in the wake of the Communist Party, or it would suffer the fate of the SPD or Labour Party. It is not a political issue that there is no party.[60]

---

58 Adorno and Horkheimer 2019, p. 64.
59 Adorno and Horkheimer 2019, p. 69.
60 Adorno and Horkheimer 2019, pp. 72–3. Regarding the 'fate of the SPD', Adorno writes Horkheimer in 1966 of his plan 'to write a critique of the Godesberger Programme' (letter from Adorno to Horkheimer, 8 December 1966 [Adorno and Horkheimer 2006, p. 783]) in which the SPD reformed itself into a *Volkspartei*, or big-tent party. While Adorno has started work on this plan, he expresses 'very serious doubts' as to whether it is 'the right point in time' for the critique: 'To attack the SPD today – as this work would, however it is put together – is to deliver grist to the mills of everyone who wants to rock the badly damaged democracy. ... I have to admit to you that political instinct has forsaken me. On the one hand, it is apparent that the grand coalition entails the danger that the SPD will deprive itself of a near certain chance of an election victory in 1969 with the result that a right-wing conservative course *à la* [Franz Josef] Strauß will emerge as the saviour from neo-Nazism, even though this course would be quite similar to what it claims to

As they again attempt to compose a manifesto in the style of Marx and
Engels, the fact that neither Adorno nor Horkheimer reflect upon their previous discussions on the topic – that neither in 1945 nor 1956 do they mention
that they already had similar conversations, and that these conversations produced neither a manifesto nor progress in their own insights into the matter: all
this indicates a theoretical standstill within Critical Theory, or at least as practiced by Adorno and Horkheimer between 1939 and 1956, concerning central
questions of the critique of political economy.

Schmid Noerr's comment that the final group of conversations is also concerned 'not least with what form of writing is appropriate to the present'[61]
can certainly be expanded. In all three groups of conversations, Adorno and
Horkheimer veritably slave away at the question of how to write effectively in
a time in which, on the one hand, reality is no longer dressed up in ideology
but rather exposed for all to see, yet on the other, all texts are received with an
apathetic mildness depriving every appeal of its spur. In a September 1941 letter
to Horkheimer, Adorno refers to a note he had written two years prior, which
in his words 'at least shows how much I am aware of my own helplessness. I
admittedly tend towards the view that this is not merely a matter of my failure,
but rather also one of a real antinomy'.[62] This note reads as follows:

> The prohibitive difficulty of theory today is revealed in language. Lan-
> guage no longer allows anything to be said as it is experienced. Either it
> is reified, commodity-language, a language which is banal and partially
> falsifies thoughts. Or it is fleeing from banality, ceremonial without cere-
> mony, empowered without power, validated by its own account. ... That
> the violence of facts has become so outrageous that all theory, and even
> true theory, makes a mockery of them – this is burned like a mark into
> the organ of theory itself, language. The practice which takes away the-
> ory's power emerges as an element of destruction within theory, without

---

be the saviour from. On the other hand, I see in the grand coalition the genuine chance
for a transition to a two-party system ... and with that, for the exclusion of the [neo-Nazi]
NPD. So please lend me some sage advice; and it would be wonderful if you wouldn't delay
too long in doing so' (letter from Adorno to Horkheimer, 8 December 1966 [Adorno and
Horkheimer 2006, pp. 783–4]). Horkheimer discouraged Adorno (cf. letter from Adorno to
Horkheimer, 15 December 1966 [Adorno and Horkheimer 2006, p. 785]), who dropped the
plan. As a result of the federal election in 1969, a social-liberal coalition government was
formed under Willy Brandt, who served as Germany's first Social Democratic chancellor.

61   Cf. Schmid Noerr 1996, p. 33.

62   Letter from Adorno to Horkheimer, 4 September 1941 (Adorno and Horkheimer 2004,
      p. 224); cf. Müller-Doohm 2008, pp. 37–8, n. 37.

regards for potential practice. In fact, nothing more can be said. Action is the only form which remains in theory.[63]

This is the curse which afflicts writing when 'the objective presuppositions are lacking for such forms as the leaflet or the manifesto', as Adorno observes they were in 1959: 'Those who imitate them are only acting as secret worshippers of power, parading their own impotence'.[64] After all,

> the notion that through the theory, and through the enunciation of the theory, one can immediately stir people and arouse them to action has become doubly impossible. This results from the disposition of men who, as is well known, can no longer be aroused by theory in any way, and results from the form of reality which excludes the possibility of such actions which for Marx seemed to be just around the corner. If today one behaved as if one could change the world tomorrow, then one would be a liar.[65]

Today, appeals are no longer composed to appeal, but rather to demonstrate that one has composed an appeal. Every text which wants to immediately intervene is now only a documentation of itself. Until further notice, the linguistic mediation between theory and practice addressed at the outset of this chapter no longer exists. If Critical Theory wants to become practical in spite of this, in times in which the mediation between emancipatory theory and practice is socially truncated, then every utterance aiming towards practice inevitably presents itself solely as a testimony of individual nonconformity which in turn can be dismissed as quirkiness. The social stupidity which speaks from language is essential to that practice which calls to be changed. If theory is to avoid succumbing to this stupidity, it requires a mode of speaking which is different from the merely communicative. However, this mode of speaking would no longer be understood by the masses to whom manifestos and leaflets are usually addressed – at least not insofar as 'understanding' is understood as a content-related category rather than a cognitive one. At best, the contents of leaflets are perceived as something artificial or artistic – as literature – and at worst, as impotent requests to speak issued by irrelevant parties. Either way, they are not understood as suggestions of how life could be better: here as well, cultural absorption has been completed. Whoever wants to read elaborate

63   Adorno 1995b, p. 7.
64   Adorno 2019a, p. 301.
65   Adorno cited in Dahrendorf 1976, pp. 128–9, cf. editorial note by Tiedemann (Adorno 2008, pp. 227–8, n. 17).

social critique in leaflet form is better off looking in the exhibits of specialised museums than on the streets. All that remains is to criticise the social process in its own right, including as it manifests itself in the degeneration of 'language as the organon of thought'.[66]

---

66   Adorno 2007b, p. 56.

PART 3

∵

CHAPTER 10

?? Did He Read Marx?

> Only then could the whole be better and more prudently connected
> with the individual parts.
>
> ECKHARD HENSCHEID, Rossmann, Rossmann …

∴

1   Priority of Economy or Society

Generally speaking, Adorno's renewed turn towards Marx in the post-war period came about for two reasons: first, his work on his magnum opus, *Negative Dialectics*, and second, his elaboration of a meta-economic social critique,
which he developed in continuous dialogue with his students. Moreover, these
areas were not separate from each other: on the contrary, Adorno worked out
Negative Dialectics in engagement with the audience of his courses, with whom
he shared his work as it progressed.[1]

Starting with the winter semester of 1957–8, Adorno held a two-semester
seminar titled 'Wirtschaft und Gesellschaft' ('Economy and Society'),[2] which
Horkheimer also co-taught on occasion. This seminar marked the first time
in his teaching that he 'explicitly and exhaustively covered Marxian theory'.[3]
Adorno identified the 'primary task' of the seminar as the attempt to 'assemble
the building blocks of a politico-economic theory beyond the division of economy and sociology, and in doing so, to prevent the de-economisation of sociology from rendering it a psychology in disguise',[4] such as Freud envisioned it.[5]

---

1 'Work on *Negative Dialectics* occupied Adorno from 1959–66, and was closely bound up with
   his teaching during this time' (Demirović 1999a, p. 633).
2 An overview of Adorno's lecture and seminar courses can be found in Müller-Doohm 2003,
   pp. 944–50.
3 Demirović 1999a, p. 460.
4 Adorno 2021a, vol. 2, p. 51.
5 'If anyone were in a position to show in detail the way in which these different factors – the
   general inherited human disposition, its racial variations and its cultural transformations –
   inhabit and promote one another under the conditions of social rank, profession and earning
   capacity – if anyone were able to do this, he would have supplemented Marxism so that it was

According to Alex Demirović, the Institute for Social Research sociologist Man-fred Teschner[6] literally had to 'convince Adorno to finally offer a course on this topic'.[7] The syllabus for the seminar spanning the winter semester of 1957–58 and the summer semester of 1958 contained a list of subjects to be presented and discussed: 'Marxist Theory of Modern Imperialism', 'Economy and Society: The Contribution of Neoliberalism', 'On the Relationship Between Economy and Society in Max Weber's Work', 'On the Relationship Between Economy and Society in Talcott Parsons's Work', 'Sombart's Humanities-Based Social Eco-nomy', 'Problems of the Subjectivist Value Theory of National Economy', 'On the Use of the Term "Society" in Contemporary National Economy', 'Basics of the Development of Soviet Russian Society', 'State and Economy in the United States' and 'Excursus: On Ralf Dahrendorf's Theory of Social Classes'.[8]

As preserved in the transcripts, Adorno's introduction to the seminar reads as follows:

> The overlap between the topic and the title of Max Weber's magnum opus shall by no means determine the work. It is much rather the case that the goal of the seminar is to reflect on society as a totality, and on the rela-tionship of economy and sociology in a narrower sense. The attempt will be made to illuminate society in its entirety while focusing on a few areas in particular, to recognise what holds society together and reproduces it.[9]

---

made into a genuine social science. For sociology too, dealing as it does with the behaviour of people in society, cannot be anything but applied psychology. Strictly speaking there are only two sciences: psychology, pure and applied, and natural science' (Freud 2001b, p. 179).

6 Among other things, Teschner composed a monograph titled *Politik und Gesellschaft im Unterricht* [*Politics and Society in Teaching*] and contributed to a study by the Institute for Social Research titled *Betriebsklima. Eine insudstiesoziologische Untersuchung aus dem Ruhrgebiet* (*Business Climate: An Industrial-Sociological Investigation from the Ruhr Region*) for which Adorno wrote the preface (cf. Adorno 2003ae, pp. 642–3). Both appeared in *Frankfurter Beiträge zur Soziologie*, a book series published by the Institute at the time.

7 Demirović 1999a, p. 460, n. 380.

8 Universitätsarchiv Frankfurt am Main, Abt. 139 Nr. 3, 'Prof. Adorno / Soziologisches Haupt-seminar, WS 1957/58 und SS 1958 / "Wirtschaft und Gesellschaft"'. This plan is attached to the corresponding transcripts and presentations from both semesters. During Horkheimer's trip from Chicago to the American west coast in the spring of 1957, Adorno writes to him the fol-lowing from Frankfurt: 'In Los Angeles you will ... probably meet all kinds of VIPs, such as Talcott Parsons. I don't need you to say anything about him as an intellectual figure, but his authority in America and now also here (Dahrendorf!) is so great that it would be good if you could maintain friendly contact with him, provided that you can do this without falling asleep from boredom. It's hard to make a living' (letter from Adorno to Horkheimer, 14 March 1957 [Adorno and Horkheimer 2006, p. 422]).

9 Adorno 2021a, vol. 2, p. 49.

Indeed, as the seminar progresses, the treatment of Weber recedes into the background in favour of that of Marx: while Adorno concedes that Weber made 'the last great attempt to grasp the essence of society as a whole',[10] he criticises the latter precisely for missing what is essential about society.

Already in the summer semester of 1954, Adorno had held a seminar titled 'Max Webers wissenschaftlich-theoretische Schriften' ('Max Weber's Writings on the Theory of Science'), which made quite clear his preference for Marxian theory, particularly with regards to society's economically determined cohesion. In preparation for this seminar, Adorno again engaged with Weber's *Gesammelte Aufsätze zur Wissenschaftslehre* (*Collected Essays on the Theory of Science*),[11] and immediately took issue with Weber's interpretation of Marx. In *Gesammelte Aufsätze*, Weber writes that 'the idea of something "objectively" valid – that is to say: <u>something which *ought to* be</u> – has, from Scholasticism to <u>Marxist theory</u>, been intertwined with an abstraction derived from the empirical process of price formation. And this idea: that the "value" of commodities <u>*ought* to</u> be regulated according to certain principles of "natural law" has had immense importance for the development not just of medieval culture – an importance that still persists'.[12] A note from Adorno in the margin next to this passage reads as follows: '?? did he read Marx? K[arl] M[arx] criticised precisely the exchange of equivalents!'[13] Later in the seminar itself, Adorno explains that

Weber 'viewed the question of objective essence as external to science. ... On what the idea type's formation was based, Weber left to chance.' Therein lies his decisive failure and the difference between him and Marx.[14]

---

10   Adorno 2021a, vol. 2, p. 50.

11   Adorno's library contains a copy of this book published in Tübingen by J.C.B. Mohr in 1922. A handwritten note by Adorno therein makes clear that all the marginalia and marks within it were in fact made in 1954, the year of his first seminar on Weber (TWA, NB 2428, p. 192).

12   Weber 2012, p. 128, underlinings by Adorno (TWA, NB 2428, p. 196).

13   TWA, NB 2428, p. 196. Another handwritten note by Adorno is at the top of the page: 'idea + ideal type'.

14   Adorno 2021a, vol. 1, p. 227; cf. Demirović 1999a, p. 442. A similar comment can be found in *Jargon of Authenticity*: 'What is essential in phenomena, and what is accidental, hardly ever springs straightforwardly out of the phenomena. In order to be determined in its objectivity, it has first to be reflected on subjectively. Certainly, at first glance, it seems more essential to a worker that he has to sell his [labour-power], that the means of production do not belong to him, that he produces material goods, than that he is a member of a suburban gardening club; although the worker himself may think that the latter is more essential. However, as soon as the question directs itself to so central a concept as

Adorno acknowledges some common elements in Weber's and Marx's respective analyses of capitalism.[15] However, 'what makes the entire difference',
Adorno argues, is the position of these elements within the overall analysis:

> whether these [elements] are listed and summarized in a kind of defin-
> ition, by an interpreting, analytical, descriptive sociology in the older
> positivist style ... or whether they are developed ... from certain basic
> categories; and whether they give rise to what Marx himself, in the fam-
> ous letter of his youth, called the 'grotesque, precipitous melody [*groteske
> Felsenmelodie*]' of Hegel's thought, that awesome and overwhelming phe-
> nomenon of a compelling coherence between the so-called attributes,
> which are not simply orientated towards a conceptual core, but are each
> derived from the other. And the hellish, compulsive character of the
> whole from which we all suffer is demonstrated in such thought in a quite
> different way than in the descriptive, interpretative kind of sociology to be
> found in Weber. You may see from this that even when the different meth-
> odological approaches yield the same thing, that thing is not the same
> after all, but carries an entirely different weight.[16]

capitalism, Marx and the verbal definitions of Max Weber say something extremely different from each other. In many cases the distinction between essential and inessential,
between authentic and inauthentic, lies with the arbitrariness of definition, without in
the least implying the relativity of truth' (Adorno 1973, pp. 122–3).

15   In his 1968 lecture course *Introduction to Sociology*, Adorno argues that '[c]ertain basic
structures of society do manifest themselves in the most diverse methods. If, for example,
you consider the qualities Max Weber attributed, very much in the manner of subjective
sociology, to the "ideal type" of capitalism, and compare them with the Marxian theory
against which Weber's sociology was largely conceived, you will find a large number of
moments in common: for example, the equivalent form, the market, rationality, calculation and suchlike concepts' (Adorno 2000a, p. 83). However, as he claims in his 1960 lecture
course *Philosophie und Soziologie* (*Philosophy and Sociology*), 'the concept of rationality
in Max Weber seems rather naive about it insofar as it fails to recognize the problematic character of thisrationality even in a supposedly rational form of exchange society.
In other words, if I may appeal to an old and famous formulation, in the world that we
inhabit, with its prevailing structure of exchange, the relations between human beings are
reflected back to us as if these relations were really properties of things, and the objective
reason why the world appears to us in a thing-like way lies precisely in the reified character
of our own experience' (Adorno 2022, p. 67).

16   Adorno 2000a, p. 84. In a letter from November 1837, Marx writes his father that 'the grotesque craggy melody [*groteske Felsenmelodie*]' of Hegel's philosophy does not appeal to
him (Marx 1975b, p. 18).

When Weber uses action theory to define categories of economic sociology, he draws on concepts such as 'utility' and 'scarcity'.[17] In doing so, he defines the economy subjectively, or according to the intentions of actors: 'Action will be called "economically-*oriented*" inasmuch as its intended meaning is oriented to meeting a desire for utilities. "Economic activity" will refer to a *peaceful* exercise of power of disposition *primarily* oriented to "rational economic action", which action is primarily rational by virtue of being directed to a purpose, and hence is *planfully* oriented to economic ends'.[18] From the perspective of the theory of economy, this subjectivism leads to the marginal utility of neoclassical economics,[19] whose assumption that capitalism's specific preconditions are transhistorical is shared by Weber: 'Economic action emerges in Weber's work as a paradigm of rational action. This in turn invites the question of where in fact the difference between rational and economic action lies'.[20] Ultimately, Weber's economic theory expresses the 'historically particular capitalist version of competition through an historically unspecific calculus of scarcity'[21] while disregarding the fact that this calculus is itself the product[22] of capitalist forms of intercourse – forms which the calculus itself is supposed to explain.

The 1957–8 seminar thus seeks to focus on the question 'of the priority of economy or society'.[23] Whereas in *Dialectic of Enlightenment*, Adorno and Horkheimer 'had not clearly established whether exchange results from domination and a predominant form of thought which aims at the domination of nature, or whether, conversely, exchange determines the forms of thought and of domination over nature and human beings',[24] Adorno now rejects this question as undialectical:

> The task of a truly critical theory must be to liquidate of a question of this kind. What's important is not to demonstrate the primacy of one of the two, but rather their unity.

17   Cf. Bader, Berger, Ganßmann and von dem Knesebeck 1976, pp. 196–7.
18   Weber 2019 p. 143.
19   Cf. Bader, Berger, Ganßmann and von dem Knesebeck 1976, p. 209.
20   Bader, Berger, Ganßmann and von dem Knesebeck 1976, p. 199.
21   Bader, Berger, Ganßmann and von dem Knesebeck 1976, p. 201.
22   In the margin next to Weber's claim in *Gesammelte Aufsätze zur Wissenschaftslehre* that 'the essential' is what is *'permanently valuable'* (Weber 2012, p. 129), a note by Adorno reads 'ouch' (TWA, NB Adorno 2428, p. 199).
23   Adorno 2021a, vol. 2, p. 79.
24   Demirović 1999a, p. 467.

The concept of political economy itself, if consequently elaborated, would mean – were it to be taken seriously – the unity of exchange economy and social process.[25]

Alex Demirović notes that this formulation 'remains unclear' because 'on the one hand, exchange is an economic concept, and on the other, a dialectical theory must say the same for each of its concepts – it always concerns elements which mediate the whole', whereas 'Adorno privileges a view according to which the social whole is in fact determined by exchange, social labour and surplus-value'.[26] However, precisely through its determination by these elements, Adorno understands the social whole to be determined by domination: noting that 'the priority of economy' in Marx's work is the 'result of the actual attempt to derive all power relations from immanent, purely economic factors',[27] he comments that this 'hypostatisation of the economy is quite problematic. Insofar as there can only be "economy" in the sense of a developed exchange economy, it is also questionable to what extent a theory which reduces power relations to economic factors can be applied to relations predating exchange at all'.[28] The supremacy of economy over (political) domination in the theory of Marx and Engels is viewed by Adorno as a consequence of the political imperative of their time to pragmatically 'draw a battle line against anarchism',[29] which 'sought social injustice in rule as such without reflecting on the economic. Against this, it needed to be shown that power relations were already mediated, as Engels did in *Anti-Dühring*'.[30] Adorno makes a similar point in his lecture course *Fragen der Dialektik* (*Questions of Dialectics*) from the winter semester of 1963–4. After acknowledging 'the countless anarchist tendencies' which Marx 'certainly had to fight against given the demands of the political situation', Adorno adds that Marx

dealt with these in a way which, I would think, is only really exacting its full vengeance today, in the real historical situation. The Marxian centralism, which initially emerged in its vision of a strictly organised party,

---

25   Adorno 2021a, vol. 2, p. 79; cf. Demirović 1999a, p. 467; cf. also Adorno's critique of mono-causal analyses of society in Adorno 2007b, p. 269.

26   Demirović 1999a, pp. 467–8.

27   Adorno 2021a, vol. 2, p. 81

28   Adorno 2021a, vol. 2., p. 80

29   Adorno 2021a, vol. 2, p. 80

30   Ibid. 'Adorno sees the reason for the primacy of economic analysis in Marx's polemical position against anarchism, which was only abstractly concerned with change because it was merely political. In contrast, Marx and Engels located political change in a change

was inherited by Lenin and then ultimately turned into a new state social-ism – this Marxian centralism grew precisely out of an hostility towards anarchism. This hostility falls into our set of problems insofar as it really represents the attempt to realise the aspect of use-value, or the recovery of human immediacy, through the medium of immediacy, or specific-ally through the appropriation of individual factories by the proletariat. It does this without considering that all the misery of bourgeois society criticised by Marx would then have to reproduce itself. This misery was summed up by Marx in one expression which, not without reason, spe-cifically evokes anarchism: 'anarchy of production'. ... One can say that everywhere – and this is only one of the most central problems of materi-alist dialectics in general – the tendency has emerged for the unavoidably rational synthetic or centralist element inherent in materialist dialectics to blow back in repression within itself. This is because such rational plan-ning is linked with domination in its very essence. Conversely, and this certainly has to be said, the appeal to the pure immediacy of nature and the renunciation of this rationality especially only serves as a pretext for the powerful to assert their interests, which indeed are almost always – think of the Third Reich – presented as natural, as the powers of irration-ality or whatever such concepts may be.[31]

The question of whether economy or society is primary comes into focus dur-ing a seminar session from May 1958 at which Horkheimer is also present. Emphasising that 'exchange as a key category first had its breakthrough in bourgeois society', Horkheimer claims that 'in no previous era of society were human relationships so decisively shaped by exchange relations as they are today'. According to him, while it is only under capitalism that exchange en-tered into *all* human relationships, there is no doubting its historically univer-sal significance: 'Forms of exchange existed in all ages, even though exchange's significance varied in particular historical periods. ... The only invariant valid for all of prehistory is the category of exchange!'[32] One seminar participant objects to this that

the actual exchange society only arose with bourgeois society, and ... only since then can one speak of a strict dependence of society on the eco-

---

in economy. The process of exchange assumes class-relations. It implicitly contains their acceptance and an element of the fetishistic' (Adorno 2021a, vol. 4, p. 233).

31 Adorno 2021b, pp. 268–9.
32 Adorno 2021a, vol. 2, p. 127.

nomy. The sole orientation of this problem on the exchange-relation is too narrow. In historical materialism, which not without reason emerged in the bourgeois era, the analysis of the exchange-relation is supposed to reveal particular relationships between classes. The apologetic study of economy transforms into a critical one once it shatters the appearance of fair exchange, and provides evidence of very specific class-relations which characterise both bourgeois and pre-capitalist society. So by ana-lysing bourgeois society, it's possible draw conclusions for dependency relations in pre-bourgeois societies. But what is important, in addition to relationships of exchange, are traditional power- and class-relations!

The sole focus on the exchange-relation strikes this participant as 'merely a detour which ultimately must lead to the fundamental phenomenon existing in all eras of society and not emerging only from relationships of exchange, but also from the facts of previous societies: namely, the existence of classes'.[33] Adorno responds that he finds this outlook to be unrealistic: 'One must not hypostatise class-relations and attempt to reduce history to them, independ-ently of the economy. On the contrary, one has to derive class-divisions from economic conditions'.[34] In a session from another seminar at the end of 1965, Adorno affirms the position he had already taken in 'Reflections on Class The-ory': given that class-relations are assumed by the production of surplus-value, which depends on the consumption of the commodity of labour-power, this production 'implicitly contains their acceptance and an element of the fetish-istic'.[35] After all, the acceptance of class-relations as transhistorical facts misses that these relations 'reproduce [themselves] by way of the [exchange] of equi-valents'.[36] This claim again indicates that history for Adorno cannot simply be viewed as the history of class struggles. Class struggles do not take precedence

---

33   Adorno 2021a, vol. 2, p. 124.

34   Ibid.

35   Adorno 2021a, vol. 4, p. 233.

36   Adorno 2007b, p. 166. 'The process of increasing social rationalization, of universal exten-
      sion of the market system, is not something that takes place beyond the specific social
      conflicts and antagonisms, or in spite of them. It works through those antagonisms them-
      selves, the latter at the same time tearing society apart in the process. For the institution of
      exchange there is created and reproduced that antagonism which could at any time bring
      organized society to ultimate catastrophe and destroy it. The whole business keeps creak-
      ing and groaning on, at unspeakable human cost, only on account of the profit motive and
      the interiorization by individuals of the breach torn in society as a whole' (Adorno 1989,
      p. 272).

over economy, but rather are themselves an element of economy. Although the primacy of economy always dominates given that 'human beings have wanted to live at all times', Adorno continues in the 1958 seminar,

> it is nevertheless not entirely correct, not even in the case of primitive societies, to speak of an unambiguous dependency of society on the economy – not even in a time when there was neither a fully formed economy nor society. Back then, rational economic elements [such as exchange] existed only in a rudimentary form, and self-preservation was overgrown with religious elements. Everything was in a state of becoming, and the dependence of society on the economy was also something which produced itself historically.[37]

Here, Adorno apparently has in mind an economic system which already obeys a certain rationality. Horkheimer also then warns against

> offhandedly conflating economy with exchange economy, for many equivocations are possible with the phrase 'economy through exchange'. Above all, economic exchange is confused with economic competition. Whoever wants to explain social processes on the basis of, or put them in the context of economic competition, could only do so for the latest phase of bourgeois society, since the phenomenon of economic competition first emerges in this late phase.

Horkheimer claims that 'to achieve a particular concept of economy ...', it is necessary to investigate whether exchange' – described by Adorno as 'the fundamental category of all of economy' – 'has in fact been the hallmark of economy since its beginnings. In primitive tribes, in groups of hunters and gatherers who fed themselves by catching fish or collecting mussels, exchange does not appear to have played a decisive role'. Adorno objects to this: 'Even in primitive society, exchange was present. The primitive human being wanted the good he did not have'.[38] Thus, while Horkheimer warns against conflating economy in general with exchange in light of the marginal status of exchange in subsistence economies, Adorno avoids this problem by invoking an ideal-typical anthropological desire. However, simply desiring the good does not make the 'primitive' human being a participant in exchange – a desire is not

---

37   Adorno 2021a, vol. 2, p. 124.
38   Adorno 2021a, vol. 2, p. 129.

an action. Furthermore, the mere prehistoric existence of desire certainly does not mean that subsistence economies were exchange economies, for the desire to acquire something must not necessarily bring about exchange as a mode of acquisition which structures society.

As the seminar transcripts show, subsequent speculation on this issue remains vague in its generality. Once again, Horkheimer voices his doubts regarding the equation of exchange and subsistence economy:

> As to whether the genuinely economic can be equated with the principle of exchange, one must take into account ... that the slave economy of the Greeks and Romans was not the only form of economy at that time. In relatively isolated countries such as Persia, which was surrounded by mountains, people had to provide for themselves with the means at their disposal for processing nature. In these countries, the economy essentially had to do with self-sustenance. However, this form of sustenance, or economy, is not the same as when human beings sustain themselves through the profit motive.[39]

Adorno mentions slavery in antiquity: 'Exchange also played a role for the Greeks: when they received materials from the barbarians, these would certainly have been more valuable than what they gave up for them. And getting more than one gives is teleologically immanent in the principle of exchange'.[40]

To this is as well, Horkheimer objects that '[n]ot even in Greek or Roman society was exchange typical'.[41] After all,

> [w]hat the Greeks wanted was: to live well, to have as many slaves as possible and to not be disturbed by anyone. Their economy was created in such a way that it was essentially carried out by slaves. For this form of economy, exchange is not characteristic. The consciousness of the Greeks, or of the Romans, who had their slaves fetch for them from the Sicilian mines what they needed for their own use, was essentially different from the consciousness of the merchant.[42]

---

39   Adorno 2021a, vol. 2, p. 130
40   Adorno 2021a, vol. 2, p. 129
41   Ibid.
42   Adorno 2021a, vol. 2, pp. 129–30

Horkheimer does concede to Adorno that 'exchanging ... probably has an extremely deep human history'. Yet to illustrate this thesis – one of the central theses of *Dialectic of Enlightenment* – Horkheimer makes use not of economic-historical argumentation, but instead cites the Bible, deriving the historical universality of the principle of exchange from the state of consciousness of ancient Judaism:

> The Old Testament saying of 'an eye for an eye and a tooth for a tooth' means a regulation of barbaric punishment, which was fundamentally a moderation, because previously there had been no fixed sentence at all. So when it says that nothing more will be done to you than what you have done yourself – that this is the price you have to pay – this assumes the principle of exchange. All of jurisprudence at the time was based on exchange: to this extent, Professor Adorno's theory is confirmed.[43]

With this comment, Horkheimer underhandedly grants domination primacy over economy. Adorno responds to Horkheimer's historical argument by qualifying his own argument that exchange 'also played a role for the [ancient] Greeks':

> The slave economy was not an economic relation in a strict sense, but much more of a social relation maintained through the exercise of power and control, which kept in check what one could call the process of production. The difference becomes clear when one realises that the essence of the economic principle lies in the fact that this principle itself is not contingent on social power, but rather creates social power from itself. In the rule over slaves, society has primacy over economy. The slave economy does not emerge from the apparatus of production; rather, it emerges when a group of people has acquired power. However, this immediate relation of power cannot be described as an economic relation in the sense of the theories of Engels.[44]

---

43   Adorno 2021a, vol. 2, p. 130. After this passage in the transcript, the following comment appears: '(In this context, Westermann's book on moral concepts is referenced)'. This was probably a misunderstanding on the part of the transcriber: what was likely mentioned was the book *The Origin and Development of the Moral Ideas* by Edvard Westermarck, which is also referred to in *Dialectic of Enlightenment* (see Adorno and Horkheimer and Adorno 2002, p. 251, n. 21).

44   Adorno 2021a, vol. 2, pp. 130–1.

Nor can it be described as such in the sense used by Adorno, who maintains that 'economy is actually only present where there is exchange',[45] where there is already a division of labour which guarantees social reproduction. 'If we want to understand social life, we have to first explain how this life comes into being: it only exists because humans have to eat. Thus, *the reproduction of life in society must logically and genetically have priority over social forms*'.[46]

2   ultima philosophia

Adorno and Horkheimer's seminar discussion of whether historical or logical priority belongs to the realm of the economic, or rather to that of the social, that is, to domination, ultimately remains fruitless. Evidently, it lacks the dialectical mediation necessary to conceive of domination and economy as two sides of the very same principle. In any case, Adorno neglects his prior insight – articulated independently of Horkheimer – that 'the question of whether domination or economy comes first' already contains something 'of the delusion of the nineteenth century' which maintained that 'everything which exists can be explained based on what came first'.[47] In contrast to this delusion, Adorno writes elsewhere that 'one of the most important goals of materialist dialectics' seems to him to be 'to liquidate the idea of *prima philosophia* and ... to replace it with an *ultima philosophia*':[48] 'the original sin of *prima philosophia*', he argues, is that '[m]erely in order to gain continuity and completeness' – to achieve a closed system of representation – it 'must cut out of its sphere of judgment whatever does not fit'.[49] Against this, Adorno emphasises that 'one cannot deduce the entire world from exchange, as with some naïve scientific method, and as taught beyond the eastern border, in a very simple and obvious systematic approach'.[50]

---

45   Adorno 2021a, vol. 2, p. 130.

46   Adorno 2021a, vol. 2., p. 132.

47   Adorno 2021a, vol. 2, p. 86.

48   Letter from Adorno to Sohn-Rethel, 3 November 1936 (Adorno and Sohn-Rethel 1991, p. 11). 'Adorno frequently attempted to formulate the deeply unsatisfactory nature of all traditional philosophy, its inappropriateness to its subject, its repudiation by the worldly wise. He hoped to lead thought along the "only critical path that remains open", by identifying such fallacies as "thinking of a first philosophy", "origin" thinking, the primacy of subjectivity, the universal rule of domination – and also as the constitution of method' (Tiedemann 2008, pp. xii–xiii).

49   Adorno 1978c, p. 82.

50   Adorno 2019i, p. 104.

In the *Encyclopedia of the Philosophical Sciences*, Hegel describes development as a process of unfolding:

> The movement of the *concept* is ... *development*, by means of which that alone is posited that is already on hand in itself. In nature it is the organic life, which corresponds to the stage of the concept. Thus, for example, the plant develops itself out of its seed [*Keimzelle*]. This seed contains the entire plant in itself already, but in an ideal manner and so one should not construe its development as if the various parts of the plant, root, stem, leaves and so forth were already *really* in the seed yet merely in utterly miniature fashion. This is the so-called 'Chinese box hypothesis', the deficiency of which consists in the fact that what is only on hand initially in an ideal manner is considered as already concretely existing. What is right in this hypothesis is, by contrast, this: that the concept, in its process, remains with itself and that nothing new is posited by this means with respect to the content. Instead only an alteration of form is brought forth.[51]

On the basis of Hegel's use of metaphor in this passage, some theorists who attempt to interpret Marx with recourse to Hegel have envisioned the commodity as a *Keimzelle* – a seed, or more precisely, a germ cell – 'whose unfolding will reproduce the whole internal structure of the capitalist society'. For example, Karl Kosík argues that the commodity is '"an absolute reality" because it is the unity of all determinations, the germ of all contradictions, and as such can be characterized in Hegelian terms as the unity of being and not-being, of the differentiated and the undifferentiated, of identity and non-identity'.[52] Here, Kosík conceives of the commodity as a totality which simply has to unfold itself in the process of capital, and before the discerning theorist. By viewing the thinker or theorist as someone who reveals social being by helping to theoretically unfold the commodity,[53] this position applies the 'objective-idealist principle of the identity of thought and being'[54] to the analysis of the commodity-form – a principle in Hegel's work which has been criticised by Jindřich Zelený. At the same time, it either disregards socially constitutive practice, or understands such practice as the result of a truly 'unfolded' commodity-form. Kosík seeks to avoid the accusation of reductionism, emphasising that '[d]ialectics is

---

51   Hegel 2010a, p. 234.
52   Kosík 1976, p. 16.
53   Cf. Ritsert 1973, p. 13.
54   Zelený 1980, p. 33.

not a method of reduction, but a method of spiritual and intellectual reproduction of society, a method of unfolding and explicating social phenomena on the basis of the objective activity of the historical man'.[55] Yet indeed, he accounts for only *one* activity, namely the activity of producing commodities – in keeping with the metaphor of the germ cell, all other social actions are already conflated with the commodity. Against this, Marx himself observes that commodities 'cannot themselves go to market'.[56] The commodity requires human action beyond its production, for it cannot mediate itself. The metaphor of the germ cell may seem trivial, but as Jürgen Ritsert comments, it actually leads to a substantial pitfall in the reading of Marx:

> Among other things, the faulty metaphor of the 'germ cell' causes one to overlook a further barrier to comparisons with Hegel on the problem of origin. In *Science of Logic*, Hegel writes that advancement in philosophy actually consists in a 'a retrogression and a grounding, only by virtue of which it then follows as result that that, with which the beginning was made, was not just an arbitrary assumption but was in fact *the truth*, and *the first truth* at that'. ... Yet Marx's conception of capitalism as a whole does not return to the point of origin the way it came. The commodity ... is not what the elaborated representation would designate as the *central* element of society, its ensemble of dominant relations or qualities, its *principium synthesis* or some other such phenomenon to which society fundamentally goes back.[57]

Philosophising in systems – systematic thinking in general – takes concepts established by identity thinking and severs from them what does not acquiesce to the system. 'The reduction of quality to quantity – the ability to master social and natural processes – is equated with the progress of knowledge *qua* the progress of the object. But this very process, as a process of abstraction, is one that *distances* itself from the objects'[58] – that is, from the qualitative compositions of objects.

Undated notes[59] from a conversation between Adorno and Horkheimer contain the following dialogue:

55   Kosík 1976, p. 17.
56   Marx 1982a, p. 178.
57   Ritsert 1973, pp. 15–6; quoted from Hegel 2010b, p. 48.
58   Adorno 2008, p. 127.
59   These notes exist as a two-page typescript titled 'Notizen aus Gesprächen' ('Notes from Conversations'). Adorno and Horkheimer are denoted respectively with 'T' for Teddie and 'M' for Max (Adorno and Horkheimer, 'Notizen aus Gesprächen', TWA, Ts 52535–6).

ADORNO: Is there a totality of the system?

HORKHEIMER: According to Marx, totality means that when I change something, this changes the whole.

ADORNO: Is the relationship between the individual and the whole not significantly deeper? Because there is no system, the power of the whole in general has been transferred to the individual. The individual is not only a representative of the whole; rather, the dialectical power lies in the split-off individual.[60]

Reality is not a system insofar as it is not a reconciled whole in which each element 'receives its function and derives its meaning'. However, society is a system 'in the sense of a real yet abstract assemblage of what is in no way immediately or "organically" united'.[61] In place of successful mediation between the universal and the particular, which would require observance of the qualitative, the implementation of this system consolidates the individuals who maintain it into a 'radically societalized society'.[62] Theoretically formed systems are therefore not simply methodologically questionable depictions of reality, but rather manifestations precisely of '[b]ourgeois ratio, as an exchange principle', which 'brought *reality* closer and closer to the system, leaving less and less outside'.[63] Adorno contrasts this form of rationality with 'dialectical contradiction', which he argues

> expresses the real antagonisms which do not become visible within the logical-scientistic system of thought. For positivists, the system, according to the logical-deductive model, is something worth striving for, something 'positive'. For dialecticians, in real no less than in philosophical terms, it is the core of what has to be criticised.[64]

'Furthermore', Adorno claims in his seminar on Weber,

> such deductions of this kind, of what existed first, lack a certain stringency. Statements about primal history usually have a speculative character; behind one alleged first, another can always be discovered. The question of the *prius* – economy or domination – is more of an ideal-

---

60 Adorno and Horkheimer, 'Notizen aus Gesprächen', TWA, Ts 52536.
61 Adorno 1976a, p. 37.
62 Adorno 1993a, p. 27.
63 Adorno 2008, p. 129.
64 Adorno 1976a, p. 26.

istic question which goes against dialectical thought. As the apparatus of production has become increasingly independent over the course of history, so too have relations of production become ever more decisive for the forms of human coexistence. In the exchange society, the economy has a far greater weight than in the feudal system. Contrary to Engels, the question of the relationship between economy and society cannot be formulated in this ontological way. Instead, it comes down much more to analysing the relationship between economy and society in concrete historical eras, and particularly in the present.[65]

In the second part of the seminar, held during the summer semester of 1958, Adorno argues more decisively for the primacy of economy over society, emphasising that 'not only today does the economy have priority over society, but that this priority was present at all times – albeit in varying degrees of strength'.[66] That being said, he once again claims that economy and society determine each other and cannot be viewed apart from each other: 'One can only speak of society since something like rational economic activity has been present – since the reproduction of human life was no longer left to mere chance of whatever conditions may have existed'.[67] The primacy of economy, he continues, must by no means be blindly hypostasised:

> It's important ... that one doesn't fall victim to apologetic thinking and try to produce evidence of economic supremacy since times of yore [*zu Olims Zeiten*]. What's interesting in this problem is the question of the respective degree of independence of society from the economy in various eras of social development. In other words, it's important not to turn historical tendencies and this question into an anthropological one. With this problem regarding the dynamics of society, one should not try to orient oneself on a static model *of* the human being, for human, society and economy are historically realised.
>
> In order to be able to speak of a primacy of economy over society at all, it has to be assumed that society not only represents the totality of the relationships between human beings and their institutions, but that the economy forms a unity consolidated as a whole in its own right. This is at least the case in a fully developed exchange economy.[68]

---

65   Adorno 2021a, vol. 2, pp. 86–7.
66   Adorno 2021a, vol. 2, p. 123.
67   Adorno 2021a, vol. 2, p. 127.
68   Adorno 2021a, vol. 2, p. 123.; cf. Demirović 1999a, pp. 469–70. '*Quam olim Abrahae promisisti*

In his study on the genesis and development of the so-called *neue Marx-Lektüre*, or New German Reading of Marx, a school of interpretation of Marx's work with origins in 1960s West Germany,[69] Ingo Elbe writes that 'the representatives of the classical Frankfurt tradition, like the whole of Western Marxism, hardly went beyond a hidden orthodoxy in matters of economy criticism'.[70] In a chart titled 'Overview of the Marxisms', Elbe identifies the 'Theses on Feuerbach', the *1844 Manuscripts*, 'On the Jewish Question' and 'The German Ideology' as the 'Central Reference Texts of Marx/Engels' for the Frankfurt School, and argues that the latter claimed Marx's '[h]umanist early works as [an] interpretative framework for the "scientific" later works'.[71] However, as far as Adorno's reception and understanding of Marx is concerned, the opposite is actually the case – discounting Elbe's positioning of 'The German Ideology' in the chart. The 'Theses on Feuerbach' are regarded by Adorno as invalidated

---

ex semini eius. What God promised to Abraham and to his seed is now remembered and called for by those praying. Yet there is no mistaking a secret frivolousness here. The Latin word *olim* refers to a very distant past. When it came to a statute of limitations, [German-speaking] lawyers in the early twentieth century would speak in a quasi-personifying manner of "Olim's times" [*Olims Zeiten*]' (Mayer 1997, p. 137).

69   The *neue Marx-Lektüre* owes substantially to Hans-Georg Backhaus and Helmut Reichelt, whose respective texts 'On the Dialectics of the Value-Form' from 1969 (Backhaus 1980) and *Zur logischen Struktur des Kapitalbegriffs bei Karl Marx* [*On the Logical Structure of Marx's Concept of Capital*] from 1971 (Reichelt 2001; Reichelt's book draws upon Backhaus's essay as well as Alfred Schmidt's earlier work *The Concept of Nature in Marx*, see p. 25) revived Marxian value-form analysis in the German-speaking world and beyond (cf. Psychopedis 2000, pp. 266–7). According to Elbe (2008, p. 32), the *neue Marx-Lektüre* can be viewed in both a broad and narrow sense: 'Whereas the former was an international phenomenon, the latter was confined primarily to West Germany. If the former still remained predominantly trapped within Engelsian dogma with regard to the critique of political economy, the latter foregrounded the revision of previous historicist or empiricist interpretations of Marx's form analysis. In terms of content, a threefold abandonment of central topoi of traditional Marxism was consummated in the main threads of the debate …: a move away from a substantialist theory of value; abandonment of manipulative-instrumental conceptions of the state; and a move away from labor movement-centric interpretations of the critique of political economy, or interpretations based on a "labor-ontological" revolutionary theory (or even upon revolutionary theory as such). This new reading articulates its theoretical efforts in the form of a reconstruction of Marx's theory' (Elbe 2013). The name *neue Marx-Lektüre* is something of a paradox. Rather than a self-designation, it retrospectively designates a tradition which is already experiencing its own historiography. Understood in this way, Backhaus's book *Dialektik der Wertform* – which both brings together for the first time essays relevant to this tradition and recounts the creation of this 'new' view of Marx – can be understood simultaneously as both a collection of seminal texts for the *neue Marx-Lektüre* and as the tradition's testament.

70   Elbe 2008, p. 68.

71   Elbe 2008, p. 29; partially reproduced in English in Elbe 2013.

by history after Marx, the *Paris Manuscripts* were never important to him and
'On the Jewish Question' is only mentioned in one passage in his writings.[72]
Moreover, he explicitly rejects the real humanism of the 'young Marx'. Marx's
later economic writings provide an 'interpretative framework' – to use a turn of
phrase – for Adorno's own theory, although the latter certainly does not accept
this framework as a limitation.

At any rate, the term 'hidden orthodoxy' is taken from Habermas, who claims
that '[a]mong the older scholars' who are 'still bound to the Marxist tradition',
social critique as cultural critique

> frequently take[s] on the form of a *hidden orthodoxy*: the categories of the
> Marxist labor theory of value are revealed in their application to cultural
> critique, without being explicitly named as such. In the esoteric fabric of
> aesthetic reflection lingers something like the echo of a Critique of Polit-
> ical Economy. The less these are explicitly stated, the more their canon
> can, tacitly and intangibly, be made the underlying basis.[73]

Yet Adorno's 'Marxist orthodoxy'[74] is not hidden – in his university courses at
any rate, it is discussed extensively – and Adorno himself is not so orthodox
that he conceives of economy as separate from society and its culture. For him,
'an adequate concept of the critique of political economy' had much more to
do with 'how he elaborated the "unity of the exchange economy and the social
process" in a seminar'.[75] Any new reading of Marx whose main ambition – put
bluntly – were to show that economic substance does not assume the form
most people imagine would have been rejected by Adorno, it may be presumed,
as an economisation of the critique of political economy.

---

72   See Adorno 2009a, p. 17; see also letter from Adorno to Horkheimer, Summer Semester
     1954 (Adorno and Horkheimer 2006, p. 269); an implicit mention of 'On the Jewish Ques-
     tion' occurs in Adorno and Horkheimer 2002, p. 165.
73   Habermas 1988, pp. 202–3.
74   Habermas 1988, p. 203.
75   Grigat 2007, p. 135; quoted from Demirović 1999a, p. 467.

Eating and Being Eaten

> HAMM: Nature has forgotten us.
> CLOV: There's no more nature.
> HAMM: No more nature! You exaggerate.
> CLOV: In the vicinity.
>
> SAMUEL BECKETT, Endgame

∴

1 The Moment

If Adorno's second, post-1945 intensive engagement with Marx was externally motivated insofar as it was prompted by his students, it also followed the development of his own theory, and particularly his work on *Negative Dialectics*. According to Rolf Tiedemann, this text 'crystallised from a lecture course Adorno held in the winter semester of 1960–1 under the title "Ontology and Dialectics"; a series of lectures of the same title delivered by Adorno at the Collège de France in March 1961 formed the first version of the first section of *Negative Dialectics* .... Subsequently from 1964–6, Adorno successively taught no fewer than three courses on subjects or topics which are also at the center of *Negative Dialectics*, which he was working on intensively at the time'.[1] These were the lecture courses *History and Freedom* in the winter semester of 1964–5, *Metaphysics: Concept and Problems* in the summer semester of 1965 and a course from the winter semester of 1965–6 bearing the title of the end result of Adorno's efforts: *Negative Dialectics*.[2]

'Philosophy, which once seemed obsolete, lives on because the moment to realize it was missed. The summary judgment that it had merely interpreted the

---

1 Tiedemann 2007, p. 158; cf. also Wiggershaus 1995, p. 599. The diary kept by Adorno during his stay in Paris has been published under the title 'Reise im Frühjahr 1961' ('Trip in Spring 1961') (Adorno 2003y).

2 These lectures have been published as *Ontology and Dialectics: 1960/61* (Adorno 2019h), *History and Freedom: Lectures 1964–1965* (Adorno 2006a), *Metaphysics: Concept and Problems* (Adorno 2000b) and *Lectures on Negative Dialectics: Fragments of a Lecture Course 1965/1966* (Adorno 2008).

world, that resignation in the face of reality had crippled it in itself, becomes a defeatism of reason after the attempt to change the world miscarried'.[3] These introductory sentences from *Negative Dialectics* invoke the critique of philosophy articulated by Marx in his introduction to 'A Contribution to the Critique of Hegel's Philosophy of Right'[4] and 'Theses on Feuerbach'.[5] At the same time, this prelude is also a rejection of Lukács's attempt to heal – with an act of theoretical violence – the schism between theory and practice, which appears to Adorno as irreparable for the time being.

'The transition that Marx believed was just round the corner, in 1848 or thereabouts, did not take place. The qualitative leap that would change the world did not occur. And the proletariat failed to constitute itself as the subject-object of history, as it was supposed to according to Marx's own theory'.[6] Therefore,

> today we simply cannot think any more as Marx thought, namely that the revolution was imminent – simply because, on the one hand, the proletariat in his day was not integrated in bourgeois society and, on the other hand, bourgeois society did not yet possess the vast instruments of power, both actual physical instruments of power and also psychological instruments in the broadest sense, that it now has. Both factors, together with the increasing process of integration, have come together to make the concept of a revolution highly problematic nowadays.[7]

According to Adorno, the 'Theses on Feuerbach', the eleventh of which he alludes to in the prelude of *Negative Dialectics*,

> cannot be correctly understood *in abstracto*, or severed from the historical dimension. They take on their meaning only in the context of the expectation of imminent revolution which existed at that time; without such an expectation they degenerate into mumbo-jumbo. Once this given possibility failed to be realized, Marx spent decades in the British Museum writing a theoretical work on national economy. That he did so without having engaged in much praxis in reality is not a matter of mere biographical accident; an historical [element] is imprinted even in this.[8]

---

3   Adorno 2007b, p. 3.
4   Cf. Marx 2007, pp. 64–5.
5   Cf. Demirović 1999a, p. 634.
6   Adorno 2008, pp. 42–3.
7   Adorno 2008, p. 45.
8   Adorno 2000a, p. 150. 'Marx demanded as little as any other philosopher that the shape of

Where the 'moment to realise' philosophy – a moment 'at which, as Adorno suspected, liberation was once possible'[9] – is missed, yet no new possibility to realise philosophy is visible even from afar, there exists either a practice which acts as though the revolution were immediately pending, as though revolution were now only that 'litany of the unmediated unity of theory and practice'[10] which Adorno sees at work in Soviet Marxism, or as though it were 'infinitely delayed'. After all, '[t]heory cannot prolong the moment its critique depended on'.[11]

Whereas Marx, 'who thought his own era was ripe to redeem the theoretical promise of historical materialism',[12] could still anticipate the proletarian revolution which would cause philosophy to be superseded by a transformed practice and supposedly thereby liberate theory from a locked-up and base totality, it is no longer possible for Adorno to ground his theory in a practically effective non-identical. Following Lukács, Adorno envisioned as late as the 1930s a revolution on the part of the proletariat. However, this never materialised, and 'the progressive implications of the contradiction' between society and the working class 'disappeared',[13] as Adorno and Horkheimer note several times in their discussions on whether and how to write a manifesto. As early as 1948, Adorno describes the changes resulting from the new situation for theory itself in a long letter to Herbert Marcuse:

> I'd like to avoid the misunderstanding that I want to rescue the traditional pre-Marxian concept of philosophy – that is, the ontological concept, the concept of *prima philosophia* in the broadest sense. Rather, I only want to stick to a strict enough concept ... of what counts as 'theory and real theory'. By philosophy, I mean nothing else. But what's at issue is more than a merely terminological argument (unlike the philosophy professors, I don't believe at all in merely terminological quarrels; rather, every philosophical concept has, by virtue of its historical dimension, an irreplaceable quality which cannot be solved by reference to synonyms).

---

thought should be measured according to practice, that it be tailored to practical needs at the expense of truth. Marx spoke contemptuously of scholars who sacrifice something of their knowledge for the sake of a practical thesis to be demonstrated, of achieving some effect: he called them "wretches" [*Lumpen*]' (Adorno and Horkheimer 2003a, pp. 654–5). On Marx's use of the term 'wretch' see Marx 1975a, p. 112.

9   Demirović 1998, p. 89.
10   Adorno 2019b, p. 213.
11   Adorno 2007b, p. 3.
12   Bremer 1998, p. 92.
13   Lindner 1983, p. 73.

Instead, my motif is that we must face the situation that we are theorists, for God's sake, and not immediate practitioners. Theory needs to account for this in some way if it doesn't want to make the revolutionary action into a *deus ex machina* and a *captatio benevolentiae* – 'well I'm a theorist, but actually I mean practice, so I'm not really a theorist but rather have theory-practice and stand righteously before Lenin even when I *don't* have practice'. I think practice is too damn serious for that. Unless there is a truly transparent dialectical relationship between practice and theory, it seems to me that theory has no right to cognitively invoke practice. Instead, it must stand on its own two legs, that is, prove itself theoretically, and in a strong sense at that – this is philosophy, after all. Just because true theory is practice doesn't mean that theory can already become practice on its own. It can't claim to be practice and no longer philosophy. At the same time, the repeated separation of theory and practice to which we find ourselves opposed must itself be theoretically determined. I ... think we have to face, on the one hand, what became of the labour movement, without which the strong concept of practice turns into pragmatism – and by no means in the strong sense – and on the other, the chemical changes to which the concept of practice in society as a whole is subjected. Under liberalism, theory was ideology, and practice – the proletarian kind – stood immediately opposed to it. Theory no longer exists in the world today. ... In other words, ideology, the lie in service of perpetuating what exists, has gone over to practice in the broadest sense, in whose name, that of socialist build-up, theory is liquidated beyond the Iron Curtain as well. No longer is there any sentence whatsoever to which a *cui bono* isn't affixed. The relationship between action and contemplation stands in the same dialectic. The theses against Feuerbach are no longer valid; every professor will shout to us that the point is to change the world, but to first interpret the world again is something no one wants to do anymore. What resists ideology has gone over solely to what does not play along, simply helps the matter – without arranging it according to goals and thereby forcing it to conform to one of the powers (*einer der Mächte gleichzuschalten*)[14] – to express itself in a way which the entire world order otherwise precludes. That is, it has gone over precisely to 'pure' thought, yet not in the sense of apriorism, but rather in the sense of maintaining one's

---

14   Translator's note: *Gleichschaltung* ('coordination') was a term used to designate official state policy of forced conformity of all aspects of German society to the Nazi regime.

purity against swearing an oath on something existing. I am well aware that this means, in a certain way, a regression against Marx – back to the Stoics, if you will – but this is precisely the regression of the society from which we, particularly as Marxists, are not independent. And if we have no other recourse anymore, then we should at least not speak as if the workers' battalions were booming behind our books. I believe that only by becoming conscious of this entire situation in all its complexity, and of its profound dubiousness and the danger of quietism, can we contribute our powerlessness so that the situation might change. I don't have to assure you that I do not ... advocate the resurrection of metaphysics just because the barricades are closed due to construction. And if against me you object that such adherence to philosophy is threatened by a relapse into conformity, I am the last who would dispute this – with the one caveat that there is simply no thought and no attitude today not faced with this threat, precisely because the world is converging into a total system and thereby tending to absorb everything. All we can do is resist this absorption – above all, I think, through language. ... I mean something ... difficult to express, but very dialectical – that in the moment they happen, the decisive actions always have an aspect of hopelessness, of 'impossibility' – this is exactly the threshold to positivism, indeed to all bourgeois reason. God knows, this is not to say that these actions are *objectively* hopeless – then they would be pure martyrdom, which I'd want to idolise as little as you. But the absurd, 'subjective' *aspect* in them cannot be skipped over. Otherwise, it would be in the bag, and the all-important qualitative leap is exactly what one does not, not ever, under absolutely any circumstances have in the bag. But seriously pursuing these things really leads to a sphere about which one can talk but not correspond.[15]

At any rate, as Helmuth Plessner has established, Adorno 'has over Marx' – and one might add over the Lukács of *History and Class Consciousness* – 'the advantage of historical perspective', having seen how proletarian revolutions

> put new industry bureaucrats in the saddle and kindled endless quarrels about true communism, analogous to the patristic-scholastic disputes following Christ. The liberation of the working class did not put an end to the interpretation of this class, but rather enlivened it to an unforeseen

---

15   Letter from Adorno to Marcuse, 18 July 1948 (TWA, Br 969/11–12).

degree. The situation of the interregnum which philosophy has gotten into – that is, philosophy surviving its death, not uncontested yet also not illegitimate – is where Adorno begins.[16]

For Adorno, '[r]eflection about why a practical change did *not* take place', the exceeding of theory in practice – 'in other words, why practice finds itself in these difficulties or in this standstill situation' – is now the order of the day. And 'such reflection is itself an important part of what we can call philosophy today. In a certain sense, then, because the predicted transition from theory to practice did not take place, the interaction between theory and practice must revert to theory'.[17]

One scholarly attempt to introduce *Negative Dialectics* describes the claim Adorno asserts on philosophy therein as follows: 'The fact that "the moment to realize" philosophy "was missed" should be able to be determined *ex negativo* as a condition of possibility for philosophy's survival'.[18] Yet this and other such descriptions are hardly half the truth. Adorno does not want to show the *possibility* of philosophy, but rather *the necessity* of turning to philosophy in times when revolutionary practice is impossible. 'Practice endlessly postponed can no longer serve as an appellate court against philosophy. – The process of reflection about why this did not happen *is* philosophy'.[19] In other words, the point of philosophy should be to revise Marx's eleventh thesis on Feuerbach, to reflect on why the possibility of changing the world is temporarily foreclosed. Critique as a theoretical possibility is, for the time being, the only remaining possibility to address society as a whole.

Settling for this is difficult at times, for '[d]istance from praxis is disreputable in the eyes of everyone. Anyone who does not take immediate action and who is not willing to get his hands dirty is the subject of suspicion; it is felt that his antipathy toward such action was not legitimate, and further that his view has even been distorted by the privileges he enjoys'[20] – that is, by the fact that many must 'get their hands dirty' so that a select few do not have to do so. However, if practice is pitted against the only theory currently on offer, then the concept of practice simultaneously becomes ideologically limited to 'increased production of the means of production', such as was the case in the Soviet Union – where the 'only criticism still tolerated was that people still were not working hard

---

16   Plessner 1970, p. 508.
17   Adorno 2008, p. 56.
18   Naeher 1984, p. 165.
19   Adorno 2008, p. 55.
20   Adorno 1978b, p. 165; on Adorno's concept of praxis (or practice) cf. also Braunstein 2009.

enough'. In this way, Adorno believes, 'the subordination of theory to praxis results in the support of renewed repression'.[21]

What remains is a philosophy which does not affirmatively build on the most advanced form it had reached before Marx – for Adorno, this form is present in Hegel's philosophy 'with its attempt to comprehend the non-identical, albeit to comprehend it by *identifying* with it'.[22] 'Having broken its pledge to be as one with reality', which it made in Hegel's work, 'or at the point of [reality's] realization', which it made in the work of Marx, 'philosophy is obliged ruthlessly to criticize itself'.[23]

Adorno elaborates near the beginning of *Negative Dialectics*:

> Contradiction is not what Hegel's absolute idealism was bound to transfigure it into: it is not of the essence in a Heraclitean sense. It indicates the untruth of identity, the fact that the concept does not exhaust the thing conceived. Yet the appearance of identity is inherent in thought itself, in its pure form. To think is to identify. Conceptual order is content to screen what thinking seeks to comprehend.[24]

'We shall see', he claims in *Lectures on Negative Dialectics*,

---

21   Adorno 1978b, p. 166.

22   Adorno 2008, p. 59. 'The assertion of the identity of being and thought, which stands behind the entire philosophical tradition, has succumbed irrevocably to the protests against it. If the world were truly at one with spirit, if it were the product of spirit, permeated with spirit, this would mean with inexorable necessity that the world would be meaningful in its current form. However, that very fact, the very assertion that, as people put it, the world has a meaning, can simply not be maintained in the light of all that we have experienced in our own epoch of history. A philosophy that blinds itself to these experiences and that clings instead to the thesis of meaningfulness in epistemology and the related realm of metaphysics, without allowing itself to be deterred by the truth that the world really does not have a meaning any more – such a philosophy really would sink to the level of idle chatter and professional reassurance worthy only of the contempt held in readiness by certain philosophical trends such as the positivists, as well as the common or garden opinions of the ordinary man' (ibid.).

23   Adorno 2007b, p. 3. 'On the other hand, it has to be said that the fact that the transition to practice that has been implicit in philosophy ever since Hegel has failed, contains the further implication that philosophy itself should be subjected to the most rigorous process of self-criticism, a self-criticism that must self-evidently take its lead from the latest forms assumed by philosophy. (I am not thinking here of a critique of the countless irrelevant studies that appear every year as products of the academic industry and seem to have no difficulty in finding publishers and printers)' (Adorno 2008, p. 57).

24   Adorno 2007b, p. 5.

that the thesis of the identity of concept and thing is in general the vital nerve of idealist thought, and indeed traditional thought in general. Furthermore, this assertion of the identity of concept and thing is inextricably intertwined with the structure of reality itself. And negative dialectics as critique means above all criticism of precisely this claim to identity – a claim that cannot of course be tested on every single object in a kind of bad infinity, but which certainly can be applied to the essential structures confronting philosophy either directly or as mediated through the themes of philosophy. Furthermore, dialectics as critique implies the criticism of any hypostatization of the mind as the primary thing, the thing that underpins everything else.[25]

This criticism wants to 'break immanently, in its own measure the appearance of total identity' within the 'totality of cogitative definitions'. However,

> [s]ince that totality is structured to accord with logic, ... whose core is the principle of the excluded middle, whatever will not fit this principle, whatever differs in quality, comes to be designated as a contradiction. Contradiction is nonidentity under the aspect of identity; the dialectical [primacy] of the principle of contradiction makes the thought of unity the measure of heterogeneity. As the heterogenous collides with its limit it exceeds itself.
> Dialectics is the consistent sense of nonidentity.[26]

Adorno does not believe that identity should be thought of as a final principle in whose name all contradictions should ultimately be transcended. After all, according to its own concept, identity is itself necessarily mediated by what it is not: by the non-identical:

> Identity and contradiction of thought are welded together. Total contradiction is nothing but the manifested untruth of total identification. Contradiction is nonidentity under the rule of law that affects the nonidentical as well.
> This law is not a cogitative law, however. It is real.[27]

---

25   Adorno 2008, pp. 21–2.
26   Adorno 2007b, p. 5.
27   Adorno 2007b, p. 6.

It is the law of identity which establishes the norms for all thought and action in developed exchange society. The very rationality which this identity embodies, 'unconscious like the transcendental subject and establishing identity by [exchange], remains incommensurable with the subjects it reduces to the same denominator: the subject as the subject's foe'.[28] Consequently, Adorno defines theory as critical self-reflection on the part of the subject, without which it suffers from a 'constriction of ... abundance' of mental experience.

> Theory and mental experience need to interact. Theory does not contain answers to everything; it reacts to the world, which is faulty to the core. What would be free from the spell of the world is not under theory's jurisdiction.[29]

Ultimately, it is in this sense which 'philosophical theory means that its own end lies in its realization'.[30]

2   A Being for the Other

'In other words, one could say that the principle of identity is a principle of thought itself', Adorno claims in *Philosophische Terminologie* (*Philosophical Terminology*), a lecture course held in the summer semester of 1962 and winter semester of 1962–3. He continues: 'I would not hesitate to say that every principle, every tenet which can be appealed to, under which all variety is subsumed, or from which all variety can be derived, is necessarily a principle of thought. The recourse to a first (and the stem *principium* means first), the reduction to an all-inclusive unity, is always the recourse or reduction to thought'.[31] With this, Adorno returns to a set of considerations already undertaken in *Against Epistemology: A Metacritique* regarding demystification through identification. In a passage from that work, which according to Rolf Tiedemann 'counts among the sharpest he ever wrote',[32] Adorno comments as follows:

---

28   Adorno 2007b, p. 10.
29   Adorno 2007b, p. 31.
30   Adorno 2007b, p. 29.
31   Adorno 1974a, p. 83.
32   Tiedemann 1998, p. 29.

Since the philosophical first must always already contain everything, spirit confiscates what is unlike itself and makes it the same, its property. Spirit inventories it. Nothing may slip through the net. The principle must guarantee completeness. ... In the concept of the first already belongs the number series. Wherever a πρῶτον becomes thematic in the concept of being in Aristotelian metaphysics, number and computability are also thought. ... [W]ithout the Idea of the Many, that of the One could never be specified. In numbers is reflected the opposition of organizing and retentive spirit to what it faces. First spirit reduces it to indeterminacy, in order to make it the same as itself, and then determines it as the Many. Of course, spirit does not yet say it is identical with or reducible back to itself. But the two are already similar. As a set of unities the Many forfeits its particular qualities .... Numbers are an arrangement for making the non-identical, dubbed 'the Many', commensurable with the subject, the model of unity. They bring the manifold of experience to its abstraction.[33]

Counting is a process of quantification – a process which disregards the qualities of what is counted in order to transform the being-in-itself of things into a controllable being-for-others.[34] However, the principle of being-for-another is precisely the genuine principle of all economy, pre-capitalist and capitalist alike. What is new under capital compared to previous economic systems is the total assertion of this principle as 'the absolute being for the other of the commodity world'.[35] '[S]ociety has become the total functional context which liberalism used to think it was: to be is to be relative to other persons and things, and to be irrelevant in oneself'.[36]

Already in *Dialectic of Enlightenment*, Horkheimer and Adorno note that '[e]verything has value only in so far as it can be exchanged, not in so far as it is something in itself'.[37] This functionality of value, whose concept is 'formed in the exchange relationship, a being for the other',[38] is generalised by Adorno

---

33   Adorno 2013, pp. 9–10. 'In this view, thinking in numbers, a longing for demythologisation, turns into "myth" and becomes the antithesis of enlightenment. "Myth" ..., which wants to "establish", for which philosophy is "homesickness", manifests itself as the greatest antithesis not only to enlightenment, but also to Adorno's dialectical philosophy in general, whose home is "not the lost state of old", but rather the "state of having escaped"' (Müller-Strömsdörfer 1960 p. 85; cf. Adorno and Horkheimer 2002, pp. 60–1).

34   Cf. Tiedemann 1998, p. 28.

35   Adorno 2003n, p. 255.

36   Adorno 2007b, p. 65.

37   Adorno and Horkheimer 2002, p. 128.

38   Adorno 1976c, p. 117.

into the universal principle of exchange society: in this society, 'everything is heteronomously defined'.[39] This principle stymies the mature development of subjects, who adhere to 'the promise of security offered by logic: identity and the absence of contradiction'.[40] 'The criterion of the irrefutable, a property which shall not be able to be wrested away from a person, takes the place of the weight of insight. Its means, indeed the methods, become ends in themselves in accordance with a society-wide tendency to give the for-the-other, exchange-value, primacy over every in-itself, every purpose'.[41] With that,

> [o]bjective bourgeois spirit has risen up as a replacement for philosophy. One cannot fail to recognize in this the *parti pris* for the exchange principle, abstracted to the norm of being-for-another, with which the criterion of empathetic reconstructability and the concept of communication, ultimately formed in the culture industry, comply as the measure of all that is intellectual.[42]

Where philosophical experience once existed, there emerges a common sense[43] which is not only linguistically related to what the National Socialists referred to as the *gesundes Volksempfinden* – literally the 'healthy sense of the *Volk*', of the racially defined people[44] – but also 'chooses ideological formulas which ensure subjective security, which always already have ready for everything a coherent and declarative answer'.[45]

For Adorno, the totality of the principle of exchange on which society is based establishes the *a priori* of the commodity-form's logic, according to which all things are potentially quantifiable and thus exchangeable for equivalents. Because of this *a priori*, things need not first 'prove themselves on the

---

39   Adorno 2002a, p. 226; cf. Adorno 2007b, p. 73: 'Society has become the total functional context which liberalism used to think it was: to be is to be relative to other persons and things, and to be irrelevant in oneself'.

40   Tiedemann 1983, p. 72. 'The people from the old Hegelian tradition here are the only ones immune to the spook of the void. Out of a kind of perverted need for security, all of the young ones all fall for it. Some security, that *a* equals *a* and not equals not *a*!' (letter from Adorno to Horkheimer, 30 October 1936 [Adorno and Horkheimer 2006, p. 209]).

41   Adorno 2003j, p. 264.

42   Adorno 1976a, p. 57.

43   'And if one has to choose between the paranoid fantasy about a paranoid reality or the stupidity of common sense, one is always going to get further with paranoia' (letter from Adorno to Horkheimer, 12 November 1952 [Adorno and Horkheimer 2006, p. 67]).

44   Translator's note: *Gesundes Volksempfinden* was a legal term in Nazi Germany: one could be prosecuted for actions viewed as going against the *gesundes Volksempfinden*.

45   Demirović 1999a, p. 644.

market', as the saying goes.[46] Rather, it is far more essential that things possess use-value and value – in other words, that in addition to the qualitative state of their existence, they are also quantifiable. Under capital, which valorises virtually *everything*, this logic applies to all matters. Seen in this way, history up until now presents itself as a progression towards the totality that is universal quantification. 'The tit for tat of history[,] as well as the totality-bound principle of equivalence in the social relation between individual subjects, both proceed according to the logicity which Hegel is said merely to interpret into them'.[47] What cannot be measured does not let itself be subsumed under identity, is not supposed to exist, have ever existed or ever come into existence – history remains prehistory, and as such, it approaches a standstill.

Where abstraction as a universal principle must sever everything from things which impedes their commensurability, the non-identical remainder is left over as a waste product of this process of abstraction. Yet insofar as abstraction a conceptual condition of the possibility of rational knowledge – and insofar as the concept itself is a condition thereof – the only viable way to unregulated knowledge is that utopian way of 'unseal[ing] the non-conceptual with concepts, without making it their equal'.[48]

> The object itself is literally a concept, a concept in itself. Yet it is not a concept in the sense of being the life of the absolute, but rather in the sense that it – that is, the objectively consolidated society – essentially and constitutively contains within itself a conceptual element, namely that of exchange. To this extent, one can really say in an ironic sense that the world in which we live is a subject-object, meaning that precisely the objectivity to which we stand opposed – the entity which appears to us as heteronomous and unintelligible, and at whose mercy we stand –

---

46   'Although Adorno repeatedly spoke about the exchange society, he should not be described – as he so often wrongly is – as a theorist of an exchange society in the economic sense. The essence of Adorno's critical theory lies in the very fact that he understands the capitalist economy as an inverted reality in which individuals no longer "interact with one another" on the market as rationally acting subjects, as the idea of the exchange economy suggests. Adorno criticises such a concept as "social nominalism". Rather, individuals act as executors of constraints generated and reproduced by themselves, which are implemented in and through their conscious actions, yet without these being consciously accessible to them. This is what the strong concept of totality means .... Totality is not a methodological postulate, but rather the concept of a real "becoming autonomous" [*Verselbständigung*]' (Reichelt 2007, pp. 4–5). On the problem of 'social nominalism', cf. Adorno 2018c, pp. 154–5.
47   Adorno 2007b, p. 317.
48   Adorno 2007b, p. 10.

this objectivity has become what it is precisely by modelling, supporting, levelling and abstracting itself out according to a conceptuality, indeed, according to the principle of exchange.[49]

However, the non-identical does not wait unrecognised for its discovery. As long as the 'insatiable identity principle'[50] prevails, 'the nonidentical has no positive existence'.[51] The non-identical is the governor of a knowledge which does not need to violently whip objects into shape in order to adjust itself. As long as this possibility of knowledge is not realised, everything which could possibly be different will appear as 'just how it's always been'[52] – with all the forthright consent implied by that saying.

As Adorno writes in *Negative Dialectics,*

> [w]hat appears as the formlessness of [an existence] modeled solely after subjective reason is in fact that which enslaves the subjects: the pure principle of being-for-something-else, of being [a commodity]. For the sake of universal equivalence and comparability this principle depreciates qualitative definitions everywhere; its tendency is to bring all things down to one level. Yet the same [commodity] character – the indirect rule of men over other men – consolidates the subjects' state of tutelage. Their coming of age and their freedom to think qualitatively would go together.[53]

However, the mediation of subjects by other subjects is also a condition of individualisation, and a virtually necessary one at that:

> Although all elements on the side of the universal process of exchange are made commensurable with each other, individuality is only possible given this relationship. After all, individuality is not a pure being-for-itself, but rather becomes one in relationship to another. Thus, the process of levelling is at the same time itself a process of differentiation and also of individualisation. Individuality as differentiation emerges through comparability with others.[54]

---

49   Adorno 2021b, p. 271.
50   Adorno 2007b, p. 142.
51   Adorno 2002a, p. 73.
52   Cf. Adorno 1973, p. 11.
53   Adorno 2007b, p. 94.
54   Adorno 2021a, vol. 4, p. 213.

In other words, being 'irrelevant in oneself' is the price the individualised subject has to pay for its individuality, a concept which in turn is verging on irrelevance: if the common denominator of all subjects is their mere irrelevance, this contradicts the very notion of a strong concept of individuality. From the perspective of the valorisation process, individuality is now merely the valorisable form of an arbitrary substance. The individual subsists as the embodiment of its labour-power, or as the owner of capital – in short, as a functionary of its respective class in the capitalist process of reproduction. By this, Adorno does not mean to suggest that the state in which individuals exist is completely socially determined. Rather, he refers to individuality as a *form* of subjects' existence, given that it is *subjects* who are socially cultivated in order to fulfil social objectives. 'The act of differentiating' subjects from each other 'is in itself one such act of socialisation; individuation and individuality are thus an element of society'.[55]

A footnote underlined as many as seven times in Adorno's copy of *Capital*[56] reads as follows:

> In a certain sense, a man is in the same situation as a commodity. As he neither enters into the world in possession of a mirror, nor as a Fichtean philosopher who can say 'I am I', a man first sees and recognizes himself in another man. Peter only relates to himself as a man through his relation to another man, Paul, in whom he recognizes his likeness. With this, however, Paul also becomes from head to toe, in his physical form as Paul, the form of appearance of the species man for Peter.[57]

For Marx, the human being is not constituted as a species in its relationship to the other. Adorno himself – for whom this passage perhaps first became relevant because of his interest in Marx's concept of alienation – would subsequently go beyond its mediation between epistemology and intersubjectivity, analysing individuality itself as the result of economic relations.

> Bourgeois individuality is the actual 'substrate' of Marxian thought on social phenomena. To this extent, Marx himself is a bourgeois individualist and a product of his time. The notion that the category of the individual itself is socially produced did not yet occur to him at all. He

---

55   Ibid.
56   1932 edition (TWA, NB 279).
57   Marx 1982a, p. 144, n. 19.

believed that something like free and fair exchange between individuals – an ideology in liberalism – could be realised if people would simply
behave rationally, and if production took place for society as a whole. In
this vision of the individual, and of the rational behaviour of all, there is
of course no room for the concept of authority as a problem. Marx did
not yet recognise the whole coercive mechanism to which rationality is
subjected.[58]

Instead, Marx envisioned

> the individual as an invariant. Presumably only covered up by the coercive
> relations of exchange, it could be set free again through their eradication.
> In this respect, Marx was a bourgeois liberal.[59]

When Adorno elaborated these thoughts in a seminar, his interpretation of
Marx's concept of the individual was met at the time with audible scepticism:[60]

> Regarding several objections as to whether the individual is in fact con-
> ceived of as a constant in Marx's work with no dialectical breakthrough,
> Adorno responded that Marx could not yet have seen the development
> in which everything individual in concept was being functionalised. For
> him, the individual is simply bound by ties which a rational practice could
> loosen again. In this, Marx ignored the dialectic of individualisation, that

---

58   Adorno 2021a, vol. 3, p. 462. Regarding a student presentation to be held on Marx's concept
      of the individual in his seminar from the 1964 summer semester, Adorno comments 'that
      Marx hardly talks explicitly about the problem of the individual, so the presentation can-
      not completely clarify the status of the individual in Marxian theory. It is much rather the
      case that the individual in Marx's work is concealed behind other concepts, such as that
      of spontaneity, which means the actions of individuals insofar as their whole existence is
      not identical with society's existence' (Adorno 2021a, vol. 4, p. 43).
59   Adorno 2021a, vol. 4, p. 231.
60   This scepticism was justified, for Marx in fact criticises the establishment of the individual
      as a transhistorical point of departure for social development as 'simple-mindedness'.
      According to him, for 'the eighteenth-century prophets ... this eighteenth-century indi-
      vidual – the product on one side of the dissolution of the feudal forms of society, on the
      other side of the new forces of production developed since the sixteenth century – appears
      as an ideal, whose existence they project into the past. Not as a historic result but as his-
      tory's point of departure. As the Natural Individual appropriate to their notion of human
      nature, not arising historically, but posited by nature. This illusion has been common to
      each new epoch to this day' (Marx 1993, pp. 83–4).

the individual itself could only be the product of an historical development rather than its precondition.[61]

Rather than view the individual as a piece of nature to be freed from its social transformation, Adorno instead foregrounds the mediation between society and nature, which he also views as the mediation between the identifying concept and what evades identification, the non-identical: identification is domination of nature.

3   The Usefulness of a Thing

In *The Concept of Nature in Marx*, a dissertation written in the late 1950s under the supervision of Adorno and Horkheimer,[62] the philosopher Alfred Schmidt elaborates the thesis that although Marx did not view nature and society as two separate spheres which only seldom come into contact, he nevertheless considered nature to be '"the primary source of all instruments and objects of labour", i.e. he saw nature from the beginning in relation to human activity'.[63] However, this insight alone does not sufficiently define nature, but simply names the precondition for knowledge of nature: nature can only be grasped as socially mediated. Marx advocates (along with Engels) – granted, 'with the critical reservation that any such priority could only exist within mediation'[64] – a 'priority of external nature'.[65] However, a pre-eminence of social subjects paradoxically results from this priority, because insofar as nature is viewed as 'the material of human activity',[66] it is yet again primarily assigned the status of an instrumentality, of a being-for-another, which exists namely for the subject. In Marx's work, the mediacy between nature and society finds expression in the dichotomy between use-value and value.

Marx claims on the one hand that use-value is realised 'in use or consumption' – that is, that use or consumption forms the *entire* intent and purpose of use-value. On the other, he argues that '[i]n the form of society to be con-

61   Adorno 2021a, vol. 4, pp. 234–5.
62   Cf. the foreword to the published edition of Schmidt's dissertation, which appeared in the book series *Frankfurter Beiträge zur Soziologie* (*Frankfurt Contributions to Sociology*) (Adorno and Horkheimer 2003a); cf. letter from Horkheimer to Adorno, 2 March 1962 (Adorno and Horkheimer 2006, pp. 672–3).
63   Schmidt 2013, p. 15; quoted from Marx 2010a, p. 341.
64   Schmidt 2013, pp. 26–7.
65   Marx and Engels 1976, p. 40.
66   Schmidt 2013, p. 27.

sidered here, [use-values] are also the material bearers of ... exchange-value'.[67]
Moreover, he views use-value as the element of a commodity in which the value
of another commodity expresses itself in the exchange-relation.[68]

Precisely at this point of the account in *Capital*, in which it should be
emphasised that 'the relationship between exchange-value and use-value is not
one of subsumption but rather of mutual preconditions and exclusions – a dialectical relationship, so to speak'[69] – Marx proceeds remarkably undialectically
by claiming that use-value and exchange-value have no inner relationship to
each other, and that the former falls outside of the realm of economic analysis.[70]

The contradictions which necessarily result from the identification of use-
value with the utility of the product of labour can only be resolved by viewing
use-value as the qualitative social element of the commodity – as opposed to
value, its quantitative social element. Whereas the 'exchange values of commodities must be reduced to a common element, of which they represent a
greater or a lesser quantity'[71] – whereas these values are purely quantitative –
the use-value of a commodity can only be determined qualitatively. This situation becomes clear when Marx uses the abstraction of use-values from commodities to extrapolate the substance of their values as 'labour, human labour
in the abstract'. 'If then we disregard the use-value of commodities', he claims,
'only one property remains, that of being products of labour'.[72] If, as in Marx's
work, use-value is regarded as utility, then once the utility of the commodities
is disregarded, their useless elements still remain – elements which compose a

---

67   Marx 1982a, p. 126, brackets in original.
68   'By means of the value-relation, therefore, the natural form of commodity B becomes the
      value-form of commodity A, in other words the physical body of commodity B becomes
      a mirror for the value of commodity A. Commodity A, then, in entering into a relation
      with commodity B as an object of value, as a materialization of human labour, makes the
      use-value B into the material through which its own value is expressed. The value of com-
      modity A, thus expressed in the use-value of commodity B, has the form of relative value'
      (Marx 1982a, p. 144).
69   Hafner 1993, p. 69.
70   'Use value in this indifference to the determined economic form, i.e. use value as such,
      lies outside the sphere of investigation of political economy. It belongs in this sphere only
      when it is itself a determinate form' (Marx 1987a, p. 270). Fritz Reusswig and Jürgen Ritsert
      have commented on the ambiguous 'role or non-role of use-values in the Marxian critique
      of political economy'. Against its frequently alleged functional unambiguity, including by
      Marx himself, they ask: 'How is use-value related to *utility* and/or *expediency*?' (Reusswig
      and Ritsert 1991, p. 22).
71   Marx 1982a, p. 127.
72   Marx 1982a, p. 128.

multiplicity of properties in their own right. Yet on the other hand, if use-value is simply taken to be the qualitative element itself in the commodity, then 'a property' in fact resulting from abstraction – the property of 'being a product of labour' – underhandedly becomes a qualitative property again, that is, one which does not determine value. However, there is a third possibility: if use-value is seen as a qualitative commodity-form which is specific to capitalism – a form which commodities must inevitably assume in addition to the value-form – then the 'usefulness of a thing' can be defined by the fact that the benefit of a commodity consists of both its ability to be consumed, and of its ability to represent the value of another commodity. If one then disregards the 'use-value of commodities' understood in this way, the only property use-value still has is the property of being a value.

In the course of the 'irritations'[73] produced by Marx's ambiguous definition of use-value, orthodox Marxism endeavoured in a 'use-value oriented' manner to free an allegedly ontological use-value from exchange-value.[74] However, in doing so, it overlooked that use-value 'only becomes a "general utility" through the self-valorisation of money',[75] that is, through capital. The notion that the production of use-values is principally the production of innocent, needs-fulfilling, potentially emancipatory goods amounts to the claim that the production and circulation of commodities would be morally desirable if they were not accompanied by the existence of (manipulative, fraudulent) exchange-values. In this way, use-value becomes a subjective-functional concept. The notion of an emancipatory 'use-value orientation' must evidently assume that *every* commodity per se comes with an 'emancipatory use-value', that is, with the possibility of providing a non-capitalist utility. Yet the utility of weapons, deportation centres, instruments of torture and the like is based not only on the production of death, suffering and horror, but also on maintaining and entrenching the dominant order. No theory of reification is needed to recognise this,[76] for all these aspects of utility are germane to the production of these commodities: they are produced to kill, deport and torture people.

---

73   Brentel 1981, p. 20.

74   Along these lines, Helmut Brentel – certainly no representative of traditional labour-movement Marxism in his day – argues that the telos of the critique of political economy should be the 'use-value-oriented and nature-incorporating *delimitation* of the concept of socialisation' from what he terms 'the logic of labour-values' (Brentel 1981, p. 27). However, the 'logic of labour-values' is also the 'logic of use-values' which allows the law of value to claim validity in the first place.

75   Kurz 1992, p. 137.

76   Cf. Hafner 1993, p. 61.

The association (or even equation) of use-value and utility forecloses the possibility of inquiring into the concrete substance of 'utility' while necessitating the categorical establishment of a 'utility-in-itself'. However, this latter kind of utility

> not only does not exist, but also cannot exist, for it contradicts what the concept of utility designates. This concept is constituted as a *relation* with two sides: a *particular* need and a *particular* quality of an object, which bears the title of use-object because of this quality. Just as different human needs are qualitatively different in substance from each other, the use-objects for satisfying *these* needs differ from each other in their usefulness.[77]

The Marxian definition of use-value – as the 'usefulness of a thing'[78] – is only accurate in a value-producing society whose precondition and result are use-values themselves. Joan Robinson notes the mediacy between use-value and exchange-value when she claims that '[u]*tility* is a metaphysical concept of impregnable circularity; *utility* is the quality in commodities that makes individuals want to buy them, and the fact that individuals want to buy commodities shows that they have *utility*'.[79] Even Marx's statement that various use-values correspond to 'different forms of useful labour'[80] does not lead out of this logical dilemma, for the utility of labour would be that it produces use-values which are useful in the first place. Labour, which is supposed to explain the utility of use-value, can itself only be identified as useful in reference to the use-value of labour-power; the use-value of labour-power is that it produces use-values.

Exchange-value and use-value determine each other: 'A commodity can only ... become a use value if it is realised as an exchange value, while it can only be

---

77 Dunn 1984, p. 5. 'Tellingly, the notion of pure utility visible in the utilitarian theories first develops when the production of commodities has more or less asserted itself in society and the last remainder of Aristotelianism, in the sense of the notion of a determination inherent in the specific thing, has disappeared' (Hafner 1993, pp. 64–5).

78 Marx 1987a, p. 126.

79 Robinson 1974, p. 48. Michael Heinrich uses this quotation (Heinrich 1999, p. 68, n. 14) to dismantle the topos of economic marginalism, namely the possibility of estimating individual utility based on existing relationships of exchange: 'Tracing exchange-value back to utility is simply a claim which cannot be proved. Fundamentally, the theory of marginal utility says nothing more than that someone expects more from an exchange he enters into than from one he refuses' (Heinrich 1999, p. 68).

80 Marx 1982a, p. 132.

realised as an exchange value if it is alienated and functions as a use value'.[81] Therefore, the fetishisation of the exchange-value is at the same time also the fetishisation of use-value:

> The salient point of fetishism is that both sides can always only be super-seded at the same time. ... Use-value as well is simultaneously an abstraction of a commodity .... The entire dichotomous concept should be abolished for the benefit of something which can only be created in the process of abolition.[82]

Formulated differently, use-value and exchange-value are historically specific elements of capitalist society, which is why 'even the analysis of the use-value of the commodity must already make use of *others as functional concepts*, and on this level is already dependent on the categories of *essence* and *appearance*'.[83] Specifically, this analysis relies on the distinction between the capitalist essence of use-value and the manifestation of use-value as usefulness, which appears to hold out for the prospect of a world beyond the exchange of commodities. Kornelia Hafner's accusation of 'use-value fetishism'[84] is thus quite justified. After all, if commodities possess the 'form of a use-value ... by nature' ('it is their natural form'), this is the case 'only for another commodity',[85] that is, only in the exchange relation, which in turn requires the existence of exchange-values. Use-value 'does not have a real existence as such, but rather an existence *only within the opposition of use-value and value*'.[86]

Although he does not draw the decisive consequences, Marx too is thoroughly aware the historicity of use-value as such: 'If "the value" of the com-

---

81   Marx 1987a, p. 284.
82   Stoetzler 1998, p. 5. In relation to Adorno's concept of the fetish-character in music, this
      also means that music's emancipatory power to 'contradict the enchained society through
      unchained art' (Adorno 2007c, p. 82) cannot be regained by 'redeeming' use-value from the
      commodity.
83   Backhaus 1997, p. 24, emphasis added.
84   In light of the belief in 'a dimension of innocent utility in the products of capitalist indus-
      triousness', Kornelia Hafner asks whether the lesson of 'the school of Lukács, Horkheimer,
      Adorno and Marcuse' – that is, the 'critique of reification, of the universal commodifica-
      tion of human productivity, of the historical formation and deformation of inner nature' –
      has been imparted only 'to be forgotten again' (Hafner 1993, p. 61). However, she under-
      stands use-value fetishism as based on a commodity-mediated manipulation of socialised
      individuals, not as a needs-independent, immanently necessary result of the relationship
      between labour power expended and commodity produced.
85   Marx 1983, p. 32.
86   Pohrt 1995, p. 40, emphasis added.

modity is only a specific historical form of something which exists in all forms of society, then so is the ... "use-value" of the commodity'.[87] Consequently, 'use-value' as a manifestation is also the historical form of an essentially social form. Material substance as such is not use-value; rather, use-value merely contains a 'natural element'.[88] The only things which can meaningfully be described as use-values are those whose utility constitutes an element of society,[89] which is to say that use-value is itself a purely formal concept with an arbitrary relationship to the various qualities to which it is applied. Its 'discovery' is 'the work of history',[90] as is claimed *Capital*. Use-value is not only 'use value as such', but is also 'determined economic *form*', and as such, it again enters into the 'sphere of investigation of political economy'.[91]

4 Metabolism

Adorno addresses the problems involved with the Marxian concept of nature in *Philosophische Terminologie*. According to him, this concept

> necessarily relates to nature in Marx's work, although the concept of 'nature' in which productivity is executed itself remains undeveloped in its own right, just as it does in the famous expression 'metabolism with nature'. It may well be assumed that Marx, with quite considerable reason, paused in his dialectical reflection precisely when confronted with the concept of nature in order to avoid grasping this concept – which for him designated the element which cannot purely be dissolved into the subject, that is, into human labour – as yet again constituted by humans. He apparently did not want to draw it into identity thinking again. While there is no natural philosophy from Marx per se, nature itself still has a philosophical meaning for him, I would in any case assume.[92]

---

87   Marx 2010b, p. 249.

88   Marx 1987a, p. 278.

89   Uli Krug has reached a quite similar conclusion, albeit via another path: '*Use-value is possessed not by the world preserved in its natural or habitual state, but rather by the one made useful, whose potentiality was awakened from its Sleeping Beauty slumber. Capital itself sets use-value*' (Krug 1999, p. 46).

90   Marx 1982a, p. 125.

91   Marx 1987a, p. 270, emphasis added.

92   Adorno 1974a, p. 268.

Adorno takes specific issue with the term 'metabolism with nature' – according to which it is necessary to bring nature under 'collective control instead of being dominated by it as a blind power; accomplishing it with the least expenditure of energy and in conditions most worthy and appropriate for their human nature'.[93] He 'cannot positively accept' it, as for him, '[a] society is first humane when it no longer stands under the law of metabolism'.[94] Here, 'metabolism' means the social deterioration of nature, the social process which is 'neither purely social nor purely natural' but rather 'an exchange between man and nature – a permanent interaction between the two'.[95]

Adorno himself depicts the inner connection between society and nature in a highly remarkable passage in *Negative Dialectics*:

> the ineffable part of utopia is that what defies subsumption under identity – the 'use-value', in Marxist terminology – is necessary anyway if life is to go on at all, even under the prevailing circumstances of production. The utopia extends to the sworn enemies of its realization. Regarding the concrete utopian possibility, dialectics is the ontology of the wrong state of things. The right state of things would be free of it: neither a system nor a contradiction.[96]

This passage constitutes a relatively late addition in the writing of the text, one revised by Adorno only once – a departure from his usual writing habits.[97] It

---

93   Marx 1991, p. 959. Marx continues as follows: 'But this always remains a realm of necessity. The true realm of freedom, the development of human powers as an end in itself, begins beyond it, though it can only flourish with this realm of necessity as its basis. The reduction of the working day is the basic prerequisite' (ibid.).

94   Adorno 2021a, vol. 4, p. 64.

95   Adorno 1961, p. 33.

96   Adorno 2007b, p. 11.

97   The revision of the passage looks as follows (italics correspond to handwritten additions, strike-throughs were also made by hand): '~~The~~ Antagonistic generality / ... / Generality is the ~~expression~~ *product* of particular interests. ~~This motivates, beyond philosophy,~~ *This is why a* ~~p~~*P*philosophical critique of identity~~,~~ *transcends philosophy*. But the ineffable part of the utopia is that what defies subsumption under identity – the use-value in Marxist terminology – ~~must exist~~ *is necessary* ~~nevertheless~~ *Aanyway* if life is to ~~survive~~ *go on* at all, *even under the prevailing circumstances of production*. The utopia extends to the sworn enemies of its realization. ~~According to~~ *Regarding* the concrete utopian possibility, dialectics is the ontology of the wrong state of things. The right state of things would be free of it: neither a system nor a contradiction~~, but rather the preserved and reconciled life of difference~~' (TWA, Ts 12542. From a bundle of writings TWA, Ts 12531–603: 'Third transcript 15.3.1966. / ~~Philosophy after the fall of Hegel still possible?~~ / Introduction'). At the very top of the page is a handwritten heading: '*On the possibility of philosophy*' (TWA, Ts 12531).

is remarkable because at first glance, it suggests that Marx's use-value and the non-identical could be defined in reference to each other, even though the non-identical is precisely supposed to resist all positive definitions.[98]

In his essay 'Rien ne va plus – Wolfgang Pohrts *Theorie des Gebrauchswerts*' ('Nothing Goes Anymore – Wolfgang Pohrt's *Theory of Use-Value*'),[99] Kolja Lindner addresses this apparent conflation of the non-identical and use-value when he comments that in Adorno's work, use-value is incorrectly but nevertheless 'consequently regarded as what does not let itself be subsumed under identity'.[100] In fact, the situation is precisely the opposite. Adorno does not derive use-value from the non-identical, but rather takes the 'use' in Marx's concept of use-value as a model for how his own concept of the non-identical should be understood. This certainly constitutes a derivation from Marx's employment of the concept of use-value, in spite of Adorno's claims to the contrary. However, this means neither that Adorno identifies the non-identical with use-value, nor that he lacks a specifically economic understanding of use-value. Rather, it appears he does not consider that the concept of use-value is only conditionally suited as a model of the non-identical. Insofar as use-value stands opposed to exchange-value as a non-quantifiable, purely qualitative element, it can indeed be viewed as occupying an analogous position to the non-identical in the latter's relationship to the identical. That being said, use-value designates what is qualitative in commodities under capitalist relations of production, whereas the non-identical – an epistemological category – applies to all possibly conceivable things, not only to those things which first became commodities under capital. The analogy between use-value and the non-identical completely fails when the former is regarded as the embodiment of usefulness, as it is by Marx when he claims in *A Contribution to the Critique of Political Economy* that '[o]ne

---

98   A quite similar statement can be in the 1965 lecture 'Functionalism Today' when Adorno speaks of the 'bit of freedom' living '[e]ven in the false needs of a human being', a freedom 'expressed in what economic theory once called the "use value" as opposed to the [abstract] "exchange value"' (Adorno 1997, p. 14).

99   Although Lindner's essay bears the subtitle 'Wolfgang Pohrts *Theorie des Gebrauchswerts*', ['Wolfgang Pohrt's *Theory of Use-Value*'] Lindner assumes that Pohrt had adopted the views of (especially Adorno's) Critical Theory. In doing so, he often lumps together the theories of Pohrt and Adorno so that at times it is hard to distinguish whether which one is meant, or whether both are meant at the same time. Lindner's text is methodologically prototypical as well, insofar as he simply measures Pohrt against Marx only to criticise the former when he deviates from the latter. For example, one passage argues that Pohrt's 'speculative Marx philology turns out here to be simply irreconcilable with the Marxian text' (Lindner 2007, p. 235). Whether this might indicate a deficiency of Marxian theory seems at least to be debatable, and not something which can be dictated from on high.

100   Lindner 2007, p. 215.

and the same use value can be used in various ways', but that 'the extent of its possible applications is limited by its existence as an object with distinct properties'.[101] That being said, 'applications' are exactly what Adorno does not have in mind when he invokes the non-identical. For him, if one wants to do justice to a thing, then subsuming this thing into the 'extent of its possible applications' is precisely what one cannot do. Opposed to this, Adorno's non-identical designates the element which eludes fungibility.

Here, Adorno vacillates between two definitions of use-value. On the one hand, in analogy to the non-identical, use-value is construed as non-substantive. Yet on the other, Adorno suggests that use-value as a 'part of nature'[102] is in a certain sense co-opted by exchange-value. This latter construal backslides into the critique of political economy's capitalism-specific concept of exchange, whereas the reference to the difference between the identical and the non-identical demands the meta-economic, extra-capitalist concept of exchange already employed elsewhere by Adorno. Contrary to Lindner, *Negative Dialectics* does not conceptualise 'identity logic as the capitalist form of thought par excellence, one whose model is exchange'.[103] Although Adorno does claim that the principle of exchange 'is fundamentally akin to the principle of identification' and that exchange itself is 'the social model of the principle',[104] the exchange presented by Adorno as a model here is not the specifically capitalist exchange-relation. Rather, it is meta-economic exchange in general. Like the logic of identity, exchange does not first come into being with capitalism, but instead exists as the 'age-old myth' of 'an eye for an eye, a

---

101   Marx 1987a, p. 269.
102   Adorno 2002a, p. 70.
103   Lindner 2007, p. 215.
104   Adorno 2007b, p. 146. Adorno's thesis in this passage – 'it is through exchange that nonidentical individuals and performances become commensurable and identical' (ibid.) – is the subject of a vehement critique by Kornelia Hafner: 'Opposed to Marx, whose argumentation here gives itself to over the power of negativity by showing that this commensurability is appearance, by destroying this appearance and thereby coming to the realisation that what is primary is not commodity exchange, as liberal models suggest, but rather money as a universal commodity, as necessarily the result and precondition of the exchange process, Adorno adamantly adheres to the "exchange principle" and claims commensurability is something manufactured, even if it is something which is wrong and coercive towards humans and things under its authority. The proliferation of this principle constrains the entire world to the identical, to totality' (Hafner 2005, p. 152). However, nowhere in the passage is mention made of an 'exchange principle' moulding the world into an identical totality – what is at issue is the principle of identity, or with respect to the economy, the principle of equivalence. Moreover, Adorno is not interested here in whether commodities could be exchanged for other commodities of money, but rather in the fact *that* exchange takes place, and that it is *equivalent*.

quid pro quo'.[105] It has the same origin as the logic of identity insofar as both are mediated by each other in the quid pro quo: neither is possible nor even conceivable without the other. In his lecture course *Kant's 'Critique of Pure Reason'*, Adorno emphasises that in myth – defined as the 'idea that nothing new should come into being' – the exchange-relation is already established, also with respect to knowledge. In other words, in the 'equation of binding truth with timeless or eternal knowledge',[106] the notion comes into effect that

> the act of cognition is a kind of exchange in which equivalents, namely efforts and products, are exchanged so that debts are settled and the sums work out. There is a relationship of equivalence such that in principle nothing can emerge without entering into it, that is, nothing that does not have to be paid for by whatever has first been *posited*. And in the process only this exchange relation of knowledge, that is, the effort, the exchange between the labour of thinking and the object which thought then appropriates, and the products of this process, namely the fact that the ideas *work out* – only this becomes the thing that endures, the lasting product.[107]

In *Philosophische Terminologie*, Adorno wagers a definition of use-value in spite of his scepticism towards such practices: 'Use-value is the value which some object in its concrete form has for human beings'. However, as he immediately elaborates, 'you will later see that this concept, which could possibly be described as a system-transcendent concept of value, takes a highly surprising turn'.[108] Adorno designates use-value as 'system-transcendent' – in distinction to exchange-value, which 'could be referred to as a "system-immanent" concept of value'[109] – because in Marx's work, it functions among other ways by binding the system, or capitalist society, to nature.

When Adorno speaks of the 'highly surprising turn' taken by use-value, a turn which consists of the fact that the use-value of the commodity of labour-power can explain the production of surplus-value, he thereby indicates the difficulties caused by regarding use-value as a product of transforming what is external to society, namely nature. The commodity of labour-power is the only commodity which emerges and reproduces itself in the consumption of

---

105 Adorno 2019f, p. 425.
106 Adorno 2001c, p. 26.
107 Adorno 2001c, p. 27.
108 Adorno 1974a, p. 269.
109 Adorno 1974a, p. 260.

use-values. However, rather than being immediately given, these use-values are themselves products of society, manufactured by the very labour-power they nourish. The attempt to establish the dependence of use-values on a nature external to society becomes lost in an infinite regression.[110]

Adorno elaborates further with the help of a quotation from *Capital*:

> The product of the process of labour is a use-value, a natural substance adopted to human needs through a change in form. Here, the concept of nature is indeed already grasped in the sense of, one could say philosophically, a *constitutum*. Something similarly tangible, similarly present, is for example the object of the natural sciences, where reflection about this object's constitution itself is either severed or has already been discarded *ab ovo*. There again, this reflection is namely itself conceptualised as a function of the process of labour. 'Labour has become bound up in its object', namely with this natural substance: 'labour has been objectified, the object has been worked on. What on the side of the worker appeared in the form of unrest now appears, on the side of the product, in the form of being, as a fixed, immobile characteristic. The worker has spun, and the product is a spinning'. As an aside, here you can see very clearly what is meant by Marxian materialism's constantly recurring concept of congealed or objectified labour. Yet at the same time, fully in keeping with Hegel, this congealed labour is not conceived of as something purely subjective, but as something already mediated by subject and object. It is conceived as something which contains in itself the labour of the subject as well as the natural material on which this labour is performed. This became extraordinary important in Marx's polemic against the Lassalleans, who misappropriated exactly this natural element. Marx polemicised against the famous saying that labour is the source of all wealth in 'Critique of the Gotha Programme'.[111]

---

110   'Although a use-value emerges from the labour process, in the form of a product, other use-values, products of previous labour, enter into it as means of production. The same use-value is both the product of a previous process, and a means of production in a later process. Products are therefore not only results of labour, but also its essential conditions' (Marx 1982a, p. 287). This passage is underlined in Adorno's copy of *Capital* (TWA, NB 280).

111   Adorno 1974a, p. 270, quoted from Marx 1982a, p. 287. Marx writes as follows: 'Labour is *not the source* of all wealth. Nature is just as much the source of use-values (and surely these are what make up material wealth!) as labour. Labour is itself only the manifestation of a force of nature, human labour power. This phrase can be found in any children's primer; it is correct in so far as it is *assumed* that labour is performed with the objects and instruments necessary to it. A socialist programme, however, cannot allow such bourgeois

In 'Critique of the Gotha Programme', Marx correctly asserts against the 'customary litany of [vulgar] socialists' that labour is 'not the sole source of social wealth'. In doing so, Adorno argues in *Negative Dialectics*,

> he was philosophically – at a time when the official philosophical thematics lay already behind him – saying no less than that labor could not be hypostatized in any form, neither in the form of diligent hands nor in that of mental production. Such hypostasis merely extends the illusion of the predominance of the productive principle. It comes to be true only in relation to that nonidentical [element] which Marx in his disdain for epistemology called first by the crude, too narrow name of 'nature', later on by that of 'natural material' and by other less incriminated terms.[112]

Adorno continues in *Philosophische Terminologie* with another quotation from *Capital*:

> 'If we look at the whole process from the point of view of its result, the product, it is plain that both the instruments and the object of labour' – not only the hammer, but also the raw material – 'are means of production and that the labour itself is productive labour'. I can only present the central materialist element in this without drawing out its full consequences and essentially philosophical meaning. Productive labour in Marx's work means first of all only labour which produces material goods of one kind or another, because according to Marx's definition, labour must be done to a natural material, that is, to something non-conscious.[113]

---

formulations to silence the *conditions* which give them the only meaning they possess. Man's labour only becomes a source of use-values, and hence also of wealth, if his relation to nature, the primary source of all instruments and objects of labour, is one of ownership from the start, and if he treats it as belonging to him. There is every good reason for the bourgeoisie to ascribe *supernatural creative power* to labour, for when a man has no property other than his labour power it is precisely labour's dependence on nature that forces him, in all social and cultural conditions, to be the slave of other men who have taken the objective conditions of labour into their own possession. He needs their permission to work, and hence their permission to live' (Marx 2010a, p. 341).

112   Adorno 2007b, pp. 177–8; cf. Adorno 1993a, p. 23.
113   Adorno 1974a, pp. 270–1; quoted from Marx 1982a, p. 287. Adorno continues as follows: 'There are passages in *Capital* which take this materialist motif, I want to say, to the limits of the absurd, to the limits of paradoxical, by using productive worker to refer only to someone who in the most narrow sense is engaged in the productive apparatus of material goods'. For Adorno, in contemporary society, these questions are 'rife with problems of the most difficult kind. Due to the neurotisation undergone by consciousness

Nevertheless, Adorno maintains that 'in the form of science, even spirit has become a force of production' and 'intervenes in the historical process. Those who claim Marx dismissed spirit as a chimera must be opposed'.[114] According to Adorno, Marx in his own time 'opposed idealism by asserting that it is not consciousness which determines being but being consciousness, and that the truth about society is to be found not in its idealistic notions of itself but in its economy'.[115] In doing so, Marx exposed the discourse about autonomy of spirit as ideology. In his lecture course *Philosophie und Soziologie (Philosophy and Sociology)* from the summer semester of 1960, Adorno comments that within the alleged autonomy of spirit,

> the class character of society itself is here ignored or repressed, so that the actually existing relations of domination are legitimated through the intrinsic and unconditional right of the mind to control or subjugate all that is. Thus among the arguments offered in defence of the existing relations of production you will constantly encounter the idea that it just happens there are clever people and stupid people, and the supposedly clever people, namely the ones with better minds, have justifiably higher claims and expectations than the others. These arguments, and others like

---

in response to Marx, they have still not really been addressed' (Adorno 1974a, pp. 271–2; cf. Behrens 2005, p. 7). 'I believe', Adorno comments earlier in *Philosophie und Soziologie*, 'it would be a no less riveting task, if one wanted to seriously take it up someday, to pursue what the materialist motif is in Marx's work itself, and how it differs from vulgar materialist views. Today, all of this is almost fully covered over. In the East, one has developed out of Marx something like a materialist worldview which strictly contradicts the texts. As a reaction against this, and certainly to a very great extent, it has been attempted in the Western sphere to do away with the actual materialist element. In Marx's work, this element is really quite difficult to define; I wouldn't take up the task myself, unless a special study were available. The attempt made above all with the aid of Marx's early writings – the *Economic and Philosophical Manuscripts* and "The German Ideology" – to attribute to him something like an anthropology simply stands in contradiction to him, whose writings against Feuerbach reject exactly this anthropological intention. Under this false alternative, the problem of what the concept of materialism in Marx's work actually is has been fully covered up until now. To realise this problem by getting to work on the texts themselves, without apologetic intentions towards one side or the other, would be a first step. Yet it's like things are jinxed with Marx; there is apparently no human being who can simply take hold of these texts without them starting to totter either to the right or left, and a genuine relationship to these texts, according to their own truth content, is an extraordinary rare breed' (Adorno 1974a, p. 256).

114   Adorno 2021a, vol. 1, p. 466.
115   Adorno and Horkheimer 2002, p. 175.

them, are the last remaining dregs, as it were, from this momentous historical process in which the mind has asserted its complete independence of physical labour. And since these dregs are all that remain, the thesis in question looks like an extremely suspect and problematic one which has been well and truly contaminated in the process.[116]

Among other ways, Marx and Engels responded to this thesis with the assertion that '[c]onsciousness [*das Bewusstsein*] can never be anything else than conscious being [*das bewusste Sein*], and the being of men is their actual life-process'.[117]

Describing the situation as it appeared to him at the end of the 1940s, Adorno writes that 'the definition of consciousness in terms of being has become a means of dispensing with all consciousness which does not conform to existence. The objectivity of truth, without which the dialectic is inconceivable, is tacitly replaced by vulgar positivism and pragmatism – ultimately, that is, by bourgeois subjectivism'.[118] For him, in the rigid 'opposition of base and superstructure, of material and mind', there is already 'an element of stasis, and indeed of reification ... which Marx criticises as ideological'.[119]

Adorno argues that Marx's concept of productive labour, the concept to which the discourse on forces of production refers, is in fact 'quite complicated because it is already taken from the rules of the game of bourgeois society, and one could almost say that it is a parody of what Marx himself might have imagined as productivity'.[120] After all,

[w]hereas the concept of productivity in bourgeois society, one may say here, is ideologised, glorifying of labour, this concept of productivity is in reality only limited to valorisability. In contrast, on the one hand, Marx wrests labour away from this ideology, yet while he himself does not perceive labour according to its valorisability, he does perceive it according to its utility: this utility, however – this is extraordinarily important, and I point it out to you as a great heresy against official Marxism – must not be a utility at all. To illustrate this, I present to you one of the most altogether astounding passages I am familiar with in Marx's work, a passage which

---

116   Adorno 2022, pp. 98–9.
117   Marx and Engels 1976, p. 36.
118   Adorno 1988c, p. 29.
119   Adorno 2021a, vol. 1, p. 468.
120   Adorno 1974a, p. 259.

was just pointed out to me a few days ago. Here, you can see behind the scenes, so to speak, and recognise what is actually meant by this materialism.[121]

Adorno then cites a passage from Marx's 'Results of the Immediate Process of Production':

'From the foregoing it is evident that for *labour to be designated productive*, qualities are required' – always system-immanent qualities – 'which are utterly unconnected with the *specific content* of the labour, with its particular utility or the use-value in which it is objectified' – so, this is quite different from how productive labour was defined in *Capital*. 'Hence labour with *the same content* can be either productive or unproductive'. And now comes the astounding part: 'For instance, Milton, who wrote *Paradise Lost*, was an unproductive worker' – this means he created no exchange-value by doing so, that it wasn't valorisable. 'On the other hand, a writer who turns out work for his publisher in factory style' – so for example, the writer of trash films who produces some wretched scripts for Hollywood which are completely ideological and worthless – 'is a productive worker. Milton produced *Paradise Lost* as a silkworm produces silk, as the activation of *his own* nature. He later sold his product for £5 and thus became a merchant. But the literary proletarian of Leipzig who produces books, such as compendia on political economy, at the behest of his publisher is pretty nearly a productive worker since his production is taken over by capital and only occurs in order to increase it. A singer who sings like a bird is an unproductive worker. If she sells her song for money, she is to that extent a wage-labourer or merchant. But if the same singer is engaged by an entrepreneur who makes her sing to make money, then she becomes a productive worker, since she *produces* capital directly'. From this passage, it really emerges that all the categories of bourgeois society, represented here by productivity in the sense understood by the principle of exchange – so in other words, the whole system which Marx develops – is not supposed to be a system of the absolute or of truth. It is much rather the case that Marx wants to show that in fact the whole ... is the untrue. Hence, it is an utter perversion that out of so-called dialectical materialism, something like a system has been made in the name of *Diamat*.[122]

---

121   Adorno 1974a, p. 275.
122   Translator's note: Stalinist shorthand for dialectical materialism.

I would say that the question of understanding Marx first begins where this curious refraction re-emerges. It is however evident that behind the Marxian concept of productivity, there is a notion which does in fact go far beyond the concept of mere material production.[123]

5   Total Mediation

That the Marxian concept of productivity cannot be reduced to material production becomes evident in view of the concepts of first and second nature. Alfred Schmidt summarises these concepts as follows:

> Hegel describes first nature, a world of things existing outside men, as blind conceptless occurrence. The world of men as it takes shape in the state, law, society, and the economy, is for him 'second nature', manifested reason, objective spirit. Marxist analysis opposes to this the view that Hegel's 'second nature' should rather be described in the terms he applied to the first: namely, as the area of conceptlessness, where blind necessity and blind chance coincide. The 'second nature' is still the 'first'.[124]

By contrast, having adopted the concept of 'second nature' from Lukács (who himself adopted it from Hegel), Adorno does not simply define 'second nature' as 'first'. Rather, he insists on the 'immanence of first and second nature'[125] given that 'a pure nature – that is to say, a nature that has not gone through the mediation processes of society – does not exist'.[126] At the same time, this also means that 'first nature' is already 'second nature':

> Hegel already gave a rating of greater substantiality to the results of abstraction. Under the same *topos* he deals with matter, also with the

---

123   Adorno 1974a, pp. 276–7; quoted from Marx 1982b, p. 1044. Along these lines, Adorno speaks in a seminar of 'Marx, who referred to socially useful labour as that which is paid for on the market. According to the laws of the market, however, Milton would not have performed socially useful labour for his work *Paradise Lost* sold for absurdly little money. Through this example, Marx immediately places the concepts functional and dysfunctional under irony. He delivers immanent criteria for what is organic and non-organic to a society' (Adorno 2021a, vol. 4, p. 63). On the consequences of this concept of productivity for art, cf. Adorno 2002a, pp. 227–8.

124   Schmidt 2013, pp. 12–3.

125   Schweppenhäuser 1973, p. 76.

126   Adorno 2018a, p. 77.

transition to existence. That its concept is indefinite, that as a concept it lacks precisely what is meant by it, is supposed to be why all light is cast on its form. Hegel fits this into Western metaphysics, at its outermost limits; Engels saw that, but came to the opposite, equally undialectical conclusion: that matter is the first Being.

Dialectical criticism is due [to] the concept of the first Being itself.[127]

No first nature is in sight as long as history is natural history, and in this respect prehistory. The fact that nature no longer exists also means that everything, even society itself, is only nature – that even the non-identical does not positively exist, is only negatively recognisable. Since the human beings have existed – that is, since the separation between subject and object – nature has been available for them to dominate.[128] However, theoretically speaking, this means that *all* nature is available for them. In practical terms, this availability is expanded by technological advancement, which knows neither unavailability nor non-identity – this also explains the 'difficulty of positively defining first nature'.[129]

But the second nature, philosophically raised again for the first time in Lukács' theory of the novel, remains the negation of any nature that might be conceived as the first. What is truly θέσει – produced by the functional context of individuals, if not by themselves – usurps the insignia of that which a bourgeois consciousness regards as nature and as natural. To that consciousness nothing appears as being outside any more; in a certain sense there actually is nothing outside any more, nothing unaffected by total mediation. What is trapped within, therefore, comes to appear to itself as its own otherness – a primal phenomenon of idealism. The

---

127   Adorno 2007b, p. 121. 'Adorno's critique of Hegel builds on his own concept – oriented on Lukács's theory of the novel – of "second nature" as is elaborated in his early manifesto for the philosophy of history, "The Idea of Natural History". There it is claimed that "[s]econd nature is, in truth, first nature"' (Müller 2006, p. 142; quoted from Adorno 1984, p. 124).

128   Between November 1932 and August 1933, Adorno wrote the libretto for a light opera he was planning titled *Der Schatz des Indianer-Joe* [*The Treasure of Indian Joe*] (cf. Tiedemann 1979, p. 120). In one scene, a protagonist named Young Tom looks out of the entrance of an enormous dripstone cave and says, '[h]ow the forest outside looks through the grey gate before the cave. Completely different. As if it were artificially depicted. Like no real forest [*richtiger Wald*] at all' (Adorno 1979, p. 76). Tiedemann offers a convincing interpretation of this passage: 'That there is no right life [*richtiges Leben*] in the wrong one is expressed thusly in *Indianer-Joe*: "there is no real nature where society is false"' (Tiedemann 1979, p. 135).

129   Duarte 1989, p. 68.

more relentlessly socialization commands all moments of human and interhuman immediacy, the smaller the capacity of men to recall that this web has evolved, and the more irresistible its natural appearance. The appearance is reinforced as the distance between human history and nature keeps growing: nature turns into an irresistible parable of imprisonment.

The youthful Marx expressed the unending entwinement of the two elements with an extremist vigor bound to irritate dogmatic materialists: 'We know only a single science, the science of history. History can be considered from two sides, divided into the history of nature and the history of mankind. Yet there is no separating the two sides; as long as men exist, natural and human history will qualify each other.' The traditional antithesis of nature and history is both true and false – true insofar as it expresses what happened to the natural element; false insofar as, by means of conceptual reconstruction, it apologetically repeats the concealment of history's natural growth.[130]

When Adorno refers to 'wars or similar natural catastrophes of society',[131] he decisively appropriates 'Marx's polemical concept of natural [law]'[132] which characterises capitalist production. In the introduction to *Capital*, Marx writes the following:

> Even when a society has begun to track down the natural laws of its movement – and it is the ultimate aim of this work to reveal the economic law of motion of modern society – it can neither leap over the natural phases of its development nor remove them by degree. But it can shorten and lessen the birth-pangs. ... I do not by any means depict the capitalist and the landowner in rosy colours. But individuals are dealt with here only in so far as they are the personifications of economic categories, the bearers of particular class-relations and interests. My standpoint, from which the development of the economic formation of society is viewed as a process of natural history, can less than any other make the individual responsible for relations whose creature he remains, socially speaking, however much he may subjectively raise himself above them.[133]

---

130   Adorno 2007b, pp. 357–8; quoted from Marx and Engels 1976, pp. 28–9.
131   Adorno 2000a, p. 144.
132   Adorno 2007b, p. 355.
133   Marx 1982, p. 92. Adorno cites this passage in *Negative Dialectics* (Adorno 2007b, p. 354).

'What is meant here', Adorno comments, 'is certainly not Feuerbach's an-thropological concept of nature, against which Marx aimed dialectical materi-alism in the sense of a Hegelian reprise against the Left Hegelians. The so-called law of nature that is merely one of capitalist society, after all, is therefore called "mystification" by Marx'[134] when he refers to the 'law of capitalist accumula-tion, mystified by the economists into a supposed law of nature'.[135] 'There is a contradiction here: on the one hand, Marx speaks with the scientist's passion of the inexorable laws of nature, in particular of the evolution of the laws of economics. At the same time, however, these laws are shown to be a mystifica-tion, an illusion'.[136] After all, the 'organic nature of capitalist society is both an actuality *and* at the same time a socially necessary illusion. The illusion signi-fies that within this society laws can only be implemented as natural processes over people's heads, while their validity arises from the form of the relations of production within which production takes place'.[137]

This means that 'natural history' in Marx's work, '[i]n contrast to the natural-ist approach of vulgar Marxism, ... is a *critical* concept':[138] 'Human history, the history of the progressing mastery of nature, continues the unconscious history of nature, of devouring and being devoured. / Ironically, Marx was a Social Dar-winist: what the Social Darwinists praised, and what they would like to go by,

---

134   Adorno 2007b, p. 354.
135   Marx 1982a, p. 771.
136   Adorno 2006a, pp. 117–18.
137   Adorno 2006a, p. 118.
138   Adorno 2006a, p. 116. 'There is a passage from *Foundations of Political Economy* that leaves no doubt that [Marx's] view of natural history was critical in essence: "Much as the whole of this motion appears as a social process, much as the single moments of this motion take their departure from the conscious will and from particular purposes of individuals – the totality of the process does appear as an objective context arising by natural growth. It is indeed due to the interaction of conscious individuals, but neither seated in their con-sciousness nor subsumed under them as a whole." / Such a social concept of nature has a dialectic of its own. The thesis that society is subject to natural laws is ideology if it is hypostatized as immutability given by nature. But this legality is real as a law of motion for the unconscious society, as [*Capital*], in a phenomenology of the anti-spirit, traces it from the analysis of the [commodity-]form to the theory of collapse. The changes from each constitutive economic form to the next occurred like those of the animal types that rose and died out over millions of years. The fetish chapter's "theological quirks of [the com-modity]" mock the false consciousness in which the social relation of the exchange value is reflected to contradicting parties as a quality of things-in-themselves; but those quirks are also as true as the practice of bloody idolatry was once a fact. For the constitutive forms of socialization, of which that mystification is one, maintain their absolute supremacy over mankind as if they were divine Providence' (Adorno 2007b, pp. 355–6; quoted from Marx 1993, pp. 196–7, Marx 1983, p. 44).

is to him the negativity [which, within itself, awakens] the chance of voiding [itself]'.[139] Social Darwinism, the 'hopeless rhythm of coming to be and passing away – or of eating and being eaten', is a rhythm in which '[n]othing changes': 'The historical link between predator and prey is essentially unhistorical'.[140] In the words of Adorno from one of his seminars, the 'brilliance of Marx lies in the fact that although he conceives of history as a continuation of natural history, he opposes precisely the condition in which Darwinism becomes elevated to a worldview. His critique of political economy is one of the heteronomous domination of relations of production, a domination from which human beings should liberate themselves'.[141]

However, this liberation would not deliver human beings to infinitely redeemed use-values, but rather from capitalism altogether – including from its elementary categories of value and use-value. Thus, Kolja Lindner concedes to Critical Theory – again referring to Adorno –

> that in spite of all logic of subsumption, the diagnosis of a use-value fully incorporated by capital remains ambivalent. This is not only due to the various versions and contexts in which it has been presented in over twenty five years of theoretical work, but also Adorno's iridescent conception of society. Society is said to be a totality that subsumes use-value, ... yet also an 'ongoing antagonism' ... which entails the possibility of overcoming totality .... For the context in question here, this is important insofar as there exists in Adorno's work the hope that social confrontation might topple the existing totality of relations of production and release use-values form their social bracketing, bringing the emancipatory potential of use-values to bear – as long as they have such potential, in the sense of something which serves the well-being of humanity.[142]

From this, Lindner concludes that 'for Adorno, the idea of freedom first emerges in a certain capitalist stage in the development of the forces of production, namely after necessary labour has been reduced to a vanishingly small minimum, potentially eradicating humanity's material deprivation'.[143]

---

139 Adorno 2007b, p. 355. 'With considerations such as these, Adorno stands in pointed contrast to Marx. Although the latter was not the enthusiastic proponent of industrialism some would like to declare him to be, domination over nature appeared to him, at least in his later years, to be necessary and largely unproblematic' (Schiller 1993a, p. 46).

140 Adorno 1961, p. 49.

141 Adorno 2021a, vol. 2, p. 88.

142 Lindner 2007, p. 216.

143 Lindner 2007, p. 216, n. 3.

Insofar as Lindner means by this that only under the above circumstances does the *possibility* of freedom exist for Adorno, he is incorrect. The opposite is the case: already in his seminar from the winter semester of 1957–8, Adorno rejects the 'assumption that the increase in goods on the side of use-value could make social antagonisms inoperative', arguing that 'what counts is not increasing the quantity of goods as such: what's decisive is much rather the relation between the terms *c*, *v* and *s* which characterise capitalist production'.[144] As is shown by the discussion of the economically unproductive labour which Milton performed with *Paradise Lost*, Adorno makes the Marxian 'punchline'[145] of this exposition his own. This punchline reads as follows:

> productive labour, according to the prevailing capitalist system, is only that labour which falls into the capitalist valorisation process, which produces exchange-value. What does not produce exchange-value – however much use-value it might produce, however productive it may be in a higher sense – is indeed, according to the rules of the game of society, in spite of all the ideals society professes, precisely not productive labour.[146]

---

144   Adorno 2021a, vol. 2, pp. 84–5. Marx uses *c* to denote constant capital, which is composed of the means of production, *v* to denote variable capital and *s* to denote surplus value. Production occurs not for the sake of surplus values, and certainly not for the sake of fulfilling human needs, but rather for the sake of profit, whose rate *s'* can be calculated from these three variables: $p' = s / (c + v)$ (see Marx 1991, p. 141).

145   Adorno 1974a, p. 274.

146   Ibid. 'The order in which these vast quantities of goods are produced is subject to the exchange principle. Moreover, the competitive principle makes the compulsion to produce unavoidable: it is precisely these laws of motion which should be affected by the theory, not the variable phenomena of massively increased production' (Adorno 2021a, vol. 2, p. 85).

CHAPTER 12

Point of Indifference

> Or might it even concern something like the
> central=heating of the whole?
>
> ARNO SCHMIDT, Sitara und der Weg dorthin

∴

1   A Gap

According to Marx, labour, or labour-power, is the only 'total exclusion of objective wealth'.[1] In Hegelian terms, it is the negation of capital,[2] the *'real non-capital'* and thus the 'only *use value which can present an opposite and a complement to money as capital'*.[3] As a commodity, it gains use-value as a consequence of being consumed to create value. 'The opposite of capital as the independent, firmly self-sufficient objectified labour is living labour capacity itself, and so the only exchange by means of which money can become capital is the exchange between the possessor of capital and the possessor of the living labour capacity, i.e. the worker'.[4] Labour-capacity, or labour-power,[5] has use-value insofar as it is a condition for the possibility of labour. From this it follows that actually performed labour – labour which produces commodities and hence value – is the realisation of labour-power's use-value.[6]

As physiological potential, human labour-power is simultaneously both nature and value. 'This value is equal to the labour time required to produce the means of subsistence necessary for the reproduction of labour capacity, or to

---

1 Marx 1993, p. 296.
2 Cf. Friedrich 2000, pp. 210–11.
3 Marx 1987b, p. 503.
4 Marx 1987b, p. 502.
5 Marx uses the terms 'labour-power' (*Arbeitskraft*) and 'labour-capacity' (*Arbeitsvermögen*) synonymously: 'We mean by labour-power, or labour-capacity, the aggregate of those mental and physical capabilities existing in the physical form, the living personality of a human being, capabilities which he sets in motion whenever he produces a use-value of any kind' (Marx 1982a, p. 270).
6 Cf. Marx 1987b, p. 506.

the price of the means of subsistence necessary for the existence of the worker as a worker'.[7] When the capitalist purchases the commodity of labour-power, he also acquires the right to use it, and by productively employing labour-power, he creates value with it. Indeed, he uses labour-power to create more value than what it cost him, which is to say, he has labour-power perform more labour than is necessary to produce the commodities he will need to reproduce his labour-power. By all means, equivalents are exchanged throughout this process: the total value of the commodity of labour-power is remunerated in accordance with the society-wide average.[8] The accruing surplus-value does not arise from circulation (for example, from unfair exchange), but rather from production: it is a product of wage-labour. 'This discovery', Walter Tuchscheerer argues, 'is one of the greatest in the field of political economy', for '[i]t forms the key with which Marx goes on to solve all the contradictions in which economists prior to him had gotten entangled. As long as it was assumed that the capitalist paid the "value of labour" [and not the value of labour-capacity], why the "value of labour" – the wage – does not equal the value produced by labour, why a particular quantity of objectified labour is exchanged, had to remain an insoluble contradiction'.[9] This discovery allows the existence of surplus-value – and therefore also the self-movement of capital – to be explained not in spite of, but on the basis of the exchange of equivalents.

'Labour power', Adorno claims, 'is the source of surplus-value because it is at the same time use-value and exchange-value',[10] and therefore a commodity. Because workers as subjects are both a part of society and nature – or more precisely, because society and nature are actually one with each other – labour is not limited to producing commodities; as it produces commodities, it can also produce surplus-value. As a part of what is usually designated as 'first nature', labour-power expresses itself as labour existing both under and for capital,

---

7 Marx 1988, p. 353. This is an ambiguous definition of the amount of value of the commodity of labour-power, a fact which Michael Heinrich has criticised as a failure of Marx: 'What Marx can be accused of is not sufficiently emphasising the particularity the definition of labour-power's value. ... For the analysis of a particular capitalist society, a narrower definition of the value of labour-power, the level of reproduction and the mode of reproduction is naturally of decisive importance' (Heinrich 1999, p. 261).

8 'This seems paradox and contrary to everyday observation. It is also paradox that the earth moves round the sun, and that water consists of two highly inflammable gases. Scientific truth is always paradox, if judged by everyday experience, which catches only the delusive appearance of things' (Marx 1985, p. 127).

9 Tuchscheerer 1968, p. 399. However, wages do not equal the value of labour because the latter's price-form, the labour-value, indeed has value-form.

10 Adorno 2018c, p. 161.

while capital in turn exists as (and for) 'second nature'. 'The capitalist epoch is therefore characterized by the fact that labour-power, in the eyes of the worker himself, takes on the form of a commodity which is his property; his labour consequently takes on the form of wage-labour. On the other hand, it is only from this moment that the commodity-form of the products of labour becomes universal'[11] by capital becoming the *'totality of commodities'*.[12]

Here, Adorno largely follows Marxian theory: 'The illusion in the process of exchange lies in the concept of surplus-value',[13] a concept which is based on the appropriation of surplus-value by the purchasers of labour-power in compliance with the exchange of equivalents. He suggests that also at the point of indifference – between nature and society, as well as between classes – everything is in keeping with like for like. Both classes appear equal from the perspective of exchange, and nothing in their formal equality suggests that the class-relation first constitutes itself in the exchange of labour-power for wages.

> In order to understand the concept of surplus value, two time-spans have to be compared: the time which is necessary for the production of labour-power and the time that the worker gives in labour. One must not start with the commodity produced by the worker, rather it is a matter of an exchange process: the worker sells his labour-time for which he receives his equivalent. But the time he gives and the time that is needed for the reproduction of his labour-power are different.[14]

The equality in this exchange manifests itself in the fact that the capitalist can say to the worker: 'Please, you're expending such-and-such amount of labour-power, I'm going to give you just enough to reproduce this labour-power'. Meanwhile, the inequality lies on the one hand in the difference between the 'reproduction costs of the average social labour-power expended by the worker', and on the other in 'the labour-power calculated in the labour-hours which the worker spends in the apparatus of production'.[15]

'The result of this disparity, which is constitutive for surplus-value, is that the worker's labour does not belong to him, that he cannot have at his disposal

11   Marx 1982a, p. 274, n. 4.
12   Marx 1993, p. 262.
13   Adorno 2018c, p. 160.
14   Adorno 2018c, p. 162.
15   Adorno 1974a, p. 262. The concepts of the worker and the capitalist, whereby the former sells his labour-power to the latter for wages, should 'not be seen, say, as descriptions of individual processes, but rather from the perspective of society as a whole' (ibid.).

the products of his labour. His products are foreign to him, which means that there must be someone else, someone more powerful, who is stealing them from him'.[16] Domination is no longer immediate, something exerted by some human beings over others. Rather, it is social, or in a manner of speaking, structural. Domination over 'first nature', which is exerted by human beings seeking to free themselves from being dominated by nature, results in humans being dominated by 'second nature' instead. Additionally, Adorno sees an 'increasing anonymisation' of domination being 'enacted in the capitalist system':

> With the increase in capital's concentration and the enormous increase in importance of the administrative apparatus, the power relations on the side of capital increasingly recede into the background. This is why it is difficult to identify those who actually have capital at their disposal. Nevertheless, there is a dominant group. Although they do not compose a class when viewed quantitatively ... (if the concept of class demands a certain quantity). However, keeping in mind that Marx defines the concept of class according to the position of human beings in the production process, it can be said that that there are absolutely still classes today, even though levelling tendencies are becoming manifest in subjective consciousness.[17]

For Adorno, precisely in the exchange of labour-power for wages,

> the dialectical power of Marxian thought can be more adequately perceived ... than in the frequently invoked oppositions between factors relating to being and factors relating to consciousness, between forces and relations of production. After all, for Marx, exchange in bourgeois society exhibits a strictly dialectical character insofar as it both is and isn't the exchange of equivalents, as can be demonstrated by the substitution relationship between wage and labour. Specifically, because a commodity's value is determined by the labour-time which is socially necessary for its production, yet the production of the commodity of labour consists of its social reproduction, this commodity is paid for according to its value, even when the worker only recovers the costs of its reproduction while handing over its full use-value. The objects of exchange – the amount of labour expended by the worker, and the means for his reproduction as paid out in money – are in other words, according to the meas-

16   Adorno 2021a, vol. 4, p. 329.
17   Adorno 2021a, vol. 3, p. 463.

ure of labour-value, equal. Yet on the other hand, because labour is the only commodity which not only has value, but also creates value, they are also unequal insofar as the average expenditure of labour-time which the worker needs to produce his means of reproduction is smaller than what he in fact sells to the entrepreneur.[18]

In this passage from a transcript taken in his seminar from the 1955–6 winter semester, Adorno still conflates the terms 'labour' and 'labour-time' – just as Lukács does in *History and Class Consciousness*. Later, however, he adheres much more closely to Marxian terminology when he claims that

labour disaggregates into two parts: wages, which are necessary for the reproduction of labour-power, and in surplus labour. Marx would measure this difference according to the average socially necessary labour-time. The average labour-time spent by the worker at the site of production is greater than the labour-time necessary for his preservation.[19]

'The surplus-value of the entrepreneur', Adorno claims, 'emerges where a gap is revealed in equivalent exchange, and indeed, where what the worker gets for his own commodity – labour-power, which also reproduces itself – is less than what he gives'.[20] Here, where 'exchange is by no means pure circulation anymore' but instead 'immediately relates to production',[21] exchange under capitalist conditions of production is revealed to be both just and unjust at the same time. 'Adorno sought the origin of the real difference between concrete and abstract, the particular and the general, ultimately in the process of production as well. ... Therefore, for him, exchange is ultimately an exchange between wage-labour and capital which is realised in production as a unity of real differences: the concrete process of labour, and the abstract process of valorisation'.[22] As the exchange of wages for labour-power, exchange encroaches on production, thereby becoming totalised throughout society.

Although Adorno and Horkheimer are often blindly declared to be 'founding fathers of circulation Marxism',[23] Adorno is actually acutely aware of the site at which exchange, as society's constitutive principle, involves production:

---

18   Adorno 2021a, vol. 1, p. 373.
19   Adorno 2021a, vol. 4, p. 329.
20   Adorno 2021a, vol. 2, p. 62.
21   Adorno 2021a, vol. 4, p. 267.
22   Backhaus 2004a, p. 58.
23   Hanloser und Reitter 2008, p. 14. The authors continue as follows: 'Particularly with

namely, that site at which, precisely 'because everything fits, something doesn't fit',[24] at which 'the principle of equivalence ... is violated by being upheld'.[25]

Ingo Elbe has taken issue specifically with this statement:

> Marx's point of explaining the emergence of profit on the basis of the exchange of equivalents is not based on setting up a statement and showing how it is contradicted by the process of exchange. Rather, it shows that the real conditions of freedom and equality *in exchange* are interactively bound up with conditions of heteronomy and exploitation *on another level*, that of the immediate process of production as a process of consumption of labour-power. By this, Marx criticises both the projection of the conditions of exchange onto the entire process of capital's reproduction, and the misconception that these conditions are a mere structural *element* of capital. Thus, Adorno's engagement with the dialectical character of Marx's critical account of economy remains crude.[26]

However, in the passage where Adorno makes this statement, he is engaging neither with the dialectical character of Marx's critical account of economy, nor with exchange as a structural element of economy. His point, rather, is that the 'concept of the exchange society ... should be seen as an immanently critical concept'. Exchange, in whose concept 'the principle of equivalence is co-posited',[27] can systematically correspond neither to the concept of equivalence, nor therefore to its own. The exchange of equivalents is not actually an exchange of equivalents, but rather an 'ideological illusion'.[28]

Yet indeed, it is also more than this.

Adorno, it is less the case that he interprets the Marxian definitions as socio-economic categories, and far more the case he plumbs the depths of their epistemological and epistemo-critical potential' (ibid.). Almost aside from the phrase regarding plumbing the depths of potential: in its vagueness, this statement may or may not pertain to some of Adorno's texts; it certainly does not pertain to Adorno's social critique, as it misses the indissoluble connection between the critique of socio-economy and of knowledge in Adorno's work.

24   Adorno 1974a, p. 262.
25   Adorno 2021a, vol. 4, p. 267.
26   Elbe 2008, p. 124.
27   Adorno 2021a, vol. 4, p. 267.
28   Adorno 2021a, vol. 4, p. 329. However, this illusion does not become immediately visible to the worker in the sale of labour-power, but rather only later once he has to finance his life with the wages received. 'The merchant presents [the workers]', Horkheimer and Adorno write in 'Elements of Anti-Semitism', 'with the promissory note they have signed on behalf

2   The Truth of the Expansion

'In an exchange, something is the same and simultaneously not the same; it is and at the same time is not above-board': the discovery of this principle by Marx confirms for Adorno that the former 'takes dialectics seriously and [does not simply coquet] with its terminology'.[29] The dialectical upshot which Adorno sees recognised by Marx is that the 'assertion of the equivalence of what is exchanged, the basis of all exchange', is 'repudiated' precisely 'by its consequences'.[30] Although Marx may have 'left behind no class theory', Adorno maintains that

> the theory of surplus-value implies one. If one views the appropriation of alien labour ... as the core of the formation of class, as does Marx, this means that the position of human beings in the process of production determines their fate, for only those who control the means of production can appropriate surplus-value. According to Marx, the precondition of the realisability of surplus-value are class-relations.[31]

Adorno regards the Marxian theory of surplus-value as the 'actual conceptual model of Marxism'.[32] After all, this theory is concerned not only with the intersection of production and consumption – that is, with economy – but also with the 'social dynamic which keeps the whole together, producing social conflicts and conditions. The theory of surplus-value should be understood economically as well as socially, as a point of indifference of economy and society'.[33]

---

of the manufacturer. The merchant is the bailiff for the whole system, taking upon himself the odium due to others. That the circulation sphere is responsible for exploitation is a socially necessary illusion' (Adorno and Horkheimer 2002, pp. 142–3).

29   Adorno 2018c, p. 158.

30   Adorno 1976a, p. 25.

31   Adorno 2021a, vol. 3, p. 494.

32   Adorno 2021a, vol. 2, p. 62; cf. Demirović 1999a, p. 463; cf. also Adorno 2003q, p. 115, where Adorno refers to the theory of surplus-value as the 'centerpiece of Marxian theory'.

33   Adorno 2021a, vol. 2, p. 60; cf. Demirović 1999a, p. 463. Here, in the social pursuit of profit, Adorno sees on the one hand a synthesising element, and on the other, a 'tragic element' (Adorno 2021a, vol. 2, p. 55) in a society organised around the profit motive: 'in order for society to survive, it must expand; insofar as it does this, it drives towards its own downfall. Here we have the innermost principle of the Marxian theory of the connection between economy and society in capitalism. Sombart and Max Weber also repeatedly emphasised this: the dynamism of capitalist society in contrast to the stasis of feudalism' (ibid.).

However, according to Adorno, social antagonisms do not just exist between and within classes. Rather, they perpetuate themselves not only in class-divisions, but also within every single individual.

> Precisely because the antagonisms are necessary, and indeed in this way indicate the irrationality of the system, they make a final rational mastery of the social whole impossible. The discomfort in the individual consciousness, the universality of neuroses as a consequence of internalised antagonisms, is predetermined by society. The irrational danger of the system exploding is constantly raised by these conscious dispositions, which retrospectively leads to the formation in individuals of a universal fear. Marx had not yet gone so far in his theory. His concept of the class individual prevented him from relating the antagonisms of the system as a whole to the consciousness of all individuals.[34]

The proletarian is just as much of a character mask as is the capitalist.

The production of surplus-value as the result and purpose of the exchange of wages for labour-power is

> where Hegel's philosophy of history coincides with classical economic theory and also with Marx – the fact that people pursue their own individual interests makes them at the same time the exponents and executors of that same historical objectivity that is ready to turn against their interests at any moment and thus may assert itself over their heads. There is a contradiction here since it is claimed that what asserts itself despite people's own efforts does so by virtue of them, by virtue of their own interests. But since the society in which we live is antagonistic, and since the course of the world to which we are harnessed is antagonistic too, what we might term this logical contradiction should not be thought of as merely a contradiction, merely the product of an inadequate formulation. It is a contradiction that arises from the situation.[35]

Critical Theory has been criticised for allegedly containing 'an enduring tension between respective diagnoses of totality and antagonism' – a tension which is said to be 'clearly unsatisfactory' insofar as 'Adorno's focus on totality occasionally causes him to lose sight of the class-character of capitalist society'.[36]

---

34   Adorno 2021a, vol. 3, p. 462; cf. Marx and Engels 1976, pp. 78–9.
35   Adorno 2006a, pp. 26–7.
36   Lindner 2007, p. 217.

Yet following Adorno, it could be objected that social totality survives only *by means of* contradictions. In his work, as in that of Marx, the fundamental antagonism is that of class; the diagnosis of social totality implies social contradictions and vice versa. 'Society stays alive, not despite its antagonism, but by means of it'.[37] Given that individuals can only reproduce themselves though the capital-relation, they also inevitably reproduce this 'imposed form of society' by which 'each of us is devoured ... from head to toe'.[38] All are compelled by the threat of personal ruin to fulfil their function in the capital process, and as long as society is constituted by this opposition in the first place, so too will the objective class-opposition persist. 'Down to the present day life has succeeded in perpetuating itself only because of this division in society, because a number of people in control confront others who have been separated from the means of production'.[39]

According to this understanding, classes cannot be scaled according to measurable quantities (such as income). Rather, they designate the qualitative opposition between the purchasers and sellers of labour-power, or between the owners of the means of productions and the producers of surplus-value. Adorno insists that this 'dynamic class theory and its knife-edged economic expression' not be 'diluted by substituting the simpler antithesis of rich and poor'.[40] – 'The antagonisms continue; they are not directly visible, often not even indirectly visible as contrasts of lifestyle or contrasts between terrible poverty and abundant wealth, but they continue in the shape of an antagonism of social power and social powerlessness that has reached an extreme level, and ... this contrast of power and powerlessness prevails today precisely because of the increasing integration of society as a whole'.[41]

---

37   Adorno 2007b, p. 320. 'I shall say here only that the essence of this model of an antagonistic society is that it is not a society *with* contradictions or *despite* its contradictions, but *by virtue of* its contradictions. In other words, a society based on profit necessarily contains this division in society because of the objective existence of the profit motive. This profit motive which divides society and potentially tears it apart is also the factor by means of which society reproduces its own existence' (Adorno 2008, pp. 8–9).

38   Adorno 2019i, p. 68.

39   Adorno 2006a, p. 51. Adorno continues as follows: 'And given this reality, the needs of human beings, the satisfaction of human beings, is never more than a sideshow and in great measure no more than ideology. If it is said that everything exists only for human beings, it sounds hollow because in reality production is for profit and people are planned in as consumers from the outset. In short, it sounds hollow because of this built-in conflict' (ibid.).

40   Adorno 2007b, p. 32.

41   Adorno 2019i, p. 67.

Furthermore, 'factory hands'[42] – individuals who possess little more than their labour-power, which they are often compelled to sell in precarious 'employment relationships' – are still needed, and indeed still exist. In the 'modern' or even 'postmodern vagabond' employee, it is not difficult to recognise the terminologically flexibilised proletarian of former times if one takes into account 'how close anarchy is to conformism, how ambivalent both are, how little the integration of the integral society succeeded'.[43] The social relations which seek to make the worker appear as autonomous and independent need him, economically speaking, to be an individual with a yet-to-be-realised potential for producing surplus-value – that is, if they still need him to be anything other than a mere consumer, a role which of course cannot be fulfilled for long by someone without money due to lack of wage-labour. In order to avoid depriving the concept of class of its socio-critical content, neither should 'the proletariat (in the sense of a blanket identification of subjective and objective situation) be fetishised, nor should the category of "class" simply be abandoned and replaced by that of the "underprivileged"'.[44] When in 'a sociological discussion in which someone makes use of the word "class"', someone objects '[i]n no time at all ... that you can no longer used the word "class"' – that 'nowadays you have to talk about different strata, and these strata have to be defined very precisely, and so forth' – it 'becomes clear that what used to be an attempt to make more careful distinctions has ended up as the wish to sabotage the critical function of concepts by claiming that their negative aspect simply does not exist'.[45]

3 Surplus-Value Continues to Be Appropriated

Like Marx, Adorno champions a concept of class which disregards all subjective elements[46] and is 'objectively deduced'[47] from the 'relation of its members to the means of production'.[48] That being said, he views class-consciousness is 'a secondary product' which

42   Engels 2010, p. 134.
43   Adorno and Jaerisch 2003, p. 164.
44   Adorno 2021a, vol. 4, p. 544.
45   Adorno 2006a, p. 139.
46   Cf. Hobsbawm 1971, p. 6.
47   Adorno 2021a, vol. 4, p. 332.
48   Adorno 2003q, p. 114.

is not produced automatically by the historical process. Contrary to Marx's prognosis, and to the situation in the middle of the last century, class-consciousness is tending to diminish. This diminution is caused by phenomena which are described as integrative by the predominant academic sociology, and their existence cannot be denied simply because they conflict with sacrosanct beliefs.[49]

Adorno acknowledges that

> [p]lausible explanations for the absence of class consciousness are scarcely lacking. We have, for example, the fact that the workers were not becoming pauperized but were increasingly being integrated into bourgeois society and its views, a development that was not to be foreseen during and immediately after the Industrial Revolution, when the industrial proletariat was recruited from the ranks of the paupers and still found themselves halfway outside society. It is not the case that social existence directly creates class consciousness ....[50]

At the same time, Adorno also claims that 'the so-called phenomena of integration are essentially subjective, namely phenomena of consciousness among the workers, and ... their objective significance should therefore not be overestimated'. On this point, he highlights 'how thin this crust of an integrated society actually is', going 'almost' so far as to say that this integration 'is merely a form of clothing worn by society and that, if one takes off those clothes, in the very place where one would expect nature to begin, the class system now becomes drastically evident'.[51] This indeed means nothing less than that 'this integration is not true', but instead owes to a 'semblance of freedom that is created only be a certain visible satisfaction of needs, without any change to one's real status in the production process'.[52]

The objective concept of class is valid for the simple reason that 'surplus-value continues to be appropriated. When it appears as if surplus-value no longer plays the role of dividing classes because of how much bifurcation has increased in society as a whole today (pensions and social services), one should make sure that the multitude of bifurcations doesn't underhandedly become

---

49 Adorno 2000a, p. 23.
50 Adorno 2003q, pp. 114–15.
51 Adorno 2019i, p. 60.
52 Adorno 2019i, p. 71.

a veil which surplus-value disappears behind'.[53] Here, Adorno adheres to his thesis from 'Reflections on Class Theory', according to which those who dominate society give workers a 'handout'[54] so that they can continue to work while being dominated. 'A portion of surplus-value is returned to the workers in order to prevent crises. This occurs within the framework and for the maintenance of the existing system'.[55] Adorno believes that technological advance 'makes labour objectively superfluous to a large extent, that is, the superfluity is more one of labourers than of labour'. Nevertheless, the economy of society 'remains a matter of appropriating surplus value, even with a minimum of workers'. Through 'a kind of mercy'[56] – the 'handout' composed of redistributed surplus-value – 'we are all increasingly dependent on surplus-value, tending to become benefit recipients'.[57]

Yet even though the objective concept of class must be separated from class-consciousness, Adorno sees in the latter's disappearance a problem which does not leave class theory in general unaffected:

> If there really is a gradual process whereby those who are objectively defined, according to some threshold value, as proletarians are no longer conscious of themselves as such, and even whereby they emphatically reject such a consciousness, then, as a tendency, no proletarian will finally be left knowing he is a proletarian. In that case, despite the objective situation, the use of the traditional concept of class can easily become a dogma or a fetish. There comes a point – and I believe that this is a case in which the empirical aspect of sociology comes into its own – where a concept such as class-consciousness must be simply confronted with the reality of individual consciousness. Of course, classes are not defined by class-consciousness. But if the proletarians, who allegedly have everything to gain and nothing to lose but their chains, no longer even know that they are proletarians, the practical appeal to them takes on an ideological [element]. Sociological knowledge must, unquestionably, take account of this.[58]

---

53   Adorno 2021a, vol. 3, pp. 436–4.
54   Adorno 2003x, p. 105.
55   Adorno 2021a, vol. 4, p. 265.
56   Adorno 2019i, p. 126.
57   Adorno 2021a, vol. 3, p. 696.
58   Adorno 2000a, p. 23.

The political function of the proletariat has indeed changed. More ana-chronistic today than the formerly 'famous term "class consciousness"'[59] is talk of the proletariat itself, which now prefers to be referred to as 'the workforce' in collective negotiations and similar contexts. The proletarians, who 'hardly feel themselves to be more than that',[60] no longer want to call themselves by that name, and simply do not allow themselves to be named anymore – the designation 'proletarian', like the word 'prole' especially, is an insult, associated with lack of education, anti-sociality and – worst of all – poverty.[61] The pro-letariat has dissolved itself out into a mass of individualised employees. 'The provisional result of the history of capital in its advanced zones presents itself as a classless class society, in which the old workers' milieu has been dissolved into a generalized wage-dependency: everywhere proletarianized individuals, nowhere the proletariat'.[62] All who are individualised in this way accommodate themselves to their allegedly or in some instances genuinely secure circum-stances, defined by 'Nationwide, lawnmowers, gameshows and Statutory Sick Pay'.[63] The relative prosperity of the Western industrial societies has 'lifted' large sections of the proletariat into the middle class. Taking this into account, the German sociologist Helmut Schelsky proposed abandoning the concept of class in the 1950s, advocating instead a discourse on the 'levelled middle-class society' (*nivellierten Mittelstandsgesellschaft*).[64]

On the contrary, numerous Marxist authors have invariably fallen back on the proletariat as the guarantors of their own revolutionary hopes, only to become embittered when real proletarians have not lived up to expectations. Some have expressed their disappointment over the fact that, rather than ful-fil its 'class-specific mission', the working class has preferred to make itself at home within the status quo, that indeed, '[a]n entire "society" has made a career: from the destitute factory worker to the internet-competent jobseeker,

59   Adorno 2019i, p. 60.
60   Adorno and Jaerisch 2003, p. 187.
61   'Here, it does not help matters at all that the label [proletarian] is not at all supposed to designate the moral qualities of someone, but rather a materially inferior *status* which the system of wage labour forces upon its "dependent employees": precisely because everyone hears a critique of the social status of the great mass of society, this critique of this is rejec-ted as a violation of mores in the name of those who are consigned to this status' (Decker and Hecker 2002, p. 8).
62   Friends of the Classless Society 2010.
63   Bruhn, Dahlmann and Nachtmann 2000, p. 7.
64   The relevant essays can now be found in Schelsky 1979. Heinz Bude writes that Schel-sky's efforts were primarily restorative in nature because 'with concepts such as "com-munity of fate" [*Schicksalsgemeinschaft*] and "levelled middle-class society" [*nivellierte Mittelstandsgesellschaft*], he lent expression to the existential feeling [*Lebensgefühl*] of

from the collective lacking rights to the consummate bourgeois and company employee, from the starveling to the courted consumer. Two hundred years after its first world-historical appearance, the proletariat is simply *beyond all recognition*.[65] However, Adorno rejects this view. To him, it appears

> quite unjustified to blame the workers for thinking the way people think if they have more to lose than their chains. For that is not a betrayal; rather, such accusations against the workers in particular usually amount to agreement with those whose only response to the concerns of the labour movement is to reach for the truncheon. If the workers do indeed have more to lose than their chains, then that may be painful for the theory, but it is initially very good for the workers.[66]

After all,

> [o]bviously, every improvement within the work process, everything that constitutes itself in the everyday struggle of the trade unions ..., is something good and positive and must be supported without reservation; and naturally this also includes the work climate. Anyone who wanted to prevent this for the sake of maintaining a purity of class relationships, as it were, would be both a fool and a reactionary – a reactionary simply because every form of independent understanding and autonomy is tied to a certain freedom from the most pressing daily needs, which can be achieved precisely by means of these improvements.[67]

When a critical theory disregards that in many respects, circumstances faced by human beings today are better than they were in Marx's time, it ultimately fails to 'incorporate those aspects where the way things have so far gone materially has not actually resulted in the extreme situation predicted by Marx'.[68] As a consequence, this theory 'itself becomes a fetish' insofar as it 'neglects the state in which human beings find themselves'.[69]

---

a collective people [*Volkskollektivs*] affected by war, captivity, fleeing and expulsion. In the Federal Republic of Germany, all the rhetoric of the welfare state appertains to coping with the consequences of war, whereby an integrative social sense beyond its political articulation was always present' (Bude 2004, p. 9).

65   Decker and Hecker 2002, p. 5.
66   Adorno 2019i, pp. 49–50.
67   Adorno 2019i, p. 63.
68   Adorno 2019i, p. 50.
69   Adorno 2021a, vol. 3, p. 492.

In light of 'findings such as that subjectively, no proletarian class-consciousness is present (class-for-itself)', Adorno views it as distinctly possible that 'the theory of the objectivity of class approaches the mythological. Therefore, he finds it difficult, in spite of his adherence to a critical theory of class, to continue to operate with the concept of the proletariat'.[70] However, in spite of all levelling tendencies, he nevertheless argues that the total integration of the proletariat has yet to succeed:

> Let me tell you from my experience in empirical social research that there have been times which the so-called integration process was considerably overestimated on the subjective side too; that is, several studies – including ones for which I was responsible – have shown that there are more substantial differences between the consciousness of the workers in a narrower sense and that of the bourgeoisie in the usual sense, which must include the white-collar proletarians, the employees, than the theory of the so-called levelled middle-class society would lead one to expect.[71]

After all, the 'more bourgeois the workers feel in their own subjective consciousness, the more they will view one another as competitors, just as other groups in society do'.[72] Adorno regards the 'concept of the white-collar proletarian' (*Stehkragenproletarier*) as a 'key anthropological category' insofar as he sees it as showing that the individual is defined by its class affiliation: 'The bourgeois is a human being who cannot change classes. His class is his individuality. It is the true guarantor of his estate. Here lies the actual key for the whole of fascism'.[73] Along these lines, in one of Adorno's seminars,

> the potential difference between objective social tendencies, and the subjective self-understanding of the classes in which changes take place, was

---

70 Adorno 2021a, vol. 4, p. 553. 'Adorno illustrated how much critical theory has been affected thusly: at the moment when no worker feels it necessity to transform society anymore, and when it cannot be made plausible to him that existing society must be transformed, then the status of the proletariat, as assigned to the proletariat by Marx, certainly becomes extraordinarily problematic as well. Already twenty years ago (1948), Adorno posed the following question in *Minima Moralia*: "where is the proletariat?" Not only critical theory will become a real force when it seizes the masses, as Marx and Engels say; false consciousness will become a force too, if it spreads among the masses' (ibid.).

71 Adorno 2019i, pp. 52–3. Here, Adorno is referring primarily to the study by the Institute for Social Research on business climate (see Chapter 10, n. 6 of the present study).

72 Adorno 2019i, p. 37.

73 Adorno 2004a, p. 474.

discussed using the example of salaried employees [*Angestellten*]. The claim that workers are passing into a 'new middle class' (reference to the economic dependence on a labour contract as opposed to the economic freedom of the bourgeois) was rejected, as was the claim that the impoverished bourgeois strata will not become proletarians, although their situation is not objectively different from that of the workers. As a substitute for class solidarity, National Socialists then skilfully deploy race and nation for their own ends.[74]

On the eve of the Third Reich's rise, Siegfried Kracauer attempted to answer the question of the position of salaried employees in his work *The Salaried Masses*. Already in the nineteenth century,

> the term 'new middle class' [*neuer Mittelstand*] was coined for the 'middle strata' [*Zwischenschicht*] of salaried employees. Because the breakdown of an old bourgeoisie dispossessed by war, inflation and surges in rationalisation allowed this middle strata to grow into a mass in the 1920s, and because the salaried employees ... ultimately composed the core of modern, mass-cultural audience, they were naturally thought of as the 'middle' of Weimar society. However, Kracauer exposes this notion as illusory.[75]

In 'Shelter for the Homeless',[76] a chapter in *The Salaried Masses* whose title Adorno later appropriated as the heading of an aphorism in *Minima Moralia*,[77] Kracauer compares salaried employees with the proletariat. 'The average worker, upon whom so many lowly salaried employees like to look down,

---

74   Adorno 2021a, vol. 2, p. 76.
75   Mülder-Bach 2006, p. 385; translator's note: cf. Mülder-Bach 1998, p. 6. In a letter from shortly after the appearance of *The Salaried Masses*, Kracauer writes the following to Adorno: 'Very interesting: all these people are getting annoyed with me for getting rid of the [salaried employees'] class consciousness and ranking it with the proletariat. This is a sensitive point. The democratic unions of white-collar workers are of course the most furious with me – they are a particularly crummy band of petty-bourgeois types' (letter from Kracauer to Adorno, 20 April 1930, [Adorno and Kracauer 2020, p. 136]).
76   Kracauer 1998, pp. 88–95. The corresponding aphorism by Adorno ends with the famous saying '[w]rong life cannot be lived rightly' (*Es gibt kein richtiges Leben im falschen*) (Adorno 2005b, p. 39). Translator's note: on the problems of translating this sentence into English, see Chapter 1, footnote 10 of the present study.
77   Translator's note: the original German title, *Asyl für Obdachslose*, is translated as 'Refuge for the Homeless' in the standard print translation of *Minima Moralia* (Adorno 2005b, p. 38). *Asyl* can be translated as asylum, refuge or shelter.

often enjoys not merely a material but also an existential superiority over them'. After all, while the life of the 'class-conscious proletarian' is at least still 'roofed over with vulgar-Marxist concepts', the 'mass of salaried employees' is 'spiritually homeless'[78] in comparison. 'Economically proletarianized, fervently bourgeois in their ideology', salaried employees 'contributed a sizable contingent to the mass basis of fascism',[79] Adorno argues. Although definitively a product of and objectively belonging to the proletariat, these employees were led to believe that 'they were something special', and thereby made to 'toe the bourgeois line'. Meanwhile, regarding the established 'culture of employees' of his own time, Adorno describes it as having 'become the universal ideology of a society which mistakes itself for a unified middle class' thanks to a 'lasting market boom'.[80]

Alex Demirović expresses scepticism concerning Adorno's interpretation of the Marxian theory of value. For Demirović, the former and the latter are 'only compatible to a limited extent because Marx takes the view that no deception occurs in the capitalist form of the exchange of equivalents: on average, the full value of labour-power is remunerated, and with that, equality is already realised'.[81] Yet this is precisely also the view of Adorno, who recognises that the realisation of equality in exchange reproduces the inequality of individuals.

> In the concept of exchange, the principle of equivalence is co-posited. Yet the analysis of political economy shows that the principle of equivalence is violated at its very origin by being upheld. The concept of the exchange society should be seen as an immanently critical concept. The exchange of labour-power is already no longer an equivalent exchange. In a non-exploitative society, exchange could be realised as equivalent.[82]

Demirović objects to Adorno that Marx 'makes clear in his analyses how the problem of a standard for equality is solved by the market-mediated formation

---

78   Kracauer 1998, p. 88.
79   Adorno 2019l, p. 341.
80   Adorno 1973, p. 20. According to Adorno and Hanns Eisler, every culture is 'supposedly high-class entertainment, accessible to recipients of small pay checks, yet presented in such a way that nothing seems too good or too expensive for them. It is a pseudo-democratic luxury, which is neither luxurious nor democratic, for the people who walk on heavily carpeted stairways into the marble palaces and glamorous castles of moviedom are incessantly frustrated without being aware of it' (Adorno and Eisler 2005, p. 52).
81   Demirović 2004, pp. 22–3.
82   Adorno 2021a, vol. 4, p. 267.

of an average of socially necessary labour'.[83] However, Adorno establishes along with Marx that this standard negates itself precisely through its application in exchange.

> This is the decisive turn in Marx's work – that unlike some primitive socialist or primitive anarchist who opposes bourgeois society, he doesn't simply claim: this is all untrue. Rather, he claims: in order to be able to transform this tremendous apparatus in the first place, we want to use its own power to set it in motion. In a passage on subjective logic, Hegel had already described how it is the task of dialectics to absorb the power of one's opponent into one's own argumentation and use it against him. This Hegelian principle is paid extraordinary heed by Marx, and taken extraordinarily seriously. Instead of simply rejecting bourgeois society's claim to achieve harmony, he takes it completely seriously and asks: is the society which you theorise really identical with your concept? Does your world of free and just exchange really correspond, as you claim, to a free and just society? He also stays faithful to the principle of dia-lectics when he says that it does and it doesn't. He shows that in this society, everything fits with equivalents genuinely being exchanged, yet that there is one decisive area – namely, what concerns the commod-ity of labour-power – where, because everything fits, something doesn't fit.[84]

In other words,

> [t]he assertion of the equivalence of what is exchanged, the basis of all exchange, is repudiated by its consequences. As the principle of exchange, by virtue of its immanent dynamics, extends to the living labours of human beings it changes compulsively into objective inequality, namely that of social classes. Forcibly stated, the contradiction is that exchange takes place justly and unjustly.[85]

According to Adorno, it is just as evident *that* equivalents are exchanged as it is that 'the exchange rate is itself a calculation: the mathematical form of the equation of exchanged goods in a socially prevailing exchange'.[86] For him,

---

83   Demirović 2004, p. 23.
84   Adorno 1974a, pp. 261–2.
85   Adorno 1976a, p. 25.
86   Adorno 2019i, p. 20. In the 'calculatory equation' which 'relates the same with the same',

there is no doubt as to the mathematical operationalisability of exchange, for 'to exchange commodities [is] to cancel one act by another; it is, thus, an essentially timeless activity although it takes place in time – not unlike a mathematical operation which is also, in its essential nature, out of time'.[87] With precisely this mathematical exactness, Adorno argues, Marx could call liberalism to account insofar as 'Marx's system is also a critique of political economy, that is, also a critique of the liberal field of national economy':[88] 'Marx already formulated the economic laws mathematically, but in contrast to the devoutly mathematical positivism, he used them sardonically'[89] – that is, not like 'national economy, which focuses in mathematized fashion on states within established market society',[90] but rather in a way 'that attacked the undoubtedly mathematisable fiction of pure exchange, and in a sense calculated the failure of liberalism based on its own concepts'.[91] The mathematisation of economic laws, Adorno claims, follows 'deductively from the exchange of equivalents; it is not statistics'.[92]

'Marx did explain in the preface to *Capital* that he only coquetted with Hegelian language. However, if dialectics are taken seriously in practice, then it must be possible to develop the whole of Marx's theory from any point therein – that is, in its own movement, the dialectical thought must pass into the concrete'.[93] That being said, Adorno does not advocate the exact mathematical quantification of the findings of Marxian theory. For him, this would be the goal of a 'positive' economic theory focused on 'exact market laws, the mathematical calculability of supply and demand' – a goal he rejects precisely because '[m]arket is already a construct!' Because positive economic theory 'dispenses with all foundational problems', Adorno argues it is insufficient: 'The ultimate concern cannot be to express system-immanent processes in formulas. Rather, the deeper problem is to determine the significance of an economic phenomenon in society'.[94] There will 'necessarily be a distance between mental

---

Adorno discovers in the ideological yet at the same time also real equality an emancipatory element 'which has founded the difference between bourgeois society and feudalism' (Adorno 2018c, p. 156).

87   Adorno 1961, p. 41.
88   Adorno 2021a, vol. 2, p. 65.
89   Adorno 2021a, vol. 3, p. 333.
90   Adorno 2019i, p. 125.
91   Adorno 2021a, vol. 3, p. 333.
92   Adorno 2019i, p. 20.
93   Adorno 2021a, vol. 2, pp. 61–2.
94   Adorno 2021a, vol. 2. p. 97.

models and empirical data if theory is to be more than a reproduction of facts with the help of concepts. Marx did not want to create an operational theory, but rather a theory of society as a whole – and the whole of society can never be fully empirically grasped in the way it is possible to do so with individual sectors'.[95]

4   The Service of Abstraction

'[E]xchange takes place', Adorno claims, 'through money as the equivalent form'.[96] At the same time, 'the true unit which stands behind money as the equivalent form is the average necessary amount of social labour time, which is modified, of course, in keeping with the specific social relationships governing the exchange'.[97] Adorno thus concludes 'that two commodities become commensurable with each other precisely on the basis of the average social labour-time invested in them – that is, without regard to their specific determinants'.[98]

Insofar as exchange takes place according to equivalence, it is assumed that objects of exchange have a common measure. Because objects are qualities, 'the objects to be exchanged must be commensurable with each other, their specific and naturally occurring qualities having been forgotten, sanded away by abstraction, while nothing remains beyond the abstract unit of labour-time applied to them, according to which they are exchangeable'.[99] Yet this means nothing other than that the exchange process is itself 'a process of abstraction'.[100] 'The exchange of materially different things in the exchange society demands the service of abstraction'.[101] Adorno emphasises the 'implicit element of reflection in the exchange process',[102] which possesses '[an element] of

---

95   Adorno 2021a, vol. 2, p. 65.

96   Adorno 2000a, p. 31; cf. also notes made by Adorno following a discussion with Sohn-Rethel: 'The abstractness of exchange and its categories by no means spontaneously becomes conscious, but rather can become so only by means of money as that which synthesises an infinity of exchanges, represents a totality of the mediacy of the connection of individuals to each other and to nature' (Adorno and Sohn-Rethel 1989, p. 221).

97   Adorno 2000a, pp. 31–2.

98   Adorno 2021b, p. 272; cf. Adorno 2018c, p. 159: 'What makes commodities exchangeable is the unity of socially necessary abstract labour-time'.

99   Adorno 2021b, p. 128.

100   Adorno 2018c, p. 156.

101   Adorno 2021a, vol. 2, p. 50.

102   Adorno 1974a, p. 215.

conceptuality',[103] as 'the category of exchange ... is itself also something conceptual, mental'.[104] '[W]hether human beings know it or not, by entering into a relationship of exchange and reducing different use-values to labour-value they actualise a real conceptual operation socially': 'Even if a single human being had not had the idea of this absolute exchange, there would objectively still be a process of abstraction in the objective reduction to the same, a process of abstraction which amounts to the objectivity of the conceptual [element]'.[105] However, this process of abstraction '*distances* itself from the objects. And it is false in itself because qualities do not simply disappear in the course of exchange but are also retained'.[106] 'The exchange of equivalents, of exchange-values equal to each other, requires – as Marx very extensively showed – that one can disregard the particular use-value quality founded upon the sensuous immediacy of the individual things or objects to be exchanged. Exchange-value, exchange in general, only exists insofar as there is a concept: to this extent, the element of the concept – that is, the immaterial element – lies not only in the construction of concepts, and not merely in the observer, but just as much in the fact of social objectivity itself, which Marx attempts to analyse'.[107] Mediated through this conceptuality, so too is 'the concept of society ... a mental fact'.[108]

Adorno defines the ability to abstract not as an anthropological invariant, but rather as something acquired – as something which has developed over the course of human history. Human beings, he claims, had to endure a 'very painstaking and lengthy journey' in order to 'first lean to abstract, that is, to emancipate themselves from external nature. Abstraction is only possible at a certain state of history: "As a rule, the most general abstractions arise only in the midst of the richest possible concrete development, where one thing appears as common to many, to all"'.[109] In arguing that pre-Socratic writings already bear witness to this process, Adorno again recapitulates the motif of

---

103   Adorno 2018c, p. 156.
104   Adorno 1974a, p. 22.
105   Adorno 2018c, p. 156.
106   Adorno 2008, p. 127, paragraph break omitted.
107   Adorno 1974a, pp. 22–3.
108   Adorno 2021a, vol. 2, p. 497. Hence, according to Adorno, Marx also 'cannot be called a nominalist when he asserts the primacy of the totality before the realities collected within it' (ibid.). It is much rather the case that 'the Marxian approach contains a kind of autonomy of the concept, which would be entirely foreign to a primitive materialist nominalism' (Adorno 1974a, p. 262).
109   Adorno 2021a, vol. 4, p. 541; quoted from Marx 1993, p. 104.

an historical continuity from prehistory to the present. In *Fragen der Dialektik*
(*Questions of Dialectics*), he claims that rationalism has an element of untruth
precisely insofar as

> in order to produce consciousness from identity between the matter and
> the idea, it trimmed the latter, cut away at it – just as already occurs in
> one of the myths from the circle of Heracles, and in the final instance in
> the model of the exchange economy .... All rational thought really does
> have something of this exchange process. Not for nothing can formula-
> tions of an exchange of like for like according to the arrangement of time
> already be found in the earliest pre-Socratic drafts of a rational explana-
> tion of the world – in the work of Anaximander as well as of Heraclitus,
> who followed the former.[110]

Here, Adorno returns to a consideration from a few years earlier regarding a
'proto-bourgeois'[111] saying by Anaximander. In the English translation by Kathleen Freeman – which is itself based on a German translation by Hermann
Diels, the standard during Adorno's time – this quotation reads as follows: 'The
Non-Limited is the original material of existing things; further, the source from
which existing things derive their existence is also that to which they return
at their destruction, according to necessity; for they give justice and make
reparation to one another for their injustice, according to the arrangement of
Time'.[112]

For Adorno, 'Anaximander's curse'[113] points to aspects of 'archaic legal vin-
dictiveness'[114] which were mythologically legitimated: 'The law that defined
itself as punishment for lawlessness comes to resemble it and itself becomes
lawlessness, a order for destruction: that, however, is the nature of myth as it
is echoed in pre-Socratic thought'.[115] At the same time, this saying describes
the dynamic which blindly reproduces 'the same pattern over and over again',
perpetuating it into the present.

> As long as men were not completely in control, either of themselves, or
> of society, the social process would continue in irrational cycles, in spite

---

110   Adorno 2021b, p. 128.
111   Adorno 1993d, p. 86.
112   Quoted from Freeman 1948, p. 19.
113   Adorno 2013, p. 25.
114   Adorno 2007b, p. 267.
115   Adorno 2009a, p. 107.

of all rationalizations. For Marx and, before him, Hegel, the dialectical movement of history could, in a sense, be summed up as permanent transition or unchanging change. With a kind of hope born of despair, Marx applied the term 'prehistory' to no less than the entire stretch of history known to him – to what had been, and was, the realm of bondage.

Hence, 'the dialectical process had to be described in terms of perennial categories, which needed only to be modified to apply, for instance, to the modern, rational, form of society. This is why, in Marx, such expressions as "wage slavery", which he applied to free wage labor, are something more than metaphors'.[116] Rather, they are the expression of the historical constant of relations of dominance and exploitation, from slavery to wage-labour.[117]

In his lecture course *Philosophical Elements of a Theory of Society* from the summer semester of 1964, Adorno accounts 'for exchange as a social rather than an economic phenomenon'[118] – that is, as a phenomenon within existing society. In doing so, he works out a view he describes as 'completely heretical from the perspective of Marxist theory, as Marx believed that power ... could be derived from the exchange relationship'.[119] To clarify this view, Adorno refers to the saying 'leonine contract',[120] which is based on Aesop's fable 'The Lion, the Cow, the She-Goat, and the Sheep':[121]

> *An alliance made with the high and mighty can never be trusted. This little fable proves my point.*
> A cow and a she-goat and a long-suffering sheep decided to become the lion's companions. They went into the forest together and there they caught an extremely large stag which they divided into four portions. Then the lion said, 'I claim the first portion by right of my title, since I am called the king; the second portion you will give me as your partner;

---

116 Adorno 1961, p. 45. In writings which are more polemical than scientific, Marx at times refers to 'capital and wage slavery' (Marx 2010c, p. 212).

117 'What distinguishes the various economic formations of society – the distinction between for example a society based on slave-labour and a society based on wage-labour – is the form in which this surplus labour is in each case extorted from the immediate producer, the worker' (Marx 1982a, p. 325).

118 Adorno 2019i, p. 57.

119 Adorno 2019i, p. 58.

120 See Adorno 2019i, pp. 57–8.

121 Also titled 'The Lion's Share' in some translations; numerous variations on this fable exist. This title corresponds to Laura Gibbs's translation (Aesop 2002).

then, because I am strongest, the third portion is mine – and woe betide anyone who dares to touch the fourth!' In this way the wicked lion carried off all the spoils for himself.[122]

From this point of reference, Adorno goes on to describe exchange in capitalist society as follows:

> the exchange of labour power for wages that is required of every worker may be a free contractual relationship in formal terms, with complete parity between the two sides, but in reality, of course, the workers will face hunger and have nothing to live on if they do not enter into the contract, and are thus forced by objective circumstances to sign the contract far more than is the entrepreneur, who – viewed as an overall class, at least – can generally wait until the worker sees reason, as the saying goes, namely subjective reason, and accepts these terms. If, for a second, you do not take what I am conveying to you as individually as I have presented it but, rather, extrapolate to the conditions of society as a whole, what this means is quite simply that the decisive exchange act, namely the act of exchanging live labour for wages, in fact presupposes the class system; and it is decisively modified and modelled by this class system in such a way that the semblance of freedom for all parties which is created by the legal contract of the wage agreement is, in reality, nothing but that: a semblance.[123]

Initially, this view is anything but a heresy against Marxism, for at various points, Marx also emphasises that classes must have already had to exist before the capital-relation could develop. Among other places, this claim can be found in *Capital*:

> The capital-relation presupposes a complete separation between the workers and the ownership of the conditions for the realization of their labour. As soon as capitalist production stands on its own feet, it not only maintains this separation, but reproduces it on a constantly extending scale. The process, therefore, which creates the capital-relation can be nothing other than the process which divorces the worker from the ownership of the conditions of his own labour; it is a process which operates

---

122   Aesop 2002, p. 14.
123   Adorno 2019i, pp. 57–8.

two transformations, whereby the social means of subsistence and production are turned into capital, and the immediate producers are turned
into wage-labourers. So-called primitive accumulation, therefore, is nothing else than the historical process of divorcing the producer from the
means of production. It appears as 'primitive' because it forms the prehistory of capital, and of the mode of production corresponding to capital.[124]

Yet in his subsequent lecture course from the winter semester of 1964–5, *History and Freedom*, Adorno does formulate an independent theory of class.
When Adorno speaks of the hindrance of genuine progress by the principle
of exchange, this theory goes beyond that of Marx:

> Bourgeois society created the concept of progress, and the convergence of
> the concept with the negation of progress originates in the principle gov-
> erning society, namely the principle of exchange. Exchange is the rational
> form of mythical eternal sameness. In the tit for tat of every exchange,
> each act revokes the other; it's a zero-sum game. If the exchange was fair,
> then nothing has happened, everything stays as it was, people are quits,
> things are just as they were before. At the same time, the assertion of pro-
> gress, which conflicts with this principle, is true to the extent that the
> doctrine of tit for tat is a lie. It always was a lie, and not just since the so-
> called capitalist appropriation of surplus value in the course of which the
> commodity of labour power is exchanged for the costs of its reproduc-
> tion. For one of the parties to the transaction, the more powerful party,
> always received more than the other. Thanks to this injustice, one that
> had been codified as early as Aesop's fable about the lion, something novel
> takes place in the course of the exchange; the process that proclaims its
> own stasis becomes dynamic. We might say, then, that progress origin-
> ates in the fact that the justice that amounts to a repetition of sameness
> is unmasked as injustice and perpetual inequality. The truth of the expan-
> sion feeds on the lie of the equality. Social actions are supposed to cancel
> each other out in the overall system and yet they do not. Where bourgeois
> society satisfies the concept it cherishes of itself it knows no progress;
> where it knows progress it sins against its own law in which this offence
> is already present, and with this inequality it perpetuates the wrong that
> progress is supposed to transcend. ... Zarathustra proclaims that man will

---

124   Marx 1982a, pp. 874–3; cf. Marx 1992, p. 114 and Marx 1987b, p. 509.

be freed from revenge, or, rather, he does not proclaim it, he preaches that man shall be freed from revenge. For revenge is the mythical prototype of exchange; as long as domination persists through exchange, the myth will continue to prevail too.[125]

This passage once again reveals that the meta-economic principle of domination via equivalence and identity (which has become total under capital) is central to Adorno's work. Furthermore, it also demonstrates that class analysis – which Adorno allegedly 'hints at only aphoristically and relegates to the periphery of his thought"[126] – is in truth at the centre of both his critique of economy and his Critical Theory as a whole.

---

125   Adorno 2006a, pp. 170–1. This passage is almost identical to a passage from Adorno's article 'Progress', cf. Adorno 2005f, p. 159. *Thus Spoke Zarathustra* contains the following: 'For *that mankind be redeemed from revenge*: that to me is the bridge to the highest hope and a rainbow after long thunderstorms' (Nietzsche 2006, p. 77).

126   Kreimeier 1983, p. 43.

CHAPTER 13

Something's Missing

To put the subject by, / 'The rest next time –'
'It *is* next time!'

LEWIS CARROLL, Alice's Adventures in Wonderland

∴

1   Actually This Has Always Been Possible

'In a sense', notes Rolf Tiedemann,

> *Negative Dialectics* is the attempt, one already made in *Against Epistem-ology*, to enable logic *to speak*, instead of continuing to translate speech into logic. The concept of 'concept', which is what is at issue here, would be 'fulfilled' at best through the name, if one were to be had; a name would make it possible to reap the reward that philosophy had vainly sought under the heading of 'intellectual intuition': namely, the non-identical determinate thing, the inextinguishable colour of the concrete. In *The Origin of German Tragic Drama*, Benjamin claimed for philosophy Adam's action of naming things, 'the word ... reclaiming its name-giving rights'. Adorno did not follow him down this road.[1]

The positive-theological philosophy of language presented by Benjamin in 'On Language as Such and the Language of Man'[2] is something Adorno cannot claim for himself. For Adorno, who in contrast to Benjamin appears 'to have

---

1   Editorial note by Tiedemann (Adorno 2008, p. 229, n. 5; quoted from Adorno 2013, p. 40 and Benjamin 2009, p. 37). Adorno writes to Elisabeth Lenk that he has 'tried so hard, my whole life long, to make logic speak, as I once described it' (letter from Adorno to Lenk, 18 May 1967 [Adorno and Lenk 2015, p. 137]).

2   If this essay can be said to have a quintessence, then this can be seen at its end: 'The language of an entity is the medium in which its mental being is communicated. The uninterrupted flow of this communication runs through the whole of nature, from the lowest forms of existence to man and from man to God. Man communicates himself to God through name, which

had instilled little faith in the image-world of childhood',[3] it is instead animals which exist 'without any purpose recognizable to men'. In this existence, animals 'hold out, as if for expression, their own names, utterly impossible to exchange. This make[s] them so beloved [by] children, their contemplation so blissful. "I am a rhinoceros", signifies the [shape] of the rhinoceros."[4] Here, Adorno sees play[5] and 'purposeless activity'[6] as honouring what his philosophy – 'an effort toward that intentionless thing for which the inadequate word "name" was chosen'[7] – seeks to develop on the level of society.

Thomas Mann once lamented to his 'honoured friend' Adorno that the latter's work contains not even 'a single positive word ... that vouchsafed even the vaguest glimpse of the true society which we are forced to postulate'.[8] In his response, Adorno refuses to construe for Mann – or for himself – what a better state might look like:

> If anything in Hegel, and in those who turned him right way up, has become part of my very flesh and blood, it is an asceticism with regard to any unmediated expression of the positive. This truly is a case of asceticism, believe me, since the opposite impulse, a tendency to the unfettered expression of hope, really lies much closer to my own nature. But I have

---

he gives to nature and (in proper names) to his own kind; and to nature he gives names according to the communication that he receives from her, for the whole of nature, too, is imbued with a nameless, unspoken language, the residue of the creative word of God, which is preserved in man as the cognizing names and above man as the judgment suspended over him. The language of nature is comparable to a secret password that each sentry passes to the next in his own language, but the meaning of the password is the sentry's language itself. All higher language is a translation of lower ones, until in ultimate clarity the word of God unfolds, which is the unity of this movement made up of language' (Benjamin 2004d, p. 74).

3 Tiedemann 1998, p. 9.
4 Adorno 2005b, p. 228; cf. Adorno 2002a, p. 112.
5 'Just because [the playing child] deprives the things with which he plays of their mediated usefulness, he seeks to rescue in them what is benign towards men and not what subserves the exchange relation that equally deforms men and things. The little trucks travel nowhere and the tiny barrels on them are empty; yet they remain true to their destiny by not performing, not participating in the process of abstraction that levels down that destiny, but instead abide as allegories of what they are specifically for. Scattered, it is true, but not ensnared, they wait to see whether society will finally remove the social stigma on them; whether the vital process between men and things, praxis, will cease to be practical' (Adorno 2005b, p. 228).
6 Ibid.
7 Adorno 2009b, p. 140.
8 Letter from Mann to Adorno, 30 October 1952, (Adorno and Mann 2006, p. 93).

the constant feeling that we are merely encouraging the cause of untruth if we turn prematurely to the positive and fail to persevere in the negative.[9]

Adorno bristles at all 'adductions about a "future" society':

Not only have all upstanding human beings regarded this point with a kind of taboo – and not least Marx, who left the depiction of the society of the future to Bebel. I don't want to say that this exercise should be abandoned – the vision of a just society has to be the centre of force endowing every sentence written about sociology with light. But it is not beneficial to look at the sun.[10]

Referring to the ban on images,[11] which 'occupies a position of central importance in the religions that believe in salvation',[12] Adorno argues that to 'speak directly of the ultimate things' is no longer possible: 'The impotent word that calls them by name weakens them. Both naiveté and a defiant casualness in expressing metaphysical ideas reveal their lack of grounding'.[13] The positivity of what is given is only 'an *aspect*' of it, one which 'cannot be reduced'[14] to things as they are. Otherwise, Hegel's statement that '[w]hat is rational is actual; and what is actual is rational'[15] would simply be a call 'to capitulate before reality',[16] while the establishment of positivity would be the last possible act of any theory.[17] If this were the case, Adorno notes, one would effectively have to 'chose between theology', that is, between the idea that what exists is more than itself, 'and tautology', or the idea that what exists is all that there is. 'In this case', Adorno admits, 'I would prefer theology',[18] even though this choice would mean abandoning the knowledge that no non-identical has a

---

9   Letter from Adorno to Mann, 1 December 1952 (Adorno and Mann 2006, p. 97).

10   Letter from Adorno to Ernst Kux, 26 January 1955 (TWA, Br 853/28). Horkheimer had already criticised Bebel's vision of revolution in 'The Authoritarian State' (see Horkheimer 1973, p. 12).

11   In the Old Testament, primarily Exodus 20:4 and Deuteronomy 4:15–19; cf. Bernhardt 1962, p. 249.

12   Adorno 2008, p. 26.

13   Adorno 2019k, p. 186.

14   Adorno 2008, p. 22.

15   Hegel 1991, p. 20.

16   Adorno 2005a, p. 282.

17   Cf. Braunstein 2008.

18   Adorno 2003k, p. 38.

positive existence: 'Utopia amounts to representing a non-identical as a being, that is, to representing it immediately, and there is a fraudulent element in the objective substance of the philosophy which does this',[19] – that is, if this philosophy does not simply outright indulge in affirmation through description.

Apropos 'ban on images', it is worth noting that Adorno at times refers to certain motifs from Judaism, including this motif – something not unusual for a thinker in the German context whose philosophy emerged at a time in which there was still a German Jewry able to contribute to public debate. For this reason, several authors have regarded Adorno as a Jew as well, including Martin Jay: 'And yet, the German Jew in Adorno did not die with his father's name. Even in exile in America, his manners remained those of the cultured Central European *haut bourgeois*'[20] – voilà, a German Jew in Adorno! In a conversation between Micha Brumlik and Eveline Goodman-Thau, one which is not exactly sparing in its deployment of clichés, Goodman-Thau wants clarity on this matter: 'But what is Jewish about Adorno? Where is he a German thinker, where is he a Jewish thinker?' Brumlik answers that Adorno is a Jewish thinker simply because 'he affirms again and again the Biblical metaphor of the ban on images'.[21] Setting aside the fact that the Biblical ban on images is not in fact a metaphor, but rather a literal command, the claim that someone who refers to this ban in his philosophy thinks Jewishly appears especially dubious given that the Old Testament carries religious significance not only in Judaism. Yet if the existence of specifically Jewish (religious) motifs is accepted but that of a Jewish mode of thinking rejected, the question of whether or not Adorno is a Jew is more or less irrelevant. According to the Halakhic definition, Adorno was certainly not a Jew, as his mother was a Catholic and his father a baptised Protestant. Furthermore, Adorno neither refers to himself as a Jew in existing sources, nor did he practise any form of religious Judaism.[22] For much of his life, the Jewish community was as foreign to him as any other religious community. In a 1937 letter to Horkheimer written during a voyage across the Atlantic, Adorno describes some of the Jewish passengers with a malice which at the time could still be regarded as anti-religious polemic:

> The ship was overflowing with Eastern European Jews eating with their yarmulkes on their heads, extruding religious ululations and committing

19   Adorno 2003k, p. 29.
20   Jay 1969, p. 62.
21   Brumlik and Goodman-Thau 2007, p. 226.
22   Cf. Brumlik 2003, p. 75.

racial defilement through their overall behaviour. On Saturday, one of their medicine men or ritual murderers gave a long speech in Yiddish in the public reading room. By the way, he looked a little bit like Trotsky ....[23]

Only after the war does Adorno reach a kind of negative identification with Judaism as a community of fate.[24] When his father complains about the manners of some Jews whom he encountered while visiting New York, Adorno answers him as follows:

I am reluctant to correspond with you about the Jews .... After 6 million have been murdered, it goes against my instincts to dwell on the manners of those few who survived, whom I incidentally do not need to like. In addition to that, the 50% goy in me feels somehow responsible for the Jewish persecution, so I am therefore quite especially allergic to everything that is said against the chosen people.[25]

In raising this issue, the point is not to imply that an affiliation with Judaism is somehow contemptuous – that this even has to be emphasised to avoid misunderstandings is a disgrace. Rather, the point is that it is noteworthy that Adorno is constantly associated with Judaism by others.[26] He himself formulates this succinctly when he says about himself that he 'escaped by accident' and 'by rights should have been killed'.[27] The right (*Recht*) of which he speaks here is the governing law (*Recht*) of the Third Reich, in which Germans defined who was a Jew, and hence to be murdered. As long as to be a Jew is to be tainted with the whiff of what does not fully belong, the *designation* 'Jew' is always still, whether intentionally or unintentionally, a criterion of exclusion containing all the associated clichés.[28] In any case, it is illegitimate to engage in the same practice as those who, as a matter of law, arbitrarily decided who was a Jew and who was not. When it came to the matter of religion

---

23   Letter from Adorno to Horkheimer, 6 July 1937 (Adorno and Horkheimer 2003, p. 375).
24   Cf. Brumlik 2003, p. 76.
25   Letter from Adorno to his parents, 11 March 1946 (Adorno 2006b, p. 248); cf. Gumbrecht 2004, p. 118; on the designation of the Jews as the 'chosen people' cf. Adorno and Horkheimer 2002, p. 137.
26   For example, this has recently been done by Carl Djerassi (see Djerassi 2008).
27   Adorno 2007b, p. 363.
28   Tellingly, Peter Bürger describes Adorno, '[t]he Jewish intellectual who escaped extermination', as being '[c]onstantly on the run', guided by 'hatred' and 'deal[ing] blows to all sides' (Bürger 2003, pp. 27–8). Of course, what is meant here are not literally blows, but merely Adorno's harsh yet thoroughly substantive criticisms of Heidegger.

itself, Adorno was always aware 'that the struggle against magic waged by both Christianity and Judaism is itself magical through and through, magic against magic'.[29]

In a surprisingly conciliatory conversation between Adorno and Bloch[30] from 1964, the two consider the relationship between society and utopia:

> BLOCH: There would not have been a French Revolution, as Marx stated, without the heroic illusions that natural law engendered. Of course, they did not become real, and what did become real of them, the free market of the bourgeoisie, is not at all that which was dreamed of, [thought of,] wished for, hoped, demanded, as utopia. Thus now, if a world were to emerge that is hindered for apparent reasons, but that is entirely possible, one could say, it is astonishing that it [does] not [exist] – if such a world, in which hunger and immediate wants were eliminated, entirely in contrast to death, if this world would finally just 'be allowed to breathe' and were set free, there would not only be platitudes that would come out at the end and gray prose and a complete lack of prospects and perspectives in regard to existence here and over there, but there would also be freedom from earning instead of freedom to earn, and this would provide some space for such richly prospective doubt and the decisive incentive toward utopia that is the meaning of Brecht's short sentence, 'Something's missing.' What exactly is missing, is unknown. This sentence, which is in *Mahoganny*, is one of the most profound sentences that Brecht ever wrote, and it is in two words.[31] What is this 'something'? If it is not allowed

---

29   Letter from Adorno to Marie Luise Kaschnitz, 11 June 1965 (TWA, Br 727/23).
30   Surprising insofar as the history of their friendship – if it ever was one – readily reveals itself as characterised by mutual misunderstandings (cf. Schmid Noerr 2001; cf. also Bloch's 'hostile' (ibid.) and at times outrageous remarks in Bloch and Reinicke 1976).
31   In Brecht's 'opera' about the 'paradise city' or 'golden city' of Mahoganny (Brecht 2007, p. 8), the protagonist Paul Ackermann wants to leave the city because nothing there is worth staying for:
      'JAKE: Paul, why are you running away?
      PAUL: Well, what is there to keep me here?
      ...
      JOE: Haven't you got gin and cheap whisky?
      PAUL: They're too cheap!
      HARRY: And peace and concord?
      PAUL: It's too peaceful!
      JAKE: If you feel like eating fish / you can go catch one
      PAUL: That won't make me happy.

to be cast in a picture, then I shall portray it as in the process of being (*seiend*). But one should not be allowed to eliminate it as if it [were not really, in a practical sense, what one could describe as being 'what really counts'].

ADORNO: ... We have come strangely close to the ontological proof of God, Ernst ...

BLOCH: That surprises me!

ADORNO: All of this comes from what you said when you used the phrase borrowed from Brecht – something's missing – a phrase that we actually cannot have if seeds or ferment of what this phrase denotes were not possible.

Actually I would think that unless there is no kind of trace of truth in the ontological proof of God, that is, unless the element of its reality is also already conveyed in the power of the concept itself, there could not only be no utopia but there could also not be any thinking.[32]

JOE: You can smoke.
PAUL: You can smoke.
HARRY: You can nod off.
PAUL: You can sleep.
JAKE: You can swim.
PAUL: You can pick a banana!
JOE: You can look at the water
PAUL: *just shrugs his shoulders*
HARRY: You can forget.
PAUL: But something is missing'
BRECHT 2007, pp. 20–1

32   Adorno and Bloch 1989, pp. 15–16; cf. also Thaidigsmann 1995; on the ontological proof of God cf. a note by Adorno titled 'Facit' ('Conclusion'): 'My experience with metaphysics began with the Lukácsian theory of epochs imbued with meaning [from *Theory of the Novel*], where the glorification of meaning and the horror at its loss appears as the guarantor of its *truth*, and the *loss* of objective reason remains unnoticed. In this, there already lies the notion of the loss of the middle, in which the West and the developing countries so happily conform to each other [*sich gleichschalten* – translator's note: *Gleichschaltung* (coordination) was a term used to designate official state policy of forced conformity of all aspects of German society to the Nazi regime]. That things were *better* in the presence of an immanent or transcendental meaning comes to guarantee the latter's truth. This is precisely the argument of necessity criticised by Nietzsche – it is basically already present in the Kantian critique of the ontological proof of God. But isn't something being forgotten? Isn't there ultimately something to every argument? Can such a radical distinction be made between the idea of a utopian state and the idea of truth upon which this state is based? Wouldn't that be two different truths? Is there a difference between the truth of meaning in itself and the truth of the state in which meaning would be a necessary

The hope that if a concept for something exists, then there also exists a 'trace' of what it describes – that is, that there also exists the real possibility of this concept being realised – is affirmed by Adorno in his lecture course *History and Freedom*. Therein, he claims that it is only possible to 'speak meaningfully of freedom because there are concrete possibilities of freedom, because freedom can be achieved in reality. And in contrast to the entire dialectical tradition of Hegel and Marx, I would almost go so far as to say that actually this has always been possible, that it has been possible at every moment'.[33] After all, he claims elsewhere,

> If there is something bourgeois and anti-dialectical, it is the belief in an only-afterwards-relation in essential matters. The banal thought comes to one's mind that humanity 'is not yet mature [enough] for socialism'. ... The thinking of the classless society has to shake off the logic of this only-afterwards, the embodiment of sanity and reason and human's notion of time, or it remains in a bad sense traditionalistic.[34]

2   Paradise with Its Bloody Hands

Adorno's preferred theology, at least if he were faced with a choice between theology and tautology, would be a negative, godless theology. The messiah, whom Adorno – doubtless following Benjamin[35] – often borrowed from the

---

condition? Would right life be right if what it necessarily required were wrong? Doesn't what was once meaningful here – even negatively meaningful – say something about the truth of meaning? Kant's refutation of the ontological proof of God is true but also not – with the first sentence, do I not posit the absolute by postulating its truth? And because the elements of every concept come from something which exists – where should I take the strong concept from? Or is this all fallacy? To think through this – with and against Kant – is my task, and the task of philosophy. I only know one thing: if this isn't it, then everything amounts to nothing. Right?' (Adorno 2003k, p. 22).

33   Adorno 2006a, p. 181; cf. Tiedemann 1997, p. 126. Here, Adorno comes close to Benjamin's notion of 'now-time', which is 'shot through with splinters of messianic time', and in which 'every second' is 'the small gateway in time through which the Messiah might enter' (Benjamin 2006b, p. 397).

34   Adorno 2017b, pp. 291–2.

35   In a preparatory note to his theses 'On the Concept of History', Benjamin writes that '[i]n the concept of the classless society, Marx secularized the concept of the messianic age' (Benjamin 2001d, p. 1231, translation from Tiedemann 1983, p. 83). 'The Messiah, redemption, the angel and the Antichrist appear in the theses as images, analogies, and parables, not literally. Benjamin does not for a moment think of undertaking the representation of

Jewish religion as the epitome of realised utopia, has yet to arrive. Thus, in potentially 'crypto-theological'[36] statements, Adorno invokes a state of salvation which knows neither God nor the messiah, but which amounts to the realisation of the messianic idea. 'There is not', Adorno claims, 'a natural-scientific truth and a revelatory truth, but rather – insofar as something has been revealed about intra-worldly things – this truth must be an absolutely valid truth which cannot be divided into a merely a natural-scientific part and a merely revelatory part. In this, I really believe that ... hardheaded orthodoxy is more experienced with the decisive problem here than is all philosophy of religion, but the consequence I draw from this is that I say, *non credo*'.[37] Salvation would be 'an event which takes place publicly, on the stage of history and within the community. It is an occurrence which takes in the visible world and which cannot be conceived apart from such a visible appearance'.[38] As Joseph Ratzinger recapitulated in his role as Pope Benedict XVI in the encyclical *Spe Salvi*, Adorno not only 'firmly upheld this total rejection of images, which naturally meant the exclusion of any "image" of a loving God',[39] he never came remotely close to imagining – out of an unfulfilled desire for salvation – a God who would promise to one day grant human beings the experience of justice. 'The unbearable today which never seems to end is given solace by the promise of a recon-

---

what Marx ultimately achieved in theory and what the working class movement preserved in practice' (Tiedemann 1983, p. 83).

36   Schmid Noerr 2001, p. 29.

37   Adorno and Kogon 1958, p. 489.

38   Scholem 1995, p. 1.

39   Ratzinger 2007. In a tangent during his introductory lecture course on epistemology from the winter semester of 1957–8, Adorno suggests to his listeners that they should not leave ostensibly religious questions to be answered by those ostensibly responsible for them: 'A poster is hanging in our university for a lecture titled "God and Immortality", or "Death and Immortality", or something along those lines. And as I caught sight of the poster, I knew immediately without even having looked closer that this could only be the event of either a Catholic or Protestant student organisation. I then checked, and it really was the event of a Catholic student organisation. And the fact that I guessed this immediately ... actually really shocked me, namely because it shows that this ... has really also been commandeered, occupied by the administrative division of the world. That is, death and immortality – we all of course die in the end, and somehow we indeed probably all hope for immortality – if not for one's own, then for the immorality of the human beings we love .... Such a question only appears at all anymore in the – I would almost say – corporate, or at any rate organisationally defined section of a kind of student organisation which spends its time on such things, just as a democratic student organisation would probably host a lecture titled "Crisis of Parliamentarianism?" with a question mark, or a socialist organisation a lecture titled "Is Marxism Still Relevant Today?" I believe that what actually matters, and what really constitutes the relevance of philosophy, ... is that the epistemological or

ciled tomorrow'[40] – solace which is similar to the belief that one will be justly
rewarded after death, and which therefore only veils the reasons for the *need*
for consolation. As opposed to this, Adorno is not concerned with solace, but
with a place where no one has ever been, because it has not yet existed. He
seeks neither to return to God – for him, the 'unmediated identification of the
rational society with the kingdom of God' is 'one of the most dangerous manip-
ulations'[41] – nor does he long for the arrival of the messiah. Rather, the goal
of his social critique is the abolition of a society which prevents its members
from entering into a humanity[42] which would be worthy of its concept. 'The
maturation of human beings', Adorno claims in a seminar, 'can only mean the
end of a prehistory in which there has never been anything like a paradisiacal
state'.[43] The phrase 'paradisiacal state' indicates that while Adorno indeed sec-
ularises religious utopia, he does so without profaning it. In this, he seeks to
bring out its best, which is nothing other than the longing for a state in which,
finally, 'all, all [would be] well'.[44] In such a state, religious belief would probably
have to be given over to the population of heaven, but the world itself arranged
like the place which belief envisions heaven to be. Hence, negative utopia can
only be expressed in theological categories simply because realised utopia has
no immediate existence. That being said, what today appears as theological-
utopian could be the most mundane thing in a reconciled world.

For Adorno, the 'most profound reason, the metaphysical reason' that 'one
can actually talk about utopia only in a negative way' lies in the existence of
death. 'Every attempt to describe or portray utopia in a simple way, i.e., it will
be like this, would be an attempt to avoid the antinomy of death and to speak
about the elimination of death as if death did not exist'.[45] This antinomy is
also described by Jean Améry as 'the rejection of all dialectic: the negation of a
negation of a negation'[46] which comes along with the 'totally bad tidings, the

---

generally philosophical way of thinking allows one to move beyond the deplorable har-
dening into branches, beyond this administration of the most important things by which-
ever experts, who now even present themselves as experts for God and immortality ...,
and that one in fact sees that questions on topics such as death and immortality are not
something which can be administered by licensed and calibrated people' (Adorno 2018b,
pp. 201–3).

40   Demirović 2005, p. 143.
41   Letter from Adorno to Horkheimer, 17 February 1944 (Adorno and Horkheimer 2004,
     p. 312).
42   Cf. Demirović 2003a, p. 22.
43   Adorno 2021a, vol. 2, p. 82.
44   von Eichendorff 1966, p. 111; on the utopian substance of this passage cf. Löhr 2003, p. 440.
45   Adorno in Adorno and Bloch 1989, p. 10.
46   Améry 1994, p. 110.

annunciation of the end'.[47] All progress beyond the existing state of affairs is negated by death. Before death, which always has the final say, everything is the same; all which exists is ultimately all there is. What would appear as happiness in the 'light of redemption'[48] is the shame of all past and future generations before the darkness of the inevitable. Having 'repressed all that is "horrific" in death'[49] – whose 'scandalous imposition' is 'a humiliation without compare, that we put up with, not in humility, but as the humiliated'[50] – bourgeois civilisation tries 'either to ennoble it or to corral it with hygiene. The futility of false life must not be allowed to enter consciousness through the ghastliness that death reveals – nor the fact that death is an offence to human beings, one that should be abolished rather than celebrated in the name of tragedy',[51] as it is in the fundamental ontology of Heidegger and his followers.[52] In view of the injustice 'which death does to every single individual',[53] 'surrendering to the inevitable ... becomes its recommendation'.[54] This afflicts every utopia which 'enlists the services of theology' in hopes of overcoming death while treating theology as something which 'has to be kept out of sight'.[55] In view of the 'universally' practised distancing from utopia – ' "Oh, that's just utopian; oh, that's possible only in the Land of Cockaigne. [And in fact,] that shouldn't [exist] at all" '[56] – Adorno's notion that death is 'avoidable and criticizable, or at any rate the precise opposite of what thinking should actually identify with',[57] leads to the denial of the wish that all suffering be overcome. Against this, Adorno takes the view that 'the question about the elimination of death is indeed the crucial point', something which he argues 'can be ascertained very easily':

---

47   Améry 1994, p. 101.

48   Adorno 1984, p. 120.

49   Letter from Adorno to Mann, 18 January 1954 (Adorno and Mann 2006, p. 102).

50   Améry 1994, p. 128.

51   Letter from Adorno to Mann, 18 January 1954 (Adorno and Mann 2006, p. 102).

52   'Lesser authentics raise their eyes reverently before death, but their spiritual attitude, infatuated with the living, disregards death. The thorn in theology, without which salvation is unthinkable, is removed. According to the concept of theology, nothing natural has gone through death without metamorphosis. In the man-to-man relationship there can be no eternity now and here, and certainly not in the relationship of man to God, a relationship that seems to pat Him on the shoulder' (Adorno 1973, pp. 16–17).

53   Adorno 2003s, p. 346.

54   Adorno 2003af, p. 424.

55   Benjamin 2006b, p. 389.

56   Adorno in Adorno and Bloch 1989, p. 4.

57   Adorno 2008, p. 104.

you only have to speak about the elimination of death some time with a so-called well-disposed person ['*wohlgesinnten*' *Menschen*] .... Then you will get an *immediate* reaction .... Yes, if death were eliminated, if people would no longer die, that would be the most terrible and most horrible thing. I would say that it is precisely this form of reaction that actually opposes the utopian consciousness most of the time. The identification with death is that which goes beyond the identification of people with the existing social conditions and in which they are extended.

Utopian consciousness means a consciousness for which the *possibility* that people no longer have to die does not have anything horrible about it, but is, on the contrary, *that* which one actually wants.[58]

Thoughts such as these, which by all means take 'theological risks',[59] 'immediately provoke the well-known controversies – the "yes buts" – and there is nothing in the world, however bad, for which there are not the strongest possible arguments that it must be so and cannot under any circumstances be changed'.[60] Given that such arguments often present themselves as scholarly nuance – that 'this "but" is the very dogma of positivist social science in our own day'[61] – it is no surprise that 'some social scientists inspired by Critical Theory fear that the elevation of theological motifs in this mode of thinking only comes at the price of non-committal, of empty generality and thus also of affirmation'.[62] A radical utopia as socially critical theory's point of refuge can only be imagined by sociology as resignation in view of the worst, and never as the opposite of resignation, for

even utopia is not immune to the imperatives of the cultural environment. It is characteristic of modern culture that it constantly devours its

---

58   Adorno in Adorno and Bloch 1989, p. 8; on the '*wohlgesinnten*' *Menschen* – the 'well-disposed person', or the person with a 'benevolent attitude' – cf. Adorno 1973, p. 22.

59   Adorno 2007b, p. 77.

60   Adorno 2000a, p. 16.

61   Adorno 2022, p. 23. 'After all, a scientific discipline concerned with its own continued existence could allow itself to incorporate into its very categories of inquiry fear of death, reflection upon it, the struggle for its elimination and the need for happiness – regarding these preconditions of Critical Theory, the late Horkheimer said the following: "To not merely come to know the world from the perspective of something so self-evident [expiration] and that which immediately precedes it [inescapable loneliness], but rather to come to know one's self and one's own goals from this perspective, would not be something like cynicism, but rather the beginning of knowledge about the identity of a blind life with inexorable reality"' (Schmid Noerr 1997, p. 81, brackets in original; quoted from Horkheimer 1988a, p. 124).

62   Brumlik 1994, p. 231.

own images, even the image of apocalypse itself. If it is difficult to appreciate the urgency of the cultural criticism of the 1920s and 1930s, it is not
because it has become less meaningful, but because the catastrophe has
become a permanent fixture – the apocalypse is boring. Worse, its image
is ubiquitous in the culture industry.

The sheer weight of the apocalypse obliterates utopia. The catastrophe
no longer conjures up images of redemption. Instead it produces cynicism, which is no less ideological. Cynicism is the total embrace of the
power of reality as fate, or as a joke, the 'unhappy consciousness' of powerlessness.[63]

Against this, the ubiquitous fear of death owing to the fact that life no longer
lives is only apparently paradoxical. After all,

> the less people really live – or, perhaps more correctly, the more they
> become aware that they have not really lived – the more abrupt and fright-
> ening death becomes for them, and the more it appears as a misfortune.
> It is as if ... they were corpses from the first. ... The terror of death today
> is largely the terror of seeing how much the living resemble it.[64]

The identification with death can be seen as the desire for an end to this terror
which life causes. It is a longing directed towards an end to suffering, but one
which can only imagine suffering's end as abstract negation – not as the abolition of terror in this world. 'If human beings are measured by their utopia, by
their hope, then it's safe to say that as their standards have increased, they have
become extremely modest'.[65] Horkheimer and Adorno oppose this, claiming
that they 'want to make sure not to affirm the entire historical process along
with Marx by claiming, for example, that revolution leads to harmony. Humanity cannot realise paradise with its bloody hands'.[66] This categorical rejection

---

63   Rabinbach 1985, p. 124.
64   Adorno 2000b, p. 136.
65   Horkheimer 1988a, p. 54; cf. Adorno in Adorno and Bloch 1989, pp. 3–4: 'Whatever uto-
      pia is, whatever can be imagined as utopia, this is the transformation of the totality. ...
      It seems to me that what people have lost subjectively in regard to consciousness is very
      simply the capability to imagine the totality as something that could be completely dif-
      ferent'.
66   Adorno and Horkheimer, TWA, T8 52531. Along these lines, the protagonist in Italo Svevo's
      novel *Zeno's Conscience* says the following to a newborn: 'The minutes now passing may
      actually be pure, but all the centuries that prepared for your coming were certainly not'

of a better society in the future to be paid for as the price of history up to the present – the assurance that while this society might be better, it would hardly be reconciled – runs throughout the entirety of Adorno's work. In a 1949 letter to Horkheimer, Adorno writes of the unbearable notion of a progress 'based on the terrible agonies of previous generations which could not have had any idea that they served, in a certain sense, as history's "guinea pigs", so that in the most distant future, things might be better for the species'.[67] In his lecture course *History and Freedom* from the winter semester of 1964–5, Adorno would revisit this problem:

> The identification with the universal enters deeply into the fibre of Marxism notwithstanding the much cruder epistemological positions of Marx and the Marxists. For there you find something like the belief that, when ultimately the universal takes over and the concept is victorious, individuals will indeed come into their own – and this factor will ensure that all the suffering and the wasted individuality of history will somehow be made good. This is an issue that to the best of my knowledge was first commented on critically by Ivan Turgenev in the nineteenth century. Turgenev maintained that even the prospect of a completely classless society could not console him for the fate of all those who had suffered to no purpose and had fallen by the wayside.[68]

For reconciliation to succeed, it would need to embrace the unreconciled dead.

3 Moved to Different Places

For Adorno,

> utopia is essentially ... in the [determinate] negation of that which merely is, and [yet] by concretizing itself as something false, it always points at the same time to what should be. ... Falsum – the false thing – index sui et veri. That means that the true thing determines itself via the false thing,

---

(Svevo 2003, p. 6). The momentary happiness of the individual is sullied by the prior unhappiness of countless others.
67   Letter from Adorno to Horkheimer, 28 May 1949 (Adorno and Horkheimer 2005, p. 264).
68   Adorno 2006a, pp. 43–4.

or via that which makes itself falsely known. And insofar as ... we do not know what the correct thing would be, we know exactly, to be sure, what the false thing is.[69]

Because 'utopia only expresses itself in configurations of elements of what is and not immediately',[70] it can 'only be grasped as the answer to particular questions, not in a free-floating manner, but rather only as the moment of dialectical reversal'.[71] This is the reason for the ban on images, which Adorno also refers to in *Negative Dialectics* when he criticises a 'deficiency in Kantian theory' he claims owes to 'the elusive, abstract side of the intelligible character'. However, Adorno also argues that this deficiency

> has a touch of the truth of the anti-image ban which post-Kantian philosophers – including Marx – extended to all concepts of positivity.
> Like freedom, the intelligible character as a subjective possibility is a thing that comes to be, not a thing that is. It would be a betrayal to incorporate it in existence by description, even by the most cautious description. In the right condition, as in the Jewish *theologoumenon*, all things would differ only a little from the way they are; but [how things would then be cannot be conceived even in the slightest].[72]

Adorno invokes this theologoumenon as early as 1942 in a letter to Edward M. David, the translator of the English version of his essay on Spengler,[73] in order to clarify a difficult passage of the text: 'Think of the Jewish legend: when the [Messiah] comes everything will be exactly as it is today, but the whole will be a very very little different'.[74] Adorno apparently adopts this motif

---

69   Adorno in Adorno and Bloch 1989, p. 12; cf. Adorno 2008, p. 28 and editorial note by Tiedemann (Adorno 2008, p. 219, n. 13).
70   Adorno 2003l, p. 92.
71   Adorno in Adorno and Horkheimer 1985a, p. 465.
72   Adorno 2007b, pp. 298–9. Wiebrecht Ries notes 'that Kant as well was deeply influenced by the Old Testament ban on images. In the *Critique of Judgment*, he praises the demand that "[t]hou shalt not make unto thyself any graven image, nor any likeness" as the most sublime sentence in the Bible' (Ries 1976, p. 76; quoted from Kant 2007, p. 156).
73   See Adorno 1941.
74   Letter from Adorno to David, 3 July 1941 (MHA VI, 1B.95). This motif also emerges in *Minima Moralia* as the subject of a childhood memory: 'To a child returning from a holiday, home seems new, fresh, festive. Yet nothing has changed there since he left. Only because duty has now been forgotten, of which each piece of furniture, window, lamp, was otherwise a reminder, is the house given back this sabbath peace, and for minutes one is at home in a never-returning world of rooms, nooks and corridors in a way that makes the

from Benjamin, who in his work on Kafka refers to the poem 'Das bucklige Männlein' ('The Little Hunchbacked Man') from *Des Knaben Wunderhorn* (*The Boy's Magic Horn*), an early nineteenth-century collection of German folk poems:[75] 'This little man is at home in distorted life; he will disappear with the coming of the Messiah, who (a great rabbi once said) will not wish to change the world by force but will merely make a slight adjustment in it'.[76] Bloch also invokes this saying by a 'wise rabbi'[77] in *Traces*, a collection of aphorisms published in 1930, prompting Scholem to claim to Benjamin that '[t]he great rabbi with the profound dictum on the messianic kingdom who appears in Bloch is none other than *I* myself; what a way to achieve fame!! It was one of my first ideas about the Kabbalah'.[78]

However, it appears that Scholem's memory deceives him both here and when he subsequently claims that the appropriation of his saying revealed to him 'what honors one can garner for oneself with an apocryphal sentence',[79] for 'Benjamin and Bloch's attributions were not actually wrong': the saying really did come from a rabbi, the tzaddik rabbi Nachman of Breslov, 'who knew how to tell the tale of exchange and change to something only very slightly different'.[80] The theologoumenon which evidently made such an impression

---

rest of life there a lie. No differently will the world one day appear, almost unchanged, in its constant feast-day light, when it stands no longer under the law of labour, and when for home-comers duty has the lightness of holiday play' (Adorno 2005b, p. 112; cf. also Adorno 2002a, p. 6).

75   See von Arnim and Brentano 2003, pp. 1136–7; on the significance of this poem for Benjamin cf. Siepmann 1990, pp. 21–2.

76   Benjamin 2005a, p. 811; the reference here comes from Scholem (see letter from Scholem to Benjamin, 9 July 1934 [Benjamin and Scholem 1992, pp. 123–5]). Benjamin uses this motif as early as a 1932 'thought-image' (*Denkbild*) titled 'In the Sun': 'The Hasidim have a saying about the world to come. Everything there will be arranged just as it is with us. The room we have now will be just the same in the world to come; where our child lies sleeping, it will sleep in the world to come. The clothes we are wearing we shall also wear in the next world. Everything will be the same as here – only a little bit different' (Benjamin 2005b, p. 664).

77   'Another rabbi, a true Kabbalist, once said: To bring about the kingdom of freedom, it is not necessary that everything be destroyed, and [an entirely] new world begin; rather, this cup, or that bush, or that stone, and so all things must only be shifted a little. Because this "a little" is hard to do, and its measure so hard to find, humanity cannot do it in this world; instead this is why the Messiah comes. [In saying this, this wise rabbi too] spoke out not for creeping progress but completely for the leap of the lucky glimpse and the [lucky] hand' (Bloch 2006, p. 158; cf. Schiller 1993a, p. 52).

78   Letter from Scholem to Benjamin, 9 July 1934 (Benjamin and Scholem 1992, p. 123).

79   Letter from Scholem to Benjamin, 9 July 1934 (Benjamin and Scholem 1992, p. 123, n. 5).

80   Brocke 1985, p. 284.

on Adorno in fact has its origin in Nachman's tale 'The Exchanged Children',[81] which contains the following passage:

> They showed him the throne and he saw that it was extremely tall .... He went over to the throne and gazed at it. ... The late king had devised each detail with such wisdom that no person could understand its significance until an extraordinarily wise person came along, who would understand the concept .... He would then know how to exchange and arrange all things correctly.
>
> [He then saw that] the same was true of the bed. He understood that it had to be moved somewhat, and the lamp likewise had to have its position adjusted. The birds and animals also had to be moved to different places. Thus, a bird would have to be taken from one place and set in another place. ...
>
> [All the animals and birds] then began to sing a very wonderful melody. Each one functioned properly.[82]

The social totality cannot be negated as a whole, which is to say it cannot be negated abstractly. The only way it could be changed would be through the determinate negation of its elements. Where the social totality quantifies everything, variability can only be hoped for in what universal quantification rejects as rubbish. This in turn leads to the non-identical – to 'the other, exempt from the mechanism of the social process of production and reproduction[, not subjected to the reality principle]',[83] or in other words, to what 'falls through the net': 'the most minute thing', a thing containing what actually 'cries out for philosophical explanation',[84] what wants through philosophical explanation to transcend the totality from within this minute thing.[85] And it is by no means inevitable that the ultimate revolution – for this is what is at issue here – would arrive with a bang. Triumph over the whole does not have to be accompan-

---

81   First translated into German by Martin Buber under the title 'The King's Son and the Son of the Maid' (the English edition of Buber's version of this tale is located in Buber 1956, pp. 95–114).

82   Nachman of Breslov 1983, pp. 272–4; on Benjamin, Bloch and Adorno's reception of this tale, cf. Ebach 2001, p. 83, n. 30 and Faber 2002, p. 32.

83   Adorno 2002a, p. 311.

84   Adorno 2008, p. 70.

85   In view of 'compactly dovetailed reality' (Adorno 2007b, p. 347), the 'smallest intramundane traits would be of relevance to the absolute, for the micrological view cracks the shells of what, measured by the subsuming cover concept, is helplessly isolated and explodes its identity, the delusion that it is but a specimen' (Adorno 2007b, p. 408).

ied by enormous noise. To stay with the metaphor, what would fall would not clatter, for what would fall to determinate negation would no longer be falling: there would be no impact; the revolution would come on velvet paws. Were this triumph to succeed, then indeed, 'virtually nothing [would have] made all well',[86] as Adorno writes in the libretto of his light opera *Der Schatz des Indianer Joe* (*The Treasure of Indian Joe*) – evidently in view of the Hasidic motif cited above.

4   Realisation Alone Would Transcend Exchange

Adorno criticises exchange as 'the rational form of mythical ever-sameness', as a constant cycle of giving and taking in which 'every act … revokes the other'.[87] Through the 'unjust' exchange of labour-power for wages – that is, where production and circulation come into contact, where 'exchange is by no means pure circulation anymore' and 'the sphere of production itself is already competition or circulation'[88] – labour puts something new into circulation, while the stasis of the system is guaranteed by its perpetual internal dynamics.

Adorno agues that for exchange to make 'all well', it would have to live up to a *further* possibility enabled by its descent from the principle of identity: it would have to become just. '[I]n society as it ought to be, [exchange] would be not only abolished but fulfilled'.[89] Although 'humanness requires that the law of an eye for an eye, a quid pro quo, be brought to an end; that the infamous exchange of equivalents, in which age-old myth is recapitulated in rational economics, cease', it is also the case that this process 'has its dialectical crux in the requirement that what rises above exchange not fall back behind it; that the suspension of exchange not once again cost human beings, as the objects of order, the full fruits of their labor. The abolition of the exchange of equivalents would be its fulfillment; as long as equality reigns as law, the individual is cheated of equality'.[90] In this fulfilment, each would finally 'receive' what 'exchange essentially always only promised to them, only to let them down'.[91]

---

86   Adorno 1979, p. 95; cf. Tiedemann 1979, pp. 135–6.
87   Adorno 2005f, p. 159.
88   Adorno 2021a, vol. 4, p. 267.
89   Adorno 2007b, p. 296.
90   Adorno 2019f, p. 425.
91   Adorno 2003v, p. 163. 'As pathetic as it is to have something from someone, so too is a
      relationship hollowed out when it is only nourished by memory and no longer yields hap-

If workers were no longer deprived of their real earnings by the owners of capital for whom they work, then 'the category of exchange would abolish itself' because 'the exchange of equivalents would become truth'.[92] This would also cause the disintegration of the system of all other economic categories such as class, commodity, money and capital – exchange would no longer be economic, and humanity would be liberated from '[just] exchange by [exchange] fulfil[ling] itself [justly]'.[93] However, this insight does not lead Adorno to desire something along the lines of an abstract negation of the principle of equality on which exchange is based. After all, 'if we proclaimed, to the greater glory of the irreducibly qualitative, that parity should no longer be the ideal rule', we would simply 'be creating excuses for recidivism into ancient injustice. From olden times, the main characteristic of the exchange of equivalents has been that unequal things would be exchanged in its name, that the surplus value of labour would be appropriated'.[94] 'If reason were to skip over individual interests in an abstract way', that is, through blind negation, this

---

piness; the demand for happiness is legitimate, one doesn't want to be bored with human beings. Hence, my thesis that exchange in a humane society would not only be eliminated but also fulfilled appears to extend into the private realm, but indeed, in this it becomes a disgrace. This thesis instructs as to how much the immediacy of the private is an illusion' (Adorno 2003k, p. 35). Cf. also Adorno 2019g, p. 128: 'The world beyond exchange would be one in which no one participating in an exchange would be cheated of what belonged to him. If reason were to skip over individual interests in an abstract way, without Aristotelian equity [*Billigkeit*], it would violate justice, and universality itself would reproduce particularity in the bad sense. Dwelling on – lingering with – the concrete is an inextinguishable aspect of anything that frees itself from particularity. At the same time, that moment of emancipation shows the specificity of particularity to be just as limited as the blind domination of a totality that does not respect particularity'.

92   Adorno 2021a, vol. 2, p. 138.
93   Adorno 1973, p. 152.
94   Adorno 2007b, p. 146. Along these lines, Adorno claims the following in his lecture course *Fragen der Dialektik* (*Questions of Dialectics*): 'For example, it is simple, or certainly fairly evident to determine – and indeed, we have done this quite abundantly in this course – that the universality of the principle of exchange, and hence the reduction to an abstract general concept, is actually the vehicle of identification in the real society in which we live. In other words, we non-identical individual beings become identical, that is, commensurable, by means of exchange, and in this way, so too does the entire world become an identical, that is, a totality. Yet if it were now claimed that, well, in light of this, this principle of exchange must simply be done away with – that in other words, things must no longer be determined by like for like – then this would be a regression behind the principle of exchange. That is, this would then simply mean that no standard of comparison would exist at all anymore, and that in the place of the rationality contained in this principle of exchange, forms of the immediate appropriation, the immediate viol-

would reproduce particularity in the bad sense. Dwelling on – lingering with – the concrete is an inextinguishable aspect of anything that frees itself from particularity. At the same time, that moment of emancipation shows the specificity of particularity to be just as limited as the blind domination of a totality that does not respect particularity.[95]

While exchange in existing society is mediated by value, an Adornian solution to this cannot be the replacement of the exchange of equivalents with an *immediate* exchange which is unjust. As Adorno argues in *Negative Dialectics*, echoing a point he makes in 'Reflections on Class Theory', '[i]f comparability as a category of measure were simply annulled, the rationality which is inherent in the [exchange] principle – as ideology, of course, but also as a promise – would give way to direct appropriation, to force, and nowadays to the naked privilege of monopolies and cliques'.[96] Given his belief that '[it certainly cannot be said that] exchange will have ceased to take place'[97] in a post-capitalist society, it is much rather the case that in Adorno's utopia, every exchange would be just in itself, without particular justice being annulled by a totality superordinate to all individuals.

Adorno claims that

> [w]hen we criticize the [exchange] principle as the identifying principle of thought, we want to realize the ideal of free and just [exchange]. To date, this ideal is only a pretext. Its realization alone would transcend [exchange]. [If] critical theory has shown it up for what it is – as exchange of things that are equal and yet unequal – our critique of the inequality within equality aims at equality too, for all our skepticism of the rancor involved in the bourgeois egalitarian ideal that tolerates no qualitative difference. If no man had part of his labor withheld from him any more,

---

ence – whatever you want to call it – of the privilege of the monopoly would now assert themselves. So the critique of the principle of exchange as an identifying principle of thought should absolutely be augmented with the clause that actually in general, the ideal of free and just exchange must first be fulfilled anyway for the world to be delivered from exchange, or from revenge, as it is called quite analogously in Nietzsche's work' (Adorno 2021b, p. 308.).

95   Adorno 2019g, p. 128.
96   Adorno 2007b, pp. 146–7. By 'comparability as a category of measure', Adorno does not refer to money or some other de facto means of measure, but rather the principle of equality, which first makes measurement possible and creates the 'necessity of exchanging like for like' (Adorno 2000a, p. 32) to begin with (cf. Demirović 2003a, p. 22).
97   Adorno 2000a, p. 31.

rational identity would be a fact, and society would have transcended the identifying mode of thinking.[98]

If the principle of identity were to disappear, so too would the objective dialectic between the identical and the non-identical.

As Tiedemann claims, this precisely does not mean that happiness 'is a plurale tantum – happiness is either happiness of the species, or it does not exist'.[99] The 'image of happiness without shame'[100] shows a human being who, as an individual both phylogenetically and socially tied to the species, would no longer be a mere specimen – yet one who would not stand opposed to society as an outcast:[101] Utopia would be the 'subject's nonidentity without sacrifice'.[102] Equality in the bad sense, which propagates the 'familiar argument of tolerance'[103] according to which all human beings are said to be equal,[104] would be transcended in a society 'in which people could be different without fear'. It 'would not be a unitary state, but the realization of universality in the reconciliation of differences'[105] – a 'state of differentiation without domination, with the differentiated participating in each other'.[106]

---

98   Adorno 2007b, p. 147.

99   Tiedemann 1998, p. 10.

100   Adorno 2001b, p. 16.

101   For a comprehensive study on this question which has been written in the meantime, see Duckheim 2014.

102   Adorno 2007b, p. 281; cf. Hintz 2004, pp. 37–8.

103   Adorno 2005b, p. 102.

104   'Humanity becomes the most general and empty form of privilege. It is strictly suited to a form of consciousness which no longer suffers any privileges yet which finds itself under the spell of privilege. Such universal humanity, however, is ideology. It caricatures of the equal rights everything which bears a human face, since it hides from men the unalleviated discriminations of societal power: differences between hunger and overabundance, between spirit and docile idiocy. Chastely moved, man lets himself be addressed through Man: it doesn't cost anyone anything' (Adorno 1973, p. 66).

105   Adorno 2005b, p. 103.

106   Adorno 2005d, p. 247. 'Only once the totality dissolves – a totality which exists as long as a whole raises itself up as a such by creating and excluding something non-identical, foreign, other – will humanity exist. Accordingly, humanity does not represent something which already exists in principle, but rather is understood here as an entirely new and unique stage of history, of acting and of thinking. After all, humanity is beyond all totality conceived so comprehensively; it is "plurality, an association of free, individual human beings"' (Demirović 2004, pp. 30–1; quoted from Adorno 2003i, p. 586). On the other hand, '[c]ommunity for community's sake is no ideal. Declaring togetherness as such the goal indicates that one has forgotten about the substance of community: a humane arrangement of the world. The cult of community as an end-in-itself belongs to the National Socialists and the people's democracies in the Russian style. It is essentially totalitarian:

'For a liberated humanity, the qualitative diversity of the bygone and obsolete would be absolved'.[107]

Adorno's 'criticism [of] the ideal of equality is directed at a state of richness in which it would be [repressive to count the beefsteaks which everyone eats] because everyone [could] eat as much as they want [anyway], whereas [some might be ashamed to keep eating meat] in such a situation. As long as [that] time has not come the vulgar-materialist phrase of sharing is right'.[108] Until then, there is 'tenderness only in the coarsest demand: that no-one shall go hungry any more'.[109]

In several places, Adorno points to the already existing possibilities for emancipation enabled by the contemporary state of the forces of production.[110] Yet possibilities alone are not enough to bring about the establishment of a truly emancipated society. After all, the fact that overabundance is produced while deprivation of the most basic necessities prevails is not an administrative problem; rather, the former results from the latter. Even if capitalism were overcome and the forces of production liberated, this would not suffice to reconcile society, that is, to reconcile the contradiction between the universal and particular. The material sustenance of all would not preclude a new form of domination, nor would it alone be the guarantor of a 'happiness of mankind that would be the happiness of individuals'.[111] Already in 1944, Adorno writes that one can at least say 'that in today's objective situation the thought of a necessary transitional period to absolute-socialism contradicts the status of the [material forces of production] so much that it almost sounds like an excuse for the [domination which is becoming entrenched. Even so, to be fair], one has to say that even the most thoughtful of all Marxists, those who in fact [are Marxists no longer], imagined the first phase much shorter than the Christians the

---

within it, the tendency towards the oppression of the individual constantly resonates. However, a real community would be one of free human beings' (Adorno 2003g, p. 438).

107   Adorno 2003k, p. 14. Here, Wayne Whitson Floyd recognises 'Adorno's eschatological vision: diversity without domination' (Floyd 1993, p. 544).

108   Adorno 2017b, p. 300.

109   Adorno 2005b, p. 156.

110   See for example Adorno 2003i, p. 585: 'the forces of production, the material forces of production, have today developed such that if society were arranged rationally, material hardship would no longer be necessary. That such a state could be produced, and indeed throughout the world in tellurian measure, would have been written off as crassly utopian in the nineteenth century. ... Because the objective possibilities have been so infinitely expanded, the kind of critique of the concept of utopia which oriented itself on continued shortage actually has no more currency'. Adorno elaborates the same thought with a slightly different choice of words in *History and Freedom*: cf. Adorno 2006a, p. 67.

111   Adorno 2007b, p. 352.

time between the birth of Jesus and the *Parousia*, a period of time which covers the whole of temporality'.[112]

Just exchange, therefore, does not indicate a standard of action to be observed in the future. Rather, it names the precondition for the possibility of overcoming injustice and the compulsion of identity. Only simultaneously can the compulsive action and the principle on which it is based be superseded.

> The notion that deprivation shall not exist, that no one in the world shall go hungry anymore – in other words, the notion that the abolition of distress be fulfilled – itself requires an increase in the forces of production, and thus the domination of nature. Not only is this increase deeply entwined with the anti-materialist principle, it is only conceivable in the first place insofar as human beings – who, in their domination of external nature, are supposed to learn to dominate themselves – are constantly subjected to disallowances. The conception of a state without disallowances, the unfettering of the forces of production, the elimination of distress. That is, to be possible at all, the utopian element of unlimited fulfilment indeed requires – in order to be possible at all according to its own sense – limitation, asceticism, a particular element of repression, of oppression.

For Adorno, the continued history of humanity will be decided by 'whether it will succeed in getting out of this terrible bind: what the alternative means, and what shall lead to the alternative in order to realise itself, develops within itself the principle against which it turns. Thus, this alternative stands in constant danger of regressing back into myth'.[113] The increase in society's productive capacity extends domination, whatever its form, and thus perpetually constitutes a 'change which is necessary for everything to stay the same'.[114] In spite of all dynamics internal to society, the whole of society 'always remain[s] the same – the persistence of "pre-history"' which is 'realized as constantly different, unforeseen, exceeding all expectations, the faithful shadow of developing productive forces'.[115] The constant development of the forces of production,[116]

---

112   Adorno 2017b, p. 297.

113   Adorno 1974a, p. 187.

114   Demirović 2005, p. 144.

115   Adorno 2005b, p. 234.

116   Regarding the idea of the 'unleashing of productive forces', Adorno suggests that the 'very word "unleashed" [*entfesselt*] has undertones of menace' (Adorno 2007b, p. 307).

itself an expression of the 'reckless domination of nature',[117] is a blind element of ever-sameness, of what Adorno grasps as myth. For him, Marx as well fails to escape the 'metaphysics of the forces of production',[118] as he presupposes 'something like the metaphysical substantiality of ... productive forces' – which is 'reminiscent of the Hegelian World Spirit'. The consequence of this, Adorno argues, is

> the persistence in Marx of a highly dubious theorem of German idealism. We find it explicitly stated, above all by Engels in the *Anti-Dühring*. This is the assertion that freedom really amounts to doing consciously what is necessary, something that is of course meaningful only if what is necessary, the World Spirit, the development of the forces of production is in the right a priori and its victory is guaranteed. This belief is one that has led to some catastrophic consequences – in particular, all the anti-liberal and authoritarian perversions to which the doctrine of Marx and Engels had been subjected with its installation in the states of the Eastern bloc.[119]

Although Adorno believes that Marx 'in principle thought dialectically', he maintains that 'the forces of production nonetheless gain a certain metaphysical character in Marx's work', something which the Marx 'adopted directly from Saint-Simon'. Moreover, Adorno argues, Marx was 'forced' by his 'historical optimism' to 'give the forces of production the final say'.[120] Additionally,

---

117   Adorno 1974a, p. 187.
118   Adorno 2008, p. 96. As Adorno says in the same passage, this expression was coined by Alfred Seidel, a friend from his youth (cf. editorial note by Tiedemann [Adorno 2008, p. 240, n. 12]): 'To be able to give a unified account of history, Marx, like Hegel, had to assume *one* agent of history. Yet Marx rejected the Hegelian metaphysics of spirit, and replaced it, realist that he was, with economy .... So it was that the agent of history could only be an economic agent, and indeed the factors which summon or increase the productivity of labour – that is, the "forces of production". ... Because these were supposed to be the agent of history, they were absolutised and elevated to a metaphysical entity, albeit an immanently metaphysical one, in unconscious analogy with the religious-metaphysical, that is, the transcendent-metaphysical philosophy of history from the Old Testament to Hegel' (Seidel 1927, pp. 209–10).
119   Adorno 2008, pp. 96–7; cf. Adorno 1974a, p. 22; regarding Engels cf. Engels 1987a, p. 105; cf. editorial note by Tiedemann (Adorno 2008, p. 240, n. 14).
120   Adorno 2021a, vol. 3, p. 691. Claude-Henri de Rouvroy, comte de Saint-Simon (1760–1825), in his day a friend and teacher of Auguste Comte, was an early sociologist now considered to be among the founding fathers of the discipline. With the 'pathos of revolutionary eighteenth-century bourgeois culture' (Adorno 2022, p. 14), he represented progress in the sense of the 'unfolding of the technical forces of production' (Adorno 2022, p. 17). 'The most important question in connection with Saint-Simon is the question of whether

Adorno claims 'that *Marx* tended to see the forces of production as the stronger factor relating to his teleological understanding of history, while *Weber* tended to emphasise the key importance of the relations of production in society. This difference may express … not least the distinct historical phase in which Weber lived as opposed to Marx: now, the objective forms of society have consolidated infinitely, confidence in the primacy of productive forces in social development shaken'.[121]

Adorno turns against this tendency in his oft-cited aphorism 'Sur l'eau' in *Minima Moralia*, the closest he comes to positively describing a fulfilled utopia.[122] This utopia would consist precisely of a human existence beyond production's coercion:

> The naive supposition of an unambiguous development towards increased production is itself a piece of that bourgeois outlook which permits development in only one direction because, integrated into a totality, dominated by quantification, it is hostile to qualitative difference. If we imagine emancipated society as emancipation from precisely such totality, then vanishing-lines come into view that have little in common with increased production and its human reflections. If uninhibited people are by no means the most agreeable or even the freest, a society rid of its fetters might take thought that even the forces of production are not the deepest substratum of man, but represent his historical form adapted to the production of commodities. Perhaps the true society will grow tired of development and, out of freedom, leave possibilities unused, instead of storming under a confused compulsion to the conquest of strange stars. A mankind which no longer knows want will begin to have an inkling of the delusory, futile nature of all the arrangements hitherto made in order to escape want, which used wealth to reproduce want on a larger scale.[123]

---

harmony might actually be enabled by an ever-intensifying development of the forces of production: in the meantime, this belief has passed away, its antithesis formulated in the theories of class in which the totality of society is viewed as the self-moving and actively self-reproducing contradiction. Simplified, "dialectics" for Marx means the development of the forces of production through the class-opposition, only the elimination of which can lead to harmony' (Adorno 2021a, vol. 3, p. 327; cf. also Adorno 2018c, pp. 163–4.

121   Adorno 2021a, vol. 3, pp. 690–1.
122   A more extensive interpretation of this aphorism is located in Schweppenhäuser 2009, pp. 87–90.
123   Adorno 2005b, pp. 156–7.

Here, Adorno refers to the Marxian discourse on relations of production as a
'fetter' on the mode of production. In a central passage in *Capital*, Marx writes –
not without pathos – of the centralisation of capitals, placing his trust in a kind
of historico-philosophical anomaly which finds no support in his actual critique of political economy:

> One capitalist always strikes down many others. Hand in hand with this
> centralization, or this expropriation of many capitalists by a few, other
> developments take place on an ever-increasing scale, such as the growth
> of the co-operative form of the labour process, the conscious technical
> application of science, the planned exploitation of the soil, the transform-
> ation of the means of labour into forms in which they can only be used
> in common, the economizing of all means of production by their use as
> the means of production of combined, socialized labour, the entangle-
> ment of all peoples in the net of the world market, and, with this, the
> growth of the international character of the capitalist regime. Along with
> the constant decrease in the number of capitalist magnates, who usurp
> and monopolize all the advantages of this process of transformation, the
> mass of misery, oppression, slavery, degradation and exploitation grows;
> but with this there also grows the revolt of the working class, a class con-
> stantly increasing in numbers, and trained, united and organized by the
> very mechanism of the capitalist process of production. The monopoly
> of capital becomes a fetter upon the mode of production which has flour-
> ished alongside and under it. The centralization of the means of produc-
> tion and the socialization of labour reach a point at which they become
> incompatible with their capitalist integument. This integument is burst
> asunder. The knell of capitalist private property sounds. The expropriat-
> ors are expropriated.[124]

To conceive of growth in the forces of production and in material wealth as
progress is itself the product of a conception of history which Adorno refuses
to abide. As long as human beings must dominate nature, it will also dominate them, for in their attempt to elevate themselves over nature, socialised
individuals only become further entangled in it. If nature no longer needed to
be dominated, humanity would no longer stand powerlessly at its mercy. At
that point, nature, the progenitor of the human being which 'posits' itself as
non-nature, would perhaps be reconciled as totality in such a way that human

---

124   Marx 1982a, p. 929.

being – who would now be an element of nature instead of an appendage –
could shape nature's history, which would no longer be prehistory, in accordance with a reason no longer conceived of as distinct from and opposed to
nature. As the result of determinate negation, the reconciliation between subject and object hoped for by Adorno would affect not only subjects. Reconciliation does not mean a return to nature, but rather a transcendence of the
dichotomy between nature and society, or between 'first' and 'second nature'.
Reconciliation between subject and object, the 'theological archetype'[125] of
Adorno's utopia,

> would release the nonidentical, would rid it of coercion, including spir-
> itualized coercion; it would open the road to the multiplicity of different
> things and strip dialectics of its power over them. Reconcilement would
> be [thinking] of [multiplicity] as no longer inimical, a [thinking] that
> is anathema to subjective reason. Dialectics serves the end of reconcile-
> ment.[126]

'The qualities would simply fall into the lap' only of a reconciled social process,
one which has been 'freed from exchange'.[127]

For Adorno, negative dialectics means 'to recognize and accept the object,
the Other, the alien'. For him, this is the only way to move beyond the object's
negative primacy, which is to say, beyond 'domination over powerless individuals by social forces that [have] become autonomous – society's condition when
it lack[s] an overall subject'.[128] Although 'the nonidentical has no positive existence' as long as 'the spell of universal identity'[129] prevails, it can be accessed by a
mode of thinking which respects 'that which is to be thought – the object – even
where the object does not heed the rules of thinking'.[130] 'Concepts alone can
achieve what the concept prevents. Cognition is a τρώσας ἰάσεται',[131] or in other
words: a means to heal the wounds which it itself strikes.[132] 'The determinable

---

125   Tiedemann 1997, p. 126.
126   Adorno 2007b, p. 6.
127   Adorno 2008, p. 127.
128   Wiggershaus 1995, pp. 602–3.
129   Adorno 2002a, p. 73.
130   Adorno 2007b, p. 141; cf. Wiggershaus 1987, pp. 36–7.
131   Adorno 2007b, p. 53.
132   This phrase comes from the Greek myth of the Arcadian (and mythical founder of Per-
      gamon) Telephus, who was wounded by Achilles and (depending on the version of the
      narration) then later healed by him: '[O]nly the spear which strikes the wound can heal

flaw in every concept makes it necessary to cite others; [in this arise those constellations which were the sole inheritors] of some of the hope of the name. The
language of philosophy approaches that name by [negating itself]'.[133] Under
the spell of identity, the non-identical can only be recognised as something
negative whose outline is traced by the borders of positive concepts. Where
the latter do not reach, the former is to be located.

> Thus in philosophy we are obliged to make use *of* concepts in order to
> talk *about* concepts. And this means that what we are concerned with in
> philosophy – namely, the non-conceptual, that which the concepts refer
> to – is excluded from philosophy from the outset. Thus by virtue of its own
> methodology philosophy bars its own way to what it wishes to achieve,
> namely, to be in a position to judge matters that are not itself, that are
> not concepts. And I would like to suggest quite simply as a programme
> ... that philosophy should reflect conceptually on this process in which
> it deals only with concepts and, by raising it to the level of the concept,
> should revise it and reverse it again, in so far as this can be achieved with
> conceptual methods.[134]

Only in this way, Adorno believes, could philosophy realise what he considers to
be its genuine task: to 'say what *cannot* be said. Against Wittgenstein'.[135] Adorno
pays just as little heed to Wittgenstein's premise that '[t]he world is all that is
the case'[136] as he does to the imperative derived from it: 'What we cannot speak
about we must pass over in silence'.[137] For Adorno, it is nothing less than 'car-
dinal untruth, having recognized an existence to be bad, to present it as truth
simply because it has been recognized'.[138] – 'The task of philosophy, I would
like just to say, is the complete opposite of what is postulated in the famous
saying by Wittgenstein which concludes his *Tractatus*'.[139]

---

it – and vice versa. Only the cure can also be the poison, and as such, can function as a cure
again. To metaphysics, spear and pharmakon are metaphysical language itself' (Hecker
2001, p. 229).

133   Adorno 2007b, p. 53.
134   Adorno 2008, p. 62.
135   Adorno 2008, p. 66.
136   Wittgenstein 2001, p. 5.
137   Wittgenstein 2001, p. 89.
138   Adorno 2005b, p. 98.
139   Adorno 1974a, p. 183; cf. Wiggershaus 2000.

5   This Core

In his 'Hornberger Letter' from 1935, Adorno writes Benjamin that a 'restoration of theology, or better still, a radicalization of dialectic introduced into the glowing heart of theology, would simultaneously require the utmost intensification of the social-dialectical, and indeed economic, motifs'.[140]

Adorno's philosophy is always also the attempt to pin down this economic motif. Economy here means neither merely capitalism, nor social production as such. Rather, it concerns how subjects deal with themselves and with other subjects or objects; it aims – and this is the critical element of Adorno's philosophy, inseparable from its material – at the possibility of human togetherness in view of the impossibility of immediate unity. Although Adorno sees the world as under the 'spell of universal identity',[141] this does not lead him to quietism, that '"we can't do anything about it"-mentality'[142] which is the practical consequence[143] of what his theory criticises. He does not think that 'because we ruthlessly define the blocked state and disproportionate power relationships of the present situation, we should therefore be branded with quietism or resignation. For anyone who shrinks back from analysing the existing structure for the sake of a thesis to be demonstrated or a goal to be achieved thereby betrays both truth and theory; and that is quite certainly not what has ever been meant by the unity of theory and practice'.[144]

Even though Adorno engages – more intensively following the Second World War – with the Marxian critique of political economy, he is never exclusively concerned with the critique of the capitalist mode of production in particular. Rather, he views this mode of production as emerging in an historical phase in which the meta-economy became an economy in the narrower sense – a 'special case of'[145] the more general phenomenon of economy. He is concerned with a negative philosophy of history – that is, with a history without a 'total subject, however construable',[146] and precisely for this reason remains a prehistory in which human beings, in spite of all attempts to gain control, remain fatefully trapped in nature. Adorno's social critique seeks to reconcile contradictions through determinate negation, which has no positive upshot as long

140   Letter from Adorno to Benjamin, 2–4 August 1935 (Adorno and Benjamin 1999, p. 108).
141   Adorno 2002a, p. 73.
142   Letter from Adorno to Lotte Tobisch, 27 November 1968 (Adorno and Tobisch 2003, p. 264).
143   'The practical consequence of the bourgeois "Nothing to be done" ... is precisely the perfidious "you must adjust" of the totalitarian Brave New World' (Adorno 1988a, p. 114).
144   Adorno 2000a, p. 28.
145   Adorno 2003x, p. 100.
146   Adorno 2007b, p. 304.

as the principle of identity prevails – a principle expressed economically in the exchange of like for like, and in a broader sense leads to the rupture between object and subject.

Adorno's critique of political economy is the critique of a society which is still the constant result of an historical progression – a progression which, in all of its immanent dynamics, remains a static whole insofar as it does not move beyond itself, but rather is always only a means to its own end: progress-in-and-for-itself. Adorno recognises that the weakness of the critique of economy as practiced by Marx is that it falls back into a 'reified and often truly "economistic" mode of thinking', and thereby falls victim to a 'fetishisation of the sphere of economy'.[147] Against this, Adorno seeks

> to bring out the dialectical core of Marxian economy – which it contains, so to speak, in spite of itself – and to show that the decisive concepts such as commodity, forces of production, and rate of profit really do 'move themselves'. Yet this is only possible if they are not conceived of as a system of national economy, not even as the representation of the capitalist economy's laws of development, as Marx himself intended, but rather as objectively controlled by the critical intention at their conceptual core. Marx did not want to describe the dynamics of free and just exchange; rather, he plays the melody to 'Se vuol ballare': you speak of free and just exchange – fine, you shall have it, but in the process it will be revealed that precisely by fulfilling its concept, it becomes the opposite of free and just exchange, that its sense namely includes the appropriation of surplus-value. Put less economistically: elevated to a totality, the exchange-relation results in the class-relation. Equal is unequal. And this core, which is of course the last thing orthodox exegetes of Marx will admit, we indeed regard as dialectical.[148]

Although the capitalist mode of production represents a radical break with all previous relations of production, this mode of production itself ultimately remains within the continuity of subjects' domination over objects. For Ador-

---

147   Letter from Adorno to Jürgen von Kempski, 27 January 1950 (Braunstein 2010a, p. 256).

148   Ibid. While 'Se vuol ballare' ('If you want to dance, my little count') – an aria from Mozart's *Marriage of Figaro* – is also cited by Marx and Engels in an article in the *Neue Rheinische Zeitung* from 12 August 1848 (Marx and Engels 1977, p. 384), Adorno was probably made aware of the phrase by the introduction of the 'Critique of Hegel's Philosophy of Right', according to which the 'petrified conditions must be made to dance by singing to them their own melody' (Marx 2007, p. 60).

no, the primary principle of all domination is that of identity, whose economic derivative is equivalence, the index of all measurement.

Adorno's critique of economy is a critique of economy in general, which, as a thing-in-itself, is the universal rationality for all, a rationality present in those meta-economic principles around which the world is forcibly arranged. Because negative utopia is just as all-encompassing as its 'positive' inverse, material critique, it sustains 'all its hopes as worries'.[149] Its rigidity owes to the desire to transcend critique and utopia in one: in the reconciled state, both would no longer be necessary.

Something's missing, and not something which can already be conceived, let alone articulated, in the here and now. Just as realised utopia does not await its emanation from beyond, neither can an image or concept of this utopia be revealed. Between what currently exists and realised utopia there would necessarily be a rupture, yet this rupture would be accomplished by a continuity with what exists,[150] and ensured by determinate negation, without which it cannot happen. For Adorno, what follows this rupture is not a 'positive absolute',[151] as Horkheimer hopes in his late phase, but rather something which can only be created by human beings. Precisely for this reason, hope does not rely on a notion of will understood as akin to a divinity. Instead, hope attaches itself to the determinate negation of what exists by virtue of a practice whose possibility must nevertheless first be established.

---

149   Schuh 2006, p. 327.
150   Precisely this strength of the Adornian concept of utopia – its refusal to bow down to what appears possible in the here and now for the sake of practical expedience – is lamented by Kracauer in a letter to Löwenthal, and characterised as a weakness: according to Kracauer, the concept of utopia in Adorno's work is 'entirely impermissible' insofar as it is 'used as a pure limiting concept (*Grenzbegriff*) which lacks even the slightest substance. Ah, he doesn't see utopia' (letter from Kracauer to Löwenthal, 15 February 1960 [Löwenthal and Kracauer 2003, p. 227]).
151   Horkheimer 1985b, p. 386; cf. Ries 1976, p. 71.

CHAPTER 14

Raison d'être

> A series of sliding transitions leads from the sacrifice of one's own
> mother, which is supposed to deliver to the future sorcerer his rack-
> et, to the dissertation at universities by which the adept individual
> proves that his thinking, feeling and speaking had irrevocably adop-
> ted the forms of the academic racket.
>
> HORKHEIMER, Die Rackets und der Geist

∴

As a philosopher, sociologist, musicologist, theorist of art and – unjustifiably –
above all as a cultural critic,[1] Adorno has become enshrined in death as a classic representative of European intellectual life. This has not only occurred in
academia, but also in the cultural sector itself. However, the vast majority of
references reduce the fact that he was a radical critic of the relations of production to a footnote. Even well-meaning commentators either dispute his engagement with economics, or trivialise it relative to his achievements in other areas.
Adorno was never bothered with political economy, it is alleged.[2] Given that
scholarship on Adorno has pursued a remarkable variety of issues, thoroughly
typical assessments such as these give rise to the suspicion that scholars have
sheepishly turned a blind eye to their subject's critique of political economy.
Ironically, it was Jürgen Habermas who sensed a 'hidden orthodoxy' in Adorno's
work: 'In the esoteric fabric of aesthetic reflections lingers something like the
echo of a Critique of Political Economy'.[3] Yet what Habermas himself failed to
mention was that this was not a matter of an embarrassing return of a repressed
theoretical inheritance, but rather of an historically (and theoretically) justified re-appropriation: an ongoing and – in the 1950s and 1960s – even intensive
engagement with the Marxian critique of economy. Adorno might qualify as

---

1 'I shudder to find myself referred to as a cultural critic. This really does remind one a bit of
   the profession of a pimp, for a cultural critic in fact really is someone who lives from what he
   exploits and simultaneously abuses. I'd like nothing to do with this' (Adorno 1964, p. 56).
2 Cf. Habermas 1991, p. 109; see Chapter 1 of the present study.
3 Habermas 1988, p. 203; see Chapter 10 of the present study.

orthodox insofar as for him, the 'production paradigm'[4] rejected by Habermas formed the centre to which every one of his own most popularly cited judgements on art, culture and society referred – even though this centre was not unalterably fixed, but rather had to be constantly defined anew, precisely in relation to art, culture and society. Given what the present study has shown, the supposed hiddenness of Adorno's orthodoxy – perhaps one reason why even Marxist commentators generally underestimate the significance of the critique of economy for Adorno's Critical Theory – can be interpreted as stemming from the fact that up until now, numerous texts which prove that this orthodoxy is anything but hidden have either not been published at all, or have only been published on a modest scale. For this reason in particular, this study has quoted extensively from still largely unknown writings and notes.

Adorno's Critical Theory cannot be understood apart from his critique of economy. Adorno did not attack culture, incidentally an extremely easy target, without offending the powers with which cultural critics in particular all too readily make common cause; he criticised society while at the same time conceiving of culture as its defective product and potential antithesis. The materialist critique of society to which he aspired necessarily includes a critique of the relations of production. Accordingly, Adorno's works in philosophy, sociology and art theory, as well as his writings on music and literary theory and his essays on psychoanalysis, should above all be viewed as models of a critique of political economy developed in the manner of a social theory. An interpretation which seeks to reduce them to this alone would certainly fall short, whereas one which omits this central motif goes astray. This thesis inevitably implies that Adorno did in fact deal specifically with economic issues as well: not with the kinds of questions which fall under the domain of the scholarly discipline referred to as economics (*Wirtschaftswissenschaften*) yet indeed with the sociotheoretically elementary meaning of economy (*Ökonomie*) in a broader sense.

Adorno's reception of Marxian writings was actually always orthodox – yet certainly not in the sense of respecting the Marxian critique of economy as either an ineluctable or ultimate state of knowledge with universal applicability. In his engagement with the capitalist mode of production in general and the late-capitalist society of his time in particular, Adorno did not accept the authority of scripture, and he at times contradicted not only schools of Marxist thought, but also Marx himself. Here as well, Adorno underwent a development and certainly progressed in his own understanding – a comparison of his early work with his later writings shows this. Just as there is no one Ador-

---

4 Cf. Habermas 1998.

nian Marxism which reached maturity at a particular point in time, so too is
there no eternally valid programme of Critical Theory which was set down
at a particular point in time and only fleshed out in later years. If one recognises in Adorno's 1931 inaugural lecture something of the 'dreamlike anticipation'[5] which Adorno himself retrospectively identified in his early writings,
one should surely assume that the work, which was drafted there in a dreamlike manner, still had to be done. While on the journey supposedly mapped out
in his early writings, it need not be said that Adorno was forced to take heed
of historical reality. Yet history also took place in the theory which he appropriated and advanced – and the critique of economy which Adorno engaged
with repeatedly from the 1930s onward, and from which he conceived of novel
interventions in seemingly remote areas such as language and literature, must
be viewed in particular as leading the way in this history. The development
of Adorno's Critical Theory can only be understood in view of his progressive
examination of economy, in whose rationality he discovered the 'formula used
to bewitch the world'.[6]

The still widespread view that the recourse in Adorno's work to Marx, and
especially to Marx's critique of political economy, represents a relic from short-
lived stages in the development of Adorno's own theory – a relic which Adorno
dragged along on his return from America as if it were a valuable antique – can
be refuted on the basis of relevant textual documents. This is also true of the
common assumption that Adorno never engaged especially intensively with
the Marxian critique of political economy in any case. With Adorno's career
as a theorist serving as point of reference, this study has shown in detail what
prompted him to grapple with respective aspects of the critique of political economy, and how this strongly influenced his further theoretical work in turn.

Not least due to his study of Marx, Adorno perceived as contingent the
allegedly eternal, including what economy represents: the metabolism within
society as well as between society and nature, a metabolism whose purpose is
society's own reproduction. He accepted as eternal constants neither this metabolism, nor nature under the spell of the total society – just as he refused to
accept the total society itself. The lie contained within the claim of equivalence
and identity, a lie which leads to originary philosophy (*Ursprungsphilosophie*)
and systems-thinking, asserts itself in society as the principle of exchange,
the principle mediating and perpetuating domination. Revolutionary practice,
which would need to transcend the society recognised as false, was viewed

---

5   Letter from Adorno to Ernst Bloch, 1962 (Tiedemann 2003a, p. 384); translation from Buck-
    Morss 1977, p. xii.
6   Adorno 1976d, p. 80.

by Adorno as indefinitely postponed, rendered immediately impossible by the totality of political economy. The horizon against which Adorno's social critique – that is, his critique of political economy – first comes into view at all constitutes something which for its own part can never again be rationalised: the other of the total immanence of what exists. Where everything is wrong, what would alone be right is not present, and cannot be depicted: a negative utopia as the 'raison d'être of *raison*'.[7] The frequent question of whether emancipatory reforms should then generally be rejected compels the tautological answer that a better world would be better than a worse one, even if the former were itself not yet good. For Adorno in any case, the indefinite foreclosure of the path to a liberated society was no reason to reject any and all practice out of resignation.[8] Participation is betrayal, but whoever does nothing flees into the quietism urged from all sides. Adorno's efforts were directed towards preventing the worst while hoping for the best. The claim that there is no right life in wrong life means one must fight within the wrong life, against one's own powerlessness, for a right life. According to both Adorno and the existing state of affairs, this is a fight which would be able to be most effectively waged with a critical social theory. 'Today, precisely the overwhelming supremacy of that which now simply exists has become blindness, ideology, and what I mean is that it is up to the responsible spirit to wage resistance precisely at this site, in the sense meant by Marx when he spoke of the ruthless criticism of all that exists more than a century ago. It seems to me that the duty to do so grows proportionally to the irresistibility of what simply exists'.[9]

7 Adorno 2002a, p. 331; cf. Schwarz 1980, p. 457.
8 Be it noted that Adorno was not merely a resident of the ivory tower, but attempted over the course of approximately 600 speeches, public conversations and interviews to bring his Critical Theory into effect (cf. Schwarz 2009, p. 15).
9 Letter from Adorno to Konrad Körte, 26 March 1968, TWA, Br. 782/5. In 1843, Marx wrote of the '*ruthless criticism of all that exists*' (Marx 1975c, p. 142). In multiple passages in his own work, Adorno makes recourse to this Marxian phrase to elaborate his own understanding of critique, something he does succinctly in 'Kritik des Musikanten': 'Not everything which goes to the extreme in one dimension or another is radical. Rather, only that is radical which, in "ruthless critique of what exists", attacks the negative condition at its root' (Adorno 2003p, p. 92).

Bibliography

Archives

MHA   Estate of Max Horkheimer in the Archivzentrum der Universitätsbibliothek J.C. Senckenberg, Frankfurt am Main.
TWA   Theodor W. Adorno Archiv, Frankfurt am Main.

Works

Adorno, Gretel and Walter Benjamin 2008 [2005], *Correspondence 1930–1940*, edited by Henri Lonitz and Christoph Gödde, translated by Wieland Hoban, Cambridge: Polity.

Adorno, Theodor W. 1938, 'Über den Fetischcharakter in der Musik und die Regression des Hörens', *Zeitschrift für Sozialforschung*, 7, 3: 321–56.

Adorno, Theodor W. 1939, 'On Kierkegaard's Doctrine of Love', *Studies in Philosophy and Social Science* [*Zeitschrift für Sozialforschung*], 8, 3: 413–29.

Adorno, Theodor W. 1941, 'Spengler Today', *Studies in Philosophy and Social Science* [*Zeitschrift für Sozialforschung*], 9, 2: 305–25.

Adorno, Theodor W. 1961, '"Static" and "Dynamic" as Sociological Categories', translated by H. Kaal, *Diogenes*, 9, 33: 28–49.

Adorno, Theodor W. 1964, 'Laienkunst – organisierte Banausie?', in *Europa-Gespräch 1963. Die Europäische Groß-Stadt. Licht und Irrlicht*, edited by 'Amt für Kultur, Volksbildung und Schulverwaltung der Stadt Wien', Vienna: Verlag für Jugend und Volk.

Adorno, Theodor W. 1967 [1955], 'Sociology and Psychology (Part I)', translated by Irving N. Wohlfarth, *New Left Review* I/46: 67–80.

Adorno, Theodor W. 1972 [1954], 'Ideology', in *Aspects of Sociology*, edited by the Frankfurt Institute for Social Research, translated by John Viertel, Boston: Beacon.

Adorno, Theodor W. 1973 [1964], *The Jargon of Authenticity*, translated by Knut Tarnowski and Frederic Will, Evanston: Northwestern University Press.

Adorno, Theodor W. 1974a, *Philosophische Terminologie. Zur Einleitung*, Volume 2, edited by Rudolf zur Lippe, Frankfurt am Main: Suhrkamp.

Adorno, Theodor W. 1974b [1957], 'The Stars Down to Earth: The *Los Angeles Times* Astronomy Column', *Telos*, 19: 13–90.

Adorno, Theodor W. 1975 [1967], 'Culture Industry Reconsidered', translated by Anson G. Rabinbach, *New German Critique*, 6: 12–19.

Adorno, Theodor W. 1976a [1969], 'Introduction', in Theodor W. Adorno, Hans Albert, Ralf Dahrendorf, Jürgen Habermas, Harald Pilot and Karl R. Popper, *The Positivist*

Dispute in German Sociology, translated by Glyn Adey and David Frisby, London: Heinemann.

Adorno, Theodor W. 1976b [1962], *Introduction to the Sociology of Music*, translated by E.B. Ashton, New York: Seabury.

Adorno, Theodor W. 1976c [1962], 'On the Logic of the Social Sciences', in Theodor W. Adorno, Hans Albert, Ralf Dahrendorf, Jürgen Habermas, Harald Pilot and Karl R. Popper, *The Positivist Dispute in German Sociology*, translated by Glyn Adey and David Frisby, London: Heinemann.

Adorno, Theodor W. 1976d [1969], 'Sociology and Empirical Research', in Theodor W. Adorno, Hans Albert, Ralf Dahrendorf, Jürgen Habermas, Harald Pilot and Karl R. Popper, *The Positivist Dispute in German Sociology*, translated by Glyn Adey and David Frisby, London: Heinemann.

Adorno, Theodor W. 1977 [1974], 'The Actuality of Philosophy', translated by Benjamin Snow, *Telos*, 31: 120–33.

Adorno, Theodor W. 1978a [1960], 'Culture and Administration', translated by Wes Blomster, *Telos*, 37: 93–111.

Adorno, Theodor W. 1978b [1969], 'Resignation', translated by Wes Blomster, *Telos*, 35: 165–8.

Adorno, Theodor W. 1978c [1956], 'The Metacritique of Epistemology', translated by Michael B. Allen, *Telos*, 38: 77–103.

Adorno, Theodor W. 1979, *Der Schatz des Indianer-Joe. Singspiel nach Mark Twain*, Frankfurt am Main: Suhrkamp.

Adorno, Theodor W. 1984 [1973], 'The Idea of Natural History', translated by Robert Hullot-Kentor, *Telos*, 60: 111–24.

Adorno, Theodor W. 1988a [1951], 'Aldous Huxley and Utopia', in *Prisms*, translated by Samuel and Shierry Weber, Cambridge, MA: MIT Press.

Adorno, Theodor W. 1988b [1950], 'A Portrait of Walter Benjamin', in *Prisms*, translated by Samuel and Shierry Weber, Cambridge, MA: MIT Press.

Adorno, Theodor W. 1988c [1955], 'Cultural Criticism and Society', in *Prisms*, translated by Samuel and Shierry Weber, Cambridge, MA: MIT Press.

Adorno, Theodor W. 1988d [1955], 'Notes on Kafka', in *Prisms*, translated by Samuel and Shierry Weber, Cambridge, MA: MIT Press.

Adorno, Theodor W. 1988e [1953], 'Perennial Fashion – Jazz', in *Prisms*, translated by Samuel and Shierry Weber, Cambridge, MA: MIT Press.

Adorno, Theodor W. 1988f [1953], 'The Sociology of Knowledge and Its Consciousness', in *Prisms*, translated by Samuel and Shierry Weber, Cambridge, MA: MIT Press.

Adorno, Theodor W. 1989 [1966], 'Society', translated by F.R. Jameson, in *Critical Theory and Society: A Reader*, edited by Stephen Eric Bronner and Douglas MacKay Kellner, London: Routledge.

Adorno, Theodor W. 1993a [1963], 'Aspects of Hegel's Philosophy', in *Hegel: Three Studies*, translated by Shierry Weber Nicholsen, Cambridge, MA: MIT Press.

Adorno, Theodor W. 1993b, 'Der Begriff der Philosophie. Vorlesung Wintersemester 1951/52. Mitschrift von Kraft Bretschneider', in *Frankfurter Adorno Blätter*, Volume II, edited by Rolf Tiedemann, Munich: edition text+kritik.

Adorno, Theodor W. 1993c [1963], 'Skoteinos, or How to Read Hegel', in *Hegel: Three Studies*, translated by Shierry Weber Nicholsen, Cambridge, MA: MIT Press.

Adorno, Theodor W. 1993d [1963], 'The Experiential Content of Hegel's Philosophy', in *Hegel: Three Studies*, translated by Shierry Weber Nicholsen, Cambridge, MA: MIT Press.

Adorno, Theodor W. 1995a, 'Adornos Seminar vom Sommersemester 1932 über Benjamins *Ursprung des deutschen Trauerspiels*. Protokolle', in *Frankfurter Adorno Blätter*, Volume IV, edited by Rolf Tiedemann, Munich: edition text+kritik.

Adorno, Theodor W. 1995b, 'Aus einem Schulheft ohne Deckel. Bar Harbor, Sommer 1939', in *Frankfurter Adorno Blätter*, Volume IV, edited by Rolf Tiedemann, Munich: edition text+kritik.

Adorno, Theodor W. 1996 [1960], *Mahler: A Musical Physiognomy*, translated by Edmund Jephcott, Chicago: The University of Chicago Press.

Adorno, Theodor W. 1997 [1967], 'Functionalism Today', translated by Jane Newman and John Smith, in *Rethinking Architecture: A Reader in Cultural Theory*, edited by Neil Leach, London: Routledge.

Adorno, Theodor W. 1998, 'Das Problem des Idealismus. Stichworte zur Vorlesung vom Wintersemester 1953/54 und Fragmente einer Nachschrift', in *Frankfurter Adorno Blätter*, Volume V, edited by Rolf Tiedemann, Munich: edition text+kritik.

Adorno, Theodor W. 1999a [1933], *Kierkegaard: Construction of the Aesthetic*, translated by Robert Hullot-Kentor, Minneapolis: University of Minnesota Press.

Adorno, Theodor W. 1999b [1932], 'Some Ideas on the Sociology of Music', in *Sound Figures*, translated by Rodney Livingstone, Stanford: Stanford University Press.

Adorno, Theodor W. 2000a [1968], *Introduction to Sociology*, edited by Christoph Gödde, translated by Edmund Jephcott, Stanford: Stanford University Press.

Adorno, Theodor W. 2000b [1998], *Metaphysics: Concept and Problems*, edited by Rolf Tiedemann, translated by Edmund Jephcott, Cambridge: Polity.

Adorno, Theodor W. 2000c [1996], *Problems of Moral Philosophy*, edited by Thomas Schröder, translated by Rodney Livingstone, Cambridge: Polity.

Adorno, Theodor W. 2001a [1969], 'Free Time', translated by James Gordon Finlayson and Nicholas Walker, in *The Culture Industry: Selected Essays on Mass Culture*, edited by J.M. Bernstein, London: Routledge.

Adorno, Theodor W. 2001b, 'Graeculus (1). Musikalische Notizen', in *Frankfurter Adorno Blätter*, Volume VII, edited by Rolf Tiedemann, Munich: edition text+kritik.

Adorno, Theodor W. 2001c [1995], *Kant's 'Critique of Pure Reason'*, edited by Rolf Tiedemann, translated by Rodney Livingstone, Cambridge: Polity.

Adorno, Theodor W. 2001d [1981], 'The Schema of Mass Culture', translated by Nicholas Walker, in *The Culture Industry: Selected Essays*, edited by J.M. Bernstein, London: Routledge.

Adorno, Theodor W. 2001e, *Zur Lehre von der Geschichte und von der Freiheit (1964/65)* [*Nachgelassene Schriften*, Section IV: *Vorlesungen*, Volume 13], edited by Rolf Tiedemann, Frankfurt am Main: Suhrkamp.

Adorno, Theodor W. 2002a [1970], *Aesthetic Theory*, edited by Gretel Adorno and Rolf Tiedemann, translated by Robert Hullot-Kentor, New York: Continuum.

Adorno, Theodor W. 2002b [1969], 'Who's Afraid of the Ivory Tower? A Conversation with Theodor W. Adorno', translated by Gerhard Richter, *Monatshefte*, 94, 1: 10–23.

Adorno, Theodor W. 2003a [1986], 'Ad Lukács', in *Gesammelte Schriften*, Volume 20.1, *Vermischte Schriften I*, edited by Rolf Tiedemann, Frankfurt am Main: Suhrkamp.

Adorno, Theodor W. 2003b [1972], 'Anmerkungen zum sozialen Konflikt heute. Nach zwei Seminaren', in *Gesammelte Schriften*, Volume 8, *Soziologische Schriften I*, edited by Rolf Tiedemann, Frankfurt am Main: Suhrkamp.

Adorno, Theodor W. 2003c, 'Aus einem Entwurf "Zur Neuausgabe" der *Dialektik der Aufklärung*. Frankfurt a.M., Februar 1969', in *Frankfurter Adorno Blätter*, Volume VIII, edited by Rolf Tiedemann, Munich: edition text+kritik.

Adorno, Theodor W. 2003d [1954], 'Bemerkungen über Politik und Neurose', in *Gesammelte Schriften*, Volume 8, *Soziologische Schriften I*, edited by Rolf Tiedemann, Frankfurt am Main: Suhrkamp.

Adorno, Theodor W. 2003e [1940], 'Carl E. Seashore, Psychology of Music', in *Gesammelte Schriften*, Volume 19, *Musikalische Schriften VI*, edited by Rolf Tiedemann, Frankfurt am Main: Suhrkamp.

Adorno, Theodor W. 2003f [1973], *Der Begriff des Unbewußten in der transzendentalen Seelenlehre*, in *Gesammelte Schriften*, Volume 1, *Philosophische Frühschriften*, edited by Rolf Tiedemann, Frankfurt am Main: Suhrkamp.

Adorno, Theodor W. 2003g [1963], *Der getreue Korrepetitor. Lehrschriften zur musikalischen Praxis*, in *Gesammelte Schriften*, Volume 15, *Komposition für den Film/Der getreue Korrepetitor*, edited by Rolf Tiedemann, Frankfurt am Main: Suhrkamp.

Adorno, Theodor W. 2003h [1973], *Die Transzendenz des Dinglichen und Noematischen in Husserls Phänomenologie*, in *Gesammelte Schriften*, Volume 1, *Philosophische Frühschriften*, edited by Rolf Tiedemann, Frankfurt am Main: Suhrkamp.

Adorno, Theodor W. 2003i [1972], 'Diskussionsbeitrag zu "Spätkapitalismus oder Industriegesellschaft?"', in *Gesammelte Schriften*, Volume 8, *Soziologische Schriften I*, edited by Rolf Tiedemann, Frankfurt am Main: Suhrkamp.

Adorno, Theodor W. 2003j [1967], 'Einleitung zu Emile Durkheim, *Soziologie und Philosophie*', in *Gesammelte Schriften*, Volume 8, *Soziologische Schriften I*, edited by Rolf Tiedemann, Frankfurt am Main: Suhrkamp.

Adorno, Theodor W. 2003k, 'Graeculus (II). Notizen zu Philosophie und Gesellschaft 1943–1969', in *Frankfurter Adorno Blätter*, Volume VIII, edited by Rolf Tiedemann, Munich: edition text+kritik.

Adorno, Theodor W. 2003l [1954], 'Individuum und Organisation. Einleitungsvortrag zum Darmstädter Gespräch 1953', in *Gesammelte Schriften*, Volume 8, *Soziologische Schriften I*, edited by Rolf Tiedemann, Frankfurt am Main: Suhrkamp.

Adorno, Theodor W. 2003m [1986], 'Karl Korn, Die Sprache in der verwalteten Welt', in *Gesammelte Schriften*, Volume 20.2, *Vermischte Schriften II*, edited by Rolf Tiedemann, Frankfurt am Main: Suhrkamp.

Adorno, Theodor W. 2003n [1963], 'Kierkegaard noch einmal', in *Kierkegaard. Konstruktion des Ästhetischen* [*Gesammelte Schriften*, Volume 2], edited by Rolf Tiedemann, Frankfurt am Main: Suhrkamp.

Adorno, Theodor W. 2003o [1969], 'Konzeption eines Wiener Operntheaters', in *Gesammelte Schriften*, Volume 19, *Musikalische Schriften VI*, edited by Rolf Tiedemann, Frankfurt am Main: Suhrkamp.

Adorno, Theodor W. 2003p [1954], 'Kritik des Musikanten', in *Gesammelte Schriften*, Volume 14, *Dissonanzen/Einleitung in die Musiksoziologie*, edited by Rolf Tiedemann, Frankfurt am Main: Suhrkamp.

Adorno, Theodor W. 2003q [1969], 'Late Capitalism or Industrial Society? The Fundamental Question of the Present Structure of Society', in *Can One Live After Auschwitz? A Philosophical Reader*, edited by Rolf Tiedemann, translated by Rodney Livingstone, Stanford: Stanford University Press.

Adorno, Theodor W. 2003r [1951], *Minima Moralia. Reflexionen aus dem beschädigten Leben* [*Gesammelte Schriften*, Volume 4], edited by Rolf Tiedemann, Frankfurt am Main: Suhrkamp.

Adorno, Theodor W. 2003s [1962], 'Nachruf auf einen Organisator', in *Gesammelte Schriften*, Volume 10.1, *Kulturkritik und Gesellschaft I*, edited by Rolf Tiedemann, Frankfurt am Main: Suhrkamp.

Adorno, Theodor W. 2003t [1962], 'Notiz', in *Kierkegaard. Konstruktion des Ästhetischen* [*Gesammelte Schriften*, Volume 2], edited by Rolf Tiedemann, Frankfurt am Main: Suhrkamp.

Adorno, Theodor W. 2003u [1965], 'Notiz über sozialwissenschaftliche Objektivität', in *Gesammelte Schriften*, Volume 8, *Soziologische Schriften I*, edited by Rolf Tiedemann, Frankfurt am Main: Suhrkamp.

Adorno, Theodor W. 2003v [1965], 'Offener Brief an Max Horkheimer', in *Gesammelte Schriften*, Volume 20.1, *Vermischte Schriften I*, edited by Rolf Tiedemann, Frankfurt am Main: Suhrkamp.

Adorno, Theodor W. 2003w, 'Pontius als Reichsstatthalter', in *Adorno. Eine Bildmonographie*, edited by the Theodor W. Adorno Archive, Frankfurt am Main: Suhrkamp.

Adorno, Theodor W. 2003x [1972], 'Reflections on Class Theory', in *Can One Live After*

Auschwitz? A Philosophical Reader, edited by Rolf Tiedemann, translated by Rodney Livingstone, Stanford: Stanford University Press.

Adorno, Theodor W. 2003y, 'Reise im Frühjahr 1961', in *Adorno. Eine Bildmonographie*, Frankfurt am Main: Suhrkamp.

Adorno, Theodor W. 2003z, *"So müßte ich ein Engel und kein Autor sein". Adorno und seine Frankfurter Verleger. Der Briefwechsel mit Peter Suhrkamp und Siegfried Unseld*, edited by Wolfgang Schopf, Frankfurt am Main: Suhrkamp.

Adorno, Theodor W. 2003aa [1957], 'Teamwork in der Sozialforschung', in *Gesammelte Schriften*, Volume 8, *Soziologische Schriften I*, edited by Rolf Tiedemann, Frankfurt am Main: Suhrkamp.

Adorno, Theodor W. 2003ab, 'Theorie der Gesellschaft. Stichworte und Entwürfe zur Vorlesung 1949/50', in *Frankfurter Adorno Blätter*, Volume VIII, edited by Rolf Tiedemann, Munich: edition text+kritik.

Adorno, Theodor W. 2003ac [1973], 'Thesen gegen die musikpädagogische Musik', in *Gesammelte Schriften*, Volume 14, *Dissonanzen/Einleitung in die Musiksoziologie*, edited by Rolf Tiedemann, Frankfurt am Main: Suhrkamp.

Adorno, Theodor W. 2003ad [1938], 'Über den Fetischcharakter der Musik und die Regression des Hörens', in *Gesammelte Schriften*, Volume 14, *Dissonanzen/Einleitung in die Musiksoziologie*, edited by Rolf Tiedemann, Frankfurt am Main: Suhrkamp.

Adorno, Theodor W. 2003ae [1986], 'Vorworte, Vorreden und Vorbemerkungen zu den "Frankfurter Beiträgen zur Soziologie"', in *Gesammelte Schriften*, Volume 20.2, *Vermischte Schriften II*, edited by Rolf Tiedemann, Frankfurt am Main: Suhrkamp.

Adorno, Theodor W. 2003af [1967], 'Wien, nach Ostern 1967', in *Gesammelte Schriften*, Volume 10.1, *Kulturkritik und Gesellschaft I*, edited by Rolf Tiedemann, Frankfurt am Main: Suhrkamp.

Adorno, Theodor W. 2004a, 'Ad Chaplin und Hitler', in Theodor W. Adorno and Max Horkheimer, *Briefwechsel 1938–1944*, [Theodor Adorno, *Briefe und Briefwechsel*, Volume 4.II], edited by Christoph Gödde and Henri Lonitz, Frankfurt am Main: Suhrkamp.

Adorno, Theodor W. 2004b [1981], 'The Schema of Mass Culture', translated by Nicholas Walker, in *The Culture Industry: Selected Essays*, edited by J.M. Bernstein, London: Routledge.

Adorno, Theodor W. 2005a [1969], 'Critique', in *Critical Models: Interventions and Catchwords*, translated by Henry W. Pickford, New York: Columbia University Press.

Adorno, Theodor W. 2005b [1951], *Minima Moralia: Reflections from Damaged Life*, translated by E.F.N. Jephcott, London: Verso.

Adorno, Theodor W. 2005c [1951], *Minima Moralia: Reflections from Damaged Life*, translated by Dennis Redmond, available at: https://www.marxists.org/reference/archive/adorno/1951/mm/ch01.htm.

Adorno, Theodor W. 2005d [1977], 'On Subject and Object', in *Critical Models: Interven-*

tions and Catchwords, translated by Henry W. Pickford, New York: Columbia University Press.

Adorno, Theodor W. 2005e [1962], 'Philosophy and Teachers', in *Critical Models: Interventions and Catchwords*, translated by Henry W. Pickford, New York: Columbia University Press.

Adorno, Theodor W. 2005f [1969], 'Progress', in *Critical Models: Interventions and Catchwords*, translated by Henry W. Pickford, New York: Columbia University Press.

Adorno, Theodor W. 2005g [1969], 'Prologue to Television', in *Critical Models: Interventions and Catchwords*, translated by Henry W. Pickford, New York: Columbia University Press.

Adorno, Theodor W. 2005h [1969], 'Scientific Experiences of a European Scholar in America', in *Critical Models: Interventions and Catchwords*, translated by Henry W. Pickford, New York: Columbia University Press.

Adorno, Theodor W. 2005i [1959], 'The Meaning of Working Through the Past', in *Critical Models: Interventions and Catchwords*, translated by Henry W. Pickford, New York: Columbia University Press.

Adorno, Theodor W. 2006a [2001], *History and Freedom: Lectures 1964–1965*, edited by Rolf Tiedemann, translated by Rodney Livingstone, Cambridge: Polity.

Adorno, Theodor W. 2006b [2003], *Letters to his Parents 1939–1951*, edited by Christoph Gödde and Henri Lonitz, translated by Wieland Hoban, Cambridge: Polity.

Adorno, Theodor W. 2006c [1958], 'Reconciliation under Duress', in Theodor W. Adorno, Walter Benjamin, Ernst Bloch, Bertolt Brecht and Georg Lukács, *Aesthetics and Politics*, London: Verso.

Adorno, Theodor W. 2006d [2001], *Towards a Theory of Musical Reproduction: Notes, a Draft and Two Schemata*, edited by Henri Lonitz, translated by Wieland Hoban, Cambridge: Polity.

Adorno, Theodor W. 2007a [1993], *Beethoven: The Philosophy of Music*, edited by Rolf Tiedemann, translated by Edmund Jephcott, Cambridge: Polity.

Adorno, Theodor W. 2007b [1966], *Negative Dialectics*, translated by E.B. Ashton, New York: Continuum.

Adorno, Theodor W. 2007c [1949], *Philosophy of New Music*, translated by Robert Hullot-Kentor, Minneapolis: University of Minnesota Press.

Adorno, Theodor W. 2007d [1973], 'Theses on the Language of the Philosopher', translated by Samir Gandesha and Michael K. Palamarek, in *Adorno and the Need in Thinking: New Critical Essays*, edited by Donald A. Burke, Colin J. Campbell, Kathy Kiloh, Michael K. Palamarek, and Jonathan Short, Toronto: University of Toronto Press.

Adorno, Theodor W. 2008 [2003], *Lectures on Negative Dialectics: Fragments of a lecture course 1965/1966*, edited by Rolf Tiedemann, translated by Rodney Livingstone, Cambridge: Polity.

Adorno, Theodor W. 2009a [1952], *In Search of Wagner*, translated by Rodney Livingstone, London: Verso.

Adorno, Theodor W. 2009b [1953], 'On the Contemporary Relationship of Philosophy and Music', translated by Susan H. Gillespie, in *Essays on Music*, edited by Richard Leppert, Berkeley: University of California Press.

Adorno, Theodor W. 2009c [1938], 'On the Fetish-Character in Music and the Regression of Listening', translated by Maurice Goldbloom, in *Essays on Music*, edited by Richard Leppert, Berkeley: University of California Press.

Adorno, Theodor W. 2009d [1932], 'On the Social Situation of Music', translated by Wes Blomster, in *Essays on Music*, edited by Richard Leppert, Berkeley: University of California Press.

Adorno, Theodor W. 2009e [1955], 'The Aging of the New Music', translated by Robert Hullot-Kentor and Frederic Will, in *Essays on Music*, edited by Richard Leppert, Berkeley: University of California Press.

Adorno, Theodor W. 2013 [1956], *Against Epistemology: A Metacritique*, translated by Willis Domingo, Cambridge: Polity.

Adorno, Theodor W. 2017a [2010], *An Introduction to Dialectics*, edited by Christoph Ziermann, translated by Nicholas Walker, Cambridge: Polity.

Adorno, Theodor W. 2017b [2004], 'Contra Paulum', translated by Bryan Wagoner, in Bryan Wagoner, *Prophetic Interruptions: Critical Theory, Emancipation, and Religion in Paul Tillich, Theodor Adorno, and Max Horkheimer (1929–1944)*, Macon: Mercer University Press.

Adorno, Theodor W. 2017c [1972], 'Theses on Need', translated by Martin Shuster and Iain Macdonald, *Adorno Studies*, 1, 1: 101–4.

Adorno, Theodor W. 2018a [2009], *Aesthetics*, edited by Eberhard Ortland, translated by Wieland Hoban, Cambridge: Polity

Adorno, Theodor W. 2018b [unauthorised publication in 1973], *Erkenntnistheorie (1957/58)* [*Nachgelassene Schriften*, Section IV: *Vorlesungen*, Volume 1], edited by Karel Markus, Frankfurt am Main: Suhrkamp.

Adorno, Theodor W. 2018c [1997], 'Theodor W. Adorno on "Marx and the Basic Concepts of Sociological Theory": From a Seminar Transcript in the Summer Semester of 1962', translated by Verena Erlenbusch-Anderson and Chris O'Kane, *Historical Materialism*, 26, 1: 154–64.

Adorno, Theodor W. 2019a [1965], 'Bibliographical Musings', in *Notes to Literature*, edited by Rolf Tiedemann, translated by Shierry Weber Nicholsen, New York: Columbia University Press.

Adorno, Theodor W. 2019b [1960], 'Ernst Bloch's *Spuren*: On the Revised Edition of 1959', in *Notes to Literature*, edited by Rolf Tiedemann, translated by Shierry Weber Nicholsen, New York: Columbia University Press.

Adorno, Theodor W. 2019c [1955], 'Introduction to Benjamin's *Schriften*', in *Notes to*

Literature, edited by Rolf Tiedemann, translated by Shierry Weber Nicholsen, New York: Columbia University Press.

Adorno, Theodor W. 2019d [1965], 'Morals and Criminality: On the Eleventh Volume of the Works of Karl Kraus', in *Notes to Literature*, edited by Rolf Tiedemann, translated by Shierry Weber Nicholsen, New York: Columbia University Press.

Adorno, Theodor W. 2019e [1936], 'On Jazz', in *Night Music: Essays on Music*, edited by Rolf Tiedemann, translated by Wieland Hoban, Kolkata: Seagull Books.

Adorno, Theodor W. 2019f [1967], 'On the Classicism of Goethe's *Iphigenie*', in *Notes to Literature*, edited by Rolf Tiedemann, translated by Shierry Weber Nicholsen, New York: Columbia University Press.

Adorno, Theodor W. 2019g [1959], 'On the Final Scene of Faust', in *Notes to Literature*, edited by Rolf Tiedemann, translated by Shierry Weber Nicholsen, New York: Columbia University Press.

Adorno, Theodor W. 2019h [2002], *Ontology and Dialectics: 1960/61*, edited by Rolf Tiedemann, translated by Nicholas Walker, Cambridge: Polity.

Adorno, Theodor W. 2019i [2008], *Philosophical Elements of a Theory of Society*, edited by Tobias ten Brink and Marc Phillip Nogueira, translated by Wieland Hoban, Cambridge: Polity

Adorno, Theodor W. 2019j, 'Presuppositions: On the Occasion of Reading by Hans G. Helms', in *Notes to Literature*, edited by Rolf Tiedemann, translated by Shierry Weber Nicholsen, New York: Columbia University Press.

Adorno, Theodor W. 2019k [1958], 'Short Commentaries on Proust', in *Notes to Literature*, edited by Rolf Tiedemann, translated by Shierry Weber Nicholsen, New York: Columbia University Press.

Adorno, Theodor W. 2019l [1964], 'The Curious Realist: On Siegfried Kracauer', in *Notes to Literature*, edited by Rolf Tiedemann, translated by Shierry Weber Nicholsen, New York: Columbia University Press.

Adorno, Theodor W. 2019m [1965], 'The Handle, the Pot, and Early Experience', in *Notes to Literature*, edited by Rolf Tiedemann, translated by Shierry Weber Nicholsen, New York: Columbia University Press.

Adorno, Theodor W. 2019n [1961], 'Trying to Understand Endgame', in *Notes to Literature*, edited by Rolf Tiedemann, translated by Shierry Weber Nicholsen, New York: Columbia University Press.

Adorno, Theodor W. 2019o [1961], 'Valéry's Deviations', in *Notes to Literature*, edited by Rolf Tiedemann, translated by Shierry Weber Nicholsen, New York: Columbia University Press.

Adorno, Theodor W. 2021a, *Die Frankfurter Seminare Theodor W. Adornos. Gesammelte Sitzungsprotokolle 1949–1969*, four volumes, edited by Dirk Braunstein, Berlin: De Gruyter.

Adorno, Theodor W. 2021b, *Fragen der Dialektik*, edited by Christoph Ziermann, Frankfurt am Main: Suhrkamp.

Adorno, Theodor W. 2022 [2011], *Philosophy and Sociology*, edited by Dirk Braunstein, translated by Nicholas Walker, Cambridge: Polity.

Adorno, Theodor W., Günther Anders, Bertolt Brecht, Hanns Eisler, Max Horkheimer, Herbert Marcuse, Ludwig Marcuse, Nbg., Friedrich Pollock, Hans Reichenbach, Berthold Viertel 1985, 'Diskussionen aus einem Seminar über die Theorie der Bedürfnisse', in Max Horkheimer, *Gesammelte Schriften*, Volume 12, *Nachgelassene Schriften 1931–1949*, edited by Gunzelin Schmid Noerr, Frankfurt am Main: Fischer.

Adorno, Theodor W. and Walter Benjamin 1999 [1994], *The Complete Correspondence, 1928–1940*, edited by Henri Lonitz, translated by Nicholas Walker, Cambridge: Polity.

Adorno, Theodor W. and Alban Berg 2005 [1997], *Correspondence 1925–1935*, edited by Henri Lonitz, translated by Wieland Hoban, Cambridge: Polity.

Adorno, Theodor W. and Ernst Bloch 1989 [1978], 'Something's Missing: A Discussion between Ernst Bloch and Theodor W. Adorno on the Contradictions of Utopian Longing', in Ernst Bloch, *The Utopian Function of Art and Literature: Selected Essays*, translated by Jack Zipes and Frank Mecklenburg, Cambridge, MA: MIT Press.

Adorno, Theodor W. and Erich Doflein 2006, *Briefwechsel. Mit einem Radiogespräch von 1951 und drei Aufsätzen Erich Dofleins*, edited by Andreas Jacob, Hildesheim: Olms.

Adorno, Theodor W. and Hanns Eisler 2005 [1947], *Composing for the Films*, New York: Continuum.

Adorno, Theodor W., Hans-Georg Gadamer and Max Horkheimer 1989, 'Über Nietzsche und uns. Zum 10. Todestag des Philosophen', in Max Horkheimer, *Gesammelte Schriften*, Volume 14, *Nachgelassene Schriften 1949–1972*, edited by Gunzelin Schmid Noerr, Frankfurt am Main: Fischer.

Adorno, Theodor W. and Max Horkheimer 1985a, 'Diskussion über die Differenz zwischen Positivismus und materialistischer Dialektik', in Max Horkheimer, *Gesammelte Schriften*, Volume 12, *Nachgelassene Schriften 1931–1949*, edited by Gunzelin Schmid Noerr, Frankfurt am Main: Fischer.

Adorno, Theodor W. and Max Horkheimer 1985b, 'Diskussion über Sprache und Erkenntnis, Naturbeherrschung am Menschen, politische Aspekte des Marxismus', in Max Horkheimer, *Gesammelte Schriften*, Volume 12, *Nachgelassene Schriften 1931–1949*, edited by Gunzelin Schmid Noerr, Frankfurt am Main: Fischer.

Adorno, Theodor W. and Max Horkheimer 2002 [1948], *Dialectic of Enlightenment: Philosophical Fragments*, edited by Gunzelin Schmid Noerr, translated by Edmund Jephcott, Stanford: Stanford University Press.

Adorno, Theodor W. and Max Horkheimer 2003a [1962], 'Alfred Schmidt, Der Begriff der Natur in der Lehre von Marx', in Theodor W. Adorno, *Gesammelte Schriften*, Volume 20.1, *Vermischte Schriften II*, edited by Rolf Tiedemann, Frankfurt am Main: Suhrkamp.

Adorno, Theodor W. and Max Horkheimer 2003b, *Briefwechsel*, Volume I, 1927–1937

[Theodor W. Adorno, *Briefe und Briefwechsel*, Volume 4.i], edited by Christoph Gödde and Henri Lonitz, Frankfurt am Main: Suhrkamp.

Adorno, Theodor W. and Max Horkheimer 2004, *Briefwechsel*, Volume ii, *1938–1944* [Theodor Adorno, *Briefe und Briefwechsel*, Volume 4.ii], edited by Christoph Gödde and Henri Lonitz, Frankfurt am Main: Suhrkamp.

Adorno, Theodor W. and Max Horkheimer 2005, *Briefwechsel*, Volume iii, *1945–1949* [Theodor W. Adorno, *Briefe und Briefwechsel*, Volume 4.iii], edited by Christoph Gödde and Henri Lonitz, Frankfurt am Main: Suhrkamp.

Adorno, Theodor W. and Max Horkheimer 2006, *Briefwechsel*, Volume iv, *1950–1969* [Theodor W. Adorno, *Briefe und Briefwechsel*, Volume 4.iv], edited by Christoph Gödde and Henri Lonitz, Frankfurt am Main: Suhrkamp.

Adorno, Theodor W. and Max Horkheimer 2019 [1989], *Towards a New Manifesto*, translated by Rodney Livingstone, London: Verso.

Adorno, Theodor W. and Ursula Jaerisch 2003 [1968], 'Anmerkung zum sozialen Konflikt heute', in *Gesammelte Schriften*, Volume 8, *Soziologische Schriften I*, Frankfurt am Main: Suhrkamp.

Adorno, Theodor W. and Eugen Kogon 1958, 'Offenbarung oder autonome Vernunft', *Frankfurter Hefte*, 13, 7: 484–98.

Adorno, Theodor W. and Siegfried Kracauer 2020 [2008], *Correspondence*, translated by Susan Reynolds and Michael Winkler, Cambridge: Polity.

Adorno, Theodor W. and Ernst Krenek 1974, *Briefwechsel*, edited by Wolfgang Rogge, Frankfurt am Main: Suhrkamp.

Adorno, Theodor W. and Elisabeth Lenk 2015 [2001], *The Challenge of Surrealism: The Correspondence of Theodor W. Adorno and Elisabeth Lenk*, edited and translated by Susan H. Gillespie, Minneapolis: University of Minnesota Press.

Adorno, Theodor W. and Leo Löwenthal 1984, 'Briefwechsel Leo Löwenthal – Theodor W. Adorno', in Leo Löwenthal, *Schriften*, Volume 4, edited by Helmut Dubiel, Frankfurt am Main: Suhrkamp.

Adorno, Theodor W. and Thomas Mann 2006 [2002], *Correspondence 1943–1955*, edited by Christoph Gödde and Thomas Sprecher, translated by Nicholas Walker, Cambridge: Polity.

Adorno, Theodor W. and Alfred Sohn-Rethel 1989, 'Notizen von einem Gespräch zwischen Th.W. Adorno und A. Sohn-Rethel am 16.4.1965', in Alfred Sohn-Rethel, *Geistige und körperliche Arbeit. Zur Epistemologie der abendländischen Geschichte. Revidierte und ergänzte Neuauflage*, Weinheim: vch.

Adorno, Theodor W. and Alfred Sohn-Rethel 1991, *Briefwechsel*, edited by Christoph Gödde, Munich: edition text+kritik.

Adorno, Theodor W. and Lotte Tobisch 2003, *Der private Briefwechsel*, edited by Bernhard Kraller and Heinz Steinert, Graz: Droschl.

Adorno, Theodor W. and Peter von Haselberg 1983 [1965], 'On the Historical Adequacy of Consciousness', translated by Wes Blomster, *Telos*, 56: 97–103.

Aesop 2002, *The Complete Fables*, translated by Laura Gibbs, Oxford: Oxford University Press.

Alker, Andrea Barbara 2007, *Das Andere im Selben. Subjektivitätskritik und Kunstphilosophie bei Heidegger und Adorno*, Würzburg: Königshausen & Neumann.

Altvater, Elmar 1978 [1972], 'Some Problems of State Interventionism', in *State and Capital: A Marxist Debate*, edited by John Holloway and Sol Picciotto, London: Edward Arnold.

Améry, Jean 1994 [1968], *On Aging: Revolt and Resignation*, translated by John D. Barlow, Bloomington: Indiana University Press.

Anderson, Perry 1987 [1976], *Considerations on Western Marxism*, London: Verso.

Arato, Andrew 1978, 'Introduction', in *The Essential Frankfurt School Reader*, edited by Andrew Arato and Eike Gebhardt, Oxford: Bloomsbury.

Auer, Dirk, Thorsten Bonacker and Stefan Müller-Doohm 1999, 'Entdeckungen in der Tradition – Ein Literaturbericht über aktuelle Aspekte der kritischen Theorie', *Zeitschrift für kritische Theorie*, 5, 8: 113–31.

Backhaus, Hans-Georg 1980 [1969], 'On the Dialectics of the Value-Form', *Thesis Eleven*, 1, 1: 99–120.

Backhaus, Hans-Georg 1997, 'Zuvor. Die Anfänge der neuen Marx-Lektüre', in *Dialektik der Wertform. Untersuchungen zur marxschen Ökonomiekritik*, Freiburg in Breisgau: ça ira.

Backhaus, Hans-Georg 2004a, 'Adorno und die metaökonomische Kritik der positivistischen Nationalökonomie', in *Die Lebendigkeit der kritischen Gesellschaftstheorie. Dokumentation der Arbeitstagung aus Anlaß des 100. Geburtstages von Theodor W. Adorno 4.–6. Juli 2003 an der Johann Wolfgang Goethe-Universität, Frankfurt am Main*, edited by Andreas Gruschka and Ulrich Oevermann. Wetzlar: Büchse der Pandora.

Backhaus, Hans-Georg 2004b, 'Der "fiktive Kommunismus" als die aporetische Grundlage der akademischen Makroökonomie', in *Vereinigung freier Individuen. Kritik der Tauschgesellschaft und gesellschaftliches Gesamtsubjekt bei Theodor W. Adorno*, edited by Jens Becker and Heinz Brakemeier, Hamburg: VSA.

Bader, Veit Michael, Johannes Berger, Heiner Ganßmann, Jost von dem Knesebeck 1976, *Einführung in die Gesellschaftstheorie I. Gesellschaft, Wirtschaft und Staat bei Marx und Weber*, Frankfurt am Main: Campus.

Bahr, Erhard 2007, *Weimar on the Pacific. German Exile Culture in Los Angeles and the Crisis of Modernism*, Berkeley: University of California Press.

Bauermann, Rolf and Hans-Jochen Rötscher 1971, 'Zur Marxverfälschung der "kritischen Theorie" der Frankfurter Schule', *Deutsche Zeitschrift für Philosophie*, 19, 12: 1440–59.

Behrens, Diethard 2005, 'Einleitung', in *Materialistische Theorie und Praxis. Zum Verhältnis von Kritischer Theorie und Kritik der Politischen Ökonomie*, edited by Diethard Behrens, Freiburg in Breisgau: ça ira.

Behrens, Diethard and Kornelia Hafner 1993, 'Totalität und Kritik', in *Gesellschaft und Erkenntnis. Zur materialistischen Erkenntnis- und Ökonomiekritik*, edited by Diethard Behrens, Freiburg in Breisgau: ça ira.

Benjamin, Walter 1999, *Gesammelte Briefe*, Volume V, 1935–1937, edited by Christoph Gödde and Henri Lonitz, Frankfurt am Main: Suhrkamp.

Benjamin, Walter 2001a [1929], 'Bücher, die lebendig geblieben sind', in *Gesammelte Schriften*, Volume III, *Kritiken und Rezensionen*, edited by Hella Tiedemann-Bartels, Frankfurt am Main: Suhrkamp.

Benjamin, Walter 2001b [1932], 'Der Irrtum des Aktivismus. Zu Kurt Hillers Essaybuch "Der Sprung ins Helle"', in *Gesammelte Schriften*, Volume III, edited by Hella Tiedemann-Bartels, Frankfurt am Main: Suhrkamp.

Benjamin, Walter 2001c [1982], 'Exposé Paris – Die Hauptstadt des XIX. Jahrhunderts', in *Gesammelte Schriften*, Volume V.2, *Das Passagenwerk*, edited by Rolf Tiedemann, Frankfurt am Main: Suhrkamp.

Benjamin, Walter 2001d [1974], *Gesammelte Schriften*, Volume I.3, *Abhandlungen*, Volume 3, edited by Rolf Tiedemann and Hermann Schweppenhäuser, Frankfurt am Main: Suhrkamp.

Benjamin, Walter 2001e [1989], *Gesammelte Schriften*, Volume VII.1, *Nachträge*, edited by Rolf Tiedemann and Hermann Schweppenhäuser, Frankfurt am Main: Suhrkamp.

Benjamin, Walter 2001f [1936], 'L'œuvre d'art à l'epoque de sa reproduction méchanisée', in *Gesammelte Schriften*, Volume I.2, *Abhandlungen*, Volume 2, edited by Rolf Tiedemann and Hermann Schweppenhäuser, Frankfurt am Main: Suhrkamp.

Benjamin, Walter 2001g [1982], 'Paris, Capitale du XIXème siècle', in *Gesammelte Schriften*, Volume V.2, *Das Passagenwerk*, edited by Rolf Tiedemann, Frankfurt am Main: Suhrkamp.

Benjamin, Walter 2002a [1982], 'Paris, the Capital of the Nineteenth Century 'Exposé of 1935'', in *The Arcades Project*, edited by Rolf Tiedemann, translated by Howard Eiland and Kevin McLaughlin, Cambridge, MA: Belknap.

Benjamin, Walter 2002b [1982], 'Paris, Capital of the Nineteenth Century 'Exposé of 1939'', in *The Arcades Project*, edited by Rolf Tiedemann, translated by Howard Eiland and Kevin McLaughlin, Cambridge, MA: Belknap.

Benjamin, Walter 2002c [1982], *The Arcades Project*, edited by Rolf Tiedemann, translated by Howard Eiland and Kevin McLaughlin, Cambridge, MA: Belknap.

Benjamin, Walter 2002d [1982], 'The Ring of Saturn or Some Remarks on Iron Construction', in *The Arcades Project*, edited by Rolf Tiedemann, translated by Howard Eiland and Kevin McLaughlin, Cambridge, MA: Belknap.

Benjamin, Walter 2004a [1921], 'Fate and Character', translated by Edmund Jephcott, in *Walter Benjamin: Selected Writings*, Volume 1, *1913–1926*, edited by Marcus Bullock and Michael W. Jennings, Cambridge, MA: Belknap.

Benjamin, Walter 2004b [1924–5], 'Goethe's *Elective Affinities*', translated by Stanley Corngold, in *Walter Benjamin: Selected Writings*, Volume 1, *1913–1926*, edited by Marcus Bullock and Michael W. Jennings, Cambridge, MA: Belknap.

Benjamin, Walter 2004c [1928], 'One-Way Street', translated by Edmund Jephcott, in *Walter Benjamin: Selected Writings*, Volume 1, *1913–1926*, edited by Marcus Bullock and Michael W. Jennings, Cambridge, MA: Belknap.

Benjamin, Walter 2004d [1977], 'On Language as Such and the Language of Man', translated by Edmund Jephcott, in Walter Benjamin, *Selected Writings*, Volume 1, *1913–1926*, edited by Marcus Bullock and Michael W. Jennings, Cambridge, MA: Belknap.

Benjamin, Walter 2005a [1934], 'Franz Kafka: On the Tenth Anniversary of His Death', translated by Harry Zohn, in *Selected Writings*, Volume 2, part 2, *1931–1934*, edited by Michael W. Jennings, Howard Eiland and Gary Smith, Cambridge, MA: Belknap.

Benjamin, Walter 2005b [1932], 'In the Sun', translated by Rodney Livingstone, in *Selected Writings*, Volume 2, part 2, *1931–1934*, edited by Michael W. Jennings, Howard Eiland and Gary Smith, Cambridge, MA: Belknap.

Benjamin, Walter 2005c [1933], 'Kierkegaard: The End of Philosophical Idealism', translated by Rodney Livingstone, in *Walter Benjamin: Selected Writings*, Volume 2, part 2, *1931–1934*, edited by Michael W. Jennings, Howard Eiland and Gary Smith, Cambridge, MA: Belknap.

Benjamin, Walter 2005d [1929], 'On the Image of Proust', translated by Harry Zohn, in *Selected Writings*, Volume 2, part 1, *1927–1930*, edited by Michael W. Jennings, Howard Eiland and Gary Smith, Cambridge, MA: Belknap.

Benjamin, Walter 2005e [1934], 'The Present Social Situation of the French Writer', translated by Rodney Livingstone, in *Walter Benjamin: Selected Writings*, Volume 2, part 2, *1931–1934*, edited by Michael W. Jennings, Howard Eiland and Gary Smith, Cambridge, MA: Belknap.

Benjamin, Walter 2006a [1939], 'On Some Motifs in Baudelaire', translated by Harry Zohn, in *Walter Benjamin: Selected Writings*, Volume 4, *1938–1940*, edited by Howard Eiland and Michael W. Jennings, Cambridge, MA: Belknap.

Benjamin, Walter 2006b [1942], 'On the Concept of History', translated by Harry Zohn, in *Walter Benjamin: Selected Writings*, Volume 4, *1938–1940*, edited by Howard Eiland and Michael W. Jennings, Cambridge, MA: Belknap.

Benjamin, Walter 2006c [1974], 'The Paris of the Second Empire in Baudelaire', translated by Harry Zohn, in *Walter Benjamin: Selected Writings*, Volume 4, *1938–1940*, edited by Howard Eiland and Michael W. Jennings, Cambridge, MA: Belknap.

Benjamin, Walter 2006d [1936], 'The Work of Art in the Age of Its Technological Reproducibility: Second Version', translated by Edmund Jephcott and Harry Zohn, in *Walter Benjamin: Selected Writings*, Volume 3, *1935–1938*, edited by Howard Eiland and Michael W. Jennings, Cambridge, MA: Belknap.

Benjamin, Walter 2006e [1939], 'The Work of Art in the Age of Its Technological Reproducibility: Third Version', translated by Harry Zohn and Edmund Jephcott, in *Walter Benjamin: Selected Writings, Volume 3, 1935–1938*, edited by Howard Eiland and
Michael W. Jennings, Cambridge, MA: Belknap.

Benjamin, Walter 2009 [1928], *The Origin of German Tragic Drama*, translated by John
Osborne, London: Verso.

Benjamin, Walter 2012 [1966], *The Correspondence of Walter Benjamin 1910–1940*, edited
Gershom Scholem and Theodor W. Adorno, translated by Manfred R. Jacobson and
Evelyn M. Jacobson, Chicago: University of Chicago Press.

Benjamin, Walter and Gershom Scholem 1992 [1980], *The Correspondence of Walter
Benjamin and Gershom Scholem*, edited by Gershom Scholem, translated by Gary
Smith and Andre Lefevere, Cambridge, MA: Harvard University Press.

Benl, Andreas 1999, '/anti/ /deutsche/ /wert/ /arbeit/ oder: *Französisch*, ein Kauder-
welsch mit undurchsichtigen Grammatik- und Vorfahrtsregeln (titanic)', *karoshi* 4:
66–75.

Bernhardt, Karl-Heinz 1962, 'Bild', in *Biblisch-historisches Handwörterbuch. Landes-
kunde, Geschichte, Religion, Kultur, Literatur*, Volume 1, edited by Bo Reicke and
Leonhard Rost, Göttingen: Vandenhoeck & Ruprech.

Blank, Hans-Joachim 2002, 'Zur Marx-Rezeption bei Horkheimer I', in *Materialistische
Theorie und Praxis. Zum Verhältnis von Kritischer Theorie und Kritik der Politischen
Ökonomie*, edited by Diethard Behrens, Freiburg in Breisgau: ça ira.

Bloch, Ernst 1975, 'War Allende zuwenig Kältestrom? Ein Gespräch mit Arno Münster
1975', in *Gespräche mit Ernst Bloch*, edited by Rainer Traub and Harald Wieser, Frankfurt am Main: Suhrkamp.

Bloch, Ernst 2006 [1930], *Traces*, translated by Anthony A. Nassar, Stanford: Stanford
University Press.

Bloch, Ernst 2020 [1923], 'Actuality and Utopia: On Lukács' *History and Class Consciousness* (1923)', translated by Cat Moir, in Cat Moir, 'The Archimedian Point: Consciousness, Praxis, and the Present in Lukács and Bloch', *Thesis Eleven*, 157, 1: 3–23.

Bloch, Ernst, Iring Fetscher and Georg Lukács 1975, 'Erbschaft aus Dekadenz? Ein
Gespräch mit Iring Fetscher und Georg Lukács 1967', in *Gespräche mit Ernst Bloch*,
edited by Rainer Traub and Harald Wieser, Frankfurt am Main: Suhrkamp.

Bloch, Ernst and Helmut Reinicke 1979, 'Gespräch: Sokratisches zu Berufsverbot und
Studentenbewegung', in *Revolution der Utopie. Texte von und über Ernst Bloch*, edited
by Helmut Reinicke, Frankfurt am Main: Campus.

Blumentritt, Martin 1992, 'Die Diktatur der Idee des Proletariats. Differenzen in der
Hegelkritik des jungen Lukács und Adorno', in *Hegel-Jahrbuch 1992 [Hegel im Kon-
text der Wirkungsgeschichte. Zweiter Teil]*, edited by Heinz Kimmerle and Wolfgang
Lefèvre, Bochum: Germinal.

Böckelmann, Frank 1998 [1972], *Über Marx und Adorno. Schwierigkeiten der spätmar-
xistischen Theorie*, Freiburg in Breisgau: ça ira.

Bolte, Gerhard 2003, *Flaschenpost. Thesen und Essays zur Kritischen Theorie der Gesellschaft*, Münster: Oktober.

Brandt, Gerhard 1981, 'Ansichten kritischer Sozialforschung 1930–1980', in *Gesellschaftliche Arbeit und Rationalisierung. Neuere Studien aus dem Institut für Sozialforschung in Frankfurt am Main*, edited by the Institute for Social Research, Wiesbaden: Springer.

Braeuer, Walter 1954, 'Henryk Grossmann als Nationalökonom', *Arbeit und Wirtschaft*, 8: 149–51.

Braunstein, Dirk 2008, 'Kritik üben', in *Theorie als Kritik*, edited by Fabian Kettner and Paul Mentz, Freiburg in Breisgau; ça ira.

Braunstein, Dirk 2009, 'Adorno nicht. Kritik als Praxis in Zeiten deren Unmöglichkeit', in *Erkenntnis und Kritik. Zeitgenössische Positionen*, edited by Devi Dumbadze, Johannes Geffers, Jan Haut, Arne Klöpper, Vanessa Lux and Irene Pimminger, Bielefeld: transcript.

Braunstein, Dirk 2010a, '"Gleich ist zugleich nicht gleich". Adornos rettende Kritik des Tausches', in *Der sich selbst entfremdete und wiedergefundene Marx*, edited by Helmut Lethen, Birte Löschenkohl and Falko Schmieder, Munich: Wilhelm Fink.

Braunstein, Dirk 2010b, *Herrschaft und Ökonomie bei Theodor W. Adorno* [*Helle Panke Philosophische Gespräche*, Volume 17], Berlin: Helle Panke.

Braunstein, Dirk 2015, 'Die Erfahrung der Gesellschaft. Grundsätzliches zur philosophischen Erkenntnis', in *Unreglementierte Erfahrung*, edited by Devi Dumbadze and Christoph Hesse, Freiburg in Breisgau: ça ira.

Braunstein, Dirk and Simon Duckheim 2015, 'Adornos Lukács – Ein Lektürebericht', in *Jahrbuch der Internationalen Georg-Lukács-Gesellschaft*, Volume 14/15, edited by Rüdiger Dannemann, Bielefeld: Aisthesis.

Brecht, Bertolt 1993, *Journals 1934–1955*, edited by John Willett, translated by Hugh Rorrison, London: Methuen.

Brecht, Bertolt 2007 [1955], *Rise and Fall of the City of Mahoganny*, translated by Steve Giles, London: Meuthen.

Bredtmann, Bastian 2015, 'Westlicher Marxismus und kritische Theorie', in *Klasse Geschichte Bewußtsein. Was bleibt von Georg Lukács' Theorie?*, edited by Hanno Plass, Berlin: Verbrecher.

Breines, Paul 1973, 'Introduction to Horkheimer's "The Authoritarian State"', *Telos*, 15: 2.

Bremer, Rainer 1998, 'Zur Aktualität Marxens', *Zeitschrift für kritische Theorie*, 4, 6: 91–9.

Brentel, Helmut 1989, *Soziale Form und ökonomisches Objekt. Studien zum Gegenstands- und Methodenverständnis der Kritik der politischen Ökonomie*, Opladen: vs.

Breuer, Stefan 1985, *Aspekte totaler Vergesellschaftung*, Freiburg in Breisgau: ça ira.

Brocke, Michael 1985, 'Kommentar', in Nachman von Bratzlaw, *Die Erzählung des Rabbi Nachman von Bratzlaw*, translated into German by Michael Brocke, Munich: Hanser.

Brodersen, Momme 1986, '"Ein Idealist mit Einschränkung". Ein Seminar zu Walter

Benjamins *Ursprung des deutschen Trauerspiels*, die tageszeitung (*magazin*), 4 March 1986: 12–13.

Bröckling, Ulrich 2006, 'Kritik oder Die Umkehrung des Genitivs', *Mittelweg 36. Zeitschrift des Hamburger Instituts für Sozialforschung*, 15, 4: 93–100.

Brömsel, Sven 2000, 'Antisemitismus', in *Nietzsche Handbuch. Leben – Werk – Wirkung*, edited by Henning Ottmann, Stuttgart: Metzler.

Bruch, Michael 2003, 'Leblose Lebendigkeit. Zur Bedeutung von Organisation, Wissen, und Norm im Konzept der verwalteten Welt', in *Modelle kritischer Gesellschaftstheorie. Traditionen und Perspektiven der Kritischen Theorie*, edited by Alex Demirović, Stuttgart: Metzler.

Bruhn, Joachim, Manfred Dahlmann and Clemens Nachtmann, 'Johannes Agnoli zum 75. Geburtstag', in *Kritik der Politik. Johannes Agnoli zum 75. Geburtstag*, Freiburg in Breisgau: ça ira.

Brumlik, Micha 1994, 'Theologie und Messianismus im Denken Adornos', in *Messianismus zwischen Mythos und Macht. Jüdisches Denken in der europäischen Geistesgeschichte*, Berlin: Akademie.

Brumlik, Micha 2003, 'Verborgene Tradition und messianisches Licht. Arendt, Adorno und ihr Judentum', in *Arendt und Adorno*, edited by Dirk Auer, Lars Rensmann and Julia Schulze Wessel, Frankfurt am Main: Suhrkamp.

Brumlik, Micha and Eveline Goodman-Thau 2007, 'Zerbrochene Schalen und Bilderverbot. Adorno als jüdischer Denker', *Zeitschrift für kritische Theorie*, 13, 24–5: 220–39.

Buber, Martin 1956 [1908], *The Tales of Rabbi Nachman*, translated by Maurice Friedman, New York: Horizon.

Buckel, Sonja 2008, 'Zwischen Schutz und Maskerade – Kritik(en) des Rechts', in *Kritik und Materialität*, edited by Alex Demirović, Münster: Westfälisches Dampfboot.

Buck-Morss, Susan 1977, *The Origin of Negative Dialectics: Theodor W. Adorno, Walter Benjamin, and the Frankfurt Institute*, New York: The Free Press.

Bude, Heinz 2004, 'Das Phänomen der Exklusion. Der Widerstreit zwischen gesellschaftlicher Erfahrung und soziologischer Rekonstruktion', in *Mittelweg 36. Zeitschrift des Hamburger Instituts für Sozialforschung*, 4: 3–15.

Bürger, Peter 2003, 'Die Kraft der Sehnsucht und die Zeit des Nachher. Der Essay bei Lukács und Adorno', *Neue deutsche Literatur. Zeitschrift für deutschsprachige Literatur*, 5: 21–32.

Bung, Jochen 2007, 'Stichwort: Rechtskritik', in *Normativität und Rechtskritik. Tagungen des Jungen Forums Rechtsphilosophie (JFR) in der Internationalen Vereinigung für Rechts- und Sozialphilosophie (IVR) im September 2006 in Würzburg und im März 2007 in Frankfurt am Main*, edited by Jochen Bung, Brian Valerius and Sascha Zimmermann, Stuttgart: Franz Steiner.

Busch, Fritzi 2008, 'Philip Roth – *Exit Ghost*', *Konkret*, 3: 51.

Claussen, Detlev 2008 [2003], *Theodor W. Adorno: One Last Genius*, translated by Rodney Livingstone, Cambridge, MA: Belknap.

Dahrendorf, Ralf 1976 [1962], 'Remarks on the Discussion', in Theodor W. Adorno, Hans Albert, Ralf Dahrendorf, Jürgen Habermas, Harald Pilot and Karl R. Popper, *The Positivist Dispute in German Sociology*, translated by Glyn Adey and David Frisby, London: Heinemann.

Dahrendorf, Ralf 1995, *LSE. A History of the London School of Economics and Political Science 1895–1995*, Oxford: Oxford University Press.

Dannemann, Rüdiger 1997, *Georg Lukács zu Einführung*, Hamburg: Junius.

Dauvé, Gilles 2002, 'Um noch einmal auf die Situationistische Internationale zurückzukommen ...', *Wildcat-Zirkular*, 62: 37–41.

Deborin, A. 1924, 'Lukács und seine Kritik des Marxismis', *Arbeiter-Literatur*, 10: 615–40.

Decker, Peter und Konrad Hecker 2002, *Das Proletariat*, Munich: GegenStandpunkt.

Demirović, Alex 1989, 'Zwischen Nihilismus und Aufklärung. Publizistische Reaktionen auf die *Minima Moralia*', in *Kritische Theorie und Kultur*, edited by Rainer Erd, Dietrich Hoß, Otto Jacobi and Peter Noller, Frankfurt am Main: Suhrkamp.

Demirović, Alex 1998, 'Ökonomiekritik und kritische Gesellschaftstheorie', *Zeitschrift für kritische Theorie*, 4, 6: 83–90.

Demirović, Alex 1999a, *Der nonkonformistische Intellektuelle. Die Entwicklung der kritischen Theorie zur Frankfurter Schule*, Frankfurt am Main: Suhrkamp.

Demirović, Alex 1999b, 'Spannungsgeschichte Nähe. Zum Verhältnis von Frankfurter Schule und Leo Kofler', *Mitteilungen der Leo-Kofler-Gesellschaft*, 3: 34–45.

Demirović, Alex 2001, 'Geistige und körperliche Arbeit', in *Historisch-kritisches Wörterbuch des Marxismus*, Volume 5, edited by Wolfgang Fritz Haug, Hamburg: Argument.

Demirović, Alex 2003a, 'Kritische Gesellschaftstheorie und Gesellschaft', in *Modelle kritischer Gesellschaftstheorie. Traditionen und Perspektiven der Kritischen Theorie*, Stuttgart: Metzler.

Demirović, Alex 2003b, 'Vorwort', in *Modelle kritischer Gesellschaftstheorie. Traditionen und Perspektiven der Kritischen Theorie*, edited by Alex Demirović, Stuttgart: Metzler.

Demirović, Alex 2004, 'Freiheit und Menschheit', in *Vereinigung freier Individuen. Kritik der Tauschgesellschaft und gesellschaftliches Gesamtsubjekt bei Theodor W. Adorno*, edited by Jens Becker and Heinz Brakemeier, Hamburg: VSA.

Demirović, Alex 2005, 'Zur Dialektik von Utopie und bestimmter Negation. Eine Diskussionsbemerkung', in *Kritische Wissenschaften im Neoliberalismus*, edited by Christina Kaindl, Marburg: Bund demokratischer Wissenschaftlerinnen und Wissenschaftler.

Demirović, Alex 2007, *Nicos Poulantzas. Aktualität und Probleme materialistischer Staatstheorie*, Münster: Westfälisches Dampfboot.

Djerassi, Carl 2008, *Four Jews on Parnassus – A Conversation: Benjamin, Adorno, Scholem, Schönberg*, New York: Columbia University Press.

Dorn, Thea 2003, 'Einkuscheln bei "Teddie"', *Kölnische Rundschau*, 11 September 2003, available at: https://www.rundschau-online.de/interview--einkuscheln-bei--teddie--11650102.

Dowe, Dieter and Klaus Tenfelde 1980, 'Zur Rezeption Eugen Dührings in der deutschen Arbeiterbewegung in den 1870er Jahren', *Schriften aus dem Karl-Marx-Haus Trier*, 24: 25–8.

Doyé, Sabine 2005, 'Rationalität und Verdinglichung. Georg Lukács' *Geschichte und Klassenbewusstsein*, die Rekonstruktion der Marxschen Ideologienlehre und Adornos "Verrat" an den Quellen eines undogmatischen Marxismus', in *Jahrbuch der Internationalen Georg-Lukács-Gesellschaft*, Volume 9, edited by Frank Benseler and Werner Jung, Bielefeld: Aisthesis.

Droste, Wiglaf 1995, 'Mit Nazis reden', in *Das Wörterbuch des Gutmenschen*, Volume 11, *Zur Kritik von Plapperjargon und Gesinnungssprache*, edited by Wiglaf Droste and Kaus Bittermann, Berlin: Edition Tiamat.

Droste, Wiglaf 2007, *Will denn in China gar kein Sack Reis mehr umfallen?* Berlin: Bittermann.

Duarte, Rodrigo Antonio de Paiva 1989, *Zum Begriff Naturbeherrschung bei Theodor W. Adorno*, Universität Kassel, doctoral dissertation: University of Kassel.

Dubiel, Helmut 1975, 'Einleitung des Herausgebers. Kritische Theorie und politische Ökonomie', in Friedrich Pollock, *Stadien des Kapitalismus*, edited by Helmut Dubiel, Munich: C.H. Beck.

Dubiel, Helmut 1981, 'Der Marxismus in der frühen Kritischen Theorie', in *Soziologie in der Gesellschaft. Referate aus den Veranstaltungen der Sektionen der Deutschen Gesellschaft für Soziologie, der Ad-hoc-Gruppen und des Berufsverbandes Deutscher Soziologen beim 20. Deutschen Soziologentag Bremen, 16. bis 19. September 1980*, edited by Werner Schulte, Bremen: University of Bremen.

Duckheim, Simon 2014, *Auf der Suche nach der versprengten Spur. Glück und Hoffnung bei Adorno und Benjamin*, Würzburg: Königshausen & Neumann.

Dunn, Malcolm 1984, *Kampf um Malakka. Eine wirtschaftsgeschichtliche Studie über den portugiesischen und niederländischen Kolonialismus in Südostasien*, Wiesbaden: Franz Steiner.

Durkheim, Emile 1982 [1895], *The Rules of Sociological Method*, edited by Steven Lukes, translated by W.D. Halls, New York: The Free Press.

Ebach, Jürgen 2001, 'Zeit als Frist. Zur Lektüre der Apokalypsen-Abschnitte in der *Abendländischen Eschatologie*', in *Abendländische Eschatologie. Ad Jacob Taubes*, edited by Richard Faber, Eveline Goodman-Thau and Thomas Macho, Würzburg: Königshausen & Neumann.

Elbe, Ingo 2008, *Marx im Westen. Die neue Marx-Lektüre in der Bundesrepublik seit 1965*, Berlin: De Gruyter.

Elbe, Ingo 2009, '(K)ein Staat zu machen? Die sowjetische Rechts- und Staatsdebatte auf dem Weg zum adjektivischen Sozialismus', in *Staatsfragen. Einführungen in die materialistische Staatskritik*, edited by associazione delle talpe and Rosa Luxemburg Initiative Bremen, available at: https://www.rosalux.de/fileadmin/rls_uploads/pdfs/rls_papers/rls-papers_Staatsfragen_0911t.pdf.

Elbe, Ingo 2013 [2006], 'Between Marx, Marxism, and Marxisms – Ways of Reading Marx's Theory', translated by Alexander Locascio, *Viewpoint Magazine*, 21 October 2013, available at: https://www.viewpointmag.com/2013/10/21/between-marx-marxism-and-marxisms-ways-of-reading-marxs-theory/.

Engels, Friedrich 1987a [1878], *Anti-Dühring: Herr Eugen Dühring's Revolution in Science*, translated by Emile Burns, in *Marx/Engels Collected Works*, Volume 25, London: Lawrence and Wishart.

Engels, Friedrich 1987b [1962], 'From Engels' Preparatory Writings for *Anti-Dühring*', translated by Emile Burns, in *Marx/Engels Collected Works*, Volume 25, London: Lawrence and Wishart.

Engels, Friedrich 1989 [1880], 'Socialism: Utopian and Scientific', translated by Edward Aveling, in *Marx/Engels Collected Works*, Volume 24, London: Lawrence and Wishart.

Engels, Friedrich 2001, *Marx/Engels Collected Works*, Volume 49, *Engels: 1890–92*, London: Lawrence and Wishart.

Engels, Friedrich 2010 [1845], *The Condition of the Working-Class in England in 1892*, translated by Florence Kelley Wischnewetzky, Cambridge: Cambridge University Press.

Engster, Frank 2006, 'Das Verhältnis von Utopie, Wissenschaft und Kritik – bei Marx, Lukács, Adorno und Derrida', *Schriftenreihe der freien Akademie*, 26: 129–54.

Engster, Frank 2009, *Sohn-Rethel und das Problem einer Einheit von Gesellschafts- und Erkenntniskritik* [*Helle Panke Philosophische Gespräche*, Volume 15], Berlin: Helle Panke.

Erckenbrecht, Ulrich 1976, *Das Geheimnis des Fetischismus. Grundmotive der Marxschen Erkenntniskritik*, Frankfurt am Main: Europäische Verlagsanstalt.

Ette, Wolfram 1998, 'Warenkunst. Prolegomena zu einer marxistischen Theorie der Kunst', in *Mit den Ohren denken. Adornos Philosophie der Musik*, edited by Richard Klein and Claus-Steffen Mahnkopf, Frankfurt am Main: Suhrkamp.

Faber, Richard 2002, '*Sagen lassen sich die Menschen nichts, aber erzählen lassen sie sich alles.' Über Grimm-Hebelsche Erzählung, Moral und Utopie in Benjaminscher Perspektive*, Würzburg: Königshausen & Neumann.

Fabri, Albrecht 2000, 'Sätze', in *Der schmutzige Daumen. Gesammelte Schriften*, edited by Ingeborg Fabri and Martin Weinmann, Frankfurt am Main: Zweitausendeins.

Fahlbusch, Markus 2006a, 'Über Jazz', in *Schlüsseltexte der Kritischen Theorie*, edited by Axel Honneth, Wiesbaden: vs Verlag für Sozialwissenschaften.

Fahlbusch, Markus 2006b, 'Über den Fetischcharakter in der Musik und die Regression des Hörens', in *Schlüsseltexte der Kritischen Theorie*, edited by Axel Honneth, Wiesbaden: vs Verlag für Sozialwissenschaften.

Feher, Ferenc 1985, 'Lukács and Benjamin: Parallels and Contrasts', *New German Critique*, 34: 125–38.

Fekete, Éva and Éva Karáci 1981, *György Lukacs: His Life in Pictures and Documents*, translated by Peter Balaban with revisions by Kenneth McRobbie, Budapest: Corvina.

Fetscher, Iring 1971 [1969], 'Ein Kämpfer ohne Illusionen', *Theodor W. Adorno zum Gedächtnis. Eine Sammlung*, edited by Hermann Schweppenhäuser, Frankfurt am Main: Suhrkamp.

Fischer, Karsten 1999, *'Verwilderte Selbsterhaltung'. Zivilisationstheoretische Kulturkritik bei Nietzsche, Freud, Weber und Adorno*, Berlin: Akademie.

Floyd, Wayne Whitson 1993, 'Transcendence in the Light of Redemption: Adorno and the Legacy of Rosenzweig and Benjamin', *Journal of the American Academy of Religion*, 61, 3: 539–51.

Freeman, Kathleen 1948, *Ancilla to The Pre-Socratic Philosophers: A complete translation of the Fragments in Diels, 'Fragmente der Vorsokratiker'*, Oxford: Basil Blackwell.

Freud, Sigmund 2001a [1916], *Introductory Lectures on Psycho-Analysis (Parts I and II)*, in *The Standard Edition of the Complete Psychological Works of Sigmund Freud*, Volume XV, 1915–1916, translated and edited by James Strachey, London: Vintage.

Freud, Sigmund 2001b [1933], *New Introductory Lectures on Psycho-Analysis*, in *The Standard Edition of the Complete Psychological Works of Sigmund Freud*, Volume XXII, edited and translated by James Strachey, London: Vintage.

Freud, Sigmund 2001c [1911], *Psycho-Analytic Notes on an Autobiographical Account of a Case of Paranoia (Dementia Paranoides)*, in *The Standard Edition of the Complete Psychological Works of Sigmund Freud*, Volume XII, translated and edited by James Strachey, London: Vintage.

Freud, Sigmund 2016 [1905], *Three Essays on the Theory of Sexuality: The 1905 Edition*, translated by Ulrike Kistner, edited by Philippe Van Haute and Herman Westerink, London: Verso.

Freytag, Carl 1992, 'Der Angriff der Osterhasen. Zu den Phantasmagorien des Warentauschs', *Widerspruch. Münchner Zeitschrift für Philosophie*, 12: 145–8.

Freytag, Carl 2006, 'Die Sprache der Dinge. Alfred Sohn-Rethels "Zwischenexistenz" in Positano (1924–1927)', in *Geld und Geltung. Zu Alfred Sohn-Rethels soziologischer Erkenntnistheorie*, edited by Rudolf Heinz and Jochen Hörisch, Würzburg: Königshausen & Neumann.

Friedrich, Horst 2000, *Hegels 'Wissenschaft der Logik'. Ein marxistischer Kommentar. Erster Teil*, Berlin: Dietz.

Friends of the Classless Society 2010 [2007], '28 Theses on Class Society', *Kosmoprolet*, 25 June 2010, available at: https://www.kosmoprolet.org/en/28-theses-class-society.

Funke, Manfred 2004, '"Behemoth" war die erste Strukturanalyse des Dritten Reiches', *Die Politische Meinung*, 421, 12: 79–81.

Gangl, Manfred 1987, *Politische Ökonomie und Kritische Theorie. Ein Beitrag zur theoretischen Entwicklung der Frankfurter Schule*, Frankfurt am Main: Campus.

García Düttmann, Alexander 2004, *So ist es. Ein philosophischer Kommentar zu Adornos Minima Moralia*, Frankfurt am Main: Suhrkamp.

Glasenapp, Jörn 2006, 'Kulturindustrie als Status Quo-Industrie. Adorno und das Populäre', in *Unterhaltungskultur*, edited by Werner Faulstich and Karin Knop, Munich: Wilhelm Fink.

Gmünder, Ulrich 1985, *Kritische Theorie. Horkheimer, Adorno, Marcuse, Habermas*, Stuttgart: Metzler.

Gödde, Christoph and Henri Lonitz 2006, 'Das Institut für Sozialforschung/Gretel Adorno, Adorno und Horkheimer', in *Benjamin Handbuch. Leben – Werk – Wirkung*, edited by Burkhardt Lindner, Stuttgart: Metzler.

Gramsci, Antonio 2000 [1988], *The Gramsci Reader: Selected Writings 1916–1935*, edited by David Forgacs, New York: New York University Press.

Grenz, Friedemann 1974, *Adornos Philosophie in Grundbegriffen. Auflösung einiger Deutungsprobleme*, Frankfurt am Main: Suhrkamp.

Grigat, Stephan 2007, *Fetisch und Freiheit. Über die Rezeption der Marxschen Fetischkritik, die Emanzipation von Staat und Kapital und die Kritik des Antisemitismus*, Freiburg in Breisgau: ça ira.

Gross, Lucas 2003, 'Das vermeintlich von Geschichte und Gesellschaft befreite Jetzt. 100 Jahre Theodor W. Adorno – Im Sinne einer Aktualität seiner Gesellschaftstheorie', *soz:mag. Das Soziologie Magazin*, 4: 46–50.

Grünberg, Carl 1986 [1924], 'Inaugural Address on the Opening of the Institute of Social Research at the University of Frankfurt/Main 22 June 1924', translated by Michael Bodemann, *Insurgent Sociologist*, 13, 3: 4–9.

Gumbrecht, Hans Ulrich 2004, '"Euer altes Kind Teddie"', *Deutsche Zeitschrift für Philosophie*, 52, 1: 117–19.

Gurland, A.R.L. 1941, 'Technological Trends and Economic Structure under National Socialism', *Studies in Philosophy and Social Science [Zeitschrift für Sozialforschung]*, 9, 2: 226–63.

Habermas, Jürgen 1988 [1963], 'Between Philosophy and Science: Marxism as Critique', in *Theory and Practice*, translated by John Viertel, Boston: Beacon.

Habermas, Jürgen 1991 [1971], *Philosophical-Political Profiles*, translated by Frederick G. Lawrence, Cambridge: Polity.

Habermas, Jürgen 1993 [1991], 'Notes on the Developmental History of Horkheimer's Work', translated by Mark Ritter, *Theory, Culture & Society*, 10, 2: 61–77.

Habermas, Jürgen 1998 [1985], 'Excursus on the Obsolescence of the Production Paradigm', in *The Philosophical Discourse of Modernity: Twelve Lectures*, translated by Frederick G. Lawrence, Cambridge: Polity.

Hafner, Kornelia 1993, 'Gebrauchswertfetischismus', in *Gesellschaft und Erkenntnis. Zur materialistischen Erkenntnis- und Ökonomiekritik.* edited by Diethard Behrens, Freiburg in Breisgau: ça ira.

Hafner, Kornelia 2005, '"Daß der Bann sich löse". Annäherungen an Adornos Marx-Rezeption', in *Materialistische Theorie und Praxis. Zum Verhältnis von Kritischer Theorie und Kritik der Politischen Ökonomie,* edited by Diethard Behrens, Freiburg in Breisgau: ça ira.

Hanloser, Gerhard and Karl Reitter 2008, *Der bewegte Marx. Eine einführende Kritik des Zirkulationsmarxismus,* Münster: Unrast.

Haug, Wolfgang Fritz 1986 [1971], *Critique of Commodity Aesthetics: Appearance, Sexuality, and Advertising in Capitalist Society,* translated by Robert Bock, Cambridge: Polity.

Haug, Wolfgang Fritz 2004, 'Hegemonie', in *Historisch-kritisches Wörterbuch des Marxismus,* Volume 6/I, edited by Wolfgang Fritz Haug, Hamburg: Argument.

Haustein, Heinz-Dieter 2004, *Quellen der Meßkunst. Zu Maß und Zahl, Geld und Gewicht.* Berlin: de Gruyter.

Hecker, Achim 2001, *Übergänge. Metaphysikkritik auf den Spuren Heideggers und Derridas,* doctoral dissertation: University of Freiburg in Beisgau, available at: https://freidok.uni-freiburg.de/data/252.

Hecker, Rolf 2000, *Erfolgreiche Kooperation: Das Frankfurter Institut für Sozialforschung und das Moskauer Marx-Engels-Institut (1924–1928),* Hamburg: Argument.

Hedeler, Wladislaw 1997, 'A.M. Deborin – eine biographische Skizze', in *David Borisovič Rjazanov und die erste MEGA. Beiträge zur Marx-Engels-Forschung,* edited by Carl-Erich Vollgraf, Richard Sperl and Rolf Hecker, Hamburg: Argument.

Hegel, Georg Wilhelm Friedrich 1977 [1801], *The Difference Between Fichte's and Schelling's System of Philosophy,* translated by H.S. Harris and Walter Cerf, Albany: SUNY Press.

Hegel, Georg Wilhelm Friedrich 1991 [1820], *Elements of the Philosophy of Right,* translated by H.B. Nisbet, Cambridge: Cambridge University Press.

Hegel, Georg Wilhelm Friedrich 2010a [1817], *Encyclopedia of the Philosophical Sciences in Basic Outline: Part 1: Science of Logic,* translated by Klaus Brinkmann and Daniel O. Dahlstrom, Cambridge: Cambridge University Press.

Hegel, Georg Wilhelm Friedrich 2010b [1812–16], *The Science of Logic,* edited and translated by George di Giovanni, Cambridge: Cambridge University Press.

Hegel, Georg Wilhelm Friedrich 2018 [1807], *Phenomenology of Spirit,* translated by Terry Pinkard, Cambridge: Cambridge University Press.

Heidegger, Martin and Ernst Jünger 2016 [2008]: Correspondence 1949–1975, translated by Timothy Sean Quinn, London, New York: Rowman & Littlefield international.

Heiniger, Jörg 1990, 'Lukács', in *Literaturlexikon,* Volume 7, edited by Walther Killy, Munich: C. Bertelsmann.

Heinrich, Michael 1999, *Die Wissenschaft vom Wert. Die Marxsche Kritik der politischen*

Ökonomie zwischen wissenschaftlicher Revolution und klassischer Tradition, Münster: Westfälisches Dampfboot.

Heinrich, Michael 2003, 'Geld und Kredit in der Kritik der politischen Ökonomie', *Das Argument. Zeitschrift für Philosophie und Sozialwissenschaft*, 45, 3: 397–409.

Heinrich, Michael 2007, 'Profit ohne Ende', *Jungle World*, 12 Juli 2007: 17.

Heinrich, Michael 2009, 'Grenzen des "idealen Durchschnitts". Zum Verhältnis von Ökonomiekritik und Staatsanalyse bei Marx', in *Staatsfragen. Einführungen in die materialistische Staatskritik*, edited by associazione delle talpe and Rosa Luxemburg Initiative Bremen, available at: https://www.rosalux.de/fileadmin/rls_uploads/pdfs/rls_papers/rls-papers_Staatsfragen_0911t.pdf.

Heinrich, Michael 2012 [2004], *An Introduction to the Three Volumes of Karl Marx's Capital*, translated by Alexander Locascio, New York: Monthly Review Press.

Heinrich, Michael 2021 [2008], *How to Read Marx's Capital: Commentary and Explanations on the Beginning Chapters*, translated by Alexander Locascio, New York: Monthly Review Press.

Heißenbüttel, Helmut 2006, 'Helmut Heißenbüttel, Radioredakteur. Aus den Korrespondenzen mit Theodor W. Adorno, Arno Schmidt und Hans Magnus Enzensberger', *Schreibheft*, 67: 163–89.

Helmes-Conzett, Cornelius and Dorothee Knab 1999, 'Ein Briefwechsel', in *Kritisierte Gesellschaft. Gabi Althaus zum 61. Geburtstag*, edited by Henrik Ghanaat, Holger Andreas Leidig, Carsten Otte and Tilman Reitz, Berlin: Metropol.

Helvétius, Claude Adrien 1810 [1773], *A Treatise on Man; His Intellectual Faculties and His Education*, translated by William Hooper, London: Albion.

Henscheid, Eckhard 1993, *Dummdeutsch*. Stuttgart: Reclam.

Henscheid, Eckhard 1999, 'Schönheit Musik? Kunstform Oper? Ach was! Eine entschiedene Gesamtbetrachtung', in *Meine Jahre mit Sepp Herberger. Neue Feuilletons*, Berlin: Edition Tiamat.

Henscheid, Eckhard 2003, *Sudelblätter*, in *Gesammelte Werke in Einzelausgaben*, Volume 3, Frankfurt am Main: Zweitausendeins.

Henscheid, Eckhard 2005, 'Fetisch Beethoven. Faseln mit Adorno', in *Gesammelte Werke in Einzelausgaben*, Volume 7, Frankfurt am Main: Zweitausendeins.

Henscheid, Eckhard 2007, 'Scene-Deutsch: Fluch oder Segen? Nachwort zu einem Wörterbuch', in *Gesammelte Werke in Einzelausgaben*, Volume 9, Frankfurt am Main: Zweitausendeins.

Henschel, Gerhard 2008, *Neidgeschrei. Antisemitismus und Sexualität*, Hamburg: Hoffmann und Campe.

Henschel, Gerhard 2010, *Menetekel. 3000 Jahre Untergang des Abendlandes*, Frankfurt am Main: Eichborn.

Hentschel, Rüdiger 2006, '"Ein Korrespondent aus Ost-Berlin". Zum Briefwechsel Alfred Sohn-Rethel – Ekkehard Schwarzkopf 1964–1972', in *Geld und Geltung. Zu Alfred*

Sohn-Rethels soziologischer Erkenntnistheorie, edited by Rudolf Heinz and Jochen Hörisch, Würzburg: Königshausen & Neumann.

Herrschaft, Felicia 2009, 'Soziologische Lehrveranstaltungen 1949–1973: Archivbestände der Goethe-Universität Frankfurt', available at: https://wiki.studiumdigitale.uni -frankfurt.de/SOZFRA/index.php?title=Soziologische_Lehrveranstaltungen_vo n_1949-1973_-_Archivbestaende_der_Goethe-Universitaet_Frankfurt.

Herrschaft, Felicia 2010a, 'Die Gestalt der soziologische Lehre in Frankfurt', *UniReport. Goethe-Universität. Frankfurt am Main*, 43, 1: 4.

Herrschaft, Felicia 2010b, 'Die Lehrgestalt der Frankfurter Soziologie in den 1950er und 1960er Jahren. Theorie und Praxis', in *Soziologie in Frankfurt. Eine Zwischenbilanz*, edited by Felicia Herrschaft and Klaus Lichtblau, Wiesbaden: Springer VS.

Hesse, Christoph 2006, *Filmform und Fetisch*, Bielefeld: Aisthesis.

Hilferding, Rudolf 1981 [1910], *Finance Capital: A Study of the Latest Phase of Capitalist Development*, edited by Tom Bottomore, translated by Morris Watnick and Sam Gordon, London: Routledge.

Hintz, Michael 2004, 'Paradoxale Wandlungsprozesse kritischer Gesellschaftstheorie – der Stachel Adorno', in *Vereinigung freier Individuen. Kritik der Tauschgesellschaft und gesellschaftliches Gesamtsubjekt bei Theodor W. Adorno*, edited by Jens Becker and Heinz Brakemeier, Hamburg: VSA.

Hobsbawm, E.J. [Eric] 1971, 'Class Consciousness in History', in *Aspects of History and Class Consciousness*, edited by István Mészáros, London: Routledge & Kegan Paul.

Hobsbawm, E.J. 1995 [1994], *The Age of Extremes: A History of the World 1914–1991*, London: Abacus.

Höge, Helmut 2008, 'Geld und Geist/Licht (35)', *Hier spricht der Aushilfshausmeister* [*taz blogs*], 4 December 2008, available at: http://blogs.taz.de/hausmeisterblog/200 8/12/04/geld_und_geistlicht/.

Hörisch, Jochen 1978, 'Identitätszwang und Tauschabstraktion. Alfred Sohn-Rethels soziogenetische Erkenntnistheorie', *Philosophische Rundschau*, 25, 1: 42–54.

Hofmann, Jürgen 1999, 'Zum Umgang mit deutscher Zweistaatlichkeit. Anmerkungen zu einer notwendigen Debatte über die "Doppelbiographie" der Bundesrepublik', *Utopie kreativ. Diskussion sozialistischer Alternativen*, 106: 46–53.

Hohendahl, Peter Uwe 1981, 'Autonomy of Art: Looking Back at Adorno's *Ästhetische Theorie*', *The German Quarterly*, 54, 2: 133–48.

Horkheimer, Max 1941a, 'Preface', *Studies in Philosophy and Social Science* [*Zeitschrift für Sozialforschung*], 9, 2: 195–9.

Horkheimer, Max 1941b, 'The End of Reason', *Studies in Philosophy and Social Science* [*Zeitschrift für Sozialforschung*], 9, 3: 366–88.

Horkheimer, Max 1973 [1942], 'The Authoritarian State', translated by the People's Translation Service, mediated by Elliot Eisenberg, *Telos*, 15: 3–20.

Horkheimer, Max 1985a, 'Aufzeichnungen und Entwürfe zur *Dialektik der Aufklärung 1939–1942*', in *Gesammelte Schriften*, Volume 12, *Nachgelassene Schriften 1931–1949*, edited by Gunzelin Schmid Noerr, Frankfurt am Main: Fischer.

Horkheimer, Max 1985b [1970], 'Die Sehnsucht nach dem ganz Anderen' [Gespräch mit Helmut Gumnoir], in *Gesammelte Schriften*, Volume 7, *Vorträge und Aufzeichnungen 1949–1973*, edited by Gunzelin Schmid Noerr, Frankfurt am Main: Fischer.

Horkheimer, Max 1987, *Gesammelte Schriften*, Volume 12, *Dialektik der Aufklärung*, edited by Gunzelin Schmid Noerr, Frankfurt am Main: Fischer.

Horkheimer, Max 1988a, 'Nachgelassene Notizen 1949–1969' in *Gesammelte Schriften*, Volume 14, *Nachgelassene Schriften 1949–1972*, edited by Gunzelin Schmid Noerr, Frankfurt am Main: Fischer.

Horkheimer, Max 1988b, 'Späne. Notizen über Gespräche mit Max Horkheimer, in unverbindlicher Formulierung aufgeschrieben von Friedrich Pollock', in *Gesammelte Schriften*, Volume 14, *Nachgelassene Schriften 1949–1972*, edited by Gunzelin Schmid Noerr, Frankfurt am Main: Fischer.

Horkheimer, Max 1989 [1939], 'The Jews and Europe', translated by Max Ritter, in *Critical Theory and Society: A Reader*, edited by Stephen Eric Bronner and Douglas MacKay Kellner, London: Routledge.

Horkheimer, Max 1993a [1930], 'Beginnings of the Bourgeois Philosophy of History', in *Between Philosophy and Social Science: Selected Early Writings*, translated by G. Frederick Hunter, Matthew S. Kramer and John Torpey, Cambridge, MA: MIT Press.

Horkheimer, Max 1993b [1933], 'Materialism and Morality', in *Between Philosophy and Social Science: Selected Early Writings*, translated by G. Frederick Hunter, Matthew S. Kramer and John Torpey, Cambridge, MA: MIT Press.

Horkheimer, Max 1995a, 'Aktennotiz vom 24.12.1935', in *Gesammelte Schriften*, Volume 15, *Briefwechsel 1913–1936*, edited by Gunzelin Schmid Noerr, Frankfurt am Main: Fischer.

Horkheimer, Max 1995b, *Gesammelte Schriften*, Volume 15, *Briefwechsel 1913–1936*, edited by Gunzelin Schmid Noerr, Frankfurt am Main: Fischer.

Horkheimer, Max 1995c, *Gesammelte Schriften*, Volume 16, *Briefwechsel 1937–1940*, edited by Gunzelin Schmid Noerr, Frankfurt am Main: Fischer.

Horkheimer, Max 1996a, *Gesammelte Schriften*, Volume 17, *Briefwechsel 1941–1948*, edited by Gunzelin Schmid Noerr, Frankfurt am Main: Fischer.

Horkheimer, Max 1996b, *Gesammelte Schriften*, Volume 19, *Nachträge, Verzeichnisse und Register*, edited by Gunzelin Schmid Noerr, Frankfurt am Main: Fischer.

Horkheimer, Max 2002 [1937], 'Traditional and Critical Theory', in *Critical Theory: Selected Essays*, translated by Matthew J. O'Connell, New York: Continuum.

Horkheimer, Max 2004 [1947], *Eclipse of Reason*, London: Continuum.

Horkheimer, Max 2007, *A Life in Letters: Selected Correspondence*, edited and translated by Manfred R. Jacobson and Evelyn M. Jacobson, Lincoln, NE: University of Nebraska Press.

Horkheimer, Max 2014, 'Max Horkheimer's critique of Marxist Positivism in Henryk Grossmann', translated by Frederik van Gelder, available at: https://amsterdam-ador no.net/fvg2014_T_mh_grossmann_letter.html.

Horkheimer, Max 2016, 'On the Sociology of Class Relations', *nonsite.org* 18, available at: https://nonsite.org/the-tank/max-horkheimer-and-the-sociology-of-class-relati ons.

Horkheimer, Max 2019 [1985], 'On the Problem of Needs', translated by Iain Macdonald, in Theodor W. Adorno and Max Horkheimer, *Towards a New Manifesto*, translated by Rodney Livingstone, London: Verso.

Hullot-Kentor, Robert 2009 [2006], 'Introduction', in Theodor W. Adorno, *Current of Music: Elements of a Radio Theory*, edited by Robert Hullot-Kentor, Cambridge: Polity.

Iber, Christian 2005, *Grundzüge der Marx'schen Kapitalismustheorie*, Berlin: Parega.

Initiative Sozialistisches Forum 2000, *Der Theoretiker ist der Wert. Eine ideologiekritische Skizze der Wert- und Krisentheorie der Krisis-Gruppe*, Freiburg in Breisgau: ça ira.

Iorio, Marco 2003, *Karl Marx – Geschichte, Gesellschaft, Politik. Eine Ein- und Weiterführung*, Berlin: De Gruyter

Jäger, Lorenz 2004, *Adorno: A Political Biography*, translated by Stewart Spencer, New Haven: Yale University Press.

Jay, Martin 1969, 'The Permanent Exile of Theodor W. Adorno', *Midstream*, 15: 62–7.

Jay, Martin 1977, 'The Concept of Totality in Lukács and Adorno', *Telos*, 32: 117–37.

Jay, Martin 1979, 'Kurt Mandelbaum: His Decade at the Institute of Social Research', *Development and Change*, 10, 4: 545–52.

Jay, Martin 1981, 'Positive and Negative Totalities: Implicit Tensions in Critical Theory's Vision of Interdisciplinary Research', *Thesis Eleven*, 3: 72–87.

Jay, Martin 1984, *Adorno*, Cambridge, MA: Harvard University Press.

Jay, Martin 1996 [1973], *The Dialectical Imagination*, Berkeley: University of California Press.

Johannes, Rolf 1995, 'Das ausgesparte Zentrum. Adornos Verhältnis zur Ökonomie', in *Soziologie im Spätkapitalismus: Zur Gesellschaftstheorie Theodor W. Adornos*, edited by Gerhard Schweppenhäuser, Darmstadt: Darmstadt Wissenschaftliche Buchgesellschaft.

Jornitz, Sieglinde 2003, 'Blick zurück nach vorn – Ein Nachtrag zum "Adorno-Jahr"', *Pädagogische Korrespondenz. Zeitschrift für kritische Zeitdiagnostik in Pädagogik und Gesellschaft*, 31: 101–2.

Kager, Reinhard 1988, *Herrschaft und Versöhnung. Einführung in das Denken Theodor W. Adornos*, Frankfurt am Main: Campus.

Kant, Immanuel 1998 [1781], *Critique of Pure Reason*, edited and translated by Paul Guyer and Allen W. Wood, Cambridge: Cambridge University Press.

Kant, Immanuel 2007 [1790], *Critique of the Power of Judgment*, edited by Paul Guyer, translated by Paul Guyer and Eric Matthews, Cambridge: Cambridge University Press.

Kapferer, Norbert 1993, 'Das philosophische Vorspiel zum Kalten Krieg. Die Jaspers-Lukácz-Kontroverse in Genf 1946', in *Jahrbuch der Österreichischen Karl-Jaspers-Gesellschaft*, Volume 6, edited by Kurt Salamun, Wien: StudienVerlag.

Kapielski, Thomas 1999, *Danach war schon. Gottesbeweise I–VIII*, Berlin: Merve.

Kaufmann, Harald 1993, *Von innen und außen. Schriften über Musik, Musikleben und Ästhetik*, edited by Werner Grünzweig and Gottfried Krieger, Hofheim: Wolke.

Kaulen, Heinrich 1995, 'Walter Benjamin und Asja Lacis. Eine biographische Konstellation und ihre Folgen', *Deutsche Vierteljahrsschrift für Literatur und Geistesgeschichte*, 69, 1: 99–122.

Kausch, Michael 1988, *Kulturindustrie und Populärkultur. Kritische Theorie der Massenmedien*, Frankfurt am Main: Fischer.

Kierkegaard, Søren 1987 [1885], *Either/Or: Part II*, edited and translated by Howard V. Hong and Edna H. Hong, Princeton: Princeton University Press.

Kirchheimer, Otto 1939, 'Criminal Law in National-Socialist Germany', *Studies in Philosophy and Social Science [Zeitschrift für Sozialforschung]*, 8, 3: 444–63.

Klein, Richard 2006, '"Versuch über Wagner"', in *Schlüsseltexte der Kritischen Theorie*, edited by Axel Honneth, Wiesbaden: Springer.

Kluth, Heinz 1969, 'Protokoll der Diskussion', in *Spätkapitalismus oder Industriegesellschaft? Verhandlungen des 16. Deutschen Soziologentages*, edited by Theodor W. Adorno, Stuttgart: Ferdinand Enke.

König, Thomas and Florian Markl 2001, 'Totalität and Gesellschaftskritik', *Streifzüge*, 1: 18–22.

Kolpinskij, Nikita Jurevič 1997, 'Rjazanov – Gelehrter, Wissenschaftsorganisator und Politiker', in *David Borisovic Rjazanov und die erste MEGA*, edited Rolf Hecker, Richard Sperl and Carl-Erich Vollgraf, Hamburg: Argument.

Koltan, Michael T. 1999, 'Adorno gegen seine Liebhaber verteidigt', in *Kritische Theorie und Poststrukturalismus. Theoretische Lockerungsübungen*, edited by Jochen Baumann, Elfriede Müller and Stefan Vogt, Hamburg: Argument.

Kornelius, Stefan 2008, 'Offen, aber nicht notwendig tolerant', *Süddeutsche Zeitung*, 17 July 2008: 13.

Korsch, Karl 2001, *Briefe 1908–1938*, edited by Michael Buckmiller, Michel Prat and Meike G. Werner, Hannover: Offizin.

Kosík, Karel 1976 [1963], *Dialectics of the Concrete: A Study on Problems of Man and World*, translated by Karel Kovanda and James Schmidt, Boston: D. Reidel.

Kracauer, Siegfried 1998 [1929], *The Salaried Masses: Duty and Distraction in Weimar Germany*, translated by Quintin Hoare, London: Verso.

Krätke, Michael 2004, 'Mythos Markt oder Wo der gesellschaftliche Verstand (nicht) zu haben ist', in *Vereinigung freier Individuen?' Kritik der Tauschgesellschaft und gesellschaftliches Gesamtsubjekt bei Theodor W. Adorno*, edited by Jens Becker and Heinz Brakemeier, Hamburg: VSA.

Kraus, Karl 1986 [1912], *Pro domo et mundo*, in *Schriften*, Volume 8, edited by Christian Wagenknecht, Frankfurt am Main: Suhrkamp.

Kraus, Karl 2020 [1952], *The Third Walpurgis Night*, translated by Fred Bridgham and Edward Timms, New Haven: Yale University Press.

Kreimeier, Klaus 1971, 'Grundsätzliche Überlegungen zu einer materialistischen Theorie der Massenmedien', *Kunst und Gesellschaft*, 7: 61–85.

Kreimeier, Klaus 1983 [1971], 'Fundamental Reflections on a Materialist Theory of the Mass Media', translated by Robert Peck, *Media, Culture & Society*, 5, 1: 37–47.

Krings, Hermann 1953, 'Grenze der Dialektik. Zu Th.W. Adornos "Minima Moralia"', *Hochland. Monatsschrift für alle Gebiete des Wissens, der Literatur und Kunst*, 46, 4: 362–6.

Krug, Uli 1999, 'Gebrauchswert und Wertkritik. Ein Marx teilt sich nicht in zwei', *Bahamas*, 28: 43–8.

Kuczynski, Thomas 1990, 'Was wird auf dem Arbeitsmarkt verkauft?', in *Auf der Suche nach dem Kompaß. Politische Ökonomie als Bahnsteigkarte fürs 21. Jahrhundert*, edited by Dorothee Wolf, Kai Eicker-Wolf and Sabine Reiner, Cologne: Papyrossa.

Küpper, Thomas and Timo Skrandies 2006, 'Rezeptionsgeschichte', in *Benjamin Handbuch. Leben – Werk – Wirkung*, edited by Burkhardt Lindner, Stuttgart: Metzler.

Kürnberger, Ferdinand 1985 [1855], *Der Amerikamüde*, Berlin: Volk und Welt.

Kurz, Robert 1987, 'Die Herrschaft der toten Dinge. Kritische Anmerkungen zur neueren Produktivkraft-Kritik und Entgesellschaftungs-Ideologie', *Marxistische Kritik*, 2: 7–68.

Kurz, Robert 1992, 'Geschlechtsfetischismus. Anmerkungen zur Logik von Weiblichkeit und Männlichkeit', *Krisis. Beiträge zur Kritik der Warengesellschaft*, 12: 117–68.

Kurzbein, Uwe 2003, 'Am Anfang steht die Initiative', *Graswurzelrevolution*, 279: 10–11.

Kwiet, Konrad 1998 [1997], 'Judenstern', in *Enzyklopädie des Nationalsozialismus*, edited by Wolfgang Benz, Hermann Graml and Hermann Weiß, Stuttgart: Klett-Cotta.

Lacis, Asja 1976 [1971], *Revolutionär im Beruf. Berichte über proletarisches Theater, über Meyerhold, Brecht, Benjamin und Piscator*, edited by Hildegard Brenner, Munich: Rogner & Bernhard.

Lang, Peter Christian 1995, 'Adorno, Theodor W. (= Wiesengrund)', *Metzler Philosophen Lexikon. Von den Vorsokratikern bis zu den Neuen Philosophen*, edited by Bernd Lutz, Stuttgart: Metzler.

Lange, Ernst Michael 1978, 'Wertformanalyse, Geldkritik und die Konstruktion des Fetischismus bei Marx', *Neue Hefte für Philosophie*, 13: 1–46.

Lazarsfeld, Paul F. 1969, 'An Episode in the History of Social Research: A Memoir', in *The Intellectual Migration: Europe and America, 1930–1960*, edited by Donald Fleming and Bernard Bailyn, Cambridge, MA: Belknap.

Lehr, Andreas 2000, *Kleine Formen. Adornos Kombinationen: Konstellation/Konfiguration, Montage und Essay*, doctoral dissertation: University of Freiburg in Breisgau, available at: https://freidok.uni-freiburg.de/data/27.

Lenin, Vladimir I. 1972 [1918], '"Left-Wing" Childishness', in *Collected Works*, Volume 27, translated by Clemens Dutt, edited by Robert Daglish, Moscow: Progress Publishers.

Lenin, Vladimir I. 1973a [1922], 'The Role and Functions of the Trade Unions Under the New Economic Policy', in *Collected Works*, Volume 33, edited by David Skvirsky and George Hanna, Moscow: Progress Publishers.

Lenin, Vladimir I. 1973b [1921], 'The Tax in Kind', in *Collected Works*, Volume 32, edited by Yuri Sdobnikov, Moscow: Progress Publishers.

Lenin, Vladimir I. 1973c [1921], 'Third Congress of the Communist International, June 22–July 12, 1921', in *Collected Works*, Volume 32, edited by Yuri Sdobnikov, Moscow: Progress Publishers.

Lenin, Vladimir I. 1992 [1918], *The State and Revolution*, translated by Robert Service, London: Penguin.

Levin, Thomas Y. and Michael von der Linn 1994, 'Elements of a Radio Theory: Adorno and the Princeton Radio Project', *The Musical Quarterly*, 78, 2: 316–24.

Liessmann, Konrad Paul 1998, 'Hot Potatoes. Zum Briefwechsel zwischen Günther Anders und Theodor W. Adorno', *Zeitschrift für kritische Theorie*, 4, 6: 29–38.

Liessmann, Konrad Paul 2003, 'Ein Moment des Glücks', *Der Freitag*, 5 September 2003: 16.

Lindemann, Kai 2000, 'Der Racketbegriff als Gesellschaftskritik. Die Grundform der Herrschaft bei Horkheimer', *Zeitschrift für kritische Theorie*, 6, 11: 63–81.

Lindner, Burkhardt 1972, 'Brecht/Benjamin/Adorno – Über Veränderungen der Kunstproduktion im wissenschaftlich-technischen Zeitalter', in *Bertolt Brecht I*, edited by Heinz Ludwig Arnold, Munich: edition text+kritik.

Lindner, Burkhardt 1983 [1977], 'Herrschaft als Trauma. Adornos Gesellschaftstheorie zwischen Marx und Benjamin', in *Theodor W. Adorno*, edited by Heinz Ludwig Arnold, Munich: edition text+kritik.

Lindner, Burkhardt 1985 [1978], 'Habilitationsakte Benjamin. Über ein "akademisches Trauerspiel" und über ein Vorkapitel der "Frankfurter Schule" (Horkheimer, Adorno)', in *Walter Benjamin im Kontext*, edited by Burkhardt Lindner, Königstein im Taunus: Athenäum.

Lindner, Kolja 2007, 'Rien ne va plus – Wolfgang Pohrts *Theorie des Gebrauchswerts*', *Beiträge zur Marx-Engels-Forschung. Neue Folge*, 2007: 212–46.

Löhr, Katja 2003, *Sehnsucht als poetologisches Prinzip bei Joseph von Eichendorff*, Würzburg: Königshausen & Neumann.

Löwenthal, Leo and Siegfried Kracauer 2003, *In steter Freundschaft. Briefwechsel 1921–1966*, edited by Peter-Erwin Jansen and Christian Schmidt, Springe: zu Klampen.

Lohmann, Hans-Martin 2006, 'Kritische Theorie', in *Freud-Handbuch. Leben – Werk – Wirkung*, edited by Hans-Martin Lohmann and Joachim Pfeiffer, Stuttgart: Metzler.

Lukács, Georg 1949 [1947], 'Heidegger redivivus (Martin Heidegger: Platons Lehre von der Wahrheit, mit einem Brief über "Humanismus". A. Franke. Bern 1947)', *Sinn und Form. Beiträge zur Literatur*, 3: 37–62.

Lukács, Georg 1972a [1968], *History and Class Consciousness: Studies in Marxist Dialectics*, translated by Rodney Livingstone, Cambridge, MA: MIT Press.

Lukács, Georg 1972b [1968], 'Preface to the new edition (1967)', in *History and Class Consciousness: Studies in Marxist Dialectics*, translated by Rodney Livingstone, Cambridge, MA: MIT Press.

Lukács, Georg 1974 [1920], *The Theory of the Novel: A historico-philosophical essay on the forms of great epic literature*, translated by Anna Bostock, Cambridge, MA: MIT Press.

Lukács, Georg 1980 [1954], *The Destruction of Reason*, translated by Peter Palmer, London: Merlin.

Lukács, Georg 2004, 'Gehört Nietzsche dem Faschismus', in *Jahrbuch der Internationalen Georg-Lukács-Gesellschaft*, Volume 8, edited by Frank Benseler and Werner Jung, Bielefeld: Aisthesis.

Maaser, Michael 2003, 'Eine Brücke über die Senckenberganlage. Adorno und die Universität Frankfurt', *Forschung Frankfurt*, 21, 3–4: 48–51.

Magritte, René 2016, *Selected Writings*, edited by Kathleen Rooney and Eric Plattner, translated by Jo Levy and Adam Elgar, Minneapolis: University of Minnesota Press.

Mandelbaum, Kurt and Gerhard Meyer 1934, 'Zur Theorie der Planwirtschaft', *Zeitschrift für Sozialforschung*, 3, 2: 228–62.

Maras, Konstadinos 2002, *Vernunft- und Metaphysikkritik bei Adorno und Nietzsche*, Tübingen: University of Tübingen (doctoral dissertation), available at: https://publikationen.uni-tuebingen.de/xmlui/bitstream/handle/10900/46175/pdf/Dissertation.PDF?sequence=1&isAllowed=y.

Marcuse, Herbert 1973 [1948], 'Sartre's Existentialism', in *Studies in Critical Philosophy*, translated by Joris de Bres, Boston: Beacon.

Marcuse, Herbert 2009 [1979], 'The Struggle Against Liberalism in the Totalitarian View of the State', in *Negations: Essays on Critical Theory*, translated by Jeremy J. Shapiro, London: MayFlyBooks.

Marramao, Giacomo 1975 [1973], 'Political Economy and Critical Theory', *Telos*, 24: 56–80.

Martens, René 1995, 'Authentizität', in *Das Wörterbuch des Gutmenschen, Volume II, Zur Kritik von Plapperjargon und Gesinnungssprache*, edited by Wiglaf Droste and Klaus Bittermann, Berlin: Edition Tiamat.

Martin, Kurt [Kurt Mandelbaum] 1981, 'Staatskapitalismus? Probleme der Planbarkeit der kapitalistischen Gesellschaft – Ein Rückblick auf die Diskussionen im alten Frankfurter Institut für Sozialforschung', in *Soziologie in der Gesellschaft. Referate aus den Veranstaltungen der Sektionen der Deutschen Gesellschaft für Soziologie, der Ad-hoc-Gruppen und des Berufsverbandes Deutscher Soziologen beim 20. Deutschen Soziologentag Bremen, 16. bis 19. September 1980*, Schulte, edited by Werner Schulte, Bremen: Universität Bremen.

Marx, Karl 1975a [1843], 'Comments on the Latest Prussian Censorship Instruction', translated by Clemens Dutt, in *Marx-Engels Collected Works*, Volume 1, *Marx: 1835–1843*, London: Lawrence and Wishart.

Marx, Karl 1975b [1897], 'Letter from Marx to His Father in Trier', translated by Clemens Dutt, in *Marx/Engels Collected Works*, Volume 1, *Marx: 1835–1843*, London: Lawrence and Wishart.

Marx, Karl 1975c [1844], 'Letters from the *Deutsch-Französische Jahrbücher*', translated by Clemens Dutt, in *Marx/Engels Collected Works*, Volume 3, London: Lawrence and Wishart.

Marx, Karl 1976 [1847], *The Poverty of Philosophy: Answer to the* Philosophy of Poverty *by M. Proudhon*, translated by the Institute of Marxism-Leninism, in *Marx/Engels Collected Works*, Volume 6, London: Lawrence and Wishart.

Marx, Karl 1977, 'Reflection', in *Marx-Engels-Gesamtausgabe*, Section 1, Volume 10, Berlin: Dietz.

Marx, Karl 1982a [1867], *Capital: A Critique of Political Economy, Volume One*, translated by Ben Fowkes, London: Penguin.

Marx, Karl 1982b [1933], 'Results of the Immediate Process of Production', in *Capital: A Critique of Political Economy*, Volume One, translated by Ben Fowkes, London: Penguin.

Marx, Karl 1983 [1867], *Das Kapital. Kritik der politischen Ökonomie. Erster Band. Hamburg 1867*, [*Marx/Engels Gesamtausgabe*, Volume II.5], Berlin: Dietz.

Marx, Karl 1985 [1898], 'Value, Price and Profit', in *Marx/Engels Collected Works*, Volume 20, London: Lawrence and Wishart.

Marx, Karl 1987a [1859], *A Contribution to the Critique of Political Economy*, translated by Salo Ryazanskaya, in *Marx/Engels Collected Works*, Volume 29, London: Lawrence and Wishart.

Marx, Karl 1987b [1980], *The Original Text of the Second and the Beginning of the Third Chapter of 'A Contribution to the Critique of Political Economy'*, translated by Yuri Sdobnikov, in *Marx/Engels Collected Works*, Volume 29, London: Lawrence and Wishart.

Marx, Karl 1988 [1905], 'The Physiocrats' [from *Theories of Surplus Value*], translated by Emile Burns, in *Marx/Engels Collected Works*, Volume 30, London: Lawrence and Wishart.

Marx, Karl 1989 [1910], 'Opposition to the Economists (Based on the Ricardian Theory)' [from *Theories of Surplus Value*], in *Marx/Engels Collected Works*, Volume 32,
translated by Emile Burns, Renate Simpson and Jack Cohen, London: Lawrence and
Wishart.

Marx, Karl 1991 [1894], *Capital: A Critique of Political Economy*, Volume Three, translated
by David Fernbach, London: Penguin.

Marx, Karl 1992 [1885], *Capital: A Critique of Political Economy*, Volume Two, translated
by David Fernbach, London: Penguin.

Marx, Karl 1993 [1939], *Grundrisse: Foundations of the Critique of Political Economy
(Rough Draft)*, translated by Martin Nicolaus, London: Penguin.

Marx, Karl 2007 [1844], 'A Contribution to the Critique of Hegel's Philosophy of Right:
Introduction', in *Marx: Early Political Writings*, edited and translated by Joseph
O'Malley with Richard A. Davis, Cambridge: Cambridge University Press.

Marx, Karl 2010a [1891], 'Critique of the Gotha Programme', translated by Joris de Bres,
in *The First International and After* [*Political Writings*, Volume 3], edited by David
Fernbach, London: Verso

Marx, Karl 2010b [1962], '"Notes" on Adolph Wagner', in *Marx: Later Political Writings*, edited and translated by Terrell Carver, Cambridge: Cambridge University
Press.

Marx, Karl 2010c [1871], 'The Civil War in France: Address of the General Council', in *The
First International and After* [*Political Writings*, Volume 3], edited by David Fernbach,
London: Verso.

Marx, Karl and Friedrich Engels 1975 [1845], *The Holy Family, Or Critique of Critical Criti-
cism: Against Bruno Bauer and Company*, translated by Richard Dixon and Clemens
Dutt, in *Marx/Engels Collected Works*, Volume 4: 1844–1845, London: Lawrence and
Wishart.

Marx, Karl and Friedrich Engels 1976 [1932], *The German Ideology*, translated by Clemens Dutt, W. Lough and C.P. Magill, in *Marx/Engels Collected Works*, Volume 5,
London: Lawrence and Wishart.

Marx, Karl and Friedrich Engels 1977 [1848], 'The German Citizenship and the Prussian
Police', translated by Kai Schoenhals, in *Marx/Engels Collected Works*, Volume 7, London: Lawrence and Wishart.

Marx, Karl and Friedrich Engels 1982, *Marx/Engels Collected Works*, Volume 38, *Letters
1844–1851*, London: Lawrence and Wishart.

Marx, Karl and Friedrich Engels 1985, *Marx/Engels Collected Works*, Volume 41, *Letters 1860–1864*, translated by Peter and Betty Ross, London: Lawrence and Wishart.

Marx, Karl and Friedrich Engels 2010 [1848], 'Manifesto of the Communist Party', translated by Samuel Moore, in Karl Marx, *Political Writings*, Volume 1, *The Revolutions of
1848*, edited by David Fernbach, London: Verso.

Marxhausen, Thomas 1999, 'Fetischcharakter der Ware', in *Historisch-kritisches Wörter-buch des Marxismus*, Volume 4, edited by Wolfgang Fritz Haug, Hamburg: Argument.

Mattfeld, Julius 1966, 'Musik im amerikanischen Rundfunk und Fernsehen', in *Die Musik in Geschichte und Gegenwart. Allgemeine Enzyklopädie der Musik*, Volume 13, edited by Friedrich Blume, Kassel: Bärenreiter.

Mauss, Marcel 2002 [1950], *The Gift: The Form and Reason for Exchange in Archaic Societies*, London: Routledge.

Mayer, Hans 1971, *Der Repräsentant und der Märtyrer. Konstellationen der Literatur*, Frankfurt am Main: Suhrkamp.

Mayer, Hans 1997, *Reisen nach Jerusalem: Erfahrungen 1968 bis 1995*, Frankfurt am Main: Suhrkamp.

Mayer, Hans 1998, 'Bemerkungen zu einer kritischen Musiktheorie (1)', in *Mit den Ohren denken. Adornos Philosophie der Musik*, edited by Richard Klein and Claus-Steffen Mahnkopf, Frankfurt am Main: Suhrkamp.

Menke, Bettine 2006, '*Ursprung des deutschen Trauerspiels*', in *Benjamin Handbuch. Leben – Werk – Wirkung*, edited by Burkhardt Lindner with assistance from Thomas Küpper and Timo Skrandies, Stuttgart: Metzler.

Mentzos, Stavros 1984, *Neurotische Konfliktverarbeitung. Einführung in die psychoanalytische Neurosenlehre unter Berücksichtigung neuer Perspektiven*, Frankfurt am Main: Fischer.

Migdal, Ulrike 1981, *Die Frühgeschichte des Frankfurter Instituts für Sozialforschung*, Frankfurt am Main: Campus.

Montinari, Mazzino 2003 [1982], 'Nietzsche between Alfred Bäumler and Georg Lukács', in *Reading Nietzsche*, translated by Greg Whitlock, Champaign, IL: University of Illinois Press.

Morrison, David E. 1978, 'Kultur and Culture: The Case of Theodor W. Adorno and Paul F. Lazarsfeld', *Social Research*, 45, 2: 331–55.

Müller, Ulrich 2006, *Theodor W. Adornos 'Negative Dialektik'*, Darmstadt: Wissenschaftliche Buchgesellschaft.

Mülder-Bach, Inka 1998, 'Introduction', in Siegfried Kracauer, *The Salaried Masses: Duty and Distraction in Weimar Germany*, translated by Quintin Hoare, London: Verso.

Mülder-Bach, Inka 2006, 'Nachbemerkung und editorische Notiz', in Siegfried Kracauer, *Werke*, Volume 1, edited by Inka Mülder-Bach, Frankfurt am Main: Suhrkamp.

Müller-Doohm, Stefan 2000 [1996], *Die Soziologie Theodor W. Adornos. Eine Einführung*, Frankfurt am Main: Campus.

Müller-Doohm, Stefan 2003, *Adorno. Eine Biographie*, Frankfurt am Main, Suhrkamp.

Müller-Doohm, Stefan 2006, '"Die Aktualität der Philosophie"', in *Schlüsseltexte der Kritischen Theorie*, edited by Axel Honneth, Wiesbaden: Springer.

Müller-Doohm, Stefan 2008, 'Sagen, was einem aufgeht. Sprache bei Adorno – Adornos

Sprache' in *Wozu Adorno? Beiträge zur Kritik und zum Fortbestand einer Schlüsseltheorie des 20. Jahrhunderts*, edited by Georg Kohler and Stefan Müller-Doohm, Weilerswist: Velbrück.

Müller-Doohm, Stefan 2009 [2003], *Adorno: A Biography*, translated by Rodney Livingstone, Cambridge: Polity.

Müller-Schöll, Nikolaus 2006, 'Bertolt Brecht', in *Benjamin Handbuch. Leben – Werk – Wirkung*, edited by Burkhardt Lindner, Stuttgart: Metzler.

Müller-Strömsdörfer, Ilse 1960, 'Die "helfende Kraft bestimmter Negation"', *Philosophische Rundschau*, 8, 2/3: 81–104.

Münz-Koenen, Inge 1997, *Konstruktion des Nirgendwo. Die Diskursivität des Utopischen bei Bloch, Adorno, Habermas*, Berlin: Akademie.

Naeher, Jürgen 1984, '"Unreduzierte Erfahrung" – "Verarmung der Erfahrung". Die Einleitung der *Negativen Dialektik* (13–66)', in *Die Negative Dialektik Adornos. Einführung – Dialog*, Opladen: vs.

Neumann, Franz 2009 [1942], *Behemoth: The Structure and Praxis of National Socialism 1933–1944*, Chicago: Ivan R. Dee.

Niemann, Heinz 1999, 'Linkssozialismus in der Weimarer Republik. Anmerkungen zu Konzept und Politik eines "dritten Weges"', *Utopie kreativ. Diskussion sozialistischer Alternativen*, 107: 11–22.

Nietzsche, Friedrich 1968, *The Will to Power*, edited by Walter Kaufmann, translated by Walter Kaufmann and R.J. Hollingdale, London: Weidenfeld and Nicolson.

Nietzsche, Friedrich 1995 [1878], *Human, All Too Human, I: A Book for Free Spirits*, translated by Gary Handwerk, Stanford: Stanford University Press.

Nietzsche, Friedrich 1999, *Kritische Studienausgabe*, Volume 13, *Nachgelassene Fragmente 1887–1889*, edited by Giorgio Colli and Mazzino Montinari, Munich: dtv.

Nietzsche, Friedrich 2001 [1882], *The Gay Science: With a Prelude in German Rhymes and an Appendix of Songs*, edited by Bernard Williams, translated by Josefine Nauckhoff and Adrian Del Caro, Cambridge: Cambridge University Press.

Nietzsche, Friedrich 2006 [1883], *Thus Spoke Zarathustra: A Book for All and None*, edited by Adrian Del Caro, translated by Robert B. Pippin, Cambridge: Cambridge University Press.

Nietzsche, Friedrich 2007 [1888], 'The Case of Wagner: A Musician's Problem', in *The Anti-Christ, Ecce Homo, Twilight of the Idols, and Other Writings*, edited by Aaron Ridley, translated by Judith Norman, Cambridge: Cambridge University Press.

Nitschke, Wolfgang 1999, 'Guido Knopp und Die wilde 13. "Hitlers Helfer – Täter und Vollstrecker" von Guido Knopp', in *Bestsellerfressen. Eine literarische Schlachtplatte*, Berlin: Edition Tiamat.

Olle, Werner 1974, 'Zur Theorie des Staatskapitalismus – Probleme von Theorie und Geschichte in Theorien der Übergangsgesellschaft', *Probleme des Klassenkampfs. Zeitschrift für politische Ökonomie und sozialistische Politik*, 4, 1, 11/12: 91–144.

Ottmann, Henning 1984, 'Anti-Lukács. Eine Kritik der Nietzsche-Kritik von Georg Lukács', *Nietzsche-Studien. Internationales Jahrbuch für die Nietzsche-Forschung*, 13: 571–86.

Ottmann, Henning 1985, 'Nietzsches Stellung zur antiken und modernen Aufklärung' in *Nietzsche und die philosophische Tradition*, Volume 2, edited by Josef Simon, Würzburg: Königshausen & Neumann.

Overesch, Manfred 1983, *Das Dritte Reich. 1939–1945*, Düsseldorf: Droste.

Palmier, Jean-Michel 2006, *Walter Benjamin: Le Chiffonnier, l'Ange et le Petit Bossu*, Paris: Klincksieck.

Pettazzi, Carlo 1983 [1977], 'Studien zu Leben und Werk Adornos bis 1938', translated by Carlo Pettazzi, in *Theodor W. Adorno*, edited by Heinz-Ludwig Arnold, Munich: edition text+kritik.

Phelps, Christoph and Paul Sweezy 1999, 'An Interview with Paul Sweezy', *Monthly Review* 51, 1: 31–51.

Plessner, Helmuth 1970, 'Adornos Negative Dialektik. Ihr Thema mit Variationen', *Kant-Studien*, 61, 4: 507–19.

Pocai, Romano 2006, '*Kierkegaard. Konstruktion des Ästhetischen*', in *Schlüsseltexte der Kritischen Theorie*, edited by Axel Honneth, Wiesbaden: Springer.

Pohrt, Wolfgang 1995 [1976], *Theorie des Gebrauchswerts. Über die Vergänglichkeit der historischen Voraussetzungen, unter denen allein das Kapital Gebrauchswert setzt*, Berlin: Edition Tiamat.

Pollock, Friedrich 1932, 'Die gegenwärtige Lage des Kapitalismus und die Aussichten einer planwirtschaftlichen Neuordnung', *Zeitschrift für Sozialforschung*, 1, 1: 8–27.

Pollock, Friedrich 1933, 'Bemerkungen zur Wirtschaftskrise', *Zeitschrift für Sozialforschung*, 2, 3: 321–54.

Pollock, Friedrich 1941a, 'Is National Socialism a New Order?', *Studies in Philosophy and Social Science* [*Zeitschrift für Sozialforschung*], 9, 3: 440–55.

Pollock, Friedrich 1941b, 'State Capitalism: Its Possibilities and Limitations', *Studies in Philosophy and Social Science* [*Zeitschrift für Sozialforschung*], 9, 2: 200–25.

Pollock, Friedrich 1957 [1956], *Automation: A Study of its Economic and Social Consequences*, translated by W.O. Henderson and W.H. Chaloner, New York: Frederick A. Praeger.

Postman, Neil 2005 [1985], *Amusing Ourselves to Death: Public Discourse in the Age of Show Business*, London: Penguin.

Postone, Moishe 2003 [1993], *Time, Labor, and Social Domination: A Reinterpretation of Marx's Critical Theory*, Cambridge: Cambridge University Press.

Ponzi, Mauro 2004, 'Kunstproduktion und Simulation im post-auratischen Zeitalter', *Zeitschrift für kritische Theorie*, 18/19: 116–32.

Psychopedis, Kosmas 2000, 'Das politische Element in der Darstellung dialektischer Kategorien', in *Kritik der Politik. Johannes Agnoli zum 75. Geburtstag*, edited by Joachim Bruhn, Manfred Dahlmann and Clemens Nachtmann, Freiburg in Breisgau: ça ira.

Pütz, Peter 1981 [1973], 'Nietzsche and Critical Theory', *Telos*, 50: 103–14.

Puttnies, Hans and Gary Smith 1991, *Benjaminiana. Eine biographische Recherche*, Gießen: Anabas.

Rabinbach, Anson 1985, 'Between Enlightenment and Apocalypse: Benjamin, Bloch and Modern German Jewish Messianism', *New German Critique*, 34: 78–124.

Ratzinger, Joseph 2007, *Encyclical Letter* SPE SALVI *of the Supreme Pontiff Benedict* XVI *to the Bishops, Priests and Deacons, Men and Women Religious, and all the Lay Faithful on Christian Hope*, available at: http://www.vatican.va/content/benedict-xvi/en/encyclicals/documents/hf_ben-xvi_enc_20071130_spe-salvi.html.

Raulff, Ulrich 2003, 'Die *Minima Moralia* nach fünfzig Jahren. Ein philosophisches Volksbuch im Spiegel seiner frühen Kritik', in *Theodor W. Adorno. 'Minima Moralia' neu gelesen*, edited by Andreas Bernard and Ulrich Raulff, Frankfurt am Main: Suhrkamp.

Reemtsma, Jan Philipp 1995, 'Nicht Kösteins Paradox. Zur *Dialektik der Aufklärung*', in *Frankfurter Adorno Blätter*, Volume IV, edited by Rolf Tiedemann, Munich: edition text+kritik.

Reichelt, Helmut 2001 [1971], *Zur logischen Struktur des Kapitalbegriffs bei Karl Marx*, Freiburg in Breisgau: ça ira.

Reichelt, Helmut 2007 [2001], 'Marx's Critique of Economic Categories: Reflections on the Problem of Validity in the Dialectical Method of Presentation in *Capital*', translated by Werner Strauss, edited by Jim Kincaid, *Historical Materialism*, 15, 4: 3–52.

Reuss, Vasco 2007, *Eine Kritik der juristischen Vernunft. Rezeptionsversuche der Negativen Dialektik Adornos für die Dogmatik des Strafrechts*, Frankfurt am Main: Peter Lang.

Reusswig, Fritz and Jürgen Ritsert 1991, 'Marxsche Dialektik. Stichworte zu einer unendlichen Geschichte' [materials from a 1991–92 winter semester seminar on *Negative Dialectics* at Goethe University of Frankfurt], available at: http://ritsert-online.de/materialien.htm.

Ries, Wiebrecht 1976, '"Die Rettung des Hoffnungslosen". Zur "theologia occulta" in d. Spätphilosophie Horkheimers u. Adornos', *Zeitschrift für philosophische Forschung*, 30, 1: 69–81.

Ritsert, Jürgen 1973, *Probleme politisch-ökonomischer Theoriebildung*, Frankfurt am Main: Athenäum.

Ritsert, Jürgen 1998, 'Realabstraktion. Ein zu recht abgewertetes Thema der kritischen Theorie?', in *Kein Staat zu machen. Zur Kritik der Sozialwissenschaften*, edited by Christoph Görg and Roland Roth, Münster: Westfälisches Dampfboot.

Robelin, Jean 1988, 'Staatskapitalismus', translated by Michael Krätke, in *Kritisches Wörterbuch des Marxismus*, Volume 7, edited by Georges Labica, Hamburg: Argument.

Robinson, Joan 1974 [1962], *Economic Philosophy*, Harmondsworth: Pelican.

Rudel, Gerd 1981, *Die Entwicklung der marxistischen Staatstheorie in der Bundesrepublik*, Frankfurt am Main: Campus.

Rudolf, Michael 2007, *Atmo. Bingo. Credo. Das ABC der Kultdeutschen*, Berlin: Bittermann.

Sablowski, Thomas 2003, 'Entwicklungstendenzen und Krisen des Kapitalismus', in *Modelle kritischer Gesellschaftstheorie. Traditionen und Perspektiven der Kritischen Theorie*, edited by Alex Demirović, Stuttgart: Metzler.

Schandl, Franz 2001, 'Manisch Germanisch. Ausufernde Anmerkungen zur Trennung im Kritischen Kreis', *Streifzüge*, 3/2001: 42–9.

Scheible, Hartmut 1999 [1989], *Theodor W. Adorno*, Reinbeck: Rowohlt.

Scheit, Gerhard 2003, 'Verrannt und talmudistisch: Adornos Philosophie des Nichtidentischen', *Risse. Analyse und Subversion*, 5: 21–5.

Schenk, Heinz 1992, 'Die Autonomen machen keine Fehler, sie sind der Fehler!!!' in *Feuer und Flamme 2. Kritiken, Reflexionen und Anmerkungen zur Lage der Autonomen*, edited by Geronimo, Tecumseh and Richard Proletario, Berlin: Edition ID-Archiv.

Schiller, Hans-Ernst 1993a, 'Selbstkritik der Vernunft. Zu einigen Motiven der Dialektik bei Adorno', in *An unsichtbarer Kette. Stationen Kritischer Theorie*, Lüneburg: zu Klampen.

Schiller, Hans-Ernst 1993b, 'Zergehende Transzendenz. Theologie und Gesellschaftskritik bei Adorno', in *An unsichtbarer Kette. Stationen Kritischer Theorie*, Lüneburg: zu Klampen.

Schlette, Magnus 2000, 'Flaneur', in *Historisch-kritisches Wörterbuch des Marxismus*, Volume 4, edited by Wolfgang Fritz Haug, Hamburg: Argument.

Schmider, Christine and Michael Werner 2006, 'Das Baudelaire-Buch', in *Benjamin Handbuch. Leben – Werk – Wirkung*, edited by Burkhardt Lindner, Stuttgart: Metzler.

Schmid Noerr, Gunzelin 1987, 'Die philosophischen Frühschriften. Grundzüge der Entwicklung des Horkheimerschen Denkens von der Dissertation bis zur "Dämmerung"', in Max Horkheimer, *Gesammelte Schriften*, Volume 2, *Philosophische Frühschriften 1922–1932*, edited by Gunzelin Schmid Noerr, Frankfurt am Main: Fischer.

Schmid Noerr, Gunzelin 1995, 'Max Horkheimers Gesammelte Schriften und Briefe – Zum Abschluß der Edition', *Mitteilungen*, 6: 69–78.

Schmid Noerr, Gunzelin 1996, 'Editorische Vorbemerkung', in Max Horkheimer, *Gesammelte Schriften*, Volume 19, *Nachträge, Verzeichnisse und Register*, edited by Gunzelin Schmid Noerr, Frankfurt am Main: Fischer.

Schmid Noerr, Gunzelin 1997, 'Gesten aus Begriffen. Interdisziplinärer Materialismus und das Verhältnis von Philosophie und Wissenschaften im Briefwechsel Max Horkheimers', in *Gesten aus Begriffen. Konstellationen der Kritischen Theorie*, Frankfurt am Main: Fischer.

Schmid Noerr, Gunzelin 2001, 'Bloch und Adorno – bildhafte und bilderlose Utopie', *Zeitschrift für kritische Theorie*, 7, 13: 25–56.

Schmid Noerr, Gunzelin 2002 [1987], 'The Position of "Dialectic of Enlightenment" in the Development of Critical Theory', in Theodor W. Adorno and Max Horkheimer, *Dialectic of Enlightenment: Philosophical Fragments*, translated by Edmund Jephcott, Stanford, CA: Stanford University Press.

Schmidt, Alfred 1963, 'Zur Frage der Dialektik in Nietzsches Erkenntnistheorie', in *Zeugnisse. Theodor W. Adorno zum sechzigsten Geburtstag*, edited by Max Horkheimer, Frankfurt am Main: Europäische Verlagsanstalt.

Schmidt, Alfred 1983, 'Begriff des Materialismus bei Adorno', in *Adorno-Konferenz 1983*, edited by Ludwig von Friedeburg and Jürgen Habermas, Frankfurt am Main: Suhrkamp.

Schmidt, Alfred 1988, 'Nachwort des Herausgebers zu den Bänden 3 und 4', in Max Horkheimer, *Gesammelte Schriften*, Volume 4, *Schriften 1936–1941*, edited by Alfred Schmidt, Frankfurt am Main: Fischer.

Schmidt, Alfred 2013 [1962], *The Concept of Nature in Marx*, translated by Ben Fowkes, London: Verso.

Schmidt, Arno 1990, 'Das Geheimnis von Finnegans Wake', in *Dialoge 2 [Bargfelder Ausgabe*, Work Group II, Volume 2], edited by the Arno Schmidt Stiftung, Frankfurt am Main: Suhrkamp.

Schneider, Manfred 2006, 'Aufzeichnungen', in *Benjamin Handbuch. Leben – Werk – Wirkung*, edited by Burkhardt Lindner, Stuttgart: Metzler.

Schöttker, Detlev 2007, 'Kommentar', in Walter Benjamin, *Das Kunstwerk im Zeitalter seiner technischen Reproduzierbarkeit* [student's edition], Frankfurt am Main: Suhrkamp.

Schöttker, Detlev and Erdmut Wizisla 2006, 'Hannah Arendt und Walter Benjamin. Konstellationen, Debatten, Vermittlungen', in *Arendt und Benjamin. Texte, Briefe, Dokumente*, edited by Detlev Schöttker and Erdmut Wizisla, Frankfurt am Main: Suhrkamp.

Scholem, Gershom 1995 [1963], 'Toward an Understanding of the Messianic Idea in Judaism', translated by Michael A. Meyer, in *The Messianic Idea in Judaism and Other Essays on Jewish Spirituality*, New York: Schocken.

Schopenhauer, Arthur 2010 [1818], *The World as Will and Representation*, Volume 1, edited and translated by Judith Norman, Alistair Welchman and Christopher Janaway, Cambridge: Cambridge University Press.

Schürmann, Volker 2003 [2001], *Muße*, Bielefeld: transcript.

Schütrumpf, Jörn 2008 [2006], 'Between Love and Anger: Rosa Luxemburg', in *Rosa Luxemburg or: The Price of Freedom*, edited by Jörn Schütrumpf, Berlin: Dietz.

Schuh, Franz 2006, *Schwere Vorwürfe, schmutzige Wäsche*, Vienna: Zsolnay.

Schulz, Frank 2008, *Morbus fonticuli oder Die Sehnsucht des Laien*, Zürich: Eichborn.

Schulte, Günter 1991, *Kennen Sie Marx? Kritik der proletarischen Vernunft*, Frankfurt am Main: Campus.

Schwarz, Michael 2009, 'Die Frankfurter Schule on Air' [interview with Michael Angele], *Der Freitag*, 6 August 2019: 15.

Schwarz, Ulrich 1980, 'Entfesselung der Produktivkräfte und ästhetische Utopie. Zu Adornos geschichtsphilosophischer Fundierung der ästhetischen Theorie', in *Materialien zur ästhetischen Theorie Theodor W. Adornos. Konstruktion der Moderne*, edited by Burkhardt Lindner and W. Martin Lüdke, Frankfurt am Main: Suhrkamp.

Schweppenhäuser, Gerhard 2009 [1996], *Theodor W. Adorno: An Introduction*, translated by James Rolleston, Durham, NC: Duke University Press.

Schweppenhäuser, Hermann 1973, 'Negativität und Intransigenz. Wider eine Reidealisierung Adornos', in Traugott Koch, Klaus-Michael Kodalle and Hermann Schweppenhäuser, *Negative Dialektik und die Idee der Versöhnung. Eine Kontroverse über Theodor W. Adorno*, Stuttgart: Kohlhammer.

Schweppenhäuser, Hermann 2003, 'Dialektischer Bildbegriff und "dialektisches Bild" in der Kritischen Theorie', *Zeitschrift für kritische Theorie*, 9, 16: 7–46.

Seel, Martin 2006, 'Minima Moralia. Reflexionen aus dem beschädigten Leben', in *Schlüsseltexte der kritischen Theorie*, edited by Axel Honneth, Wiesbaden: Springer.

Seidel, Alfred 1927, *Bewusstsein als Verhängnis*, edited by Hans Prinzhorn, Bonn: Friedrich Cohen.

Siepmann, Eckhard 1990, 'Traumzeit', in *Bucklicht Männlein und Engel der Geschichte. Walter Benjamin, Theoretiker der Moderne. Ausstellung des Werkbund-Archivs im Martin-Gropius-Bau in Berlin, 28. Dezember bis 28. April 1991*, edited by Werkbund-Archiv, Gießen: Anabas.

Söllner, Alfons 1983, 'Angst und Politik. Zur Aktualität Adornos im Spannungsfeld von Politikwissenschaft und Sozialpsychologie', in *Adorno-Konferenz 1983*, edited by Ludwig von Friedeburg and Jürgen Habermas, Frankfurt am Main: Suhrkamp.

Sohn-Rethel, Alfted 1961, 'Warenform und Denkform. Versuch über den gesellschaftlichen Ursprung des reinen Verstandes', *Wissenschaftliche Zeitschrift der Humboldt-Universität zu Berlin/Gesellschafts- und sprachwissenschaftliche Reihe*, 10, 2/3: 163–179.

Sohn-Rethel, Alfted 1985, *Soziologische Theorie der Erkenntnis*, Frankfurt am Main: Suhrkamp.

Sohn-Rethel, Alfted 1987 [1973], *The Economy and Class Structure of German Fascism*, translated by Martin Sohn-Rethel, London: Free Association Books.

Sohn-Rethel, Alfted 1989a, 'Exposé zur Theorie der funktionalen Vergesellschaftung. Ein Brief an Theodor W. Adorno (1936)', in *Geistige und körperliche Arbeit. Zur Epistemologie der abendländischen Geschichte. Revidierte und ergänzte Neuauflage*, Weinheim: VCH.

Sohn-Rethel, Alfted 1989b, 'Vorwort', in *Geistige und körperliche Arbeit. Zur Epistemologie der abendländischen Geschichte. Revidierte und ergänzte Neuauflage*, Weinheim: VCH.

Sohn-Rethel, Alfted 2020 [1970], *Intellectual and Manual Labour: A Critique of Epistemology*, translated by Martin Sohn-Rethel, Brill: Leiden.

Sohn-Rethel, Alfred, Stefan Breuer and Bodo von Greiff 1986, 'Differenzen im Paradigmakern der Kritischen Theorie, Teil II', *Leviathan. Zeitschrift für Sozialwissenschaft*, 2: 308–20.

Steinert, Heinz 2003a [1998], *Culture Industry*, translated by Sally-Ann Spencer, Cambridge: Polity.

Steinert, Heinz 2003b [1992], *Die Entdeckung der Kulturindustrie oder: Warum Professor Adorno Jazz-Musik nicht ausstehen konnte*, Münster: Westfälisches Dampfboot.

Stock, Christian 1996, 'Statistik als Kritik', *Konkret*, 2: 37.

Stoetzler, Marcel 1998, 'Der Sonntag des Sprechens', *karoshi*, 3: 4–9.

Strohal, Richard 1959, 'Autorität und Kritik', *Studium Generale. Zeitschrift für die Einheit der Wissenschaften im Zusammenhang ihrer Begriffsbildungen und Forschungsmethoden*, 12, 7: 403–10.

Svevo, Italo 2003 [1923], *Zeno's Conscience*, translated by William Weaver, New York: Vintage.

Tertulian, Nicolas 2005, 'Lukács – Adorno: Polemiken und Missverständnisse', in *Jahrbuch der Internationalen Georg-Lukács-Gesellschaft*, Volume 9, edited by Frank Benseler and Werner Jung, Bielefeld: Aisthesis.

Thaidigsmann, Edgar 1995, 'Von der Gerechtigkeit der Wahrheit. Der ontologische Gottesbeweis bei T.W. Adorno mit einem Blick auf die Theologie Karl Barths', *Neue Zeitschrift für systematische Theologie und Religionsphilosophie*, 37: 144–64.

Theodor W. Adorno Archiv (ed.) 2003, *Adorno. Eine Bildmonographie*, Frankfurt am Main: Suhrkamp.

Tiedemann, Rolf 1979, 'Auch Narr! Auch Dichter!', in Theodor W. Adorno, *Der Schatz des Indianer-Joe. Singspiel nach Mark Twain*, Frankfurt am Main: Suhrkamp.

Tiedemann, Rolf 1983, 'Historical Materialism or Political Messianism? An Interpretation of the Theses "On the Concept of History"', translated by Barton Byg, *The Philosophical Forum*, 15, 1: 71–104.

Tiedemann, Rolf 1992, ' "Mitdichtende Einfühlung". Adornos Beiträge zum *Doktor Faustus* – noch einmal', in *Frankfurter Adorno Blätter*, Volume I, edited by Rolf Tiedemann, Munich: edition text+kritik.

Tiedemann, Rolf 1994, ' "Gegen den Trug der Frage nach dem Sinn". Eine Dokumentation zu Adornos Beckett-Lektüre', in *Frankfurter Adorno Blätter*, Volume III, edited by Rolf Tiedemann, Munich: edition text I kritik.

Tiedemann, Rolf 1997 [1993], 'Concept, Image, Name: On Adorno's Utopia of Knowledge', translated by Tom Huhn and in *The Semblance of Subjectivity: Essays in*

Adorno's Aesthetic Theory, edited by Tom Huhn and Lambert Zuidervaart, Cambridge, MA: MIT Press.

Tiedemann, Rolf 1998, '"Gegenwärtige Vorwelt". Zu Adornos Begriff des Mythischen (1)', in *Frankfurter Adorno Blätter*, Volume v, edited by Rolf Tiedemann, Munich: edition text+kritik.

Tiedemann, Rolf 2001 [1982], 'Einleitung des Herausgebers', in Walter Benjamin, *Gesammelte Schriften*, Volume v.1, *Das Passagenwerk*, Volume 1, edited by Rolf Tiedemann, Frankfurt am Main: Suhrkamp.

Tiedemann, Rolf 2002 [1982], 'Dialectics at a Standstill: Approaches to the *Passagen-Werk*', in Walter Benjamin, *The Arcades Project*, edited by Rolf Tiedemann, translated by Howard Eiland and Kevin McLaughlin, Cambridge, MA: Harvard University Press.

Tiedemann, Rolf 2003a [1973], 'Editorische Nachbemerkung', in Theodor W. Adorno, *Gesammelte Schriften*, Volume 1, *Philosophische Frühschriften*, edited by Rolf Tiedemann, Frankfurt am Main: Suhrkamp.

Tiedemann, Rolf 2003b [1971], 'Editorische Nachbemerkung', in Theodor W. Adorno, *Gesammelte Schriften*, Volume 5, *Zur Metakritik der Erkenntnistheorie/Drei Studien zu Hegel*, edited by Rolf Tiedemann, Frankfurt am Main: Suhrkamp.

Tiedemann, Rolf 2007, 'Unterwegs zur "Negativen Dialektik". Zu einigen Vorlesungen Adornos', in *Niemandsland. Studien mit und über Theodor W. Adorno*, Munich: edition text+kritik.

Tiedemann, Rolf 2008 [2003], 'Editor's Foreword', in Theodor W. Adorno, *Lectures on Negative Dialectics*, edited by Rolf Tiedemann, translated by Rodney Livingstone, Cambridge: Polity.

Tiedemann, Rolf, Christoph Gödde and Henri Lonitz (eds.) 1991 [1990], *Walter Benjamin 1892–1940. Eine Ausstellung des Theodor W. Adorno Archivs Frankfurt am Main in Verbindung mit dem Deutschen Literaturarchiv Marbach am Neckar* [*Marbacher Magazin* 55], Marbach: Deutsche Schillergesellschaft.

Tiedemann, Rolf and Hermann Schweppenhäuser 2001 [1974], 'Anmerkungen der Herausgeber', in Walter Benjamin, *Gesammelte Schriften*, Volume 1.3, *Abhandlungen*, Volume 3, Frankfurt am Main: Suhrkamp.

Tietz, Udo and Volker Caysa 2005, 'Falsche Verdinglichungsphilosophie und verkehrte Leiberinnerung. Zum Verhältnis von Verdinglichungstheorie in *Geschichte und Klassenbewußtsein* und Leibphilosophie in der *Dialektik der Aufklärung*', in *Jahrbuch der Internationalen Georg-Lukács-Gesellschaft*, Volume 9, edited by Frank Benseler and Werner Jung, Bielefeld: Aisthesis.

Trampert, Rainer 2002, 'Heimwerker', in *Sachzwang & Gemüt: Sarkastische und analytische Texte über die Republik, die Welt und unsere Nachbarn*, edited by Rainer Trampert and Thomas Ebermann, Hamburg: Konkret Literatur.

Trenkle, Norbert 1992, '"Differenz und Gleichheit". Zur Kritik eines falschen Gegensatzes', *Krisis. Beiträge zur Kritik der Warengesellschaft*, 12: 99–115.

Tuchscheerer, Walter 1968, *Bevor 'Das Kapital' entstand. Die Herausbildung und Ent-wicklung der ökonomischen Theorie von Karl Marx in der Zeit von 1843 bis 1858*, Berlin: Akademie.

Türcke, Christoph and Gerhard Bolte 1994, *Einführung in die kritische Theorie*. Darmstadt: Wissenschaftliche Buchgesellschaft.

van Reijen, Willem and Jan Bransen 2002 [1987], 'The Disappearance of Class History in *Dialectic of Enlightenment*: A Commentary on the Textual Variants (1947 and 1944)', in Theodor W. Adorno and Max Horkheimer, *Dialectic of Enlightenment: Philosophical Fragments*, translated by Edmund Jephcott, Stanford, CA: Stanford University Press.

van Reijen, Willem and Herman van Doorn 2001, *Aufenthalte und Passagen. Leben und Werk Walter Benjamins. Eine Chronik*, Frankfurt am Main: Suhrkamp.

Vialon, Martin 2004, 'Theodor W. Adorno's "Hornberg Letter" to Walter Benjamin: A Controversial Discussion of Historical Materialism', in *Theodor W. Adorno. Philosoph des beschädigten Lebens*, edited by Moshe Zuckermann, Göttingen: Wallstein.

Vollgraf, Carl-Erich 1988, *Theoriegeschichtliche Studien zur Entstehungsgeschichte des 'Anti-Dühring'. Marx' Mitarbeit am 'Anti-Dühring'*, Berlin: Institut für Marxismus-Leninismus beim Zentralkomitee der Sozialistischen Einheitspartei Deutschlands (doctoral dissertation).

von Arnim, Achim and Clemens Brentano 2003 [1806–8], *Des Knaben Wunderhorn. Alte deutsche Lieder. Gesammelt von Achim von Arnim und Clemens Brentano*, edited by Heinz Röllecke, Frankfurt am Main: Suhrkamp.

von Eichendorff, Joseph 1966 [1826], *The Life of a Good-For-Nothing*, translated by Michael Glenny, London: Blackie.

von Haselberg, Peter 1983 [1977], 'Wiesengrund-Adorno', in *Theodor W. Adorno*, edited by Heinz Ludwig Arnold, Munich: edition text+kritik.

von Wussow, Philipp 2007, *Logik der Deutung. Adorno und die Philosophie*, Würzburg: Königshausen & Neumann.

Weber, Max 2012 [1904], 'The "Objectivity of Knowledge" in Social Science and Social Policy', in *Collected Methodological Writings*, edited by Hans Henrik Bruun and Sam Whimster, translated by Hans Henrik Bruun, London: Routledge.

Weber, Max 2019 [1922], *Economy and Society: A New Translation*, edited and translated by Keith Tribe, Cambridge, MA: Harvard University Press.

Weber, Thomas 1999, 'Dialektisches Bild', in *Historisch-Kritisches Wörterbuch des Marxismus*, Volume 2, edited by Wolfgang Fritz Haug, Hamburg: Argument.

Wenzel, Eckardt and Stefan Amzoll 1997, 'Was war dieses Jahrhundert eigentlich?', *Utopie kreativ. Diskussion sozialistischer Alternativen*, 81/82: 30–48.

Wiggershaus, Rolf 1987, *Theodor W. Adorno*, Munich: Beck.

Wiggershaus, Rolf 1995 [1986], *The Frankfurt School: Its History, Theories, and Political Significance*, translated by Michael Robertson, Cambridge, MA: MIT Press.

Wiggershaus, Rolf 1998, *Max Horkheimer zur Einführung*, Hamburg: Junius.

Wiggershaus, Rolf 2000, *Wittgenstein und Adorno. Zwei Spielarten modernen Philosophierens*, Göttingen: Wallstein.

Willemsen, Roger 1999, 'Im Sendekreis des Walrosses. Ein ethnologischer Blick auf die Medienstadt Hamburg', in *Bild dir meine Meinung. Kritisches und Polemisches*, Berlin: Edition Tiamat.

Wittgenstein, Ludwig 2001 [1921], *Tractatus Logico-Philosophicus*, translated by D.F. Pears and B.F. McGuiness, London: Routledge.

Wizisla, Erdmut 2016 [2004], *Benjamin and Brecht: The Story of a Friendship*, translated by Christine Shuttleworth, London: Verso.

Wolf, Frieder Otto 1994, 'Althusser-Schule', in *Historisch-kritisches Wörterbuch des Marxismus*, Volume 1, edited by Wolfgang Fritz Haug, Hamburg: Argument.

Wolf, Winfried 1999, 'Programmdebatte. Koalitionsfähig um jeden Preis?', *Sozialistische Zeitung*, 18 March 1999: 10.

Würger-Donitza, Wolfgang 1996, *Rationalitätsmodelle und ihr Zusammenhang mit Leben und Tod. Adornos Grundlegung einer sympathetischen Vernunft*, Würzburg: Königshausen & Neumann.

Zademach, Wieland 2003, 'Leistungsdenken oder soziale Gerechtigkeit. Haben die Kirchen ihre soziale Sprache verloren?', *Utopie kreativ. Diskussion sozialistischer Alternativen*, 156: 939–48.

Zelený, Jindřich 1980 [1968], *The Logic of Marx*, edited and translated by Terrell Carver, Oxford: Basil Blackwell.

Afterword to the Second Edition

> I've already spoken out in multiple interviews for protecting the environment and for world peace. But apparently it was of no use.
>
> LOTHAR MATTHÄUS, quoted in Roger Willemsen, Kopf oder Adler

∴

The first edition of this book, which appeared in 2011 – a lightly revised version of a doctoral dissertation of the same title submitted at the Free University of Berlin – has sold out: not a bad fate for a dissertation in times in which most dissertations are destined simply to help the author obtain a doctorate, and possibly to start a so-called career, but otherwise to sleep away their time in the publishing house. That being said, the author of the present study harbours no illusions that he has achieved something extraordinary. This work was not written to sell out. The saying at the beginning of this afterword may draw a smile, yet in its childlike naiveté, it expresses what Critical Theory wants as well: to be of use, to make a difference – in a way quite distinct from the reductive sense of utilitarianism – whether it is concerned with the whole of society or not. It goes without saying that this theory barely even registers to the dominant practice of today: the times are as good for pessimists as ever. Yet against this, Adorno's famous description of the almost insoluble task of letting oneself become stupefied neither by the power of others nor by one's own powerlessness articulates the responsibility of the intellectual who desires something more than to simply produce scholarship, which in the meantime has truly become its own industry. This reality also affects the present study. Although generally well-received, it was at times accused of having an academic style, given its abundance of footnotes. The responsible party takes this accusation in stride. Academism, against which there is quite rightly much to say, is best dealt with not by breaking its rules, but rather by criticising its procedures. Yet this applies less to form than substance – and of course to its linguistic presentation thereof. In terms of substance, readers of this second edition will hardly find anything not already contained in the first. One addition – marginal in length – containing material from a more recent work was included by the author in one passage, which is noted accordingly. Otherwise, corrections were made only to typos and other small errors. Passages which no longer quite meet the author's aspirations, or which do in fact appear academistic to him, were

© FERNWOOD PUBLISHING, 2023 | DOI:10.1163/9789004525979_017

left unchanged: a second edition is not a new book, and to amend all such passages would have ultimately required writing one. In short, this is a reviewed edition, one with the immodest ambition to be reviewed, criticised and expanded upon, so that in the best case, it might be of use.

Index

www.ingramcontent.com/pod-product-compliance
Lightning Source LLC
Chambersburg PA
CBHW062112040426
42337CB00043B/3707